D0687843

ORACLE®

Oracle Press™

OCA/OCP Java® SE 7 Programmer I & II Study Guide

(Exams 1Z0-803 & 1Z0-804)

ORACLE® *Oracle Press*™

OCA/OCP Java® SE 7 Programmer I & II Study Guide

(Exams 1Z0-803 & 1Z0-804)

Kathy Sierra
Bert Bates

New York Chicago San Francisco
Athens London Madrid
Mexico City Milan New Delhi
Singapore Sydney Toronto

Cataloging-in-Publication Data is on file with the Library of Congress

McGraw-Hill Education books are available at special quantity discounts to use as premiums and sales promotions, or for use in corporate training programs. To contact a representative, please visit the Contact Us pages at www .mhprofessional.com.

OCA/OCP Java® SE 7 Programmer I & II Study Guide (Exams 1Z0-803 & 1Z0-804)

1234567890 DOC DOC 10987654

ISBN: Book p/n 978-0-07-177197-9 and CD p/n 978-0-07-177198-6
of set 978-0-07-177200-6

MHID: Book p/n 0-07-177197-2 and CD p/n 0-07-177198-0
of set 0-07- 177200-6

Sponsoring Editor
Timothy Green

Editorial Supervisor
Jody McKenzie

Project Editor
LeeAnn Pickrell

Acquisitions Coordinators
Mary Damery, Stephanie Evans

Copy Editors
Lisa McCoy, Lisa Theobald

Proofreader
Paul Tyler

Indexer
Ted Laux

Production Supervisor
Jim Kussow

Composition
Apollo Publishing

Illustration
Howie Severson, Fortuitous Publishing

Art Director, Cover
Jeff Weeks

CONTRIBUTORS

Kathy Sierra was a lead developer for the SCJP exam for Java 5 and Java 6. Kathy worked as a Sun "master trainer," and in 1997, founded JavaRanch.com, the world's largest Java community website. Her bestselling Java books have won multiple *Software Development Magazine* awards, and she is a founding member of Oracle's Java Champions program.

These days, Kathy is developing advanced training programs in a variety of domains (from horsemanship to computer programming), but the thread that ties all of her projects together is helping learners reduce cognitive load.

Bert Bates was a lead developer for many of Sun's Java certification exams, including the SCJP for Java 5 and Java 6. Bert was also one of the lead developers for Oracle's OCA 7 and OCP 7 exams. He is a forum moderator on JavaRanch.com and has been developing software for more than 30 years (argh!). Bert is the co-author of several bestselling Java books, and he's a founding member of Oracle's Java Champions program. Now that the book is done, Bert plans to go whack a few tennis balls around and once again start riding his beautiful Icelandic horse, Eyrraros fra Gufudal-Fremri.

About the Technical Review Team

This is the fourth edition of the book that we've cooked up. The first version we worked on was for Java 2. Then we updated the book for the SCJP 5, again for the SCJP 6, and now for the OCA 7 and OCP 7 exams. Every step of the way, we were unbelievably fortunate to have fantastic, JavaRanch.com-centric technical review teams at our sides. Over the course of the last 12 years, we've been "evolving" the book more than rewriting it. Many sections from our original work on the Java 2 book are still intact. On the following pages, we'd like to acknowledge the members of the various technical review teams who have saved our bacon over the years.

About the Java 2 Technical Review Team

Johannes de Jong has been the leader of our technical review teams forever and ever. (He has more patience than any three people we know.) For the Java 2 book, he led our biggest team ever. Our sincere thanks go out to the following volunteers who were knowledgeable, diligent, patient, and picky, picky, picky!

Rob Ross, Nicholas Cheung, Jane Griscti, Ilja Preuss, Vincent Brabant, Kudret Serin, Bill Seipel, Jing Yi, Ginu Jacob George, Radiya, LuAnn Mazza, Anshu Mishra, Anandhi Navaneethakrishnan, Didier Varon, Mary McCartney, Harsha Pherwani, Abhishek Misra, and Suman Das.

About the SCJP 5 Technical Review Team

Andrew

Bill M

Burk

Devender

Gian Jef Jeoren Jim

Johannes Kristin Marcelo Marilyn

Mark Mikalai Seema Valentin

We don't know who burned the most midnight oil, but we can (and did) count everybody's edits—so in order of most edits made, we proudly present our Superstars.

Our top honors go to **Kristin Stromberg**—every time you see a semicolon used correctly, tip your hat to Kristin. Next up is **Burk Hufnagel** who fixed more code than we care to admit. **Bill Mietelski** and **Gian Franco Casula** caught every kind of error we threw at them—awesome job, guys! **Devender Thareja** made sure we didn't use too much slang, and **Mark Spritzler** kept the humor coming. **Mikalai Zaikin** and **Seema Manivannan** made great catches every step of the way, and **Marilyn de Queiroz** and **Valentin Crettaz** both put in another stellar performance (saving our butts yet again).

Marcelo Ortega, **Jef Cumps** (another veteran), **Andrew Monkhouse**, and **Jeroen Sterken** rounded out our crew of Superstars—thanks to you all. **Jim Yingst** was a member of the Sun exam creation team, and he helped us write and review some of the twistier questions in the book (bwa-ha-ha-ha).

As always, every time you read a clean page, thank our reviewers, and if you do catch an error, it's most certainly because your authors messed up. And oh, one last thanks to **Johannes**. You rule, dude!

About the SCJP 6 Technical Review Team

Fred

Marc P.

Marc W.

Since the upgrade to the Java 6 exam was like a small, surgical strike we decided that the technical review team for this update to the book needed to be similarly fashioned. To that end we hand-picked an elite crew of JavaRanch's top gurus to perform the review for the Java 6 exam.

Mikalai

Christophe

Our endless gratitude goes to **Mikalai Zaikin**. Mikalai played a huge role in the Java 5 book, and he returned to help us out again for this Java 6 edition. We need to thank Volha, Anastasia, and Daria for letting us borrow Mikalai. His comments and edits helped us make huge improvements to the book. Thanks, Mikalai!

Marc Peabody gets special kudos for helping us out on a double header! In addition to helping us with Sun's new SCWCD exam, Marc pitched in with a great set of edits for this book—you saved our bacon this winter, Marc! (BTW, we didn't learn until late in the game that Marc, Bryan Basham, and Bert all share a passion for ultimate Frisbee!)

Like several of our reviewers, not only does **Fred Rosenberger** volunteer copious amounts of his time moderating at JavaRanch, he also found time to help us out with this book. Stacey and Olivia, you have our thanks for loaning us Fred for a while.

Marc Weber moderates at some of JavaRanch's busiest forums. Marc knows his stuff, and uncovered some really sneaky problems that were buried in the book. While we really appreciate Marc's help, we need to warn you all to watch out—he's got a Phaser!

Finally, we send our thanks to **Christophe Verre**—if we can find him. It appears that Christophe performs his JavaRanch moderation duties from various locations around the globe, including France, Wales, and most recently Tokyo. On more than one occasion Christophe protected us from our own lack of organization. Thanks for your patience, Christophe! It's important to know that these guys all donated their reviewer honorariums to JavaRanch! The JavaRanch community is in your debt.

The OCA 7 and OCP 7 Team

Contributing Authors

Tom Jeanne

The OCA 7 exam is primarily a useful repackaging of some of the objectives from the SCJP 6 exam. On the other hand, the OCP 7 exam introduced a vast array of brand-new topics. We enlisted several talented Java gurus to help us cover some of the new topics on the OCP 7 exam. Thanks and kudos to **Tom McGinn** for his fantastic work in creating the massive JDBC chapter. Several reviewers told us that Tom did an amazing job channeling the informal tone we use throughout the book. Next, thanks to **Jeanne Boyarsky**. Jeanne was truly a renaissance woman on this project. She contributed to several OCP chapters, she wrote some questions for the master exams, she performed some project management activities, and as if that wasn't enough, she was one of our most energetic technical reviewers. Jeanne, we can't thank you enough. Our thanks go to **Matt Heimer** for his excellent work on the Concurrent chapter. A really tough topic, nicely handled! Finally, **Roel De Nijs** and **Roberto Perillo** made some nice contributions to the book *and* helped out on the technical review team—thanks, guys!

Technical Review Team

Roel, what can we say? Your work as a technical reviewer is unparalleled. Roel caught so many technical errors, it made our heads spin. Between the printed book and all the material on the CD, we estimate that there are over 1,500 pages of "stuff" here. It's huge! Roel grinded through page after page, never lost his focus, and made this book better in countless ways. Thank you, Roel!

Roel

Mikalai

In addition to her other contributions, **Jeanne** provided one of the most thorough technical reviews we received. (We think she enlisted her team of killer robots to help her!)

It seems like no K&B book would be complete without help from our old friend **Mikalai Zaikin**. Somehow, between earning 812 different Java certifications, being a husband and father (thanks to **Volha**, **Anastasia**, **Daria**, and **Ivan**), and being a "theoretical fisherman" [sic], Mikalai made substantial contributions to the quality of the book; we're honored that you helped us again, Mikalai.

Vijitha

Roberto

Next up, we'd like to thank **Vijitha Kumara**, JavaRanch moderator and tech reviewer extraordinaire. We had many reviewers help out during the long course of writing this book, but Vijitha was one of the few who stuck with us from Chapter 1 all the way through the master exams and on to Chapter 15. Vijitha, thank you for your help and persistence!

Finally, thanks to the rest of our review team: **Roberto Perillo** (who also wrote some killer exam questions), **Jim Yingst** (was this your fourth time?), other repeat offenders: **Fred Rosenberger**, **Christophe Verre**, **Devaka Cooray**, **Marc Peabody**, and newcomer **Amit Ghorpade**—thanks, guys!

For Andi

For Bob

CONTENTS AT A GLANCE

CONTENTS

ACKNOWLEDGMENTS

Kathy and Bert would like to thank the following people:

- All the incredibly hard-working folks at McGraw-Hill Education: Tim Green (who's been putting up with us for 12 years now), LeeAnn Pickrell (and team), and Jim Kussow. Thanks for all your help, and for being so responsive, patient, flexible, and professional, and the nicest group of people we could hope to work with.
- All of our friends at Kraftur (and our other horse-related friends) and most especially to Sherry, Steinar, Stina and the girls, Jec, Lucy, Cait, and Jennifer, Leslie and David, Annette and Bruce, Kacey, DJ, Gabrielle, and Mary. Thanks to Pedro and Ely, who can't believe it can take so long to finish a book.
- Some of the software professionals and friends who helped us in the early days: Tom Bender, Peter Loerincs, Craig Matthews, Leonard Coyne, Morgan Porter, and Mike Kavenaugh.
- Dave Gustafson for his continued support, insights, and coaching.
- Our new, wonderful, and talented team at Oracle: Linda Brown, Julia Johnson, Peter Fernandez, and Harold Green.
- The crew at Oracle who worked hard to build these exams: Tom McGinn, Matt Heimer, Mike Williams, Stuart Marks, Cindy Church, Kenny Somerville, Raymond Gallardo, Stacy Thurston, Sowmya Kannan, Jim Holmlund, Mikalai Zaikin, Sharon Zakhour, Lawrence Chow, and Yamuna Santhakumari.
- Our old wonderful and talented certification team at Sun Educational Services, primarily the most persistent get-it-done person we know, Evelyn Cartagena.
- Our great friends and gurus, Simon Roberts, Bryan Basham, and Kathy Collina.

- Stu, Steve, Burt, and Eric for injecting some fun into the process.
- To Eden and Skyler, for being horrified that adults—out of school—would study this hard for an exam.
- To the JavaRanch Trail Boss Paul Wheaton, for running the best Java community site on the Web, and to all the generous and patient JavaRanch moderators.
- To all the past and present Sun Ed Java instructors for helping to make learning Java a fun experience, including (to name only a few) Alan Petersen, Jean Tordella, Georgianna Meagher, Anthony Orapallo, Jacqueline Jones, James Cubeta, Teri Cubeta, Rob Weingruber, John Nyquist, Asok Perumainar, Steve Stelting, Kimberly Bobrow, Keith Ratliff, and the most caring and inspiring Java guy on the planet, Jari Paukku.
- Our furry and feathered friends Eyra, Kara, Draumur, Vafi, Boi, Niki, and Bokeh.
- Finally, to Eric Freeman and Beth Robson for your continued inspiration.

PREFACE

This book's primary objective is to help you prepare for and pass Oracle's OCA Java SE 7 and OCP Java SE 7 Programmer I & II certification exams.

If you already have an SCJP certification, all of the topics covered in the OCP 7 Upgrade exam are covered here as well. And, if for some reason it's appropriate for you to obtain an OCPJP 5 or OCPJP 5 Java certification, the contents of the book and the bonus material on the CD-ROM will help you cover all those bases.

This book follows closely both the breadth and the depth of the real exams. For instance, after reading this book, you probably won't emerge as a regex guru, but if you study the material and do well on the Self Tests, you'll have a basic understanding of regex, and you'll do well on the exam. After completing this book, you should feel confident that you have thoroughly reviewed all of the objectives that Oracle has established for these exams.

In This Book

This book is organized in two parts to optimize your learning of the topics covered by the OCA 7 exam in Part I and the OCP 7 exam in Part II. Whenever possible, we've organized the chapters to parallel the Oracle objectives, but sometimes we'll mix up objectives or partially repeat them in order to present topics in an order better suited to learning the material.

Serialization was a topic on the old SCJP 5 and SCJP 6 exams, and recently (as of the summer of 2014), Oracle reintroduced serialization for the OCP 7 exam. Please see the CD-ROM included with this book for in-depth, complete chapter coverage of serialization, right down to a Self Test. In addition to fully covering the OCA 7 and OCP 7 exams, we have included on the CD-ROM one bonus chapter that covers OCPJP 5 and OCPJP 6 topics, and eight chapters that cover important aspects of Oracle's Java SE 6 Developer exam.

In Every Chapter

We've created a set of chapter components that call your attention to important items, reinforce important points, and provide helpful exam-taking hints. Take a look at what you'll find in every chapter:

- Every chapter begins with the **Certification Objectives**—what you need to know in order to pass the section on the exam dealing with the chapter topic. The Certification Objective headings identify the objectives within the chapter, so you'll always know an objective when you see it!

exam watch

***Exam Watch** notes call attention to information about, and potential pitfalls in, the exam. Since we were on the team that created these exams, we know what you're about to go through!*

on the job

- **On the Job** callouts discuss practical aspects of certification topics that might not occur on the exam, but that will be useful in the real world.
- **Exercises** are interspersed throughout the chapters. They help you master skills that are likely to be an area of focus on the exam. Don't just read through the exercises; they are hands-on practice that you should be comfortable completing. Learning by doing is an effective way to increase your competency with a product.
- **From the Classroom** sidebars describe the issues that come up most often in the training classroom setting. These sidebars give you a valuable perspective into certification- and product-related topics. They point out common mistakes and address questions that have arisen from classroom discussions.
- The **Certification Summary** is a succinct review of the chapter and a restatement of salient points regarding the exam.
- ✓ The **Two-Minute Drill** at the end of every chapter is a checklist of the main points of the chapter. It can be used for last-minute review.
- Q&A The **Self Test** offers questions similar to those found on the certification exam, including multiple choice and pseudo drag-and-drop questions. The answers to these questions, as well as explanations of the answers, can be found at the end of every chapter. By taking the Self Test after completing each chapter, you'll reinforce what you've learned from that chapter, while becoming familiar with the structure of the exam questions.

INTRODUCTION

Organization

This book is organized in such a way as to serve as an in-depth review for the OCA Java SE 7 Programmer I and OCP Java SE 7 Programmer II exams for both experienced Java professionals and those in the early stages of experience with Java technologies. Each chapter covers at least one major aspect of the exam, with an emphasis on the "why" as well as the "how to" of programming in the Java language. The CD-ROM included with the book also includes two chapters that complete the coverage necessary for the OCP 7, OCPJP 6, and OCPJP 5 certifications, and an in-depth review of the essential ingredients for a successful assessment of a project submitted for the Oracle Java SE 6 Developer exam.

Throughout this book and CD-ROM, you'll find support for six exams:

- OCA Java SE 7 Programmer I
- OCP Java SE 7 Programmer II
- Upgrade to Java SE 7 Programmer
- OCP Java SE 6 Programmer
- OCP Java SE 5 Programmer
- Java SE 6 Developer

Finally, the CD-ROM contains practice exam software with the equivalent of four practice exams: two 60-question exams for OCA candidates and two 85-question exams for OCP candidates.

What This Book Is Not

You will not find a beginner's guide to learning Java in this book. All 1,000+ pages of this book are dedicated solely to helping you pass the exams. If you are brand new to Java, we suggest you spend a little time learning the basics. You should not start with this book until you know how to write, compile, and run simple Java programs. We do not, however, assume any level of prior knowledge of the individual topics covered. In other words, for any given topic (driven exclusively by the actual exam objectives), we start with the assumption that you are new to that topic. So we assume you're new to the individual topics, but we assume that you are not new to Java.

We also do not pretend to be both preparing you for the exam and simultaneously making you a complete Java being. This is a certification exam study guide, and it's very clear about its mission. That's not to say that preparing for the exam won't help you become a better Java programmer! On the contrary, even the most experienced Java developers often claim that having to prepare for the certification exam made them far more knowledgeable and well-rounded programmers than they would have been without the exam-driven studying.

On the CD-ROM

For more information on the CD-ROM, please see the Appendix.

Some Pointers

Once you've finished reading this book, set aside some time to do a thorough review. You might want to return to the book several times and make use of all the methods it offers for reviewing the material:

1. *Re-read all the Two-Minute Drills, or have someone quiz you.* You also can use the drills as a way to do a quick cram before the exam. You might want to make some flash cards out of 3 × 5 index cards that have the Two-Minute Drill material on them.
2. *Re-read all the Exam Watch notes.* Remember that these notes are written by authors who helped create the exam. They know what you should expect—and what you should be on the lookout for.
3. *Re-take the Self Tests.* Taking the tests right after you've read the chapter is a good idea because the questions help reinforce what you've just learned. However, it's an even better idea to go back later and do all the questions in the book in one sitting. Pretend that you're taking the live exam. (Whenever you take the Self Tests, mark your answers on a separate piece of paper. That way, you can run through the questions as many times as you need to until you feel comfortable with the material.)
4. *Complete the exercises.* The exercises are designed to cover exam topics, and there's no better way to get to know this material than by practicing. Be sure you understand why you are performing each step in each exercise. If there is something you are not clear on, re-read that section in the chapter.

5. *Write lots of Java code.* We'll repeat this advice several times. When we wrote this book, we wrote hundreds of small Java programs to help us do our research. We have heard from hundreds of candidates who have passed the exam, and in almost every case, the candidates who scored extremely well on the exam wrote lots of code during their studies. Experiment with the code samples in the book, create horrendous lists of compiler errors—put away your IDE, crank up the command line, and write code!

Introduction to the Material in the Book

The OCP 7 exam is considered one of the hardest in the IT industry, and we can tell you from experience that a large chunk of exam candidates goes in to the test unprepared. As programmers, we tend to learn only what we need to complete our current project, given the insane deadlines we're usually under.

But this exam attempts to prove your complete understanding of the Java language, not just the parts of it you've become familiar with in your work.

Experience alone will rarely get you through this exam with a passing mark, because even the things you think you know might work just a little differently than you imagined. It isn't enough to be able to get your code to work correctly; you must understand the core fundamentals in a deep way, and with enough breadth to cover virtually anything that could crop up in the course of using the language.

The Oracle Java SE 6 Developer Exam (covered in chapters that are contained on the CD-ROM) is unique to the IT certification realm because it actually evaluates your skill as a developer rather than simply your knowledge of the language or tools. Becoming a Certified Java Developer is, by definition, a development experience.

Who Cares About Certification?

Employers do. Headhunters do. Programmers do. Passing this exam proves three important things to a current or prospective employer: you're smart; you know how to study and prepare for a challenging test; and, most of all, you know the Java language. If an employer has a choice between a candidate who has passed the exam and one who hasn't, the employer knows that the certified programmer does not have to take time to learn the Java language.

But does it mean that you can actually develop software in Java? Not necessarily, but it's a good head start. To really demonstrate your ability to develop (as opposed to just your knowledge of the language), you should consider pursuing the Developer Exam, where you're given an assignment to build a program, start to finish, and submit it for an assessor to evaluate and score.

Taking the Programmer's Exam

In a perfect world, you would be assessed for your true knowledge of a subject, not simply how you respond to a series of test questions. But life isn't perfect, and it just isn't practical to evaluate everyone's knowledge on a one-to-one basis.

For the majority of its certifications, Oracle evaluates candidates using a computer-based testing service operated by Pearson VUE. To discourage simple memorization, Oracle exams present a potentially different set of questions to different candidates. In the development of the exam, hundreds of questions are compiled and refined using beta testers. From this large collection, questions are pulled together from each objective and assembled into many different versions of the exam.

Each Oracle exam has a specific number of questions, and the test's duration is designed to be generous. The time remaining is always displayed in the corner of the testing screen. If time expires during an exam, the test terminates, and incomplete answers are counted as incorrect.

exam watch

Many experienced test-takers do not go back and change answers unless they have a good reason to do so. Only change an answer when you feel you may have misread or misinterpreted the question the first time. Nervousness may make you second-guess every answer and talk yourself out of a correct one.

After completing the exam, you will receive an email from Oracle telling you that your results are available on the Web. As of summer 2014, your results can be found at certview.oracle.com. If you want a printed copy of your certificate, you must make a specific request.

Question Format

Oracle's Java exams pose questions in multiple-choice format.

Multiple-Choice Questions

In earlier versions of the exam, when you encountered a multiple-choice question, you were not told how many answers were correct, but with each version of the exam, the questions have become more difficult, so today, each multiple-choice question tells you how many answers to choose. The Self Test questions at the end of each chapter closely match the format, wording, and difficulty of the real exam questions, with two exceptions:

- Whenever we can, our questions will *not* tell you how many correct answers exist (we will say "Choose all that apply"). We do this to help you master the material. Some savvy test-takers can eliminate wrong answers when the number of correct answers is known. It's also possible, if you know how many answers are correct, to choose the most plausible answers. Our job is to toughen you up for the real exam!
- The real exam typically numbers lines of code in a question. Sometimes we do not number lines of code—mostly so that we have the space to add comments at key places. On the real exam, when a code listing starts with line 1, it means that you're looking at an entire source file. If a code listing starts at a line number greater than 1, that means you're looking at a partial source file. When looking at a partial source file, assume that the code you can't see is correct. (For instance, unless explicitly stated, you can assume that a partial source file will have the correct import and package statements.)

exam watch

When you find yourself stumped answering multiple-choice questions, use your scratch paper (or whiteboard) to write down the two or three answers you consider the strongest, then underline the answer you feel is most likely correct. Here is an example of what your scratch paper might look like when you've gone through the test once:

- 21. <u>B</u> or C
- 33. A or <u>C</u>

This is extremely helpful when you mark the question and continue on. You can then return to the question and immediately pick up your thought process where you left off. Use this technique to avoid having to re-read and rethink questions. You will also need to use your scratch paper during complex, text-based scenario questions to create visual images to better understand the question. This technique is especially helpful if you are a visual learner.

Tips on Taking the Exam

The number of questions and passing percentages for every exam are subject to change. Always check with Oracle before taking the exam, at www.Oracle.com.

You are allowed to answer questions in any order, and you can go back and check your answers after you've gone through the test. There are no penalties for wrong answers, so it's better to at least attempt an answer than to not give one at all.

A good strategy for taking the exam is to go through once and answer all the questions that come to you quickly. You can then go back and do the others. Answering one question might jog your memory for how to answer a previous one.

Be very careful on the code examples. Check for syntax errors first: count curly braces, semicolons, and parentheses and then make sure there are as many left ones as right ones. Look for capitalization errors and other such syntax problems before trying to figure out what the code does.

Many of the questions on the exam will hinge on subtleties of syntax. You will need to have a thorough knowledge of the Java language in order to succeed.

This brings us to another issue that some candidates have reported. The testing center is supposed to provide you with sufficient writing implements so that you can work problems out "on paper." In some cases, the centers have provided inadequate markers and dry-erase boards that are too small and cumbersome to use effectively. We recommend that you call ahead and verify that you will be supplied with a sufficiently large whiteboard, sufficiently fine-tipped markers, and a good eraser. What we'd really like to encourage is for everyone to complain to Oracle and Pearson VUE and have them provide actual pencils and at least several sheets of blank paper.

Tips on Studying for the Exam

First and foremost, give yourself plenty of time to study. Java is a complex programming language, and you can't expect to cram what you need to know into a single study session. It is a field best learned over time, by studying a subject and then applying your knowledge. Build yourself a study schedule and stick to it, but be reasonable about the pressure you put on yourself, especially if you're studying in addition to your regular duties at work.

One easy technique to use in studying for certification exams is the 15-minutes-per-day effort. Simply study for a minimum of 15 minutes every day. It is a small but significant commitment. If you have a day where you just can't focus, then give up at 15 minutes. If you have a day where it flows completely for you, study longer. As long as you have more of the "flow days," your chances of succeeding are excellent.

We strongly recommend you use flash cards when preparing for the programmer's exams. A flash card is simply a 3 × 5 or 4 × 6 index card with a question on the front and the answer on the back. You construct these cards yourself as you go through a chapter, capturing any topic you think might need more memorization or practice time. You can drill yourself with them by reading the question, thinking through the answer, and then turning the card over to see if you're correct. Or you can get another person to help you by holding up the card with the question facing you and then verifying your answer. Most of our students have found these to be tremendously helpful, especially because they're so portable that while you're in study mode, you can take them everywhere. Best not to use them while driving, though, except at red lights. We've taken ours everywhere—the doctor's office, restaurants, theaters, you name it.

Certification study groups are another excellent resource, and you won't find a larger or more willing community than on the JavaRanch.com Big Moose Saloon certification forums. If you have a question from this book, or any other mock exam question you may have stumbled upon, posting a question in a certification forum will get you an answer in nearly all cases within a day—usually, within a few hours. You'll find us (the authors) there several times a week, helping those just starting out on their exam preparation journey. (You won't actually think of it as anything as pleasant sounding as a "journey" by the time you're ready to take the exam.)

Finally, we recommend that you write a lot of little Java programs! During the course of writing this book, we wrote hundreds of small programs, and if you listen to what the most successful candidates say (you know, those guys who got 98 percent), they almost always report that they wrote a lot of code.

Scheduling Your Exam

You can purchase your exam voucher from Oracle or Pearson VUE. Visit Oracle.com (follow the training/certification links) or visit PearsonVue.com for exam scheduling details and locations of test centers.

Arriving at the Exam

As with any test, you'll be tempted to cram the night before. Resist that temptation. You should know the material by this point, and if you're groggy in the morning, you won't remember what you studied anyway. Get a good night's sleep.

Arrive early for your exam; it gives you time to relax and review key facts. Take the opportunity to review your notes. If you get burned out on studying, you can usually start your exam a few minutes early. We don't recommend arriving late. Your test could be cancelled, or you might not have enough time to complete the exam.

When you arrive at the testing center, you'll need to provide current, valid photo identification. Visit PearsonVue.com for details on the ID requirements. They just want to be sure that you don't send your brilliant Java guru next-door-neighbor who you've paid to take the exam for you.

Aside from a brain full of facts, you don't need to bring anything else to the exam room. In fact, your brain is about all you're allowed to take into the exam!

All the tests are closed book, meaning you don't get to bring any reference materials with you. You're also not allowed to take any notes out of the exam room. The test administrator will provide you with a small marker board. If you're allowed to, we do recommend that you bring a water bottle or a juice bottle (call ahead for details of what's allowed). These exams are long and hard, and your brain functions much better when it's well hydrated. In terms of hydration, the ideal approach is to take frequent, small sips. You should also verify how many "bio-breaks" you'll be allowed to take during the exam!

Leave your pager and telephone in the car, or turn them off. They only add stress to the situation, since they are not allowed in the exam room, and can sometimes still be heard if they ring outside of the room. Purses, books, and other materials must be left with the administrator before entering the exam.

Once in the testing room, you'll be briefed on the exam software. You might be asked to complete a survey. The time you spend on the survey is *not* deducted from your actual test time—nor do you get more time if you fill out the survey quickly. Also, remember that the questions you get on the exam will *not* change depending on how you answer the survey questions. Once you're done with the survey, the real clock starts ticking and the fun begins.

The testing software allows you to move forward and backward between questions. Most important, there is a Mark check box on the screen—this will prove to be a critical tool, as explained in the next section.

Test-Taking Techniques

Without a plan of attack, candidates can become overwhelmed by the exam or become sidetracked and run out of time. For the most part, if you are comfortable with the material, the allotted time is more than enough to complete the exam. The trick is to keep the time from slipping away during any one particular problem.

Your obvious goal is to answer the questions correctly and quickly, but other factors can distract you. Here are some tips for taking the exam more efficiently.

Size Up the Challenge

First, take a quick pass through all the questions in the exam. "Cherry-pick" the easy questions, answering them on the spot. Briefly read each question, noticing the type of question and the subject. As a guideline, try to spend less than 25 percent of your testing time in this pass.

This step lets you assess the scope and complexity of the exam, and it helps you determine how to pace your time. It also gives you an idea of where to find potential answers to some of the questions. Sometimes the wording of one question might lend clues or jog your thoughts for another question.

If you're not entirely confident in your answer to a question, answer it anyway, but check the Mark box to flag it for later review. In the event that you run out of time, at least you've provided a "first guess" answer, rather than leaving it blank.

Second, go back through the entire test, using the insight you gained from the first go-through. For example, if the entire test looks difficult, you'll know better than to spend more than a minute or two on each question. Create a pacing with small milestones—for example, "I need to answer 10 questions every 15 minutes."

At this stage, it's probably a good idea to skip past the time-consuming questions, marking them for the next pass. Try to finish this phase before you're 50 to 60 percent through the testing time.

Third, go back through all the questions you marked for review, using the Review Marked button in the question review screen. This step includes taking a second look at all the questions you were unsure of in previous passes, as well as tackling the time-consuming ones you deferred until now. Chisel away at this group of questions until you've answered them all.

If you're more comfortable with a previously marked question, unmark the Review Marked button now. Otherwise, leave it marked. Work your way through the time-consuming questions now, especially those requiring manual calculations. Unmark them when you're satisfied with the answer.

By the end of this step, you've answered every question in the test, despite having reservations about some of your answers. If you run out of time in the next step, at least you won't lose points for lack of an answer. You're in great shape if you still have 10 to 20 percent of your time remaining.

Review Your Answers

Now you're cruising! You've answered all the questions, and you're ready to do a quality check. Take yet another pass (yes, one more) through the entire test (although you'll probably want to skip a review of the drag-and-drop questions!), briefly re-reading each question and your answer.

Carefully look over the questions again to check for "trick" questions. Be particularly wary of those that include a choice of "Does not compile." Be alert for last-minute clues. You're pretty familiar with nearly every question at this point, and you may find a few clues that you missed before.

The Grand Finale

When you're confident with all your answers, finish the exam by submitting it for grading. After you finish your exam, you'll receive an e-mail from Oracle giving you a link to a page where your exam results will be available. As of this writing, you must ask for a hard copy certificate specifically or one will not be sent to you.

Retesting

If you don't pass the exam, don't be discouraged. Try to have a good attitude about the experience, and get ready to try again. Consider yourself a little more educated. You'll know the format of the test a little better, and you'll have a good idea of the difficulty level of the questions you'll get next time around.

If you bounce back quickly, you'll probably remember several of the questions you might have missed. This will help you focus your study efforts in the right area.

Ultimately, remember that Oracle certifications are valuable because they're hard to get. After all, if anyone could get one, what value would it have? In the end, it takes a good attitude and a lot of studying, but you can do it!

Objectives Map

The following four tables—one for the OCA Java SE 7 Programmer I Exam, one for the OCP Java SE 7 Programmer II Exam, one for the Upgrade to Java SE 7 Programmer Exam, and one for the OCP Java Programmer 5 and OCP Java Programmer 6 exams—describe the objectives and where you will find them in the book.

Oracle Certified Associate Java SE 7 Programmer (Exam 1Z0-803)

Official Objective	Study Guide Coverage
Java Basics	
Define the scope of variables (1.1)	Chapter 3
Define the structure of a Java class (1.2)	Chapter 1
Create executable Java applications with a main method (1.3)	Chapter 1
Import other Java packages to make them accessible in your code (1.4)	Chapter 1
Working with Java Data Types	
Declare and initialize variables (2.1)	Chapters 1 and 3
Differentiate between object reference variables and primitive variables (2.2)	Chapter 2
Read or write to object fields (2.3)	Whole book
Explain an object's lifecycle (creation, "dereference," and garbage collection) (2.4)	Chapters 2 and 3
Call methods on objects (2.5)	Whole book
Manipulate data using the StringBuilder class and its methods (2.6)	Chapter 5
Create and manipulate Strings (2.7)	Chapter 5
Using Operators and Decision Constructs	
Use Java operators (3.1)	Chapter 4
Use parentheses to override operator precedence (3.2)	Chapter 4
Test equality between Strings and other objects using == and equals() (3.3)	Chapter 4
Create if and if/else constructs (3.4)	Chapter 6
Use a switch statement (3.5)	Chapter 6
Creating and Using Arrays	
Declare, instantiate, initialize and use a one-dimensional array (4.1)	Chapter 5
Declare, instantiate, initialize and use multi-dimensional array (4.2)	Chapter 5
Declare and use an ArrayList (4.3)	Chapter 5

OCA Java SE 7 Objectives (*cont.*)

Official Objective	Study Guide Coverage
Using Loop Constructs	
Create and use while loops (5.1)	Chapter 6
Create and use for loops including the enhanced for loop (5.2)	Chapter 6
Create and use do/while loops (5.3)	Chapter 6
Compare loop constructs (5.4)	Chapter 6
Use break and continue (5.5)	Chapter 6
Working with Methods and Encapsulation	
Create methods with arguments and return values (6.1)	Chapters 2 and 3
Apply the static keyword to methods and fields (6.2)	Chapter 1
Create an overloaded method (6.3)	Chapter 2
Differentiate between default and user defined constructors (6.4)	Chapter 2
Create and overload constructors (6.5)	Chapter 2
Apply access modifiers (6.6)	Chapter 1
Apply encapsulation principles to a class (6.7)	Chapter 2
Determine the effect upon object references and primitive values when they are passed into methods that change the values (6.8)	Chapter 3
Working with Inheritance	
Implement inheritance (7.1)	Chapter 2
Develop code that demonstrates the use of polymorphism (7.2)	Chapter 2
Differentiate between the type of a reference and the type of an object (7.3)	Chapter 2
Determine when casting is necessary (7.4)	Chapter 2
Use super and this to access objects and constructors (7.5)	Chapter 2
Use abstract classes and interfaces (7.6)	Chapters 1 and 2
Handling Exceptions	
Differentiate among checked exceptions, RuntimeExceptions, and Errors (8.1)	Chapter 6
Create a try-catch block and determine how exceptions alter normal program flow (8.2)	Chapter 6
Describe what exceptions are used for in Java (8.3)	Chapter 6
Invoke a method that throws an exception (8.4)	Chapter 6
Recognize common exception classes and categories (8.5)	Chapter 6

Oracle Certified Professional Java SE 7 Programmer II (Exam IZ0-804)

Although the OCP objectives are not specifically listed in Part I of the book, many of them are covered in those chapters, as detailed here, as material is duplicated across the two exams.

Official Objective	Study Guide Coverage
Java Class Design	
Use access modifiers: private, protected, and public (1.1)	Chapter 1
Override methods (1.2)	Chapter 2
Overload constructors and methods (1.3)	Chapter 2
Use the instanceof operator and casting (1.4)	Chapter 2
Use virtual method invocation (1.5)	Chapters 2 and 10
Override the hashcode, equals, and toString methods from the Object class to improve the functionality of your class (1.6)	Chapter 11
Use package and import statements (1.7)	Chapter 1
Advanced Class Design	
Identify when and how to apply abstract classes (2.1)	Chapter 1
Construct abstract Java classes and subclasses (2.2)	Chapters 1 and 2
Use the static and final keywords (2.3)	Chapter 1
Create top level and nested classes (2.4)	Chapters 1–3, 12
Use enumerated types (2.5)	Chapter 1
Object-Oriented Design Principles	
Write code that declares, implements, and/or extends interfaces (3.1)	Chapters 1 and 2
Choose between interface inheritance and class inheritance (3.2)	Chapter 2
Apply cohesion, low-coupling, IS-A, and HAS-A principles (3.3)	Chapters 2 and 10
Apply object composition principles (including HAS-A relationships) (3.4)	Chapters 2 and 10
Design a class using a singleton design pattern (3.5)	Chapter 10
Write code to implement the Data Access Object (DAO) (3.6)	Chapter 10
Design and create objects using a factory and use factories from the API (3.7)	Chapter 10
Generics and Collections	
Create a generic class (4.1)	Chapter 11
Use the diamond syntax to create a collection (4.2)	Chapter 11
Analyze the interoperability of collections that use raw and generic types (4.3)	Chapter 11

OCP Java SE 7 Objectives (*cont.*)

Official Objective	Study Guide Coverage
Use wrapper classes and autoboxing (4.4)	Chapter 11
Create and use a List, a Set, and a Deque (4.5)	Chapters 11 and 14
Create and use a Map (4.6)	Chapter 11
Use java.util.Comparator and java.lang.Comparable (4.7)	Chapter 11
Sort and search arrays and lists (4.8)	Chapter 11
String Processing	
Search, parse, and build strings (including Scanner, StringTokenizer, StringBuilder, String, and Formatter) (5.1)	Chapter 8
Search, parse, and replace strings by using regular expressions, using expression patterns for matching limited to . (dot), * (star), + (plus), ?, \d, \D, \s, \S, \w, \W, \b, \B, [], and (). (5.2)	Chapter 8
Format strings using the formatting parameters %b, %c, %d, %f, and %s in format strings. (5.3)	Chapter 8
Exceptions and Assertions	
Use throw and throws statements (6.1)	Chapters 6 and 7
Develop code that handles multiple Exception types in a single catch block (6.2)	Chapter 7
Develop code that uses try-with-resources statements (including classes that implement the AutoCloseable interface) (6.3)	Chapter 7
Create custom exceptions (6.4)	Chapters 6 and 7
Test invariants by using assertions (6.5)	Chapter 7
Java I/O Fundamentals	
Read and write data from the console (7.1)	Chapter 9
Use streams to read from and write to files by using classes in the java.io package, including BufferedReader, BufferedWriter, File, FileReader, FileWriter, DataInputStream, DataOutputStream, ObjectOutputStream, ObjectInputStream, and PrintWriter (7.2)	Chapter 9 and CD-ROM
Java File I/O (NIO.2)	
Operate on file and directory paths with the Path class (8.1)	Chapter 9
Check, delete, copy, or move a file or directory with the Files class (8.2)	Chapter 9
Read and change file and directory attributes, focusing on the BasicFileAttributes, DosFileAttributes, and PosixFileAttributes interfaces (8.3)	Chapter 9
Recursively access a directory tree using the DirectoryStream and FileVisitor interfaces (8.4)	Chapter 9
Find a file with the PathMatcher interface (8.5)	Chapter 9
Watch a directory for changes with the WatchService interface (8.6)	Chapter 9

Official Objective	Study Guide Coverage
Building Database Applications with JDBC	
Describe the interfaces that make up the core of the JDBC API (including the Driver, Connection, Statement, and ResultSet interfaces and their relationships to provider implementations) (9.1)	Chapter 15
Identify the components required to connect to a database using the DriverManager class (including the JDBC URL) (9.2)	Chapter 15
Submit queries and read results from the database (including creating statements; returning result sets; iterating through the results; and properly closing result sets, statements, and connections) (9.3)	Chapter 15
Use JDBC transactions (including disabling auto-commit mode, committing and rolling back transactions, and setting and rolling back to savepoints) (9.4)	Chapter 15
Construct and use RowSet objects using the RowSetProvider class and the RowSetFactory interface (9.5)	Chapter 15
Create and use PreparedStatement and CallableStatement objects (9.6)	Chapter 15
Threads	
Create and use the Thread class and the Runnable interface (10.1)	Chapter 13
Manage and control thread lifecycle (10.2)	Chapter 13
Synchronize thread access to shared data (10.3)	Chapter 13
Identify code that may not execute correctly in a multithreaded environment (10.4)	Chapter 13
Concurrency	
Use collections from the java.util.concurrent package with a focus on the advantages over and differences from the traditional java.util collections (11.1)	Chapter 14
Use Lock, ReadWriteLock, and ReentrantLock classes in the java.util.concurrent.locks package to support lock-free thread-safe programming on single variables (11.2)	Chapter 14
Use Executor, ExecutorService, Executors, Callable, and Future to execute tasks using thread pools (11.3)	Chapter 14
Use the parallel Fork/Join Framework (11.4)	Chapter 14
Localization	
Read and set the locale using the Locale object (12.1)	Chapter 8
Build a resource bundle for each locale (12.2)	Chapter 8
Call a resource bundle from an application (12.3)	Chapter 8
Format dates, numbers, and currency values for localization with the NumberFormat and DateFormat classes (including number format patterns) (12.4)	Chapter 8
Describe the advantages of localizing an application (12.5)	Chapter 8
Define a locale using language and country codes (12.6)	Chapter 8

Upgrade to Java SE 7 Programmer (Exam IZ0-805)

Official Objective	Study Guide Coverage
Language Enhancements	
Develop code that uses String objects in switch statements (1.1)	Chapter 6
Develop code that uses binary literals and numeric literals with underscores (1.2)	Chapter 3
Develop code that uses try-with-resources statements (including classes that implement the AutoCloseable interface) (1.3)	Chapter 7
Develop code that handles multiple exception types in a single catch block (1.4)	Chapter 7
Develop code that uses the diamond with generic declarations (1.5)	Chapter 11
Design Patterns	
Design a class using a singleton design pattern (2.1)	Chapter 10
Apply object composition principles (including HAS-A relationships) (2.2)	Chapters 2 and 10
Write code to implement the Data Access Object (DAO) (2.3)	Chapter 10
Design and create objects using a factory pattern (2.4)	Chapter 10
Database Applications with JDBC	
Describe the interfaces that make up the core of the JDBC API (including the Driver, Connection, Statement, and ResultSet interfaces and their relationships to provider implementations) (3.1)	Chapter 15
Identify the components required to connect to a database using the DriverManager class (including the JDBC URL) (3.2)	Chapter 15
Construct and use RowSet objects using the RowSetProvider class and the RowSetFactory interface (3.3)	Chapter 15
Use JDBC transactions (including disabling auto-commit mode, committing and rolling back transactions, and setting and rolling back to savepoints) (3.4)	Chapter 15
Submit queries and read results from the database (including creating statements; returning result sets; iterating through the results; and properly closing result sets, statements, and connections) (3.5)	Chapter 15
Create and use PreparedStatement and CallableStatement objects (3.6)	Chapter 15
Concurrency	
Identify code that may not execute correctly in a multithreaded environment (4.1)	Chapter 13
Use collections from the java.util.concurrent package with a focus on the advantages over and differences from the traditional java.util collections (4.2)	Chapter 14
Use Lock, ReadWriteLock, and ReentrantLock classes in the java.util.concurrent.locks package to support lock-free thread-safe programming on single variables (4.3)	Chapter 14
Use Executor, ExecutorService, Executors, Callable, and Future to execute tasks using thread pools (4.4)	Chapter 14
Use the parallel Fork/Join Framework (4.5)	Chapter 14

Official Objective	Study Guide Coverage
Localization	
Describe the advantages of localizing an application (5.1)	Chapter 8
Define a locale using language and country codes (5.2)	Chapter 8
Read and set the locale by using the Locale object (5.3)	Chapter 8
Build a resource bundle for each locale (5.4)	Chapter 8
Call a resource bundle from an application (5.5)	Chapter 8
Format dates, numbers, and currency values for localization with the NumberFormat and DateFormat classes (including number format patterns) (5.6)	Chapter 8
Java File I/O (NIO.2)	
Operate on file and directory paths with the Path class (6.1)	Chapter 9
Check, delete, copy, or move a file or directory with the Files class (6.2)	Chapter 9
Read and change file and directory attributes, focusing on the BasicFileAttributes, DosFileAttributes, and PosixFileAttributes interfaces (6.3)	Chapter 9
Recursively access a directory tree using the DirectoryStream and FileVisitor interfaces (6.4)	Chapter 9
Find a file with the PathMatcher interface (6.5)	Chapter 9
Watch a directory for changes with the WatchService interface (6.6)	Chapter 9

Java SE 5 Programmer and OCP Java Programmer 6

Official Objective	Study Guide Coverage
1. Declarations, Initialization and Scoping	**Chapters 1–3, 5, and 12**
2. Flow Control	Chapters 6 and 7
3. API Contents	Chapters 5, 8, 9, and 11
4. Concurrency	Chapter 13
5. OO Concepts	Chapters 2 and 10
6. Collections/Generics	Chapter 11
7. Fundamentals	Chapters 1–4, Classpaths and JARs chapter on CD-ROM

Part I

OCA and OCP

CHAPTERS

1

Declarations and Access Control

CERTIFICATION OBJECTIVES

- Identifiers and Keywords
- javac, java, main(), and Imports
- Declare Classes and Interfaces
- Declare Class Members
- Declare Constructors and Arrays
- Create static Class Members
- Use enums
- ✓ Two-Minute Drill
- Q&A Self Test

We assume that because you're planning on becoming certified, you already know the basics of Java. If you're completely new to the language, this chapter—and the rest of the book—will be confusing; so be sure you know at least the basics of the language before diving into this book. That said, we're starting with a brief, high-level refresher to put you back in the Java mood, in case you've been away for a while.

Java Refresher

A Java program is mostly a collection of *objects* talking to other objects by invoking each other's *methods*. Every object is of a certain *type*, and that type is defined by a *class* or an *interface*. Most Java programs use a collection of objects of many different types. Following is a list of a few useful terms for this object-oriented (OO) language:

- **Class** A template that describes the kinds of state and behavior that objects of its type support.
- **Object** At runtime, when the Java Virtual Machine (JVM) encounters the `new` keyword, it will use the appropriate class to make an object that is an instance of that class. That object will have its own state and access to all of the behaviors defined by its class.
- **State (instance variables)** Each object (instance of a class) will have its own unique set of instance variables as defined in the class. Collectively, the values assigned to an object's instance variables make up the object's state.
- **Behavior (methods)** When a programmer creates a class, she creates methods for that class. Methods are where the class's logic is stored and where the real work gets done. They are where algorithms get executed and data gets manipulated.

Identifiers and Keywords

All the Java components we just talked about—classes, variables, and methods—need names. In Java, these names are called *identifiers*, and, as you might expect, there are rules for what constitutes a legal Java identifier. Beyond what's *legal*, though, Java (and Oracle) programmers have created *conventions* for naming methods, variables, and classes.

Like all programming languages, Java has a set of built-in *keywords*. These keywords must *not* be used as identifiers. Later in this chapter we'll review the details of these naming rules, conventions, and the Java keywords.

Inheritance

Central to Java and other OO languages is the concept of *inheritance*, which allows code defined in one class to be reused in other classes. In Java, you can define a general (more abstract) superclass, and then extend it with more specific subclasses. The superclass knows nothing of the classes that inherit from it, but all of the subclasses that inherit from the superclass must explicitly declare the inheritance relationship. A subclass that inherits from a superclass is automatically given accessible instance variables and methods defined by the superclass, but the subclass is also free to override superclass methods to define more specific behavior. For example, a `Car` *super*class could define general methods common to all automobiles, but a `Ferrari` *sub*class could override the `accelerate()` method that was already defined in the `Car` class.

Interfaces

A powerful companion to inheritance is the use of interfaces. Interfaces are like a 100-percent abstract superclass that defines the methods a subclass must support, but not *how* they must be supported. In other words, for example, an `Animal` interface might declare that all `Animal` implementation classes have an `eat()` method, but the `Animal` interface doesn't supply any logic for the `eat()` method. That means it's up to the classes that implement the `Animal` interface to define the actual code for how that particular `Animal` type behaves when its `eat()` method is invoked.

Finding Other Classes

As we'll see later in the book (for you OCP candidates), it's a good idea to make your classes *cohesive*. That means that every class should have a focused set of responsibilities. For instance, if you were creating a zoo simulation program, you'd want to represent aardvarks with one class and zoo visitors with a different class. In addition, you might have a `Zookeeper` class and a `PopcornVendor` class. The point is that you don't want a class that has both Aardvark *and* PopcornVendor behaviors (more on that in Chapter 10).

Even a simple Java program uses objects from many different classes: some that *you* created, and some built by others (such as Oracle's Java API classes). Java organizes classes into *packages* and uses *import* statements to give programmers a consistent way to manage naming of, and access to, classes they need. The exam covers a *lot* of concepts related to packages and class access; we'll explore the details throughout the book.

CERTIFICATION OBJECTIVE

Identifiers and Keywords (OCA Objectives 1.2 and 2.1)

1.2 *Define the structure of a Java class.*

2.1 *Declare and initialize variables.*

Remember that when we list one or more Certification Objectives in the book, as we just did, it means that the following section covers at least some part of that objective. Some objectives will be covered in several different chapters, so you'll see the same objective in more than one place in the book. For example, this section covers declarations and identifiers, but *using* the things you declare is covered primarily in later chapters.

So, we'll start with Java identifiers. The two aspects of Java identifiers that we cover here are

- **Legal identifiers** The rules the compiler uses to determine whether a name is legal.
- **Oracle's Java Code Conventions** Oracle's recommendations for naming classes, variables, and methods. We typically adhere to these standards throughout the book, except when we're trying to show you how a tricky exam question might be coded. You won't be asked questions about the Java Code Conventions, but we strongly recommend that you use them.

Legal Identifiers

Technically, legal identifiers must be composed of only Unicode characters, numbers, currency symbols, and connecting characters (such as underscores). The exam doesn't dive into the details of which ranges of the Unicode character set are considered to qualify as letters and digits. So, for example, you won't need to know that Tibetan digits range from `\u0420` to `\u0f29`. Here are the rules you *do* need to know:

- Identifiers must start with a letter, a currency character (`$`), or a connecting character such as the underscore (_). Identifiers cannot start with a digit!

- After the first character, identifiers can contain any combination of letters, currency characters, connecting characters, or numbers.
- In practice, there is no limit to the number of characters an identifier can contain.
- You can't use a Java keyword as an identifier. Table 1-1 lists all of the Java keywords.
- Identifiers in Java are case-sensitive; `foo` and `FOO` are two different identifiers.

Examples of legal and illegal identifiers follow. First some legal identifiers:

```
int _a;
int $c;
int ______2_w;
int _$;
int this_is_a_very_detailed_name_for_an_identifier;
```

The following are illegal (it's your job to recognize why):

```
int :b;
int -d;
int e#;
int .f;
int 7g;
```

Oracle's Java Code Conventions

Oracle estimates that over the lifetime of a standard piece of code, 20 percent of the effort will go into the original creation and testing of the code, and 80 percent of the effort will go into the subsequent maintenance and enhancement of the code.

TABLE 1-1 Complete List of Java Keywords (`assert` added in 1.4, `enum` added in 1.5)

abstract	boolean	break	byte	case	catch
char	class	const	continue	default	do
double	else	extends	final	finally	float
for	goto	if	implements	import	instanceof
int	interface	long	native	new	package
private	protected	public	return	short	static
strictfp	super	switch	synchronized	this	throw
throws	transient	try	void	volatile	while
assert	enum				

Agreeing on, and coding to, a set of code standards helps to reduce the effort involved in testing, maintaining, and enhancing any piece of code. Oracle has created a set of coding standards for Java and published those standards in a document cleverly titled "Java Code Conventions," which you can find if you start at `java.oracle.com`. It's a great document, short, and easy to read, and we recommend it highly.

That said, you'll find that many of the questions in the exam don't follow the code conventions because of the limitations in the test engine that is used to deliver the exam internationally. One of the great things about the Oracle certifications is that the exams are administered uniformly throughout the world. To achieve that, the code listings that you'll see in the real exam are often quite cramped and do not follow Oracle's code standards. To toughen you up for the exam, we'll often present code listings that have a similarly cramped look and feel, often indenting our code only two spaces as opposed to the Oracle standard of four.

We'll also jam our curly braces together unnaturally, and we'll sometimes put several statements on the same line...ouch! For example:

```
 1. class Wombat implements Runnable {
 2.   private int i;
 3.   public synchronized void run() {
 4.     if (i%5 != 0) { i++; }
 5.     for(int x=0; x<5; x++, i++)
 6.       { if (x > 1) Thread.yield(); }
 7.     System.out.print(i + " ");
 8.   }
 9.   public static void main(String[] args) {
10.     Wombat n = new Wombat();
11.     for(int x=100; x>0; --x) { new Thread(n).start(); }
12. } }
```

Consider yourself forewarned—you'll see lots of code listings, mock questions, and real exam questions that are this sick and twisted. Nobody wants you to write your code like this—not your employer, not your coworkers, not us, not Oracle, and not the exam creation team! Code like this was created only so that complex concepts could be tested within a universal testing tool. The only standards that *are* followed as much as possible in the real exam are the naming standards. Here are the naming standards that Oracle recommends and that we use in the exam and in most of the book:

- **Classes and interfaces** The first letter should be capitalized, and if several words are linked together to form the name, the first letter of the inner words should be uppercase (a format that's sometimes called "CamelCase"). For classes, the names should typically be nouns. Here are some examples:

```
Dog
Account
PrintWriter
```

For interfaces, the names should typically be adjectives, like these:

```
Runnable
Serializable
```

- **Methods** The first letter should be lowercase, and then normal CamelCase rules should be used. In addition, the names should typically be verb-noun pairs. For example:

```
getBalance
doCalculation
setCustomerName
```

- **Variables** Like methods, the CamelCase format should be used, but starting with a lowercase letter. Oracle recommends short, meaningful names, which sounds good to us. Some examples:

```
buttonWidth
accountBalance
myString
```

- **Constants** Java constants are created by marking variables `static` and `final`. They should be named using uppercase letters with underscore characters as separators:

```
MIN_HEIGHT
```

CERTIFICATION OBJECTIVE

Define Classes (OCA Objectives 1.2, 1.3, 1.4, 6.6, and 7.6)

1.2 Define the structure of a Java class.

1.3 Create executable Java applications with a main method.

1.4 *Import other Java packages to make them accessible in your code.*

6.6 *Apply access modifiers.*

7.6 *Use abstract classes and interfaces.*

When you write code in Java, you're writing classes or interfaces. Within those classes, as you know, are variables and methods (plus a few other things). How you declare your classes, methods, and variables dramatically affects your code's behavior. For example, a `public` method can be accessed from code running anywhere in your application. Mark that method `private`, though, and it vanishes from everyone's radar (except the class in which it was declared).

For this objective, we'll study the ways in which you can declare and modify (or not) a class. You'll find that we cover modifiers in an extreme level of detail, and although we know you're already familiar with them, we're starting from the very beginning. Most Java programmers think they know how all the modifiers work, but on closer study they often find out that they don't (at least not to the degree needed for the exam). Subtle distinctions are everywhere, so you need to be absolutely certain you're completely solid on everything in this section's objectives before taking the exam.

Source File Declaration Rules

Before we dig into class declarations, let's do a quick review of the rules associated with declaring classes, `import` statements, and `package` statements in a source file:

- There can be only one `public` class per source code file.
- Comments can appear at the beginning or end of any line in the source code file; they are independent of any of the positioning rules discussed here.
- If there *is* a `public` class in a file, the name of the file must match the name of the `public` class. For example, a class declared as `public class Dog { }` must be in a source code file named `Dog.java`.
- If the class is part of a package, the `package` statement must be the first line in the source code file, before any `import` statements that may be present.
- If there are `import` statements, they must go *between* the `package` statement (if there is one) and the class declaration. If there isn't a `package` statement, then the `import` statement(s) must be the first line(s) in the source code file.

If there are no `package` or `import` statements, the class declaration must be the first line in the source code file.

- `import` and `package` statements apply to *all* classes within a source code file. In other words, there's no way to declare multiple classes in a file and have them in different packages or use different imports.
- A file can have more than one nonpublic class.
- Files with no `public` classes can have a name that does not match any of the classes in the file.

Using the javac and java Commands

In this book, we're going to talk about invoking the `javac` and `java` commands about 1000 times. Although in the **real world** you'll probably use an integrated development environment (IDE) most of the time, you could see a few questions on the exam that use the command line instead, so we're going to review the basics. (By the way, we did NOT use an IDE while writing this book. We still have a slight preference for the command line while studying for the exam; all IDEs do their best to be "helpful," and sometimes they'll fix your problems without telling you. That's nice on the job, but maybe not so great when you're studying for a certification exam!)

Compiling with javac

The `javac` command is used to invoke Java's compiler. You can specify many options when running `javac`. For example, there are options to generate debugging information or compiler warnings. Here's the structural overview for `javac`:

```
javac [options] [source files]
```

There are additional command-line options called `@argfiles`, but they're rarely used, and you won't need to study them for the exam. Both the `[options]` and the `[source files]` are optional parts of the command, and both allow multiple entries. The following are both legal `javac` commands:

```
javac -help
javac -version Foo.java Bar.java
```

The first invocation doesn't compile any files, but prints a summary of valid options. The second invocation passes the compiler an option (`-version`, which prints the version of the compiler you're using), and passes the compiler two `.java` files to compile (`Foo.java` and `Bar.java`). Whenever you specify multiple options and/or files, they should be separated by spaces. (Note: If you're studying for the OCP 7, in Chapter 7 we'll talk about the assertion mechanism and when you might use the `-source` option when compiling a file.)

Launching Applications with java

The `java` command is used to invoke the Java Virtual Machine (JVM). Here's the basic structure of the command:

```
java [options] class [args]
```

The `[options]` and `[args]` parts of the `java` command are optional, and they can both have multiple values. (Of the two exams, only the OCP 7 will use `[options]`.) You must specify exactly one class file to execute, and the `java` command assumes you're talking about a `.class` file, so you don't specify the `.class` extension on the command line. Here's an example:

```
java -version MyClass x 1
```

This command can be interpreted as "Show me the version of the JVM being used, and then launch the file named `MyClass.class` and send it two String *arguments* whose values are `x` and `1`." Let's look at the following code:

```
public class MyClass {
  public static void main(String[] args) {
    System.out.println(args[0] + " " + args[1]);
  }
}
```

It's compiled and then invoked as follows:

```
java MyClass x 1
```

The output will be

```
x 1
```

We'll be getting into arrays in depth later, but for now it's enough to know that args—like all arrays—uses a zero-based index. In other words, the first command line argument is assigned to `args[0]`, the second argument is assigned to `args[1]`, and so on.

Note: Again, for the OCP 7 candidates, in Chapter 7 we'll talk about the assertion mechanism and when you might use flags such as `-ea` or `-da` when launching an application.

Using public static void main(String[] args)

The use of the `main()` method is implied in most of the questions on the exam, and on the OCA exam it is specifically covered. For the .0001% of you who don't know, `main()` is the method that the JVM uses to start execution of a Java program.

First off, it's important for you to know that naming a method `main()` doesn't give it the superpowers we normally associate with `main()`. As far as the compiler and the JVM are concerned, the **only** version of `main()` with superpowers is the `main()` with this signature:

```
public static void main(String[] args)
```

Other versions of `main()` with other signatures are perfectly legal, but they're treated as normal methods. There is some flexibility in the declaration of the "special" `main()` method (the one used to start a Java application): the order of its modifiers can be altered a little, the `String` array doesn't have to be named `args`, and as of Java 5 it can be declared using var-args syntax. The following are all legal declarations for the "special" `main()`:

```
static public void main(String[] args)
public static void main(String... x)
static public void main(String bang_a_gong[])
```

For the OCA exam, the only other thing that's important for you to know is that `main()` **can be overloaded**. We'll cover overloading in detail in the next chapter.

Import Statements and the Java API

There are a gazillion Java classes in the world. The Java API has thousands of classes and the Java community has written the rest. We'll go out on a limb and contend that all Java programmers everywhere use a combination of classes they wrote and classes that other programmers wrote. Suppose we created the following:

```
public class ArrayList {
  public static void main(String[] args) {
    System.out.println("fake ArrayList class");
  }
}
```

This is a perfectly legal class, but as it turns out, one of the most commonly used classes in the Java API is also named `ArrayList`, or so it seems.... The API version's actual name is `java.util.ArrayList`. That's its *fully qualified name*. The use of fully qualified names is what helps Java developers make sure that two versions of a class like `ArrayList` don't get confused. So now let's say that I want to use the `ArrayList` class from the API:

```
public class MyClass {
  public static void main(String[] args) {
    java.util.ArrayList<String> a =
      new java.util.ArrayList<String>();
  }
}
```

(First off, trust us on the `<String>` syntax; we'll get to that later.) While this is legal, it's also a LOT of keystrokes. Since we programmers are basically lazy (there, we said it), we like to use other people's classes a LOT, AND we hate to type. If we had a large program, we might end up using `ArrayLists` many times.

`import` statements to the rescue! Instead of the preceding code, our class could look like this:

```
import java.util.ArrayList;
public class MyClass {
  public static void main(String[] args) {
    ArrayList<String> a = new ArrayList<String>();
  }
}
```

We can interpret the `import` statement as saying, "In the Java API there is a package called 'util', and in that package is a class called 'ArrayList'. Whenever you see the word 'ArrayList' in this class, it's just shorthand for: 'java.util.ArrayList'." (Note: Lots more on packages to come!) If you're a C programmer, you might think that the `import` statement is similar to an `#include`. Not really. All a Java `import` statement does is save you some typing. That's it.

As we just implied, a package typically has many classes. The `import` statement offers yet another keystroke-saving capability. Let's say you wanted to use a few different classes from the `java.util` package: `ArrayList` and `TreeSet`. You can add a wildcard character (`*`) to your `import` statement that means, "If you see a reference to a class you're not sure of, you can look through the entire package for that class," like so:

```
import java.util.*;
public class MyClass {
  public static void main(String[] args) {
    ArrayList<String> a = new ArrayList<String>();
    TreeSet<String> t = new TreeSet<String>();
  }
}
```

When the compiler and the JVM see this code, they'll know to look through `java.util` for `ArrayList` and `TreeSet`. For the exam, the last thing you'll need to remember about using `import` statements in your classes is that you're free to mix and match. It's okay to say this:

```
ArrayList<String> a = new ArrayList<String>();
java.util.ArrayList<String> a2 = new java.util.ArrayList<String>();
```

Static Import Statements

Dear Reader, We really struggled with when to include this discussion of static imports. From a learning perspective this is probably not the ideal location, but from a reference perspective, we thought it made sense. As you're learning the material for the first time, you might be confused by some of the ideas in this section. If that's the case, we apologize. Put a sticky note on this page and circle back around after you're finished with Chapter 3. On the other hand, once you're past the learning stage and you're using this book as a reference, we think putting this section here will be quite useful. Now, on to static imports.

Sometimes classes will contain **static members**. (We'll talk more about static class members later, but since we were on the topic of imports we thought we'd toss in static imports now.) Static class members can exist in the classes you write and in a lot of the classes in the Java API.

As we said earlier, ultimately the only value import statements have is that they save typing and they can make your code easier to read. In Java 5, the import statement was enhanced to provide even greater keystroke-reduction capabilities, although some would argue that this comes at the expense of readability. This feature is known as *static imports*. Static imports can be used when you want to "save typing" while using a class's static members. (You can use this feature on classes in the API and on your own classes.) Here's a "before and after" example using a few static class members provided by a commonly used class in the Java API, `java.lang.Integer`. This example also uses a static member that you've used a thousand times, probably without ever giving it much thought; the `out` field in the `System` class.

Before static imports:

```
public class TestStatic {
  public static void main(String[] args) {
    System.out.println(Integer.MAX_VALUE);
    System.out.println(Integer.toHexString(42));
  }
}
```

After static imports:

```
import static java.lang.System.out;              // 1
import static java.lang.Integer.*;               // 2
public class TestStaticImport {
  public static void main(String[] args)  {
    out.println(MAX_VALUE);                      // 3
    out.println(toHexString(42));                // 4
  }
}
```

Both classes produce the same output:

```
2147483647
2a
```

Let's look at what's happening in the code that's using the static import feature:

1. Even though the feature is commonly called "static import" the syntax MUST be `import static` followed by the fully qualified name of the `static` member you want to import, or a wildcard. In this case, we're doing a static import on the `System` class `out` object.
2. In this case we might want to use several of the `static` members of the `java.lang.Integer` class. This static import statement uses the wildcard to say, "I want to do static imports of ALL the `static` members in this class."
3. Now we're finally seeing the *benefit* of the static import feature! We didn't have to type the `System` in `System.out.println`! Wow! Second, we didn't have to type the `Integer` in `Integer.MAX_VALUE`. So in this line of code we were able to use a shortcut for a `static` method AND a constant.
4. Finally, we do one more shortcut, this time for a method in the `Integer` class.

We've been a little sarcastic about this feature, but we're not the only ones. We're not convinced that saving a few keystrokes is worth possibly making the code a little harder to read, but enough developers requested it that it was added to the language.

Here are a couple of rules for using static imports:

- You must say `import static`; you can't say `static import`.
- Watch out for ambiguously named `static` members. For instance, if you do a static import for both the `Integer` class and the `Long` class, referring to `MAX_VALUE` will cause a compiler error, since both `Integer` and `Long` have a `MAX_VALUE` constant, and Java won't know which `MAX_VALUE` you're referring to.
- You can do a static import on `static` object references, constants (remember they're `static` and `final`), and `static` methods.

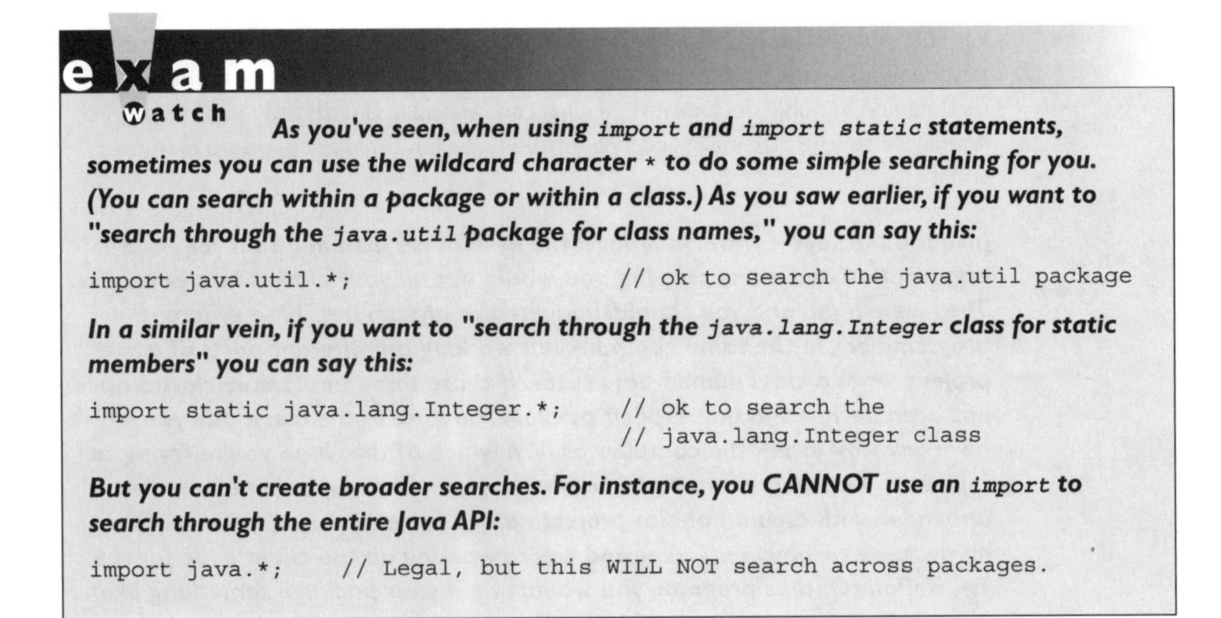

exam watch

As you've seen, when using `import` and `import static` statements, sometimes you can use the wildcard character `*` to do some simple searching for you. (You can search within a package or within a class.) As you saw earlier, if you want to "search through the `java.util` package for class names," you can say this:

```
import java.util.*;                    // ok to search the java.util package
```

In a similar vein, if you want to "search through the `java.lang.Integer` class for static members" you can say this:

```
import static java.lang.Integer.*;     // ok to search the
                                       // java.lang.Integer class
```

But you can't create broader searches. For instance, you CANNOT use an `import` to search through the entire Java API:

```
import java.*;    // Legal, but this WILL NOT search across packages.
```

Class Declarations and Modifiers

The class declarations we'll discuss in this section are limited to top-level classes.

Although nested classes (often called inner classes) are included on the OCP exam, we'll save nested class declarations for Chapter 12. If you're an OCP candidate, you're going to love that chapter. No, really. Seriously.

The following code is a bare-bones class declaration:

```
class MyClass { }
```

This code compiles just fine, but you can also add modifiers before the class declaration. In general, modifiers fall into two categories:

- Access modifiers (`public`, `protected`, `private`)
- Nonaccess modifiers (including `strictfp`, `final`, and `abstract`)

We'll look at access modifiers first, so you'll learn how to restrict or allow access to a class you create. Access control in Java is a little tricky, because there are four access *controls* (levels of access) but only three access *modifiers*. The fourth access control level (called *default* or *package* access) is what you get when you don't use any of the three access modifiers. In other words, *every* class, method, and instance variable you declare has an access *control*, whether you explicitly type one or not. Although all four access *controls* (which means all three *modifiers*) work for most method and variable declarations, a class can be declared with only `public` or *default* access; the other two access control levels don't make sense for a class, as you'll see.

on the Job

Java is a package-centric language; the developers assumed that for good organization and name scoping, you would put all your classes into packages. They were right, and you should. Imagine this nightmare: Three different programmers, in the same company but working on different parts of a project, write a class named `Utilities`. If those three `Utilities` classes have not been declared in any explicit package, and are in the classpath, you won't have any way to tell the compiler or JVM which of the three you're trying to reference. Oracle recommends that developers use reverse domain names, appended with division and/or project names. For example, if your domain name is `geeksanonymous.com`, and you're working on the client code for the TwelvePointOSteps program, you would name your package something like `com.geeksanonymous.steps.client`. That would essentially change the name of your class to `com.geeksanonymous.steps.client.Utilities`. You might still have name collisions within your company if you don't come up with your own naming schemes, but you're guaranteed not to collide with classes developed outside your company (assuming they follow Oracle's naming convention, and if they don't, well, Really Bad Things could happen).

Class Access

What does it mean to access a class? When we say code from one class (class A) has access to another class (class B), it means class A can do one of three things:

- Create an *instance* of class B.
- *Extend* class B (in other words, become a subclass of class B).
- *Access* certain methods and variables within class B, depending on the access control of those methods and variables.

In effect, access means *visibility*. If class A can't *see* class B, the access level of the methods and variables within class B won't matter; class A won't have any way to access those methods and variables.

Default Access A class with default access has *no* modifier preceding it in the declaration! It's the access control you get when you don't type a modifier in the class declaration. Think of *default* access as *package*-level access, because a class with default access can be seen only by classes within the same package. For example, if class A and class B are in different packages, and class A has default access, class B won't be able to create an instance of class A or even declare a variable or return type of class A. In fact, class B has to pretend that class A doesn't even exist, or the compiler will complain. Look at the following source file:

```
package cert;
class Beverage { }
```

Now look at the second source file:

```
package exam.stuff;
import cert.Beverage;
class Tea extends Beverage { }
```

As you can see, the superclass (`Beverage`) is in a different package from the subclass (`Tea`). The `import` statement at the top of the `Tea` file is trying (fingers crossed) to import the `Beverage` class. The `Beverage` file compiles fine, but when we try to compile the `Tea` file, we get something like this:

```
Can't access class cert.Beverage. Class or interface must be public, in same
package, or an accessible member class.
import cert.Beverage;
```

`Tea` won't compile because its superclass, `Beverage`, has default access and is in a different package. You can do one of two things to make this work. You could put both classes in the same package, or you could declare `Beverage` as `public`, as the next section describes.

When you see a question with complex logic, be sure to look at the access modifiers first. That way, if you spot an access violation (for example, a class in package A trying to access a default class in package B), you'll know the code won't compile so you don't have to bother working through the logic. It's not as if you don't have anything better to do with your time while taking the exam. Just choose the "Compilation fails" answer and zoom on to the next question.

Public Access

A class declaration with the `public` keyword gives all classes from all packages access to the `public` class. In other words, *all* classes in the Java Universe (JU) have access to a `public` class. Don't forget, though, that if a `public` class you're trying to use is in a different package from the class you're writing, you'll still need to import the `public` class.

In the example from the preceding section, we may not want to place the subclass in the same package as the superclass. To make the code work, we need to add the keyword `public` in front of the superclass (`Beverage`) declaration, as follows:

```
package cert;
public class Beverage { }
```

This changes the `Beverage` class so it will be visible to all classes in all packages. The class can now be instantiated from all other classes, and any class is now free to subclass (extend from) it—unless, that is, the class is also marked with the nonaccess modifier `final`. Read on.

Other (Nonaccess) Class Modifiers

You can modify a class declaration using the keyword `final`, `abstract`, or `strictfp`. These modifiers are in addition to whatever access control is on the class, so you could, for example, declare a class as both `public` and `final`. But you can't always mix nonaccess modifiers. You're free to use `strictfp` in combination with `final`, for example, but you must never, ever, ever mark a class as both `final` *and* `abstract`. You'll see why in the next two sections.

You won't need to know how `strictfp` works, so we're focusing only on modifying a class as `final` or `abstract`. For the exam, you need to know only that `strictfp` is a keyword and can be used to modify a class or a method, but never a variable. Marking a class as `strictfp` means that any method code in the class will conform to the IEEE 754 standard rules for floating points. Without that modifier, floating points used in the methods might behave in a platform-dependent way. If you don't declare a class as `strictfp`, you can still get `strictfp` behavior on a method-by-method basis, by declaring a method as `strictfp`. If you don't know the IEEE 754 standard, now's not the time to learn it. You have, as they say, bigger fish to fry.

Final Classes

When used in a class declaration, the `final` keyword means the class can't be subclassed. In other words, no other class can ever extend (inherit from) a `final` class, and any attempts to do so will result in a compiler error.

So why would you ever mark a class `final`? After all, doesn't that violate the whole OO notion of inheritance? You should make a `final` class only if you need an absolute guarantee that none of the methods in that class will ever be overridden. If you're deeply dependent on the implementations of certain methods, then using `final` gives you the security that nobody can change the implementation out from under you.

You'll notice many classes in the Java core libraries are `final`. For example, the `String` class cannot be subclassed. Imagine the havoc if you couldn't guarantee how a `String` object would work on any given system your application is running on! If programmers were free to extend the `String` class (and thus substitute their new `String` subclass instances where `java.lang.String` instances are expected), civilization—as we know it—could collapse. So use `final` for safety, but only when you're certain that your `final` class has indeed said all that ever needs to be said in its methods. Marking a class `final` means, in essence, your class can't ever be improved upon, or even specialized, by another programmer.

There's a benefit of having nonfinal classes is this scenario: Imagine that you find a problem with a method in a class you're using, but you don't have the source code. So you can't modify the source to improve the method, but you can extend the class and override the method in your new subclass and substitute the subclass everywhere the original superclass is expected. If the class is `final`, though, you're stuck.

Let's modify our `Beverage` example by placing the keyword `final` in the declaration:

```
package cert;
public final class Beverage {
  public void importantMethod() { }
}
```

Now let's try to compile the `Tea` subclass:

```
package exam.stuff;
import cert.Beverage;
class Tea extends Beverage { }
```

We get an error—something like this:

```
Can't subclass final classes: class
cert.Beverage class Tea extends Beverage{
1 error
```

In practice, you'll almost never make a final class. A final class obliterates a key benefit of OO—extensibility. So unless you have a serious safety or security issue, assume that someday another programmer will need to extend your class. If you don't, the next programmer forced to maintain your code will hunt you down and <insert really scary thing>.

Abstract Classes An `abstract` class can never be instantiated. Its sole purpose, mission in life, raison d'être, is to be extended (subclassed). (Note, however, that you can compile and execute an `abstract` class, as long as you don't try to make an instance of it.) Why make a class if you can't make objects out of it? Because the class might be just too, well, *abstract*. For example, imagine you have a class `Car` that has generic methods common to all vehicles. But you don't want anyone actually creating a generic, abstract `Car` object. How would they initialize its state? What color would it be? How many seats? Horsepower? All-wheel drive? Or more importantly, how would it behave? In other words, how would the methods be implemented?

No, you need programmers to instantiate actual car types such as `BMWBoxster` and `SubaruOutback`. We'll bet the Boxster owner will tell you his car does things the Subaru can do "only in its dreams." Take a look at the following `abstract` class:

```
abstract class Car {
   private double price;
   private String model;
   private String year;
   public abstract void goFast();
   public abstract void goUpHill();
   public abstract void impressNeighbors();
   // Additional, important, and serious code goes here
}
```

The preceding code will compile fine. However, if you try to instantiate a `Car` in another body of code, you'll get a compiler error something like this:

```
AnotherClass.java:7: class Car is an abstract
class. It can't be instantiated.
      Car x = new Car();
1 error
```

Notice that the methods marked `abstract` end in a semicolon rather than curly braces.

Look for questions with a method declaration that ends with a semicolon, rather than curly braces. If the method is in a class—as opposed to an interface—then both the method and the class must be marked `abstract`. You might get a question that asks how you could fix a code sample that includes a method ending in a semicolon, but without an `abstract` modifier on the class or method. In that case, you could either mark the method and class `abstract` or change the semicolon to code (like a curly brace pair). Remember that if you change a method from `abstract` to nonabstract, don't forget to change the semicolon at the end of the method declaration into a curly brace pair!

We'll look at `abstract` methods in more detail later in this objective, but always remember that if even a single method is `abstract`, the whole class must be declared `abstract`. One `abstract` method spoils the whole bunch. You can, however, put nonabstract methods in an `abstract` class. For example, you might have methods with implementations that shouldn't change from Car type to Car type, such as `getColor()` or `setPrice()`. By putting nonabstract methods in an `abstract` class, you give all concrete subclasses (concrete just means not abstract) inherited method implementations. The good news there is that concrete subclasses get to inherit functionality and need to implement only the methods that define subclass-specific behavior.

(By the way, if you think we misused *raison d'être* earlier, don't send an e-mail. We'd like to see *you* work it into a programmer certification book.)

Coding with `abstract` class types (including interfaces, discussed later in this chapter) lets you take advantage of *polymorphism*, and gives you the greatest degree of flexibility and extensibility. You'll learn more about polymorphism in Chapter 2.

You can't mark a class as both `abstract` and `final`. They have nearly opposite meanings. An `abstract` class must be subclassed, whereas a `final` class must not be subclassed. If you see this combination of `abstract` and `final` modifiers used for a class or method declaration, the code will not compile.

EXERCISE 1-1

Creating an Abstract Superclass and Concrete Subclass

The following exercise will test your knowledge of `public`, default, `final`, and `abstract` classes. Create an `abstract` superclass named `Fruit` and a concrete subclass named `Apple`. The superclass should belong to a package called `food` and the subclass can belong to the default package (meaning it isn't put into a package explicitly). Make the superclass `public` and give the subclass default access.

1. Create the superclass as follows:

```
package food;
public abstract class Fruit{ /* any code you want */}
```

2. Create the subclass in a separate file as follows:

```
import food.Fruit;
class Apple extends Fruit{ /* any code you want */}
```

3. Create a directory called `food` off the directory in your class path setting.
4. Attempt to compile the two files. If you want to use the `Apple` class, make sure you place the `Fruit.class` file in the `food` subdirectory.

CERTIFICATION OBJECTIVE

Use Interfaces (OCA Objective 7.6)

7.6 Use abstract classes and interfaces.

Declaring an Interface

When you create an interface, you're defining a contract for *what* a class can do, without saying anything about *how* the class will do it. An interface is a contract. You could write an interface `Bounceable`, for example, that says in effect, "This is the `Bounceable` interface. Any class type that implements this interface must agree to write the code for the `bounce()` and `setBounceFactor()` methods."

By defining an interface for `Bounceable`, any class that wants to be treated as a `Bounceable` thing can simply implement the `Bounceable` interface and provide code for the interface's two methods.

Interfaces can be implemented by any class, from any inheritance tree. This lets you take radically different classes and give them a common characteristic. For example, you might want both a `Ball` and a `Tire` to have bounce behavior, but `Ball` and `Tire` don't share any inheritance relationship; `Ball` extends `Toy` while `Tire` extends only `java.lang.Object`. But by making both `Ball` and `Tire` implement `Bounceable`, you're saying that `Ball` and `Tire` can be treated as, "Things that can bounce," which in Java translates to, "Things on which you can invoke the `bounce()` and `setBounceFactor()` methods." Figure 1-1 illustrates the relationship between interfaces and classes.

Think of an interface as a 100-percent `abstract` class. Like an `abstract` class, an interface defines abstract methods that take the following form:

```
abstract void bounce();  // Ends with a semicolon rather than
                         // curly braces
```

FIGURE 1-1

The relationship between interfaces and classes

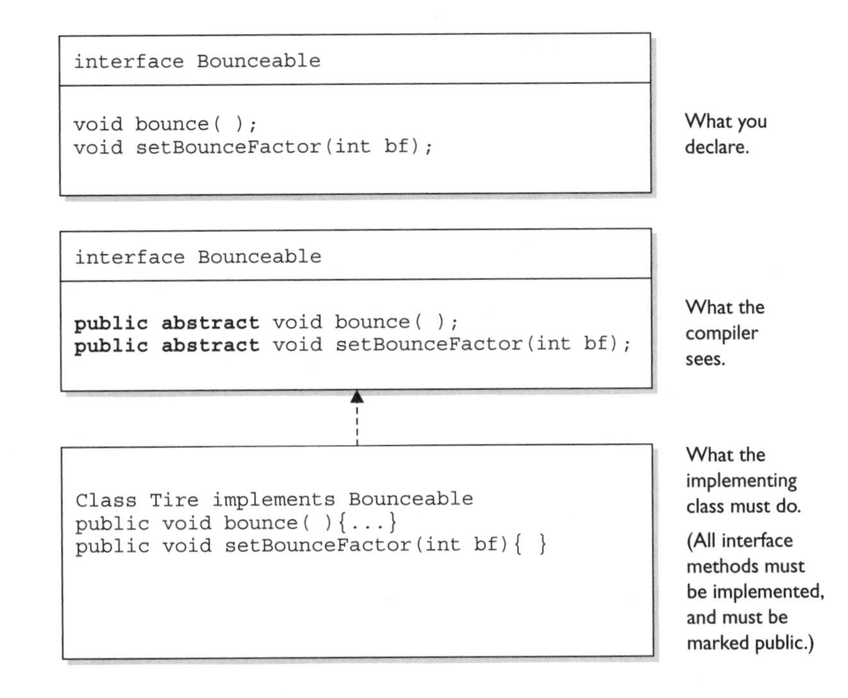
interface Bounceable
void bounce( );
void setBounceFactor(int bf);
What you declare.
interface Bounceable
public abstract void bounce( );
public abstract void setBounceFactor(int bf);
What the compiler sees.
Class Tire implements Bounceable
public void bounce( ){...}
public void setBounceFactor(int bf){ }
What the implementing class must do.
(All interface methods must be implemented, and must be marked public.)

But although an `abstract` class can define both `abstract` and nonabstract methods, an interface can have only `abstract` methods. Another way interfaces differ from `abstract` classes is that interfaces have very little flexibility in how the methods and variables defined in the interface are declared. These rules are strict:

- All interface methods are implicitly `public` and `abstract`. In other words, you do not need to actually type the `public` or `abstract` modifiers in the method declaration, but the method is still always `public` and `abstract`.
- All variables defined in an interface must be `public`, `static`, and `final`— in other words, interfaces can declare only constants, not instance variables.
- Interface methods must not be `static`.
- Because interface methods are abstract, they cannot be marked `final`, `strictfp`, or `native`. (More on these modifiers later in the chapter.)
- An interface can *extend* one or more other interfaces.
- An interface cannot extend anything but another interface.
- An interface cannot implement another interface or class.

- An interface must be declared with the keyword `interface`.
- Interface types can be used polymorphically (see Chapter 2 for more details).

The following is a legal interface declaration:

```
public abstract interface Rollable { }
```

Typing in the `abstract` modifier is considered redundant; interfaces are implicitly abstract whether you type `abstract` or not. You just need to know that both of these declarations are legal and functionally identical:

```
public abstract interface Rollable { }
public interface Rollable { }
```

The `public` modifier is required if you want the interface to have `public` rather than default access.

We've looked at the interface declaration, but now we'll look closely at the methods within an interface:

```
public interface Bounceable {
    public abstract void bounce();
    public abstract void setBounceFactor(int bf);
}
```

Typing in the `public` and `abstract` modifiers on the methods is redundant, though, since all interface methods are implicitly `public` and `abstract`. Given that rule, you can see that the following code is exactly equivalent to the preceding interface:

```
public interface Bounceable {
      void bounce();                   // No modifiers
      void setBounceFactor(int bf);    // No modifiers
}
```

You must remember that all interface methods are `public` and `abstract` regardless of what you see in the interface definition.

Look for interface methods declared with any combination of `public`, `abstract`, or no modifiers. For example, the following five method declarations, if declared within their own interfaces, are legal and identical!

```
void bounce();
public void bounce();
abstract void bounce();
public abstract void bounce();
abstract public void bounce();
```

The following interface method declarations won't compile:

```
final void bounce();          // final and abstract can never be used
                              // together, and abstract is implied
static void bounce();         // interfaces define instance methods
private void bounce();        // interface methods are always public
protected void bounce();      // (same as above)
```

Declaring Interface Constants

You're allowed to put constants in an interface. By doing so, you guarantee that any class implementing the interface will have access to the same constant. By placing the constants right in the interface, any class that implements the interface has direct access to the constants, just as if the class had inherited them.

You need to remember one key rule for interface constants. They must always be

```
public static final
```

So that sounds simple, right? After all, interface constants are no different from any other publicly accessible constants, so they obviously must be declared `public`, `static`, and `final`. But before you breeze past the rest of this discussion, think about the implications: **Because interface constants are defined in an interface, they don't have to be *declared* as `public`, `static`, or `final`. They must be `public`, `static`, and `final`, but you don't actually have to declare them that way.** Just as interface methods are always `public` and `abstract` whether you say so in the code or not, any variable defined in an interface must be—and implicitly is—a `public` constant. See if you can spot the problem with the following code (assume two separate files):

```
interface Foo {
  int BAR = 42;
  void go();
}

class Zap implements Foo {
  public void go() {
     BAR = 27;
  }
}
```

You can't change the value of a constant! Once the value has been assigned, the value can never be modified. The assignment happens in the interface itself (where the constant is declared), so the implementing class can access it and use it, but as a read-only value. So the `BAR = 27` assignment will not compile.

exam watch

Look for interface definitions that define constants, but without explicitly using the required modifiers. For example, the following are all identical:

```
public int x = 1;                  // Looks non-static and non-final,
                                   // but isn't!
int x = 1;                         // Looks default, non-final,
                                   // non-static, but isn't!
static int x = 1;                  // Doesn't show final or public
final int x = 1;                   // Doesn't show static or public
public static int x = 1;           // Doesn't show final
public final int x = 1;            // Doesn't show static
static final int x = 1             // Doesn't show public
public static final int x = 1;     // what you get implicitly
```

Any combination of the required (but implicit) modifiers is legal, as is using no modifiers at all! On the exam, you can expect to see questions you won't be able to answer correctly unless you know, for example, that an interface variable is `final` and can never be given a value by the implementing (or any other) class.

CERTIFICATION OBJECTIVE

Declare Class Members (OCA Objectives 2.1, 2.2, 2.3, 2.4, 2.5, 4.1, 4.2, 6.2, and 6.6)

2.1 *Declare and initialize variables.*

2.2 *Differentiate between object reference variables and primitive variables.*

2.3 *Read or write to object fields.*

2.4 *Explain an object's lifecycle.*

2.5 *Call methods on objects.*

4.1 *Declare, instantiate, initialize, and use a one-dimensional array.*

4.2 *Declare, instantiate, initialize, and use a multidimensional array.*

6.2 *Apply the static keyword to methods and fields.*

6.6 *Apply access modifiers.*

We've looked at what it means to use a modifier in a class declaration, and now we'll look at what it means to modify a method or variable declaration.

Methods and instance (nonlocal) variables are collectively known as *members*. You can modify a member with both access and nonaccess modifiers, and you have more modifiers to choose from (and combine) than when you're declaring a class.

Access Modifiers

Because method and variable members are usually given access control in exactly the same way, we'll cover both in this section.

Whereas a *class* can use just two of the four access control levels (default or `public`), members can use all four:

- `public`
- `protected`
- default
- `private`

Default protection is what you get when you don't type an access modifier in the member declaration. The default and `protected` access control types have almost identical behavior, except for one difference that we will mentioned later.

It's crucial that you know access control inside and out for the exam. There will be quite a few questions with access control playing a role. Some questions test several concepts of access control at the same time, so not knowing one small part of access control could mean you blow an entire question.

What does it mean for code in one class to have access to a member of another class? For now, ignore any differences between methods and variables. If class A has access to a member of class B, it means that class B's member is visible to class A. When a class does not have access to another member, the compiler will slap you for trying to access something that you're not even supposed to know exists!

You need to understand two different access issues:

- Whether method code in one class can *access* a member of another class
- Whether a subclass can *inherit* a member of its superclass

The first type of access occurs when a method in one class tries to access a method or a variable of another class, using the dot operator (.) to invoke a method or retrieve a variable. For example:

```
class Zoo {
  public String coolMethod() {
    return "Wow  baby";
  }
}
class Moo {
  public void useAZoo() {
    Zoo z = new Zoo();
    // If the preceding line compiles Moo has access
    // to the Zoo class
    // But... does it have access to the coolMethod()?
    System.out.println("A Zoo says, " + z.coolMethod());
    // The preceding line works because Moo can access the
    // public method
  }
}
```

The second type of access revolves around which, if any, members of a superclass a subclass can access through inheritance. We're not looking at whether the subclass can, say, invoke a method on an instance of the superclass (which would just be an example of the first type of access). Instead, we're looking at whether the subclass *inherits* a member of its superclass. Remember, if a subclass *inherits* a member, it's exactly as if the subclass actually declared the member itself. In other words, if a subclass *inherits* a member, the subclass *has* the member. Here's an example:

```
class Zoo {
  public String coolMethod() {
    return "Wow  baby";
 }
}
class Moo extends Zoo {
  public void useMyCoolMethod() {
    // Does an instance of Moo inherit the coolMethod()?
    System.out.println("Moo says, " + this.coolMethod());
    // The preceding line works because Moo can inherit the
    // public method
    // Can an instance of Moo invoke coolMethod() on an
    // instance of Zoo?
```

```
      Zoo z = new Zoo();
      System.out.println("Zoo says, " + z.coolMethod());
      // coolMethod() is public, so Moo can invoke it on a Zoo
      // reference
    }
  }
```

Figure 1-2 compares a class inheriting a member of another class and accessing a member of another class using a reference of an instance of that class.

Much of access control (both types) centers on whether the two classes involved are in the same or different packages. Don't forget, though, that if class A *itself* can't be accessed by class B, then no members within class A can be accessed by class B.

You need to know the effect of different combinations of class and member access (such as a default class with a `public` variable). To figure this out, first look at the access level of the class. If the class itself will not be visible to another class, then none of the members will be visible either, even if the member is declared `public`. Once you've confirmed that the class is visible, then it makes sense to look at access levels on individual members.

Public Members

When a method or variable member is declared `public`, it means all other classes, regardless of the package they belong to, can access the member (assuming the class itself is visible).

Look at the following source file:

```
package book;
import cert.*;  // Import all classes in the cert package
class Goo {
  public static void main(String[] args) {
    Sludge o = new Sludge();
    o.testIt();
  }
}
```

Now look at the second file:

```
package cert;
public class Sludge {
  public void testIt() { System.out.println("sludge"); }
}
```

As you can see, `Goo` and `Sludge` are in different packages. However, `Goo` can invoke the method in `Sludge` without problems, because both the `Sludge` class and its `testIt()` method are marked `public`.

FIGURE 1-2

Comparison of inheritance vs. dot operator for member access

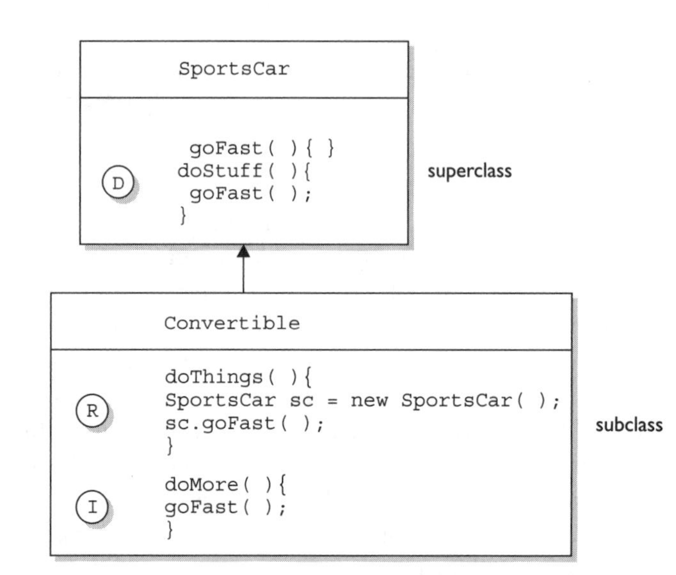

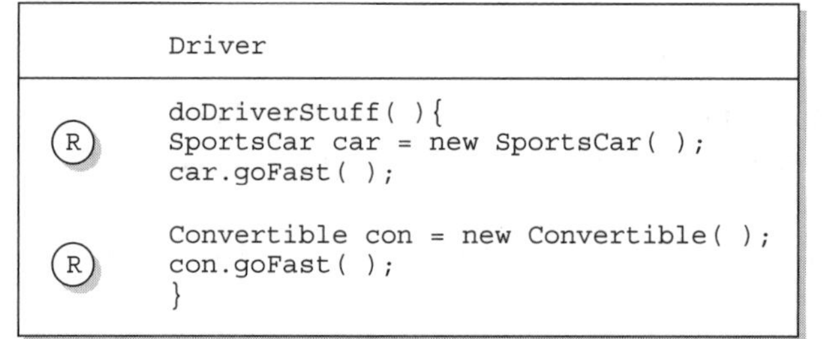

Three ways to access a method:

(D) Invoking a method declared in the same class

(R) Invoking a method using a reference of the class

(I) Invoking an inherited method

For a subclass, if a member of its superclass is declared `public`, the subclass inherits that member regardless of whether both classes are in the same package:

```
package cert;
public class Roo {
  public String doRooThings() {
    // imagine the fun code that goes here
    return "fun";
  }
}
```

The Roo class declares the doRooThings() member as public. So if we make a subclass of Roo, any code in that Roo subclass can call its own inherited doRooThings() method.

Notice in the following code that the doRooThings() method is invoked without having to preface it with a reference:

```
package notcert;    // Not the package Roo is in
import cert.Roo;
class Cloo extends Roo {
  public void testCloo() {
    System.out.println(doRooThings());
  }
}
```

Remember, if you see a method invoked (or a variable accessed) without the dot operator (.), it means the method or variable belongs to the class where you see that code. It also means that the method or variable is implicitly being accessed using the this reference. So in the preceding code, the call to doRooThings() in the Cloo class could also have been written as this.doRooThings(). The reference this always refers to the currently executing object—in other words, the object running the code where you see the this reference. Because the this reference is implicit, you don't need to preface your member access code with it, but it won't hurt. Some programmers include it to make the code easier to read for new (or non) Java programmers.

Besides being able to invoke the doRooThings() method on itself, code from some other class can call doRooThings() on a Cloo instance, as in the following:

```
class Toon {
  public static void main(String[] args) {
    Cloo c = new Cloo();
    System.out.println(c.doRooThings()); // No problem; method
                                         // is public
  }
}
```

Private Members

Members marked private can't be accessed by code in any class other than the class in which the private member was declared. Let's make a small change to the Roo class from an earlier example:

```
package cert;
public class Roo {
  private String doRooThings() {
    // imagine the fun code that goes here, but only the Roo
    // class knows
```

```
    return "fun";
  }
}
```

The `doRooThings()` method is now `private`, so no other class can use it. If we try to invoke the method from any other class, we'll run into trouble:

```
package notcert;
import cert.Roo;
class  UseARoo {
  public void testIt() {
    Roo r = new Roo(); //So far so good; class Roo is public
    System.out.println(r.doRooThings()); // Compiler error!
  }
}
```

If we try to compile `UseARoo`, we get a compiler error something like this:

```
cannot find symbol
symbol  : method doRooThings()
```

It's as if the method `doRooThings()` doesn't exist, and as far as any code outside of the `Roo` class is concerned, this is true. A `private` member is invisible to any code outside the member's own class.

What about a subclass that tries to inherit a `private` member of its superclass? When a member is declared `private`, a subclass can't inherit it. For the exam, you need to recognize that a subclass can't see, use, or even think about the `private` members of its superclass. You can, however, declare a matching method in the subclass. But regardless of how it looks, ***it is not an overriding method!*** It is simply a method that happens to have the same name as a `private` method (which you're not supposed to know about) in the superclass. The rules of overriding do not apply, so you can make this newly-declared-but-just-happens-to-match method declare new exceptions, or change the return type, or do anything else you want it to do.

```
package cert;
public class Roo {
   private String doRooThings() {
    // imagine the fun code that goes here, but no other class
    // will know
    return "fun";
   }
}
```

The doRooThings() method is now off limits to all subclasses, even those in the same package as the superclass:

```
package cert;                          // Cloo and Roo are in the same package
class  Cloo extends Roo {              // Still OK, superclass Roo is public
  public void testCloo() {
    System.out.println(doRooThings()); // Compiler error!
  }
}
```

If we try to compile the subclass Cloo, the compiler is delighted to spit out an error something like this:

```
%javac Cloo.java
Cloo.java:4: Undefined method: doRooThings()
      System.out.println(doRooThings());
1 error
```

Can a private method be overridden by a subclass? That's an interesting question, but the answer is technically no. Since the subclass, as we've seen, cannot inherit a private method, it therefore cannot override the method—overriding depends on inheritance. We'll cover the implications of this in more detail a little later in this section as well as in Chapter 2, but for now just remember that a method marked private cannot be overridden. Figure 1-3 illustrates the effects of the public and private modifiers on classes from the same or different packages.

Protected and Default Members

The protected and default access control levels are almost identical, but with one critical difference. A *default* member may be accessed only if the class accessing the member belongs to the same package, whereas a protected member can be accessed (through inheritance) by a subclass ***even if the subclass is in a different package.*** Take a look at the following two classes:

```
package certification;
public class OtherClass {
  void testIt() {   // No modifier means method has default
                    // access
    System.out.println("OtherClass");
  }
}
```

FIGURE 1-3

Effects of `public` and `private` access

The effect of private access control

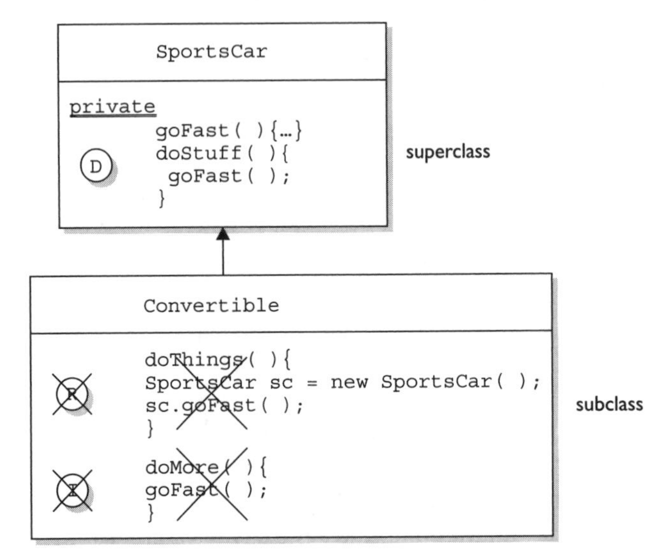

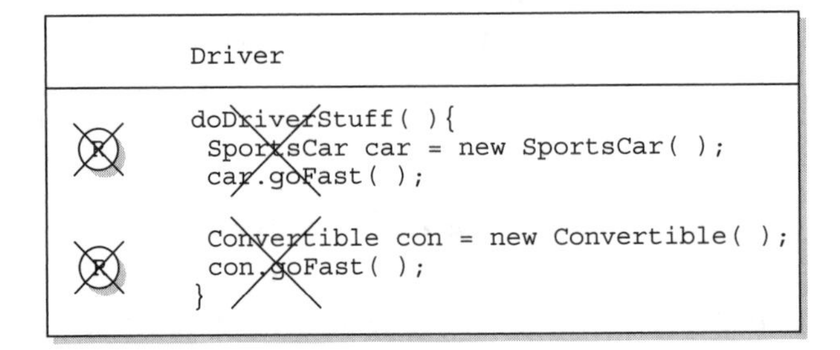

Three ways to access a method:

(D) Invoking a method declared in the same class

(R) Invoking a method using a reference of the class

(I) Invoking an inherited method

In another source code file you have the following:

```
package somethingElse;
import certification.OtherClass;
class AccessClass {
  static public void main(String[] args) {
    OtherClass o = new OtherClass();
    o.testIt();
  }
}
```

As you can see, the `testIt()` method in the first file has *default* (think *package-level*) access. Notice also that class `OtherClass` is in a different package from the `AccessClass`. Will `AccessClass` be able to use the method `testIt()`? Will it cause a compiler error? Will Daniel ever marry Francesca? Stay tuned.

```
No method matching testIt() found in class
certification.OtherClass.    o.testIt();
```

From the preceding results, you can see that `AccessClass` can't use the `OtherClass` method `testIt()` because `testIt()` has default access and `AccessClass` is not in the same package as `OtherClass`. So `AccessClass` can't see it, the compiler complains, and we have no idea who Daniel and Francesca are.

Default and protected behavior differ only when we talk about subclasses. If the `protected` keyword is used to define a member, any subclass of the class declaring the member can access it *through inheritance*. It doesn't matter if the superclass and subclass are in different packages; the `protected` superclass member is still visible to the subclass (although visible only in a very specific way as we'll see a little later). This is in contrast to the default behavior, which doesn't allow a subclass to access a superclass member unless the subclass is in the same package as the superclass.

Whereas default access doesn't extend any special consideration to subclasses (you're either in the package or you're not), the `protected` modifier respects the parent-child relationship, even when the child class moves away (and joins a new package). So when you think of *default* access, think *package* restriction. No exceptions. But when you think `protected`, think *package + kids*. A class with a `protected` member is marking that member as having package-level access for all classes, but with a special exception for subclasses outside the package.

But what does it mean for a subclass-outside-the-package to have access to a superclass (parent) member? It means the subclass inherits the member. It does not, however, mean the subclass-outside-the-package can access the member using a reference to an instance of the superclass. In other words, `protected` = inheritance. `Protected` does not mean that the subclass can treat the `protected` superclass member as though it were public. So if the subclass-outside-the-package gets a reference to the superclass (by, for example, creating an instance of the superclass somewhere in the subclass' code), the subclass cannot use the dot operator on the superclass reference to access the `protected` member. To a subclass-outside-the-package, a `protected` member might as well be default (or even `private`), when the subclass is using a reference to the superclass. **The subclass can see the `protected` member only through inheritance.**

Are you confused? Hang in there and it will all become clearer with the next batch of code examples.

Protected Details

Let's take a look at a `protected` instance variable (remember, an instance variable is a member) of a superclass.

```
package certification;
public class Parent {
   protected int x = 9; // protected access
}
```

The preceding code declares the variable `x` as `protected`. This makes the variable *accessible* to all other classes *inside* the certification package, as well as *inheritable* by any subclasses *outside* the package.

Now let's create a subclass in a different package, and attempt to use the variable `x` (that the subclass inherits):

```
package other;                              // Different package
import certification.Parent;
class Child extends Parent {
   public void testIt() {
      System.out.println("x is " + x); // No problem; Child
                                        // inherits x
   }
}
```

The preceding code compiles fine. Notice, though, that the `Child` class is accessing the `protected` variable through inheritance. Remember that any time we talk about a subclass having access to a superclass member, we could be talking about the subclass inheriting the member, not simply accessing the member through a reference to an instance of the superclass (the way any other nonsubclass would access it). Watch what happens if the subclass `Child` (outside the superclass' package) tries to access a `protected` variable using a `Parent` class reference:

```
package other;
import certification.Parent;
class Child extends Parent {
   public void testIt() {
      System.out.println("x is " + x);             // No problem; Child
                                                   // inherits x
      Parent p = new Parent();                     // Can we access x using
                                                   // the p reference?
      System.out.println("X in parent is " + p.x); // Compiler error!
   }
}
```

The compiler is more than happy to show us the problem:

```
%javac -d . other/Child.java
other/Child.java:9: x has protected access in certification.Parent
System.out.println("X in parent is " + p.x);
                                        ^
1 error
```

So far, we've established that a `protected` member has essentially package-level or default access to all classes except for subclasses. We've seen that subclasses outside the package can inherit a `protected` member. Finally, we've seen that subclasses outside the package can't use a superclass reference to access a protected member. ***For a subclass outside the package, the protected member can be accessed only through inheritance.***

But there's still one more issue we haven't looked at: What does a `protected` member look like to other classes trying to use the subclass-outside-the-package to get to the subclass' inherited `protected` superclass member? For example, using our previous `Parent/Child` classes, what happens if some other class—`Neighbor`, say—in the same package as the `Child` (subclass), has a reference to a `Child` instance and wants to access the member variable `x` ? In other words, how does that `protected` member behave once the subclass has inherited it? Does it maintain its `protected` status, such that classes in the `Child`'s package can see it?

No! Once the subclass-outside-the-package inherits the `protected` member, that member (as inherited by the subclass) becomes private to any code outside the subclass, with the exception of subclasses of the subclass. So if class `Neighbor` instantiates a `Child` object, then even if class `Neighbor` is in the same package as class `Child`, class `Neighbor` won't have access to the `Child`'s inherited (but `protected`) variable `x`. Figure 1-4 illustrates the effect of `protected` access on classes and subclasses in the same or different packages.

Whew! That wraps up `protected`, the most misunderstood modifier in Java. Again, it's used only in very special cases, but you can count on it showing up on the exam. Now that we've covered the `protected` modifier, we'll switch to default member access, a piece of cake compared to `protected`.

Default Details

Let's start with the default behavior of a member in a superclass. We'll modify the `Parent`'s member `x` to make it default.

```
package certification;
public class Parent {
  int x = 9; // No access modifier, means default
             // (package) access
}
```

FIGURE 1-4

Effects of `protected` access

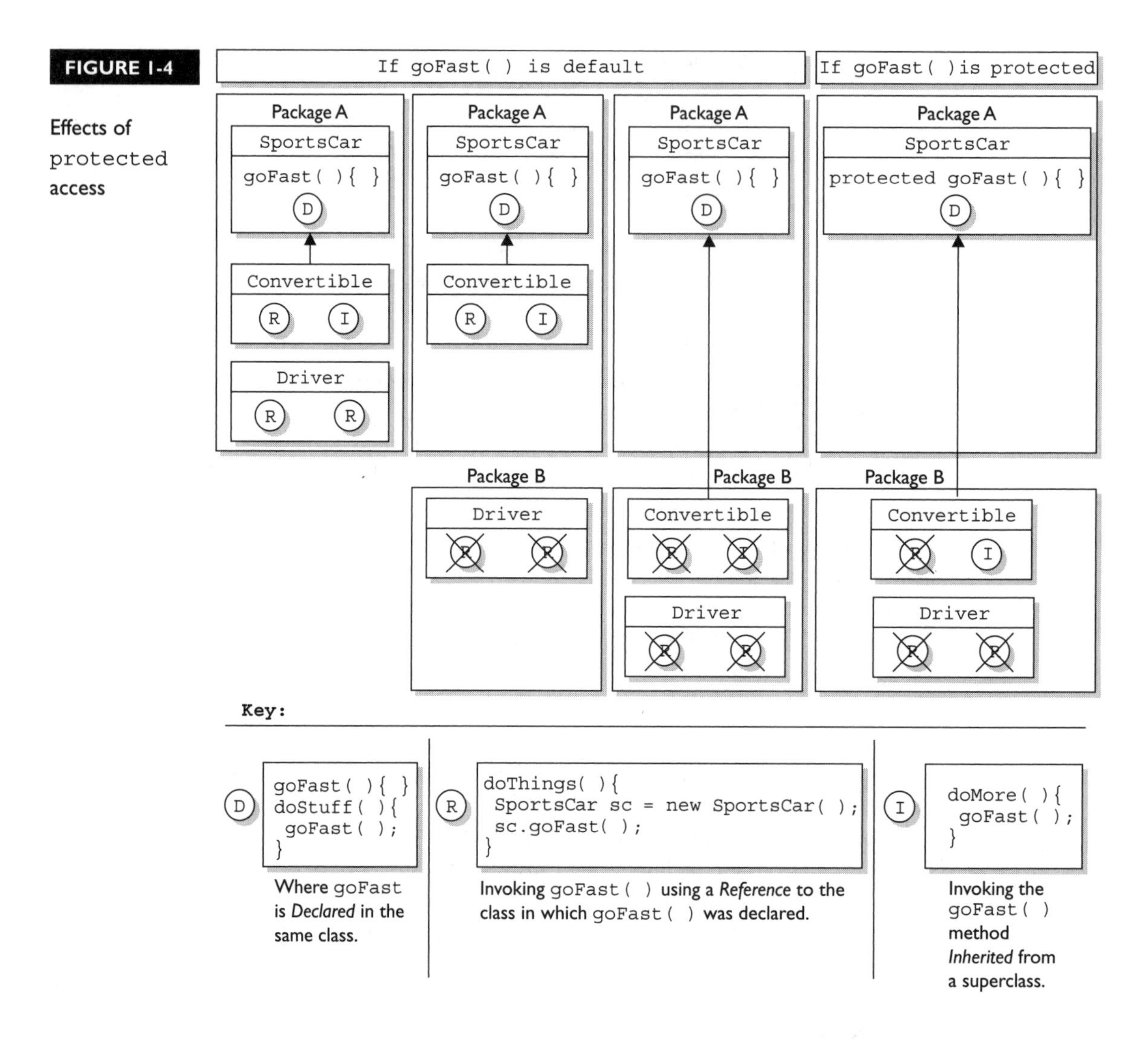

Notice we didn't place an access modifier in front of the variable `x`. Remember that if you don't type an access modifier before a class or member declaration, the access control is default, which means package level. We'll now attempt to access the default member from the `Child` class that we saw earlier.

When we try to compile the `Child.java` file, we get an error something like this:

```
Child.java:4: Undefined variable: x
      System.out.println("Variable x is " + x);
1 error
```

The compiler gives the same error as when a member is declared as `private`. The subclass `Child` (in a different package from the superclass `Parent`) can't see or use the default superclass member `x` ! Now, what about default access for two classes in the same package?

```
package certification;
public class Parent{
  int x = 9; // default access
}
```

And in the second class you have the following:

```
package certification;
class Child extends Parent{
  static public void main(String[] args) {
    Child sc = new Child();
    sc.testIt();
  }
  public void testIt() {
    System.out.println("Variable x is " + x); // No problem;
  }
}
```

The preceding source file compiles fine, and the class `Child` runs and displays the value of `x`. Just remember that default members are visible to subclasses only if those subclasses are in the same package as the superclass.

Local Variables and Access Modifiers

Can access modifiers be applied to local variables? NO!

There is never a case where an access modifier can be applied to a local variable, so watch out for code like the following:

```
class Foo {
  void doStuff() {
    private int x = 7;
    this.doMore(x);
  }
}
```

You can be certain that any local variable declared with an access modifier will not compile. In fact, there is only one modifier that can ever be applied to local variables—`final`.

That about does it for our discussion on member access modifiers. Table 1-2 shows all the combinations of access and visibility; you really should spend some time with it. Next, we're going to dig into the other (nonaccess) modifiers that you can apply to member declarations.

TABLE 1-2 Determining Access to Class Members

Visibility	Public	Protected	*Default*	Private
From the same class	Yes	Yes	Yes	Yes
From any class in the same package	Yes	Yes	Yes	No
From a subclass in the same package	Yes	Yes	Yes	No
From a subclass outside the same package	Yes	Yes, *through inheritance*	No	No
From any nonsubclass class outside the package	Yes	No	No	No

Nonaccess Member Modifiers

We've discussed member access, which refers to whether code from one class can invoke a method (or access an instance variable) from another class. That still leaves a boatload of other modifiers you can use on member declarations. Two you're already familiar with—`final` and `abstract`—because we applied them to class declarations earlier in this chapter. But we still have to take a quick look at `transient`, `synchronized`, `native`, `strictfp`, and then a long look at the Big One—`static`.

We'll look first at modifiers applied to methods, followed by a look at modifiers applied to instance variables. We'll wrap up this section with a look at how `static` works when applied to variables and methods.

Final Methods

The `final` keyword prevents a method from being overridden in a subclass, and is often used to enforce the API functionality of a method. For example, the `Thread` class has a method called `isAlive()` that checks whether a thread is still active. If you extend the `Thread` class, though, there is really no way that you can correctly implement this method yourself (it uses native code, for one thing), so the designers have made it `final`. Just as you can't subclass the `String` class (because we need to be able to trust in the behavior of a String object), you can't override many of the methods in the core class libraries. This can't-be-overridden restriction provides for safety and security, but you should use it with great caution. Preventing a subclass from overriding a method stifles many of the benefits of OO including extensibility through polymorphism. A typical `final` method declaration looks like this:

```
class SuperClass{
  public final void showSample() {
    System.out.println("One thing.");
  }
}
```

It's legal to extend `SuperClass`, since the *class* isn't marked `final`, but we can't override the `final` *method* `showSample()`, as the following code attempts to do:

```
class SubClass extends SuperClass{
  public void showSample() { // Try to override the final
                             // superclass method
    System.out.println("Another thing.");
  }
}
```

Attempting to compile the preceding code gives us something like this:

```
%javac FinalTest.java
FinalTest.java:5: The method void showSample() declared in class
SubClass cannot override the final method of the same signature
declared in class SuperClass.
Final methods cannot be overridden.
     public void showSample() { }
1 error
```

Final Arguments

Method arguments are the variable declarations that appear in between the parentheses in a method declaration. A typical method declaration with multiple arguments looks like this:

```
public Record getRecord(int fileNumber, int recNumber) {}
```

Method arguments are essentially the same as local variables. In the preceding example, the variables `fileNumber` and `recNumber` will both follow all the rules applied to local variables. This means they can also have the modifier `final`:

```
public Record getRecord(int fileNumber, final int recNumber) {}
```

In this example, the variable `recNumber` is declared as `final`, which of course means it can't be modified within the method. In this case, "modified" means reassigning a new value to the variable. In other words, a `final` argument must keep the same value that the parameter had when it was passed into the method.

Abstract Methods

An `abstract` method is a method that's been *declared* (as `abstract`) but not *implemented*. In other words, the method contains no functional code. And if you recall from the earlier section "Abstract Classes," an `abstract` method declaration doesn't even have curly braces for where the implementation code goes, but instead closes with a semicolon. In other words, *it has no method body*. You mark a method `abstract` when you want to force subclasses to provide the implementation. For example, if you write an abstract class Car with a method goUpHill(), you might want to force each subtype of Car to define its own goUpHill() behavior, specific to that particular type of car.

```
public abstract void showSample();
```

Notice that the abstract method ends with a semicolon instead of curly braces. **It is illegal to have even a single abstract method in a class that is not explicitly declared abstract!** Look at the following illegal class:

```
public class IllegalClass{
  public abstract void doIt();
}
```

The preceding class will produce the following error if you try to compile it:

```
IllegalClass.java:1: class IllegalClass must be declared
abstract.
It does not define void doIt() from class IllegalClass.
public class IllegalClass{
1 error
```

You can, however, have an abstract class with no abstract methods. The following example will compile fine:

```
public abstract class LegalClass{
   void goodMethod() {
      // lots of real implementation code here
   }
 }
```

In the preceding example, goodMethod() is not abstract. Three different clues tell you it's not an abstract method:

- The method is not marked abstract.
- The method declaration includes curly braces, as opposed to ending in a semicolon. In other words, the method has a method body.
- The method **might** provide actual implementation code inside the curly braces.

Any class that extends an abstract class must implement all abstract methods of the superclass, unless the subclass is *also* abstract. The rule is this:

The first concrete subclass of an abstract class must implement *all* abstract methods of the superclass.

Concrete just means nonabstract, so if you have an abstract class extending another abstract class, the abstract subclass doesn't need to provide implementations for the inherited abstract methods. Sooner or later, though, somebody's going to make a nonabstract subclass (in other words, a class that can be instantiated), and that subclass will have to implement all the abstract methods from up the inheritance tree. The following example demonstrates an inheritance tree with two abstract classes and one concrete class:

```
public abstract class Vehicle {
  private String type;
  public abstract void goUpHill();  // Abstract method
  public String getType() {         // Non-abstract method
    return type;
  }
}

public abstract class Car extends Vehicle {
  public abstract void goUpHill();  // Still abstract
  public void doCarThings() {
    // special car code goes here
  }
}

public class Mini extends Car {
  public void goUpHill() {
    // Mini-specific going uphill code
  }
}
```

So how many methods does class Mini have? Three. It inherits both the getType() and doCarThings() methods, because they're public and concrete (nonabstract). But because goUpHill() is abstract in the superclass Vehicle, and is never implemented in the Car class (so it remains abstract), it means class Mini—as the first concrete class below Vehicle—must implement the goUpHill() method. In other words, class Mini can't pass the buck (of abstract method implementation) to the next class down the inheritance tree, but class Car can, since Car, like Vehicle, is abstract. Figure 1-5 illustrates the effects of the abstract modifier on concrete and abstract subclasses.

Look for concrete classes that don't provide method implementations for abstract methods of the superclass. The following code won't compile:

```
public abstract class A {
  abstract void foo();
}
class B extends A {
  void foo(int I) { }
}
```

FIGURE 1-5 The effects of the `abstract` modifier on concrete and `abstract` subclasses

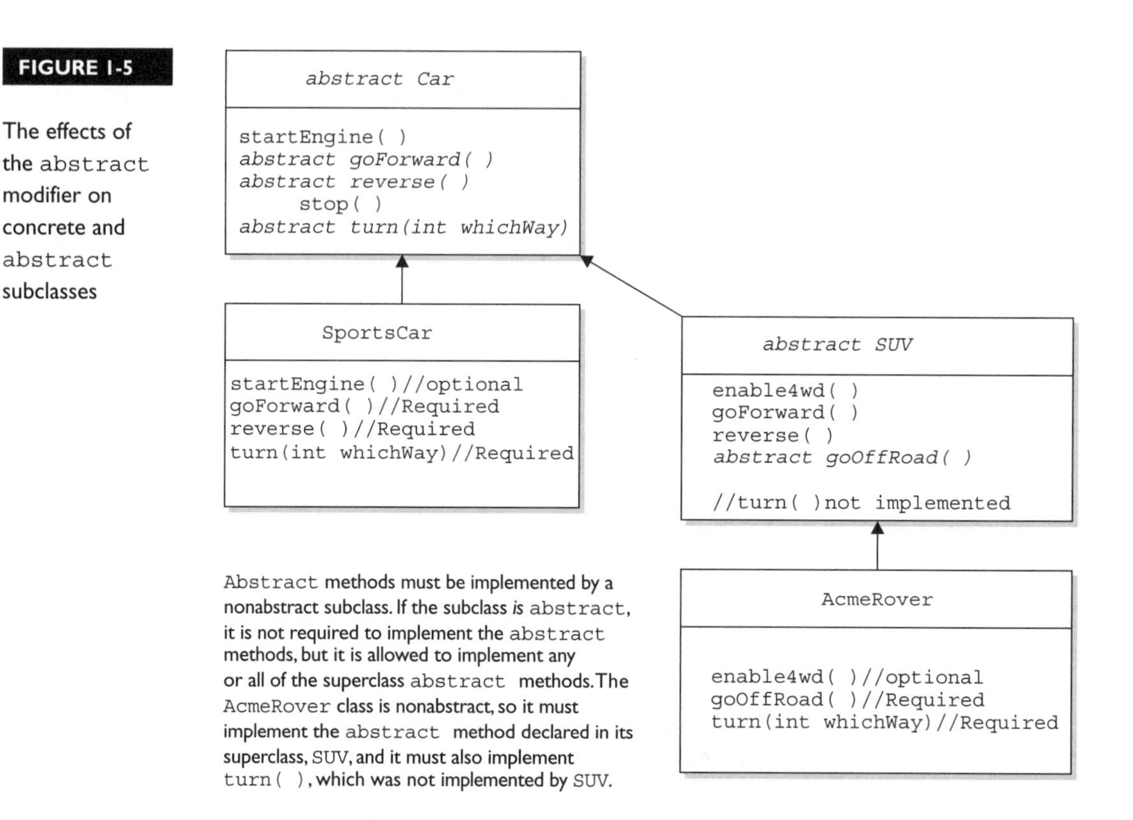

Class B won't compile because it doesn't implement the inherited `abstract` method `foo()`. Although the `foo(int I)` method in class B might appear to be an implementation of the superclass' `abstract` method, it is simply an overloaded method (a method using the same identifier, but different arguments), so it doesn't fulfill the requirements for implementing the superclass' `abstract` method. We'll look at the differences between overloading and overriding in detail in Chapter 2.

A method can never, ever, ever be marked as both `abstract` and `final`, or both `abstract` and `private`. Think about it—`abstract` methods must be implemented (which essentially means overridden by a subclass) whereas `final` and `private` methods cannot ever be overridden by a subclass. Or to phrase it another way, an `abstract` designation means the superclass doesn't know anything about how the subclasses should behave in that method, whereas a `final` designation means the superclass knows everything about how all subclasses (however far down the inheritance tree they may be) should behave in that method. The `abstract` and `final` modifiers are virtually opposites. Because `private` methods cannot even be seen by a subclass (let alone inherited), they, too, cannot be overridden, so they, too, cannot be marked `abstract`.

Finally, you need to know that—for top-level classes—the `abstract` modifier can never be combined with the `static` modifier. We'll cover `static` methods later in this objective, but for now just remember that the following would be illegal:

```
abstract static void doStuff();
```

And it would give you an error that should be familiar by now:

```
MyClass.java:2: illegal combination of modifiers: abstract and static
  abstract static void doStuff();
```

Synchronized Methods

The `synchronized` keyword indicates that a method can be accessed by only one thread at a time. We'll discuss this nearly to death in Chapter 13, but for now all we're concerned with is knowing that the `synchronized` modifier can be applied only to methods—not variables, not classes, just methods. A typical `synchronized` declaration looks like this:

```
public synchronized Record retrieveUserInfo(int id) { }
```

You should also know that the `synchronized` modifier can be matched with any of the four access control levels (which means it can be paired with any of the three access modifier keywords).

Native Methods

The `native` modifier indicates that a method is implemented in platform-dependent code, often in C. You don't need to know how to use `native` methods for the exam, other than knowing that `native` is a modifier (thus a reserved keyword) and that `native` can be applied only to *methods*—not classes, not variables, just methods. Note that a `native` method's body must be a semicolon (`;`) (like `abstract` methods), indicating that the implementation is omitted.

Strictfp Methods

We looked earlier at using `strictfp` as a class modifier, but even if you don't declare a class as `strictfp`, you can still declare an individual method as `strictfp`. Remember, `strictfp` forces floating points (and any floating-point operations) to adhere to the IEEE 754 standard. With `strictfp`, you can predict how your floating points will behave regardless of the underlying platform the JVM is running on. The downside is that if the underlying platform is capable of supporting greater precision, a `strictfp` method won't be able to take advantage of it.

You'll want to study the IEEE 754 if you need something to help you fall asleep. For the exam, however, you don't need to know anything about `strictfp` other than what it's used for, that it can modify a class or method declaration, and that a variable can never be declared `strictfp`.

Methods with Variable Argument Lists (var-args) (For OCP Candidates Only)

As of Java 5, Java allows you to create methods that can take a variable number of arguments. Depending on where you look, you might hear this capability referred to as "variable-length argument lists," "variable arguments," "var-args," "varargs," or our personal favorite (from the department of obfuscation), "variable arity parameters." They're all the same thing, and we'll use the term "var-args" from here on out.

As a bit of background, we'd like to clarify how we're going to use the terms "argument" and "parameter" throughout this book.

- **arguments** The things you specify between the parentheses when you're *invoking* a method:

```
doStuff("a", 2);   // invoking doStuff, so "a" & 2 are
                   // arguments
```

- **parameters** The things in the *method's signature* that indicate what the method must receive when it's invoked:

```
void doStuff(String s, int a) { }   // we're expecting two
                                    // parameters:
                                    // String and int
```

We'll cover using var-arg methods more in the next few chapters; for now let's review the declaration rules for var-args:

- **Var-arg type** When you declare a var-arg parameter, you must specify the type of the argument(s) this parameter of your method can receive. (This can be a primitive type or an object type.)
- **Basic syntax** To declare a method using a var-arg parameter, you follow the type with an ellipsis (...), a space, and then the name of the array that will hold the parameters received.
- **Other parameters** It's legal to have other parameters in a method that uses a var-arg.

- **Var-arg limits** The var-arg must be the last parameter in the method's signature, and you can have only one var-arg in a method.

Let's look at some legal and illegal var-arg declarations:
Legal:

```
void doStuff(int... x) { }              // expects from 0 to many ints
                                        // as parameters
void doStuff2(char c, int... x)  { }    // expects first a char,
                                        // then 0 to many ints
void doStuff3(Animal... animal) { }     // 0 to many Animals
```

Illegal:

```
void doStuff4(int x...) { }             // bad syntax
void doStuff5(int... x, char... y) { }  // too many var-args
void doStuff6(String... s, byte b) { }  // var-arg must be last
```

Constructor Declarations

In Java, objects are constructed. Every time you make a new object, at least one constructor is invoked. Every class has a constructor, although if you don't create one explicitly, the compiler will build one for you. There are tons of rules concerning constructors, and we're saving our detailed discussion for Chapter 2. For now, let's focus on the basic declaration rules. Here's a simple example:

```
class Foo {
  protected Foo() { }          // this is Foo's constructor
  protected void Foo() { }     // this is a badly named, but legal, method
}
```

The first thing to notice is that constructors look an awful lot like methods. A key difference is that a constructor can't ever, ever, ever, have a return type…ever! Constructor declarations can however have all of the normal access modifiers, and they can take arguments (including var-args), just like methods. The other BIG RULE to understand about constructors is that they must have the same name as the class in which they are declared. Constructors can't be marked `static` (they are after all associated with object instantiation), and they can't be marked `final` or `abstract` (because they can't be overridden). Here are some legal and illegal constructor declarations:

```
class Foo2 {
  // legal constructors
  Foo2() { }
  private Foo2(byte b) { }
  Foo2(int x) { }
```

```
  Foo2(int x, int... y) { }
  // illegal constructors
  void Foo2() { }              // it's a method, not a constructor
  Foo() { }                    // not a method or a constructor
  Foo2(short s);               // looks like an abstract method
  static Foo2(float f) { }     // can't be static
  final Foo2(long x) { }       // can't be final
  abstract Foo2(char c) { }    // can't be abstract
  Foo2(int... x, int t) { }    // bad var-arg syntax
}
```

Variable Declarations

There are two types of variables in Java:

- **Primitives** A primitive can be one of eight types: `char`, `boolean`, `byte`, `short`, `int`, `long`, `double`, or `float`. Once a primitive has been declared, its primitive type can never change, although in most cases its value can change.
- **Reference variables** A reference variable is used to refer to (or access) an object. A reference variable is declared to be of a specific type, and that type can never be changed. A reference variable can be used to refer to any object of the declared type or of a *subtype* of the declared type (a compatible type). We'll talk a lot more about using a reference variable to refer to a subtype in Chapter 2, when we discuss polymorphism.

Declaring Primitives and Primitive Ranges

Primitive variables can be declared as class variables (statics), instance variables, method parameters, or local variables. You can declare one or more primitives, of the same primitive type, in a single line. In Chapter 3 we will discuss the various ways in which they can be initialized, but for now we'll leave you with a few examples of primitive variable declarations:

```
byte b;
boolean myBooleanPrimitive;
int x, y, z;                   // declare three int primitives
```

On previous versions of the exam you needed to know how to calculate ranges for all the Java primitives. For the current exam, you can skip some of that detail, but it's still important to understand that for the integer types the sequence from small to big is `byte`, `short`, `int`, and `long`, and that `double`s are bigger than `float`s.

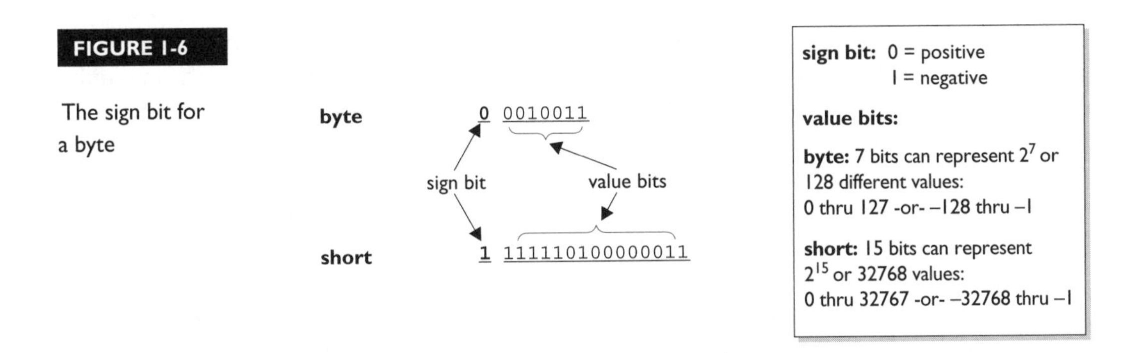

FIGURE 1-6 The sign bit for a byte

You will also need to know that the number types (both integer and floating-point types) are all signed, and how that affects their ranges. First, let's review the concepts.

All six number types in Java are made up of a certain number of 8-bit bytes and are *signed*, meaning they can be negative or positive. The leftmost bit (the most significant digit) is used to represent the sign, where a 1 means negative and 0 means positive, as shown in Figure 1-6. The rest of the bits represent the value, using two's complement notation.

Table 1-3 shows the primitive types with their sizes and ranges. Figure 1-6 shows that with a byte, for example, there are 256 possible numbers (or 2^8). Half of these are negative, and half – 1 are positive. The positive range is one less than the negative range because the number zero is stored as a positive binary number. We use the formula $-2^{(\text{bits}-1)}$ to calculate the negative range, and we use $2^{(\text{bits}-1)} - 1$ for the positive range. Again, if you know the first two columns of this table, you'll be in good shape for the exam.

The range for floating-point numbers is complicated to determine, but luckily you don't need to know these for the exam (although you are expected to know that a double holds 64 bits and a float 32).

TABLE 1-3 Ranges of Numeric Primitives

Type	Bits	Bytes	Minimum Range	Maximum Range
`byte`	8	1	-2^7	$2^7 - 1$
`short`	16	2	-2^{15}	$2^{15} - 1$
`int`	32	4	-2^{31}	$2^{31} - 1$
`long`	64	8	-2^{63}	$2^{63} - 1$
`float`	32	4	n/a	n/a
`double`	64	8	n/a	n/a

There is not a range of boolean values; a boolean can be only true or false. If someone asks you for the bit depth of a boolean, look them straight in the eye and say, "That's virtual-machine dependent." They'll be impressed.

The char type (a character) contains a single, 16-bit Unicode character. Although the extended ASCII set known as ISO Latin-1 needs only 8 bits (256 different characters), a larger range is needed to represent characters found in languages other than English. Unicode characters are actually represented by unsigned 16-bit integers, which means 2^{16} possible values, ranging from 0 to 65535 ($2^{16} - 1$). You'll learn in Chapter 3 that because a char is really an integer type, it can be assigned to any number type large enough to hold 65535 (which means anything larger than a short; although both chars and shorts are 16-bit types, remember that a short uses 1 bit to represent the sign, so fewer positive numbers are acceptable in a short).

Declaring Reference Variables

Reference variables can be declared as static variables, instance variables, method parameters, or local variables. You can declare one or more reference variables, of the same type, in a single line. In Chapter 3 we will discuss the various ways in which they can be initialized, but for now we'll leave you with a few examples of reference variable declarations:

```
Object o;
Dog myNewDogReferenceVariable;
String s1, s2, s3;                // declare three String vars.
```

Instance Variables

Instance variables are defined inside the class, but outside of any method, and are initialized only when the class is instantiated. Instance variables are the fields that belong to each unique object. For example, the following code defines fields (instance variables) for the name, title, and manager for employee objects:

```
class Employee {
  //  define fields (instance variables) for employee instances
  private String name;
  private String title,
  private String manager;
  // other code goes here including access methods for private
  // fields
}
```

The preceding `Employee` class says that each employee instance will know its own name, title, and manager. In other words, each instance can have its own unique values for those three fields. For the exam, you need to know that instance variables

- Can use any of the four access *levels* (which means they can be marked with any of the three access *modifiers*)
- Can be marked `final`
- Can be marked `transient`
- Cannot be marked `abstract`
- Cannot be marked `synchronized`
- Cannot be marked `strictfp`
- Cannot be marked `native`
- Cannot be marked static, because then they'd become class variables

We've already covered the effects of applying access control to instance variables (it works the same way as it does for member methods). A little later in this chapter we'll look at what it means to apply the `final` or `transient` modifier to an instance variable. First, though, we'll take a quick look at the difference between instance and local variables. Figure 1-7 compares the way in which modifiers can be applied to methods vs. variables.

FIGURE 1-7

Comparison of modifiers on variables vs. methods

Local Variables	Variables (non-local)	Methods
final	final public protected private static transient volatile	final public protected private static abstract synchronized strictfp native

Local (Automatic/Stack/Method) Variables

A local variable is a variable declared within a method. That means the variable is not just initialized within the method, but also declared within the method. Just as the local variable starts its life inside the method, it's also destroyed when the method has completed. Local variables are always on the stack, not the heap. (We'll talk more about the stack and the heap in Chapter 3.) Although the value of the variable might be passed into, say, another method that then stores the value in an instance variable, the variable itself lives only within the scope of the method.

Just don't forget that while the local variable is on the stack, if the variable is an object reference, the object itself will still be created on the heap. There is no such thing as a stack object, only a stack variable. You'll often hear programmers use the phrase "local object," but what they really mean is, "locally declared reference variable." So if you hear a programmer use that expression, you'll know that he's just too lazy to phrase it in a technically precise way. You can tell him we said that—unless he knows where we live.

Local variable declarations can't use most of the modifiers that can be applied to instance variables, such as `public` (or the other access modifiers), `transient`, `volatile`, `abstract`, or `static`, but as we saw earlier, local variables can be marked `final`. And as you'll learn in Chapter 3 (but here's a preview), before a local variable can be *used*, it must be *initialized* with a value. For instance:

```
class TestServer {
  public void logIn() {
    int count = 10;
  }
}
```

Typically, you'll initialize a local variable in the same line in which you declare it, although you might still need to reassign it later in the method. The key is to remember that a local variable must be initialized before you try to use it. The compiler will reject any code that tries to use a local variable that hasn't been assigned a value, because—unlike instance variables—local variables don't get default values.

A local variable can't be referenced in any code outside the method in which it's declared. In the preceding code example, it would be impossible to refer to the variable `count` anywhere else in the class except within the scope of the method `logIn()`. Again, that's not to say that the value of `count` can't be passed out of the method to take on a new life. But the variable holding that value, `count`, can't be accessed once the method is complete, as the following illegal code demonstrates:

```
class TestServer {
  public void logIn() {
    int count = 10;
  }
  public void doSomething(int i) {
    count = i;  // Won't compile! Can't access count outside
                // method logIn()
  }
}
```

It is possible to declare a local variable with the same name as an instance variable. It's known as *shadowing*, as the following code demonstrates:

```
class TestServer {
   int count = 9;         // Declare an instance variable named count
   public void logIn() {
      int count = 10;     // Declare a local variable named count
      System.out.println("local variable count is " + count);
   }
   public void count() {
      System.out.println("instance variable count is " + count);
   }
   public static void main(String[] args) {
      new TestServer().logIn();
      new TestServer().count();
   }
}
```

The preceding code produces the following output:

```
local variable count is 10
instance variable count is 9
```

Why on Earth (or the planet of your choice) would you want to do that? Normally, you won't. But one of the more common reasons is to name a parameter with the same name as the instance variable to which the parameter will be assigned.

The following (wrong) code is trying to set an instance variable's value using a parameter:

```
class Foo {
   int size = 27;
   public void setSize(int size) {
      size = size;  // ??? which size equals which size???
   }
}
```

So you've decided that—for overall readability—you want to give the parameter the same name as the instance variable its value is destined for, but how do you resolve the naming collision? Use the keyword `this`. The keyword `this` always, always, always refers to the object currently running. The following code shows this in action:

```
class Foo {
   int size = 27;
   public void setSize(int size) {
      this.size = size;  // this.size means the current object's
                         // instance variable, size. The size
                         // on the right is the parameter
   }
}
```

Array Declarations

In Java, arrays are objects that store multiple variables of the same type or variables that are all subclasses of the same type. Arrays can hold either primitives or object references, but an array itself will always be an object on the heap, even if the array is declared to hold primitive elements. In other words, there is no such thing as a primitive array, but you can make an array of primitives.

For the exam, you need to know three things:

- How to make an array reference variable (declare)
- How to make an array object (construct)
- How to populate the array with elements (initialize)

For this objective, you only need to know how to declare an array; we'll cover constructing and initializing arrays in Chapter 5.

on the Job

Arrays are efficient, but many times you'll want to use one of the Collection types from java.util (including `HashMap`, `ArrayList`, and `TreeSet`). Collection classes offer more flexible ways to access an object (for insertion, deletion, reading, and so on) and unlike arrays, can expand or contract dynamically as you add or remove elements. There are Collection types for a wide range of needs. Do you need a fast sort? A group of objects with no duplicates? A way to access a name-value pair? For OCA candidates, Chapter 5 discusses `ArrayList`, and for OCP candidates, Chapter 11 covers Collections in more detail.

Arrays are declared by stating the type of elements the array will hold (an object or a primitive), followed by square brackets to either side of the identifier.

Declaring an Array of Primitives

```
int[] key;          // Square brackets before name (recommended)
int key [];         // Square brackets after name (legal but less
                    // readable)
```

Declaring an Array of Object References

```
Thread[] threads;  // Recommended
Thread threads []; // Legal but less readable
```

on the Job

When declaring an array reference, you should always put the array brackets immediately after the declared type, rather than after the identifier (variable name). That way, anyone reading the code can easily tell that, for example, `key` is a reference to an `int` array object, and not an `int` primitive.

We can also declare multidimensional arrays, which are in fact arrays of arrays. This can be done in the following manner:

```
String[][][] occupantName;
String[] managerName [];
```

The first example is a three-dimensional array (an array of arrays of arrays) and the second is a two-dimensional array. Notice in the second example we have one square bracket before the variable name and one after. This is perfectly legal to the compiler, proving once again that just because it's legal doesn't mean it's right.

exam watch

It is never legal to include the size of the array in your declaration. Yes, we know you can do that in some other languages, which is why you might see a question or two that include code similar to the following:

```
int[5] scores;
```

The preceding code won't compile. Remember, the JVM doesn't allocate space until you actually instantiate the array object. That's when size matters.

In Chapter 5, we'll spend a lot of time discussing arrays, how to initialize and use them, and how to deal with multidimensional arrays…stay tuned!

Final Variables

Declaring a variable with the `final` keyword makes it impossible to reassign that variable once it has been initialized with an explicit value (notice we said explicit rather than default). For primitives, this means that once the variable is assigned a value, the value can't be altered. For example, if you assign 10 to the `int` variable `x`, then `x` is going to stay 10, forever. So that's straightforward for primitives, but what does it mean to have a `final` object reference variable? A reference variable marked `final` can't ever be reassigned to refer to a different object. The data within the object can be modified, but the reference variable cannot be changed. In other words, a `final` reference still allows you to modify the state of the object it refers to, but you can't modify the reference variable to make it refer to a different object. Burn this in: there are no `final` objects, only `final` references. We'll explain this in more detail in Chapter 3.

We've now covered how the `final` modifier can be applied to classes, methods, and variables. Figure 1-8 highlights the key points and differences of the various applications of `final`.

Transient Variables

If you mark an instance variable as `transient`, you're telling the JVM to skip (ignore) this variable when you attempt to serialize the object containing it. Serialization is one of the coolest features of Java; it lets you save (sometimes called "flatten") an object by writing its state (in other words, the value of its instance variables) to a special type of I/O stream. With serialization, you can save an object to a file or even ship it over a wire for reinflating (deserializing) at the other end, in another JVM. We were happy when serialization was added to the exam as of Java 5, but we're sad to say that as of Java 7, serialization is no longer on the exam.

Volatile Variables

The `volatile` modifier tells the JVM that a thread accessing the variable must always reconcile its own private copy of the variable with the master copy in memory. Say what? Don't worry about it. For the exam, all you need to know about `volatile` is that, as with `transient`, it can be applied only to instance variables. Make no mistake: the idea of multiple threads accessing an instance variable is scary stuff, and very important for any Java programmer to understand. But as you'll see in Chapter 13, you'll probably use synchronization, rather than the `volatile` modifier, to make your data thread-safe.

FIGURE 1-8

Effect of `final` on variables, methods, and classes

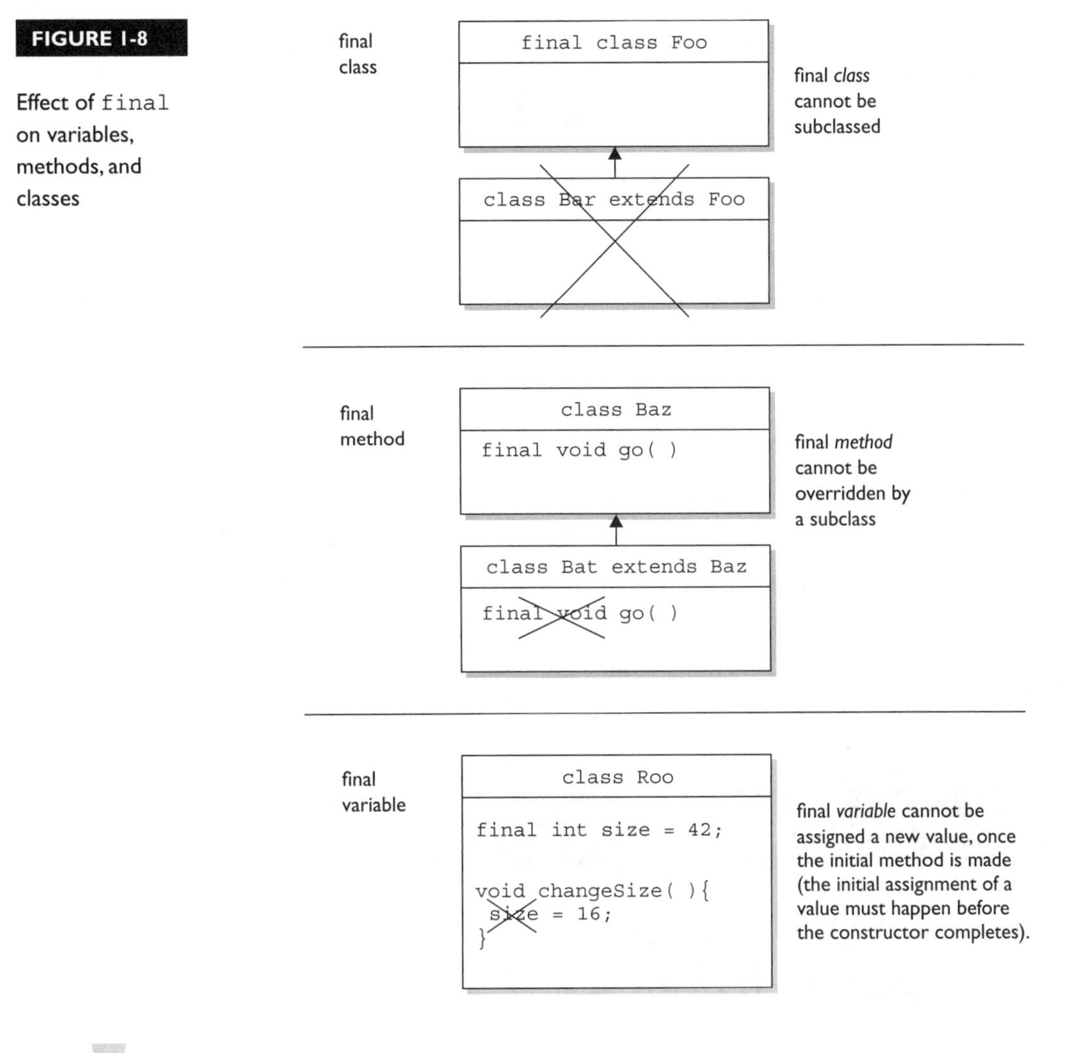
final
class
final class Foo
final class
cannot be
subclassed
class Bar extends Foo
final
method
class Baz
final void go( )
final method
cannot be
overridden by
a subclass
class Bat extends Baz
final void go( )
final
variable
class Roo
final int size = 42;
void changeSize( ){
size = 16;
}
final variable cannot be
assigned a new value, once
the initial method is made
(the initial assignment of a
value must happen before
the constructor completes).

on the
job

The `volatile` modifier may also be applied to project managers :)

Static Variables and Methods

The `static` modifier is used to create variables and methods that will exist independently of any instances created for the class. All `static` members exist before you ever make a new instance of a class, and there will be only one copy of a `static` member regardless of the number of instances of that class. In other words, all instances of a given class share the same value for any given `static` variable. We'll cover `static` members in great detail in the next chapter.

Things you can mark as `static`:

- Methods
- Variables
- A class nested within another class, but not within a method (more on this in Chapter 12)
- Initialization blocks

Things you can't mark as `static`:

- Constructors (makes no sense; a constructor is used only to create instances)
- Classes (unless they are nested)
- Interfaces (unless they are nested)
- Method local inner classes (we'll explore this in Chapter 12)
- Inner class methods and instance variables
- Local variables

CERTIFICATION OBJECTIVE

Declare and Use enums (OCA Objective 1.2 and OCP Objective 2.5)

2.5 Use enumerated types.

Note: During the creation of this book, Oracle adjusted some of the objectives for the OCA and OCP exams. We're not 100 percent sure that the topic of enums is included in the OCA exam, but we've decided that it's better to be safe than sorry, so we recommend that OCA candidates study this section. In any case, you're likely to encounter the use of enums in the Java code you read, so learning about them will pay off regardless.

Declaring enums

As of Java 5, Java lets you restrict a variable to having one of only a few predefined values—in other words, one value from an enumerated list. (The items in the enumerated list are called, surprisingly, enums.)

Using enums can help reduce the bugs in your code. For instance, in your coffee shop application you might want to restrict your CoffeeSize selections to BIG, HUGE, and OVERWHELMING. If you let an order for a LARGE or a GRANDE slip in, it might cause an error. enums to the rescue. With the following simple declaration, you can guarantee that the compiler will stop you from assigning anything to a CoffeeSize except BIG, HUGE, or OVERWHELMING:

```
enum CoffeeSize { BIG, HUGE, OVERWHELMING };
```

From then on, the only way to get a CoffeeSize will be with a statement something like this:

```
CoffeeSize cs = CoffeeSize.BIG;
```

It's not required that enum constants be in all caps, but borrowing from the Oracle code convention that constants are named in caps, it's a good idea.

The basic components of an enum are its constants (that is, BIG, HUGE, and OVERWHELMING), although in a minute you'll see that there can be a lot more to an enum. enums can be declared as their own separate class or as a class member; however, they must not be declared within a method!

Here's an example declaring an enum *outside* a class:

```
enum CoffeeSize { BIG, HUGE, OVERWHELMING }  // this cannot be
                                             // private or protected
class Coffee {
   CoffeeSize size;
}
public class CoffeeTest1 {
   public static void main(String[] args) {
      Coffee drink = new Coffee();
      drink.size = CoffeeSize.BIG;           // enum outside class
   }
}
```

The preceding code can be part of a single file. (Remember, the file must be named CoffeeTest1.java because that's the name of the public class in the file.) The key point to remember is that an enum that isn't enclosed in a class can be declared with only the public or default modifier, just like a non-inner class. Here's an example of declaring an enum *inside* a class:

```
class Coffee2 {
  enum CoffeeSize {BIG, HUGE, OVERWHELMING }
  CoffeeSize size;
}
public class CoffeeTest2 {
  public static void main(String[] args) {
    Coffee2 drink = new Coffee2();
    drink.size = Coffee2.CoffeeSize.BIG;    // enclosing class
                                            // name required
  }
}
```

The key points to take away from these examples are that enums can be declared as their own class or enclosed in another class, and that the syntax for accessing an enum's members depends on where the enum was declared.

The following is NOT legal:

```
public class CoffeeTest1 {
  public static void main(String[] args) {
    enum CoffeeSize { BIG, HUGE, OVERWHELMING } // WRONG! Cannot
                                                // declare enums
                                                // in methods
    Coffee drink = new Coffee();
    drink.size = CoffeeSize.BIG;
  }
}
```

To make it more confusing for you, the Java language designers made it optional to put a semicolon at the end of the enum declaration (when no other declarations for this enum follow):

```
public class CoffeeTest1 {
  enum CoffeeSize { BIG, HUGE, OVERWHELMING }; // <--semicolon
                                               // is optional here
  public static void main(String[] args) {
    Coffee drink = new Coffee();
    drink.size = CoffeeSize.BIG;
  }
}
```

So what gets created when you make an enum? The most important thing to remember is that enums are not Strings or ints! Each of the enumerated CoffeeSize types is actually an instance of CoffeeSize. In other words, BIG is of type CoffeeSize. Think of an enum as a kind of class that looks something (but not exactly) like this:

```
// conceptual example of how you can think
// about enums
class CoffeeSize {
    public static final CoffeeSize BIG =
                             new CoffeeSize("BIG", 0);
    public static final CoffeeSize HUGE =
                             new CoffeeSize("HUGE", 1);
    public static final CoffeeSize OVERWHELMING =
                             new CoffeeSize("OVERWHELMING", 2);

    CoffeeSize(String enumName, int index) {
       // stuff here
    }
   public static void main(String[] args) {
     System.out.println(CoffeeSize.BIG);
   }
}
```

Notice how each of the enumerated values, `BIG`, `HUGE`, and `OVERWHELMING`, is an instance of type `CoffeeSize`. They're represented as `static` and `final`, which in the Java world, is thought of as a constant. Also notice that each `enum` value knows its index or position—in other words, the order in which `enum` values are declared matters. You can think of the `CoffeeSize` enums as existing in an array of type `CoffeeSize`, and as you'll see in a later chapter, you can iterate through the values of an `enum` by invoking the `values()` method on any `enum` type. (Don't worry about that in this chapter.)

Declaring Constructors, Methods, and Variables in an enum

Because an `enum` really is a special kind of class, you can do more than just list the enumerated constant values. You can add constructors, instance variables, methods, and something really strange known as a *constant specific class body*. To understand why you might need more in your `enum`, think about this scenario: Imagine you want to know the actual size, in ounces, that map to each of the three `CoffeeSize` constants. For example, you want to know that `BIG` is 8 ounces, `HUGE` is 10 ounces, and `OVERWHELMING` is a whopping 16 ounces.

You could make some kind of a lookup table using some other data structure, but that would be a poor design and hard to maintain. The simplest way is to treat your `enum` values (`BIG`, `HUGE`, and `OVERWHELMING`) as objects, each of which can have its own instance variables. Then you can assign those values at the time the `enums` are initialized, by passing a value to the `enum` constructor. This takes a little explaining, but first look at the following code.

```
enum CoffeeSize {
    // 8, 10 & 16 are passed to the constructor
    BIG(8), HUGE(10), OVERWHELMING(16);
    CoffeeSize(int ounces) {    // constructor
      this.ounces = ounces;
    }

    private int ounces;          // an instance variable
    public int getOunces() {
      return ounces;
    }
}

class Coffee {
   CoffeeSize size;            // each instance of Coffee has an enum

   public static void main(String[] args) {
      Coffee drink1 = new Coffee();
      drink1.size = CoffeeSize.BIG;

      Coffee drink2 = new Coffee();
      drink2.size = CoffeeSize.OVERWHELMING;

      System.out.println(drink1.size.getOunces());  // prints 8
      for(CoffeeSize cs: CoffeeSize.values())
         System.out.println(cs + " " + cs.getOunces());
   }
}
```

which produces:

```
8
BIG 8
HUGE 10
OVERWHELMING 16
```

Note: Every `enum` has a static method, `values()`, that returns an array of the `enum`'s values in the order they're declared.

The key points to remember about `enum` constructors are

- You can NEVER invoke an `enum` constructor directly. The `enum` constructor is invoked automatically, with the arguments you define after the constant value. For example, `BIG(8)` invokes the `CoffeeSize` constructor that takes an `int`, passing the `int` literal 8 to the constructor. (Behind the scenes, of course, you can imagine that `BIG` is also passed to the constructor, but we don't have to know—or care—about the details.)
- You can define more than one argument to the constructor, and you can overload the `enum` constructors, just as you can overload a normal class

constructor. We discuss constructors in much more detail in Chapter 2. To initialize a `CoffeeSize` with both the number of ounces and, say, a lid type, you'd pass two arguments to the constructor as `BIG(8, "A")`, which means you have a constructor in `CoffeeSize` that takes both an `int` and a `String`.

And, finally, you can define something really strange in an enum that looks like an anonymous inner class (which we talk about in Chapter 8). It's known as a *constant specific class body*, and you use it when you need a particular constant to override a method defined in the enum.

Imagine this scenario: You want enums to have two methods—one for ounces and one for lid code (a `String`). Now imagine that most coffee sizes use the same lid code, `"B"`, but the `OVERWHELMING` size uses type `"A"`. You can define a `getLidCode()` method in the `CoffeeSize` enum that returns `"B"`, but then you need a way to override it for `OVERWHELMING`. You don't want to do some hard-to-maintain `if/then` code in the `getLidCode()` method, so the best approach might be to somehow have the `OVERWHELMING` constant override the `getLidCode()` method.

This looks strange, but you need to understand the basic declaration rules:

```
enum CoffeeSize {
     BIG(8),
     HUGE(10),
     OVERWHELMING(16) {                  // start a code block that defines
                                         // the "body" for this constant

       public String getLidCode() {      // override the method
                                         // defined in CoffeeSize
         return "A";
       }
     };     // the semicolon is REQUIRED when more code follows

     CoffeeSize(int ounces) {
       this.ounces = ounces;
     }

    private int ounces;

    public int getOunces() {
      return ounces;
    }
    public String getLidCode() {        // this method is overridden
                                        // by the OVERWHELMING constant

      return "B";                       // the default value we want to
                                        // return for CoffeeSize constants
    }
}
```

CERTIFICATION SUMMARY

After absorbing the material in this chapter, you should be familiar with some of the nuances of the Java language. You may also be experiencing confusion around why you ever wanted to take this exam in the first place. That's normal at this point. If you hear yourself asking, "What was I thinking?" just lie down until it passes. We would like to tell you that it gets easier…that this was the toughest chapter and it's all downhill from here.

Let's briefly review what you'll need to know for the exam:

There will be many questions dealing with keywords indirectly, so be sure you can identify which are keywords and which aren't.

You need to understand the rules associated with creating legal identifiers and the rules associated with source code declarations, including the use of `package` and `import` statements.

You learned the basic syntax for the `java` and `javac` command-line programs.

You learned about when `main()` has superpowers and when it doesn't.

We covered the basics of `import` and `import static` statements. It's tempting to think that there's more to them than saving a bit of typing, but there isn't.

You now have a good understanding of access control as it relates to classes, methods, and variables. You've looked at how access modifiers (`public`, `protected`, and `private`) define the access control of a class or member.

You learned that `abstract` classes can contain both `abstract` and nonabstract methods, but that if even a single method is marked `abstract`, the class must be marked `abstract`. Don't forget that a concrete (nonabstract) subclass of an `abstract` class must provide implementations for all the `abstract` methods of the superclass, but that an `abstract` class does not have to implement the `abstract` methods from its superclass. An `abstract` subclass can "pass the buck" to the first concrete subclass.

We covered interface implementation. Remember that interfaces can extend another interface (even multiple interfaces), and that any class that implements an interface must implement all methods from all the interfaces in the inheritance tree of the interface the class is implementing.

You've also looked at the other modifiers including `static`, `final`, `abstract`, `synchronized`, and so on. You've learned how some modifiers can never be combined in a declaration, such as mixing `abstract` with either `final` or `private`.

Keep in mind that there are no `final` objects in Java. A reference variable marked `final` can never be changed, but the object it refers to can be modified.

You've seen that `final` applied to methods means a subclass can't override them, and when applied to a class, the `final` class can't be subclassed.

Remember that as of Java 5, methods can be declared with a var-arg parameter (which can take from zero to many arguments of the declared type), but that you can have only one var-arg per method, and it must be the method's last parameter.

Make sure you're familiar with the relative sizes of the numeric primitives. Remember that while the values of nonfinal variables can change, a reference variable's type can never change.

You also learned that arrays are objects that contain many variables of the same type. Arrays can also contain other arrays.

Remember what you've learned about `static` variables and methods, especially that `static` members are per-class as opposed to per-instance. Don't forget that a `static` method can't directly access an instance variable from the class it's in, because it doesn't have an explicit reference to any particular instance of the class.

Finally, we covered a feature new as of Java 5: `enums`. An `enum` is a much safer and more flexible way to implement constants than was possible in earlier versions of Java. Because they are a special kind of class, `enums` can be declared very simply, or they can be quite complex—including such attributes as methods, variables, constructors, and a special type of inner class called a constant specific class body.

Before you hurl yourself at the practice test, spend some time with the following optimistically named "Two-Minute Drill." Come back to this particular drill often, as you work through this book and especially when you're doing that last-minute cramming. Because—and here's the advice you wished your mother had given you before you left for college—it's not what you know, it's when you know it.

For the exam, knowing what you can't do with the Java language is just as important as knowing what you can do. Give the sample questions a try! They're very similar to the difficulty and structure of the real exam questions and should be an eye opener for how difficult the exam can be. Don't worry if you get a lot of them wrong. If you find a topic that you are weak in, spend more time reviewing and studying. Many programmers need two or three serious passes through a chapter (or an individual objective) before they can answer the questions confidently.

✓ TWO-MINUTE DRILL

Remember that in this chapter, when we talk about classes, we're referring to non-inner classes, or *top-level* classes. For OCP 7 candidates only, we'll devote all of Chapter 12 to inner classes. **Note** on OCA 7 vs. OCP 7 objectives: Part I of this book is necessary for BOTH OCA 7 and OCP 7 candidates. Since you must now pass the OCA 7 exam before taking the OCP 7 exam, the references to objectives in the two-minute drills in the first part of the book are usually for OCA objectives only.

Identifiers (OCA Objective 2.1)

- ❑ Identifiers can begin with a letter, an underscore, or a currency character.
- ❑ After the first character, identifiers can also include digits.
- ❑ Identifiers can be of any length.

Executable Java Files and main() (OCA Objective 1.3)

- ❑ You can compile and execute Java programs using the command-line programs `javac` and `java`, respectively. Both programs support a variety of command-line options.
- ❑ The only versions of `main()` methods with special powers are those versions with method signatures equivalent to `public static void main(String[] args)`.
- ❑ `main()` can be overloaded.

Imports (OCA Objective 1.4)

- ❑ An `import` statement's only job is to save keystrokes.
- ❑ You can use an asterisk (`*`) to search through the contents of a single package.
- ❑ Although referred to as "static imports," the syntax is `import static`....
- ❑ You can import API classes and/or custom classes.

Source File Declaration Rules (OCA Objective 1.2)

- ❑ A source code file can have only one `public` class.
- ❑ If the source file contains a `public` class, the filename must match the `public` class name.
- ❑ A file can have only one `package` statement, but it can have multiple `imports`.
- ❑ The `package` statement (if any) must be the first (noncomment) line in a source file.
- ❑ The `import` statements (if any) must come after the `package` and before the class declaration.
- ❑ If there is no `package` statement, `import` statements must be the first (noncomment) statements in the source file.
- ❑ `package` and `import` statements apply to all classes in the file.
- ❑ A file can have more than one nonpublic class.
- ❑ Files with no `public` classes have no naming restrictions.

Class Access Modifiers (OCA Objective 6.6)

- ❑ There are three access modifiers: `public`, `protected`, and `private`.
- ❑ There are four access levels: `public`, `protected`, default, and `private`.
- ❑ Classes can have only `public` or default access.
- ❑ A class with default access can be seen only by classes within the same package.
- ❑ A class with `public` access can be seen by all classes from all packages.
- ❑ Class visibility revolves around whether code in one class can
  - ❑ Create an instance of another class
  - ❑ Extend (or subclass) another class
  - ❑ Access methods and variables of another class

Class Modifiers (Nonaccess) (OCA Objective 7.6)

- ❑ Classes can also be modified with `final`, `abstract`, or `strictfp`.
- ❑ A class cannot be both `final` and `abstract`.
- ❑ A `final` class cannot be subclassed.

- An `abstract` class cannot be instantiated.
- A single `abstract` method in a class means the whole class must be `abstract`.
- An `abstract` class can have both `abstract` and nonabstract methods.
- The first concrete class to extend an `abstract` class must implement all of its `abstract` methods.

Interface Implementation (OCA Objective 7.6)

- Interfaces are contracts for what a class can do, but they say nothing about the way in which the class must do it.
- Interfaces can be implemented by any class, from any inheritance tree.
- An interface is like a 100-percent `abstract` class and is implicitly abstract whether you type the `abstract` modifier in the declaration or not.
- An interface can have only `abstract` methods, no concrete methods allowed.
- Interface methods are by default `public` and `abstract`—explicit declaration of these modifiers is optional.
- Interfaces can have constants, which are always implicitly `public`, `static`, and `final`.
- Interface constant declarations of `public`, `static`, and `final` are optional in any combination.
- Note: This section uses some concepts that we HAVE NOT yet covered. Don't panic: once you've read through all of Part I of the book, this section will make sense as a reference.
  A legal nonabstract implementing class has the following properties:
  - It provides concrete implementations for the interface's methods.
  - It must follow all legal override rules for the methods it implements.
  - It must not declare any new checked exceptions for an implementation method.
  - It must not declare any checked exceptions that are broader than the exceptions declared in the interface method.
  - It may declare runtime exceptions on any interface method implementation regardless of the interface declaration.

- It must maintain the exact signature (allowing for covariant returns) and return type of the methods it implements (but does not have to declare the exceptions of the interface).

- A class implementing an interface can itself be `abstract`.
- An `abstract` implementing class does not have to implement the interface methods (but the first concrete subclass must).
- A class can extend only one class (no multiple inheritance), but it can implement many interfaces.
- Interfaces can extend one or more other interfaces.
- Interfaces cannot extend a class or implement a class or interface.
- When taking the exam, verify that interface and class declarations are legal before verifying other code logic.

Member Access Modifiers (OCA Objective 6.6)

- Methods and instance (nonlocal) variables are known as "members."
- Members can use all four access levels: `public`, `protected`, default, and `private`.
- Member access comes in two forms:
  - Code in one class can access a member of another class.
  - A subclass can inherit a member of its superclass.
- If a class cannot be accessed, its members cannot be accessed.
- Determine class visibility before determining member visibility.
- `public` members can be accessed by all other classes, even in other packages.
- If a superclass member is `public`, the subclass inherits it—regardless of package.
- Members accessed without the dot operator (`.`) must belong to the same class.
- `this.` always refers to the currently executing object.
- `this.aMethod()` is the same as just invoking `aMethod()`.
- `private` members can be accessed only by code in the same class.
- `private` members are not visible to subclasses, so `private` members cannot be inherited.

- Default and `protected` members differ only when subclasses are involved:
  - Default members can be accessed only by classes in the same package.
  - `protected` members can be accessed by other classes in the same package, plus subclasses regardless of package.
  - `protected` = package + kids (kids meaning subclasses).
  - For subclasses outside the package, the `protected` member can be accessed only through inheritance; a subclass outside the package cannot access a `protected` member by using a reference to a superclass instance. (In other words, inheritance is the only mechanism for a subclass outside the package to access a `protected` member of its superclass.)
  - A `protected` member inherited by a subclass from another package is not accessible to any other class in the subclass package, except for the subclass' own subclasses.

Local Variables (OCA Objective 2.1)

- Local (method, automatic, or stack) variable declarations cannot have access modifiers.
- `final` is the only modifier available to local variables.
- Local variables don't get default values, so they must be initialized before use.

Other Modifiers—Members (OCA Objective 6.6)

- `final` methods cannot be overridden in a subclass.
- `abstract` methods are declared with a signature, a return type, and an optional `throws` clause, but they are not implemented.
- `abstract` methods end in a semicolon—no curly braces.
- Three ways to spot a nonabstract method:
  - The method is not marked `abstract`.
  - The method has curly braces.
  - The method **MIGHT** have code between the curly braces.
- The first nonabstract (concrete) class to extend an `abstract` class must implement all of the `abstract` class' `abstract` methods.
- The `synchronized` modifier applies only to methods and code blocks.
- `synchronized` methods can have any access control and can also be marked `final`.

- ❑ `abstract` methods must be implemented by a subclass, so they must be inheritable. For that reason:
  - ❑ `abstract` methods cannot be `private`.
  - ❑ `abstract` methods cannot be `final`.
- ❑ The `native` modifier applies only to methods.
- ❑ The `strictfp` modifier applies only to classes and methods.

Methods with var-args (OCP Only, OCP Objective 1.3)

- ❑ As of Java 5, methods can declare a parameter that accepts from zero to many arguments, a so-called var-arg method.
- ❑ A var-arg parameter is declared with the syntax `type... name`; for instance: `doStuff(int... x) { }`.
- ❑ A var-arg method can have only one var-arg parameter.
- ❑ In methods with normal parameters and a var-arg, the var-arg must come last.

Variable Declarations (OCA Objective 2.1)

- ❑ Instance variables can
  - ❑ Have any access control
  - ❑ Be marked `final` or `transient`
- ❑ Instance variables can't be `abstract`, `synchronized`, `native`, or `strictfp`.
- ❑ It is legal to declare a local variable with the same name as an instance variable; this is called "shadowing."
- ❑ `final` variables have the following properties:
  - ❑ `final` variables cannot be reassigned once assigned a value.
  - ❑ `final` reference variables cannot refer to a different object once the object has been assigned to the `final` variable.
  - ❑ `final` variables must be initialized before the constructor completes.
- ❑ There is no such thing as a `final` object. An object reference marked `final` does NOT mean the object itself can't change.
- ❑ The `transient` modifier applies only to instance variables.
- ❑ The `volatile` modifier applies only to instance variables.

Array Declarations (OCA Objectives 4.1 and 4.2)

- Arrays can hold primitives or objects, but the array itself is always an object.
- When you declare an array, the brackets can be to the left or to the right of the variable name.
- It is never legal to include the size of an array in the declaration.
- An array of objects can hold any object that passes the IS-A (or `instanceof`) test for the declared type of the array. For example, if `Horse` extends `Animal`, then a `Horse` object can go into an `Animal` array.

Static Variables and Methods (OCA Objective 6.2)

- They are not tied to any particular instance of a class.
- No class instances are needed in order to use `static` members of the class.
- There is only one copy of a `static` variable/class and all instances share it.
- `static` methods do not have direct access to nonstatic members.

enums (OCA Objective 1.2 and OCP Objective 2.5)

- An `enum` specifies a list of constant values assigned to a type.
- An `enum` is NOT a `String` or an `int`; an `enum` constant's type is the `enum` type. For example, `SUMMER` and `FALL` are of the `enum` type `Season`.
- An `enum` can be declared outside or inside a class, but NOT in a method.
- An `enum` declared outside a class must NOT be marked `static`, `final`, `abstract`, `protected`, or `private`.
- `enum`s can contain constructors, methods, variables, and constant-specific class bodies.
- `enum` constants can send arguments to the `enum` constructor, using the syntax `BIG(8)`, where the `int` literal 8 is passed to the `enum` constructor.
- `enum` constructors can have arguments and can be overloaded.
- `enum` constructors can NEVER be invoked directly in code. They are always called automatically when an `enum` is initialized.
- The semicolon at the end of an `enum` declaration is optional. These are legal:
  - ```
    enum Foo { ONE, TWO, THREE}
    enum Foo { ONE, TWO, THREE};
    ```
- `MyEnum.values()` returns an array of `MyEnum`'s values.
    ```

SELF TEST

The following questions will help you measure your understanding of the material presented in this chapter. Read all of the choices carefully, as there may be more than one correct answer. Choose all correct answers for each question. Stay focused.

If you have a rough time with these at first, don't beat yourself up. Be positive. Repeat nice affirmations to yourself like, "I am smart enough to understand `enums`" and "OK, so that other guy knows `enums` better than I do, but I bet he can't <insert something you *are* good at> like me."

1. Which are true? (Choose all that apply.)

A. "X extends Y" is correct if and only if X is a class and Y is an interface.

B. "X extends Y" is correct if and only if X is an interface and Y is a class.

C. "X extends Y" is correct if X and Y are either both classes or both interfaces.

D. "X extends Y" is correct for all combinations of X and Y being classes and/or interfaces.

2. Given:

```
class Rocket {
  private void blastOff() { System.out.print("bang "); }
}
public class Shuttle extends Rocket {
  public static void main(String[] args) {
    new Shuttle().go();
  }
  void go() {
    blastOff();
    // Rocket.blastOff();   // line A
  }
  private void blastOff() { System.out.print("sh-bang "); }
}
```

Which are true? (Choose all that apply.)

A. As the code stands, the output is `bang`

B. As the code stands, the output is `sh-bang`

C. As the code stands, compilation fails.

D. If line A is uncommented, the output is `bang bang`

E. If line A is uncommented, the output is `sh-bang bang`

F. If line A is uncommented, compilation fails.

3. Given that the `for` loop's syntax is correct, and given:

```
import static java.lang.System.*;
class _ {
```

```
  static public void main(String[] __A_V_) {
    String $ = "";
    for(int x=0; ++x < __A_V_.length; )    // for loop
      $ += __A_V_[x];
    out.println($);
  }
}
```

And the command line:

```
java _ - A .
```

What is the result?

A. `-A`

B. `A.`

C. `-A.`

D. `_A.`

E. `_-A.`

F. Compilation fails

G. An exception is thrown at runtime

4. Given:

```
 1. enum Animals {
 2.   DOG("woof"), CAT("meow"), FISH("burble");
 3.   String sound;
 4.   Animals(String s) { sound = s; }
 5. }
 6. class TestEnum {
 7.   static Animals a;
 8.   public static void main(String[] args) {
 9.     System.out.println(a.DOG.sound + " " + a.FISH.sound);
10.   }
11. }
```

What is the result?

A. `woof burble`

B. Multiple compilation errors

C. Compilation fails due to an error on line 2

D. Compilation fails due to an error on line 3

E. Compilation fails due to an error on line 4

F. Compilation fails due to an error on line 9

5. Given two files:

```
1. package pkgA;
2. public class Foo {
3. int a = 5;
4. protected int b = 6;
5. public int c = 7;
6. }

3. package pkgB;
4. import pkgA.*;
5. public class Baz {
6.   public static void main(String[] args) {
7.     Foo f = new Foo();
8.     System.out.print(" " + f.a);
9.     System.out.print(" " + f.b);
10.    System.out.println(" " + f.c);
11.  }
12. }
```

What is the result? (Choose all that apply.)

A. `5 6 7`

B. `5` followed by an exception

C. Compilation fails with an error on line 7

D. Compilation fails with an error on line 8

E. Compilation fails with an error on line 9

F. Compilation fails with an error on line 10

6. Given:

```
1. public class Electronic implements Device
     { public void doIt() { } }
2.
3. abstract class Phone1 extends Electronic { }
4.
5. abstract class Phone2 extends Electronic
     { public void doIt(int x) { } }
6.
7. class Phone3 extends Electronic implements Device
     { public void doStuff() { } }
8.
9. interface Device { public void doIt(); }
```

What is the result? (Choose all that apply.)

A. Compilation succeeds
B. Compilation fails with an error on line 1
C. Compilation fails with an error on line 3
D. Compilation fails with an error on line 5
E. Compilation fails with an error on line 7
F. Compilation fails with an error on line 9

7. Given:

```
 4. class Announce {
 5.   public static void main(String[] args) {
 6.     for(int __x = 0; __x < 3; __x++) ;
 7.     int #lb = 7;
 8.     long [] x [5];
 9.     Boolean []ba[];
10.   }
11. }
```

What is the result? (Choose all that apply.)

A. Compilation succeeds
B. Compilation fails with an error on line 6
C. Compilation fails with an error on line 7
D. Compilation fails with an error on line 8
E. Compilation fails with an error on line 9

8. Given:

```
 3. public class TestDays {
 4.   public enum Days { MON, TUE, WED };
 5.   public static void main(String[] args) {
 6.     for(Days d : Days.values() )
 7.       ;
 8.     Days [] d2 = Days.values();
 9.     System.out.println(d2[2]);
10.   }
11. }
```

What is the result? (Choose all that apply.)

A. `TUE`

B. `WED`

C. The output is unpredictable
D. Compilation fails due to an error on line 4
E. Compilation fails due to an error on line 6
F. Compilation fails due to an error on line 8
G. Compilation fails due to an error on line 9

9. Given:

```
 4. public class Frodo extends Hobbit
 5.   public static void main(String[] args) {
 6.     int myGold = 7;
 7.     System.out.println(countGold(myGold, 6));
 8.   }
 9. }
10. class Hobbit {
11.   int countGold(int x, int y) { return x + y; }
12. }
```

What is the result?

A. `13`
B. Compilation fails due to multiple errors
C. Compilation fails due to an error on line 6
D. Compilation fails due to an error on line 7
E. Compilation fails due to an error on line 11

10. Given:

```
interface Gadget {
  void doStuff();
}
abstract class Electronic {
  void getPower() { System.out.print("plug in "); }
}
public class Tablet extends Electronic implements Gadget {
  void doStuff() { System.out.print("show book "); }
  public static void main(String[] args) {
    new Tablet().getPower();
    new Tablet().doStuff();
  }
}
```

Which are true? (Choose all that apply.)

A. The class `Tablet` will NOT compile
B. The interface `Gadget` will NOT compile

C. The output will be `plug in show book`

D. The `abstract` class `Electronic` will NOT compile

E. The class `Tablet` CANNOT both extend and implement

11. Given that the Integer class is in the java.lang package, and given:

```
1. // insert code here
2. class StatTest {
3.   public static void main(String[] args) {
4.     System.out.println(Integer.MAX_VALUE);
5.   }
6. }
```

Which, inserted independently at line 1, compiles? (Choose all that apply.)

A. `import static java.lang;`

B. `import static java.lang.Integer;`

C. `import static java.lang.Integer.*;`

D. `static import java.lang.Integer.*;`

E. `import static java.lang.Integer.MAX_VALUE;`

F. None of the above statements are valid import syntax

SELF TEST ANSWERS

1. ☑ **C** is correct.
   ☒ **A** is incorrect because classes implement interfaces, they don't extend them. **B** is incorrect because interfaces only "inherit from" other interfaces. **D** is incorrect based on the preceding rules. (OCA Objective 7.6)

2. ☑ **B** and **F** are correct. Since `Rocket.blastOff()` is `private`, it can't be overridden, and it is invisible to class `Shuttle`.
   ☒ **A, C, D,** and **E** are incorrect based on the above. (OCA Objective 6.6)

3. ☑ **B** is correct. This question is using valid (but inappropriate and weird) identifiers, static imports, `main()`, and pre-incrementing logic.
   ☒ **A, C, D, E, F,** and **G** are incorrect based on the above. (OCA Objective 1.2 and OCA Objectives 1.3, 1.4, and 2.1)

4. ☑ **A** is correct; `enum`s can have constructors and variables.
   ☒ **B, C, D, E,** and **F** are incorrect; these lines all use correct syntax. (OCP Objective 2.5)

5. ☑ **D** and **E** are correct. Variable `a` has default access, so it cannot be accessed from outside the package. Variable `b` has protected access in `pkgA`.
   ☒ **A, B, C,** and **F** are incorrect based on the above information. (OCA Objectives 1.4 and 6.6)

6. ☑ **A** is correct; all of these are legal declarations.
   ☒ **B, C, D, E,** and **F** are incorrect based on the above information. (OCA Objective 7.6)

7. ☑ **C** and **D** are correct. Variable names cannot begin with a #, and an array declaration can't include a size without an instantiation. The rest of the code is valid.
   ☒ **A, B,** and **E** are incorrect based on the above. (OCA Objective 2.1)

8. ☑ **B** is correct. Every `enum` comes with a `static values()` method that returns an array of the `enum`'s values, in the order in which they are declared in the `enum`.
   ☒ **A, C, D, E, F,** and **G** are incorrect based on the above information. (OCP Objective 2.5)

9. ☑ **D** is correct. The `countGold()` method cannot be invoked from a static context.
   ☒ **A, B, C,** and **E** are incorrect based on the above information. (OCA Objectives 2.5 and 6.2)

10. ☑ A is correct. By default, an interface's methods are `public` so the `Tablet.doStuff` method must be public, too. The rest of the code is valid.
☒ B, C, D, and E are incorrect based on the above. (OCA Objective 7.6)

11. ☑ C and E are correct syntax for static imports. Line 4 isn't making use of `static imports`, so the code will also compile with none of the imports.
☒ A, B, D, and F are incorrect based on the above. (OCA Objective 1.4)

2

Object Orientation

CERTIFICATION OBJECTIVES

- Describe Encapsulation
- Implement Inheritance
- Use IS-A and HAS-A Relationships (OCP)
- Use Polymorphism
- Use Overriding and Overloading
- Understand Casting
- Use Interfaces
- Understand and Use Return Types
- Develop Constructors
- Use static Members

✓ Two-Minute Drill

Q&A Self Test

Being an Oracle Certified Associate (OCA) 7 means you must be at one with the object-oriented aspects of Java. You must dream of inheritance hierarchies, the power of polymorphism must flow through you, and encapsulation must become second nature to you. (Coupling, cohesion, composition, and design patterns will become your bread and butter when you're an Oracle Certified Professional [OCP] 7.) This chapter will prepare you for all of the object-oriented objectives and questions you'll encounter on the exam. We have heard of many experienced Java programmers who haven't really become fluent with the object-oriented tools that Java provides, so we'll start at the beginning.

CERTIFICATION OBJECTIVE

Encapsulation (OCA Objectives 6.1 and 6.7)

6.1 *Create methods with arguments and return values.*

6.7 *Apply encapsulation principles to a class.*

Imagine you wrote the code for a class and another dozen programmers from your company all wrote programs that used your class. Now imagine that later on, you didn't like the way the class behaved, because some of its instance variables were being set (by the other programmers from within their code) to values you hadn't anticipated. *Their* code brought out errors in *your* code. (Relax, this is just hypothetical.) Well, it is a Java program, so you should be able just to ship out a newer version of the class, which they could replace in their programs without changing any of their own code.

This scenario highlights two of the promises/benefits of an object-oriented (OO) language: flexibility and maintainability. But those benefits don't come automatically. You have to do something. You have to write your classes and code in a way that supports flexibility and maintainability. So what if Java supports OO? It can't design your code for you. For example, imagine you made your class with `public` instance variables, and those other programmers were setting the instance variables directly, as the following code demonstrates:

```
public class BadOO {
  public int size;
  public int weight;
  ...
}
public class ExploitBadOO {
  public static void main (String [] args) {
    BadOO b = new BadOO();
    b.size = -5; // Legal but bad!!
  }
}
```

And now you're in trouble. How are you going to change the class in a way that lets you handle the issues that come up when somebody changes the `size` variable to a value that causes problems? Your only choice is to go back in and write method code for adjusting `size` (a `setSize(int a)` method, for example), and then insulate the `size` variable with, say, a private access modifier. But as soon as you make that change to your code, you break everyone else's!

The ability to make changes in your implementation code without breaking the code of others who use your code is a key benefit of encapsulation. You want to hide implementation details behind a public programming interface. By *interface*, we mean the set of accessible methods your code makes available for other code to call—in other words, your code's API. By hiding implementation details, you can rework your method code (perhaps also altering the way variables are used by your class) without forcing a change in the code that calls your changed method.

If you want maintainability, flexibility, and extensibility (and of course, you do), your design must include encapsulation. How do you do that?

- Keep instance variables protected (with an access modifier, often `private`).
- Make `public` accessor methods, and force calling code to use those methods rather than directly accessing the instance variable. These so-called accessor methods allow users of your class to **set** a variable's value or **get** a variable's value.
- For these accessor methods, use the most common naming convention of `set<someProperty>` and `get<someProperty>`.

Figure 2-1 illustrates the idea that encapsulation forces callers of our code to go through methods rather than accessing variables directly.

We call the access methods *getters* and *setters*, although some prefer the fancier terms *accessors* and *mutators*. (Personally, we don't like the word "mutate.") Regardless of what you call them, they're methods that other programmers must go

FIGURE 2-1 The nature of encapsulation

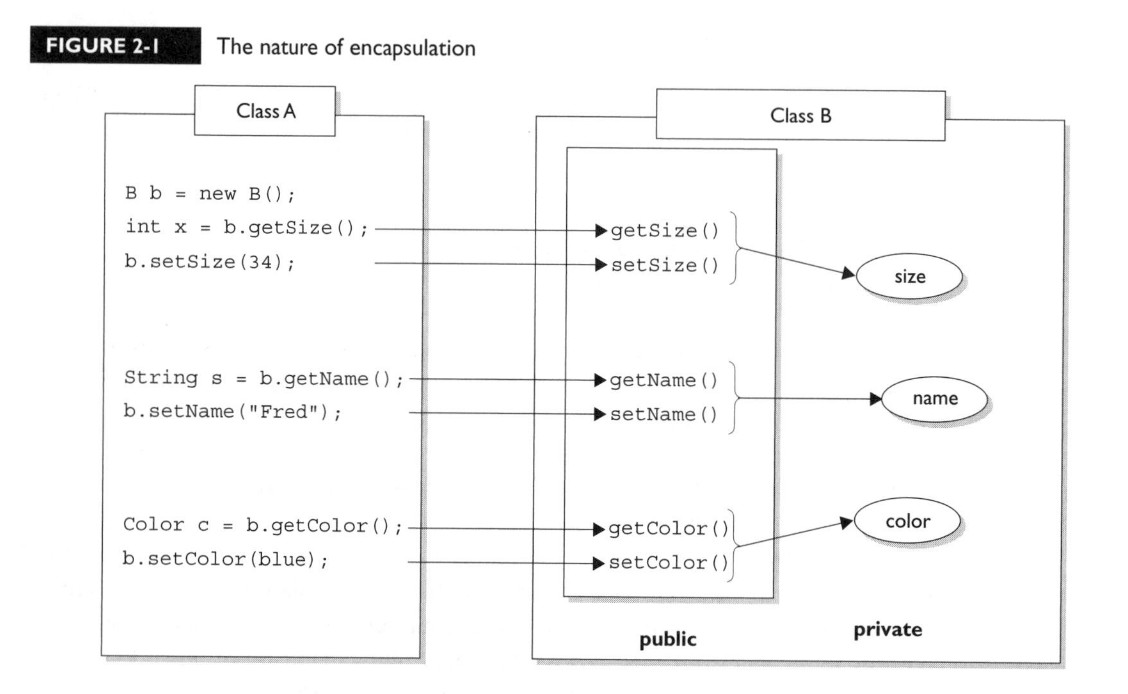

through in order to access your instance variables. They look simple, and you've probably been using them forever:

```
public class Box {
  // protect the instance variable; only an instance
  // of Box can access it
  private int size;
  // Provide public getters and setters
  public int getSize() {
    return size;
  }
  public void setSize(int newSize) {
    size = newSize;
  }
}
```

Wait a minute. How useful is the previous code? It doesn't even do any validation or processing. What benefit can there be from having getters and setters that add no functionality? The point is, you can change your mind later and add more code to your methods without breaking your API. Even if today you don't think you really need validation or processing of the data, good OO design dictates that you plan for the future. To be safe, force calling code to go through your methods rather than going directly to instance variables. *Always.* Then you're free to rework your method implementations later, without risking the wrath of those dozen programmers who know where you live.

Note: In Chapter 5 we'll be revisiting the topic of encapsulation as it applies to instance variables that are also reference variables. It's trickier than you might think, so stay tuned! (Also, we'll wait until Chapter 5 to challenge you with encapsulation-themed mock questions.)

exam watch

Look out for code that appears to be asking about the behavior of a method, when the problem is actually a lack of encapsulation. Look at the following example, and see if you can figure out what's going on:

```
class Foo {
  public int left = 9;
  public int right = 3;
  public void setLeft(int leftNum) {
    left = leftNum;
    right = leftNum/3;
  }
  // lots of complex test code here
}
```

Now consider this question: Is the value of right always going to be one-third the value of left? It looks like it will, until you realize that users of the `Foo` class don't need to use the `setLeft()` method! They can simply go straight to the instance variables and change them to any arbitrary `int` value.

CERTIFICATION OBJECTIVE

Inheritance and Polymorphism (OCA Objectives 7.1, 7.2, and 7.3)

7.1 Implement inheritance.

7.2 Develop code that demonstrates the use of polymorphism.

7.3 Differentiate between the type of a reference and the type of an object.

Inheritance is everywhere in Java. It's safe to say that it's almost (almost?) impossible to write even the tiniest Java program without using inheritance. To explore this topic, we're going to use the `instanceof` operator, which we'll discuss in more detail in Chapter 5. For now, just remember that `instanceof` returns `true` if the reference variable being tested is of the type being compared to. This code

```
class Test {
  public static void main(String [] args) {
    Test t1 = new Test();
    Test t2 = new Test();
    if (!t1.equals(t2))
      System.out.println("they're not equal");
    if (t1 instanceof Object)
      System.out.println("t1's an Object");
  }
}
```

produces this output:

```
they're not equal
t1's an Object
```

Where did that `equals` method come from? The reference variable `t1` is of type `Test`, and there's no `equals` method in the `Test` class. Or is there? The second `if` test asks whether `t1` is an instance of class `Object`, and because it *is* (more on that soon), the `if` test succeeds.

Hold on...how can `t1` be an instance of type `Object`, when we just said it was of type `Test`? I'm sure you're way ahead of us here, but it turns out that every class in Java is a subclass of class `Object` (except of course class `Object` itself). In other words, every class you'll ever use or ever write will inherit from class `Object`. You'll always have an `equals` method, a `clone` method, `notify`, `wait`, and others available to use. Whenever you create a class, you automatically inherit all of class `Object`'s methods.

Why? Let's look at that `equals` method for instance. Java's creators correctly assumed that it would be very common for Java programmers to want to compare instances of their classes to check for equality. If class `Object` didn't have an `equals` method, you'd have to write one yourself—you and every other Java programmer. That one `equals` method has been inherited billions of times. (To be fair, `equals` has also been *overridden* billions of times, but we're getting ahead of ourselves.)

For the exam, you'll need to know that you can create inheritance relationships in Java by *extending* a class. It's also important to understand that the two most common reasons to use inheritance are

- To promote code reuse
- To use polymorphism

Let's start with reuse. A common design approach is to create a fairly generic version of a class with the intention of creating more specialized subclasses that inherit from it. For example:

```
class GameShape {
  public void displayShape() {
    System.out.println("displaying shape");
  }
  // more code
}

class PlayerPiece extends GameShape {
  public void movePiece() {
    System.out.println("moving game piece");
  }
  // more code
}


public class TestShapes {
  public static void main (String[] args) {
    PlayerPiece shape = new PlayerPiece();
    shape.displayShape();
    shape.movePiece();
  }
}
```

outputs:

```
displaying shape
moving game piece
```

Notice that the `PlayerPiece` class inherits the generic `displayShape()` method from the less-specialized class `GameShape` and also adds its own method, `movePiece()`. Code reuse through inheritance means that methods with generic functionality—such as `displayShape()`, which could apply to a wide range of different kinds of shapes in a game—don't have to be reimplemented. That means all specialized subclasses of `GameShape` are guaranteed to have the capabilities of the more generic superclass. You don't want to have to rewrite the `displayShape()` code in each of your specialized components of an online game.

But you knew that. You've experienced the pain of duplicate code when you make a change in one place and have to track down all the other places where that same (or very similar) code exists.

The second (and related) use of inheritance is to allow your classes to be accessed polymorphically—a capability provided by interfaces as well, but we'll get to that in a minute. Let's say that you have a `GameLauncher` class that wants to loop through a list of different kinds of `GameShape` objects and invoke `displayShape()` on each of them. At the time you write this class, you don't know every possible kind of `GameShape` subclass that anyone else will ever write. And you sure don't want to have to redo *your* code just because somebody decided to build a dice shape six months later.

The beautiful thing about polymorphism ("many forms") is that you can treat any *subclass* of `GameShape` as a `GameShape`. In other words, you can write code in your `GameLauncher` class that says, "I don't care what kind of object you are as long as you inherit from (extend) `GameShape`. And as far as I'm concerned, if you extend `GameShape`, then you've definitely got a `displayShape()` method, so I know I can call it."

Imagine we now have two specialized subclasses that extend the more generic `GameShape` class, `PlayerPiece` and `TilePiece`:

```
class GameShape {
  public void displayShape() {
    System.out.println("displaying shape");
  }
  // more code
}

class PlayerPiece extends GameShape {
  public void movePiece() {
    System.out.println("moving game piece");
  }
  // more code
}

class TilePiece extends GameShape {
  public void getAdjacent() {
```

```
    System.out.println("getting adjacent tiles");
  }
  // more code
}
```

Now imagine a test class has a method with a declared argument type of `GameShape`, which means it can take any kind of `GameShape`. In other words, any subclass of `GameShape` can be passed to a method with an argument of type `GameShape`. This code

```
public class TestShapes {
  public static void main (String[] args) {
    PlayerPiece player = new PlayerPiece();
    TilePiece tile = new TilePiece();
    doShapes(player);
    doShapes(tile);
  }

  public static void doShapes(GameShape shape) {
    shape.displayShape();
  }
}
```

outputs:

```
displaying shape
displaying shape
```

The key point is that the `doShapes()` method is declared with a `GameShape` argument but can be passed any subtype (in this example, a subclass) of `GameShape`. The method can then invoke any method of `GameShape`, without any concern for the actual runtime class type of the object passed to the method. There are implications, though. The `doShapes()` method knows only that the objects are a type of `GameShape`, since that's how the parameter is declared. And using a reference variable declared as type `GameShape`—regardless of whether the variable is a method parameter, local variable, or instance variable—means that *only* the methods of `GameShape` can be invoked on it. The methods you can call on a reference are totally dependent on the *declared* type of the variable, no matter what the actual object is, that the reference is referring to. That means you can't use a `GameShape` variable to call, say, the `getAdjacent()` method even if the object passed in *is* of type `TilePiece`. (We'll see this again when we look at interfaces.)

IS-A and HAS-A Relationships (*OCP Objective 3.3)

Note: As of the Spring of 2014, the OCA 7 exam won't ask you **directly** about IS-A and HAS-A relationships. But, understanding IS-A and HAS-A relationships will help OCA 7 candidates with many of the questions on the exam.

Given the above, for the OCP exam you need to be able to look at code and determine whether the code demonstrates an IS-A or HAS-A relationship. The rules are simple, so this should be one of the few areas where answering the questions correctly is almost a no-brainer.

IS-A

In OO, the concept of IS-A is based on class inheritance or interface implementation. IS-A is a way of saying, "This thing is a type of that thing." For example, a Mustang is a type of Horse, so in OO terms we can say, "Mustang IS-A Horse." Subaru IS-A Car. Broccoli IS-A Vegetable (not a very fun one, but it still counts). You express the IS-A relationship in Java through the keywords `extends` (for *class* inheritance) and `implements` (for *interface* implementation).

```
public class Car {
  // Cool Car code goes here
}

public class Subaru extends Car {
  // Important Subaru-specific stuff goes here
  // Don't forget Subaru inherits accessible Car members which
  // can include both methods and variables.
}
```

A Car is a type of Vehicle, so the inheritance tree might start from the `Vehicle` class as follows:

```
public class Vehicle { ... }
public class Car extends Vehicle { ... }
public class Subaru extends Car { ... }
```

In OO terms, you can say the following:

`Vehicle` is the superclass of `Car`.
`Car` is the subclass of `Vehicle`.
`Car` is the superclass of `Subaru`.
`Subaru` is the subclass of `Vehicle`.
`Car` inherits from `Vehicle`.
`Subaru` inherits from both `Vehicle` and `Car`.
`Subaru` is derived from `Car`.
`Car` is derived from `Vehicle`.
`Subaru` is derived from `Vehicle`.
`Subaru` is a subtype of both `Vehicle` and `Car`.

Returning to our IS-A relationship, the following statements are true:

"`Car` extends `Vehicle`" means "`Car` IS-A `Vehicle`."
"`Subaru` extends `Car`" means "`Subaru` IS-A `Car`."

And we can also say:

"`Subaru` IS-A `Vehicle`"

because a class is said to be "a type of" anything further up in its inheritance tree. If the expression (`Foo instanceof Bar`) is `true`, then class `Foo` IS-A `Bar`, even if `Foo` doesn't directly extend `Bar`, but instead extends some other class that is a subclass of `Bar`. Figure 2-2 illustrates the inheritance tree for `Vehicle`, `Car`, and `Subaru`. The arrows move from the subclass to the superclass. In other words, a class' arrow points toward the class from which it extends.

HAS-A

HAS-A relationships are based on usage, rather than inheritance. In other words, class A HAS-A B if code in class A has a reference to an instance of class B. For example, you can say the following:

A `Horse` IS-A `Animal`. A `Horse` HAS-A `Halter`.

The code might look like this:

```
public class Animal { }
public class Horse extends Animal {
  private Halter myHalter;
}
```

In this code, the `Horse` class has an instance variable of type `Halter` (a halter is a piece of gear you might have if you have a horse), so you can say that a "`Horse`

FIGURE 2-2

Inheritance tree for `Vehicle`, `Car`, `Subaru`

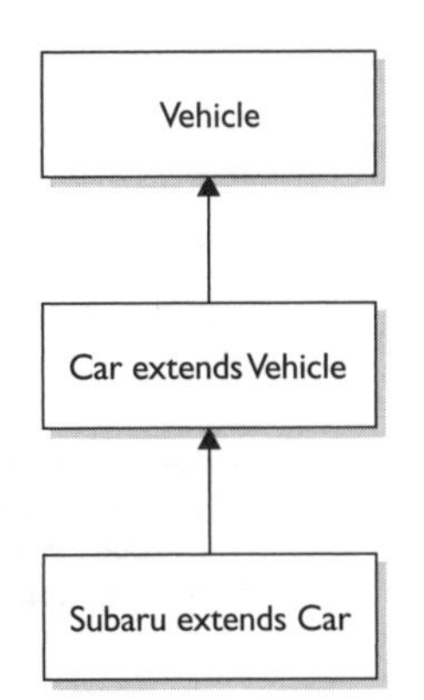

HAS-A Halter." In other words, Horse has a reference to a Halter. Horse code can use that Halter reference to invoke methods on the Halter, and get Halter behavior without having Halter-related code (methods) in the Horse class itself. Figure 2-3 illustrates the HAS-A relationship between Horse and Halter.

HAS-A relationships allow you to design classes that follow good OO practices by not having monolithic classes that do a gazillion different things. Classes (and their resulting objects) should be specialists. As our friend Andrew says, "Specialized classes can actually help reduce bugs." The more specialized the class, the more likely it is that you can reuse the class in other applications. If you put all the Halter-related code directly into the Horse class, you'll end up duplicating code in the Cow class, UnpaidIntern class, and any other class that might need Halter behavior. By keeping the Halter code in a separate, specialized Halter class, you have the chance to reuse the Halter class in multiple applications.

Users of the Horse class (that is, code that calls methods on a Horse instance) think that the Horse class has Halter behavior. The Horse class might have a tie(LeadRope rope) method, for example. Users of the Horse class should never have to know that when they invoke the tie() method, the Horse object turns around and delegates the call to its Halter class by invoking myHalter.tie(rope). The scenario just described might look like this:

```
public class Horse extends Animal {
  private Halter myHalter = new Halter();
  public void tie(LeadRope rope) {
    myHalter.tie(rope);  // Delegate tie behavior to the
                         // Halter object
   }
}
public class Halter {
  public void tie(LeadRope aRope) {
    // Do the actual tie work here
  }
}
```

FIGURE 2-3

HAS-A relationship between Horse and Halter

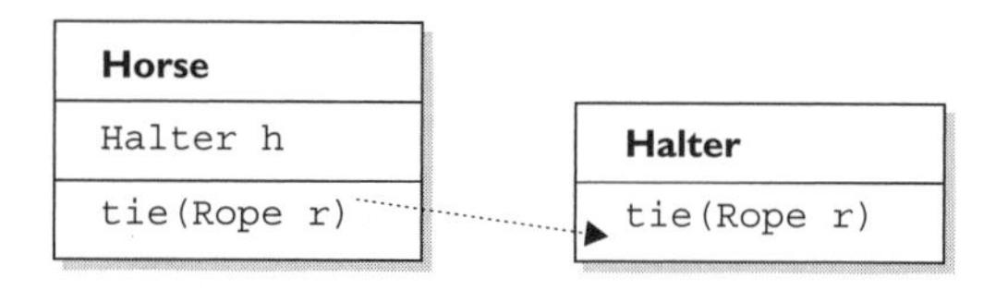

Horse class has a Halter, because Horse declares an instance variable of type Halter. When code invokes tie() on a Horse instance, the Horse invokes tie() on the Horse object's Halter instance variable.

FROM THE CLASSROOM

Object-Oriented Design

IS-A and HAS-A relationships and encapsulation are just the tip of the iceberg when it comes to OO design. Many books and graduate theses have been dedicated to this topic. The reason for the emphasis on proper design is simple: money. The cost to deliver a software application has been estimated to be as much as ten times more expensive for poorly designed programs.

Even the best OO designers (often called architects) make mistakes. It is difficult to visualize the relationships between hundreds, or even thousands, of classes. When mistakes are discovered during the implementation (code writing) phase of a project, the amount of code that has to be rewritten can sometimes mean programming teams have to start over from scratch.

The software industry has evolved to aid the designer. Visual object modeling languages, such as the Unified Modeling Language (UML), allow designers to design and easily modify classes without having to write code first, because OO components are represented graphically. This allows the designer to create a map of the class relationships and helps them recognize errors before coding begins. Another innovation in OO design is design patterns. Designers noticed that many OO designs apply consistently from project to project, and that it was useful to apply the same designs because it reduced the potential to introduce new design errors. OO designers then started to share these designs with each other. Now there are many catalogs of these design patterns both on the Internet and in book form.

Although passing the Java certification exam does not require you to understand OO design this thoroughly, hopefully this background information will help you better appreciate why the test writers chose to include encapsulation and IS-A and HAS-A relationships on the exam.

—Jonathan Meeks, Sun Certified Java Programmer

In OO, we don't want callers to worry about which class or object is actually doing the real work. To make that happen, the `Horse` class hides implementation details from `Horse` users. `Horse` users ask the `Horse` object to do things (in this case, tie itself up), and the `Horse` will either do it or, as in this example, ask something else to do it. To the caller, though, it always appears that the `Horse` object takes care of itself. Users of a `Horse` should not even need to know that there is such a thing as a `Halter` class.

CERTIFICATION OBJECTIVE

Polymorphism (OCA Objectives 7.2 and 7.3)

7.2 Develop code that demonstrates the use of polymorphism.

7.3 Differentiate between the type of a reference and the type of an object.

Remember that any Java object that can pass more than one IS-A test can be considered polymorphic. Other than objects of type `Object`, *all* Java objects are polymorphic in that they pass the IS-A test for their own type and for class `Object`.

Remember, too, that the only way to access an object is through a reference variable. There are a few key things you should know about references:

- A reference variable can be of only one type, and once declared, that type can never be changed (although the object it references can change).
- A reference is a variable, so it can be reassigned to other objects (unless the reference is declared `final`).
- A reference variable's type determines the methods that can be invoked on the object the variable is referencing.
- A reference variable can refer to any object of the same type as the declared reference, or—this is the big one—**it can refer to any *subtype* of the declared type!**
- A reference variable can be declared as a class type or an interface type. If the variable is declared as an interface type, it can reference any object of any class that *implements* the interface.

Earlier we created a `GameShape` class that was extended by two other classes, `PlayerPiece` and `TilePiece`. Now imagine you want to animate some of the shapes on the gameboard. But not *all* shapes are able to be animated, so what do you do with class inheritance?

Could we create a class with an `animate()` method, and have only *some* of the `GameShape` subclasses inherit from that class? If we can, then we could have `PlayerPiece`, for example, extend *both* the `GameShape` class and `Animatable` class, while the `TilePiece` would extend only `GameShape`. But no, this won't work! Java supports only single inheritance! That means a class can have only one immediate superclass. In other words, if `PlayerPiece` is a class, there is no way to say something like this:

```
class PlayerPiece extends GameShape, Animatable { // NO!
  // more code
}
```

A *class* cannot *extend* more than one class: that means one parent per class. A class *can* have multiple ancestors, however, since class B could extend class A, and class C could extend class B, and so on. So any given class might have multiple classes up its inheritance tree, but that's not the same as saying a class directly extends two classes.

on the Job

Some languages (such as C++) allow a class to extend more than one other class. This capability is known as "multiple inheritance." The reason that Java's creators chose not to allow multiple inheritance is that it can become quite messy. In a nutshell, the problem is that if a class extended two other classes, and both superclasses had, say, a `doStuff()` method, which version of `doStuff()` would the subclass inherit? This issue can lead to a scenario known as the "Deadly Diamond of Death," because of the shape of the class diagram that can be created in a multiple inheritance design. The diamond is formed when classes B and C both extend A, and both B and C inherit a method from A. If class D extends both B and C, and both B and C have overridden the method in A, class D has, in theory, inherited two different implementations of the same method. Drawn as a class diagram, the shape of the four classes looks like a diamond.

So if that doesn't work, what else could you do? You could simply put the `animate()` code in `GameShape`, and then disable the method in classes that can't be animated. But that's a bad design choice for many reasons—it's more error-prone, it makes the `GameShape` class less cohesive (more on cohesion in Chapter 10), and it means the `GameShape` API "advertises" that all shapes can be animated, when in fact that's not true since only some of the `GameShape` subclasses will be able to run the `animate()` method successfully.

So what *else* could you do? You already know the answer—create an `Animatable` *interface*, and have only the `GameShape` subclasses that can be animated implement that interface. Here's the interface:

```
public interface Animatable {
  public void animate();
}
```

And here's the modified PlayerPiece class that implements the interface:

```
class PlayerPiece extends GameShape implements Animatable {
  public void movePiece() {
    System.out.println("moving game piece");
  }
  public void animate() {
    System.out.println("animating...");
  }
  // more code
}
```

So now we have a PlayerPiece that passes the IS-A test for both the GameShape class and the Animatable interface. That means a PlayerPiece can be treated polymorphically as one of four things at any given time, depending on the declared type of the reference variable:

- An Object (since any object inherits from Object)
- A GameShape (since PlayerPiece extends GameShape)
- A PlayerPiece (since that's what it really is)
- An Animatable (since PlayerPiece implements Animatable)

The following are all legal declarations. Look closely:

```
PlayerPiece player = new PlayerPiece();
Object o = player;
GameShape shape = player;
Animatable mover = player;
```

There's only one object here—an instance of type PlayerPiece—but there are four different types of reference variables, all referring to that one object on the heap. Pop quiz: Which of the preceding reference variables can invoke the displayShape() method? Hint: Only two of the four declarations can be used to invoke the displayShape() method.

Remember that method invocations allowed by the compiler are based solely on the declared type of the reference, regardless of the object type. So looking at the four reference types again—Object, GameShape, PlayerPiece, and Animatable—which of these four types know about the displayShape() method?

You guessed it—both the GameShape class and the PlayerPiece class are known (by the compiler) to have a displayShape() method, so either of those reference types can be used to invoke displayShape(). Remember that to the compiler, a PlayerPiece IS-A GameShape, so the compiler says, "I see that the declared type is PlayerPiece, and since PlayerPiece extends GameShape, that means PlayerPiece inherited the `displayShape()` method. Therefore, `PlayerPiece` can be used to invoke the `displayShape()` method."

Which methods can be invoked when the `PlayerPiece` object is being referred to using a reference declared as type `Animatable`? Only the `animate()` method. Of course, the cool thing here is that any class from any inheritance tree can also implement `Animatable`, so that means if you have a method with an argument declared as type `Animatable`, you can pass in `PlayerPiece` objects, `SpinningLogo` objects, and anything else that's an instance of a class that implements `Animatable`. And you can use that parameter (of type `Animatable`) to invoke the `animate()` method but not the `displayShape()` method (which it might not even have), or anything other than what is known to the compiler based on the reference type. The compiler always knows, though, that you can invoke the methods of class `Object` on any object, so those are safe to call regardless of the reference—class or interface—used to refer to the object.

We've left out one big part of all this, which is that even though the compiler only knows about the declared reference type, the Java Virtual Machine (JVM) at runtime knows what the object really is. And that means that even if the `PlayerPiece` object's `displayShape()` method is called using a `GameShape` reference variable, if the `PlayerPiece` overrides the `displayShape()` method, the JVM will invoke the `PlayerPiece` version! The JVM looks at the real object at the other end of the reference, "sees" that it has overridden the method of the declared reference variable type, and invokes the method of the object's actual class. But there is one other thing to keep in mind:

> Polymorphic method invocations apply only to *instance methods*. You can always refer to an object with a more general reference variable type (a superclass or interface), but at runtime, the ONLY things that are dynamically selected based on the actual *object* (rather than the *reference* type) are instance methods. Not *static* methods. Not *variables*. Only overridden instance methods are dynamically invoked based on the real object's type.

Because this definition depends on a clear understanding of overriding and the distinction between static methods and instance methods, we'll cover those next.

CERTIFICATION OBJECTIVE

Overriding / Overloading (OCA Objectives 6.1, 6.3,7.2, and 7.3)

6.1 *Create methods with arguments and return values.*

6.3 *Create an overloaded method.*

7.2 *Develop code that demonstrates the use of polymorphism.*

7.3 *Differentiate between the type of a reference and the type of an object.*

The exam will use overridden and overloaded methods on many, many questions. These two concepts are often confused (perhaps because they have similar names?), but each has its own unique and complex set of rules. It's important to get really clear about which "over" uses which rules!

Overridden Methods

Any time a class inherits a method from a superclass, you have the opportunity to override the method (unless, as you learned earlier, the method is marked `final`). The key benefit of overriding is the ability to define behavior that's specific to a particular subclass type. The following example demonstrates a `Horse` subclass of `Animal` overriding the `Animal` version of the `eat()` method:

```
public class Animal {
  public void eat() {
    System.out.println("Generic Animal Eating Generically");
  }
}
class Horse extends Animal {
  public void eat() {
    System.out.println("Horse eating hay, oats, "
                          + "and horse treats");
  }
}
```

For abstract methods you inherit from a superclass, you have no choice: You *must* implement the method in the subclass ***unless the subclass is also abstract.*** Abstract methods must be *implemented* by the concrete subclass, but this is a lot like saying that the concrete subclass *overrides* the abstract methods of the superclass. So you could think of abstract methods as methods you're forced to override.

The `Animal` class creator might have decided that for the purposes of polymorphism, all `Animal` subtypes should have an `eat()` method defined in a unique, specific way. Polymorphically, when an `Animal` reference refers not to an `Animal` instance, but to an `Animal` subclass instance, the caller should be able to invoke `eat()` on the `Animal` reference, but the actual runtime object (say, a `Horse` instance) will run its own specific `eat()` method. Marking the `eat()` method abstract is the `Animal` programmer's way of saying to all subclass developers, "It doesn't make any sense for your new subtype to use a generic `eat()` method, so you have to come up with your *own* `eat()` method implementation!" A (nonabstract), example of using polymorphism looks like this:

```
public class TestAnimals {
  public static void main (String [] args) {
    Animal a = new Animal();
    Animal b = new Horse();  // Animal ref, but a Horse object
    a.eat(); // Runs the Animal version of eat()
    b.eat(); // Runs the Horse version of eat()
  }
}
class Animal {
  public void eat() {
    System.out.println("Generic Animal Eating Generically");
  }
}
class Horse extends Animal {
  public void eat() {
    System.out.println("Horse eating hay, oats, "
                       + "and horse treats");
   }
   public void buck() { }
}
```

In the preceding code, the test class uses an `Animal` reference to invoke a method on a `Horse` object. Remember, the compiler will allow only methods in class `Animal` to be invoked when using a reference to an `Animal`. The following would not be legal given the preceding code:

```
Animal c = new Horse();
c.buck();  // Can't invoke buck();
           // Animal class doesn't have that method
```

To reiterate, the compiler looks only at the reference type, not the instance type. Polymorphism lets you use a more abstract supertype (including an interface) reference to one of its subtypes (including interface implementers).

The overriding method cannot have a more restrictive access modifier than the method being overridden (for example, you can't override a method marked `public` and make it `protected`). Think about it: If the `Animal` class advertises a `public` `eat()` method and someone has an `Animal` reference (in other words, a reference declared as type `Animal`), that someone will assume it's safe to call `eat()` on the `Animal` reference regardless of the actual instance that the `Animal` reference is referring to. If a subclass were allowed to sneak in and change the access modifier on the overriding method, then suddenly at runtime—when the JVM invokes the true object's (`Horse`) version of the method rather than the reference type's (`Animal`) version—the program would die a horrible death. (Not to mention the emotional distress for the one who was betrayed by the rogue subclass.)

Let's modify the polymorphic example we saw earlier in this section:

```
public class TestAnimals {
  public static void main (String [] args) {
    Animal a = new Animal();
    Animal b = new Horse();  // Animal ref, but a Horse object
    a.eat();                 // Runs the Animal version of eat()
    b.eat();                 // Runs the Horse version of eat()
  }
}
class Animal {
  public void eat() {
    System.out.println("Generic Animal Eating Generically");
  }
}
class Horse extends Animal {
  private void eat() {      // whoa! - it's private!
    System.out.println("Horse eating hay, oats, "
                      + "and horse treats");
  }
}
```

If this code compiled (which it doesn't), the following would fail at runtime:

```
Animal b = new Horse();  // Animal ref, but a Horse
                         // object, so far so good
b.eat();                 // Meltdown at runtime!
```

The variable `b` is of type `Animal`, which has a `public eat()` method. But remember that at runtime, Java uses virtual method invocation to dynamically select the actual version of the method that will run, based on the actual instance. An `Animal` reference can always refer to a `Horse` instance, because `Horse` IS-A(n) `Animal`. What makes that superclass reference to a subclass instance possible is that the subclass is guaranteed to be able to do everything the superclass can do. Whether the `Horse` instance overrides the inherited methods of `Animal` or simply inherits them, anyone with an `Animal` reference to a `Horse` instance is free to call all accessible `Animal` methods. For that reason, an overriding method must fulfill the contract of the superclass.

Note: In Chapter 6 we will explore exception handling in detail. Once you've studied Chapter 6, you'll appreciate this handy, single list of overriding rules. The rules for overriding a method are as follows:

- The argument list must exactly match that of the overridden method. If they don't match, you can end up with an overloaded method you didn't intend.
- The return type must be the same as, or a subtype of, the return type declared in the original overridden method in the superclass. (More on this in a few pages when we discuss covariant returns.)
- The access level can't be more restrictive than that of the overridden method.
- The access level CAN be less restrictive than that of the overridden method.
- Instance methods can be overridden only if they are inherited by the subclass. A subclass within the same package as the instance's superclass can override any superclass method that is not marked `private` or `final`. A subclass in a different package can override only those non`final` methods marked `public` or `protected` (since `protected` methods are inherited by the subclass).
- The overriding method CAN throw any unchecked (runtime) exception, regardless of whether the overridden method declares the exception. (More in Chapter 6.)
- The overriding method must NOT throw checked exceptions that are new or broader than those declared by the overridden method. For example, a method that declares a `FileNotFoundException` cannot be overridden by a method that declares a `SQLException`, `Exception`, or any other non-runtime exception unless it's a subclass of `FileNotFoundException`.
- The overriding method can throw narrower or fewer exceptions. Just because an overridden method "takes risks" doesn't mean that the overriding subclass' exception takes the same risks. Bottom line: An overriding method doesn't have to declare any exceptions that it will never throw, regardless of what the overridden method declares.
- You cannot override a method marked `final`.
- You cannot override a method marked `static`. We'll look at an example in a few pages when we discuss `static` methods in more detail.

- If a method can't be inherited, you cannot override it. Remember that overriding implies that you're reimplementing a method you inherited! For example, the following code is not legal, and even if you added an `eat()` method to `Horse`, it wouldn't be an override of `Animal`'s `eat()` method.

```
public class TestAnimals {
  public static void main (String [] args) {
    Horse h =  new Horse();
    h.eat(); // Not legal because Horse didn't inherit eat()
  }
}
class Animal {
  private void eat() {
    System.out.println("Generic Animal Eating Generically");
  }
}
class Horse extends Animal { }
```

Invoking a Superclass Version of an Overridden Method

Often, you'll want to take advantage of some of the code in the superclass version of a method, yet still override it to provide some additional specific behavior. It's like saying, "Run the superclass version of the method, and then come back down here and finish with my subclass additional method code." (Note that there's no requirement that the superclass version run before the subclass code.) It's easy to do in code using the keyword `super` as follows:

```
public class Animal {
  public void eat() { }
  public void printYourself() {
    // Useful printing code goes here
  }
}
class Horse extends Animal {
  public void printYourself() {
    // Take advantage of Animal code, then add some more
    super.printYourself();  // Invoke the superclass
                            // (Animal) code
                            // Then do Horse-specific
                            // print work here
  }
}
```

Note: Using `super` to invoke an overridden method applies only to instance methods. (Remember that `static` methods can't be overridden.) And you can use `super` only to access a method in a class' superclass, not the superclass of the superclass—that is, you can't say `super.super.doStuff()`.

exam watch

If a method is overridden but you use a polymorphic (supertype) reference to refer to the subtype object with the overriding method, the compiler assumes you're calling the supertype version of the method. If the supertype version declares a checked exception, but the overriding subtype method does not, the compiler still thinks you are calling a method that declares an exception (more in Chapter 6). Let's take a look at an example:

```
class Animal {
  public void eat() throws Exception {
                     // throws an Exception
  }
}
class Dog2 extends Animal {
  public void eat() { /* no Exceptions */}
  public static void main(String [] args) {
    Animal a = new Dog2();
    Dog2 d = new Dog2();
    d.eat();            // ok
    a.eat();            // compiler error -
                        // unreported exception
  }
}
```

This code will not compile because of the Exception declared on the `Animal eat()` method. This happens even though, at runtime, the `eat()` method used would be the `Dog` version, which does not declare the exception.

Examples of Illegal Method Overrides

Let's take a look at overriding the `eat()` method of `Animal`:

```
public class Animal {
  public void eat() { }
}
```

Table 2-1 lists examples of illegal overrides of the `Animal eat()` method, given the preceding version of the `Animal` class.

TABLE 2-1 Examples of Illegal Overrides

Illegal Override Code	Problem with the Code
`private void eat() { }`	Access modifier is more restrictive
`public void eat() throws IOException { }`	Declares a checked exception not defined by superclass version
`public void eat(String food) { }`	A legal overload, not an override, because the argument list changed
`public String eat() { }`	Not an override because of the return type, and not an overload either because there's no change in the argument list

Overloaded Methods

Over*loaded* methods let you reuse the same method name in a class, but with different arguments (and, optionally, a different return type). Overloading a method often means you're being a little nicer to those who call your methods, because your code takes on the burden of coping with different argument types rather than forcing the caller to do conversions prior to invoking your method. The rules aren't too complex:

- Overloaded methods MUST change the argument list.
- Overloaded methods CAN change the return type.
- Overloaded methods CAN change the access modifier.
- Overloaded methods CAN declare new or broader checked exceptions.
- A method can be overloaded in the *same* class or in a *subclass*. In other words, if class A defines a `doStuff(int i)` method, the subclass B could define a `doStuff(String s)` method without overriding the superclass version that takes an `int`. So two methods with the same name but in different classes can still be considered overloaded if the subclass inherits one version of the method and then declares another overloaded version in its class definition.

exam watch

Less experienced Java developers are often confused about the subtle differences between overloaded and overridden methods. Be careful to recognize when a method is overloaded rather than overridden. You might see a method that appears to be violating a rule for overriding, but that is actually a legal overload, as follows:

```
public class Foo {
  public void doStuff(int y, String s) { }
  public void moreThings(int x) { }
}
class Bar extends Foo {
  public void doStuff(int y, long s) throws IOException { }
}
```

It's tempting to see the `IOException` as the problem, because the overridden `doStuff()` method doesn't declare an exception and `IOException` is checked by the compiler. But the `doStuff()` method is not overridden! Subclass `Bar` overloads the `doStuff()` method by varying the argument list, so the `IOException` is fine.

Legal Overloads

Let's look at a method we want to overload:

```
public void changeSize(int size, String name, float pattern) { }
```

The following methods are legal overloads of the `changeSize()` method:

```
public void changeSize(int size, String name) { }
private int changeSize(int size, float pattern) { }
public void changeSize(float pattern, String name)
                        throws IOException { }
```

Invoking Overloaded Methods

Note for OCP candidates: In Chapter 11 we will look at how boxing and var-args impact overloading. (You still have to pay attention to what's covered here, however.)

When a method is invoked, more than one method of the same name might exist for the object type you're invoking a method on. For example, the `Horse` class might have three methods with the same name but with different argument lists, which means the method is overloaded.

Deciding which of the matching methods to invoke is based on the arguments. If you invoke the method with a `String` argument, the overloaded version that takes a `String` is called. If you invoke a method of the same name but pass it a `float`, the overloaded version that takes a `float` will run. If you invoke the method of the same name but pass it a `Foo` object, and there isn't an overloaded version that takes a `Foo`, then the compiler will complain that it can't find a match. The following are examples of invoking overloaded methods:

```
class Adder {
  public int addThem(int x, int y) {
    return x + y;
  }

  // Overload the addThem method to add doubles instead of ints
  public double addThem(double x, double y) {
    return x + y;
  }
}
  // From another class, invoke the addThem() method
public class TestAdder {
  public static void main (String [] args) {
    Adder a = new Adder();
    int b = 27;
    int c = 3;
    int result = a.addThem(b,c);              // Which addThem is invoked?
    double doubleResult = a.addThem(22.5,9.3); // Which addThem?
  }
}
```

In this `TestAdder` code, the first call to `a.addThem(b,c)` passes two `int`s to the method, so the first version of `addThem()`—the overloaded version that takes two `int` arguments—is called. The second call to `a.addThem(22.5, 9.3)` passes two `double`s to the method, so the second version of `addThem()`—the overloaded version that takes two double arguments—is called.

Invoking overloaded methods that take object references rather than primitives is a little more interesting. Say you have an overloaded method such that one version takes an `Animal` and one takes a `Horse` (subclass of `Animal`). If you pass a `Horse` object in the method invocation, you'll invoke the overloaded version that takes a `Horse`. Or so it looks at first glance:

```
class Animal { }
class Horse extends Animal { }
class UseAnimals {
  public void doStuff(Animal a) {
    System.out.println("In the Animal version");
  }
```

```
    public void doStuff(Horse h) {
      System.out.println("In the Horse version");
    }
    public static void main (String [] args) {
      UseAnimals ua = new UseAnimals();
      Animal animalObj = new Animal();
      Horse horseObj = new Horse();
      ua.doStuff(animalObj);
      ua.doStuff(horseObj);
    }
  }
```

The output is what you expect:

```
In the Animal version
In the Horse version
```

But what if you use an `Animal` reference to a `Horse` object?

```
Animal animalRefToHorse = new Horse();
  ua.doStuff(animalRefToHorse);
```

Which of the overloaded versions is invoked? You might want to answer, "The one that takes a `Horse`, since it's a `Horse` object at runtime that's being passed to the method." But that's not how it works. The preceding code would actually print this:

```
in the Animal version
```

Even though the actual object at runtime is a `Horse` and not an `Animal`, the choice of which overloaded method to call (in other words, the signature of the method) is NOT dynamically decided at runtime.

Just remember that, the *reference* type (not the object type) determines which overloaded method is invoked! To summarize, which over*ridden* version of the method to call (in other words, from which class in the inheritance tree) is decided at *runtime* based on *object* type, but which over*loaded* version of the method to call is based on the *reference* type of the argument passed at *compile* time. If you invoke a method passing it an `Animal` reference to a `Horse` object, the compiler knows only about the `Animal`, so it chooses the overloaded version of the method that takes an `Animal`. It does not matter that at runtime a `Horse` is actually being passed.

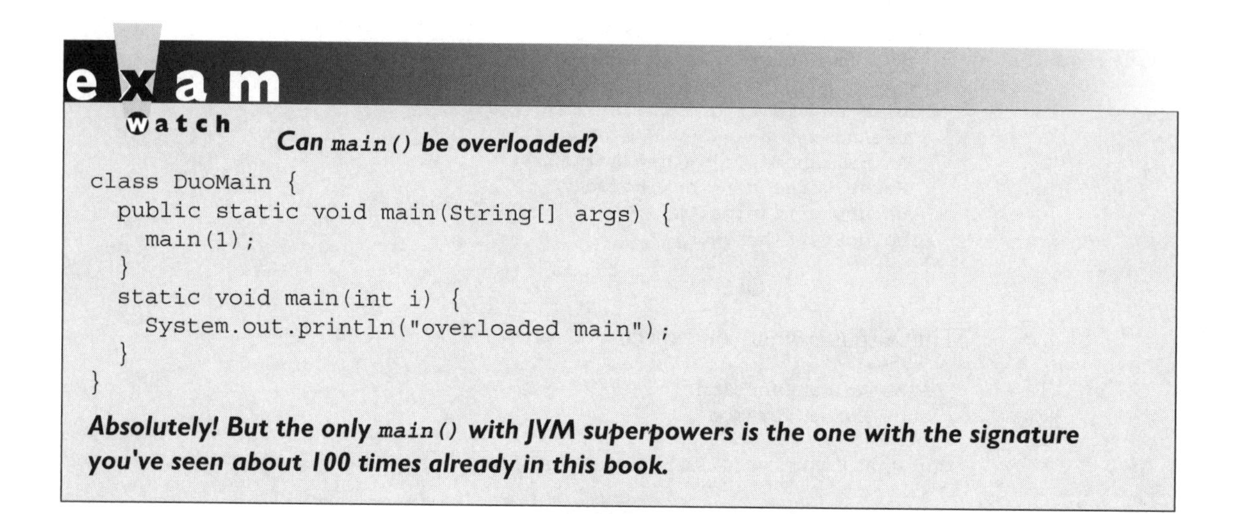

exam watch

Can `main()` be overloaded?

```
class DuoMain {
  public static void main(String[] args) {
    main(1);
  }
  static void main(int i) {
    System.out.println("overloaded main");
  }
}
```

Absolutely! But the only `main()` with JVM superpowers is the one with the signature you've seen about 100 times already in this book.

Polymorphism in Overloaded and Overridden Methods How does polymorphism work with overloaded methods? From what we just looked at, it doesn't appear that polymorphism matters when a method is overloaded. If you pass an `Animal` reference, the overloaded method that takes an `Animal` will be invoked, even if the actual object passed is a `Horse`. Once the `Horse` masquerading as `Animal` gets in to the method, however, the `Horse` object is still a `Horse` despite being passed into a method expecting an `Animal`. So it's true that polymorphism doesn't determine which overloaded version is called; polymorphism does come into play when the decision is about which overridden version of a method is called. But sometimes a method is both overloaded and overridden. Imagine that the `Animal` and `Horse` classes look like this:

```
public class Animal {
  public void eat() {
    System.out.println("Generic Animal Eating Generically");
  }
}
public class Horse extends Animal {
  public void eat() {
    System.out.println("Horse eating hay ");
  }
  public void eat(String s) {
    System.out.println("Horse eating " + s);
  }
}
```

Notice that the `Horse` class has both overloaded and overridden the `eat()` method. Table 2-2 shows which version of the three `eat()` methods will run depending on how they are invoked.

TABLE 2-2 Examples of Legal and Illegal Overrides

Method Invocation Code	Result
`Animal a = new Animal();` `a.eat();`	`Generic Animal Eating Generically`
`Horse h = new Horse();` `h.eat();`	`Horse eating hay`
`Animal ah = new` **`Horse();`** `ah.eat();`	`Horse eating hay` Polymorphism works—the actual object type (`Horse`), not the reference type (`Animal`), is used to determine which `eat()` is called.
`Horse he = new Horse();` `he.eat("Apples");`	`Horse eating Apples` The overloaded `eat(String s)` method is invoked.
`Animal a2 = new Animal();` `a2.eat("treats");`	Compiler error! Compiler sees that the `Animal` class doesn't have an `eat()` method that takes a `String`.
`Animal ah2 = new` **`Horse()`**`;` `ah2.eat("Carrots");`	Compiler error! Compiler still looks only at the reference and sees that `Animal` doesn't have an `eat()` method that takes a `String`. Compiler doesn't care that the actual object might be a `Horse` at runtime.

exam watch

Don't be fooled by a method that's overloaded but not overridden by a subclass. It's perfectly legal to do the following:

```
public class Foo {
  void doStuff() { }
}
class Bar extends Foo {
  void doStuff(String s) { }
}
```

The `Bar` class has two `doStuff()` methods: the no-arg version it inherits from `Foo` (and does not override) and the overloaded `doStuff(String s)` defined in the `Bar` class. Code with a reference to a `Foo` can invoke only the no-arg version, but code with a reference to a `Bar` can invoke either of the overloaded versions.

Table 2-3 summarizes the difference between overloaded and overridden methods.

TABLE 1-2 Differences Between Overloaded and Overridden Methods

	Overloaded Method	Overridden Method
Argument(s)	Must change.	Must not change.
Return type	Can change.	Can't change except for covariant returns. (Covered later this chapter.)
Exceptions	Can change.	Can reduce or eliminate. Must not throw new or broader checked exceptions.
Access	Can change.	Must not make more restrictive (can be less restrictive).
Invocation	*Reference* type determines which overloaded version (based on declared argument types) is selected. Happens at *compile* time. The actual *method* that's invoked is still a virtual method invocation that happens at runtime, but the compiler will already know the *signature* of the method to be invoked. So at runtime, the argument match will already have been nailed down, just not the *class* in which the method lives.	*Object* type (in other words, *the type of the actual instance on the heap*) determines which method is selected. Happens at *runtime*.

We'll cover constructor overloading later in the chapter, where we'll also cover the other constructor-related topics that are on the exam. Figure 2-4 illustrates the way overloaded and overridden methods appear in class relationships.

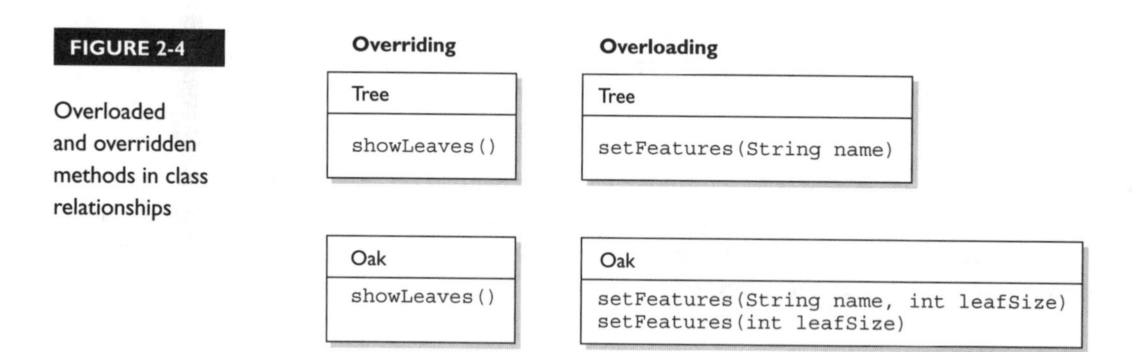

FIGURE 2-4 Overloaded and overridden methods in class relationships

CERTIFICATION OBJECTIVE

Casting (OCA Objectives 7.3 and 7.4)

7.3 *Differentiate between the type of a reference and the type of an object.*

7.4 *Determine when casting is necessary.*

You've seen how it's both possible and common to use generic reference variable types to refer to more specific object types. It's at the heart of polymorphism. For example, this line of code should be second nature by now:

```
Animal animal = new Dog();
```

But what happens when you want to use that `animal` reference variable to invoke a method that only class `Dog` has? You know it's referring to a `Dog`, and you want to do a `Dog`-specific thing? In the following code, we've got an array of `Animals`, and whenever we find a `Dog` in the array, we want to do a special `Dog` thing. Let's agree for now that all of this code is okay, except that we're not sure about the line of code that invokes the `playDead` method.

```
class Animal {
  void makeNoise() {System.out.println("generic noise"); }
}
class Dog extends Animal {
  void makeNoise() {System.out.println("bark"); }
  void playDead() { System.out.println("roll over"); }
}

class CastTest2 {
  public static void main(String [] args) {
    Animal [] a = {new Animal(), new Dog(), new Animal() };
    for(Animal animal : a) {
      animal.makeNoise();
      if(animal instanceof Dog) {
        animal.playDead();        // try to do a Dog behavior?
      }
    }
  }
}
```

When we try to compile this code, the compiler says something like this:

```
cannot find symbol
```

The compiler is saying, "Hey, class `Animal` doesn't have a `playDead()` method." Let's modify the `if` code block:

```
if(animal instanceof Dog) {
  Dog d = (Dog) animal;        // casting the ref. var.
  d.playDead();
}
```

The new and improved code block contains a cast, which in this case is sometimes called a *downcast*, because we're casting down the inheritance tree to a more specific class. Now the compiler is happy. Before we try to invoke `playDead`, we cast the `animal` variable to type `Dog`. What we're saying to the compiler is, "We know it's really referring to a `Dog` object, so it's okay to make a new `Dog` reference variable to refer to that object." In this case we're safe, because before we ever try the cast, we do an `instanceof` test to make sure.

It's important to know that the compiler is forced to trust us when we do a downcast, even when we screw up:

```
class Animal { }
class Dog extends Animal { }
class DogTest {
  public static void main(String [] args) {
    Animal animal = new Animal();
    Dog d = (Dog) animal;          // compiles but fails later
  }
}
```

It can be maddening! This code compiles! When we try to run it, we'll get an exception something like this:

```
java.lang.ClassCastException
```

Why can't we trust the compiler to help us out here? Can't it see that `animal` is of type `Animal`? All the compiler can do is verify that the two types are in the same inheritance tree, so that depending on whatever code might have come before the downcast, it's possible that `animal` is of type `Dog`. The compiler must allow things that might possibly work at runtime. However, if the compiler knows with certainty that the cast could not possibly work, compilation will fail. The following replacement code block will NOT compile:

```
Animal animal = new Animal();
Dog d = (Dog) animal;
String s = (String) animal;    // animal can't EVER be a String
```

In this case, you'll get an error something like this:

```
inconvertible types
```

Unlike downcasting, *upcasting* (casting *up* the inheritance tree to a more general type) works implicitly (that is, you don't have to type in the cast) because when you upcast you're implicitly restricting the number of methods you can invoke, as opposed to *down*casting, which implies that later on, you might want to invoke a more *specific* method. Here's an example:

```
class Animal { }
class Dog extends Animal { }

class DogTest {
  public static void main(String [] args) {
    Dog d = new Dog();
    Animal a1 = d;           // upcast ok with no explicit cast
    Animal a2 = (Animal) d;  // upcast ok with an explicit cast
  }
}
```

Both of the previous upcasts will compile and run without exception, because a `Dog` IS-A(n) `Animal`, which means that anything an `Animal` can do, a `Dog` can do. A `Dog` can do more, of course, but the point is that anyone with an `Animal` reference can safely call `Animal` methods on a `Dog` instance. The `Animal` methods may have been overridden in the `Dog` class, but all we care about now is that a `Dog` can always do at least everything an `Animal` can do. The compiler and JVM know it, too, so the implicit upcast is always legal for assigning an object of a subtype to a reference of one of its supertype classes (or interfaces). If `Dog` implements `Pet`, and `Pet` defines `beFriendly()`, then a `Dog` can be implicitly cast to a `Pet`, but the only `Dog` method you can invoke then is `beFriendly()`, which `Dog` was forced to implement because `Dog` implements the `Pet` interface.

One more thing...if `Dog` implements `Pet`, then if `Beagle` extends `Dog`, but `Beagle` does not *declare* that it implements `Pet`, `Beagle` is still a `Pet`! `Beagle` is a `Pet` simply because it extends `Dog`, and `Dog`'s already taken care of the `Pet` parts for itself, and for all its children. The `Beagle` class can always override any method it inherits from `Dog`, including methods that `Dog` implemented to fulfill its interface contract.

And just one more thing...if `Beagle` does declare that it implements `Pet`, just so that others looking at the `Beagle` class API can easily see that `Beagle` IS-A `Pet` without having to look at `Beagle`'s superclasses, `Beagle` still doesn't need to implement the `beFriendly()` method if the `Dog` class (`Beagle`'s superclass) has already taken care of that. In other words, if `Beagle` IS-A `Dog`, and `Dog` IS-A `Pet`, then `Beagle` IS-A `Pet` and has already met its `Pet` obligations for implementing the `beFriendly()` method since it inherits the `beFriendly()` method. The compiler is smart enough to say, "I know `Beagle` already IS a `Dog`, but it's okay to make it more obvious by adding a cast."

So don't be fooled by code that shows a concrete class that declares that it implements an interface but doesn't implement the *methods* of the interface. Before you can tell whether the code is legal, you must know what the superclasses of this implementing class have declared. If any superclass in its inheritance tree has already provided concrete (that is, nonabstract) method implementations, then regardless of whether the superclass declares that it implements the interface, the subclass is under no obligation to reimplement (override) those methods.

exam watch

The exam creators will tell you that they're forced to jam tons of code into little spaces "because of the exam engine." Although that's partially true, they ALSO like to obfuscate. The following code

```
Animal a = new Dog();
Dog d = (Dog) a;
d.doDogStuff();
```

can be replaced with this easy-to-read bit of fun:

```
Animal a = new Dog();
((Dog)a).doDogStuff();
```

In this case the compiler needs all of those parentheses; otherwise it thinks it's been handed an incomplete statement.

CERTIFICATION OBJECTIVE

Implementing an Interface (OCA Objective 7.6)

7.6 *Use abstract classes and interfaces.*

When you implement an interface, you're agreeing to adhere to the contract defined in the interface. That means you're agreeing to provide legal implementations for every method defined in the interface, and that anyone who knows what the interface methods look like (not how they're implemented, but how they can be called and what they return) can rest assured that they can invoke those methods on an instance of your implementing class.

For example, if you create a class that implements the `Runnable` interface (so that your code can be executed by a specific thread), you must provide the `public void run()` method. Otherwise, the poor thread could be told to go execute your `Runnable` object's code and—surprise, surprise—the thread then discovers the object has no `run()` method! (At which point, the thread would blow up and the JVM would crash in a spectacular yet horrible explosion.) Thankfully, Java prevents this meltdown from occurring by running a compiler check on any class that claims to implement an interface. If the class says it's implementing an interface, it darn well better have an implementation for each method in the interface (with a few exceptions we'll look at in a moment).

Assuming an interface, `Bounceable`, with two methods, `bounce()` and `setBounceFactor()`, the following class will compile:

```
public class Ball implements Bounceable {  // Keyword
                                           // 'implements'
  public void bounce() { }
  public void setBounceFactor(int bf) { }
}
```

Okay, we know what you're thinking: "This has got to be the worst implementation class in the history of implementation classes." It compiles, though. And it runs. The interface contract guarantees that a class will have the method (in other words, others can call the method subject to access control), but it never guaranteed a good implementation—or even any actual implementation code in the body of the method. (Keep in mind, though, that if the interface declares that a method is NOT void, your class's implementation code will have to include a return statement.) The compiler will never say to you, "Um, excuse me, but did you really mean to put nothing between those curly braces? HELLO. This is a method after all, so shouldn't it do something?"

Implementation classes must adhere to the same rules for method implementation as a class extending an `abstract` class. To be a legal implementation class, a nonabstract implementation class must do the following:

- Provide concrete (nonabstract) implementations for all methods from the declared interface.
- Follow all the rules for legal overrides, such as the following:
  - Declare no checked exceptions on implementation methods other than those declared by the interface method, or subclasses of those declared by the interface method.
  - Maintain the signature of the interface method, and maintain the same return type (or a subtype). (But it does not have to declare the exceptions declared in the interface method declaration.)

But wait, there's more! An implementation class can itself be `abstract`! For example, the following is legal for a class `Ball` implementing `Bounceable`:

```
abstract class Ball implements Bounceable { }
```

Notice anything missing? We never provided the implementation methods. And that's okay. If the implementation class is `abstract`, it can simply pass the buck to its first concrete subclass. For example, if class `BeachBall` extends `Ball`, and `BeachBall` is not `abstract`, then `BeachBall` will have to provide all the methods from `Bounceable`:

```
class BeachBall extends Ball {
  // Even though we don't say it in the class declaration above,
  // BeachBall implements Bounceable, since BeachBall's abstract
  // superclass (Ball) implements Bounceable

  public void bounce() {
  // interesting BeachBall-specific bounce code

  }
  public void setBounceFactor(int bf) {
  // clever BeachBall-specific code for setting
  // a bounce factor

  }
  // if class Ball defined any abstract methods,
  // they'll have to be
  // implemented here as well.
}
```

Look for classes that claim to implement an interface but don't provide the correct method implementations. Unless the implementing class is abstract, the implementing class must provide implementations for all methods defined in the interface.

You need to know two more rules, and then we can put this topic to sleep (or put you to sleep; we always get those two confused):

1. A class can implement more than one interface. It's perfectly legal to say, for example, the following:

   ```
   public class Ball implements Bounceable, Serializable, Runnable { ... }
   ```

You can extend only one class, but you can implement many interfaces. But remember that subclassing defines who and what you are, whereas implementing defines a role you can play or a hat you can wear, d espite how different you might be from some other class implementing the same interface (but from a different inheritance tree). For example, a Person extends HumanBeing (although for some, that's debatable). But a Person may also implement Programmer, Snowboarder, Employee, Parent, or PersonCrazyEnoughToTakeThisExam.

2. An interface can itself extend another interface, but it can never implement anything. The following code is perfectly legal:

```
public interface Bounceable extends Moveable { }   // ok!
```

What does that mean? The first concrete (nonabstract) implementation class of `Bounceable` must implement all the methods of `Bounceable`, plus all the methods of `Moveable`! The subinterface, as we call it, simply adds more requirements to the contract of the superinterface. You'll see this concept applied in many areas of Java, especially Java EE, where you'll often have to build your own interface that extends one of the Java EE interfaces.

Hold on, though, because here's where it gets strange. An interface can extend more than one interface! Think about that for a moment. You know that when we're talking about classes, the following is illegal:

```
public class Programmer extends Employee, Geek { } // Illegal!
```

As we mentioned earlier, a class is not allowed to extend multiple classes in Java. An interface, however, is free to extend multiple interfaces:

```
interface Bounceable extends Moveable, Spherical {   // ok!
  void bounce();
  void setBounceFactor(int bf);
}
interface Moveable {
  void moveIt();
}
interface Spherical {
  void doSphericalThing();
}
```

In the next example, `Ball` is required to implement `Bounceable`, plus all methods from the interfaces that `Bounceable` extends (including any interfaces those interfaces extend, and so on until you reach the top of the stack—or is it the bottom of the stack?). So `Ball` would need to look like the following:

```
class Ball implements Bounceable {

  public void bounce() { }              // Implement Bounceable's methods
  public void setBounceFactor(int bf) { }

  public void moveIt() { }              // Implement Moveable's method

  public void doSphericalThing() { }    // Implement Spherical
}
```

If class `Ball` fails to implement any of the methods from `Bounceable`, `Moveable`, or `Spherical`, the compiler will jump up and down wildly, red in the face, until it does. Unless, that is, class `Ball` is marked `abstract`. In that case, `Ball` could choose to implement any, all, or none of the methods from any of the interfaces, thus leaving the rest of the implementations to a concrete subclass of `Ball`, as follows:

```
abstract class Ball implements Bounceable {
  public void bounce() { ... }    // Define bounce behavior
  public void setBounceFactor(int bf) { ... }
  // Don't implement the rest; leave it for a subclass
}
class SoccerBall extends Ball {   // class SoccerBall must
                                  // implement the interface
                                  // methods that Ball didn't
  public void moveIt() { ... }
  public void doSphericalThing() { ... }
  // SoccerBall can choose to override the Bounceable methods
  // implemented by Ball
  public void bounce() { ... }
}
```

Figure 2-5 compares concrete and `abstract` examples of extends and implements, for both classes and interfaces.

FIGURE 2-5 Comparing concrete and `abstract` examples of extends and implements

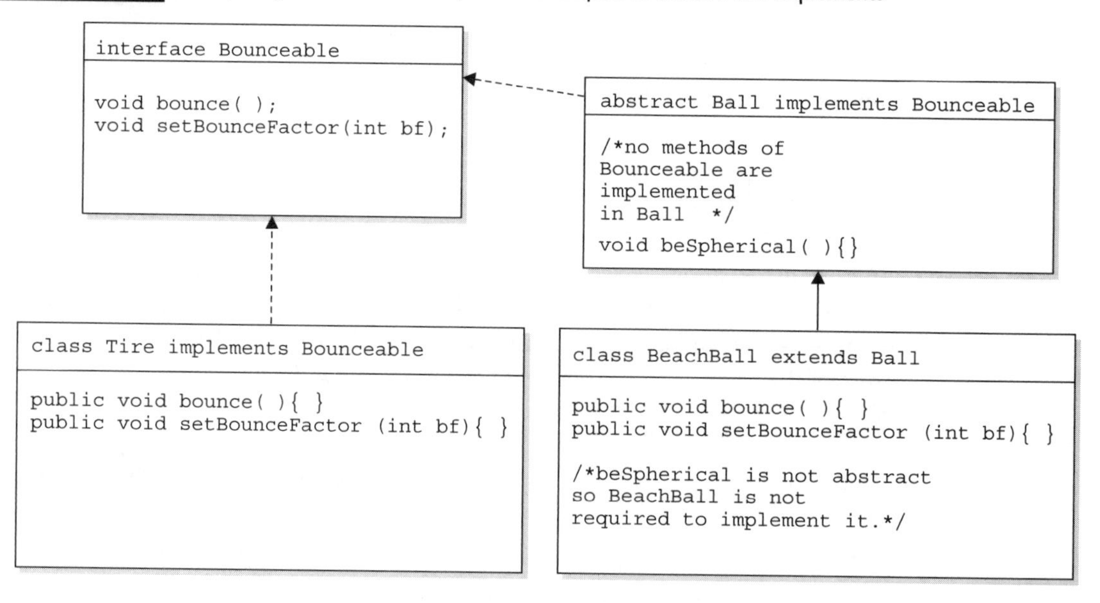

Because `BeachBall` is the first concrete class to implement `Bounceable`, it must provide implementations for all methods of `Bounceable`, except those defined in the abstract class `Ball`. Because `Ball` did not provide implementations of `Bounceable` methods, `BeachBall` was required to implement all of them.

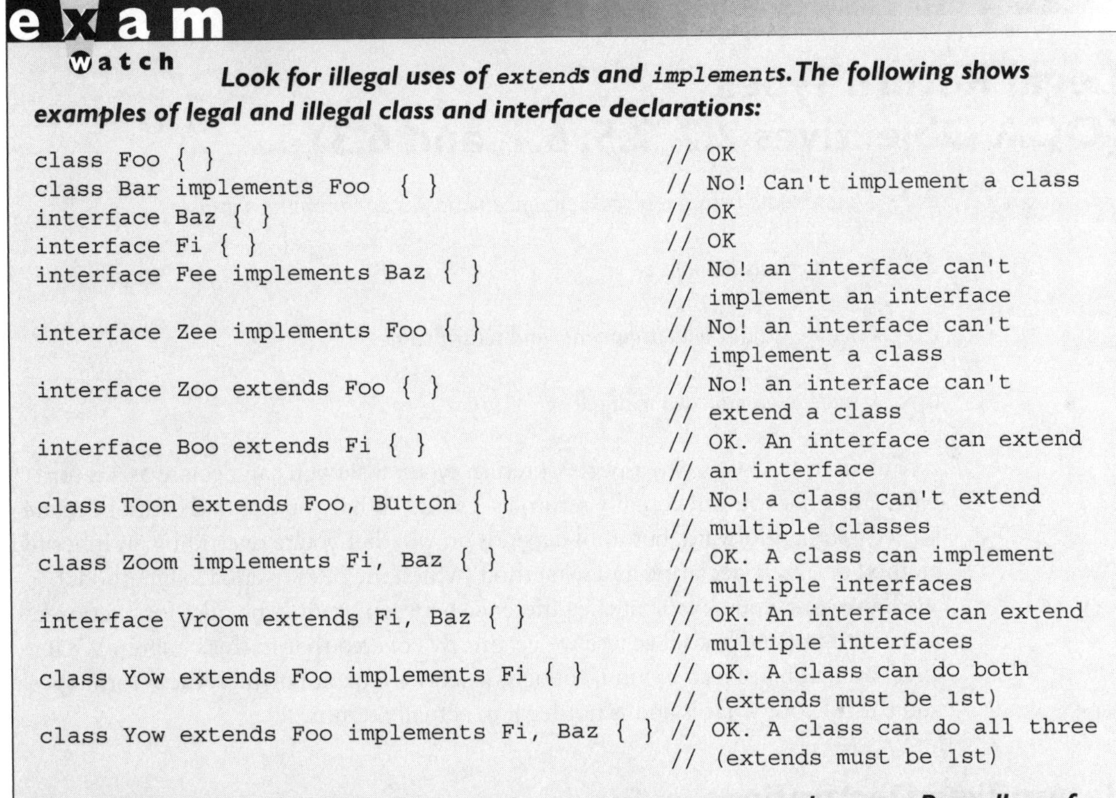

exam watch

Look for illegal uses of `extends` and `implements`. The following shows examples of legal and illegal class and interface declarations:

```
class Foo { }                                  // OK
class Bar implements Foo  { }                  // No! Can't implement a class
interface Baz { }                              // OK
interface Fi { }                               // OK
interface Fee implements Baz { }               // No! an interface can't
                                               // implement an interface
interface Zee implements Foo { }               // No! an interface can't
                                               // implement a class
interface Zoo extends Foo { }                  // No! an interface can't
                                               // extend a class
interface Boo extends Fi { }                   // OK. An interface can extend
                                               // an interface
class Toon extends Foo, Button { }             // No! a class can't extend
                                               // multiple classes
class Zoom implements Fi, Baz { }              // OK. A class can implement
                                               // multiple interfaces
interface Vroom extends Fi, Baz { }            // OK. An interface can extend
                                               // multiple interfaces
class Yow extends Foo implements Fi { }        // OK. A class can do both
                                               // (extends must be 1st)
class Yow extends Foo implements Fi, Baz { }   // OK. A class can do all three
                                               // (extends must be 1st)
```

Burn these in, and watch for abuses in the questions you get on the exam. Regardless of what the question appears to be testing, the real problem might be the class or interface declaration. Before you get caught up in, say, tracing a complex threading flow, check to see if the code will even compile. (Just that tip alone may be worth your putting us in your will!) (You'll be impressed by the effort the exam developers put into distracting you from the real problem.) (How did people manage to write anything before parentheses were invented?)

CERTIFICATION OBJECTIVE

Legal Return Types (OCA Objectives 2.2, 2.5, 6.1, and 6.3)

2.2 *Differentiate between object reference variables and primitive variables.*

2.5 *Call methods on objects.*

6.1 *Create methods with arguments and return values.*

6.3 *Create an overloaded method.*

This section covers two aspects of return types: what you can declare as a return type, and what you can actually return as a value. What you can and cannot declare is pretty straightforward, but it all depends on whether you're overriding an inherited method or simply declaring a new method (which includes overloaded methods). We'll take just a quick look at the difference between return type rules for overloaded and overriding methods, because we've already covered that in this chapter. We'll cover a small bit of new ground, though, when we look at polymorphic return types and the rules for what is and is not legal to actually return.

Return Type Declarations

This section looks at what you're allowed to declare as a return type, which depends primarily on whether you are overriding, overloading, or declaring a new method.

Return Types on Overloaded Methods

Remember that method overloading is not much more than name reuse. The overloaded method is a completely different method from any other method of the same name. So if you inherit a method but overload it in a subclass, you're not subject to the restrictions of overriding, which means you can declare any return type you like. What you can't do is change *only* the return type. To overload a method, remember, you must change the argument list. The following code shows an overloaded method:

```
public class Foo{
  void go() { }
}
public class Bar extends Foo {
  String go(int x) {
    return null;
  }
}
```

Notice that the `Bar` version of the method uses a different return type. That's perfectly fine. As long as you've changed the argument list, you're overloading the method, so the return type doesn't have to match that of the superclass version. What you're NOT allowed to do is this:

```
public class Foo{
  void go() { }
}
public class Bar extends Foo {
  String go() { // Not legal! Can't change only the return type
    return null;
  }
}
```

Overriding and Return Types, and Covariant Returns

When a subclass wants to change the method implementation of an inherited method (an override), the subclass must define a method that matches the inherited version exactly. Or, as of Java 5, you're allowed to change the return type in the overriding method as long as the new return type is a *subtype* of the declared return type of the overridden (superclass) method.

Let's look at a covariant return in action:

```
class Alpha {
  Alpha doStuff(char c) {
    return new Alpha();
  }
}

class Beta extends Alpha {
  Beta doStuff(char c) {      // legal override in Java 1.5
    return new Beta();
  }
}
```

As of Java 5, this code will compile. If you were to attempt to compile this code with a 1.4 compiler or with the source flag as follows,

```
javac -source 1.4 Beta.java
```

you would get a compiler error something like this:

```
attempting to use incompatible return type
```

(We'll talk more about compiler flags in Chapter 8.)

Other rules apply to overriding, including those for access modifiers and declared exceptions, but those rules aren't relevant to the return type discussion.

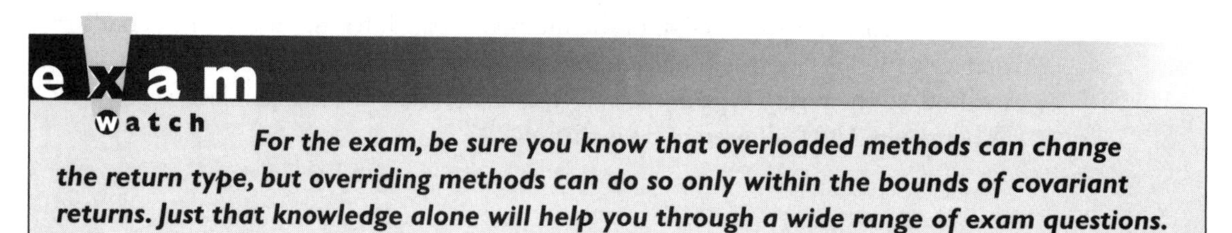

For the exam, be sure you know that overloaded methods can change the return type, but overriding methods can do so only within the bounds of covariant returns. Just that knowledge alone will help you through a wide range of exam questions.

Returning a Value

You have to remember only six rules for returning a value:

1. You can return `null` in a method with an object reference return type.

```
public Button doStuff() {
  return null;
}
```

2. An array is a perfectly legal return type.

```
public String[] go() {
  return new String[] {"Fred", "Barney", "Wilma"};
}
```

3. In a method with a primitive return type, you can return any value or variable that can be implicitly converted to the declared return type.

```
public int foo() {
  char c = 'c';
  return c;  // char is compatible with int
}
```

4. In a method with a primitive return type, you can return any value or variable that can be explicitly cast to the declared return type.

```
public int foo () {
  float f = 32.5f;
  return (int) f;
}
```

5. You must *not* return anything from a method with a void return type.

```
public void bar() {
  return "this is it";  // Not legal!!
}
```

(Although you can say `return;`)

6. In a method with an object reference return type, you can return any object type that can be implicitly cast to the declared return type.

```
public Animal getAnimal() {
  return new Horse();  // Assume Horse extends Animal
}

public Object getObject() {
  int[] nums = {1,2,3};
  return nums;         // Return an int array, which is still an object
}

public interface Chewable { }
public class Gum implements Chewable { }

public class TestChewable {
  // Method with an interface return type
  public Chewable getChewable() {
  return new Gum();  // Return interface implementer
  }
}
```

exam watch

Watch for methods that declare an abstract class or interface return type, and know that any object that passes the IS-A test (in other words, would test true using the `instanceof` operator) can be returned from that method. For example:

```
public abstract class Animal { }
public class Bear extends Animal { }
public class Test {
  public Animal go() {
    return new Bear();  // OK, Bear "is-a" Animal
  }
}
```

This code will compile, and the return value is a subtype.

CERTIFICATION OBJECTIVE

Constructors and Instantiation (OCA Objectives 6.4, 6.5, and 7.5)

6.4 *Differentiate between default and user-defined constructors.*

6.5 *Create and overload constructors.*

7.5 *Use super and this to access objects and constructors.*

Objects are constructed. You CANNOT make a new object without invoking a constructor. In fact, you can't make a new object without invoking not just the constructor of the object's actual class type, but also the constructor of each of its superclasses! Constructors are the code that runs whenever you use the keyword `new`. (Okay, to be a bit more accurate, there can also be initialization blocks that run when you say `new`, and we're going to cover `init` blocks, and their static initialization counterparts, after we discuss constructors.) We've got plenty to talk about here—we'll look at how constructors are coded, who codes them, and how they work at runtime. So grab your hardhat and a hammer, and let's do some object building.

Constructor Basics

Every class, *including abstract classes*, MUST have a constructor. Burn that into your brain. But just because a class must have a constructor doesn't mean the programmer has to type it. A constructor looks like this:

```
class Foo {
  Foo() { } // The constructor for the Foo class
}
```

Notice what's missing? There's no return type! Two key points to remember about constructors are that they have no return type and their names must exactly match the class name. Typically, constructors are used to initialize instance variable state, as follows:

```
class Foo {
  int size;
  String name;
  Foo(String name, int size) {
    this.name = name;
    this.size = size;
  }
}
```

In the preceding code example, the `Foo` class does not have a no-arg constructor. That means the following will fail to compile,

```
Foo f = new Foo();            // Won't compile, no matching constructor
```

but the following will compile:

```
Foo f = new Foo("Fred", 43);  // No problem. Arguments match
                              // the Foo constructor.
```

So it's very common (and desirable) for a class to have a no-arg constructor, regardless of how many other overloaded constructors are in the class (yes, constructors can be overloaded). You can't always make that work for your classes; occasionally you have a class where it makes no sense to create an instance without supplying information to the constructor. A `java.awt.Color` object, for example, can't be created by calling a no-arg constructor, because that would be like saying to the JVM, "Make me a new Color object, and I really don't care what color it is...you pick." Do you seriously want the JVM making your style decisions?

Constructor Chaining

We know that constructors are invoked at runtime when you say `new` on some class type as follows:

```
Horse h = new Horse();
```

But what *really* happens when you say `new Horse()`? (Assume `Horse` extends `Animal` and `Animal` extends `Object`.)

1. `Horse` constructor is invoked. Every constructor invokes the constructor of its superclass with an (implicit) call to `super()`, unless the constructor invokes an overloaded constructor of the same class (more on that in a minute).
2. `Animal` constructor is invoked (`Animal` is the superclass of `Horse`).
3. `Object` constructor is invoked (`Object` is the ultimate superclass of all classes, so class `Animal` extends `Object` even though you don't actually type "extends Object" into the `Animal` class declaration. It's implicit.) At this point we're on the top of the stack.
4. `Object` instance variables are given their explicit values. By *explicit* values, we mean values that are assigned at the time the variables are declared, such as `int x = 27`, where `27` is the explicit value (as opposed to the default value) of the instance variable.

FIGURE 2-6

Constructors on the call stack

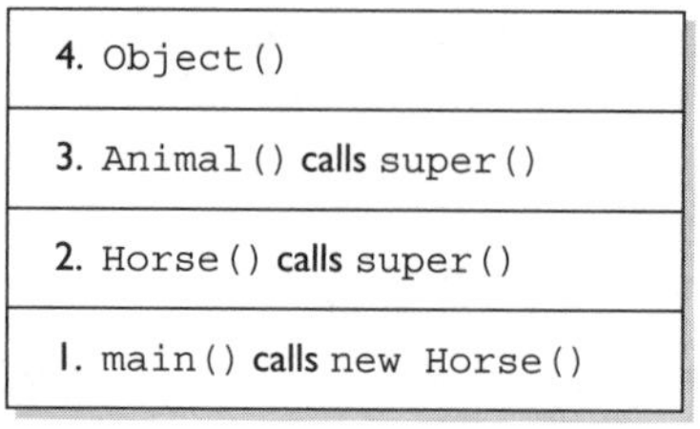

4. Object()
3. Animal() calls super()
2. Horse() calls super()
1. main() calls new Horse()

5. `Object` constructor completes.
6. `Animal` instance variables are given their explicit values (if any).
7. `Animal` constructor completes.
8. `Horse` instance variables are given their explicit values (if any).
9. `Horse` constructor completes.

Figure 2-6 shows how constructors work on the call stack.

Rules for Constructors

The following list summarizes the rules you'll need to know for the exam (and to understand the rest of this section). You MUST remember these, so be sure to study them more than once.

- Constructors can use any access modifier, including `private`. (A `private` constructor means only code within the class itself can instantiate an object of that type, so if the `private` constructor class wants to allow an instance of the class to be used, the class must provide a static method or variable that allows access to an instance created from within the class.)
- The constructor name must match the name of the class.
- Constructors must not have a return type.
- It's legal (but stupid) to have a method with the same name as the class, but that doesn't make it a constructor. If you see a return type, it's a method rather than a constructor. In fact, you could have both a method and a constructor with the same name—the name of the class—in the same class, and that's not a problem for Java. Be careful not to mistake a method for a constructor—be sure to look for a return type.
- If you don't type a constructor into your class code, a default constructor will be automatically generated by the compiler.
- The default constructor is ALWAYS a no-arg constructor.

- If you want a no-arg constructor and you've typed any other constructor(s) into your class code, the compiler won't provide the no-arg constructor (or any other constructor) for you. In other words, if you've typed in a constructor with arguments, you won't have a no-arg constructor unless you type it in yourself!
- Every constructor has, as its first statement, either a call to an overloaded constructor (`this()`) or a call to the superclass constructor (`super()`), although remember that this call can be inserted by the compiler.
- If you do type in a constructor (as opposed to relying on the compiler-generated default constructor), and you do not type in the call to `super()` or a call to `this()`, the compiler will insert a no-arg call to `super()` for you, as the very first statement in the constructor.
- A call to `super()` can either be a no-arg call or can include arguments passed to the super constructor.
- A no-arg constructor is not necessarily the default (that is, compiler-supplied) constructor, although the default constructor is always a no-arg constructor. The default constructor is the one the compiler provides! Although the default constructor is always a no-arg constructor, you're free to put in your own no-arg constructor.
- You cannot make a call to an instance method or access an instance variable until after the super constructor runs.
- Only static variables and methods can be accessed as part of the call to `super()` or `this()`. (Example: `super(Animal.NAME)` is OK, because `NAME` is declared as a static variable.)
- Abstract classes have constructors, and those constructors are always called when a concrete subclass is instantiated.
- Interfaces do not have constructors. Interfaces are not part of an object's inheritance tree.
- The only way a constructor can be invoked is from within another constructor. In other words, you can't write code that actually calls a constructor as follows:

```
class Horse {
  Horse() { } // constructor
  void doStuff() {
    Horse();  // calling the constructor - illegal!
  }
}
```

Determine Whether a Default Constructor Will Be Created

The following example shows a `Horse` class with two constructors:

```
class Horse {
  Horse() { }
  Horse(String name) { }
}
```

Will the compiler put in a default constructor for the class above? No!

How about for the following variation of the class?

```
class Horse {
  Horse(String name) { }
}
```

Now will the compiler insert a default constructor? No!

What about this class?

```
class Horse { }
```

Now we're talking. The compiler will generate a default constructor for this class, because the class doesn't have any constructors defined.

Okay, what about this class?

```
class Horse {
  void Horse() { }
}
```

It might look like the compiler won't create a constructor, since one is already in the `Horse` class. Or is it? Take another look at the preceding `Horse` class.

What's wrong with the `Horse()` constructor? It isn't a constructor at all! It's simply a method that happens to have the same name as the class. Remember, the return type is a dead giveaway that we're looking at a method, and not a constructor.

How do you know for sure whether a default constructor will be created?

Because you didn't write any constructors in your class.

How do you know what the default constructor will look like?

Because...

- The default constructor has the same access modifier as the class.
- The default constructor has no arguments.

- The default constructor includes a no-arg call to the super constructor (`super()`).

Table 2-4 shows what the compiler will (or won't) generate for your class.

TABLE 2-4 Compiler-Generated Constructor Code

Class Code (What You Type)	Compiler-Generated Constructor Code (in Bold)

class Foo { }	class Foo {
	Foo() {
	super();
	}
	}

class Foo {
Foo() { }
}
	class Foo {
	Foo() {
	super();
	}
	}

public class Foo { }	public class Foo {
	public Foo() {
	super();
	}
	}

class Foo {
Foo(String s) { }
}
	class Foo {
	Foo(String s) {
	super();
	}
	}

class Foo {
Foo(String s) {
super();
}
}
	Nothing; compiler doesn't need to insert anything.

class Foo {
void Foo() { }
}
	class Foo {
	void Foo() { }
	Foo() {
	super();
	}
	}
	(void Foo() is a method, not a constructor.)

What happens if the super constructor has arguments?

Constructors can have arguments just as methods can, and if you try to invoke a method that takes, say, an `int`, but you don't pass anything to the method, the compiler will complain as follows:

```
class Bar {
  void takeInt(int x) { }
}

class UseBar {
  public static void main (String [] args) {
    Bar b = new Bar();
    b.takeInt();  // Try to invoke a no-arg takeInt() method
  }
}
```

The compiler will complain that you can't invoke `takeInt()` without passing an `int`. Of course, the compiler enjoys the occasional riddle, so the message it spits out on some versions of the JVM (your mileage may vary) is less than obvious:

```
UseBar.java:7: takeInt(int) in Bar cannot be applied to ()
  b.takeInt();
  ^
```

But you get the idea. The bottom line is that there must be a match for the method. And by match, we mean that the argument types must be able to accept the values or variables you're passing, and in the order you're passing them. Which brings us back to constructors (and here you were thinking we'd never get there), which work exactly the same way.

So if your super constructor (that is, the constructor of your immediate superclass/parent) has arguments, you must type in the call to `super()`, supplying the appropriate arguments. Crucial point: If your superclass does not have a no-arg constructor, you must type a constructor in your class (the subclass) because you need a place to put in the call to `super()` with the appropriate arguments.

The following is an example of the problem:

```
class Animal {
  Animal(String name) { }
}

class Horse extends Animal {
  Horse() {
    super();  // Problem!
  }
}
```

And once again the compiler treats us with stunning lucidity:

```
Horse.java:7: cannot resolve symbol
symbol  : constructor Animal  ()
location: class Animal
  super();  // Problem!
  ^
```

If you're lucky (and it's a full moon), *your* compiler might be a little more explicit. But again, the problem is that there just isn't a match for what we're trying to invoke with `super()`—an `Animal` constructor with no arguments.

Another way to put this is that if your superclass does *not* have a no-arg constructor, then in your subclass you will not be able to use the default constructor supplied by the compiler. It's that simple. Because the compiler can *only* put in a call to a no-arg `super()`, you won't even be able to compile something like this:

```
class Clothing {
  Clothing(String s) { }
}
class TShirt extends Clothing { }
```

Trying to compile this code gives us exactly the same error we got when we put a constructor in the subclass with a call to the no-arg version of `super()`:

```
Clothing.java:4: cannot resolve symbol
symbol  : constructor Clothing  ()
location: class Clothing
class TShirt extends Clothing { }
^
```

In fact, the preceding `Clothing` and `TShirt` code is implicitly the same as the following code, where we've supplied a constructor for `TShirt` that's identical to the default constructor supplied by the compiler:

```
class Clothing {
  Clothing(String s) { }
}
class TShirt extends Clothing {
                // Constructor identical to compiler-supplied
                // default constructor
  TShirt() {
    super();    // Won't work!
  }             // tries to invoke a no-arg Clothing constructor
                // but there isn't one
}
```

One last point on the whole default constructor thing (and it's probably very obvious, but we have to say it or we'll feel guilty for years), ***constructors are never***

inherited. They aren't methods. They can't be overridden (because they aren't methods, and only instance methods can be overridden). So the type of constructor(s) your superclass has in no way determines the type of default constructor you'll get. Some folks mistakenly believe that the default constructor somehow matches the super constructor, either by the arguments the default constructor will have (remember, the default constructor is always a no-arg) or by the arguments used in the compiler-supplied call to `super()`.

So although constructors can't be overridden, you've already seen that they can be overloaded, and typically are.

Overloaded Constructors

Overloading a constructor means typing in multiple versions of the constructor, each having a different argument list, like the following examples:

```
class Foo {
  Foo() { }
  Foo(String s) { }
}
```

The preceding `Foo` class has two overloaded constructors: one that takes a string, and one with no arguments. Because there's no code in the no-arg version, it's actually identical to the default constructor the compiler supplies—but remember, since there's already a constructor in this class (the one that takes a string), the compiler won't supply a default constructor. If you want a no-arg constructor to overload the with-args version you already have, you're going to have to type it yourself, just as in the `Foo` example.

Overloading a constructor is typically used to provide alternate ways for clients to instantiate objects of your class. For example, if a client knows the animal name, they can pass that to an `Animal` constructor that takes a string. But if they don't know the name, the client can call the no-arg constructor and that constructor can supply a default name. Here's what it looks like:

```
 1. public class Animal {
 2.   String name;
 3.   Animal(String name) {
 4.     this.name = name;
 5.   }
 6.
 7.   Animal() {
 8.     this(makeRandomName());
 9.   }
10.
11.   static String makeRandomName() {
```

```
12.     int x = (int) (Math.random() * 5);
13.     String name = new String[] {"Fluffy", "Fido",
                                     "Rover", "Spike",
                                     "Gigi"}[x];
14.     return name;
15.   }
16.
17.   public static void main (String [] args) {
18.     Animal a = new Animal();
19.     System.out.println(a.name);
20.     Animal b = new Animal("Zeus");
21.     System.out.println(b.name);
22.   }
23. }
```

Running the code four times produces this output:

```
% java Animal
Gigi
Zeus

% java Animal
Fluffy
Zeus

% java Animal
Rover
Zeus

% java Animal
Fluffy
Zeus
```

There's a lot going on in the preceding code. Figure 2-7 shows the call stack for constructor invocations when a constructor is overloaded. Take a look at the call stack, and then let's walk through the code straight from the top.

- **Line 2** Declare a `String` instance variable name.
- **Lines 3–5** Constructor that takes a `String` and assigns it to instance variable name.

FIGURE 2-7

Overloaded constructors on the call stack

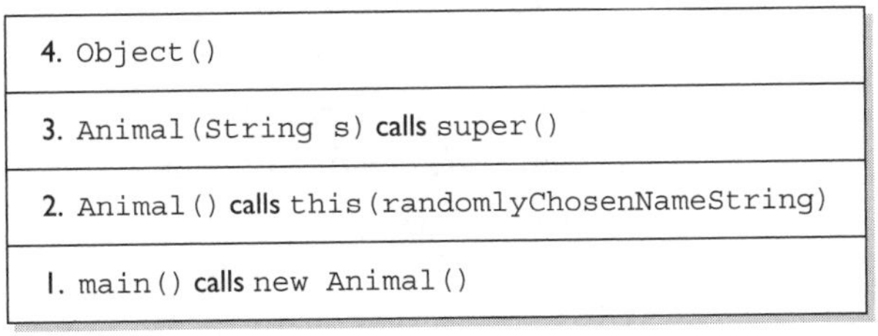

4. `Object()`
3. `Animal(String s)` calls `super()`
2. `Animal()` calls `this(randomlyChosenNameString)`
1. `main()` calls `new Animal()`

- **Line 7** Here's where it gets fun. Assume every animal needs a name, but the client (calling code) might not always know what the name should be, so you'll assign a random name. The no-arg constructor generates a name by invoking the `makeRandomName()` method.
- **Line 8** The no-arg constructor invokes its own overloaded constructor that takes a `String`, in effect calling it the same way it would be called if client code were doing a `new` to instantiate an object, passing it a `String` for the name. The overloaded invocation uses the keyword `this`, but uses it as though it were a method name `this()`. So line 8 is simply calling the constructor on line 3, passing it a randomly selected `String` rather than a client-code chosen name.
- **Line 11** Notice that the `makeRandomName()` method is marked `static`! That's because you cannot invoke an instance (in other words, nonstatic) method (or access an instance variable) until after the `super` constructor has run. And since the `super` constructor will be invoked from the constructor on line 3, rather than from the one on line 7, line 8 can use only a static method to generate the name. If we wanted all `animals` not specifically named by the caller to have the same default name, say, "Fred," then line 8 could have read `this("Fred");` rather than calling a method that returns a string with the randomly chosen name.
- **Line 12** This doesn't have anything to do with constructors, but since we're all here to learn, it generates a random integer between 0 and 4.
- **Line 13** Weird syntax, we know. We're creating a new `String` object (just a single `String` instance), but we want the string to be selected randomly from a list. Except we don't have the list, so we need to make it. So in that one line of code we
  1. Declare a `String` variable, name.
  2. Create a `String` array (anonymously—we don't assign the array itself to anything).
  3. Retrieve the string at index `[x]` (x being the random number generated on line 12) of the newly created `String` array.
  4. Assign the string retrieved from the array to the declared instance variable name. We could have made it much easier to read if we'd just written

```
String[] nameList = {"Fluffy", "Fido", "Rover", "Spike",
                     "Gigi"};

String name = nameList[x];
```

But where's the fun in that? Throwing in unusual syntax (especially for code wholly unrelated to the real question) is in the spirit of the exam. Don't be startled! (Okay, be startled, but then just say to yourself, "Whoa!" and get on with it.)

- **Line 18** We're invoking the no-arg version of the constructor (causing a random name from the list to be passed to the other constructor).
- **Line 20** We're invoking the overloaded constructor that takes a string representing the name.

The key point to get from this code example is in line 8. Rather than calling `super()`, we're calling `this()`, and `this()` always means a call to another constructor in the same class. Okay, fine, but what happens after the call to `this()`? Sooner or later the `super()` constructor gets called, right? Yes indeed. A call to `this()` just means you're delaying the inevitable. Some constructor, somewhere, must make the call to `super()`.

Key Rule: The first line in a constructor must be a call to `super()` or a call to `this()`.

No exceptions. If you have neither of those calls in your constructor, the compiler will insert the no-arg call to `super()`. In other words, if constructor `A()` has a call to `this()`, the compiler knows that constructor `A()` will not be the one to invoke `super()`.

The preceding rule means a constructor can never have both a call to `super()` and a call to `this()`. Because each of those calls must be the first statement in a constructor, you can't legally use both in the same constructor. That also means the compiler will not put a call to `super()` in any constructor that has a call to `this()`.

Thought question: What do you think will happen if you try to compile the following code?

```
class A {
  A() {
    this("foo");
  }
  A(String s) {
    this();
  }
}
```

Your compiler may not actually catch the problem (it varies depending on your compiler, but most won't catch the problem). It assumes you know what you're doing. Can you spot the flaw? Given that a `super` constructor must always be called, where would the call to `super()` go? Remember, the compiler won't put in a default constructor if you've already got one or more constructors in your class. And when the compiler doesn't put in a default constructor, it still inserts a call to `super()` in any constructor that doesn't explicitly have a call to the `super` constructor—unless, that is, the constructor already has a call to `this()`. So in the preceding code, where can `super()` go? The only two constructors in the class both have calls to `this()`, and in fact you'll get exactly what you'd get if you typed the following method code:

```
public void go() {
  doStuff();
}

public void doStuff() {
  go();
}
```

Now can you see the problem? Of course you can. The stack explodes! It gets higher and higher and higher until it just bursts open and method code goes spilling out, oozing out of the JVM right onto the floor. Two overloaded constructors both calling `this()` are two constructors calling each other. Over and over and over, resulting in this:

```
% java A
Exception in thread "main" java.lang.StackOverflowError
```

The benefit of having overloaded constructors is that you offer flexible ways to instantiate objects from your class. The benefit of having one constructor invoke another overloaded constructor is to avoid code duplication. In the `Animal` example, there wasn't any code other than setting the name, but imagine if after line 4 there was still more work to be done in the constructor. By putting all the other constructor work in just one constructor, and then having the other constructors invoke it, you don't have to write and maintain multiple versions of that other important constructor code. Basically, each of the other not-the-real-one overloaded constructors will call another overloaded constructor, passing it whatever data it needs (data the client code didn't supply).

Constructors and instantiation become even more exciting (just when you thought it was safe) when you get to inner classes, but we know you can stand to have only so much fun in one chapter, so we're holding the rest of the discussion on instantiating inner classes until Chapter 12.

Initialization Blocks

We've talked about two places in a class where you can put code that performs operations: methods and constructors. Initialization blocks are the third place in a

Java program where operations can be performed. Initialization blocks run when the class is first loaded (a static initialization block) or when an instance is created (an instance initialization block). Let's look at an example:

```
class SmallInit {
  static int x;
  int y;

  static { x = 7 ; }        // static init block
  { y = 8; }                // instance init block
}
```

As you can see, the syntax for initialization blocks is pretty terse. They don't have names, they can't take arguments, and they don't return anything. A *static* initialization block runs *once*, when the class is first loaded. An *instance* initialization block runs once *every time a new instance is created*. Remember when we talked about the order in which constructor code executed? Instance `init` block code runs right after the call to `super()` in a constructor—in other words, after all `super` constructors have run.

You can have many initialization blocks in a class. It is important to note that unlike methods or constructors, *the order in which initialization blocks appear in a class matters*. When it's time for initialization blocks to run, if a class has more than one, they will run in the order in which they appear in the class file—in other words, from the top down. Based on the rules we just discussed, can you determine the output of the following program?

```
class Init {
  Init(int x) { System.out.println("1-arg const"); }
  Init() { System.out.println("no-arg const"); }
  static { System.out.println("1st static init"); }
  { System.out.println("1st instance init"); }
  { System.out.println("2nd instance init"); }
  static { System.out.println("2nd static init"); }

  public static void main(String [] args) {
    new Init();
    new Init(7);
  }
}
```

To figure this out, remember these rules:

- `init` blocks execute in the order in which they appear.
- Static `init` blocks run once, when the class is first loaded.
- Instance `init` blocks run every time a class instance is created.
- Instance `init` blocks run after the constructor's call to `super()`.

With those rules in mind, the following output should make sense:

```
1st static init
2nd static init
1st instance init
2nd instance init
no-arg const
1st instance init
2nd instance init
1-arg const
```

As you can see, the instance `init` blocks each ran twice. Instance `init` blocks are often used as a place to put code that all the constructors in a class should share. That way, the code doesn't have to be duplicated across constructors.

Finally, if you make a mistake in your static `init` block, the JVM can throw an `ExceptionInInitializerError`. Let's look at an example:

```
class InitError {
  static int [] x = new int[4];
  static { x[4] = 5; }          // bad array index!
  public static void main(String [] args) { }
}
```

It produces something like this:

```
Exception in thread "main" java.lang.ExceptionInInitializerError
Caused by: java.lang.ArrayIndexOutOfBoundsException: 4
        at InitError.<clinit>(InitError.java:3)
```

exam watch

By convention, `init` blocks usually appear near the top of the class file, somewhere around the constructors. However, these are the OCA and OCP exams we're talking about. Don't be surprised if you find an `init` block tucked in between a couple of methods, looking for all the world like a compiler error waiting to happen!

CERTIFICATION OBJECTIVE

Statics (OCA Objective 6.2)

6.2 *Apply the static keyword to methods and fields.*

Static Variables and Methods

The `static` modifier has such a profound impact on the behavior of a method or variable that we're treating it as a concept entirely separate from the other modifiers. To understand the way a `static` member works, we'll look first at a reason for using one. Imagine you've got a utility class with a method that always runs the same way; its sole function is to return, say, a random number. It wouldn't matter which instance of the class performed the method—it would always behave exactly the same way. In other words, the method's behavior has no dependency on the state (instance variable values) of an object. So why, then, do you need an object when the method will never be instance-specific? Why not just ask the class itself to run the method?

Let's imagine another scenario: Suppose you want to keep a running count of all instances instantiated from a particular class. Where do you actually keep that variable? It won't work to keep it as an instance variable within the class whose instances you're tracking, because the count will just be initialized back to a default value with each new instance. The answer to both the utility-method-always-runs-the-same scenario and the keep-a-running-total-of-instances scenario is to use the `static` modifier. Variables and methods marked `static` belong to the class, rather than to any particular instance. In fact, you can use a `static` method or variable without having any instances of that class at all. You need only have the class available to be able to invoke a `static` method or access a `static` variable. `static` variables, too, can be accessed without having an instance of a class. But if there are instances, a `static` variable of a class will be shared by all instances of that class; there is only one copy.

The following code declares and uses a `static` counter variable:

```
class Frog {
  static int frogCount = 0;  // Declare and initialize
                             // static variable
  public Frog() {
    frogCount += 1;          // Modify the value in the constructor
  }
  public static void main (String [] args) {
    new Frog();
    new Frog();
    new Frog();
    System.out.println("Frog count is now " + frogCount);
  }
}
```

In the preceding code, the `static frogCount` variable is set to zero when the `Frog` class is first loaded by the JVM, before any `Frog` instances are created! (By the way, you don't actually need to initialize a static variable to zero; static variables get the same default values instance variables get.) Whenever a `Frog` instance is created, the `Frog` constructor runs and increments the `static frogCount` variable. When this code executes, three `Frog` instances are created in `main()`, and the result is

```
Frog count is now 3
```

Now imagine what would happen if `frogCount` were an instance variable (in other words, nonstatic):

```
class Frog {
  int frogCount = 0;  // Declare and initialize
                      // instance variable
  public Frog() {
    frogCount += 1;   // Modify the value in the constructor
  }
  public static void main (String [] args) {
    new Frog();
    new Frog();
    new Frog();
    System.out.println("Frog count is now " + frogCount);
  }
}
```

When this code executes, it should still create three `Frog` instances in `main()`, but the result is...a compiler error! We can't get this code to compile, let alone run.

```
Frog.java:11: nonstatic variable frogCount cannot be referenced
from a static context
  System.out.println("Frog count is " + frogCount);
                                        ^
  1 error
```

The JVM doesn't know which Frog object's `frogCount` you're trying to access. The problem is that `main()` is itself a `static` method and thus isn't running against any particular instance of the class; instead it's running on the class itself. A `static` method can't access a nonstatic (instance) variable because there is no instance! That's not to say there aren't instances of the class alive on the heap, but rather that even if there are, the `static` method doesn't know anything about them. The same applies to instance methods; a `static` method can't directly invoke a nonstatic method. Think static = class, nonstatic = instance. Making the method called by the JVM (`main()`) a `static` method means the JVM doesn't have to create an instance of your class just to start running code.

exam watch

One of the mistakes most often made by new Java programmers is attempting to access an instance variable (which means nonstatic variable) from the static `main()` method (which doesn't know anything about any instances, so it can't access the variable). The following code is an example of illegal access of a nonstatic variable from a `static` method:

```
class Foo {
  int x = 3;
    public static void main (String [] args) {
      System.out.println("x is " + x);
  }
}
```

Understand that this code will never compile, because you can't access a nonstatic (instance) variable from a `static` method. Just think of the compiler saying, "Hey, I have no idea which `Foo` object's `x` variable you're trying to print!" Remember, it's the class running the `main()` method, not an instance of the class.

Of course, the tricky part for the exam is that the question won't look as obvious as the preceding code. The problem you're being tested for—accessing a nonstatic variable from a `static` method—will be buried in code that might appear to be testing something else. For example, the preceding code would be more likely to appear as

```
class Foo {
  int x = 3;
  float y = 4.3f;
  public static void main (String [] args) {
     for (int z = x; z < ++x; z--, y = y + z)
     // complicated looping and branching code
  }
}
```

So while you're trying to follow the logic, the real issue is that `x` and `y` can't be used within `main()`, because `x` and `y` are instance, not `static`, variables! The same applies for accessing nonstatic methods from a `static` method. The rule is, a `static` method of a class can't access a nonstatic (instance) method or variable of its own class.

Accessing Static Methods and Variables

Since you don't need to have an instance in order to invoke a static method or access a static variable, how do you invoke or use a `static` member? What's the syntax? We know that with a regular old instance method, you use the dot operator on a reference to an instance:

```
class Frog {
  int frogSize = 0;
  public int getFrogSize() {
    return frogSize;
  }
  public Frog(int s) {
    frogSize = s;
  }
  public static void main (String [] args) {
    Frog f = new Frog(25);
    System.out.println(f.getFrogSize()); // Access instance
                                         // method using f
  }
}
```

In the preceding code, we instantiate a `Frog`, assign it to the reference variable `f`, and then use that `f` reference to invoke a method on the `Frog` instance we just created. In other words, the `getFrogSize()` method is being invoked on a specific `Frog` object on the heap.

But this approach (using a reference to an object) isn't appropriate for accessing a `static` method, because there might not be any instances of the class at all! So, the way we access a `static` method (or `static` variable) is to use the dot operator on the class name, as opposed to using it on a reference to an instance, as follows:

```
class Frog {
  static int frogCount = 0;   // Declare and initialize
                              // static variable
  public Frog() {
     frogCount += 1;          // Modify the value in the constructor
  }
}

class TestFrog {
  public static void main (String [] args) {
    new Frog();
    new Frog();
    new Frog();
    System.out.print("frogCount:"+Frog.frogCount); // Access
                                                   // static variable
  }
}
```

But just to make it really confusing, the Java language also allows you to use an object reference variable to access a `static` member:

```
Frog f = new Frog();
int frogs = f.frogCount; // Access static variable
                         // FrogCount using f
```

In the preceding code, we instantiate a `Frog`, assign the new `Frog` object to the reference variable `f`, and then use the `f` reference to invoke a `static` method! But even though we are using a specific `Frog` instance to access the `static` method, the rules haven't changed. This is merely a syntax trick to let you use an object reference variable (but not the object it refers to) to get to a `static` method or variable, but the `static` member is still unaware of the particular instance used to invoke the `static` member. In the `Frog` example, the compiler knows that the reference variable `f` is of type `Frog`, and so the `Frog` class `static` method is run with no awareness or concern for the `Frog` instance at the other end of the `f` reference. In other words, the compiler cares only that reference variable `f` is declared as type `Frog`. Figure 2-8 illustrates the effects of the `static` modifier on methods and variables.

FIGURE 2-8

The effects of `static` on methods and variables

```
class Foo

int size = 42;
static void doMore( ){
  int x = size;
}
```

`static` method cannot access an instance (non-static) variable

```
class Bar

void go(){}
static void doMore( ){
    go( );
}
```

`static` method cannot access a non-static method

```
class Baz

static int count;
static void woo( ){ }
static void doMore( ){
    woo( );
    int x = count;
}
```

`static` method *can* access a `static` method or variable

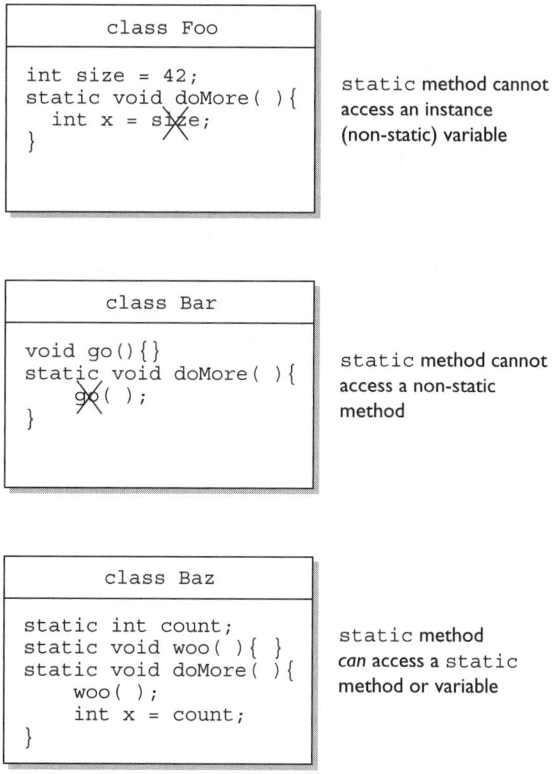

Finally, remember that `static` *methods can't be overridden*! This doesn't mean they can't be redefined in a subclass, but redefining and overriding aren't the same thing. Let's take a look at an example of a redefined (remember, not overridden) `static` method:

```
class Animal {
  static void doStuff() {
    System.out.print("a ");
  }
}
class Dog extends Animal {
  static void doStuff() {          // it's a redefinition,
                                   // not an override
    System.out.print("d ");
  }
  public static void main(String [] args) {
    Animal [] a = {new Animal(), new Dog(), new Animal()};
    for(int x = 0; x < a.length; x++) {
      a[x].doStuff();              // invoke the static method
    }
    Dog.doStuff();                 // invoke using the class name
  }
}
```

Running this code produces this output:

```
a a a d
```

Remember, the syntax `a[x].doStuff()` is just a shortcut (the syntax trick)—the compiler is going to substitute something like `Animal.doStuff()` instead. Notice also that you can invoke a `static` method by using the class name.

Notice that we didn't use the Java 5 *enhanced* for *loop* here (covered in Chapter 6), even though we could have. Expect to see a mix of both Java 1.4 and Java 5–7 coding styles and practices on the exam.

CERTIFICATION SUMMARY

We started the chapter by discussing the importance of encapsulation in good OO design, and then we talked about how good encapsulation is implemented: with private instance variables and public getters and setters.

Next, we covered the importance of inheritance, so that you can grasp overriding, overloading, polymorphism, reference casting, return types, and constructors.

We covered IS-A and HAS-A. IS-A is implemented using inheritance, and HAS-A is implemented by using instance variables that refer to other objects.

Polymorphism was next. Although a reference variable's type can't be changed, it can be used to refer to an object whose type is a subtype of its own. We learned how to determine what methods are invocable for a given reference variable.

We looked at the difference between overridden and overloaded methods, learning that an overridden method occurs when a subclass inherits a method from a superclass, and then reimplements the method to add more specialized behavior. We learned that, at runtime, the JVM will invoke the subclass version on an instance of a subclass and the superclass version on an instance of the superclass. `Abstract` methods must be "overridden" (technically, `abstract` methods must be implemented, as opposed to overridden, since there really isn't anything to override).

We saw that overriding methods must declare the same argument list and return type (or, as of Java 5, they can return a subtype of the declared return type of the superclass overridden method), and that the access modifier can't be more restrictive. The overriding method also can't throw any new or broader checked exceptions that weren't declared in the overridden method. You also learned that the overridden method can be invoked using the syntax `super.doSomething();`.

Overloaded methods let you reuse the same method name in a class, but with different arguments (and, optionally, a different return type). Whereas overriding methods must not change the argument list, overloaded methods must. But unlike overriding methods, overloaded methods are free to vary the return type, access modifier, and declared exceptions any way they like.

We learned the mechanics of casting (mostly downcasting) reference variables and when it's necessary to do so.

Implementing interfaces came next. An interface describes a *contract* that the implementing class must follow. The rules for implementing an interface are similar to those for extending an `abstract` class. Also remember that a class can implement more than one interface and that interfaces can extend another interface.

We also looked at method return types and saw that you can declare any return type you like (assuming you have access to a class for an object reference return type), unless you're overriding a method. Barring a covariant return, an overriding method must have the same return type as the overridden method of the superclass. We saw that, although overriding methods must not change the return type, overloaded methods can (as long as they also change the argument list).

Finally, you learned that it is legal to return any value or variable that can be implicitly converted to the declared return type. So, for example, a `short` can be returned when the return type is declared as an `int`. And (assuming `Horse` extends `Animal`), a `Horse` reference can be returned when the return type is declared an `Animal`.

We covered constructors in detail, learning that if you don't provide a constructor for your class, the compiler will insert one. The compiler-generated constructor is called the default constructor, and it is always a no-arg constructor with a no-arg call to `super()`. The default constructor will never be generated if even a single constructor exists in your class (regardless of the arguments of that constructor), so if you need more than one constructor in your class and you want a no-arg constructor, you'll have to write it yourself. We also saw that constructors are not inherited and that you can be confused by a method that has the same name as the class (which is legal). The return type is the giveaway that a method is not a constructor, since constructors do not have return types.

We saw how all of the constructors in an object's inheritance tree will always be invoked when the object is instantiated using `new`. We also saw that constructors can be overloaded, which means defining constructors with different argument lists. A constructor can invoke another constructor of the same class using the keyword `this()`, as though the constructor were a method named `this()`. We saw that every constructor must have either `this()` or `super()` as the first statement (although the compiler can insert it for you).

After constructors, we discussed the two kinds of initialization blocks and how and when their code runs.

We looked at `static` methods and variables. `static` members are tied to the class, not an instance, so there is only one copy of any `static` member. A common mistake is to attempt to reference an instance variable from a `static` method. Use the class name with the dot operator to access `static` members.

And, once again, you learned that the exam includes tricky questions designed largely to test your ability to recognize just how tricky the questions can be.

✓ TWO-MINUTE DRILL

Here are some of the key points from each certification objective in this chapter.

Encapsulation, IS-A, HAS-A (OCA Objective 6.7)

- Encapsulation helps hide implementation behind an interface (or API).
- Encapsulated code has two features:
  - Instance variables are kept protected (usually with the `private` modifier).
  - Getter and setter methods provide access to instance variables.
- IS-A refers to inheritance or implementation.
- IS-A is expressed with the keyword `extends` or `implements`.
- IS-A, "inherits from," and "is a subtype of" are all equivalent expressions.
- HAS-A means an instance of one class "has a" reference to an instance of another class or another instance of the same class.

Inheritance (OCA Objectives 7.1 and 7.3)

- Inheritance allows a class to be a subclass of a superclass and thereby inherit `public` and `protected` variables and methods of the superclass.
- Inheritance is a key concept that underlies IS-A, polymorphism, overriding, overloading, and casting.
- All classes (except class `Object`) are subclasses of type `Object`, and therefore they inherit `Object`'s methods.

Polymorphism (OCA Objectives 7.2 and 7.3)

- Polymorphism means "many forms."
- A reference variable is always of a single, unchangeable type, but it can refer to a subtype object.
- A single object can be referred to by reference variables of many different types—as long as they are the same type or a supertype of the object.
- The reference variable's type (not the object's type) determines which methods can be called!
- Polymorphic method invocations apply only to overridden *instance* methods.

Overriding and Overloading (OCA Objective 6.3)

- Methods can be overridden or overloaded; constructors can be overloaded but not overridden.
- With respect to the method it overrides, the overriding method
  - Must have the same argument list
  - Must have the same return type, except that, as of Java 5, the return type can be a subclass, and this is known as a covariant return
  - Must not have a more restrictive access modifier
  - May have a less restrictive access modifier
  - Must not throw new or broader checked exceptions
  - May throw fewer or narrower checked exceptions, or any unchecked exception
- `final` methods cannot be overridden.
- Only inherited methods may be overridden, and remember that private methods are not inherited.
- A subclass uses `super.overriddenMethodName()` to call the superclass version of an overridden method.
- Overloading means reusing a method name but with different arguments.
- Overloaded methods
  - Must have different argument lists
  - May have different return types, if argument lists are also different
  - May have different access modifiers
  - May throw different exceptions
- Methods from a superclass can be overloaded in a subclass.
- Polymorphism applies to overriding, not to overloading.
- Object type (not the reference variable's type) determines which overridden method is used at runtime.
- Reference type determines which overloaded method will be used at compile time.

Reference Variable Casting (OCA Objectives 7.3 and 7.4)

- There are two types of reference variable casting: downcasting and upcasting.
  - **Downcasting** If you have a reference variable that refers to a subtype object, you can assign it to a reference variable of the subtype. You must make an explicit cast to do this, and the result is that you can access the subtype's members with this new reference variable.
  - **Upcasting** You can assign a reference variable to a supertype reference variable explicitly or implicitly. This is an inherently safe operation because the assignment restricts the access capabilities of the new variable.

Implementing an Interface (OCA Objective 7.6)

- When you implement an interface, you are fulfilling its contract.
- You implement an interface by properly and concretely implementing all of the methods defined by the interface.
- A single class can implement many interfaces.

Return Types (OCA Objectives 6.1 and 6.3)

- Overloaded methods can change return types; overridden methods cannot, except in the case of covariant returns.
- Object reference return types can accept `null` as a return value.
- An array is a legal return type, both to declare and return as a value.
- For methods with primitive return types, any value that can be implicitly converted to the return type can be returned.
- Nothing can be returned from a `void`, but you can return nothing. You're allowed to simply say `return` in any method with a `void` return type to bust out of a method early. But you can't return nothing from a method with a non-`void` return type.
- Methods with an object reference return type can return a subtype.
- Methods with an interface return type can return any implementer.

Constructors and Instantiation (OCA Objectives 6.5 and 7.5)

- A constructor is always invoked when a new object is created.
- Each superclass in an object's inheritance tree will have a constructor called.
- Every class, even an abstract class, has at least one constructor.
- Constructors must have the same name as the class.
- Constructors don't have a return type. If you see code with a return type, it's a method with the same name as the class; it's not a constructor.
- Typical constructor execution occurs as follows:
  - The constructor calls its superclass constructor, which calls its superclass constructor, and so on all the way up to the `Object` constructor.
  - The `Object` constructor executes and then returns to the calling constructor, which runs to completion and then returns to its calling constructor, and so on back down to the completion of the constructor of the actual instance being created.
- Constructors can use any access modifier (even `private`!).
- The compiler will create a default constructor if you don't create any constructors in your class.
- The default constructor is a no-arg constructor with a no-arg call to `super()`.
- The first statement of every constructor must be a call either to `this()` (an overloaded constructor) or to `super()`.
- The compiler will add a call to `super()` unless you have already put in a call to `this()` or `super()`.
- Instance members are accessible only after the `super` constructor runs.
- `Abstract` classes have constructors that are called when a concrete subclass is instantiated.
- Interfaces do not have constructors.
- If your superclass does not have a no-arg constructor, you must create a constructor and insert a call to `super()` with arguments matching those of the superclass constructor.
- Constructors are never inherited; thus they cannot be overridden.
- A constructor can be directly invoked only by another constructor (using a call to `super()` or `this()`).

- Regarding issues with calls to `this()`:
  - They may appear only as the first statement in a constructor.
  - The argument list determines which overloaded constructor is called.
  - Constructors can call constructors, and so on, but sooner or later one of them better call `super()` or the stack will explode.
  - Calls to `this()` and `super()` cannot be in the same constructor. You can have one or the other, but never both.

Initialization Blocks (OCA Objective 6.5-ish)

- Use `static init` blocks—`static { /* code here */ }`—for code you want to have run once, when the class is first loaded. Multiple blocks run from the top down.
- Use normal `init` blocks—`{ /* code here }`—for code you want to have run for every new instance, right after all the super constructors have run. Again, multiple blocks run from the top of the class down.

Statics (OCA Objective 6.2)

- Use `static` methods to implement behaviors that are not affected by the state of any instances.
- Use `static` variables to hold data that is class specific as opposed to instance specific—there will be only one copy of a `static` variable.
- All `static` members belong to the class, not to any instance.
- A `static` method can't access an instance variable directly.
- Use the dot operator to access `static` members, but remember that using a reference variable with the dot operator is really a syntax trick, and the compiler will substitute the class name for the reference variable; for instance:

  ```
  d.doStuff();
  ```

  becomes

  ```
  Dog.doStuff();
  ```
- `static` methods can't be overridden, but they can be redefined.

SELF TEST

1. Given:

```
public abstract interface Frobnicate { public void twiddle(String s); }
```

Which is a correct class? (Choose all that apply.)

A.
```
public abstract class Frob implements Frobnicate {
  public abstract void twiddle(String s) { }
}
```

B.
```
public abstract class Frob implements Frobnicate { }
```

C.
```
public class Frob extends Frobnicate {
  public void twiddle(Integer i) { }
}
```

D.
```
public class Frob implements Frobnicate {
  public void twiddle(Integer i) { }
}
```

E.
```
public class Frob implements Frobnicate {
  public void twiddle(String i) { }
  public void twiddle(Integer s) { }
}
```

2. Given:

```
class Top {
  public Top(String s) { System.out.print("B"); }
}
public class Bottom2 extends Top {
  public Bottom2(String s) { System.out.print("D"); }
  public static void main(String [] args) {
    new Bottom2("C");
    System.out.println(" ");
  }
}
```

What is the result?

A. `BD`

B. `DB`

C. `BDC`

D. `DBC`

E. Compilation fails

3. Given:

```
class Clidder {
  private final void flipper() { System.out.println("Clidder"); }
}

public class Clidlet extends Clidder {
  public final void flipper() { System.out.println("Clidlet");  }
  public static void main(String [] args) {
    new Clidlet().flipper();
  }
}
```

What is the result?

A. `Clidlet`

B. `Clidder`

C. `Clidder`
`Clidlet`

D. `Clidlet`
`Clidder`

E. Compilation fails

Special Note: The next question crudely simulates a style of question known as "drag-and-drop." Up through the SCJP 6 exam, drag-and-drop questions were included on the exam. As of the Spring of 2014, Oracle DOES NOT include any drag-and-drop questions on its Java exams, but just in case Oracle's policy changes, we left a few in the book.

4. Using the **fragments** below, complete the following **code** so it compiles. Note that you may not have to fill all of the slots.

Code:

```
class AgedP {
  __________ __________ __________ __________ __________
  public AgedP(int x) {
    __________ __________ __________ __________ __________
  }
}
public class Kinder extends AgedP {
  __________ __________ __________ __________ __________ __________
  public Kinder(int x) {
    __________ __________ __________ __________ __________ ();
  }
}
```

Fragments: Use the following fragments zero or more times:

AgedP	super	this	
(		{	}
;			

5. Given:

```
class Bird {
  { System.out.print("b1 "); }
  public Bird() { System.out.print("b2 "); }
}
class Raptor extends Bird {
  static { System.out.print("r1 "); }
  public Raptor() { System.out.print("r2 "); }
  { System.out.print("r3 "); }
  static { System.out.print("r4 "); }
}
class Hawk extends Raptor {
  public static void main(String[] args) {
    System.out.print("pre ");
    new Hawk();
    System.out.println("hawk ");
  }
}
```

What is the result?

A. `pre b1 b2 r3 r2 hawk`

B. `pre b2 b1 r2 r3 hawk`

C. `pre b2 b1 r2 r3 hawk r1 r4`

D. `r1 r4 pre b1 b2 r3 r2 hawk`

E. `r1 r4 pre b2 b1 r2 r3 hawk`

F. `pre r1 r4 b1 b2 r3 r2 hawk`

G. `pre r1 r4 b2 b1 r2 r3 hawk`

H. The order of output cannot be predicted

I. Compilation fails

Note: You'll probably never see this many choices on the real exam!

6. Given the following:

```
 1. class X { void do1() { } }
 2. class Y extends X { void do2() { } }
 3.
 4. class Chrome {
 5.   public static void main(String [] args) {
 6.     X x1 = new X();
 7.     X x2 = new Y();
 8.     Y y1 = new Y();
 9.     // insert code here
10. } }
```

Which of the following, inserted at line 9, will compile? (Choose all that apply.)

A. `x2.do2();`

B. `(Y)x2.do2();`

C. `((Y)x2).do2();`

D. None of the above statements will compile

7. Given:

```
public class Locomotive {
  Locomotive() { main("hi"); }

  public static void main(String[] args) {
    System.out.print("2 ");
  }
  public static void main(String args) {
    System.out.print("3 " + args);
  }
}
```

What is the result? (Choose all that apply.)

A. `2` will be included in the output

B. `3` will be included in the output

C. `hi` will be included in the output

D. Compilation fails

E. An exception is thrown at runtime

8. Given:

```
 3. class Dog {
 4.   public void bark() { System.out.print("woof "); }
 5. }
 6. class Hound extends Dog {
 7.   public void sniff() { System.out.print("sniff "); }
 8.   public void bark() { System.out.print("howl "); }
 9. }
10. public class DogShow {
11.   public static void main(String[] args) { new DogShow().go(); }
12.   void go() {
13.     new Hound().bark();
14.     ((Dog) new Hound()).bark();
15.     ((Dog) new Hound()).sniff();
16.   }
17. }
```

What is the result? (Choose all that apply.)

A. `howl howl sniff`

B. `howl woof sniff`

C. `howl howl` followed by an exception

D. `howl woof` followed by an exception

E. Compilation fails with an error at line 14

F. Compilation fails with an error at line 15

9. Given:

```
 3. public class Redwood extends Tree {
 4.   public static void main(String[] args) {
 5.     new Redwood().go();
 6.   }
 7.   void go() {
 8.     go2(new Tree(), new Redwood());
 9.     go2((Redwood) new Tree(), new Redwood());
10.   }
11.   void go2(Tree t1, Redwood r1) {
12.      Redwood r2 = (Redwood)t1;
13.      Tree t2 = (Tree)r1;
14.   }
15. }
16. class Tree { }
```

What is the result? (Choose all that apply.)

A. An exception is thrown at runtime

B. The code compiles and runs with no output

C. Compilation fails with an error at line 8

D. Compilation fails with an error at line 9

E. Compilation fails with an error at line 12

F. Compilation fails with an error at line 13

10. Given:

```
 3. public class Tenor extends Singer {
 4.   public static String sing() { return "fa"; }
 5.   public static void main(String[] args) {
 6.     Tenor t = new Tenor();
 7.     Singer s = new Tenor();
 8.     System.out.println(t.sing() + " " + s.sing());
 9.   }
10. }
11. class Singer { public static String sing() { return "la"; } }
```

What is the result?

A. `fa fa`

B. `fa la`

C. `la la`

D. Compilation fails

E. An exception is thrown at runtime

11. Given:

```
 3. class Alpha {
 4.   static String s = " ";
 5.   protected Alpha() { s += "alpha "; }
 6. }
 7. class SubAlpha extends Alpha {
 8.   private SubAlpha() { s += "sub "; }
 9. }
10. public class SubSubAlpha extends Alpha {
11.   private SubSubAlpha() { s += "subsub "; }
12.   public static void main(String[] args) {
13.     new SubSubAlpha();
14.     System.out.println(s);
15.   }
16. }
```

What is the result?

A. `subsub`

B. `sub subsub`

C. `alpha subsub`

D. `alpha sub subsub`

E. Compilation fails

F. An exception is thrown at runtime

12. Given:

```
 3. class Building {
 4.   Building() {  System.out.print("b ");  }
 5.   Building(String name) {
 6.     this();   System.out.print("bn " + name);
 7.   }
 8. }
 9. public class House extends Building {
10.   House() {  System.out.print("h ");  }
11.   House(String name) {
12.     this();   System.out.print("hn " + name);
13.   }
14.   public static void main(String[] args) { new House("x "); }
15. }
```

What is the result?

A. `h hn x`

B. `hn x h`

C. `b h hn x`

D. `b hn x h`

E. `bn x h hn x`

F. `b bn x h hn x`

G. `bn x b h hn x`

H. Compilation fails

13. Given:

```
 3. class Mammal {
 4.   String name = "furry ";
 5.   String makeNoise() { return "generic noise"; }
 6. }
 7. class Zebra extends Mammal {
 8.   String name = "stripes ";
 9.   String makeNoise() { return "bray"; }
10. }
11. public class ZooKeeper {
12.   public static void main(String[] args) { new ZooKeeper().go(); }
13.   void go() {
14.     Mammal m = new Zebra();
15.     System.out.println(m.name + m.makeNoise());
16.   }
17. }
```

What is the result?

A. `furry bray`

B. `stripes bray`

C. `furry generic noise`

D. `stripes generic noise`

E. Compilation fails

F. An exception is thrown at runtime

14. (OCP Only) Given:

You're designing a new online board game in which `Floozels` are a type of `Jammers`, `Jammers` can have `Quizels`, `Quizels` are a type of `Klakker`, and `Floozels` can have several `Floozets`. Which of the following fragments represent this design? (Choose all that apply.)

A.
```
import java.util.*;
  interface Klakker { }
  class Jammer { Set<Quizel> q; }
  class Quizel implements Klakker { }
  public class Floozel extends Jammer { List<Floozet> f; }
  interface Floozet { }
```

B.
```
import java.util.*;
  class Klakker { Set<Quizel> q; }
  class Quizel extends Klakker { }
  class Jammer { List<Floozel> f; }
  class Floozet extends Floozel { }
      public class Floozel { Set<Klakker> k; }
```

C.
```
import java.util.*;
  class Floozet { }
  class Quizel implements Klakker { }
  class Jammer { List<Quizel> q; }
  interface Klakker { }
  class Floozel extends Jammer { List<Floozet> f; }
```

D.
```
import java.util.*;
  interface Jammer extends Quizel { }
  interface Klakker { }
  interface Quizel extends Klakker { }
  interface Floozel extends Jammer, Floozet { }
  interface Floozet { }
```

SELF TEST ANSWERS

1. ☑ **B** and **E** are correct. B is correct because an `abstract` class need not implement any or all of an interface's methods. E is correct because the class implements the interface method and additionally overloads the `twiddle()` method.
   ☒ **A, C,** and **D** are incorrect. A is incorrect because `abstract` methods have no body. C is incorrect because classes implement interfaces; they don't extend them. D is incorrect because overloading a method is not implementing it. (OCA Objectives 7.1 and 7.6)

2. ☑ **E** is correct. The implied `super()` call in `Bottom2`'s constructor cannot be satisfied because there is no no-arg constructor in `Top`. A default, no-arg constructor is generated by the compiler only if the class has no constructor defined explicitly.
   ☒ **A, B, C,** and **D** are incorrect based on the above. (OCA Objectives 6.5 and 7.5)

3. ☑ **A** is correct. Although a `final` method cannot be overridden, in this case, the method is private, and therefore hidden. The effect is that a new, accessible, method flipper is created. Therefore, no polymorphism occurs in this example, the method invoked is simply that of the child class, and no error occurs.
   ☒ **B, C, D,** and **E** are incorrect based on the preceding. (OCA Objectives 7.1 and 7.2)

   Special Note: This next question crudely simulates a style of question known as "drag-and-drop." Up through the SCJP 6 exam, drag-and-drop questions were included on the exam. As of the Spring of 2014, Oracle DOES NOT include any drag-and-drop questions on its Java exams, but just in case Oracle's policy changes, we left a few in the book.

4. Here is the answer:

```
class AgedP {
  AgedP() {}
  public AgedP(int x) {
  }
}
public class Kinder extends AgedP {
  public Kinder(int x) {
    super();
  }
}
```

   As there is no droppable tile for the variable `x` and the parentheses (in the `Kinder` constructor) are already in place and empty, there is no way to construct a call to the superclass constructor that takes an argument. Therefore, the only remaining possibility is to create a call to the no-arg superclass constructor. This is done as `super();`. The line cannot be left blank, as the parentheses are already in place. Further, since the superclass constructor called is the no-arg version, this constructor must be created. It will not be created by the compiler because another constructor is already present. (OCA Objectives 6.5, 7.1, and 7.5)
   Note: As you can see, many questions test for OCA Objective 7.1.

5. ☑ **D** is correct. Static `init` blocks are executed at class loading time; instance `init` blocks run right after the call to `super()` in a constructor. When multiple `init` blocks of a single type occur in a class, they run in order, from the top down.
☒ **A, B, C, E, F, G, H,** and **I** are incorrect based on the above. Note: You'll probably never see this many choices on the real exam! (OCA Objectives 6.5 and 7.5)

6. ☑ **C** is correct. Before you can invoke `Y`'s `do2` method, you have to cast `x2` to be of type `Y`.
☒ **A, B,** and **D** are incorrect based on the preceding. B looks like a proper cast, but without the second set of parentheses, the compiler thinks it's an incomplete statement. (OCA Objective 7.4)

7. ☑ **A** is correct. It's legal to overload `main()`. Since no instances of `Locomotive` are created, the constructor does not run and the overloaded version of `main()` does not run.
☒ **B, C, D,** and **E** are incorrect based on the preceding. (OCA Objectives 1.3 and 6.3)

8. ☑ **F** is correct. Class `Dog` doesn't have a `sniff` method.
☒ **A, B, C, D,** and **E** are incorrect based on the above information. (OCA Objectives 7.2 and 7.4)

9. ☑ **A** is correct. A `ClassCastException` will be thrown when the code attempts to downcast a `Tree` to a `Redwood`.
☒ **B, C, D, E,** and **F** are incorrect based on the above information. (OCA Objective 7.4)

10. ☑ **B** is correct. The code is correct, but polymorphism doesn't apply to `static` methods.
☒ **A, C, D,** and **E** are incorrect based on the above information. (OCA Objectives 6.2 and 7.2)

11. ☑ **C** is correct. Watch out, because `SubSubAlpha` extends `Alpha`! Since the code doesn't attempt to make a `SubAlpha`, the private constructor in `SubAlpha` is okay.
☒ **A, B, D, E,** and **F** are incorrect based on the above information. (OCA Objectives 6.5 and 7.5)

12. ☑ **C** is correct. Remember that constructors call their superclass constructors, which execute first, and that constructors can be overloaded.
☒ **A, B, D, E, F, G,** and **H** are incorrect based on the above information. (OCA Objectives 6.5 and 7.5)

13. ☑ **A** is correct. Polymorphism is only for instance methods, not instance variables.
☒ **B, C, D, E,** and **F** are incorrect based on the above information. (OCA Objectives 6.2 and 7.2)

14. ☑ **A** and **C** are correct. The phrase "type of" indicates an IS-A relationship (extends or implements), and the word "have" of course indicates a HAS-A relationship (usually instance variables).
☒ **B** and **D** are incorrect based on the above information. (OCP Objective 3.3)

3 Assignments

CERTIFICATION OBJECTIVES

- Use Class Members
- Understand Primitive Casting
- Understand Variable Scope
- Differentiate Between Primitive Variables and Reference Variables
- Determine the Effects of Passing Variables into Methods
- Understand Object Lifecycle and Garbage Collection

✓ Two-Minute Drill

Q&A Self Test

Stack and Heap—Quick Review

For most people, understanding the basics of the stack and the heap makes it far easier to understand topics like argument passing, polymorphism, threads, exceptions, and garbage collection. In this section, we'll stick to an overview, but we'll expand these topics several more times throughout the book.

For the most part, the various pieces (methods, variables, and objects) of Java programs live in one of two places in memory: the stack or the heap. For now, we're concerned about only three types of things—instance variables, local variables, and objects:

- Instance variables and objects live on the heap.
- Local variables live on the stack.

Let's take a look at a Java program and how its various pieces are created and map into the stack and the heap:

```
 1. class Collar { }
 2.
 3. class Dog {
 4.   Collar c;                          // instance variable
 5.   String name;                       // instance variable
 6.
 7.   public static void main(String [] args) {
 8.
 9.     Dog d;                           // local variable: d
10.     d = new Dog();
11.     d.go(d);
12.   }
13.   void go(Dog dog) {                 // local variable: dog
14.     c = new Collar();
15.     dog.setName("Aiko");
16.   }
17.   void setName(String dogName) {    // local var: dogName
18.     name = dogName;
19.     // do more stuff
20.   }
21. }
```

Figure 3-1 shows the state of the stack and the heap once the program reaches line 19. Following are some key points:

- Line 7—`main()` is placed on the stack.
- Line 9—Reference variable `d` is created on the stack, but there's no `Dog` object yet.

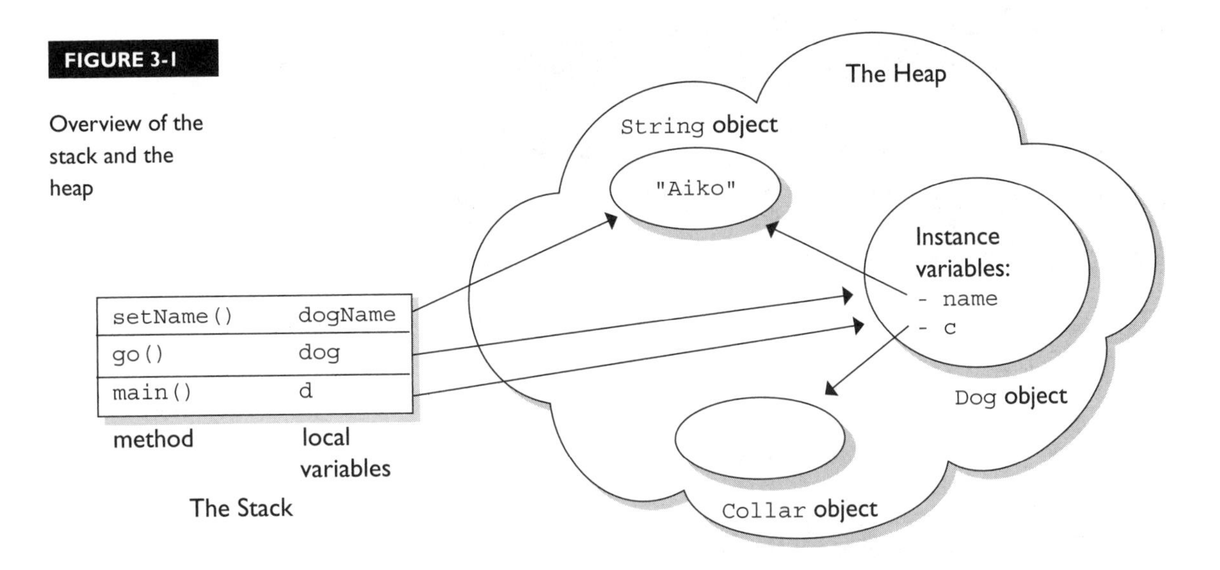

FIGURE 3-1 Overview of the stack and the heap

- Line 10—A new `Dog` object is created and is assigned to the `d` reference variable.
- Line 11—A copy of the reference variable `d` is passed to the `go()` method.
- Line 13—The `go()` method is placed on the stack, with the `dog` parameter as a local variable.
- Line 14—A new `Collar` object is created on the heap and assigned to `Dog`'s instance variable.
- Line 17—`setName()` is added to the stack, with the `dogName` parameter as its local variable.
- Line 18—The `name` instance variable now also refers to the `String` object.
- Notice that two *different* local variables refer to the same `Dog` object.
- Notice that one local variable and one instance variable both refer to the same `String Aiko`.
- After Line 19 completes, `setName()` completes and is removed from the stack. At this point the local variable `dogName` disappears, too, although the `String` object it referred to is still on the heap.

CERTIFICATION OBJECTIVE

Literals, Assignments, and Variables (OCA Objectives 2.1, 2.2, 2.3, and Upgrade Objective 1.2)

2.1 *Declare and initialize variables.*

2.2 *Differentiate between object references and primitive variables.*

2.3 *Read or write to object fields.*

Literal Values for All Primitive Types

A primitive literal is merely a source code representation of the primitive data types—in other words, an integer, floating-point number, boolean, or character that you type in while writing code. The following are examples of primitive literals:

```
'b'          // char literal
42           // int literal
false        // boolean literal
2546789.343  // double literal
```

Integer Literals

There are four ways to represent integer numbers in the Java language: decimal (base 10), octal (base 8), hexadecimal (base 16), and as of Java 7, binary (base 2). Most exam questions with integer literals use decimal representations, but the few that use octal, hexadecimal, or binary are worth studying for. Even though the odds that you'll ever actually use octal in the real world are astronomically tiny, they were included in the exam just for fun. Before we look at the four ways to represent integer numbers, let's first discuss a new feature added to Java 7, literals with underscores.

Numeric Literals with Underscores (Upgrade Exam Topic 1.2) As of Java 7, numeric literals can be declared using underscore characters (_), ostensibly to improve readability. Let's compare a pre-Java 7 declaration to an easier to read Java 7 declaration:

```
int pre7  = 1000000;       // pre Java 7 - we hope it's a million
int with7 = 1_000_000;     // much clearer!
```

The main rule you have to keep track of is that you CANNOT use the underscore literal at the beginning or end of the literal. The potential gotcha here is that you're free to use the underscore in "weird" places:

```
int i1  = _1_000_000;     // illegal, can't begin with an "_"
int i2 = 10_0000_0;       // legal, but confusing
```

As a final note, remember that you can use the underscore character for any of the numeric types (including doubles and floats), but for doubles and floats, you CANNOT add an underscore character directly next to the decimal point.

Decimal Literals Decimal integers need no explanation; you've been using them since grade one or earlier. Chances are you don't keep your checkbook in hex. (If you do, there's a Geeks Anonymous [GA] group ready to help.) In the Java language, they are represented as is, with no prefix of any kind, as follows:

```
int length = 343;
```

Binary Literals (Upgrade Exam Topic 1.2) Also new to Java 7 is the addition of binary literals. Binary literals can use only the digits 0 and 1. Binary literals must start with either `0B` or `0b`, as shown:

```
int b1 = 0B101010;    // set b1 to binary 101010 (decimal 42)
int b2 = 0b00011;     // set b2 to binary 11 (decimal 3)
```

Octal Literals Octal integers use only the digits 0 to 7. In Java, you represent an integer in octal form by placing a zero in front of the number, as follows:

```
class Octal {
  public static void main(String [] args) {
    int six = 06;       // Equal to decimal 6
    int seven = 07;     // Equal to decimal 7
    int eight = 010;    // Equal to decimal 8
    int nine = 011;     // Equal to decimal 9
    System.out.println("Octal 010 = " + eight);
  }
}
```

You can have up to 21 digits in an octal number, not including the leading zero. If we run the preceding program, it displays the following:

```
Octal 010 = 8
```

Hexadecimal Literals Hexadecimal (hex for short) numbers are constructed using 16 distinct symbols. Because we never invented single-digit symbols for the numbers 10 through 15, we use alphabetic characters to represent these digits. Counting from 0 through 15 in hex looks like this:

```
0 1 2 3 4 5 6 7 8 9 a b c d e f
```

Java will accept uppercase or lowercase letters for the extra digits (one of the few places Java is not case-sensitive!). You are allowed up to 16 digits in a hexadecimal number, not including the prefix `0x` (or `0X`) or the optional suffix extension `L`, which will be explained a bit later in the chapter. All of the following hexadecimal assignments are legal:

```
class HexTest {
  public static void main (String [] args) {
    int x = 0X0001;
    int y = 0x7fffffff;
    int z = 0xDeadCafe;
    System.out.println("x = " + x + " y = " + y + " z = " + z);
  }
}
```

Running `HexTest` produces the following output:

```
x = 1 y = 2147483647 z = -559035650
```

Don't be misled by changes in case for a hexadecimal digit or the `x` preceding it. `0XCAFE` and `0xcafe` are both legal *and have the same value.*

All four integer literals (binary, octal, decimal, and hexadecimal) are defined as `int` by default, but they may also be specified as `long` by placing a suffix of `L` or `l` after the number:

```
long jo = 110599L;
long so = 0xFFFFl;  // Note the lowercase 'l'
```

Floating-point Literals

Floating-point numbers are defined as a number, a decimal symbol, and more numbers representing the fraction. In the following example, the number 11301874.9881024 is the literal value:

```
double d = 11301874.9881024;
```

Floating-point literals are defined as `double` (64 bits) by default, so if you want to assign a floating-point literal to a variable of type `float` (32 bits), you must attach the suffix `F` or `f` to the number. If you don't do this, the compiler will complain about a possible loss of precision, because you're trying to fit a number into a (potentially) less precise "container." The F suffix gives you a way to tell the compiler, "Hey, I know what I'm doing, and I'll take the risk, thank you very much."

```
float f = 23.467890;           // Compiler error, possible loss
                               // of precision
float g = 49837849.029847F;   // OK; has the suffix "F"
```

You may also optionally attach a D or d to double literals, but it is not necessary because this is the default behavior.

```
double d = 110599.995011D; // Optional, not required
double  g = 987.897;       // No 'D' suffix, but OK because the
                           // literal is a double by default
```

Look for numeric literals that include a comma; here's an example:

```
int x = 25,343;            // Won't compile because of the comma
```

Boolean Literals

Boolean literals are the source code representation for boolean values. A boolean value can be defined only as `true` or `false`. Although in C (and some other languages) it is common to use numbers to represent `true` or `false`, this will not work in Java. Again, repeat after me: "Java is not C++."

```
boolean t = true;  // Legal
boolean  f = 0;    // Compiler error!
```

Be on the lookout for questions that use numbers where `booleans` are required. You might see an `if` test that uses a number, as in the following:

```
int x = 1;  if (x) {  } // Compiler error!
```

Character Literals

A `char` literal is represented by a single character in single quotes:

```
char a = 'a';
char b = '@';
```

You can also type in the Unicode value of the character, using the Unicode notation of prefixing the value with \u as follows:

```
char letterN = '\u004E'; // The letter 'N'
```

Remember, characters are just 16-bit unsigned integers under the hood. That means you can assign a number literal, assuming it will fit into the unsigned 16-bit range (0 to 65535). For example, the following are all legal:

```
char a = 0x892;        // hexadecimal literal
char b = 982;          // int literal
char c = (char)70000;  // The cast is required; 70000 is
                       // out of char range
char d = (char) -98;   // Ridiculous, but legal
```

And the following are not legal and produce compiler errors:

```
char e = -29;     // Possible loss of precision; needs a cast
char f = 70000;   // Possible loss of precision; needs a cast
```

You can also use an escape code (the backslash) if you want to represent a character that can't be typed in as a literal, including the characters for linefeed, newline, horizontal tab, backspace, and quotes:

```
char c = '\"';    // A double quote
char d = '\n';    // A newline
char tab = '\t';  // A tab
```

Literal Values for Strings

A string literal is a source code representation of a value of a `String` object. The following is an example of two ways to represent a string literal:

```
String s = "Bill Joy";
System.out.println("Bill" + " Joy");
```

Although strings are not primitives, they're included in this section because they can be represented as literals—in other words, they can be typed directly into code. The only other nonprimitive type that has a literal representation is an array, which we'll look at later in the chapter.

```
Thread t = ???  // what literal value could possibly go here?
```

Assignment Operators

Assigning a value to a variable seems straightforward enough; you simply assign the stuff on the right side of the = to the variable on the left. Well, sure, but don't expect to be tested on something like this:

```
x = 6;
```

No, you won't be tested on the no-brainer (technical term) assignments. You will, however, be tested on the trickier assignments involving complex expressions and casting. We'll look at both primitive and reference variable assignments. But before we begin, let's back up and peek inside a variable. What is a variable? How are the variable and its value related?

Variables are just bit holders, with a designated type. You can have an `int` holder, a `double` holder, a `Button` holder, and even a `String[]` holder. Within that holder is a bunch of bits representing the value. For primitives, the bits represent a numeric value (although we don't know what that bit pattern looks like for `boolean`, luckily, we don't care). A `byte` with a value of 6, for example, means that the bit pattern in the variable (the `byte` holder) is 00000110, representing the 8 bits.

So the value of a primitive variable is clear, but what's inside an object holder? If you say,

```
Button b = new Button();
```

what's inside the `Button` holder `b`? Is it the `Button` object? No! A variable referring to an object is just that—a *reference* variable. A reference variable bit holder contains bits representing a *way to get to the object*. We don't know what the format is. The way in which object references are stored is virtual-machine specific (it's a pointer to something, we just don't know what that something really is). All we can say for sure is that the variable's value is *not* the object, but rather a value representing a specific object on the heap. Or `null`. If the reference variable has not been assigned a value or has been explicitly assigned a value of `null`, the variable holds bits representing—you guessed it—`null`. You can read

```
Button b = null;
```

as "The `Button` variable `b` is not referring to any object."

So now that we know a variable is just a little box o' bits, we can get on with the work of changing those bits. We'll look first at assigning values to primitives and then finish with assignments to reference variables.

Primitive Assignments

The equal (=) sign is used for assigning a value to a variable, and it's cleverly named the assignment operator. There are actually 12 assignment operators, but only the 5 most commonly used assignment operators are on the exam, and they are covered in Chapter 4.

You can assign a primitive variable using a literal or the result of an expression.

Take a look at the following:

```
int x = 7;      // literal assignment
int y = x + 2; // assignment with an expression
               // (including a literal)
int z = x * y; // assignment with an expression
```

The most important point to remember is that a literal integer (such as 7) is always implicitly an `int`. Thinking back to Chapter 1, you'll recall that an `int` is a 32-bit value. No big deal if you're assigning a value to an `int` or a `long` variable, but what if you're assigning to a `byte` variable? After all, a `byte`-sized holder can't hold as many bits as an `int`-sized holder. Here's where it gets weird. The following is legal,

```
byte b = 27;
```

but only because the compiler automatically narrows the literal value to a `byte`. In other words, the compiler puts in the *cast*. The preceding code is identical to the following:

```
byte b = (byte) 27; // Explicitly cast the int literal to a byte
```

It looks as though the compiler gives you a break and lets you take a shortcut with assignments to integer variables smaller than an `int`. (Everything we're saying about `byte` applies equally to `char` and `short`, both of which are smaller than an `int`.) We're not actually at the weird part yet, by the way.

We know that a literal integer is always an `int`, but more importantly, the result of an expression involving anything `int`-sized or smaller is always an `int`. In other words, add two `byte`s together and you'll get an `int`—even if those two `byte`s are tiny. Multiply an `int` and a `short` and you'll get an `int`. Divide a `short` by a `byte` and you'll get...an `int`. Okay, now we're at the weird part. Check this out:

```
byte a = 3;     // No problem, 3 fits in a byte
byte b = 8;     // No problem, 8 fits in a byte
byte c = a + b; // Should be no problem, sum of the two bytes
                // fits in a byte
```

The last line won't compile! You'll get an error something like this:

```
TestBytes.java:5: possible loss of precision
found   : int
required: byte
    byte c = a + b;
               ^
```

We tried to assign the sum of two `bytes` to a `byte` variable, the result of which (11) was definitely small enough to fit into a `byte`, but the compiler didn't care. It knew the rule about `int`-or-smaller expressions always resulting in an `int`. It would have compiled if we'd done the *explicit* cast:

```
byte c = (byte) (a + b);
```

We were struggling to find a good way to teach this topic, and our friend, co-JavaRanch moderator, and repeat technical reviewer Marc Peabody came up with the following. We think he did a great job: It's perfectly legal to declare multiple variables of the same type with a single line by placing a comma between each variable:

```
int a, b, c;
```

You also have the option to initialize any number of those variables right in place:

```
int j, k=1, l, m=3;
```

And these variables are each evaluated in the order that you read them, left to right. It's just as if you were to declare each one on a separate line:

```
int j;
int k=1;
int l;
int m=3;
```

But the order is important. This is legal:

```
int j, k=1, l, m=k+3; // legal: k is initialized before m uses it
```

But these are not:

```
int j, k=m+3, l, m=1; // illegal: m is not initialized before k uses it
int x, y=x+1, z;      // illegal: x is not initialized before y uses it
```

Primitive Casting

Casting lets you convert primitive values from one type to another. We mentioned primitive casting in the previous section, but now we're going to take a deeper look. (Object casting was covered in Chapter 2.)

Casts can be implicit or explicit. An implicit cast means you don't have to write code for the cast; the conversion happens automatically. Typically, an implicit cast happens when you're doing a widening conversion—in other words, putting a smaller thing (say, a `byte`) into a bigger container (such as an `int`). Remember those "`possible loss of precision`" compiler errors we saw in the assignments section? Those happened when we tried to put a larger thing (say, a `long`) into a smaller container (such as a `short`). The large-value-into-small-container conversion is referred to as *narrowing* and requires an explicit cast, where you tell the compiler that you're aware of the danger and accept full responsibility.

First we'll look at an implicit cast:

```
int a = 100;
long b = a;     // Implicit cast, an int value always fits in a long
```

An explicit casts looks like this:

```
float a = 100.001f;
int b = (int)a; // Explicit cast, the float could lose info
```

Integer values may be assigned to a `double` variable without explicit casting, because any integer value can fit in a 64-bit `double`. The following line demonstrates this:

```
double d = 100L; // Implicit cast
```

In the preceding statement, a `double` is initialized with a `long` value (as denoted by the `L` after the numeric value). No cast is needed in this case because a `double` can hold every piece of information that a `long` can store. If, however, we want to assign a `double` value to an integer type, we're attempting a narrowing conversion and the compiler knows it:

```
class Casting {
  public static void main(String [] args) {
    int x = 3957.229; // illegal
  }
}
```

If we try to compile the preceding code, we get an error something like this:

```
%javac Casting.java
Casting.java:3: Incompatible type for declaration. Explicit cast
needed to convert double to int.
      int x = 3957.229; // illegal
1 error
```

In the preceding code, a floating-point value is being assigned to an integer variable. Because an integer is not capable of storing decimal places, an error occurs. To make this work, we'll cast the floating-point number to an `int`:

```
class Casting {
  public static void main(String [] args) {
    int x = (int)3957.229; // legal cast
    System.out.println("int x = " + x);
  }
}
```

When you cast a floating-point number to an integer type, the value loses all the digits after the decimal. The preceding code will produce the following output:

```
int x = 3957
```

We can also cast a larger number type, such as a `long`, into a smaller number type, such as a `byte`. Look at the following:

```
class Casting {
  public static void main(String [] args) {
    long l = 56L;
    byte b = (byte)l;
    System.out.println("The byte is " + b);
  }
}
```

The preceding code will compile and run fine. But what happens if the `long` value is larger than 127 (the largest number a `byte` can store)? Let's modify the code:

```
class Casting {
  public static void main(String [] args) {
    long l = 130L;
    byte b = (byte)l;
    System.out.println("The byte is " + b);
  }
}
```

The code compiles fine, and when we run it we get the following:

```
%java Casting
The byte is -126
```

We don't get a runtime error, even when the value being narrowed is too large for the type. The bits to the left of the lower 8 just...go away. If the leftmost bit (the sign bit) in the `byte` (or any integer primitive) now happens to be a 1, the primitive will have a negative value.

EXERCISE 3-1

Casting Primitives

Create a `float` number type of any value, and assign it to a `short` using casting.

1. Declare a `float` variable: `float f = 234.56F;`
2. Assign the `float` to a `short`: `short s = (short)f;`

Assigning Floating-point Numbers

Floating-point numbers have slightly different assignment behavior than integer types. First, you must know that every floating-point literal is implicitly a `double` (64 bits), not a `float`. So the literal `32.3`, for example, is considered a `double`. If you try to assign a `double` to a `float`, the compiler knows you don't have enough room in a 32-bit `float` container to hold the precision of a 64-bit `double`, and it lets you know. The following code looks good, but it won't compile:

```
float f = 32.3;
```

You can see that `32.3` should fit just fine into a float-sized variable, but the compiler won't allow it. In order to assign a floating-point literal to a `float` variable, you must either cast the value or append an `f` to the end of the literal. The following assignments will compile:

```
float f = (float) 32.3;
float g = 32.3f;
float h = 32.3F;
```

Assigning a Literal That Is Too Large for the Variable

We'll also get a compiler error if we try to assign a literal value that the compiler knows is too big to fit into the variable.

```
byte a = 128; // byte can only hold up to 127
```

The preceding code gives us an error something like this:

```
TestBytes.java:5: possible loss of precision
found   : int
required: byte
byte a = 128;
```

We can fix it with a cast:

```
byte a = (byte) 128;
```

But then what's the result? When you narrow a primitive, Java simply truncates the higher-order bits that won't fit. In other words, it loses all the bits to the left of the bits you're narrowing to.

Let's take a look at what happens in the preceding code. There, 128 is the bit pattern 10000000. It takes a full 8 bits to represent 128. But because the literal 128 is an `int`, we actually get 32 bits, with the 128 living in the rightmost (lower order) 8 bits. So a literal 128 is actually

00000000000000000000000010000000

Take our word for it; there are 32 bits there.

To narrow the 32 bits representing 128, Java simply lops off the leftmost (higher order) 24 bits. What remains is just the 10000000. But remember that a byte is signed, with the leftmost bit representing the sign (and not part of the value of the variable). So we end up with a negative number (the 1 that used to represent 128 now represents the negative sign bit). Remember, to find out the value of a negative number using 2's complement notation, you flip all of the bits and then add 1. Flipping the 8 bits gives us 01111111, and adding 1 to that gives us 10000000, or back to 128! And when we apply the sign bit, we end up with –128.

You must use an explicit cast to assign 128 to a byte, and the assignment leaves you with the value –128. A cast is nothing more than your way of saying to the compiler, "Trust me. I'm a professional. I take full responsibility for anything weird that happens when those top bits are chopped off."

That brings us to the compound assignment operators. This will compile:

```
byte b = 3;
b += 7;                // No problem - adds 7 to b (result is 10)
```

and it is equivalent to this:

```
byte b = 3;
b = (byte) (b + 7);  // Won't compile without the
                     // cast, since b + 7 results in an int
```

The compound assignment operator `+=` lets you add to the value of `b`, without putting in an explicit cast. In fact, `+=`, `-=`, `*=`, and `/=` will all put in an implicit cast.

Assigning One Primitive Variable to Another Primitive Variable

When you assign one primitive variable to another, the contents of the right-hand variable are copied. For example:

```
int a = 6;
int b = a;
```

This code can be read as, "Assign the bit pattern for the number 6 to the `int` variable `a`. Then copy the bit pattern in `a`, and place the copy into variable `b`."

So, both variables now hold a bit pattern for 6, but the two variables have no other relationship. We used the variable `a` *only* to copy its contents. At this point, `a` and `b` have identical contents (in other words, identical values), but if we change the contents of *either* `a or b`, the other variable won't be affected.

Take a look at the following example:

```
class ValueTest {
  public static void main (String [] args) {
    int a = 10;  // Assign a value to a
    System.out.println("a = " + a);
    int b = a;
    b = 30;
    System.out.println("a = " + a + " after change to b");
  }
}
```

The output from this program is

```
%java ValueTest
a = 10
a = 10 after change to b
```

Notice the value of `a` stayed at 10. The key point to remember is that even after you assign `a` to `b`, `a` and `b` are not referring to the same place in memory. The `a` and `b` variables do not share a single value; they have identical copies.

Reference Variable Assignments

You can assign a newly created object to an object reference variable as follows:

```
Button b = new Button();
```

The preceding line does three key things:

- Makes a reference variable named `b`, of type `Button`
- Creates a new `Button` object on the heap
- Assigns the newly created `Button` object to the reference variable `b`

You can also assign `null` to an object reference variable, which simply means the variable is not referring to any object:

```
Button c = null;
```

The preceding line creates space for the `Button` reference variable (the bit holder for a reference value), but it doesn't create an actual `Button` object.

As we discussed in the last chapter, you can also use a reference variable to refer to any object that is a subclass of the declared reference variable type, as follows:

```
public class Foo {
  public void doFooStuff() { }
}
public class Bar extends Foo {
  public void doBarStuff() { }
}
class Test {
  public static void main (String [] args) {
     Foo reallyABar = new Bar();  // Legal because Bar is a
                                  // subclass of Foo

     Bar reallyAFoo = new Foo();  // Illegal! Foo is not a
                                  // subclass of Bar

  }
}
```

The rule is that you can assign a subclass of the declared type but not a superclass of the declared type. Remember, a `Bar` object is guaranteed to be able to do anything a `Foo` can do, so anyone with a `Foo` reference can invoke `Foo` methods even though the object is actually a `Bar`.

In the preceding code, we see that `Foo` has a method `doFooStuff()` that someone with a `Foo` reference might try to invoke. If the object referenced by the `Foo` variable is really a `Foo`, no problem. But it's also no problem if the object is a `Bar`, since `Bar` inherited the `doFooStuff()` method. You can't make it work in reverse, however. If somebody has a `Bar` reference, they're going to invoke `doBarStuff()`, but if the object is a `Foo`, it won't know how to respond.

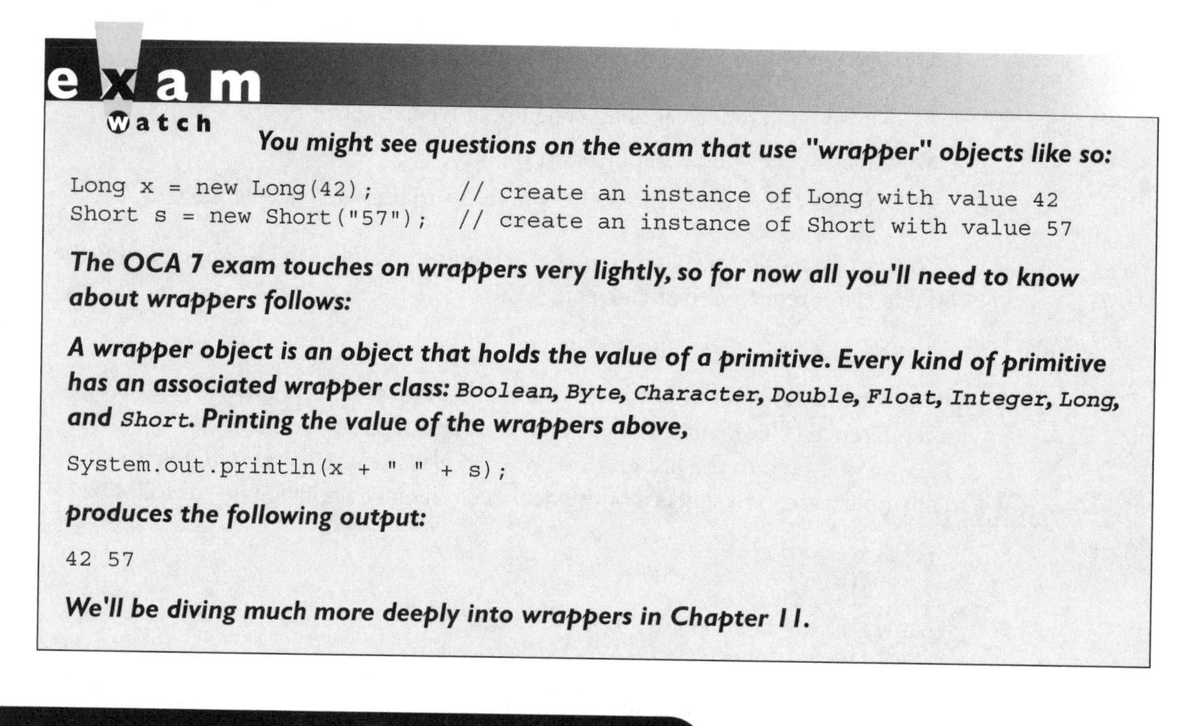

exam watch

You might see questions on the exam that use "wrapper" objects like so:

```
Long x = new Long(42);        // create an instance of Long with value 42
Short s = new Short("57");    // create an instance of Short with value 57
```

The OCA 7 exam touches on wrappers very lightly, so for now all you'll need to know about wrappers follows:

A wrapper object is an object that holds the value of a primitive. Every kind of primitive has an associated wrapper class: `Boolean`, `Byte`, `Character`, `Double`, `Float`, `Integer`, `Long`, and `Short`. Printing the value of the wrappers above,

```
System.out.println(x + " " + s);
```

produces the following output:

```
42 57
```

We'll be diving much more deeply into wrappers in Chapter 11.

CERTIFICATION OBJECTIVE

Scope (OCA Objectives 1.1 and 2.5)

1.1 *Determine the scope of variables.*

2.5 *Call methods on objects.*

Variable Scope

Once you've declared and initialized a variable, a natural question is, "How long will this variable be around?" This is a question regarding the scope of variables. And not only is scope an important thing to understand in general, it also plays a big part in the exam. Let's start by looking at a class file:

```
class Layout {                           // class
  static int s = 343;                    // static variable
  int x;                                 // instance variable
  { x = 7; int x2 = 5; }                 // initialization block
  Layout() { x += 8; int x3 = 6;}        // constructor
```

```
    void doStuff() {                      // method
      int y = 0;                          // local variable
      for(int z = 0; z < 4; z++) {        // 'for' code block
        y += z + x;
      }
    }
  }
```

As with variables in all Java programs, the variables in this program (s, x, x2, x3, y, and z) all have a scope:

- s is a static variable.
- x is an instance variable.
- y is a local variable (sometimes called a "method local" variable).
- z is a block variable.
- x2 is an init block variable, a flavor of local variable.
- x3 is a constructor variable, a flavor of local variable.

For the purposes of discussing the scope of variables, we can say that there are four basic scopes:

- Static variables have the longest scope; they are created when the class is loaded, and they survive as long as the class stays loaded in the Java Virtual Machine (JVM).
- Instance variables are the next most long-lived; they are created when a new instance is created, and they live until the instance is removed.
- Local variables are next; they live as long as their method remains on the stack. As we'll soon see, however, local variables can be alive and still be "out of scope."
- Block variables live only as long as the code block is executing.

Scoping errors come in many sizes and shapes. One common mistake happens when a variable is *shadowed* and two scopes overlap. We'll take a detailed look at shadowing in a few pages. The most common reason for scoping errors is an attempt to access a variable that is not in scope. Let's look at three common examples of this type of error.

- Attempting to access an instance variable from a static context (typically from main()):

  ```
  class ScopeErrors {
    int x = 5;
  ```

```
  public static void main(String[] args) {
    x++;    // won't compile, x is an 'instance' variable
  }
}
```

- Attempting to access a local variable from a nested method. When a method, say `go()`, invokes another method, say `go2()`, `go2()` won't have access to `go()`'s local variables. While `go2()` is executing, `go()`'s local variables are still *alive*, but they are *out of scope*. When `go2()` completes, it is removed from the stack, and `go()` resumes execution. At this point, all of `go()`'s previously declared variables are back in scope. For example:

```
class ScopeErrors {
  public static void main(String [] args) {
    ScopeErrors s = new ScopeErrors();
    s.go();
  }
  void go() {
    int y = 5;
    go2();
    y++;          // once go2() completes, y is back in scope
  }
  void go2() {
    y++;          // won't compile, y is local to go()
  }
}
```

- Attempting to use a block variable after the code block has completed. It's very common to declare and use a variable within a code block, but be careful not to try to use the variable once the block has completed:

```
void go3() {
  for(int z = 0; z < 5; z++) {
    boolean test = false;
    if(z == 3) {
      test = true;
      break;
    }
  }
  System.out.print(test);    // 'test' is an ex-variable,
                             // it has ceased to be...
}
```

In the last two examples, the compiler will say something like this:

```
cannot find symbol
```

This is the compiler's way of saying, "That variable you just tried to use? Well, it might have been valid in the distant past (like one line of code ago), but this is Internet time, baby, I have no memory of such a variable."

exam watch

Pay extra attention to code block scoping errors. You might see them in switches, try-catches, `for`, `do`, and `while` loops.

CERTIFICATION OBJECTIVE

Variable Initialization (OCA Objective 2.1)

2.1 Declare and initialize variables.

Using a Variable or Array Element That Is Uninitialized and Unassigned

Java gives us the option of initializing a declared variable or leaving it uninitialized. When we attempt to use the uninitialized variable, we can get different behavior depending on what type of variable or array we are dealing with (primitives or objects). The behavior also depends on the level (scope) at which we are declaring our variable. An instance variable is declared within the class but outside any method or constructor, whereas a local variable is declared within a method (or in the argument list of the method).

Local variables are sometimes called stack, temporary, automatic, or method variables, but the rules for these variables are the same regardless of what you call them. Although you can leave a local variable uninitialized, the compiler complains if you try to use a local variable before initializing it with a value, as we shall see.

Primitive and Object Type Instance Variables

Instance variables (also called *member* variables) are variables defined at the class level. That means the variable declaration is not made within a method, constructor, or any other initializer block. Instance variables are initialized to a default value each time a new instance is created, although they may be given an explicit value after the object's superconstructors have completed. Table 3-1 lists the default values for primitive and object types.

TABLE 3-1 Default Values for Primitives and Reference Types

Variable Type	Default Value
Object reference	null (not referencing any object)
byte, short, int, long	0
float, double	0.0
boolean	false
char	'\u0000'

Primitive Instance Variables

In the following example, the integer year is defined as a class member because it is within the initial curly braces of the class and not within a method's curly braces:

```
public class BirthDate {
  int year;                              // Instance variable
  public static void main(String [] args) {
    BirthDate bd = new BirthDate();
    bd.showYear();
  }
  public void showYear() {
    System.out.println("The year is " + year);
  }
}
```

When the program is started, it gives the variable year a value of zero, the default value for primitive number instance variables.

It's a good idea to initialize all your variables, even if you're assigning them with the default value. Your code will be easier to read; programmers who have to maintain your code (after you win the lottery and move to Tahiti) will be grateful.

Object Reference Instance Variables

When compared with uninitialized primitive variables, object references that aren't initialized are a completely different story. Let's look at the following code:

```
public class Book {
  private String title;         // instance reference variable
  public String getTitle() {
    return title;
  }
  public static void main(String [] args) {
    Book b = new Book();
    System.out.println("The title is " + b.getTitle());
  }
}
```

This code will compile fine. When we run it, the output is

```
The title is null
```

The `title` variable has not been explicitly initialized with a `String` assignment, so the instance variable value is `null`. Remember that `null` is not the same as an empty String (`""`). A `null` value means the reference variable is not referring to any object on the heap. The following modification to the `Book` code runs into trouble:

```
public class Book {
  private String title;          // instance reference variable
  public String getTitle() {
    return title;
  }
  public static void main(String [] args) {
    Book b = new Book();
    String s = b.getTitle();      // Compiles and runs
    String t = s.toLowerCase();   // Runtime Exception!
  }
}
```

When we try to run the `Book` class, the JVM will produce something like this:

```
Exception in thread "main" java.lang.NullPointerException
     at Book.main(Book.java:9)
```

We get this error because the reference variable `title` does not point (refer) to an object. We can check to see whether an object has been instantiated by using the keyword `null`, as the following revised code shows:

```
public class Book {
  private String title;          // instance reference variable
  public String getTitle() {
    return title;
  }
  public static void main(String [] args) {
    Book b = new Book();
    String s = b.getTitle();     // Compiles and runs
    if (s != null) {
      String t = s.toLowerCase();
    }
  }
}
```

The preceding code checks to make sure the object referenced by the variable `s` is not `null` before trying to use it. Watch out for scenarios on the exam where you might have to trace back through the code to find out whether an object reference will have a value of `null`. In the preceding code, for example, you look at the instance variable declaration for title, see that there's no explicit initialization, recognize that the `title` variable will be given the default value of `null`, and then realize that the variable s will also have a value of null. Remember, the value of s is a copy of the value of title (as returned by the getTitle() method), so if title is a null reference, s will be, too.

Array Instance Variables

In Chapter 5 we'll be taking a very detailed look at declaring, constructing, and initializing arrays and multidimensional arrays. For now, we're just going to look at the rule for an array element's default values.

An array is an object; thus, an array instance variable that's declared but not explicitly initialized will have a value of null, just as any other object reference instance variable. But…if the array is initialized, what happens to the elements contained *in* the array? All array elements are given their default values—the same default values that elements of that type get when they're instance variables. *The bottom line: Array elements are always, always, always given default values, regardless of where the array itself is declared or instantiated.*

If we initialize an array, object reference elements will equal null if they are not initialized individually with values. If primitives are contained in an array, they will be given their respective default values. For example, in the following code, the array year will contain 100 integers that all equal zero by default:

```
public class BirthDays {
  static int [] year = new int[100];
  public static void main(String [] args) {
    for(int i=0;i<100;i++)
      System.out.println("year[" + i + "] = " + year[i]);
  }
}
```

When the preceding code runs, the output indicates that all 100 integers in the array have a value of zero.

Local (Stack, Automatic) Primitives and Objects

Local variables are defined within a method, and they include a method's parameters.

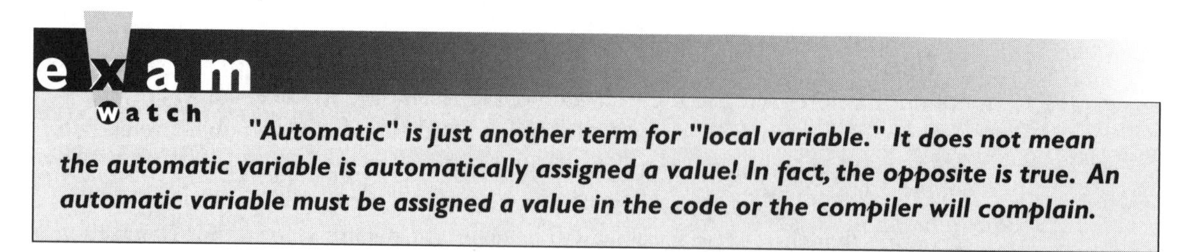

"Automatic" is just another term for "local variable." It does not mean the automatic variable is automatically assigned a value! In fact, the opposite is true. An automatic variable must be assigned a value in the code or the compiler will complain.

Local Primitives

In the following time-travel simulator, the integer `year` is defined as an automatic variable because it is within the curly braces of a method:

```
public class TimeTravel {
  public static void main(String [] args) {
    int year = 2050;
    System.out.println("The year is " + year);
  }
}
```

Local variables, including primitives, always, always, always must be initialized *before* you attempt to use them (though not necessarily on the same line of code). Java does not give local variables a default value; you must explicitly initialize them with a value, as in the preceding example. If you try to use an uninitialized primitive in your code, you'll get a compiler error:

```
public class TimeTravel {
  public static void main(String [] args) {
    int year; // Local variable (declared but not initialized)
    System.out.println("The year is " + year); // Compiler error
  }
}
```

Compiling produces output something like this:

```
%javac TimeTravel.java
TimeTravel.java:4: Variable year may not have been initialized.
          System.out.println("The year is " + year);
1 error
```

To correct our code, we must give the integer `year` a value. In this updated example, we declare it on a separate line, which is perfectly valid:

```
public class TimeTravel {
  public static void main(String [] args) {
    int year;              // Declared but not initialized
    int day;               // Declared but not initialized
    System.out.println("You step into the portal.");
    year = 2050;           // Initialize (assign an explicit value)
    System.out.println("Welcome to the year " + year);
  }
}
```

Notice in the preceding example we declared an integer called `day` that never gets initialized, yet the code compiles and runs fine. Legally, you can declare a local variable without initializing it as long as you don't use the variable—but, let's face it, if you declared it, you probably had a reason (although we have heard of programmers declaring random local variables just for sport, to see if they can figure out how and why they're being used).

on the job

The compiler can't always tell whether a local variable has been initialized before use. For example, if you initialize within a logically conditional block (in other words, a code block that may not run, such as an if block or for loop without a literal value of true or false in the test), the compiler knows that the initialization might not happen and can produce an error. The following code upsets the compiler:

```
public class TestLocal {
  public static void main(String [] args) {
    int x;
    if (args[0] != null) { // assume you know this is true
      x = 7;               // compiler can't tell that this
                           // statement will run
    }
    int y = x;             // the compiler will choke here
  }
}
```

The compiler will produce an error something like this:

```
TestLocal.java:9: variable x might not have been initialized
```

Because of the compiler-can't-tell-for-certain problem, you will sometimes need to initialize your variable outside the conditional block, just to make the compiler happy. You know why that's important if you've seen the bumper sticker, "When the compiler's not happy, ain't nobody happy."

Local Object References

Objects references, too, behave differently when declared within a method rather than as instance variables. With instance variable object references, you can get away with leaving an object reference uninitialized, as long as the code checks to make sure the reference isn't `null` before using it. Remember, to the compiler, `null` is a value. You can't use the dot operator on a `null` reference, because *there is no object at the other end of it*, but a `null` reference is not the same as an *uninitialized* reference. Locally declared references can't get away with checking for `null` before use, unless you explicitly initialize the local variable to `null`. The compiler will complain about the following code:

```
import java.util.Date;
public class TimeTravel {
  public static void main(String [] args) {
    Date date;
    if (date == null)
      System.out.println("date is null");
  }
}
```

Compiling the code results in an error similar to the following:

```
%javac TimeTravel.java
TimeTravel.java:5: Variable date may not have been initialized.
          if (date == null)
1 error
```

Instance variable references are always given a default value of `null`, until they are explicitly initialized to something else. But local references are not given a default value; in other words, *they aren't* `null`. If you don't initialize a local reference variable, then by default, its value is—well that's the whole point: it doesn't have any value at all! So we'll make this simple: Just set the darn thing to `null` explicitly, until you're ready to initialize it to something else. The following local variable will compile properly:

```
Date date = null; // Explicitly set the local reference
                  // variable to null
```

Local Arrays

Just like any other object reference, array references declared within a method must be assigned a value before use. That just means you must declare and construct the array. You do not, however, need to explicitly initialize the elements of an array. We've said it before, but it's important enough to repeat: Array elements are given their default values (`0`, `false`, `null`, `'\u0000'`, and so on) regardless of whether the array is declared as an instance or local variable. The array object itself, however, will not be initialized if it's declared locally. In other words, you must explicitly initialize an array reference if it's declared and used within a method, but at the moment you construct an array object, all of its elements are assigned their default values.

Assigning One Reference Variable to Another

With primitive variables, an assignment of one variable to another means the contents (bit pattern) of one variable are *copied* into another. Object reference variables work exactly the same way. The contents of a reference variable are a bit pattern, so if you assign reference variable `a1` to reference variable `b1`, the bit pattern in `a1` is *copied* and the new *copy* is placed into `b1`. (Some people have created a game around counting how many times we use the word *copy* in this chapter...this copy concept is a biggie!) If we assign an existing instance of an object to a new reference variable, then two reference variables will hold the same bit pattern—a bit pattern referring to a specific object on the heap. Look at the following code:

```
import java.awt.Dimension;
class ReferenceTest {
  public static void main (String [] args) {
    Dimension a1 = new Dimension(5,10);
    System.out.println("a1.height = " + a1.height);
    Dimension b1 = a1;
    b1.height = 30;
    System.out.println("a1.height = " + a1.height +
                       " after change to b");
  }
}
```

In the preceding example, a `Dimension` object `a1` is declared and initialized with a width of 5 and a height of 10. Next, `Dimension b1` is declared and assigned the value of `a1`. At this point, both variables (`a1` and `b1`) hold identical values, because the contents of `a1` were copied into `b1`. There is still only one `Dimension` object—the one that both `a1` and `b1` refer to. Finally, the `height` property is changed using the `b1` reference. Now think for a minute: is this going to change the `height` property of `a1` as well? Let's see what the output will be:

```
%java ReferenceTest
a.height = 10
a.height = 30 after change to b
```

From this output, we can conclude that both variables refer to the same instance of the `Dimension` object. When we made a change to `b1`, the `height` property was also changed for `a1`.

One exception to the way object references are assigned is `String`. In Java, `String` objects are given special treatment. For one thing, `String` objects are immutable; you can't change the value of a `String` object (lots more on this concept in Chapter 5). But it sure looks as though you can. Examine the following code:

```
class StringTest {
  public static void main(String [] args) {
    String x = "Java";  // Assign a value to x
    String y = x;       // Now y and x refer to the same
                        // String object

    System.out.println("y string = " + y);
    x = x + " Bean";    // Now modify the object using
                        // the x reference
    System.out.println("y string = " + y);
  }
}
```

You might think `String y` will contain the characters `Java Bean` after the variable `x` is changed, because `Strings` are objects. Let's see what the output is:

```
%java StringTest
y string = Java
y string = Java
```

As you can see, even though `y` is a reference variable to the same object that `x` refers to, when we change `x`, it doesn't change `y`! For any other object type, where two references refer to the same object, if either reference is used to modify the object, both references will see the change because there is still only a single object. *But any time we make any changes at all to a `String`, the VM will update the reference variable to refer to a different object.* The different object might be a new object, or it might not be, but it will definitely be a different object. The reason we can't say for sure whether a new object is created is because of the `String` constant pool, which we'll cover in Chapter 5.

You need to understand what happens when you use a `String` reference variable to modify a string:

- A new string is created (or a matching `String` is found in the `String` pool), leaving the original `String` object untouched.
- The reference used to modify the `String` (or rather, make a new `String` by modifying a copy of the original) is then assigned the brand new `String` object.

So when you say,

```
1. String s = "Fred";
2. String t = s;      // Now t and s refer to the same
                      // String object
3. t.toUpperCase();   // Invoke a String method that changes
                      // the String
```

you haven't changed the original `String` object created on line 1. When line 2 completes, both `t` and `s` reference the same `String` object. But when line 3 runs, rather than modifying the object referred to by `t` and `s` (which is the one and only `String` object up to this point), a brand new `String` object is created. And then it's abandoned. Because the new `String` isn't assigned to a `String` variable, the newly created `String` (which holds the string `"FRED"`) is toast. So although two `String` objects were created in the preceding code, only one is actually referenced, and both `t` and `s` refer to it. The behavior of `Strings` is extremely important in the exam, so we'll cover it in much more detail in Chapter 5.

CERTIFICATION OBJECTIVE

Passing Variables into Methods (OCA Objective 6.8)

6.8 *Determine the effect upon object references and primitive values when they are passed into methods that change the values.*

Methods can be declared to take primitives and/or object references. You need to know how (or if) the caller's variable can be affected by the called method. The difference between object reference and primitive variables, when passed into methods, is huge and important. To understand this section, you'll need to be comfortable with the information covered in the "Literals, Assignments, and Variables" section in the early part of this chapter.

Passing Object Reference Variables

When you pass an object variable into a method, you must keep in mind that you're passing the object *reference*, and not the actual object itself. Remember that a reference variable holds bits that represent (to the underlying VM) a way to get to a specific object in memory (on the heap). More importantly, you must remember that you aren't even passing the actual reference variable, but rather a *copy* of the reference variable. A copy of a variable means you get a copy of the bits in that variable, so when you pass a reference variable, you're passing a copy of the bits representing how to get to a specific object. In other words, both the caller and the called method will now have identical copies of the reference; thus, both will refer to the same exact (*not* a copy) object on the heap.

For this example, we'll use the `Dimension` class from the java.awt package:

```
1. import java.awt.Dimension;
2. class ReferenceTest {
3.   public static void main (String [] args) {
4.     Dimension d = new Dimension(5,10);
5.     ReferenceTest rt = new ReferenceTest();
6.     System.out.println("Before modify() d.height = "
                              + d.height);
7.     rt.modify(d);
8.     System.out.println("After modify() d.height = "
                              + d.height);
9.   }
```

```
10.   void modify(Dimension dim) {
11.     dim.height = dim.height + 1;
12.     System.out.println("dim = " + dim.height);
13.   }
14. }
```

When we run this class, we can see that the `modify()` method was indeed able to modify the original (and only) `Dimension` object created on line 4.

```
C:\Java Projects\Reference>java ReferenceTest
Before modify() d.height = 10
dim = 11
After modify() d.height = 11
```

Notice when the `Dimension` object on line 4 is passed to the `modify()` method, any changes to the object that occur inside the method are being made to the object whose reference was passed. In the preceding example, reference variables `d` and `dim` both point to the same object.

Does Java Use Pass-By-Value Semantics?

If Java passes objects by passing the reference variable instead, does that mean Java uses pass-by-reference for objects? Not exactly, although you'll often hear and read that it does. Java is actually pass-by-value for all variables running within a single VM. Pass-by-value means pass-by-variable-value. And that means pass-by-copy-of-the-variable! (There's that word *copy* again!)

It makes no difference if you're passing primitive or reference variables; you are always passing a copy of the bits in the variable. So for a primitive variable, you're passing a copy of the bits representing the value. For example, if you pass an `int` variable with the value of `3`, you're passing a copy of the bits representing `3`. The called method then gets its own copy of the value to do with it what it likes.

And if you're passing an object reference variable, you're passing a copy of the bits representing the reference to an object. The called method then gets its own copy of the reference variable to do with it what it likes. But because two identical reference variables refer to the exact same object, if the called method modifies the object (by invoking setter methods, for example), the caller will see that the object the caller's original variable refers to has also been changed. In the next section, we'll look at how the picture changes when we're talking about primitives.

The bottom line on pass-by-value: The called method can't change the caller's variable, although for object reference variables, the called method can change the object the variable referred to. What's the difference between changing the variable and changing the object? For object references, it means the called method can't reassign the caller's original reference variable and make it refer to a different object or `null`. For example, in the following code fragment,

```
void bar() {
  Foo f = new Foo();
  doStuff(f);
}
void doStuff(Foo g) {
  g.setName("Boo");
  g = new Foo();
}
```

reassigning `g` does not reassign `f`! At the end of the `bar()` method, two `Foo` objects have been created: one referenced by the local variable `f` and one referenced by the local (argument) variable `g`. Because the `doStuff()` method has a copy of the reference variable, it has a way to get to the original `Foo` object, for instance to call the `setName()` method. But the `doStuff()` method does *not* have a way to get to the `f` reference variable. So `doStuff()` can change values within the object `f` refers to, but `doStuff()` can't change the actual contents (bit pattern) of `f`. In other words, `doStuff()` can change the state of the object that `f` refers to, but it can't make `f` refer to a different object!

Passing Primitive Variables

Let's look at what happens when a primitive variable is passed to a method:

```
class ReferenceTest {
  public static void main (String [] args) {
    int a = 1;
    ReferenceTest rt = new ReferenceTest();
    System.out.println("Before modify() a = " + a);
    rt.modify(a);
    System.out.println("After modify() a = " + a);
  }
  void modify(int number) {
    number = number + 1;
    System.out.println("number = " + number);
  }
}
```

In this simple program, the variable `a` is passed to a method called `modify()`, which increments the variable by 1. The resulting output looks like this:

```
Before modify() a = 1
number = 2
After modify() a = 1
```

Notice that a did not change after it was passed to the method. Remember, it was a copy of a that was passed to the method. When a primitive variable is passed to a method, it is passed by value, which means pass-by-copy-of-the-bits-in-the-variable.

FROM THE CLASSROOM

The Shadowy World of Variables

Just when you think you've got it all figured out, you see a piece of code with variables not behaving the way you think they should. You might have stumbled into code with a shadowed variable. You can shadow a variable in several ways. We'll look at one way that might trip you up: hiding a static variable by shadowing it with a local variable.

Shadowing involves reusing a variable name that's already been declared somewhere else. The effect of shadowing is to hide the previously declared variable in such a way that it may look as though you're using the hidden variable, but you're actually using the shadowing variable. You might find reasons to shadow a variable intentionally, but typically it happens by accident and causes hard-to-find bugs. On the exam, you can expect to see questions where shadowing plays a role.

You can shadow a variable by declaring a local variable of the same name, either directly or as part of an argument:

```
class Foo {
  static int size = 7;
  static void changeIt(int size) {
    size = size + 200;
    System.out.println("size in changeIt is " + size);
  }
  public static void main (String [] args) {
    Foo f = new Foo();
    System.out.println("size = " + size);
    changeIt(size);
    System.out.println("size after changeIt is " + size);
  }
}
```

The preceding code appears to change the static `size` variable in the `changeIt()` method, but because `changeIt()` has a parameter named `size`, the local `size` variable is modified while the static `size` variable is untouched.

FROM THE CLASSROOM

Running class `Foo` prints this:

```
%java Foo
size = 7
size in changeIt is 207
size after changeIt is 7
```

Things become more interesting when the shadowed variable is an object reference, rather than a primitive:

```
class Bar {
  int barNum = 28;
}

class Foo {
  Bar myBar = new Bar();
  void changeIt(Bar myBar) {
    myBar.barNum = 99;
    System.out.println("myBar.barNum in changeIt is " + myBar.barNum);
    myBar = new Bar();
    myBar.barNum = 420;
    System.out.println("myBar.barNum in changeIt is now " + myBar.barNum);
  }
  public static void main (String [] args) {
    Foo f = new Foo();
    System.out.println("f.myBar.barNum is " + f.myBar.barNum);
    f.changeIt(f.myBar);
    System.out.println("f.myBar.barNum after changeIt is "
                      + f.myBar.barNum);
  }
}
```

The preceding code prints out this:

```
f.myBar.barNum is 28
myBar.barNum in changeIt is 99
myBar.barNum in changeIt is now 420
f.myBar.barNum after changeIt is 99
```

You can see that the shadowing variable (the local parameter `myBar` in `changeIt()`) can still affect the `myBar` instance variable, because the `myBar` parameter receives a reference to the same `Bar` object. But when the local `myBar` is reassigned a new `Bar` object, which we then modify by changing its `barNum` value, `Foo`'s original `myBar` instance variable is untouched.

CERTIFICATION OBJECTIVE

Garbage Collection (OCA Objective 2.4)

2.4 Explain an object's lifecycle.

As of Spring 2014, the official exam objectives don't use the phrases "garbage collection" or "memory management." These two concepts are implied when the objective uses the phrase "object's lifecycle."

Overview of Memory Management and Garbage Collection

This is the section you've been waiting for! It's finally time to dig into the wonderful world of memory management and garbage collection.

Memory management is a crucial element in many types of applications. Consider a program that reads in large amounts of data, say from somewhere else on a network, and then writes that data into a database on a hard drive. A typical design would be to read the data into some sort of collection in memory, perform some operations on the data, and then write the data into the database. After the data is written into the database, the collection that stored the data temporarily must be emptied of old data or deleted and re-created before processing the next batch. This operation might be performed thousands of times, and in languages like C or C++ that do not offer automatic garbage collection, a small flaw in the logic that manually empties or deletes the collection data structures can allow small amounts of memory to be improperly reclaimed or lost. Forever. These small losses are called memory leaks, and over many thousands of iterations they can make enough memory inaccessible that programs will eventually crash. Creating code that performs manual memory management cleanly and thoroughly is a nontrivial and complex task, and while estimates vary, it is arguable that manual memory management can double the development effort for a complex program.

Java's garbage collector provides an automatic solution to memory management. In most cases it frees you from having to add any memory management logic to your application. The downside to automatic garbage collection is that you can't completely control when it runs and when it doesn't.

Overview of Java's Garbage Collector

Let's look at what we mean when we talk about garbage collection in the land of Java. From the 30,000 ft. level, garbage collection is the phrase used to describe automatic memory management in Java. Whenever a software program executes (in Java, C, C++, Lisp, Ruby, and so on), it uses memory in several different ways. We're not going to get into Computer Science 101 here, but it's typical for memory to be used to create a stack, a heap, in Java's case constant pools and method areas. **The heap is that part of memory where Java objects live, and it's the one and only part of memory that is in any way involved in the garbage collection process.**

A heap is a heap is a heap. For the exam, it's important that you know that you can call it the heap, you can call it the garbage collectible heap, or you can call it Johnson, but there is one and only one heap.

So, all of garbage collection revolves around making sure that the heap has as much free space as possible. For the purpose of the exam, what this boils down to is deleting any objects that are no longer reachable by the Java program running. We'll talk more about what "reachable" means in a minute, but let's drill this point in. When the garbage collector runs, its purpose is to find and delete objects that cannot be reached. If you think of a Java program as being in a constant cycle of creating the objects it needs (which occupy space on the heap), and then discarding them when they're no longer needed, creating new objects, discarding them, and so on, the missing piece of the puzzle is the garbage collector. When it runs, it looks for those discarded objects and deletes them from memory so that the cycle of using memory and releasing it can continue. Ah, the great circle of life.

When Does the Garbage Collector Run?

The garbage collector is under the control of the JVM; JVM decides when to run the garbage collector. From within your Java program you can ask the JVM to run the garbage collector, but there are no guarantees, under any circumstances, that the JVM will comply. Left to its own devices, the JVM will typically run the garbage collector when it senses that memory is running low. Experience indicates that when your Java program makes a request for garbage collection, the JVM will usually grant your request in short order, but there are no guarantees. Just when you think you can count on it, the JVM will decide to ignore your request.

How Does the Garbage Collector Work?

You just can't be sure. You might hear that the garbage collector uses a mark and sweep algorithm, and for any given Java implementation that might be true, but the Java specification doesn't guarantee any particular implementation. You might hear that the garbage collector uses reference counting; once again maybe yes, maybe no. The important concept for you to understand for the exam is, When does an object become eligible for garbage collection? To answer this question fully, we have to jump ahead a little bit and talk about threads. (See Chapter 13 for the real scoop on threads.)

In a nutshell, every Java program has from one to many threads. Each thread has its own little execution stack. Normally, you (the programmer) cause at least one thread to run in a Java program, the one with the `main()` method at the bottom of the stack. However, as you'll learn in excruciating detail in Chapter 13, there are many really cool reasons to launch additional threads from your initial thread. In addition to having its own little execution stack, each thread has its own lifecycle. For now, all you need to know is that threads can be alive or dead.

With this background information, we can now say with stunning clarity and resolve that *an object is eligible for garbage collection when no live thread can access it.* (Note: Due to the vagaries of the `String` constant pool, the exam focuses its garbage collection questions on non-`String` objects, and so our garbage collection discussions apply to only non-`String` objects too.)

Based on that definition, the garbage collector performs some magical, unknown operations, and when it discovers an object that can't be reached by any live thread, it will consider that object as eligible for deletion, and it might even delete it at some point. (You guessed it: it also might never delete it.) When we talk about reaching an object, we're really talking about having a reachable reference variable that refers to the object in question. If our Java program has a reference variable that refers to an object, and that reference variable is available to a live thread, then that object is considered reachable. We'll talk more about how objects can become unreachable in the following section.

Can a Java application run out of memory? Yes. The garbage collection system attempts to remove objects from memory when they are not used. However, if you maintain too many live objects (objects referenced from other live objects), the system can run out of memory. Garbage collection cannot ensure that there is enough memory, only that the memory that is available will be managed as efficiently as possible.

Writing Code That Explicitly Makes Objects Eligible for Collection

In the preceding section, you learned the theories behind Java garbage collection. In this section, we show how to make objects eligible for garbage collection using actual code. We also discuss how to attempt to force garbage collection if it is necessary, and how you can perform additional cleanup on objects before they are removed from memory.

Nulling a Reference

As we discussed earlier, an object becomes eligible for garbage collection when there are no more reachable references to it. Obviously, if there are no reachable references, it doesn't matter what happens to the object. For our purposes it is just floating in space, unused, inaccessible, and no longer needed.

The first way to remove a reference to an object is to set the reference variable that refers to the object to `null`. Examine the following code:

```
1. public class GarbageTruck {
2.   public static void main(String [] args) {
3.     StringBuffer sb = new StringBuffer("hello");
4.     System.out.println(sb);
5.     // The StringBuffer object is not eligible for collection
6.     sb = null;
7.     // Now the StringBuffer object is eligible for collection
8.   }
9. }
```

The `StringBuffer` object with the value `hello` is assigned to the reference variable `sb` in the third line. To make the object eligible (for garbage collection), we set the reference variable `sb` to `null`, which removes the single reference that existed to the `StringBuffer` object. Once line 6 has run, our happy little `hello` `StringBuffer` object is doomed, eligible for garbage collection.

Reassigning a Reference Variable

We can also decouple a reference variable from an object by setting the reference variable to refer to another object. Examine the following code:

```
class GarbageTruck {
  public static void main(String [] args) {
    StringBuffer s1 = new StringBuffer("hello");
    StringBuffer s2 = new StringBuffer("goodbye");
    System.out.println(s1);
    // At this point the StringBuffer "hello" is not eligible
    s1 = s2; // Redirects s1 to refer to the "goodbye" object
    // Now the StringBuffer "hello" is eligible for collection
  }
}
```

Objects that are created in a method also need to be considered. When a method is invoked, any local variables created exist only for the duration of the method. Once the method has returned, the objects created in the method are eligible for garbage collection. There is an obvious exception, however. If an object is returned from the method, its reference might be assigned to a reference variable in the method that called it; hence, it will not be eligible for collection. Examine the following code:

```
import java.util.Date;
public class GarbageFactory {
  public static void main(String [] args) {
    Date d = getDate();
    doComplicatedStuff();
    System.out.println("d = " + d);
  }

  public static Date getDate() {
    Date d2 = new Date();
    StringBuffer now = new StringBuffer(d2.toString());
    System.out.println(now);
    return d2;
  }
}
```

In the preceding example, we created a method called `getDate()` that returns a `Date` object. This method creates two objects: a `Date` and a `StringBuffer` containing the date information. Since the method returns a reference to the `Date` object and this reference is assigned to a local variable, it will not be eligible for collection even after the `getDate()` method has completed. The `StringBuffer` object, though, will be eligible, even though we didn't explicitly set the `now` variable to `null`.

Isolating a Reference

There is another way in which objects can become eligible for garbage collection, even if they still have valid references! We call this scenario "islands of isolation."

A simple example is a class that has an instance variable that is a reference variable to another instance of the same class. Now imagine that two such instances exist and that they refer to each other. If all other references to these two objects are removed, then even though each object still has a valid reference, there will be no way for any live thread to access either object. When the garbage collector runs, it can *usually* discover any such islands of objects and remove them. As you can imagine, such islands can become quite large, theoretically containing hundreds of objects. Examine the following code:

```
public class Island {
  Island i;
  public static void main(String [] args) {

    Island i2 = new Island();
    Island i3 = new Island();
    Island i4 = new Island();

    i2.i = i3;    // i2 refers to i3
    i3.i = i4;    // i3 refers to i4
    i4.i = i2;    // i4 refers to i2

    i2 = null;
    i3 = null;
    i4 = null;

    // do complicated, memory intensive stuff
  }
}
```

When the code reaches `// do complicated`, the three `Island` objects (previously known as `i2`, `i3`, and `i4`) have instance variables so that they refer to each other, but their links to the outside world (`i2`, `i3`, and `i4`) have been nulled. These three objects are eligible for garbage collection.

This covers everything you will need to know about making objects eligible for garbage collection. Study Figure 3-2 to reinforce the concepts of objects without references and islands of isolation.

Forcing Garbage Collection (OCP 5 Candidates Only)

The first thing that we should mention here is that, contrary to this section's title, garbage collection cannot be forced. However, Java provides some methods that allow you to request that the JVM perform garbage collection.

Note: As of the Java 6 exam, the topic of using `System.gc()` has been removed from the exam. The garbage collector has evolved to such an advanced state that it's recommended that you never invoke `System.gc()` in your code—leave it to the JVM. We are leaving this section in the book in case you're studying for the OCP 5 exam.

In reality, it is possible only to suggest to the JVM that it perform garbage collection. However, there are no guarantees the JVM will actually remove all of the

FIGURE 3-2 Island objects eligible for garbage collection

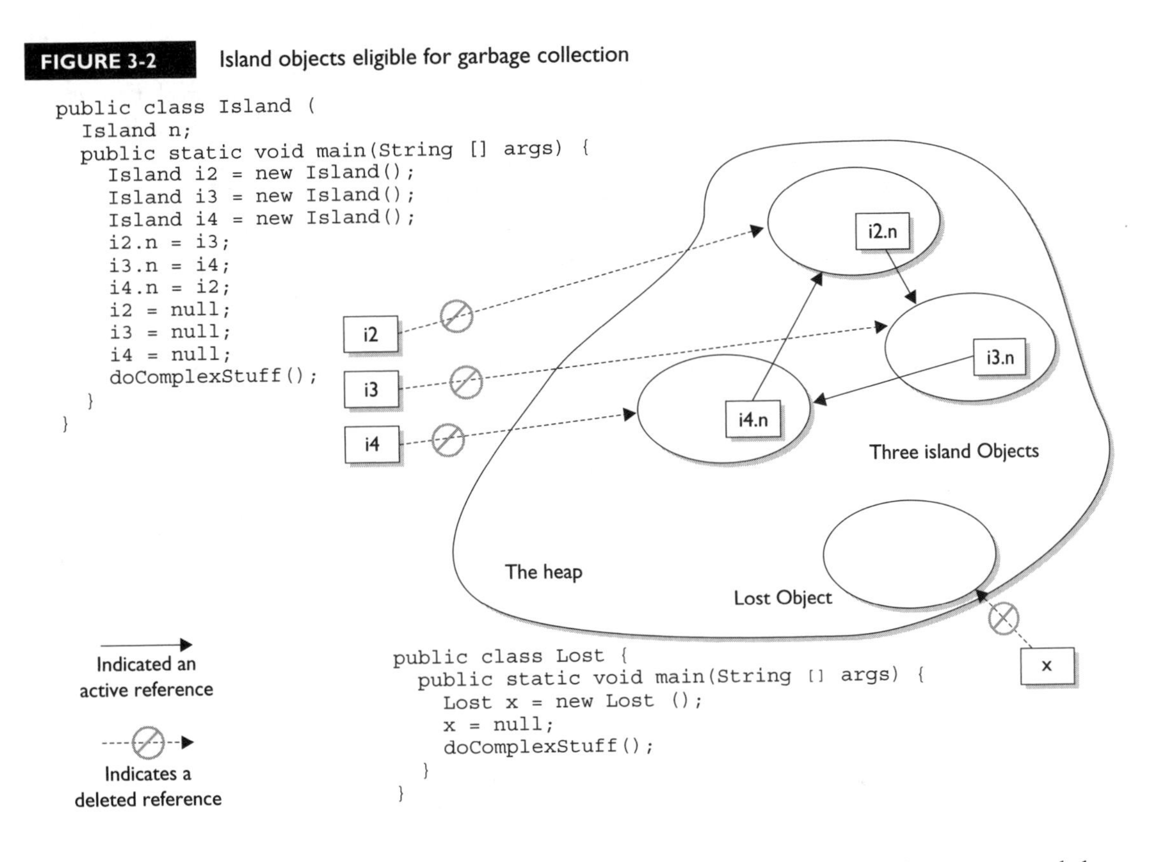
public class Island (
Island n;
public static void main(String [] args) {
Island i2 = new Island();
Island i3 = new Island();
Island i4 = new Island();
i2.n = i3;
i3.n = i4;
i4.n = i2;
i2 = null;
i3 = null;
i4 = null;
doComplexStuff();
}
}
i2
i3
i4
i2.n
i3.n
i4.n
Three island Objects
The heap
Lost Object
x
Indicated an active reference
Indicates a deleted reference
public class Lost {
public static void main(String [] args) {
Lost x = new Lost ();
x = null;
doComplexStuff();
}
}

unused objects from memory (even if garbage collection is run). It is essential that you understand this concept for the exam.

The garbage collection routines that Java provides are members of the `Runtime` class. The `Runtime` class is a special class that has a single object (a `Singleton`) for each main program. The `Runtime` object provides a mechanism for communicating directly with the virtual machine. To get the `Runtime` instance, you can use the method `Runtime.getRuntime()`, which returns the `Singleton`. Once you have the `Singleton`, you can invoke the garbage collector using the `gc()` method. Alternatively, you can call the same method on the `System` class, which has static methods that can do the work of obtaining the `Singleton` for you. The simplest way to ask for garbage collection (remember—just a request) is

```
System.gc();
```

Theoretically, after calling `System.gc()`, you will have as much free memory as possible. We say "theoretically" because this routine does not always work that way. First, your JVM may not have implemented this routine; the language specification allows this routine to do nothing at all. Second, another thread (see Chapter 13) might grab lots of memory right after you run the garbage collector.

This is not to say that `System.gc()` is a useless method—it's much better than nothing. You just can't rely on `System.gc()` to free up enough memory so that you don't have to worry about running out of memory. The Certification Exam is interested in guaranteed behavior, not probable behavior.

Now that you are somewhat familiar with how this works, let's do a little experiment to see the effects of garbage collection. The following program lets us know how much total memory the JVM has available to it and how much free memory it has. It then creates 10,000 `Date` objects. After this, it tells us how much memory is left and then calls the garbage collector (which, if it decides to run, should halt the program until all unused objects are removed). The final free memory result should indicate whether it has run. Let's look at the program:

```
 1. import java.util.Date;
 2. public class CheckGC {
 3.   public static void main(String [] args) {
 4.     Runtime rt = Runtime.getRuntime();
 5.     System.out.println("Total JVM memory: "
                          + rt.totalMemory());
 6.     System.out.println("Before Memory = "
                          + rt.freeMemory());
 7.     Date d = null;
 8.     for(int i = 0;i<10000;i++) {
 9.       d = new Date();
10.       d = null;
11.     }
12.     System.out.println("After Memory = "
                          + rt.freeMemory());
13.     rt.gc();   // an alternate to System.gc()
14.     System.out.println("After GC Memory = "
                          + rt.freeMemory());
15.   }
16. }
```

Now, let's run the program and check the results:

```
Total JVM memory: 1048568
Before Memory = 703008
After Memory = 458048
After GC Memory = 818272
```

As you can see, the JVM actually did decide to garbage collect (that is, delete) the eligible objects. In the preceding example, we suggested that the JVM to perform garbage collection with 458,048 bytes of memory remaining, and it honored our request. This program has only one user thread running, so there was nothing else going on when we called `rt.gc()`. Keep in mind that the behavior when `gc()` is called may be different for different JVMs, so there is no guarantee that the unused objects will be removed from memory. About the only thing you can guarantee is that if you are running very low on memory, the garbage collector will run before it throws an `OutOfMemoryException`.

EXERCISE 3-2

Garbage Collection Experiment

Try changing the CheckGC program by putting lines 13 and 14 inside a loop. You might see that not all memory is released on any given run of the GC.

Cleaning Up Before Garbage Collection—the finalize() Method

Java provides a mechanism that lets you run some code just before your object is deleted by the garbage collector. This code is located in a method named `finalize()` that all classes inherit from class `Object`. On the surface, this sounds like a great idea; maybe your object opened up some resources, and you'd like to close them before your object is deleted. The problem is that, as you may have gathered by now, you can never count on the garbage collector to delete an object. So, any code that you put into your class's overridden `finalize()` method is not guaranteed to run. Because the `finalize()` method for any given object might run, but you can't count on it, don't put any essential code into your `finalize()` method. In fact, we recommend that in general you don't override `finalize()` at all.

Tricky Little finalize() Gotchas

There are a couple of concepts concerning `finalize()` that you need to remember:

- For any given object, `finalize()` will be called only once (at most) by the garbage collector.
- Calling `finalize()` can actually result in saving an object from deletion.

Let's look into these statements a little further. First of all, remember that any code you can put into a normal method you can put into `finalize()`. For example, in the `finalize()` method you could write code that passes a reference to the object in question back to another object, effectively *ineligible-izing* the object for garbage collection. If at some point later on this same object becomes eligible for garbage collection again, the garbage collector can still process the object and delete it. The garbage collector, however, will remember that, for this object, `finalize()` already ran, and it will not run `finalize()` again.

CERTIFICATION SUMMARY

This chapter covered a wide range of topics. Don't worry if you have to review some of these topics as you get into later chapters. This chapter includes a lot of foundational stuff that will come into play later.

We started the chapter by reviewing the stack and the heap; remember that local variables live on the stack and instance variables live with their objects on the heap.

We reviewed legal literals for primitives and `Strings`, and then we discussed the basics of assigning values to primitives and reference variables, and the rules for casting primitives.

Next we discussed the concept of scope, or "How long will this variable live?" Remember the four basic scopes, in order of lessening life span: static, instance, local, and block.

We covered the implications of using uninitialized variables, and the importance of the fact that local variables MUST be assigned a value explicitly. We talked about some of the tricky aspects of assigning one reference variable to another and some of the finer points of passing variables into methods, including a discussion of "shadowing."

Finally, we dove into garbage collection, Java's automatic memory management feature. We learned that the heap is where objects live and where all the cool garbage collection activity takes place. We learned that in the end, the JVM will perform garbage collection whenever it wants to. You (the programmer) can request a garbage collection run, but you can't force it. We talked about garbage collection only applying to objects that are eligible, and that eligible means "inaccessible from any live thread." Finally, we discussed the rarely useful `finalize()` method and what you'll have to know about it for the exam. All in all, this was one fascinating chapter.

✓ TWO-MINUTE DRILL

Here are some of the key points from this chapter.

Stack and Heap

- ❑ Local variables (method variables) live on the stack.
- ❑ Objects and their instance variables live on the heap.

Literals and Primitive Casting (OCA Objective 2.1)

- ❑ Integer literals can be binary, decimal, octal (such as `013`), or hexadecimal (such as `0x3d`).
- ❑ Literals for `long`s end in `L` or `l`.
- ❑ Float literals end in `F` or `f`, and `double` literals end in a digit or `D` or `d`.
- ❑ The `boolean` literals are `true` and `false`.
- ❑ Literals for `char`s are a single character inside single quotes: `'d'`.

Scope (OCA Objective 1.1)

- ❑ Scope refers to the lifetime of a variable.
- ❑ There are four basic scopes:
  - ❑ Static variables live basically as long as their class lives.
  - ❑ Instance variables live as long as their object lives.
  - ❑ Local variables live as long as their method is on the stack; however, if their method invokes another method, they are temporarily unavailable.
  - ❑ Block variables (for example, in a `for` or an `if`) live until the block completes.

Basic Assignments (OCA Objectives 2.1, 2.2, and 2.3)

- ❑ Literal integers are implicitly `ints`.
- ❑ Integer expressions always result in an `int`-sized result, never smaller.
- ❑ Floating-point numbers are implicitly doubles (64 bits).
- ❑ Narrowing a primitive truncates the *high order* bits.
- ❑ Compound assignments (such as +=) perform an automatic cast.
- ❑ A reference variable holds the bits that are used to refer to an object.
- ❑ Reference variables can refer to subclasses of the declared type but not to superclasses.
- ❑ When you create a new object, such as `Button b = new Button();`, the JVM does three things:
  - ❑ Makes a reference variable named `b`, of type `Button`.
  - ❑ Creates a new `Button` object.
  - ❑ Assigns the `Button` object to the reference variable `b`.

Using a Variable or Array Element That Is Uninitialized and Unassigned (OCA Objectives 4.1 and 4.2)

- ❑ When an array of objects is instantiated, objects within the array are not instantiated automatically, but all the references get the default value of `null`.
- ❑ When an array of primitives is instantiated, elements get default values.
- ❑ Instance variables are always initialized with a default value.
- ❑ Local/automatic/method variables are never given a default value. If you attempt to use one before initializing it, you'll get a compiler error.

Passing Variables into Methods (OCA Objective 6.8)

- ❑ Methods can take primitives and/or object references as arguments.
- ❑ Method arguments are always copies.
- ❑ Method arguments are never actual objects (they can be references to objects).
- ❑ A primitive argument is an unattached copy of the original primitive.
- ❑ A reference argument is another copy of a reference to the original object.
- ❑ Shadowing occurs when two variables with different scopes share the same name. This leads to hard-to-find bugs and hard-to-answer exam questions.

Garbage Collection (OCA Objective 2.4)

- ❑ In Java, garbage collection (GC) provides automated memory management.
- ❑ The purpose of GC is to delete objects that can't be reached.
- ❑ Only the JVM decides when to run the GC; you can only suggest it.
- ❑ You can't know the GC algorithm for sure.
- ❑ Objects must be considered eligible before they can be garbage collected.
- ❑ An object is eligible when no live thread can reach it.
- ❑ To reach an object, you must have a live, reachable reference to that object.
- ❑ Java applications can run out of memory.
- ❑ Islands of objects can be garbage collected, even though they refer to each other.
- ❑ Request garbage collection with `System.gc();` (for OCP 5 candidates only).
- ❑ The `Class` object has a `finalize()` method.
- ❑ The `finalize()` method is guaranteed to run once and only once before the garbage collector deletes an object.
- ❑ The garbage collector makes no guarantees; `finalize()` may never run.
- ❑ You can ineligible-ize an object for GC from within `finalize()`.

SELF TEST

1. Given:

```
class CardBoard {
  Short story = 200;
  CardBoard go(CardBoard cb) {
    cb = null;
    return cb;
  }
  public static void main(String[] args) {
    CardBoard c1 = new CardBoard();
    CardBoard c2 = new CardBoard();
    CardBoard c3 = c1.go(c2);
    c1 = null;
    // do Stuff
} }
```

When `// do Stuff` is reached, how many objects are eligible for garbage collection?

A. 0

B. 1

C. 2

D. Compilation fails

E. It is not possible to know

F. An exception is thrown at runtime

2. Given:

```
public class Fishing {
  byte b1 = 4;
  int i1 = 123456;
  long L1 = (long)i1;        // line A
  short s2 = (short)i1;      // line B
  byte b2 = (byte)i1;        // line C
  int i2 = (int)123.456;     // line D
  byte b3 = b1 + 7;          // line E
}
```

Which lines WILL NOT compile? (Choose all that apply.)

A. Line A

B. Line B

C. Line C

D. Line D

E. Line E

3. Given:

```
public class Literally {
  public static void main(String[] args) {
    int i1 = 1_000;       // line A
    int i2 = 10_00;       // line B
    int i3 = _10_000;     // line C
    int i4 = 0b101010;    // line D
    int i5 = 0B10_1010;   // line E
    int i6 = 0x2_a;       // line F
  }
}
```

Which lines WILL NOT compile? (Choose all that apply.)

A. Line A

B. Line B

C. Line C

D. Line D

E. Line E

F. Line F

4. Given:

```
class Mixer {
  Mixer() { }
  Mixer(Mixer m) { m1 = m; }
  Mixer m1;
  public static void main(String[] args) {
    Mixer m2 = new Mixer();
    Mixer m3 = new Mixer(m2);  m3.go();
    Mixer m4 = m3.m1;          m4.go();
    Mixer m5 = m2.m1;          m5.go();
  }
  void go() { System.out.print("hi "); }
}
```

What is the result?

A. `hi`

B. `hi hi`

C. `hi hi hi`

D. Compilation fails

E. hi, followed by an exception

F. `hi hi`, followed by an exception

5. Given:

```
class Fizz {
  int x = 5;
  public static void main(String[] args) {
    final Fizz f1 = new Fizz();
    Fizz f2 = new Fizz();
    Fizz f3 = FizzSwitch(f1,f2);
    System.out.println((f1 == f3) + " " + (f1.x == f3.x));
  }
  static Fizz FizzSwitch(Fizz x, Fizz y) {
    final Fizz z = x;
    z.x = 6;
    return z;
} }
```

What is the result?

A. `true true`

B. `false true`

C. `true false`

D. `false false`

E. Compilation fails

F. An exception is thrown at runtime

6. Given:

```
public class Mirror {
  int size = 7;
  public static void main(String[] args) {
    Mirror m1 = new Mirror();
    Mirror m2 = m1;
    int i1 = 10;
    int i2 = i1;
    go(m2, i2);
    System.out.println(m1.size + " " + i1);
  }
  static void go(Mirror m, int i) {
    m.size = 8;
    i = 12;
  }
}
```

What is the result?

A. `7 10`

B. `8 10`

C. `7 12`

D. `8 12`

E. Compilation fails

F. An exception is thrown at runtime

7. Given:

```
public class Wind {
  int id;
  Wind(int i) { id = i; }
  public static void main(String[] args) {
    new Wind(3).go();
    // commented line
  }
  void go() {
    Wind w1 = new Wind(1);
    Wind w2 = new Wind(2);
    System.out.println(w1.id + " " + w2.id);
  }
}
```

When execution reaches the commented line, which are true? (Choose all that apply.)

A. The output contains `1`

B. The output contains `2`

C. The output contains `3`

D. Zero objects are eligible for garbage collection

E. One object is eligible for garbage collection

F. Two objects are eligible for garbage collection

G. Three objects are eligible for garbage collection

8. Given:

```
 3. public class Ouch {
 4.   static int ouch = 7;
 5.   public static void main(String[] args) {
 6.     new Ouch().go(ouch);
 7.     System.out.print(" " + ouch);
 8.   }
 9.   void go(int ouch) {
10.     ouch++;
11.     for(int ouch = 3; ouch < 6; ouch++)
12.       ;
13.     System.out.print(" " + ouch);
14.   }
15. }
```

What is the result?

A. `5 7`

B. `5 8`

C. `8 7`

D. `8 8`

E. Compilation fails

F. An exception is thrown at runtime

9. Given:

```
public class Happy {
  int id;
  Happy(int i) { id = i; }
  public static void main(String[] args) {
    Happy h1 = new Happy(1);
    Happy h2 = h1.go(h1);
    System.out.println(h2.id);
  }
  Happy go(Happy h) {
    Happy h3 = h;
    h3.id = 2;
    h1.id = 3;
    return h1;
  }
}
```

What is the result?

A. `1`

B. `2`

C. `3`

D. Compilation fails

E. An exception is thrown at runtime

10. Given:

```
public class Network {
  Network(int x, Network n) {
    id = x;
    p = this;
    if(n != null) p = n;
  }
  int id;
  Network p;
  public static void main(String[] args) {
    Network n1 = new Network(1, null);
    n1.go(n1);
  }
  void go(Network n1) {
    Network n2 = new Network(2, n1);
    Network n3 = new Network(3, n2);
    System.out.println(n3.p.p.id);
  }
}
```

What is the result?

A. `1`

B. `2`

C. `3`

D. `null`

E. Compilation fails

11. Given:

```
 3. class Beta { }
 4. class Alpha {
 5.   static Beta b1;
 6.   Beta b2;
 7. }
 8. public class Tester {
 9.   public static void main(String[] args) {
10.     Beta b1 = new Beta();      Beta b2 = new Beta();
11.     Alpha a1 = new Alpha();    Alpha a2 = new Alpha();
12.     a1.b1 = b1;
13.     a1.b2 = b1;
14.     a2.b2 = b2;
15.     a1 = null;  b1 = null;  b2 = null;
16.     // do stuff
17.   }
18. }
```

When line 16 is reached, how many objects will be eligible for garbage collection?

A. 0

B. 1

C. 2

D. 3

E. 4

F. 5

12. Given:

```
public class Telescope {
  static int magnify = 2;
  public static void main(String[] args) {
    go();
  }
  static void go() {
    int magnify = 3;
    zoomIn();
  }
  static void zoomIn() {
    magnify *= 5;
    zoomMore(magnify);
    System.out.println(magnify);
  }
  static void zoomMore(int magnify) {
    magnify *= 7;
  }
}
```

What is the result?

A. `2`

B. `10`

C. `15`

D. `30`

E. `70`

F. `105`

G. Compilation fails

13. Given:

```
 3. public class Dark {
 4.   int x = 3;
 5.   public static void main(String[] args) {
 6.     new Dark().go1();
 7.   }
 8.   void go1() {
 9.     int x;
10.     go2(++x);
11.   }
12.   void go2(int y) {
13.     int x = ++y;
14.     System.out.println(x);
15.   }
16. }
```

What is the result?

A. 2

B. 3

C. 4

D. 5

E. Compilation fails

F. An exception is thrown at runtime

SELF TEST ANSWERS

1. ☑ **C** is correct. Only one `CardBoard` object `(c1)` is eligible, but it has an associated `Short` wrapper object that is also eligible.
☒ **A, B, D, E,** and **F** are incorrect based on the above. (OCA Objective 2.4)

2. ☑ **E** is correct; compilation of line E fails. When a mathematical operation is performed on any primitives smaller than `ints`, the result is automatically cast to an integer.
☒ **A, B, C,** and **D** are all legal primitive casts. (OCA Objective 2.1)

3. ☑ **C** is correct; line **C** will NOT compile. As of Java 7, underscores can be included in numeric literals, but not at the beginning or the end.
☒ **A, B, D, E,** and **G** are incorrect. **A** and **B** are legal numeric literals. **D** and **E** are examples of valid binary literals, which are also new to Java 7, and **G** is a valid hexadecimal literal that uses an underscore. (OCA Objective 2.1 and Upgrade Objective 1.2)

4. ☑ **F** is correct. The `m2` object's `m1` instance variable is never initialized, so when `m5` tries to use it a `NullPointerException` is thrown.
☒ **A, B, C, D,** and **E** are incorrect based on the above. (OCA Objectives 2.1, 2.3, and 2.5)

5. ☑ **A** is correct. The references `f1`, `z`, and `f3` all refer to the same instance of `Fizz`. The `final` modifier assures that a reference variable cannot be referred to a different object, but `final` doesn't keep the object's state from changing.
☒ **B, C, D, E,** and **F** are incorrect based on the above. (OCA Objective 2.2)

6. ☑ **B** is correct. In the `go()` method, `m` refers to the single `Mirror` instance, but the `int i` is a new `int` variable, a detached copy of `i2`.
☒ **A, C, D, E,** and **F** are incorrect based on the above. (OCA Objectives 2.2 and 2.3)

7. ☑ **A, B,** and **G** are correct. The constructor sets the value of `id` for `w1` and `w2`. When the commented line is reached, none of the three `Wind` objects can be accessed, so they are eligible to be garbage collected.
☒ **C, D, E,** and **F** are incorrect based on the above. (OCA Objectives 1.1, 2.3, and 2.4)

8. ☑ **E** is correct. The parameter declared on line 9 is valid (although ugly), but the variable name `ouch` cannot be declared again on line 11 in the same scope as the declaration on line 9.
☒ **A, B, C, D,** and **F** are incorrect based on the above. (OCA Objectives 1.1, 2.1, and 2.5)

9. ☑ **D** is correct. Inside the `go()` method, `h1` is out of scope.
☒ **A, B, C,** and **E** are incorrect based on the above. (OCA Objectives 1.1 and 6.1)

10. ☑ **A** is correct. Three `Network` objects are created. The `n2` object has a reference to the `n1` object, and the `n3` object has a reference to the `n2` object. The S.O.P. can be read as, "Use the `n3` object's `Network` reference (the first `p`), to find that object's reference (`n2`), and use that object's reference (the second `p`) to find that object's (`n1`'s) `id`, and print that `id`."
☒ **B, C, D,** and **E** are incorrect based on the above. (OCA Objectives, 2.2, 2.3, and 6.4)

11. ☑ **B** is correct. It should be clear that there is still a reference to the object referred to by `a2`, and that there is still a reference to the object referred to by `a2.b2`. What might be less clear is that you can still access the other `Beta` object through the static variable `a2.b1`—because it's static.

☒ **A, C, D, E,** and **F** are incorrect based on the above. (OCA Objective 2.4)

12. ☑ **B** is correct. In the `Telescope` class, there are three different variables named `magnify`. The `go()` method's version and the `zoomMore()` method's version are not used in the `zoomIn()` method. The `zoomIn()` method multiplies the class variable `* 5`. The result (`10`) is sent to `zoomMore()`, but what happens in `zoomMore()` stays in `zoomMore()`. The S.O.P. prints the value of `zoomIn()`'s `magnify`.

☒ **A, C, D, E, F,** and **G** are incorrect based on the above. (OCA Objectives 1.1 and 6.8)

13. ☑ **E** is correct. In `go1()` the local variable `x` is not initialized.

☒ **A, B, C, D,** and **F** are incorrect based on the above. (OCA Objectives 2.1, 2.3, and 2.5)

4 Operators

CERTIFICATION OBJECTIVES

- Using Java Operators
- Use Parentheses to Override Operator Precedence
- Test Equality Between Strings and Other Objects Using == and equals( )

 Two-Minute Drill

 Self Test

If you've got variables, you're going to modify them. You'll increment them, add them together, and compare one to another (in about a dozen different ways). In this chapter, you'll learn how to do all that in Java. For an added bonus, you'll learn how to do things that you'll probably never use in the real world, but that will almost certainly be on the exam.

CERTIFICATION OBJECTIVE

Java Operators (OCA Objectives 3.1, 3.2, and 3.3)

3.1 *Use Java operators.*

3.2 *Use parentheses to override operator precedence.*

3.3 *Test equality between strings and other objects using == and equals().*

Java operators produce new values from one or more operands. (Just so we're all clear, remember that operands are the things on the right or left side of the operator.) The result of most operations is either a `boolean` or numeric value. Because you know by now that Java is not C++, you won't be surprised that Java operators aren't typically overloaded. There are, however, a few exceptional operators that come overloaded:

- The `+` operator can be used to add two numeric primitives together or to perform a concatenation operation if either operand is a `String`.
- The `&`, `|`, and `^` operators can all be used in two different ways, although on this version of the exam, their bit-twiddling capabilities won't be tested.

Stay awake. Operators are often the section of the exam where candidates see their lowest scores. Additionally, operators and assignments are a part of many questions dealing with other topics—it would be a shame to nail a really tricky threads question, only to blow it on a pre-increment statement.

Assignment Operators

We covered most of the functionality of the equal (`=`) assignment operator in Chapter 3. To summarize:

- When assigning a value to a primitive, *size* matters. Be sure you know when implicit casting will occur, when explicit casting is necessary, and when truncation might occur.
- Remember that a reference variable isn't an object; it's a way to *get* to an object. (We know all you C++ programmers are just dying for us to say, "it's a pointer," but we're not going to.)
- When assigning a value to a reference variable, *type* matters. Remember the rules for supertypes, subtypes, and arrays.

Next we'll cover a few more details about the assignment operators that are on the exam, and when we get to the next chapter, we'll take a look at how the assignment operator = works with `Strings` (which are immutable).

exam watch

Don't spend time preparing for topics that are no longer on the exam! The following topics have NOT been on the exam since Java 1.4:

bit-shifting operators
bitwise operators
two's complement
divide-by-zero stuff

It's not that these aren't important topics; it's just that they're not on the exam anymore, and we're really focused on the exam. (Note: The reason we bring this up at all is because you might encounter mock exam questions on these topics—you can ignore those questions!)

Compound Assignment Operators

There are actually 11 or so compound assignment operators, but only the 4 most commonly used (`+=`, `-=`, `*=`, and `/=`) are on the exam. The compound assignment operators let lazy typists shave a few keystrokes off their workload.

Here are several example assignments, first without using a compound operator:

```
y = y - 6;
x = x + 2 * 5;
```

Now, with compound operators:

```
y -= 6;
x += 2 * 5;
```

The last two assignments give the same result as the first two.

exam watch

Earlier versions of the exam put big emphasis on operator precedence (such as, What's the result of `x = y++ + ++x/z;`). Other than having a very basic knowledge of precedence (such as `*` and `/` are higher precedence than `+` and `-`), you won't need to study operator precedence. But you do need to know that when using a compound operator, the expression on the right side of the `=` will always be evaluated first. For example, you might expect

```
x *= 2 + 5;
```

to be evaluated like this,

```
x = (x * 2) + 5;    // incorrect precedence
```

because multiplication has higher precedence than addition. Instead, however, the expression on the right is always placed inside parentheses. It is evaluated like this:

```
x = x * (2 + 5);
```

Relational Operators

The exam covers six relational operators (`<`, `<=`, `>`, `>=`, `==`, and `!=`). Relational operators always result in a `boolean` (`true` or `false`) value. This `boolean` value is most often used in an `if` test, as follows:

```
int x = 8;
if (x < 9) {
  // do something
}
```

But the resulting value can also be assigned directly to a `boolean` primitive:

```
class CompareTest {
  public static void main(String [] args) {
    boolean b = 100 > 99;
    System.out.println("The value of b is " + b);
  }
}
```

Java has four relational operators that can be used to compare any combination of integers, floating-point numbers, or characters:

- `>` Greater than
- `>=` Greater than or equal to
- `<` Less than
- `<=` Less than or equal to

Let's look at some legal comparisons:

```
class GuessAnimal {
  public static void main(String[] args) {
    String animal = "unknown";
    int weight = 700;
    char sex = 'm';
    double colorWaveLength = 1.630;
    if (weight >= 500) { animal = "elephant"; }
    if (colorWaveLength > 1.621) { animal = "gray " + animal; }
    if (sex <= 'f') { animal = "female " + animal; }
    System.out.println("The animal is a " + animal);
  }
}
```

In the preceding code, we are using a comparison between characters. It's also legal to compare a character primitive with any number (though it isn't great programming style). Running the preceding class will output the following:

```
The animal is a gray elephant
```

We mentioned that characters can be used in comparison operators. When comparing a character with a character or a character with a number, Java will use the Unicode value of the character as the numerical value, for comparison.

"Equality" Operators

Java also has two relational operators (sometimes called "equality operators") that compare two similar "things" and return a `boolean` (`true` or `false`) that represents what's true about the two "things" being equal. These operators are

- `==` Equal (also known as equal to)
- `!=` Not equal (also known as not equal to)

Each individual comparison can involve two numbers (including `char`), two `boolean` values, or two object reference variables. You can't compare incompatible types, however. What would it mean to ask if a `boolean` is equal to a `char`? Or if a `Button` is equal to a `String` array? (This is nonsense, which is why you can't do it.) There are four different types of things that can be tested:

- Numbers
- Characters
- Boolean primitives
- Object reference variables

So what does == look at? The value in the variable—in other words, the bit pattern.

Equality for Primitives

Most programmers are familiar with comparing primitive values. The following code shows some equality tests on primitive variables:

```
class ComparePrimitives {
  public static void main(String[] args) {
    System.out.println("char 'a' == 'a'? " + ('a' == 'a'));
    System.out.println("char 'a' == 'b'? " + ('a' == 'b'));
    System.out.println("5 != 6? " + (5 != 6));
    System.out.println("5.0 == 5L? " + (5.0 == 5L));
    System.out.println("true == false? " + (true == false));
  }
}
```

This program produces the following output:

```
char 'a' == 'a'? true
char 'a' == 'b'? false
5 != 6? true
5.0 == 5L? true
true == false? false
```

As you can see, if a floating-point number is compared with an integer and the values are the same, the == operator usually returns `true` as expected.

Equality for Reference Variables

As you saw earlier, two reference variables can refer to the same object, as the following code snippet demonstrates:

```
JButton a = new JButton("Exit");
JButton b = a;
```

exam watch

Don't mistake = for == in a `boolean` expression. The following is legal:

```
11. boolean b = false;
12. if (b = true) { System.out.println("b is true");
13. } else { System.out.println("b is false"); }
```

Look carefully! You might be tempted to think the output is `b is false`, but look at the `boolean` test in line 12. The `boolean` variable `b` is not being compared to `true`; it's being set to `true`. Once `b` is set to `true`, the `println` executes and we get `b is true`. The result of any assignment expression is the value of the variable following the assignment. This substitution of = for == works only with `boolean` variables, since the `if` test can be done only on `boolean` expressions. Thus, this does not compile:

```
7. int x = 1;
8. if (x = 0) { }
```

Because `x` is an integer (and not a `boolean`), the result of `(x = 0)` is 0 (the result of the assignment). Primitive `int`s cannot be used where a `boolean` value is expected, so the code in line 8 won't work unless it's changed from an assignment (=) to an equality test (==) as follows:

```
8. if (x == 0) { }
```

After running this code, both variable `a` and variable `b` will refer to the same object (a `JButton` with the label `Exit`). Reference variables can be tested to see if they refer to the same object by using the `==` operator. Remember, the `==` operator is looking at the bits in the variable, so for reference variables, this means that if the bits in both reference variables are identical, then both refer to the same object. Look at the following code:

```
import javax.swing.JButton;
class CompareReference {
  public static void main(String[] args) {
    JButton a = new JButton("Exit");
    JButton b = new JButton("Exit");
    JButton c = a;
    System.out.println("Is reference a == b? " + (a == b));
    System.out.println("Is reference a == c? " + (a == c));
  }
}
```

This code creates three reference variables. The first two, `a` and `b`, are separate `JButton` objects that happen to have the same label. The third reference variable, `c`, is initialized to refer to the same object that `a` refers to. When this program runs, the following output is produced:

```
Is reference a == b? false
Is reference a == c? true
```

This shows us that `a` and `c` reference the same instance of a `JButton`. The `==` operator will not test whether two objects are "meaningfully equivalent," a concept we'll cover in much more detail in Chapter 11, when we look at the `equals()` *method* (as opposed to the equals *operator* we're looking at here).

Equality for Strings and java.lang.Object.equals()

We just used `==` to determine whether two reference variables refer to the same object. Because objects are so central to Java, every class in Java inherits a method from class `Object` that tests to see if two objects of the class are "equal." Not surprisingly, this method is called `equals()`. In this case of the `equals()` method, the phrase "meaningfully equivalent" should be used instead of the word "equal.". So the `equals()` method is used to determine if two objects of the same class are "meaningfully equivalent." For classes that you create, you have the option of overriding the `equals()` method that your class inherited from class `Object`, and creating your own definition of "meaningfully equivalent" for instances of your class. (There's lots more about overriding `equals()` in Chapter 11.)

In terms of understanding the `equals()` method for the OCA exam, you need to understand two aspects of the `equals()` method:

- What `equals()` means in class `Object`
- What `equals()` means in class `String`

The equals() Method in Class Object The `equals()` method in class `Object` works the same way that the `==` operator works. If two references point to the same object, the `equals()` method will return true. If two references point to different objects, even if they have the same values, the method will return false.

The equals() Method in Class String The `equals()` method in class `String` has been overridden. When the `equals()` method is used to compare two strings, it will return true if the strings have the same value, and it will return false if the strings have different values. For `String`'s `equals()` method, values ARE case sensitive.

Let's take a look at how the `equals()` method works in action (notice that the `Budgie` class did NOT override `Object.equals()`):

```
class Budgie {
  public static void main(String[] args) {
    Budgie b1 = new Budgie();
    Budgie b2 = new Budgie();
    Budgie b3 = b1;

    String s1 = "Bob";
    String s2 = "Bob";
    String s3 = "bob";                    // lower case "b"

    System.out.println(b1.equals(b2));    // false, different objects
    System.out.println(b1.equals(b3));    // true, same objects
    System.out.println(s1.equals(s2));    // true, same values
    System.out.println(s1.equals(s3));    // false, values are case sensitive
  }
}
```

which produces the output:

```
false
true
true
false
```

As we mentioned earlier, when we get to Chapter 11, we'll take a deep dive into overriding `equals()`—and its companion `hashCode()`—but for the OCA, this is all you need to know.

Equality for enums (OCP Only)

Once you've declared an `enum`, it's not expandable. At runtime, there's no way to make additional `enum` constants. Of course, you can have as many variables as you'd like, refer to a given `enum` constant, so it's important to be able to compare two `enum` reference variables to see if they're "equal"—that is, do they refer to the same `enum` constant. You can use either the `==` operator or the `equals()` method to determine whether two variables are referring to the same `enum` constant:

```
class EnumEqual {
  enum Color {RED, BLUE}                  // ; is optional
  public static void main(String[] args) {
    Color c1 = Color.RED;  Color c2 = Color.RED;
    if(c1 == c2) { System.out.println("=="); }
    if(c1.equals(c2)) { System.out.println("dot equals"); }
} }
```

(We know } } is ugly; we're prepping you.) This produces the output:

```
==
dot equals
```

instanceof Comparison

The `instanceof` operator is used for object reference variables only, and you can use it to check whether an object is of a particular type. By "type," we mean class or interface type—in other words, whether the object referred to by the variable on the left side of the operator passes the IS-A test for the class or interface type on the right side. (Chapter 2 covered IS-A relationships in detail.) The following simple example,

```
public static void main(String[] args) {
  String s = new String("foo");
  if (s instanceof String) {
    System.out.print("s is a String");
  }
}
```

prints this:

```
s is a String
```

Even if the object being tested is not an actual instantiation of the class type on the right side of the operator, `instanceof` will still return `true` if the object being compared is *assignment compatible* with the type on the right.

The following example demonstrates a common use for `instanceof`: testing an object to see if it's an instance of one of its subtypes, before attempting a downcast:

```
class A { }
class B extends A {
  public static void main (String [] args) {
    A myA = new B();
    m2(myA);
  }
  public static void m2(A a) {
    if (a instanceof B)
      ((B)a).doBstuff();      // downcasting an A reference
                              // to a B reference
  }
  public static void doBstuff() {
    System.out.println("'a' refers to a B");
  }
}
```

The code compiles and produces this output:

```
'a' refers to a B
```

In examples like this, the use of the `instanceof` operator protects the program from attempting an illegal downcast.

You can test an object reference against its own class type or any of its superclasses. This means that *any* object reference will evaluate to `true` if you use the `instanceof` operator against type `Object`, as follows:

```
B b = new B();
if (b instanceof Object) {
   System.out.print("b is definitely an Object");
}
```

This prints

```
b is definitely an Object
```

exam watch

Look for `instanceof` questions that test whether an object is an instance of an interface, when the object's class implements the interface indirectly. An indirect implementation occurs when one of an object's superclasses implements an interface, but the actual class of the instance does not. In this example,

```
interface Foo { }
class A implements Foo { }
class B extends A { }
...
A a = new A();
B b = new B();
```

the following are true:

```
a instanceof Foo
b instanceof A
b instanceof Foo  // implemented indirectly
```

An object is said to be of a particular interface type (meaning it will pass the `instanceof` test) if any of the object's superclasses implement the interface.

In addition, it is legal to test whether the `null` reference is an instance of a class. This will always result in `false`, of course. This example,

```
class InstanceTest {
   public static void main(String [] args) {
      String a = null;
      boolean b = null instanceof String;
      boolean c = a instanceof String;
      System.out.println(b + " " + c);
   }
}
```

prints this:

```
false false
```

instanceof Compiler Error

You can't use the `instanceof` operator to test across two different class hierarchies. For instance, the following will NOT compile:

```
class Cat { }
class Dog {
  public static void main(String [] args) {
    Dog d = new Dog();
    System.out.println(d instanceof Cat);
  }
}
```

Compilation fails—there's no way `d` could ever refer to a `Cat` or a subtype of `Cat`.

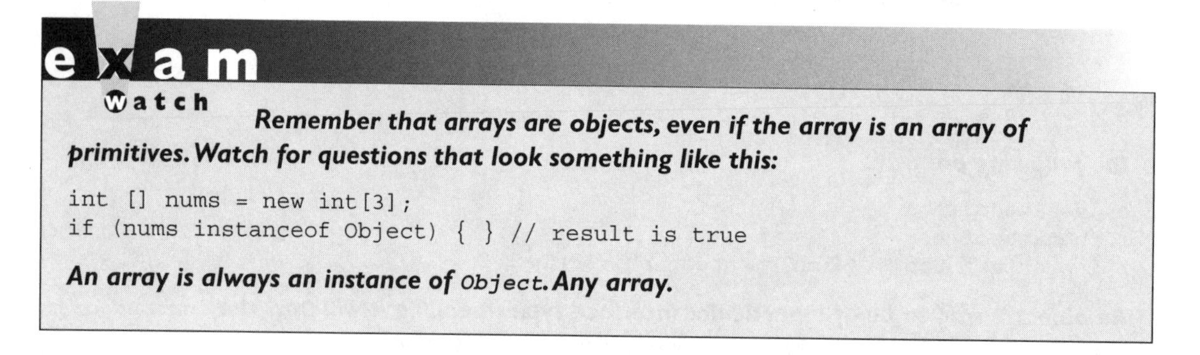

exam watch

Remember that arrays are objects, even if the array is an array of primitives. Watch for questions that look something like this:

```
int [] nums = new int[3];
if (nums instanceof Object) { } // result is true
```

An array is always an instance of `Object`. Any array.

Table 4-1 summarizes the use of the `instanceof` operator given the following:

```
interface Face { }
class Bar implements Face{ }
class Foo extends Bar { }
```

TABLE 4-1 Operands and Results Using `instanceof` Operator

First Operand (Reference Being Tested)	instanceof Operand (Type We're Comparing the Reference Against)	Result
`null`	Any class or interface type	`false`
`Foo` instance	`Foo, Bar, Face, Object`	`true`
`Bar` instance	`Bar, Face, Object`	`true`
`Bar` instance	`Foo`	`false`
`Foo [ ]`	`Foo, Bar, Face`	`false`
`Foo [ ]`	`Object`	`true`
`Foo [ 1 ]`	`Foo, Bar, Face, Object`	`true`

Arithmetic Operators

We're sure you're familiar with the basic arithmetic operators:

- `+` addition
- `–` subtraction
- `*` multiplication
- `/` division

These can be used in the standard way:

```
int x = 5 * 3;
int y = x - 4;
System.out.println("x - 4 is " +  y);   // Prints 11
```

The Remainder (%) Operator (a.k.a. the Modulus Operator)

One operator you might not be as familiar with is the remainder operator, `%`. The remainder operator divides the left operand by the right operand, and the result is the remainder, as the following code demonstrates:

```
class MathTest {
  public static void main (String [] args) {
    int x = 15;
    int y = x % 4;
    System.out.println("The result of 15 % 4 is the "
      + "remainder of 15 divided by 4. The remainder is " + y);
  }
}
```

Running class `MathTest` prints the following:

```
The result of 15 % 4 is the remainder of 15 divided by 4. The remainder is 3
```

(Remember: Expressions are evaluated from left to right by default. You can change this sequence, or *precedence*, by adding parentheses. Also remember that the `*`, `/`, and `%` operators have a higher precedence than the `+` and `-` operators.)

exam watch

When working with `ints`, the remainder operator (a.k.a. the modulus operator) and the division operator relate to each other in an interesting way:

- The modulus operator throws out **everything but** the remainder.
- The division operator throws out the remainder.

String Concatenation Operator

The plus sign can also be used to concatenate two strings together, as we saw earlier (and as we'll definitely see again):

```
String animal = "Gray " + "elephant";
```

String concatenation gets interesting when you combine numbers with `Strings`. Check out the following:

```
String a = "String";
int b = 3;
int c = 7;
System.out.println(a + b + c);
```

Will the `+` operator act as a plus sign when adding the `int` variables `b` and `c`? Or will the `+` operator treat `3` and `7` as characters, and concatenate them individually? Will the result be `String10` or `String37`? Okay, you've had long enough to think about it.

The `int` values were simply treated as characters and glued on to the right side of the `String`, giving the result:

```
String37
```

So we could read the previous code as

"Start with the value `String`, and concatenate the character `3` (the value of `b`) to it, to produce a new string `String3`, and then concatenate the character `7` (the value of `c`) to that, to produce a new string `String37`. Then print it out."

However, if you put parentheses around the two `int` variables, as follows,

```
System.out.println(a + (b + c));
```

you'll get this:

```
String10
```

Using parentheses causes the `(b + c)` to evaluate first, so the rightmost + operator functions as the addition operator, given that both operands are `int` values. The key point here is that within the parentheses, the left-hand operand is not a `String`. If it were, then the + operator would perform `String` concatenation. The previous code can be read as

"Add the values of `b and c` together, and then take the sum and convert it to a `String` and concatenate it with the `String` from variable `a`."

The rule to remember is this:

If either operand is a `String`*, the + operator becomes a* `String` *concatenation operator. If both operands are numbers, the + operator is the addition operator.*

You'll find that sometimes you might have trouble deciding whether, say, the left-hand operator is a `String` or not. On the exam, don't expect it always to be obvious. (Actually, now that we think about it, don't expect it ever to be obvious.) Look at the following code:

```
System.out.println(x.foo() + 7);
```

You can't know how the + operator is being used until you find out what the `foo()` method returns! If `foo()` returns a `String`, then `7` is concatenated to the returned `String`. But if `foo()` returns a number, then the + operator is used to add `7` to the return value of `foo()`.

Finally, you need to know that it's legal to mush together the compound additive operator (+=) and `String`s, like so:

```
String s = "123";
s += "45";
s += 67;
System.out.println(s);
```

Since both times the `+=` operator was used and the left operand was a `String`, both operations were concatenations, resulting in

```
1234567
```

exam watch

If you don't understand how `String` concatenation works, especially within a `print` statement, you could actually fail the exam even if you know the rest of the answers to the questions! Because so many questions ask, "What is the result?", you need to know not only the result of the code running, but also how that result is printed. Although at least a few questions will directly test your `String` knowledge, `String` concatenation shows up in other questions on virtually every objective. Experiment! For example, you might see a line such as this:

```
int b = 2;
System.out.println("" + b + 3);
```

It prints this:

```
23
```

But if the `print` statement changes to this:

```
System.out.println(b + 3);
```

The printed result becomes

```
5
```

Increment and Decrement Operators

Java has two operators that will increment or decrement a variable by exactly one. These operators are either two plus signs (++) or two minus signs (--):

- `++` Increment (prefix and postfix)
- `--` Decrement (prefix and postfix)

The operator is placed either before (prefix) or after (postfix) a variable to change its value. Whether the operator comes before or after the operand can change the outcome of an expression. Examine the following:

```
1. class MathTest {
2.   static int players = 0;
3.     public static void main (String [] args) {
4.       System.out.println("players online: " + players++);
5.       System.out.println("The value of players is "
                           + players);
6.       System.out.println("The value of players is now "
                           + ++players);
7.     }
8. }
```

Notice that in the fourth line of the program the increment operator is *after* the variable `players`. That means we're using the postfix increment operator, which causes `players` to be incremented by one but only *after* the value of `players` is used in the expression. When we run this program, it outputs the following:

```
%java MathTest
players online: 0
The value of players is 1
The value of players is now 2
```

Notice that when the variable is written to the screen, at first it says the value is `0`. Because we used the postfix increment operator, the increment doesn't happen until after the `players` variable is used in the `print` statement. Get it? The "post" in postfix means *after*. Line 5 doesn't increment `players`; it just outputs its value to the screen, so the newly incremented value displayed is 1. Line 6 applies the prefix increment operator to `players`, which means the increment happens *before* the value of the variable is used, so the output is `2`.

Expect to see questions mixing the increment and decrement operators with other operators, as in the following example:

```
int x = 2;  int y = 3;
if ((y == x++) | (x < ++y)) {
  System.out.println("x = " + x + " y = " + y);
 }
```

The preceding code prints this:

```
x = 3 y = 4
```

You can read the code as follows: "If 3 is equal to 2 OR 3 < 4"

The first expression compares `x` and `y`, and the result is `false`, because the increment on `x` doesn't happen until *after* the == test is made. Next, we increment `x`, so now `x` is `3`. Then we check to see if `x` is less than `y`, but we increment `y` *before* comparing it with `x`! So the second logical test is `(3 < 4)`. The result is `true`, so the `print` statement runs.

As with `String` concatenation, the increment and decrement operators are used throughout the exam, even on questions that aren't trying to test your knowledge of how those operators work. You might see them in questions on for loops, exceptions, or even threads. Be ready.

exam watch

Look out for questions that use the increment or decrement operators on a `final` variable. Because `final` variables can't be changed, the increment and decrement operators can't be used with them, and any attempt to do so will result in a compiler error. The following code won't compile:

```
final int x = 5;
int y = x++;
```

It produces this error:

```
Test.java:4: cannot assign a value to final variable x
int y = x++;
        ^
```

You can expect a violation like this to be buried deep in a complex piece of code. If you spot it, you know the code won't compile and you can move on without working through the rest of the code.

This question might seem to be testing you on some complex arithmetic operator trivia, when in fact it's testing you on your knowledge of the `final` modifier.

Conditional Operator

The conditional operator is a *ternary* operator (it has *three* operands) and is used to evaluate `boolean` expressions, much like an `if` statement, except instead of executing a block of code if the test is `true`, a conditional operator will assign a value to a variable. In other words, the goal of the conditional operator is to decide which of two values to assign to a variable. This operator is constructed using a `?` (question mark) and a `:` (colon). The parentheses are optional. Here is its structure:

```
x = (boolean expression) ? value to assign if true : value to assign if false
```

Let's take a look at a conditional operator in code:

```
class Salary {
  public static void main(String [] args) {
    int numOfPets = 3;
    String status = (numOfPets<4) ? "Pet limit not exceeded"
                    : "too many pets";
    System.out.println("This pet status is " + status);
  }
}
```

You can read the preceding code as "Set `numOfPets` equal to `3`".

Next we're going to assign a `String` to the status variable. If `numOfPets` is less than `4`, assign `"Pet limit not exceeded"` to the `status` variable; otherwise, assign `"too many pets"` to the `status` variable.

A conditional operator starts with a `boolean` operation, followed by two possible values for the variable to the left of the assignment (`=`) operator. The first value (the one to the left of the colon) is assigned if the conditional (`boolean`) test is `true`, and the second value is assigned if the conditional test is `false`. You can even nest conditional operators into one statement:

```
class AssignmentOps {
  public static void main(String [] args) {
   int sizeOfYard = 10;
   int numOfPets = 3;
   String status = (numOfPets<4)?"Pet count OK"
       :(sizeOfYard > 8)? "Pet limit on the edge"
         :"too many pets";
    System.out.println("Pet status is " + status);
  }
}
```

Don't expect many questions using conditional operators, but remember that conditional operators are sometimes confused with assertion statements, so be certain you can tell the difference. Chapter 7 covers assertions in detail.

Logical Operators

The exam objectives specify six "logical" operators (`&`, `|`, `^`, `!`, `&&`, and `||`). Some Oracle documentation uses other terminology for these operators, but for our purposes and in the exam objectives, these six are the logical operators.

Bitwise Operators (For OCJP 5 Candidates Only!)

Okay, this is going to be confusing. Of the six logical operators listed above, three of them (`&`, `|`, and `^`) can also be used as "bitwise" operators. Bitwise operators were included in previous versions of the exam, but they're NOT on the Java 6 or Java 7 exam.

Here are several legal statements that use bitwise operators:

```
byte b1 = 6 & 8;
byte b2 = 7 | 9;
byte b3 = 5 ^ 4;
System.out.println(b1 + " " + b2 + " " + b3);
```

Bitwise operators compare two variables bit-by-bit and return a variable whose bits have been set based on whether the two variables being compared had respective bits that were either both "on" (`&`), one or the other "on" (`|`), or exactly one "on" (`^`). By the way, when we run the preceding code, we get

```
0 15 1
```

Having said all this about bitwise operators, the key thing to remember is this:

BITWISE OPERATORS ARE NOT ON THE Java 6 or Java 7 EXAM!

Short-Circuit Logical Operators

Five logical operators on the exam are used to evaluate statements that contain more than one `boolean` expression. The most commonly used of the five are the two *short-circuit* logical operators:

- `&&` Short-circuit AND
- `||` Short-circuit OR

They are used to link little `boolean` expressions together to form bigger `boolean` expressions. The `&&` and `||` operators evaluate only `boolean` values. For an AND (`&&`) expression to be `true`, both operands must be `true`. For example:

```
if ((2 < 3) && (3 < 4)) { }
```

The preceding expression evaluates to `true` because *both* operand one `(2 < 3)` and operand two `(3 < 4)` evaluate to `true`.

The short-circuit feature of the `&&` operator is so named because it doesn't waste its time on pointless evaluations. A short-circuit `&&` evaluates the left side of the operation first (operand one), and if it resolves to `false`, the `&&` operator doesn't bother looking at the right side of the expression (operand two) since the `&&` operator already *knows* that the complete expression can't possibly be `true`.

```
class Logical {
  public static void main(String [] args) {
    boolean b1 = false, b2 = false;
    boolean b3 = (b1 == true) && (b2 = true);   // will b2 be set to true?
    System.out.println(b3 + " " + b2);
  }
}
```

When we run the preceding code, the **assignment** `(b2 = true)` never runs because of the short-circuit operator, so the output is

```
%java Logical
false false
```

The `||` operator is similar to the `&&` operator, except that it evaluates to `true` if EITHER of the operands is true. If the first operand in an OR operation is `true`, the result will be `true`, so the short-circuit `||` doesn't waste time looking at the right side of the equation. If the first operand is `false`, however, the short-circuit `||` has to evaluate the second operand to see if the result of the OR operation will be `true` or `false`. Pay close attention to the following example; you'll see quite a few questions like this on the exam:

```
 1. class TestOR {
 2.   public static void main(String[] args) {
 3.     if ((isItSmall(3)) || (isItSmall(7))) {
 4.       System.out.println("Result is true");
 5.     }
 6.     if ((isItSmall(6)) || (isItSmall(9))) {
 7.       System.out.println("Result is true");
 8.     }
 9.   }
10.
11.   public static boolean isItSmall(int i) {
12.     if (i < 5) {
13.       System.out.println("i < 5");
14.       return true;
15.     } else {
16.       System.out.println("i >= 5");
17.       return false;
18.     }
19.   }
20. }
```

What is the result?

```
% java TestOR
i < 5
Result is true
i >= 5
i >= 5
```

Here's what happened when the `main()` method ran:

1. When we hit line 3, the first operand in the `||` expression (in other words, the *left* side of the `||` operation) is evaluated.
2. The `isItSmall(3)` method is invoked, prints `"i < 5"`, and returns `true`.
3. Because the *first* operand in the `||` expression on line 3 is `true`, the `||` operator doesn't bother evaluating the second operand. So we never see the `"i >= 5"` that would have printed had the *second* operand been evaluated (which would have invoked `isItSmall(7)`).
4. Line 6 is evaluated, beginning with the *first* operand in the `||` expression.
5. The `isItSmall(6)` method is called, prints `"i >= 5"`, and returns `false`.
6. Because the *first* operand in the `||` expression on line 6 is `false`, the `||` operator can't skip the *second* operand; there's still a chance the expression can be `true`, if the *second* operand evaluates to `true`.
7. The `isItSmall(9)` method is invoked and prints `"i >= 5"`.
8. The `isItSmall(9)` method returns `false`, so the expression on line 6 is `false`, and thus line 7 never executes.

exam watch

The `||` and `&&` operators work only with boolean operands. The exam may try to fool you by using integers with these operators:

```
if (5 && 6) { }
```

It looks as though we're trying to do a bitwise AND on the bits representing the integers 5 and 6, but the code won't even compile.

Logical Operators (not Short-Circuit)

There are two *non-short-circuit* logical operators:

- `&` Non-short-circuit AND
- `|` Non-short-circuit OR

These operators are used in logical expressions just like the `&&` and `||` operators are used, but because they aren't the short-circuit operators, they evaluate both sides of the expression—always! They're inefficient. For example, even if the *first* operand (left side) in an `&` expression is `false`, the *second* operand will still be evaluated—even though it's now impossible for the result to be `true`! And the | is just as inefficient: if the *first* operand is `true`, the Java Virtual Machine (JVM) still plows ahead and evaluates the *second* operand even when it knows the expression will be `true` regardless.

You'll find a lot of questions on the exam that use both the short-circuit and non-short-circuit logical operators. You'll have to know exactly which operands are evaluated and which are not, since the result will vary depending on whether the second operand in the expression is evaluated. Consider this,

```
int z = 5;
if(++z > 5 || ++z > 6) z++;    // z = 7 after this code
```

versus this:

```
int z = 5;
if(++z > 5 | ++z > 6) z++;    // z = 8 after this code
```

Logical Operators ^ and !

The last two logical operators on the exam are

- `^` Exclusive-OR (XOR)
- `!` Boolean invert

The `^` (exclusive-OR) operator evaluates only `boolean` values. The `^` operator is related to the non-short-circuit operators we just reviewed, in that it always evaluates *both* the left and right operands in an expression. For an exclusive-OR (`^`) expression to be `true`, EXACTLY one operand must be `true`. This example,

```
System.out.println("xor " + ((2 < 3) ^ (4 > 3)));
```

produces this output:

```
xor false
```

The preceding expression evaluates to `false` because BOTH operand one `(2 < 3)` and operand two `(4 > 3)` evaluate to `true`.

The `!` (boolean invert) operator returns the opposite of a boolean's current value. The following statement,

```
if(!(7 == 5)) { System.out.println("not equal"); }
```

can be read "If it's not true that 7 == 5," and the statement produces this output:

```
not equal
```

Here's another example using booleans:

```
boolean t = true;
boolean f = false;
System.out.println("! " + (t & !f) + " " + f);
```

It produces this output:

```
! true false
```

In the preceding example, notice that the `&` test succeeded (printing `true`) and that the value of the `boolean` variable `f` did not change, so it printed `false`.

CERTIFICATION SUMMARY

If you've studied this chapter diligently, you should have a firm grasp on Java operators, and you should understand what equality means when tested with the `==` operator. Let's review the highlights of what you've learned in this chapter.

The logical operators (`&&`, `||`, `&`, `|`, and `^`) can be used only to evaluate two `boolean` expressions. The difference between `&&` and `&` is that the `&&` operator won't bother testing the right operand if the left evaluates to `false`, because the result of the `&&` expression can never be `true`. The difference between `||` and `|` is that the `||` operator won't bother testing the right operand if the left evaluates to `true`, because the result is already known to be `true` at that point.

The `==` operator can be used to compare values of primitives, but it can also be used to determine whether two reference variables refer to the same object.

The `instanceof` operator is used to determine whether the object referred to by a reference variable passes the IS-A test for a specified type.

The `+` operator is overloaded to perform `String` concatenation tasks and can also concatenate `Strings` and primitives, but be careful—concatenation can be tricky.

The conditional operator (a.k.a. the "ternary operator") has an unusual, three-operand syntax—don't mistake it for a complex assert statement.

The `++` and `--` operators will be used throughout the exam, and you must pay attention to whether they are prefixed or postfixed to the variable being updated.

Be prepared for a lot of exam questions involving the topics from this chapter. Even within questions testing your knowledge of another objective, the code will frequently use operators, assignments, object and primitive passing, and so on.

✓ TWO-MINUTE DRILL

Here are some of the key points from each section in this chapter.

Relational Operators (OCA Objectives 3.1 and 3.3)

- ❑ Relational operators always result in a `boolean` value (`true` or `false`).
- ❑ There are six relational operators: `>`, `>=`, `<`, `<=`, `==`, and `!=`. The last two (`==` and `!=`) are sometimes referred to as *equality operators*.
- ❑ When comparing characters, Java uses the Unicode value of the character as the numerical value.
- ❑ Equality operators
  - ❑ There are two equality operators: `==` and `!=`.
  - ❑ Four types of things can be tested: numbers, characters, booleans, and reference variables.
- ❑ When comparing reference variables, `==` returns `true` only if both references refer to the same object.

instanceof Operator (OCA Objective 3.1)

- ❑ `instanceof` is for reference variables only; it checks whether the object is of a particular type.
- ❑ The `instanceof` operator can be used only to test objects (or `null`) against class types that are in the same class hierarchy.
- ❑ For interfaces, an object passes the `instanceof` test if any of its superclasses implement the interface on the right side of the `instanceof` operator.

Arithmetic Operators (OCA Objectives 3.1 and 3.2)

- ❑ The four primary math operators are add (`+`), subtract (`-`), multiply (`*`), and divide (`/`).
- ❑ The remainder (a.k.a. modulus) operator (`%`) returns the remainder of a division.
- ❑ Expressions are evaluated from left to right, unless you add parentheses, or unless some operators in the expression have higher precedence than others.
- ❑ The `*`, `/`, and `%` operators have higher precedence than `+` and `-`.

String Concatenation Operator (OCA Objective 3.1)

- ❑ If either operand is a `String`, the `+` operator concatenates the operands.
- ❑ If both operands are numeric, the `+` operator adds the operands.

Increment/Decrement Operators (OCA Objectives 3.1 and 3.2)

- ❑ Prefix operators (for example, `++x` and `--x`) run before the value is used in the expression.
- ❑ Postfix operators (for example, `x++` and `x--`) run after the value is used in the expression.
- ❑ In any expression, both operands are fully evaluated *before* the operator is applied.
- ❑ Variables marked `final` cannot be incremented or decremented.

Ternary (Conditional) Operator (OCA Objective 3.1)

- ❑ Returns one of two values based on whether its `boolean` expression is `true` or `false`.
  - ❑ Returns the value after the `?` if the expression is `true`.
  - ❑ Returns the value after the `:` if the expression is `false`.

Logical Operators (OCA Objective 3.1)

- ❑ The exam covers six "logical" operators: `&`, `|`, `^`, `!`, `&&`, and `||`.
- ❑ Logical operators work with two expressions (except for `!`) that must resolve to boolean values.
- ❑ The `&&` and `&` operators return `true` only if both operands are `true`.
- ❑ The `||` and `|` operators return `true` if either or both operands are `true`.
- ❑ The `&&` and `||` operators are known as short-circuit operators.
- ❑ The `&&` operator does not evaluate the right operand if the left operand is `false`.
- ❑ The `||` does not evaluate the right operand if the left operand is `true`.
- ❑ The `&` and `|` operators always evaluate both operands.
- ❑ The `^` operator (called the "logical XOR") returns `true` if exactly one operand is `true`.
- ❑ The `!` operator (called the "inversion" operator) returns the opposite value of the boolean operand it precedes.

SELF TEST

1. Given:

```
class Hexy {
  public static void main(String[] args) {
    int i = 42;
    String s = (i<40)?"life":(i>50)?"universe":"everything";
    System.out.println(s);
  }
}
```

What is the result?

A. `null`

B. `life`

C. `universe`

D. `everything`

E. Compilation fails

F. An exception is thrown at runtime

2. Given:

```
public class Dog {
  String name;
  Dog(String s) { name = s; }
  public static void main(String[] args) {
    Dog d1 = new Dog("Boi");
    Dog d2 = new Dog("Tyri");
    System.out.print((d1 == d2) + " ");
    Dog d3 = new Dog("Boi");
    d2 = d1;
    System.out.print((d1 == d2) + " ");
    System.out.print((d1 == d3) + " ");
  }
}
```

What is the result?

A. `true true true`

B. `true true false`

C. `false true false`

D. `false true true`

E. `false false false`

F. An exception will be thrown at runtime

3. Given:

```
class Fork {
  public static void main(String[] args) {
    if(args.length == 1 | args[1].equals("test")) {
      System.out.println("test case");
    } else {
      System.out.println("production " + args[0]);
    }
  }
}
```

And the command-line invocation:

```
java Fork live2
```

What is the result?

A. `test case`

B. `production live2`

C. `test case live2`

D. Compilation fails

E. An exception is thrown at runtime

4. Given:

```
class Feline {
  public static void main(String[] args) {
    long x = 42L;
    long y = 44L;
    System.out.print(" " + 7 + 2 + " ");
    System.out.print(foo() + x + 5 + " ");
    System.out.println(x + y + foo());
  }
  static String foo() { return "foo"; }
}
```

What is the result?

A. `9 foo47 86foo`

B. `9 foo47 4244foo`

C. `9 foo425 86foo`

D. `9 foo425 4244foo`

E. `72 foo47 86foo`

F. `72 foo47 4244foo`

G. `72 foo425 86foo`

H. `72 foo425 4244foo`

I. Compilation fails

5. **Note**: Here's another old-style drag-and-drop question…just in case.

Place the fragments into the code to produce the output `33`. Note that you must use each fragment exactly once.

```
CODE:
class Incr {
  public static void main(String[] args) {
    Integer x = 7;
    int y = 2;

    x    ___  ___;
    ___  ___  ___;
    ___  ___  ___;
    ___  ___  ___;

    System.out.println(x);
  }
}
```

FRAGMENTS:

```
y  y  y  y

y  x  x

-=  *=  *=  *=
```

6. Given:

```
public class Cowboys {
  public static void main(String[] args) {
    int x = 12;
    int a = 5;
    int b = 7;
    System.out.println(x/a + " " + x/b);
  }
}
```

What is the result? (Choose all that apply.)

A. `2 1`

B. `2 2`

C. `3 1`

D. `3 2`

E. An exception is thrown at runtime

7. (OCP Only) Given:

```
 3. public class McGee {
 4.   public static void main(String[] args) {
 5.     Days d1 = Days.TH;
 6.     Days d2 = Days.M;
 7.     for(Days d: Days.values()) {
 8.       if(d.equals(Days.F)) break;
 9.       d2 = d;
10.     }
11.     System.out.println((d1 == d2)?"same old" : "newly new");
12.   }
13.   enum Days {M, T, W, TH, F, SA, SU};
14. }
```

What is the result?

A. `same old`

B. `newly new`

C. Compilation fails due to multiple errors

D. Compilation fails due only to an error on line 7

E. Compilation fails due only to an error on line 8

F. Compilation fails due only to an error on line 11

G. Compilation fails due only to an error on line 13

8. Given:

```
 4. public class SpecialOps {
 5.   public static void main(String[] args) {
 6.     String s = "";
 7.     boolean b1 = true;
 8.     boolean b2 = false;
 9.     if((b2 = false) | (21%5) > 2) s += "x";
10.     if(b1 || (b2 == true))        s += "y";
11.     if(b2 == true)                s += "z";
12.     System.out.println(s);
13.   }
14. }
```

Which are true? (Choose all that apply.)

A. Compilation fails

B. x will be included in the output

C. y will be included in the output

D. z will be included in the output

E. An exception is thrown at runtime

9. Given:

```
 3. public class Spock {
 4.   public static void main(String[] args) {
 5.     int mask = 0;
 6.     int count = 0;
 7.     if( ((5<7) || (++count < 10)) | mask++ < 10 )   mask = mask + 1;
 8.     if(  (6 > 8) ^ false)                           mask = mask + 10;
 9.     if( !(mask > 1) && ++count > 1)                 mask = mask + 100;
10.     System.out.println(mask + " " + count);
11.   }
12. }
```

Which two are true about the value of mask and the value of count at line 10? (Choose two.)

A. `mask` is 0

B. `mask` is 1

C. `mask` is 2

D. `mask` is 10

E. `mask` is greater than 10

F. `count` is 0

G. `count` is greater than 0

10. Given:

```
 3. interface Vessel { }
 4. interface Toy { }
 5. class Boat implements Vessel { }
 6. class Speedboat extends Boat implements Toy { }
 7. public class Tree {
 8.   public static void main(String[] args) {
 9.     String s = "0";
10.     Boat b = new Boat();
11.     Boat b2 = new Speedboat();
12.     Speedboat s2 = new Speedboat();
13.     if((b instanceof Vessel) && (b2 instanceof Toy))  s += "1";
14.     if((s2 instanceof Vessel) && (s2 instanceof Toy)) s += "2";
15.     System.out.println(s);
16.   }
17. }
```

What is the result?

A. `0`

B. `01`

C. `02`

D. `012`

E. Compilation fails

F. An exception is thrown at runtime

SELF TEST ANSWERS

1. ☑ **D** is correct. This is a ternary nested in a ternary. Both of the ternary expressions are false.

   ☒ **A, B, C, E,** and **F** are incorrect based on the above. (OCA Objective 3.1)

2. ☑ **C** is correct. The `==` operator tests for reference variable equality, not object equality.

   ☒ **A, B, D, E,** and **F** are incorrect based on the above. (OCA Objectives 3.1 and 3.3)

3. ☑ **E** is correct. Because the short circuit (`||`) is not used, both operands are evaluated. Since `args[1]` is past the `args` array bounds, an `ArrayIndexOutOfBoundsException` is thrown.

   ☒ **A, B, C,** and **D** are incorrect based on the above. (OCA Objectives 3.1 and 3.3)

4. ☑ **G** is correct. Concatenation runs from left to right, and if either operand is a `String`, the operands are concatenated. If both operands are numbers, they are added together.

   ☒ **A, B, C, D, E, F, H,** and **I** are incorrect based on the above. (OCA Objective 3.1)

5. Answer:

```
class Incr {
  public static void main(String[] args) {
    Integer x = 7;
    int y = 2;

    x *= x;
    y *= y;
    y *= y;
    x -= y;

    System.out.println(x);
  }
}
```

   Yeah, we know it's kind of puzzle-y, but you might encounter something like it on the real exam if Oracle reinstates this type of question. (OCA Objective 3.1)

6. ☑ **A** is correct. When dividing `ints`, remainders are always rounded down.

   ☒ **B, C, D,** and **E** are incorrect based on the above. (OCA Objective 3.1)

7. ☑ **A** is correct. All of this syntax is correct. The for-each iterates through the `enum` using the `values()` method to return an array. An `enum` can be compared using either `equals()` or `==`. An `enum` can be used in a ternary operator's boolean test.

   ☒ **B, C, D, E, F,** and **G** are incorrect based on the above. (OCA Objectives 3.1 and 3.3)

8. ☑ C is correct. Line 9 uses the modulus operator, which returns the remainder of the division, which in this case is `1`. Also, line 9 sets `b2` to `false`, and it doesn't test `b2`'s value. Line 10 sets `b2` to `true`, and it doesn't test its value; however, the short-circuit operator keeps the expression `b2 = true` from being executed.

   ☒ **A, B, D,** and **E** are incorrect based on the above. (OCA Objectives 3.1, 3.2, and 3.3)

9. ☑ C and **F** are correct. At line 7 the `||` keeps `count` from being incremented, but the `|` allows `mask` to be incremented. At line 8 the `^` returns true only if exactly one operand is true. At line 9 `mask` is `2` and the `&&` keeps `count` from being incremented.

   ☒ **A, B, D, E,** and **G** are incorrect based on the above. (OCA Objectives 3.1 and 3.2)

10. ☑ D is correct. First, remember that `instanceof` can look up through multiple levels of an inheritance tree. Also remember that `instanceof` is commonly used before attempting a downcast, so in this case, after line 15, it would be possible to say `Speedboat s3 = (Speedboat)b2;`.

    ☒ **A, B, C, E,** and **F** are incorrect based on the above. (OCA Objectives 3.1 and 3.2)

5

Working with Strings, Arrays, and ArrayLists

CERTIFICATION OBJECTIVES

- Create and Manipulate Strings
- Manipulate Data Using the StringBuilder Class and Its Methods
- Declare, Instantiate, Initialize, and Use a One-Dimensional Array
- Declare, Instantiate, Initialize, and Use a Multidimensional Array
- Declare and Use an ArrayList
- Use Encapsulation for Reference Variables
- ✓ Two-Minute Drill
- Q&A Self Test

CERTIFICATION OBJECTIVE

Using String and StringBuilder (OCA Objectives 2.7 and 2.6)

2.7 *Create and manipulate strings.*

2.6 *Manipulate data using the `StringBuilder` class and its methods.*

Everything you needed to know about strings in the older OCJP exams, you'll need to know for the OCA 7 and OCP 7 exams. Closely related to the `String` class are the `StringBuilder` class and the almost identical `StringBuffer` class. (For the exam, the only thing you need to know about the `StringBuffer` class is that it has exactly the same methods as the `StringBuilder` class, but `StringBuilder` is faster because its methods aren't synchronized.) Both classes, `StringBuilder` and `StringBuffer`, give you `String`-like objects that handle some of the `String` class's shortcomings (such as immutability).

The String Class

This section covers the `String` class, and the key concept for you to understand is that once a `String` object is created, it can never be changed. So, then, what is happening when a `String` object seems to be changing? Let's find out.

Strings Are Immutable Objects

We'll start with a little background information about strings. You may not need this for the test, but a little context will help. Handling "strings" of characters is a fundamental aspect of most programming languages. In Java, each character in a string is a 16-bit Unicode character. Because Unicode characters are 16 bits (not the skimpy 7 or 8 bits that ASCII provides), a rich, international set of characters is easily represented in Unicode.

In Java, strings are objects. As with other objects, you can create an instance of a string with the `new` keyword, as follows:

```
String s = new String();
```

This line of code creates a new object of class `String` and assigns it to the reference variable `s`.

So far, `String` objects seem just like other objects. Now, let's give the string a value:

```
s = "abcdef";
```

(As you'll find out shortly, these two lines of code aren't quite what they seem, so stay tuned.)

It turns out that the `String` class has about a zillion constructors, so you can use a more efficient shortcut:

```
String s = new String("abcdef");
```

And this is even more concise:

```
String s = "abcdef";
```

There are some subtle differences between these options that we'll discuss later, but what they have in common is that they all create a new `String` object, with a value of `"abcdef"`, and assign it to a reference variable `s`. Now let's say that you want a second reference to the `String` object referred to by `s`:

```
String s2 = s;   //  refer s2 to the same String as s
```

So far so good. `String` objects seem to be behaving just like other objects, so what's all the fuss about? Immutability! (What the heck is immutability?) Once you have assigned a `String` a value, that value can never change—it's immutable, frozen solid, won't budge, *fini*, done. (We'll talk about why later; don't let us forget.) The good news is that although the `String` object is immutable, its reference variable is not, so to continue with our previous example, consider this:

```
s = s.concat(" more stuff");  // the concat() method 'appends'
                              // a literal to the end
```

Now, wait just a minute, didn't we just say that `String` objects were immutable? So what's all this "appending to the end of the string" talk? Excellent question: let's look at what really happened.

The Java Virtual Machine (JVM) took the value of string `s` (which was `"abcdef"`) and tacked `" more stuff"` onto the end, giving us the value `"abcdef more stuff"`. Since strings are immutable, the JVM couldn't stuff this new value into the old `String` referenced by `s`, so it created a new `String` object, gave it the value `"abcdef more stuff"`, and made `s` refer to it. At this point in our example, we have two `String` objects: the first one we created, with the value `"abcdef"`, and the second one with the value `"abcdef more stuff"`. Technically there are now three `String` objects, because the literal argument to `concat`, `" more stuff"`, is itself a new `String` object. But we have references only to `"abcdef"` (referenced by `s2`) and `"abcdef more stuff"` (referenced by `s`).

What if we didn't have the foresight or luck to create a second reference variable for the `"abcdef"` string before we called `s = s.concat(" more stuff");`? In that case, the original, unchanged string containing `"abcdef"` would still exist in memory, but it would be considered "lost." No code in our program has any way to reference it—it is lost to us. Note, however, that the original `"abcdef"` string didn't change (it can't, remember; it's immutable); only the reference variable `s` was changed so that it would refer to a different string.

Figure 5-1 shows what happens on the heap when you reassign a reference variable. Note that the dashed line indicates a deleted reference.

To review our first example:

```
String s = "abcdef";    // create a new String object, with
                        // value "abcdef", refer s to it
String s2 = s;          // create a 2nd reference variable
                        // referring to the same String

// create a new String object, with value "abcdef more stuff",
// refer s to it. (Change s's reference from the old String
// to the new String.) (Remember s2 is still referring to
// the original "abcdef" String.)

s = s.concat(" more stuff");
```

Let's look at another example:

```
String x = "Java";
x.concat(" Rules!");
System.out.println("x = " + x);   // the output is "x = Java"
```

The first line is straightforward: Create a new `String` object, give it the value `"Java"`, and refer `x` to it. Next the JVM creates a second `String` object with the value `"Java Rules!"` but nothing refers to it. The second `String` object is instantly lost; you can't get to it. The reference variable `x` still refers to the original `String` with the value `"Java"`. Figure 5-2 shows creating a `String` without assigning a reference to it.

Let's expand this current example. We started with

```
String x = "Java";
x.concat(" Rules!");
System.out.println("x = " + x);    // the output is: x = Java
```

Now let's add

```
x.toUpperCase();
System.out.println("x = " + x);    // the output is still:
                                   // x = Java
```

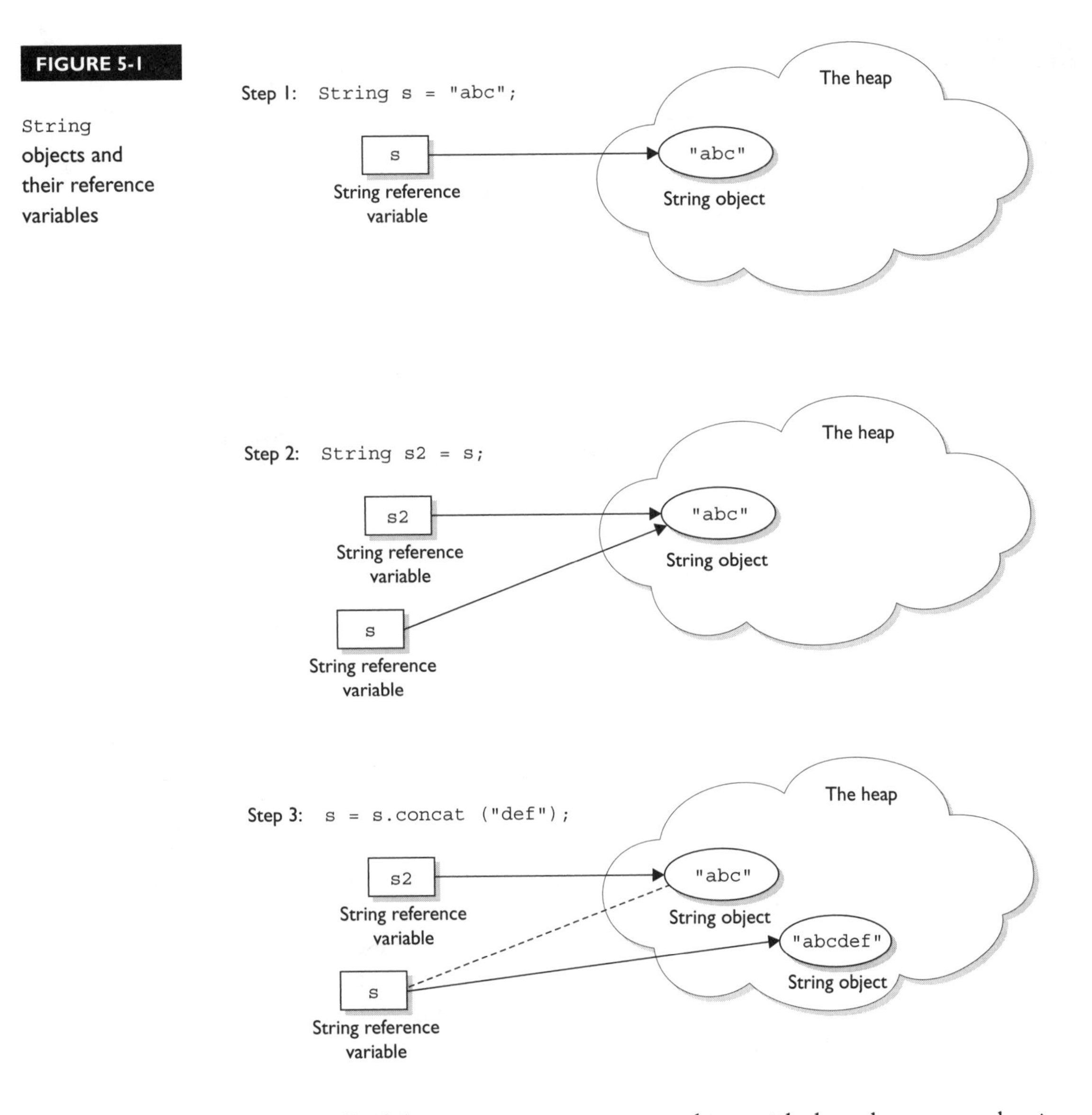

FIGURE 5-1 `String` objects and their reference variables

(We actually did just create a new `String` object with the value `"JAVA"`, but it was lost, and `x` still refers to the original, unchanged string `"Java"`.) How about adding this:

```
x.replace('a', 'X');
System.out.println("x = " + x);    // the output is still:
                                   // x = Java
```

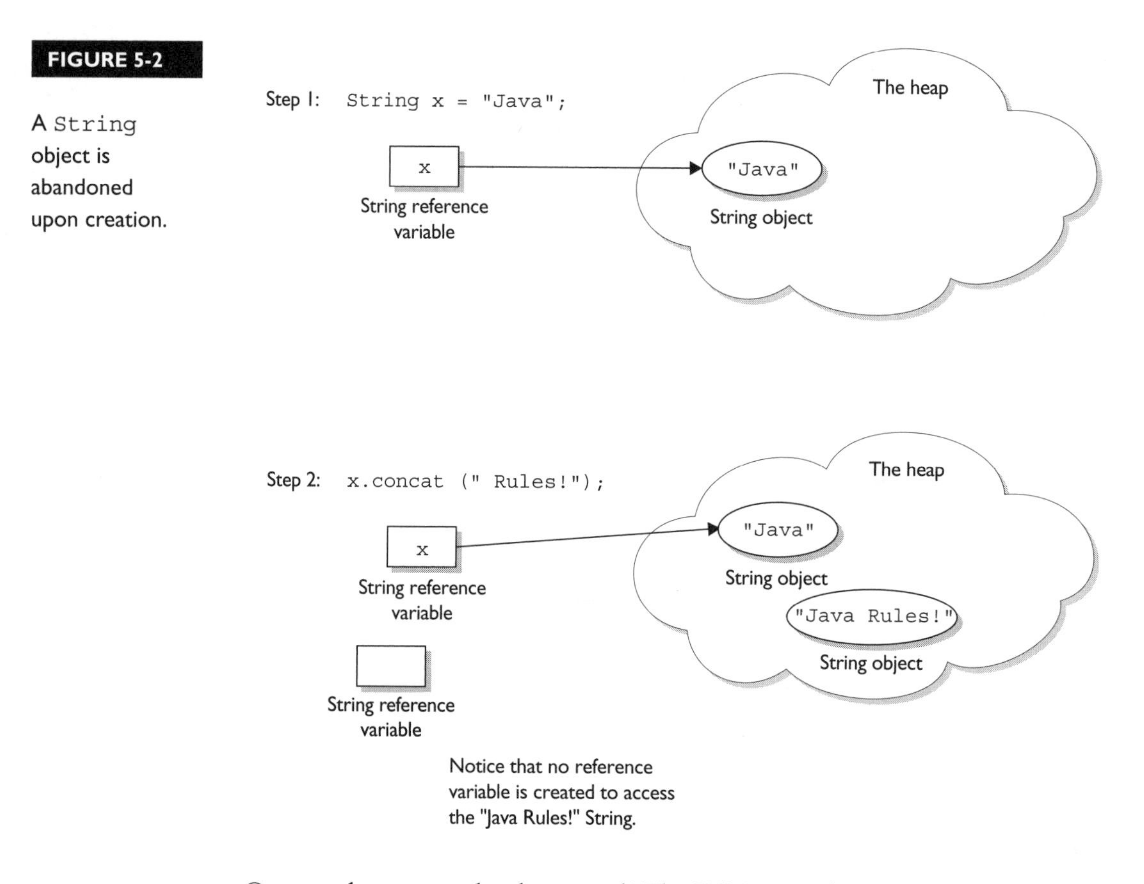

FIGURE 5-2 A `String` object is abandoned upon creation.

Can you determine what happened? The JVM created yet another new `String` object, with the value `"JXvX"`, (replacing the a's with x's), but once again this new `String` was lost, leaving `x` to refer to the original unchanged and unchangeable `String` object, with the value `"Java"`. In all of these cases, we called various string methods to create a new `String` by altering an existing `String`, but we never assigned the newly created `String` to a reference variable.

But we can put a small spin on the previous example:

```
String x = "Java";
x = x.concat(" Rules!");            // Now we're assigning the
                                    // new String to x
System.out.println("x = " + x);     // the output will be:
                                    // x = Java Rules!
```

This time, when the JVM runs the second line, a new `String` object is created with the value `"Java Rules!"`, and `x` is set to reference it. But wait...there's more—now the original `String` object, `"Java"`, has been lost, and no one is referring to it. So in both examples, we created two `String` objects and only one reference variable, so one of the two `String` objects was left out in the cold. See Figure 5-3 for a graphic depiction of this sad story. The dashed line indicates a deleted reference.

Let's take this example a little further:

```
String x = "Java";
x = x.concat(" Rules!");
System.out.println("x = " + x);      // the output is:
                                     // x = Java Rules!

x.toLowerCase();                     // no assignment, create a
                                     // new, abandoned String

System.out.println("x = " + x);      // no assignment, the output
                                     // is still: x = Java Rules!

x = x.toLowerCase();                 // create a new String,
                                     // assigned to x
System.out.println("x = " + x);      // the assignment causes the
                                     // output: x = java rules!
```

FIGURE 5-3 An old `String` object being abandoned

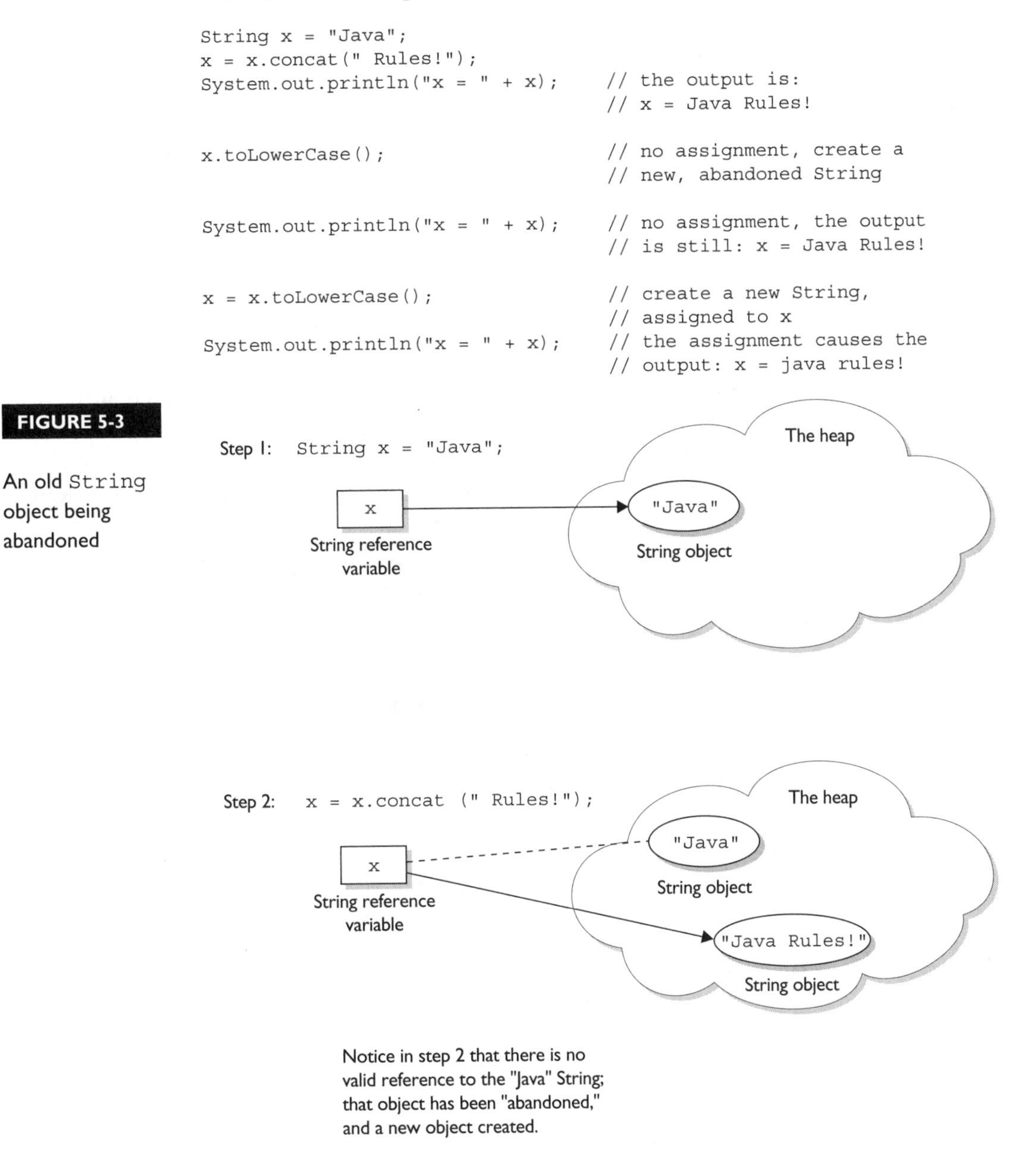

The preceding discussion contains the keys to understanding Java string immutability. If you really, really get the examples and diagrams, backward and forward, you should get 80 percent of the String questions on the exam correct.

We will cover more details about strings next, but make no mistake—in terms of bang for your buck, what we've already covered is by far the most important part of understanding how String objects work in Java.

We'll finish this section by presenting an example of the kind of devilish String question you might expect to see on the exam. Take the time to work it out on paper. (Hint: try to keep track of how many objects and reference variables there are, and which ones refer to which.)

```
String s1 = "spring ";
String s2 = s1 + "summer ";
s1.concat("fall ");
s2.concat(s1);
s1 += "winter ";
System.out.println(s1 + " " + s2);
```

What is the output? For extra credit, how many String objects and how many reference variables were created prior to the println statement?

Answer: The result of this code fragment is `spring winter spring summer`. There are two reference variables: s1 and s2. A total of eight String objects were created as follows: `"spring "`, `"summer "` (lost), `"spring summer "`, `"fall "` (lost), `"spring fall "` (lost), `"spring summer spring "` (lost), `"winter "` (lost), `"spring winter "` (at this point `"spring "` is lost). Only two of the eight String objects are not lost in this process.

Important Facts About Strings and Memory

In this section we'll discuss how Java handles String objects in memory and some of the reasons behind these behaviors.

One of the key goals of any good programming language is to make efficient use of memory. As an application grows, it's very common for string literals to occupy large amounts of a program's memory, and there is often a lot of redundancy within the universe of String literals for a program. To make Java more memory efficient, the JVM sets aside a special area of memory called the *String constant pool.* When the compiler encounters a String literal, it checks the pool to see if an identical String already exists. If a match is found, the reference to the new literal is directed to the existing String, and no new String literal object is created. (The existing String simply has an additional reference.) Now you can start to see why making

String objects immutable is such a good idea. If several reference variables refer to the same String without even knowing it, it would be very bad if any of them could change the String's value.

You might say, "Well that's all well and good, but what if someone overrides the String class functionality; couldn't that cause problems in the pool?" That's one of the main reasons that the String class is marked final. Nobody can override the behaviors of any of the String methods, so you can rest assured that the String objects you are counting on to be immutable will, in fact, be immutable.

Creating New Strings

Earlier we promised to talk more about the subtle differences between the various methods of creating a String. Let's look at a couple of examples of how a String might be created, and let's further assume that no other String objects exist in the pool. In this simple case, "abc" will go in the pool and s will refer to it:

```
String s = "abc";     //  creates one String object and one
                      //  reference variable
```

In the next case, because we used the new keyword, Java will create a new String object in normal (nonpool) memory and s will refer to it. In addition, the literal "abc" will be placed in the pool:

```
String s = new String("abc");  // creates two objects,
                               // and one reference variable
```

Important Methods in the String Class

The following methods are some of the more commonly used methods in the String class, and they are also the ones that you're most likely to encounter on the exam.

- **charAt()** Returns the character located at the specified index
- **concat()** Appends one string to the end of another (+ also works)
- **equalsIgnoreCase()** Determines the equality of two strings, ignoring case
- **length()** Returns the number of characters in a string
- **replace()** Replaces occurrences of a character with a new character
- **substring()** Returns a part of a string
- **toLowerCase()** Returns a string, with uppercase characters converted to lowercase

- **`toString()`** Returns the value of a string
- **`toUpperCase()`** Returns a string, with lowercase characters converted to uppercase
- **`trim()`** Removes whitespace from both ends of a string

Let's look at these methods in more detail.

public char charAt(int index) This method returns the character located at the `String`'s specified index. Remember, `String` indexes are zero-based—here's an example:

```
String x = "airplane";
System.out.println( x.charAt(2) );       //  output is 'r'
```

public String concat(String s) This method returns a string with the value of the `String` passed in to the method appended to the end of the `String` used to invoke the method—here's an example:

```
String x = "taxi";
System.out.println( x.concat(" cab") ); // output is "taxi cab"
```

The overloaded `+` and `+=` operators perform functions similar to the `concat()` method—here's an example:

```
String x = "library";
System.out.println( x + " card");  // output is "library card"

String x = "Atlantic";
x+= " ocean";
System.out.println( x );           // output is "Atlantic ocean"
```

In the preceding `"Atlantic ocean"` example, notice that the value of `x` really did change! Remember that the `+=` operator is an assignment operator, so line 2 is really creating a new string, `"Atlantic ocean"`, and assigning it to the `x` variable. After line 2 executes, the original string `x` was referring to, `"Atlantic"`, is abandoned.

public boolean equalsIgnoreCase(String s) This method returns a boolean value (`true` or `false`) depending on whether the value of the `String` in the argument is the same as the value of the `String` used to invoke the method. This method will return `true` even when characters in the `String` objects being compared have differing cases—here's an example:

```
String x = "Exit";
System.out.println( x.equalsIgnoreCase("EXIT"));    // is "true"
System.out.println( x.equalsIgnoreCase("tixe"));    // is "false"
```

public int length() This method returns the length of the `String` used to invoke the method—here's an example:

```
String x = "01234567";
System.out.println( x.length() );     // returns "8"
```

Arrays have an attribute (not a method) called `length`. You may encounter questions in the exam that attempt to use the `length()` method on an array or that attempt to use the `length` attribute on a `String`. Both cause compiler errors—consider these, for example:

```
String x = "test";
System.out.println( x.length );       // compiler error
```

and

```
String[] x = new String[3];
System.out.println( x.length() );    // compiler error
```

public String replace(char old, char new) This method returns a `String` whose value is that of the `String` used to invoke the method, updated so that any occurrence of the char in the first argument is replaced by the char in the second argument—here's an example:

```
String x = "oxoxoxox";
System.out.println( x.replace('x', 'X') );   // output is "oXoXoXoX"
```

public String substring(int begin) and public String substring(int begin, int end) The `substring()` method is used to return a part (or substring) of the `String` used to invoke the method. The first argument represents the starting location (zero-based) of the substring. If the call has only one argument, the substring returned will include the characters at the end of the original `String`. If the call has two arguments, the substring returned will end with the character located in the *n*th position of the original `String` where *n* is the second argument.

Unfortunately, the ending argument is not zero-based, so if the second argument is 7, the last character in the returned String will be in the original String's 7 position, which is index 6 (ouch). Let's look at some examples:

```
String x = "0123456789";                  // as if by magic, the value of each
                                          // char is the same as its index!
System.out.println( x.substring(5) );     // output is  "56789"
System.out.println( x.substring(5, 8));   // output is "567"
```

The first example should be easy: Start at index 5 and return the rest of the String. The second example should be read as follows: Start at index 5 and return the characters up to and including the 8th position (index 7).

public String toLowerCase() Converts all characters of a String to lowercase—here's an example:

```
String x = "A New Moon";
System.out.println( x.toLowerCase() );   // output is "a new moon"
```

public String toString() This method returns the value of the String used to invoke the method. What? Why would you need such a seemingly "do nothing" method? All objects in Java must have a toString() method, which typically returns a String that in some meaningful way describes the object in question. In the case of a String object, what's a more meaningful way than the String's value? For the sake of consistency, here's an example:

```
String x = "big surprise";
System.out.println( x.toString() );   // output? [reader's exercise :-) ]
```

public String toUpperCase() Converts all characters of a String to uppercase—here's an example:

```
String x = "A New Moon";
System.out.println( x.toUpperCase() );  // output is "A NEW MOON"
```

public String trim() This method returns a String whose value is the String used to invoke the method, but with any leading or trailing whitespace removed—here's an example:

```
String x = "  hi  ";
System.out.println( x + "t" );          // output is "  hi  t"
System.out.println( x.trim() + "t");    // output is "hit"
```

The StringBuilder Class

The `java.lang.StringBuilder` class should be used when you have to make a lot of modifications to strings of characters. As discussed in the previous section, `String` objects are immutable, so if you choose to do a lot of manipulations with `String` objects, you will end up with a lot of abandoned `String` objects in the `String` pool. (Even in these days of gigabytes of RAM, it's not a good idea to waste precious memory on discarded `String` pool objects.) On the other hand, objects of type `StringBuilder` can be modified over and over again without leaving behind a great effluence of discarded `String` objects.

on the job

A common use for `StringBuilders` is file I/O when large, ever-changing streams of input are being handled by the program. In these cases, large blocks of characters are handled as units, and `StringBuilder` objects are the ideal way to handle a block of data, pass it on, and then reuse the same memory to handle the next block of data.

Prefer StringBuilder to StringBuffer

The `StringBuilder` class was added in Java 5. It has exactly the same API as the `StringBuffer` class, except `StringBuilder` is not thread-safe. In other words, its methods are not synchronized. (More about thread safety in Chapter 13.) Oracle recommends that you use `StringBuilder` instead of `StringBuffer` whenever possible, because `StringBuilder` will run faster (and perhaps jump higher). So apart from synchronization, anything we say about `StringBuilder`'s methods holds true for `StringBuffer`'s methods, and vice versa. That said, for the OCA 7 and OCP 7 exams, `StringBuffer` is not tested.

Using StringBuilder (and This Is the Last Time We'll Say This: StringBuffer)

In the previous section, you saw how the exam might test your understanding of `String` immutability with code fragments like this:

```
String x = "abc";
x.concat("def");
System.out.println("x = " + x);      //  output is "x = abc"
```

Because no new assignment was made, the new `String` object created with the `concat()` method was abandoned instantly. You also saw examples like this:

```
String x = "abc";
x = x.concat("def");
System.out.println("x = " + x);    // output is "x = abcdef"
```

We got a nice new `String` out of the deal, but the downside is that the old `String "abc"` has been lost in the `String` pool, thus wasting memory. If we were using a `StringBuilder` instead of a `String`, the code would look like this:

```
StringBuilder sb = new StringBuilder("abc");
sb.append("def");
System.out.println("sb = " + sb);      // output is "sb = abcdef"
```

All of the `StringBuilder` methods we will discuss operate on the value of the `StringBuilder` object invoking the method. So a call to `sb.append("def");` is actually appending `"def"` to itself (`StringBuilder sb`). In fact, these method calls can be chained to each other—here's an example:

```
StringBuilder sb = new StringBuilder("abc");
sb.append("def").reverse().insert(3, "---");
System.out.println( sb );               // output is  "fed---cba"
```

Notice that in each of the previous two examples, there was a single call to `new`, so in each example we weren't creating any extra objects. Each example needed only a single `StringBuilder` object to execute.

So far we've seen `StringBuilders` being built with an argument specifying an initial value. `StringBuilders` can also be built empty, and they can also be constructed with a specific size or, more formally, a "capacity." For the exam, there are three ways to create a new `StringBuilder`:

```
1. new StringBuilder();        // default cap. = 16 chars
2. new StringBuilder("ab");    // cap. = 16 + arg's length
3. new StringBuilder(x);       // capacity = x (an integer)
```

The two most common ways to work with `StringBuilders` is via an `append()` method or an `insert()` method. In terms of a `StringBuilder`'s capacity, there are three rules to keep in mind when appending and inserting:

- ***If an `append()` grows a `StringBuilder` past its capacity, the capacity is updated automatically.***
- ***If an `insert()` starts within a `StringBuilder`'s capacity, but ends after the current capacity, the capacity is updated automatically.***
- ***If an `insert()` attempts to start at an index after the `StringBuilder`'s current length, an exception will be thrown.***

Important Methods in the StringBuilder Class

The `StringBuilder` class has a zillion methods. Following are the methods you're most likely to use in the real world and, happily, the ones you're most likely to find on the exam.

public StringBuilder append(String s) As you've seen earlier, this method will update the value of the object that invoked the method, whether or not the returned value is assigned to a variable. This method will take many different arguments, including `boolean`, `char`, `double`, `float`, `int`, `long`, and others, but the most likely use on the exam will be a `String` argument—for example,

```
StringBuilder sb = new StringBuilder("set ");
sb.append("point");
System.out.println(sb);        // output is "set point"
StringBuilder sb2 = new StringBuilder("pi = ");
sb2.append(3.14159f);
System.out.println(sb2);       // output is  "pi = 3.14159"
```

public StringBuilder delete(int start, int end) This method modifies the value of the `StringBuilder` object used to invoke it. The starting index of the substring to be removed is defined by the first argument (which is zero-based), and the ending index of the substring to be removed is defined by the second argument (but it is one-based)! Study the following example carefully:

```
StringBuilder sb = new StringBuilder("0123456789");
System.out.println(sb.delete(4,6));      // output is "01236789"
```

exam watch

The exam will probably test your knowledge of the difference between `String` and `StringBuilder` objects. Because `StringBuilder` objects are changeable, the following code fragment will behave differently than a similar code fragment that uses `String` objects:

```
StringBuilder sb = new StringBuilder("abc");
sb.append("def");
System.out.println( sb );
```

In this case, the output will be: `"abcdef"`

public StringBuilder insert(int offset, String s) This method updates the value of the `StringBuilder` object that invoked the method call. The `String` passed in to the second argument is inserted into the `StringBuilder` starting at the offset location represented by the first argument (the offset is zero-based). Again, other types of data can be passed in through the second argument (**`boolean`**, **`char`**, **`double`**, **`float`**, **`int`**, **`long`**, and so on), but the `String` argument is the one you're most likely to see:

```
StringBuilder sb = new StringBuilder("01234567");
sb.insert(4, "---");
System.out.println( sb );          //   output is  "0123---4567"
```

public StringBuilder reverse() This method updates the value of the `StringBuilder` object that invoked the method call. When invoked, the characters in the `StringBuilder` are reversed—the first character becoming the last, the second becoming the second to the last, and so on:

```
StringBuilder s = new StringBuilder("A man a plan a canal Panama");
sb.reverse();
System.out.println(sb); // output: "amanaP lanac a nalp a nam A"
```

public String toString() This method returns the value of the `StringBuilder` object that invoked the method call as a `String`:

```
StringBuilder sb = new StringBuilder("test string");
System.out.println( sb.toString() );  // output is "test string"
```

That's it for `StringBuilders`. If you take only one thing away from this section, it's that unlike `String` objects, `StringBuilder` objects can be changed.

exam watch

Many of the exam questions covering this chapter's topics use a tricky bit of Java syntax known as "chained methods." A statement with chained methods has this general form:

```
result = method1().method2().method3();
```

In theory, any number of methods can be chained in this fashion, although typically you won't see more than three. Here's how to decipher these "handy Java shortcuts" when you encounter them:

1. **Determine what the leftmost method call will return (let's call it `x`).**
2. **Use `x` as the object invoking the second (from the left) method. If there are only two chained methods, the result of the second method call is the expression's result.**
3. **If there is a third method, the result of the second method call is used to invoke the third method, whose result is the expression's result—for example,**

```
String x = "abc";
String y = x.concat("def").toUpperCase().replace('C','x');   //chained methods
System.out.println("y = " + y); // result is "y = ABxDEF"
```

Let's look at what happened. The literal `def` was concatenated to `abc`, creating a temporary, intermediate `String` (soon to be lost), with the value `abcdef`. The `toUpperCase()` method was called on this `String`, which created a new (soon to be lost) temporary `String` with the value `ABCDEF`. The `replace()` method was then called on this second `String` object, which created a final `String` with the value `ABxDEF` and referred `y` to it.

CERTIFICATION OBJECTIVE

Using Arrays (OCA Objectives 4.1 and 4.2)

4.1 *Declare, instantiate, initialize, and use a one-dimensional array.*

4.2 *Declare, instantiate, initialize, and use a multi-dimensional array.*

Arrays are objects in Java that store multiple variables of the same type. Arrays can hold either primitives or object references, but the array itself will always be an object on the heap, even if the array is declared to hold primitive elements. In other words, there is no such thing as a primitive array, but you can make an array of primitives. For this objective, you need to know three things:

- How to make an array reference variable (declare)
- How to make an array object (construct)
- How to populate the array with elements (initialize)

There are several different ways to do each of these, and you need to know about all of them for the exam.

on the job

Arrays are efficient, but most of the time you'll want to use one of the Collection types from java.util (including `HashMap`, `ArrayList`, `TreeSet`). Collection classes offer more flexible ways to access an object (for insertion, deletion, and so on) and unlike arrays, they can expand or contract dynamically as you add or remove elements (they're really managed arrays, since they use arrays behind the scenes). There's a Collection type for a wide range of needs. Do you need a fast sort? A group of objects with no duplicates? A way to access a name/value pair? A linked list? Chapter 11 covers collections in more detail.

Declaring an Array

Arrays are declared by stating the type of element the array will hold, which can be an object or a primitive, followed by square brackets to the left or right of the identifier.

Declaring an array of primitives:

```
int[] key;           // brackets before name (recommended)
int key [];          // brackets after name (legal but less readable)
                     // spaces between the name and [] legal, but bad
```

Declaring an array of object references:

```
Thread[] threads;  // Recommended
Thread threads[];  // Legal but less readable
```

When declaring an array reference, you should always put the array brackets immediately after the declared type, rather than after the identifier (variable name). That way, anyone reading the code can easily tell that, for example, `key` is a reference to an `int` array object and not an `int` primitive.

We can also declare multidimensional arrays, which are in fact arrays of arrays. This can be done in the following manner:

```
String[][][] occupantName;  // recommended
String[] managerName [];    // yucky, but legal
```

The first example is a three-dimensional array (an array of arrays of arrays) and the second is a two-dimensional array. Notice in the second example we have one square bracket before the variable name and one after. This is perfectly legal to the compiler, proving once again that just because it's legal doesn't mean it's right.

It is never legal to include the size of the array in your declaration. Yes, we know you can do that in some other languages, which is why you might see a question or two in the exam that include code similar to the following:

```
int[5] scores;   // will NOT compile
```

The preceding code won't make it past the compiler. Remember, the JVM doesn't allocate space until you actually instantiate the array object. That's when size matters.

Constructing an Array

Constructing an array means creating the array object on the heap (where all objects live)—that is, doing a `new` on the array type. To create an array object, Java must know how much space to allocate on the heap, so you must specify the size of the array at creation time. The size of the array is the number of elements the array will hold.

Constructing One-Dimensional Arrays

The most straightforward way to construct an array is to use the keyword `new` followed by the array type, with a bracket specifying how many elements of that type the array will hold. The following is an example of constructing an array of type `int`:

```
int[] testScores;          // Declares the array of ints
testScores = new int[4]; // constructs an array and assigns it
                           // to the testScores variable
```

The preceding code puts one new object on the heap—an array object holding four elements—with each element containing an `int` with a default value of 0. Think of this code as saying to the compiler, "Create an array object that will hold four `ints`, and assign it to the reference variable named `testScores`. Also, go ahead and set each `int` element to zero. Thanks." (The compiler appreciates good manners.)

Figure 5-4 shows the `testScores` array on the heap, after construction.

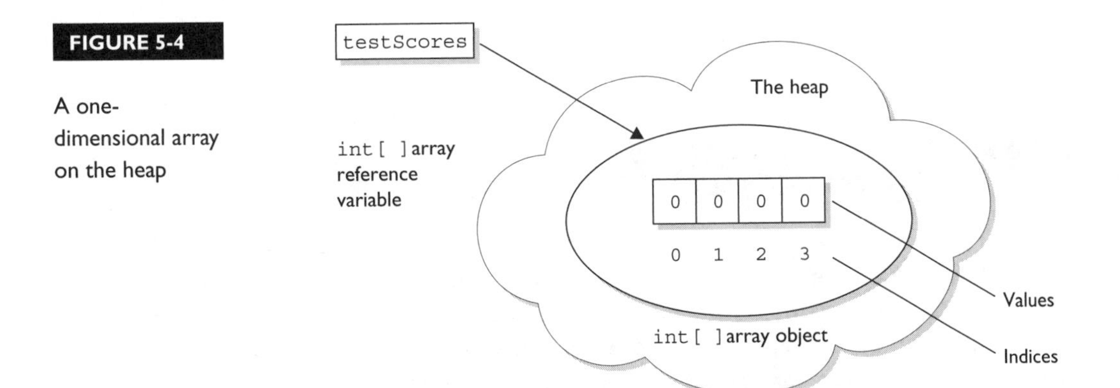

FIGURE 5-4 A one-dimensional array on the heap

You can also declare and construct an array in one statement, as follows:

```
int[] testScores = new int[4];
```

This single statement produces the same result as the two previous statements. Arrays of object types can be constructed in the same way:

```
Thread[] threads = new Thread[5];   // no Thread objects created!
                                    // one Thread array created
```

Remember that, despite how the code appears, the `Thread` constructor is not being invoked. We're not creating a `Thread` instance, but rather a single `Thread` array object. After the preceding statement, there are still no actual `Thread` objects!

exam watch

Think carefully about how many objects are on the heap after a code statement or block executes. The exam will expect you to know, for example, that the preceding code produces just one object (the array assigned to the reference variable named threads). The single object referenced by threads holds five `Thread` reference variables, but no `Thread` objects have been created or assigned to those references.

Remember, arrays must always be given a size at the time they are constructed. The JVM needs the size to allocate the appropriate space on the heap for the new array object. It is never legal, for example, to do the following:

```
int[] carList = new int[]; // Will not compile; needs a size
```

So don't do it, and if you see it on the test, run screaming toward the nearest answer marked "Compilation fails."

You may see the words "construct", "create", and "instantiate" used interchangeably. They all mean, "An object is built on the heap." This also implies that the object's constructor runs, as a result of the construct/create/instantiate code. You can say with certainty, for example, that any code that uses the keyword `new` will (if it runs successfully) cause the class constructor and all superclass constructors to run.

In addition to being constructed with new, arrays can also be created using a kind of syntax shorthand that creates the array while simultaneously initializing the array elements to values supplied in code (as opposed to default values). We'll look at that in the next section. For now, understand that because of these syntax shortcuts, objects can still be created even without you ever using or seeing the keyword new.

Constructing Multidimensional Arrays

Multidimensional arrays, remember, are simply arrays of arrays. So a two-dimensional array of type int is really an object of type int array (int []), with each element in that array holding a reference to another int array. The second dimension holds the actual int primitives.

The following code declares and constructs a two-dimensional array of type int:

```
int[][] myArray = new int[3][];
```

Notice that only the first brackets are given a size. That's acceptable in Java, since the JVM needs to know only the size of the object assigned to the variable myArray.

Figure 5-5 shows how a two-dimensional int array works on the heap.

Initializing an Array

Initializing an array means putting things into it. The "things" in the array are the array's elements, and they're either primitive values (2, x, false, and so on) or objects referred to by the reference variables in the array. If you have an array of objects (as opposed to primitives), the array doesn't actually hold the objects, just as any other nonprimitive variable never actually holds the object, but instead holds a *reference* to the object. But we talk about arrays as, for example, "an array of five strings," even though what we really mean is, "an array of five references to String objects." Then the big question becomes whether or not those references are actually pointing (oops, this is Java, we mean referring) to real String objects or are simply null. **Remember, a reference that has not had an object assigned to it is a null reference. And if you actually try to use that null reference by, say, applying the dot operator to invoke a method on it, you'll get the infamous NullPointerException.**

The individual elements in the array can be accessed with an index number. The index number always begins with zero (0), so for an array of ten objects the index numbers will run from 0 through 9. Suppose we create an array of three Animals as follows:

```
Animal [] pets = new Animal[3];
```

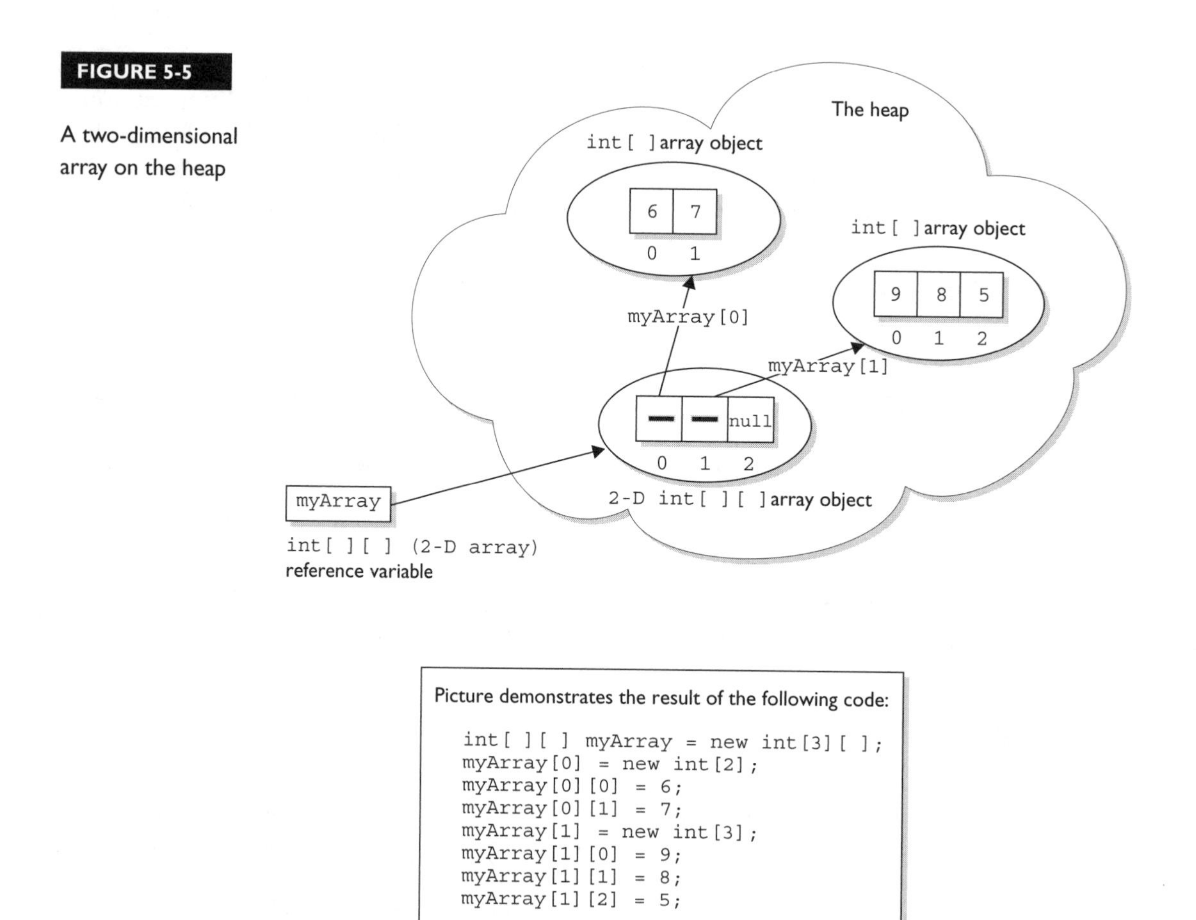
The heap
int[ ] array object
6
7
0 1
int[ ] array object
9
8
5
0 1 2
myArray[0]
myArray[1]
null
0 1 2
myArray
2-D int[ ][ ] array object
int[ ][ ] (2-D array)
reference variable
Picture demonstrates the result of the following code:
int[ ][ ] myArray = new int[3][ ];
myArray[0] = new int[2];
myArray[0][0] = 6;
myArray[0][1] = 7;
myArray[1] = new int[3];
myArray[1][0] = 9;
myArray[1][1] = 8;
myArray[1][2] = 5;

FIGURE 5-5 A two-dimensional array on the heap

We have one array object on the heap, with three `null` references of type `Animal`, but we don't have any `Animal` objects. The next step is to create some `Animal` objects and assign them to index positions in the array referenced by `pets`:

```
pets[0] = new Animal();
pets[1] = new Animal();
pets[2] = new Animal();
```

This code puts three new `Animal` objects on the heap and assigns them to the three index positions (elements) in the `pets` array.

exam

Watch

Look for code that tries to access an out-of-range array index. For example, if an array has three elements, trying to access the element `[3]` will raise an `ArrayIndexOutOfBoundsException`, because in an array of three elements, the legal index values are 0, 1, and 2. You also might see an attempt to use a negative number as an array index. The following are examples of legal and illegal array access attempts. Be sure to recognize that these cause runtime exceptions and not compiler errors!

Nearly all of the exam questions list both runtime exception and compiler error as possible answers:

```
int[] x = new int[5];
x[4] = 2;    // OK, the last element is at index 4
x[5] = 3;    // Runtime  exception. There is no element at index 5!

int[] z = new int[2];
int y = -3;
z[y] = 4;    // Runtime exception. y is a negative number
```

These can be hard to spot in a complex loop, but that's where you're most likely to see array index problems in exam questions.

A two-dimensional array (an array of arrays) can be initialized as follows:

```
int[][] scores = new int[3][];
// Declare and create an array (scores) holding three references
// to int arrays

scores[0] = new int[4];
// the first element in the scores array is an int array
// of four int elements

scores[1] = new int[6];
// the second element is an int array of six int elements

scores[2] = new int[1];
// the third element is an int array of one int element
```

Initializing Elements in a Loop

Array objects have a single public variable, `length`, that gives you the number of elements in the array. The last index value, then, is always one less than the `length`.

For example, if the `length` of an array is 4, the index values are from 0 through 3. Often, you'll see array elements initialized in a loop, as follows:

```
Dog[] myDogs = new Dog[6]; // creates an array of 6 Dog references
for(int x = 0; x < myDogs.length; x++) {
    myDogs[x] = new Dog(); // assign a new Dog to index position x
}
```

The `length` variable tells us how many elements the array holds, but it does not tell us whether those elements have been initialized.

Declaring, Constructing, and Initializing on One Line

You can use two different array-specific syntax shortcuts both to initialize (put explicit values into an array's elements) and construct (instantiate the array object itself) in a single statement. The first is used to declare, create, and initialize in one statement, as follows:

```
1.  int x = 9;
2.  int[] dots = {6,x,8};
```

Line 2 in the preceding code does four things:

- Declares an `int` array reference variable named `dots`.
- Creates an `int` array with a length of three (three elements).
- Populates the array's elements with the values 6, 9, and 8.
- Assigns the new array object to the reference variable `dots`.

The size (length of the array) is determined by the number of comma-separated items between the curly braces. The code is functionally equivalent to the following longer code:

```
int[] dots;
dots = new int[3];
int x = 9;
dots[0] = 6;
dots[1] = x;
dots[2] = 8;
```

This begs the question, "Why would anyone use the longer way?" One reason comes to mind. You might not know—at the time you create the array—the values that will be assigned to the array's elements.

With object references rather than primitives, it works exactly the same way:

```
Dog puppy = new Dog("Frodo");
Dog[] myDogs = {puppy, new Dog("Clover"), new Dog("Aiko")};
```

The preceding code creates one `Dog` array, referenced by the variable `myDogs`, with a length of three elements. It assigns a previously created `Dog` object (assigned to the reference variable `puppy`) to the first element in the array. It also creates two new `Dog` objects (`Clover` and `Aiko`) and adds them to the last two `Dog` reference variable elements in the `myDogs` array. This array shortcut alone (combined with the stimulating prose) is worth the price of this book. Figure 5-6 shows the result.

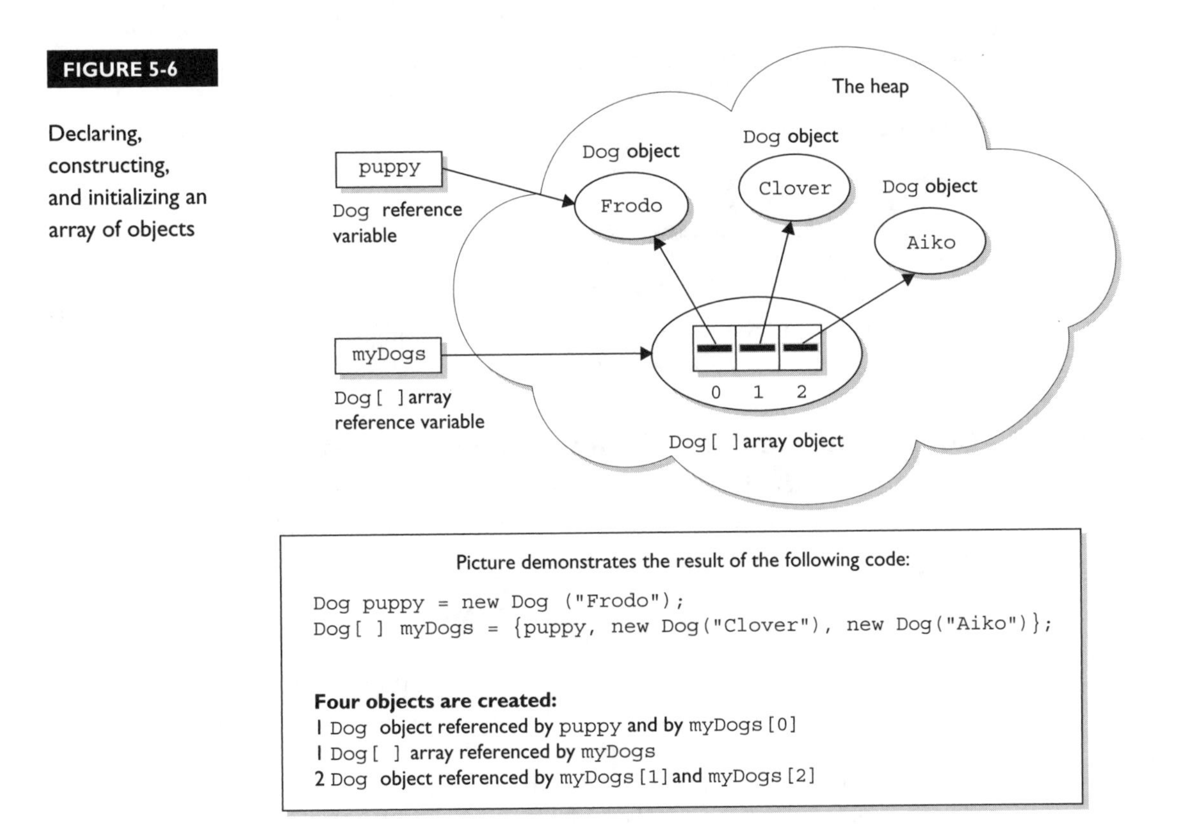
The heap
Dog object
Dog object
Dog object
puppy
Frodo
Clover
Aiko
Dog reference variable
myDogs
0 1 2
Dog[ ] array reference variable
Dog[ ] array object
Picture demonstrates the result of the following code:
Dog puppy = new Dog ("Frodo");
Dog[ ] myDogs = {puppy, new Dog("Clover"), new Dog("Aiko")};
Four objects are created:
1 Dog object referenced by puppy and by myDogs[0]
1 Dog[ ] array referenced by myDogs
2 Dog object referenced by myDogs[1] and myDogs[2]

FIGURE 5-6 Declaring, constructing, and initializing an array of objects

You can also use the shortcut syntax with multidimensional arrays, as follows:

```
int[][] scores = {{5,2,4,7}, {9,2}, {3,4}};
```

This code creates a total of four objects on the heap. First, an array of int arrays is constructed (the object that will be assigned to the scores reference variable). The scores array has a length of three, derived from the number of comma-separated items between the outer curly braces. Each of the three elements in the scores array is a reference variable to an int array, so the three int arrays are constructed and assigned to the three elements in the scores array.

The size of each of the three int arrays is derived from the number of items within the corresponding inner curly braces. For example, the first array has a length of four, the second array has a length of two, and the third array has a length of two. So far, we have four objects: one array of int arrays (each element is a reference to an int array), and three int arrays (each element in the three int arrays is an int value). Finally, the three int arrays are initialized with the actual int values within the inner curly braces. Thus, the first int array contains the values 5,2,4,7. The following code shows the values of some of the elements in this two-dimensional array:

```
scores[0]      // an array of 4 ints
scores[1]      // an array of 2 ints
scores[2]      // an array of 2 ints
scores[0][1]   // the int value 2
scores[2][1]   // the int value 4
```

Figure 5-7 shows the result of declaring, constructing, and initializing a two-dimensional array in one statement.

Constructing and Initializing an Anonymous Array

The second shortcut is called "anonymous array creation" and can be used to construct and initialize an array, and then assign the array to a previously declared array reference variable:

```
int[] testScores;
testScores = new int[] {4,7,2};
```

The preceding code creates a new int array with three elements; initializes the three elements with the values 4, 7, and 2; and then assigns the new array to the previously declared int array reference variable testScores. We call this anonymous array creation because with this syntax, you don't even need to assign the new array to anything. Maybe you're wondering, "What good is an array if you don't assign it to a reference variable?" You can use it to create a just-in-time array to use, for example, as an argument to a method that takes an array parameter. The following code demonstrates a just-in-time array argument:

```
public class JIT {
  void takesAnArray(int[] someArray) {
    // use the array parameter
  }
  public static void main (String [] args) {
    JIT j = new JIT();
    j.takesAnArray(new int[] {7,7,8,2,5});   // pass an array
  }
}
```

FIGURE 5-7

Declaring, constructing, and initializing a two-dimensional array

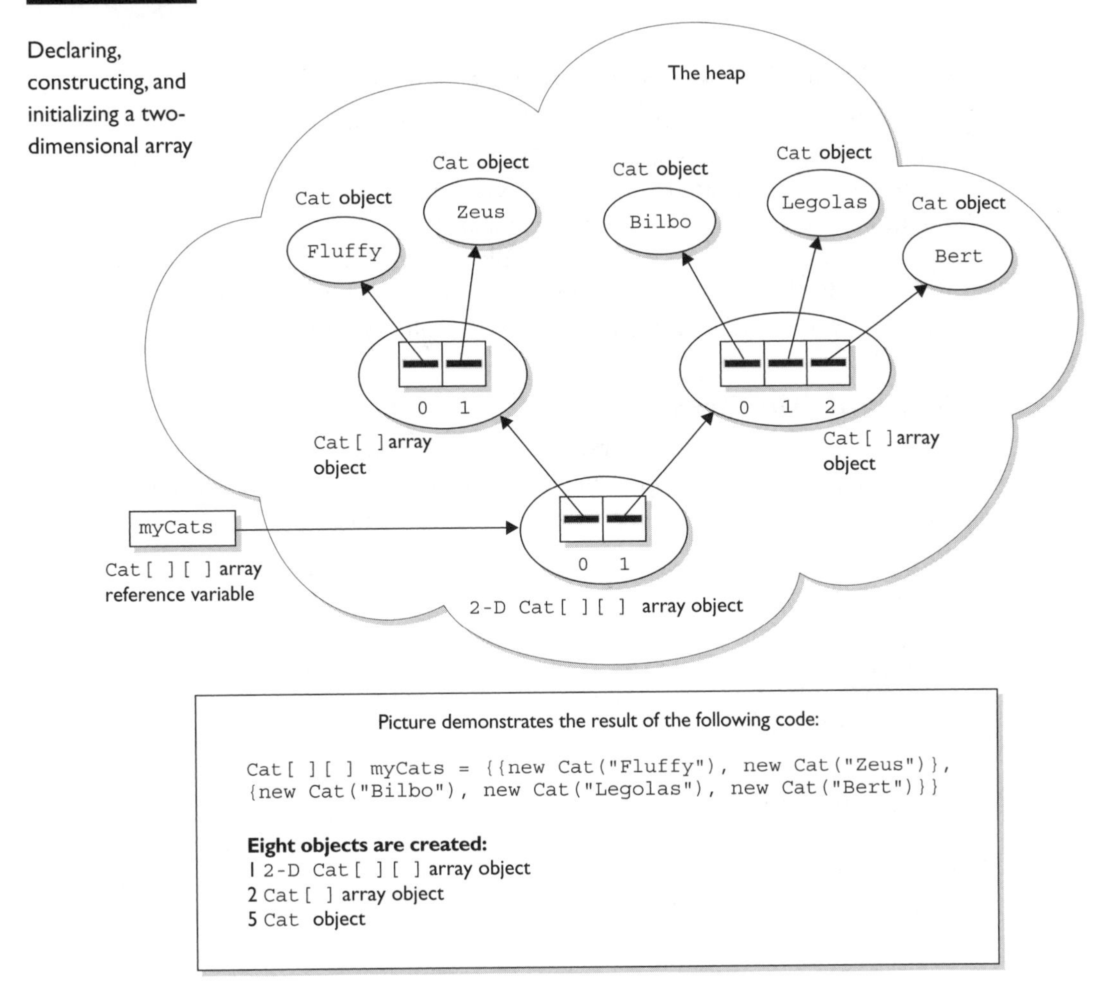

Picture demonstrates the result of the following code:

```
Cat[ ][ ] myCats = {{new Cat("Fluffy"), new Cat("Zeus")},
{new Cat("Bilbo"), new Cat("Legolas"), new Cat("Bert")}}
```

Eight objects are created:

1 2-D Cat[ ][ ] array object
2 Cat[ ] array object
5 Cat object

exam watch

Remember that you do not specify a size when using anonymous array creation syntax. The size is derived from the number of items (comma-separated) between the curly braces. Pay very close attention to the array syntax used in exam questions (and there will be a lot of them). You might see syntax such as this:

```
new Object[3] {null, new Object(), new Object()};
  // not legal; size must not be specified
```

Legal Array Element Assignments

What can you put in a particular array? For the exam, you need to know that arrays can have only one declared type (`int[]`, `Dog[]`, `String[]`, and so on), but that doesn't necessarily mean that only objects or primitives of the declared type can be assigned to the array elements. And what about the array reference itself? What kind of array object can be assigned to a particular array reference? For the exam, you'll need to know the answers to all of these questions. And, as if by magic, we're actually covering those very same topics in the following sections. Pay attention.

Arrays of Primitives

Primitive arrays can accept any value that can be promoted implicitly to the declared type of the array. For example, an `int` array can hold any value that can fit into a 32-bit `int` variable. Thus, the following code is legal:

```
int[] weightList = new int[5];
byte b = 4;
char c = 'c';
short s = 7;
weightList[0] = b;  // OK, byte is smaller than int
weightList[1] = c;  // OK, char is smaller than int
weightList[2] = s;  // OK, short is smaller than int
```

Arrays of Object References

If the declared array type is a class, you can put objects of any subclass of the declared type into the array. For example, if `Subaru` is a subclass of `Car`, you can put both `Subaru` objects and `Car` objects into an array of type `Car` as follows:

```
class Car {}
class Subaru extends Car {}
class Ferrari extends Car {}
...
Car [] myCars = {new Subaru(), new Car(), new Ferrari()};
```

It helps to remember that the elements in a `Car` array are nothing more than `Car` reference variables. So anything that can be assigned to a `Car` reference variable can be legally assigned to a `Car` array element.

If the array is declared as an interface type, the array elements can refer to any instance of any class that implements the declared interface. The following code demonstrates the use of an interface as an array type:

```
interface Sporty {
  void beSporty();
}
class Ferrari extends Car implements Sporty {
  public void beSporty() {
    // implement cool sporty method in a Ferrari-specific way
  }
}
class RacingFlats extends AthleticShoe implements Sporty {
  public void beSporty() {
    // implement cool sporty method in a RacingFlat-specific way
  }
}
class GolfClub { }
class TestSportyThings {
  public static void main (String [] args) {
    Sporty[] sportyThings = new Sporty [3];
    sportyThings[0] = new Ferrari();      // OK, Ferrari
                                          // implements Sporty
    sportyThings[1] = new RacingFlats();  // OK, RacingFlats
                                          // implements Sporty
    sportyThings[2] = new GolfClub();     // NOT ok..

        // Not OK; GolfClub does not implement Sporty
        // I don't care what anyone says
  }
}
```

The bottom line is this: Any object that passes the IS-A test for the declared array type can be assigned to an element of that array.

Array Reference Assignments for One-Dimensional Arrays

For the exam, you need to recognize legal and illegal assignments for array reference variables. We're not talking about references in the array (in other words, array elements), but rather references to the array object. For example, if you declare an `int` array, the reference variable you declared can be reassigned to any `int` array (of any size), but the variable cannot be reassigned to anything that is not an `int` array, including an `int` value. Remember, all arrays are objects, so an `int` array reference cannot refer to an `int` primitive. The following code demonstrates legal and illegal assignments for primitive arrays:

```
int[] splats;
int[] dats = new int[4];
char[] letters = new char[5];
splats = dats;     // OK, dats refers to an int array
splats = letters; // NOT OK, letters refers to a char array
```

It's tempting to assume that because a variable of type `byte`, `short`, or `char` can be explicitly promoted and assigned to an `int`, an array of any of those types could be assigned to an `int` array. You can't do that in Java, but it would be just like those cruel, heartless (but otherwise attractive) exam developers to put tricky array assignment questions in the exam.

Arrays that hold object references, as opposed to primitives, aren't as restrictive. Just as you can put a `Honda` object in a `Car` array (because `Honda` extends `Car`), you can assign an array of type `Honda` to a `Car` array reference variable as follows:

```
Car[] cars;
Honda[] cuteCars = new Honda[5];
cars = cuteCars;    // OK because Honda is a type of Car
Beer[] beers = new Beer [99];
cars = beers;       // NOT OK, Beer is not a type of Car
```

Apply the IS-A test to help sort the legal from the illegal. Honda IS-A Car, so a `Honda` array can be assigned to a `Car` array. Beer IS-A Car is not true; `Beer` does not extend `Car` (plus it doesn't make sense, unless you've already had too much of it).

The rules for array assignment apply to interfaces as well as classes. An array declared as an interface type can reference an array of any type that implements the interface. Remember, any object from a class implementing a particular interface will pass the IS-A (`instanceof`) test for that interface. For example, if `Box` implements `Foldable`, the following is legal:

```
Foldable[]  foldingThings;
Box[] boxThings = new Box[3];
foldingThings = boxThings;
// OK, Box implements Foldable, so Box IS-A Foldable
```

exam watch

You cannot reverse the legal assignments. A `Car` array cannot be assigned to a `Honda` array. A `Car` is not necessarily a `Honda`, so if you've declared a `Honda` array, it might blow up if you assigned a `Car` array to the `Honda` reference variable. Think about it: a `Car` array could hold a reference to a `Ferrari`, so someone who thinks they have an array of `Honda`s could suddenly find themselves with a `Ferrari`. Remember that the IS-A test can be checked in code using the `instanceof` operator.

Array Reference Assignments for Multidimensional Arrays

When you assign an array to a previously declared array reference, the array you're assigning must be in the same dimension as the reference you're assigning it to. For example, a two-dimensional array of `int` arrays cannot be assigned to a regular `int` array reference, as follows:

```
int[] blots;
int[][] squeegees = new int[3][];
blots = squeegees;          // NOT OK, squeegees is a
                            // two-d array of int arrays
int[] blocks = new int[6];
blots = blocks;             // OK, blocks is an int array
```

Pay particular attention to array assignments using different dimensions. You might, for example, be asked if it's legal to assign an `int` array to the first element in an array of `int` arrays, as follows:

```
int[][]  books = new int[3][];
int[] numbers = new int[6];
int aNumber = 7;
books[0] = aNumber;      // NO, expecting an int array not an int
books[0] = numbers;      // OK, numbers is an int array
```

Figure 5-8 shows an example of legal and illegal assignments for references to an array.

FIGURE 5-8 Legal and illegal array assignments

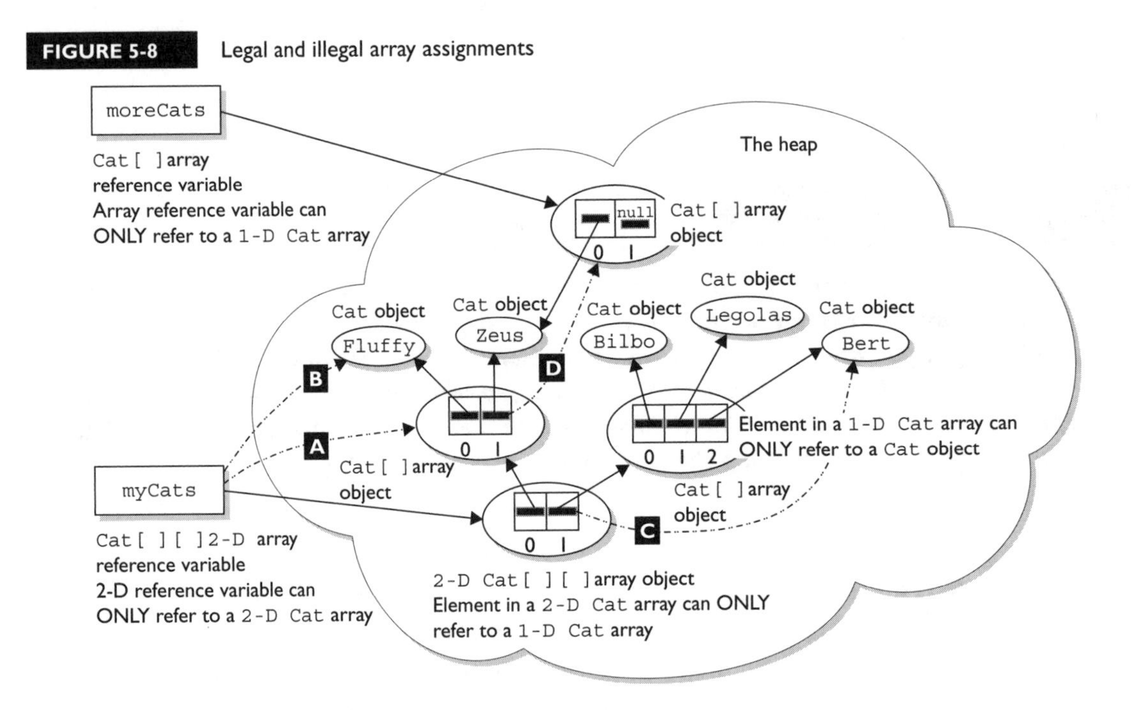

Illegal Array Reference Assignments

A `myCats = myCats[0];`
```
// Can't assign a 1-D array to a 2-D array reference
```

B `myCats = myCats[0][0];`
```
// Can't assign a nonarray object to a 2-D array reference
```

C `myCats[1] = myCats[1][2];`
```
// Can't assign a nonarray object to a 1-D array reference
```

D `myCats[0][1] = moreCats;`
```
// Can't assign an array object to a nonarray reference
// myCats[0][1] can only refer to a Cat object
```

KEY

Legal (solid arrow)

Illegal (dashed arrow)

CERTIFICATION OBJECTIVE

Using ArrayList (OCA Objective 4.3)

4.3 Declare and use an ArrayList.

Data structures are a part of almost every application you'll ever work on. The Java API provides an extensive range of classes that support common data structures such as `Lists`, `Sets`, `Maps`, *and* `Queues`. For the purpose of the OCA exam, you should remember that the classes that support these common data structures are a part of what is known as "The Collection API" (one of its many aliases). (The OCP exam covers the most common implementations of all the structures listed above, which, along with the Collection API, we'll discuss in Chapter 11.)

When to Use ArrayLists

We've already talked about arrays. Arrays seem useful and pretty darned flexible. So why do we need more functionality than arrays provide? Consider these two situations:

- You need to be able to increase and decrease the size of your list of things.
- The order of things in your list is important and might change.

Both of these situations can be handled with arrays, but it's not easy....

Suppose you want to plan a vacation to Europe? You have several destinations in mind (Paris, Oslo, Rome), but you're not yet sure in what order you want to visit these cities, and as your planning progresses you might want to add or subtract cities from your list. Let's say your first idea is to travel from north to south, so your list looks like this:

Oslo, Paris, Rome.

If we were using an array, we could start with this:

```
String[] cities = {"Oslo", "Paris", "Rome"};
```

But now imagine that you remember that you REALLY want to go to London too! You've got two problems:

- Your cities array is already full.
- If you're going from north to south, you need to insert London before Paris.

Of course, you can figure out a way to do this. Maybe you create a second array, and you copy cities from one array to the other, and at the correct moment you add London to the second array. Doable, but difficult.

Now let's see how you could do the same thing with an `ArrayList`:

```
import java.util.*;                               // ArrayList lives in .util
public class Cities {
  public static void main(String[] args) {

    List<String> c = new ArrayList<String>();  // create an ArrayList, c
    c.add("Oslo");                             // add original cities
    c.add("Paris");
    c.add("Rome");
    int index = c.indexOf("Paris");            // find Paris' index
    System.out.println(c + " " + index);
    c.add(index, "London");                    // add London before Paris
    System.out.println(c);                     // show the contents of c
  }
}
```

The output will be something like this:

```
[Oslo, Paris, Rome] 1
[Oslo, London, Paris, Rome]
```

By reviewing the code, we can learn some important facts about `ArrayLists`:

- The `ArrayList` class is in the java.util package.
- Similar to arrays, when you build an `ArrayList` you have to declare what kind of objects it can contain. In this case, we're building an `ArrayList` of `String` objects. (We'll look at the line of code that creates the `ArrayList` in a lot more detail in a minute.)
- `ArrayList` implements the List interface.
- We work with the `ArrayList` through methods. In this case we used a couple of versions of `add()`, we used `indexOf()`, and, indirectly, we used `toString()` to display the `ArrayList`'s contents. (More on `toString()` in a minute.)
- Like arrays, indexes for `ArrayLists` are zero-based.
- We didn't declare how big the `ArrayList` was when we built it.
- We were able to add a new element to the `ArrayList` on the fly.
- We were able to add the new element in the middle of the list.
- The `ArrayList` maintained its order.

As promised, we need to look at the following line of code more closely:

```
List<String> c = new ArrayList<String>();
```

First off, we see that this is a polymorphic declaration. As we said earlier, `ArrayList` implements the `List` interface (also in java.util). If you plan to take the OCP 7 exam after you've aced the OCA 7, we'll be talking a lot more about why we might want to do a polymorphic declaration in the OCP part of the book. For now, imagine that someday you might want to create a `List` of your `ArrayLists`.

Next we have this weird looking syntax with the < and > characters. This syntax was added to the language in Java 5, and it has to do with "generics." Generics aren't really included in the OCA exam, so we don't want to spend a lot of time on them here, but what's important to know is that this is how you tell the compiler and the JVM that for this particular `ArrayList` you want only `Strings` to be allowed. What this means is that if the compiler can tell that you're trying to add a "not-a-`String`" object to this `ArrayList`, your code won't compile. This is a good thing!

Also as promised, let's look at THIS line of code:

```
System.out.println(c);
```

Remember that all classes ultimately inherit from class `Object`. Class `Object` contains a method called `toString()`. Again, `toString()` isn't "officially" on the OCA exam (of course it IS in the OCP exam!), but you need to understand it a bit for now. When you pass an object reference to either `System.out.print()` or `System.out.println()`, you're telling them to invoke that object's `toString()` method. (Whenever you make a new class, you can optionally override the `toString()` method your class inherited from `Object`, to show useful information about your class's objects.) The API developers were nice enough to override `ArrayList`'s `toString()` method for you to show the contents of the `ArrayList`, as you saw in the program's output. Hooray!

ArrayLists and Duplicates

As you're planning your trip to Europe, you realize that halfway through your stay in Rome, there's going to be a fantastic music festival in Naples! Naples is just down the coast from Rome! You've got to add that side trip to your itinerary. The question is, can an `ArrayList` have duplicate entries? Is it legal to say this:

```
c.add("Rome");
c.add("Naples");
c.add("Rome");
```

And the short answer is: **Yes, ArrayLists can have duplicates**. Now if you stop and think about it, the notion of "duplicate Java objects" is actually a bit tricky. Relax, because you won't have to get into that trickiness until you study for the OCP 7.

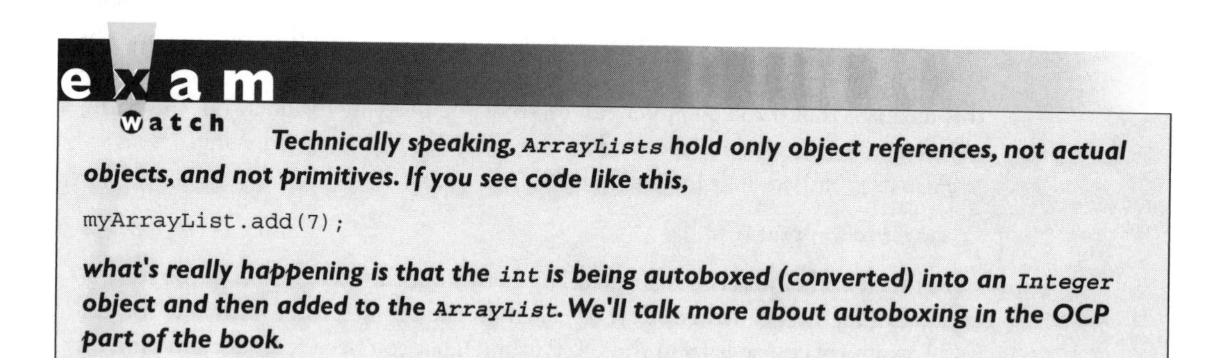

Technically speaking, `ArrayLists` hold only object references, not actual objects, and not primitives. If you see code like this,

```
myArrayList.add(7);
```

what's really happening is that the `int` is being autoboxed (converted) into an `Integer` object and then added to the `ArrayList`. We'll talk more about autoboxing in the OCP part of the book.

ArrayList Methods in Action

Let's look at another piece of code that shows off most of the `ArrayList` methods you need to know for the exam:

```
import java.util.*;
public class TweakLists {
  public static void main(String[] args) {

    List<String> myList = new ArrayList<String>();

    myList.add("z");
    myList.add("x");
    myList.add(1, "y");              // zero based
    myList.add(0, "w");              //  "     "
    System.out.println(myList);      // [w, z, y, x]

    myList.clear();                  // remove everything
    myList.add("b");
    myList.add("a");
```

```
    myList.add("c");
    System.out.println(myList);      // [b, a, c]
    System.out.println(myList.contains("a") + " " + myList.contains("x"));

    System.out.println("get 1: " + myList.get(1));
    System.out.println("index of c: " + myList.indexOf("c"));

    myList.remove(1);                // remove "a"
    System.out.println("size: " + myList.size() + " contents: " + myList);
  }
}
```

which should produce something like this:

```
[w, z, y, x]
[b, a, c]
true false
get 1: a
index of c: 2
size: 2 contents: [b, c]
```

A couple of quick notes about this code: First off, notice that `contains()` returns a boolean. This makes `contains()` great to use in "if" tests. Second, notice that `ArrayList` has a `size()` method. It's important to remember that arrays have a length attribute and `ArrayLists` have a `size()` method.

Important Methods in the ArrayList Class

The following methods are some of the more commonly used methods in the `ArrayList` class and also those that you're most likely to encounter on the exam:

- **`add(element)`** Adds this element to the **end** of the `ArrayList`
- **`add(index, element)`** Adds this element at the index point and shifts the remaining elements back (for example, what was at `index` is now at `index + 1`)
- **`clear()`** Removes all the elements from the `ArrayList`
- **`boolean contains(element)`** Returns whether the `element` is in the list
- **`Object get(index)`** Returns the `Object` located at `index`
- **`int indexOf(Object)`** Returns the (`int`) location of the element, or `-1` if the `Object` is not found
- **`remove(index)`** Removes the element at that `index` and shifts later elements toward the beginning one space

- **`remove(Object)`** Removes the **first** occurrence of the `Object` and shifts later elements toward the beginning one space
- **`int size()`** Returns the number of elements in the `ArrayList`
- To summarize, the OCA 7 exam tests only for very basic knowledge of `ArrayLists`. If you go on to take the OCP 7 exam, you'll learn a lot more about `ArrayLists` and other common, collections-oriented classes.

Encapsulation for Reference Variables

In Chapter 2 we began our discussion of the object-oriented concept of encapsulation. At that point we limited our discussion to protecting a class's primitive fields and (immutable) `String` fields. Now that you've learned more about what it means to "pass-by-copy" and we've looked at non-primitive ways of handling data such as arrays, `StringBuilders`, and `ArrayLists`, it's time to take a closer look at encapsulation.

Let's say we have some special data whose value we're saving in a `StringBuilder`. We're happy to share the value with other programmers, but we don't want them to change the value:

```
class Special {
  private StringBuilder s = new StringBuilder("bob");   // our special data
  StringBuilder getName() { return s; }
  void printName() { System.out.println(s); }           // verify our special
                                                        // data
}
public class TestSpecial {
  public static void main(String[] args) {
    Special sp = new Special();
    StringBuilder s2 = sp.getName();
    s2.append("fred");
    sp.printName();
  }
}
```

When we run the code we get this:

```
bobfred
```

Uh oh! It looks like we practiced good encapsulation techniques by making our field private and providing a "getter" method, but based on the output, it's clear that we didn't do a very good job of protecting the data in the `Special` class. Can you figure out why? Take a minute....

Okay—just to verify your answer—**when we invoke `getName()`, we do in fact return a copy, just like Java always does**. But, we're **not** returning a copy of the `StringBuilder` object; **we're returning a copy of the reference variable** that points to (I know) the one-and-only `StringBuilder` object we ever built. So, at the point that `getName()` returns, we have one `StringBuilder` object and two reference variables pointing to it (`s` and `s2`).

For the purpose of the OCA exam, the key point is this: When encapsulating a mutable object like a `StringBuilder`, or an array, or an `ArrayList`, if you want to let outside classes have a copy of the object, you must actually copy the object and return a reference variable to the object that is a copy. If all you do is return a copy of the original object's reference variable, you **DO NOT** have encapsulation.

CERTIFICATION SUMMARY

The most important thing to remember about `String`s is that `String` objects are immutable, but references to `String`s are not! You can make a new `String` by using an existing `String` as a starting point, but if you don't assign a reference variable to the new `String` it will be lost to your program—you will have no way to access your new `String`. Review the important methods in the `String` class.

The `StringBuilder` class was added in Java 5. It has exactly the same methods as the old `StringBuffer` class, except `StringBuilder`'s methods aren't thread-safe. Because `StringBuilder`'s methods are not thread-safe, they tend to run faster than `StringBuffer` methods, so choose `StringBuilder` whenever threading is not an issue. Both `StringBuffer` and `StringBuilder` objects can have their value changed over and over without your having to create new objects. If you're doing a lot of string manipulation, these objects will be more efficient than immutable `String` objects, which are, more or less, "use once, remain in memory forever." Remember, these methods ALWAYS change the invoking object's value, even with no explicit assignment.

The next topic was arrays. We talked about declaring, constructing, and initializing one-dimensional and multidimensional arrays. We talked about anonymous arrays and the fact that arrays of objects are actually arrays of references to objects.

Finally, we discussed the basics of `ArrayList`s. `ArrayList`s are like arrays with superpowers that allow them to grow and shrink dynamically and to make it easy for you to insert and delete elements at locations of your choosing within the list.

✓ TWO-MINUTE DRILL

Here are some of the key points from the certification objectives in this chapter.

Using String and StringBuilder (OCA Objectives 2.6 and 2.7)

- ❑ `String` objects are immutable, and `String` reference variables are not.
- ❑ If you create a new `String` without assigning it, it will be lost to your program.
- ❑ If you redirect a `String` reference to a new `String`, the old `String` can be lost.
- ❑ `String` methods use zero-based indexes, except for the second argument of `substring()`.
- ❑ The `String` class is `final`—it cannot be extended.
- ❑ When the JVM finds a `String` literal, it is added to the `String` literal pool.
- ❑ Strings have a *method* called `length()`—arrays have an *attribute* named `length`.
- ❑ `StringBuilder` objects are mutable—they can change without creating a new object.
- ❑ `StringBuilder` methods act on the invoking object, and objects can change without an explicit assignment in the statement.
- ❑ Remember that chained methods are evaluated from left to right.
- ❑ `String` methods to remember: `charAt()`, `concat()`, `equalsIgnoreCase()`, `length()`, `replace()`, `substring()`, `toLowerCase()`, `toString()`, `toUpperCase()`, and `trim()`.
- ❑ `StringBuilder` methods to remember: `append()`, `delete()`, `insert()`, `reverse()`, and `toString()`.

Using Arrays (OCA Objectives 4.1 and 4.2)

- ❑ Arrays can hold primitives or objects, but the array itself is always an object.
- ❑ When you declare an array, the brackets can be to the left or right of the name.
- ❑ It is never legal to include the size of an array in the declaration.
- ❑ You must include the size of an array when you construct it (using `new`) unless you are creating an anonymous array.
- ❑ Elements in an array of objects are not automatically created, although primitive array elements are given default values.
- ❑ You'll get a `NullPointerException` if you try to use an array element in an object array, if that element does not refer to a real object.

- Arrays are indexed beginning with zero.
- An `ArrayIndexOutOfBoundsException` occurs if you use a bad index value.
- Arrays have a `length` attribute whose value is the number of array elements.
- The last index you can access is always one less than the length of the array.
- Multidimensional arrays are just arrays of arrays.
- The dimensions in a multidimensional array can have different lengths.
- An array of primitives can accept any value that can be promoted implicitly to the array's declared type—for example, a `byte` variable can go in an `int` array.
- An array of objects can hold any object that passes the IS-A (or `instanceof`) test for the declared type of the array. For example, if `Horse` extends `Animal`, then a `Horse` object can go into an `Animal` array.
- If you assign an array to a previously declared array reference, the array you're assigning must be the same dimension as the reference you're assigning it to.
- You can assign an array of one type to a previously declared array reference of one of its supertypes. For example, a `Honda` array can be assigned to an array declared as type `Car` (assuming `Honda` extends `Car`).

Using ArrayList (OCA Objective 4.3)

- `ArrayLists` allow you to resize your list and make insertions and deletions to your list far more easily than arrays.
- For the OCA 7 exam, the only `ArrayList` declarations you need to know are of this form:

```
ArrayList<type> myList = new ArrayList<type>();
List<type> myList2 = new ArrayList<type>();  // polymorphic
```

- `ArrayLists` can hold only objects, not primitives, but remember that autoboxing can make it look like you're adding primitives to an `ArrayList` when in fact you're adding a wrapper version of a primitive.
- An `ArrayList`'s index starts at 0.
- `ArrayLists` can have duplicate entries. Note: Determining whether two objects are duplicates is trickier than it seems and doesn't come up until the OCP 7 exam.
- `ArrayList` methods to remember: `add(element)`, `add(index, element)`, `clear()`, `contains()`, `get(index)`, `indexOf()`, `remove(index)`, `remove(object)`, and `size()`.

SELF TEST

1. Given:

```
public class Mutant {
  public static void main(String[] args) {
    StringBuilder sb = new StringBuilder("abc");
    String s = "abc";
    sb.reverse().append("d");
    s.toUpperCase().concat("d");
    System.out.println("." + sb + ". ." + s + ".");
  }
}
```

Which two substrings will be included in the result? (Choose two.)

A. `.abc.`

B. `.ABCd.`

C. `.ABCD.`

D. `.cbad.`

E. `.dcba.`

2. Given:

```
public class Hilltop {
  public static void main(String[] args) {
    String[] horses = new String[5];
    horses[4] = null;
    for(int i = 0; i < horses.length; i++) {
      if(i < args.length)
        horses[i] = args[i];
      System.out.print(horses[i].toUpperCase() + " ");
    }
  }
}
```

And, if the code compiles, the command line:

```
java Hilltop eyra vafi draumur kara
```

What is the result?

A. `EYRA VAFI DRAUMUR KARA`

B. `EYRA VAFI DRAUMUR KARA null`

C. An exception is thrown with no other output

D. `EYRA VAFI DRAUMUR KARA`, and then a `NullPointerException`

E. `EYRA VAFI DRAUMUR KARA`, and then an `ArrayIndexOutOfBoundsException`

F. Compilation fails

3. Given:

```
public class Actors {
  public static void main(String[] args) {
    char[] ca = {0x4e, \u004e, 78};
    System.out.println((ca[0] == ca[1]) + " " + (ca[0] == ca[2]));
  }
}
```

What is the result?

A. `true true`

B. `true false`

C. `false true`

D. `false false`

E. Compilation fails

4. Given:

```
1. class Dims {
2.   public static void main(String[] args) {
3.     int[][] a = {{1,2}, {3,4}};
4.     int[] b = (int[]) a[1];
5.     Object o1 = a;
6.     int[][] a2 = (int[][]) o1;
7.     int[] b2 = (int[]) o1;
8.     System.out.println(b[1]);
9. } }
```

What is the result? (Choose all that apply.)

A. `2`

B. `4`

C. An exception is thrown at runtime

D. Compilation fails due to an error on line 4

E. Compilation fails due to an error on line 5

F. Compilation fails due to an error on line 6

G. Compilation fails due to an error on line 7

5. Given:

```
import java.util.*;
public class Sequence {
  public static void main(String[] args) {
    ArrayList<String> myList = new ArrayList<String>();
    myList.add("apple");
    myList.add("carrot");
    myList.add("banana");
    myList.add(1, "plum");
    System.out.print(myList);
  }
}
```

What is the result?

A. `[apple, banana, carrot, plum]`

B. `[apple, plum, carrot, banana]`

C. `[apple, plum, banana, carrot]`

D. `[plum, banana, carrot, apple]`

E. `[plum, apple, carrot, banana]`

F. `[banana, plum, carrot, apple]`

G. Compilation fails

6. Given:

```
 3. class Dozens {
 4.   int[] dz = {1,2,3,4,5,6,7,8,9,10,11,12};
 5. }
 6. public class Eggs {
 7.   public static void main(String[] args) {
 8.     Dozens [] da = new Dozens[3];
 9.     da[0] = new Dozens();
10.     Dozens d = new Dozens();
11.     da[1] = d;
12.     d = null;
13.     da[1] = null;
14.     // do stuff
15.   }
16. }
```

Which two are true about the objects created within `main()`, and which are eligible for garbage collection when line 14 is reached?

A. Three objects were created
B. Four objects were created
C. Five objects were created
D. Zero objects are eligible for GC
E. One object is eligible for GC
F. Two objects are eligible for GC
G. Three objects are eligible for GC

7. Given:

```
public class Tailor {
  public static void main(String[] args) {
    byte[][] ba = {{1,2,3,4}, {1,2,3}};
    System.out.println(ba[1].length + " " + ba.length);
  }
}
```

What is the result?

A. `2 4`
B. `2 7`
C. `3 2`
D. `3 7`
E. `4 2`
F. `4 7`
G. Compilation fails

8. Given:

```
 3. public class Theory {
 4.   public static void main(String[] args) {
 5.     String s1 = "abc";
 6.     String s2 = s1;
 7.     s1 += "d";
 8.     System.out.println(s1 + " " + s2 + " " + (s1==s2));
 9.
10.     StringBuilder sb1 = new StringBuilder("abc");
11.     StringBuilder sb2 = sb1;
12.     sb1.append("d");
13.     System.out.println(sb1 + " " + sb2 + " " + (sb1==sb2));
14.   }
15. }
```

Which are true? (Choose all that apply.)

A. Compilation fails

B. The first line of output is `abc abc true`

C. The first line of output is `abc abc false`

D. The first line of output is `abcd abc false`

E. The second line of output is `abcd abc false`

F. The second line of output is `abcd abcd true`

G. The second line of output is `abcd abcd false`

9. Given:

```
public class Mounds {
  public static void main(String[] args) {
    StringBuilder sb = new StringBuilder();
    String s = new String();
    for(int i = 0; i < 1000; i++) {
      s = " " + i;
      sb.append(s);
    }
    // done with loop
  }
}
```

If the garbage collector does NOT run while this code is executing, approximately how many objects will exist in memory when the loop is done?

A. Less than 10

B. About 1000

C. About 2000

D. About 3000

E. About 4000

10. Given:

```
 3. class Box {
 4.   int size;
 5.   Box(int s) { size = s; }
 6. }
 7. public class Laser {
 8.   public static void main(String[] args) {
 9.     Box b1 = new Box(5);
10.     Box[] ba = go(b1, new Box(6));
11.     ba[0] = b1;
```

```
12.     for(Box b : ba) System.out.print(b.size + " ");
13.   }
14.   static Box[] go(Box b1, Box b2) {
15.     b1.size = 4;
16.     Box[] ma = {b2, b1};
17.     return ma;
18.   }
19. }
```

What is the result?

A. `4 4`

B. `5 4`

C. `6 4`

D. `4 5`

E. `5 5`

F. Compilation fails

11. Given:

```
public class Hedges {
  public static void main(String[] args) {
    String s = "JAVA";
    s = s + "rocks";
    s = s.substring(4,8);
    s.toUpperCase();
    System.out.println(s);
  }
}
```

What is the result?

A. `JAVA`

B. `JAVAROCKS`

C. `rocks`

D. `rock`

E. `ROCKS`

F. `ROCK`

G. Compilation fails

12. Given:

```
 1. import java.util.*;
 2. class Fortress {
 3.   private String name;
 4.   private ArrayList<Integer> list;
 5.   Fortress() { list = new ArrayList<Integer>(); }
 6.
 7.   String getName() { return name; }
 8.   void addToList(int x) { list.add(x); }
 9.   ArrayList getList() { return list; }
10. }
```

Which lines of code (if any) break encapsulation? (Choose all that apply.)

A. Line 3

B. Line 4

C. Line 5

D. Line 7

E. Line 8

F. Line 9

G. The class is already well encapsulated

SELF TEST ANSWERS

1. ☑ A and D are correct. The `String` operations are working on a new (lost) `String` not `String s`. The `StringBuilder` operations work from left to right.
   ☒ B, C, and E are incorrect based on the above. (OCA Objectives 2.6 and 2.7)

2. ☑ D is correct. The `horses` array's first four elements contain `Strings`, but the fifth is null, so the `toUpperCase()` invocation for the fifth element throws a `NullPointerException`.
   ☒ A, B, C, E, and F are incorrect based on the above. (OCA Objectives 2.7 and 4.1)

3. ☑ E is correct. The Unicode declaration must be enclosed in single quotes: `'\u004e'`. If this were done, the answer would be A, but knowing that equality isn't on the OCA exam.
   ☒ A, B, C, and D are incorrect based on the above. (OCA Objectives 2.1 and 4.1)

4. ☑ C is correct. A `ClassCastException` is thrown at line 7 because `o1` refers to an `int[][]`, not an `int[]`. If line 7 were removed, the output would be 4.
   ☒ A, B, D, E, F, and G are incorrect based on the above. (OCA Objectives 4.2 and 7.4)

5. ☑ B is correct. `ArrayList` elements are automatically inserted in the order of entry; they are not automatically sorted. `ArrayLists` use zero-based indexes and the last `add()` inserts a new element and shifts the remaining elements back.
   ☒ A, C, D, E, F, and G are incorrect based on the above. (OCA Objective 4.3)

6. ☑ C and F are correct. `da` refers to an object of type "Dozens array" and each `Dozens` object that is created comes with its own "`int` array" object. When line 14 is reached, only the second `Dozens` object (and its "`int` array" object) are not reachable.
   ☒ A, B, D, E, and G are incorrect based on the above. (OCA Objectives 4.1 and 2.4)

7. ☑ C is correct. A two-dimensional array is an "array of arrays." The length of `ba` is 2 because it contains two, one-dimensional arrays. Array indexes are zero-based, so `ba[1]` refers to `ba`'s second array.
   ☒ A, B, D, E, F, and G are incorrect based on the above. (OCA Objective 4.2)

8. ☑ D and F are correct. Although `String` objects are immutable, references to `Strings` are mutable. The code `s1 += "d";` creates a new `String` object. `StringBuilder` objects are mutable, so the append() is changing the single `StringBuilder` object to which both `StringBuilder` references refer.
   ☒ A, B, C, E, and G are incorrect based on the above. (OCA Objectives 2.6 and 2.7)

9. ☑ B is correct. `StringBuilders` are mutable, so all of the `append()` invocations are acting upon the same `StringBuilder` object over and over. `Strings`, however, are immutable, so every `String` concatenation operation results in a new `String` object. Also, the string `" "` is created once and reused in every loop iteration.
   ☒ A, C, D, and E are incorrect based on the above. (OCA Objectives 2.6 and 2.7)

10. ☑ A is correct. Although `main()`'s `b1` is a different reference variable than `go()`'s `b1`, they refer to the same `Box` object.
☒ B, C, D, E, and F are incorrect based on the above. (OCA Objectives 4.1, 6.1, and 6.8)

11. ☑ D is correct. The `substring()` invocation uses a zero-based index and the second argument is exclusive, so the character at index 8 is NOT included. The `toUpperCase()` invocation makes a new `String` object that is instantly lost. The `toUpperCase()` invocation does NOT affect the `String` referred to by `s`.
☒ A, B, C, E, F, and G are incorrect based on the above. (OCA Objectives 2.6 and 2.7)

12. ☑ F is correct. When encapsulating a mutable object like an `ArrayList`, your getter must return a reference to a copy of the object, not just the reference to the original object.
☒ A, B, C, D, E, and G are incorrect based on the above. (OCA Objective 6.7)

6

Flow Control and Exceptions

CERTIFICATION OBJECTIVES

- Use if and switch Statements
- Develop for, do, and while Loops
- Use break and continue Statements
- Use try, catch, and finally Statements
- State the Effects of Exceptions
- Recognize Common Exceptions
- ✓ Two-Minute Drill
- Q&A Self Test

Can you imagine trying to write code using a language that didn't give you a way to execute statements conditionally? Flow control is a key part of most any useful programming language, and Java offers several ways to accomplish it. Some statements, such as `if` statements and `for` loops, are common to most languages. But Java also throws in a couple of flow control features you might not have used before—exceptions and assertions. (We'll discuss assertions in the next chapter.)

The `if` statement and the `switch` statement are types of conditional/decision controls that allow your program to behave differently at a "fork in the road," depending on the result of a logical test. Java also provides three different looping constructs—`for`, `while`, and `do`—so you can execute the same code over and over again depending on some condition being true. Exceptions give you a clean, simple way to organize code that deals with problems that might crop up at runtime.

With these tools, you can build a robust program that can handle any logical situation with grace. Expect to see a wide range of questions on the exam that include flow control as part of the question code, even on questions that aren't testing your knowledge of flow control.

CERTIFICATION OBJECTIVE

Using if and switch Statements (OCA Objectives 3.4 and 3.5—also Upgrade Objective 1.1)

3.4 *Create if and if-else constructs.*

3.5 *Use a switch statement.*

The `if` and `switch` statements are commonly referred to as decision statements. When you use decision statements in your program, you're asking the program to evaluate a given expression to determine which course of action to take. We'll look at the `if` statement first.

if-else Branching

The basic format of an `if` statement is as follows:

```
if (booleanExpression) {
  System.out.println("Inside if statement");
}
```

The expression in parentheses must evaluate to (a `boolean`) `true` or `false`. Typically you're testing something to see if it's true, and then running a code block (one or more statements) if it is true and (optionally) another block of code if it isn't. The following code demonstrates a legal `if-else` statement:

```
if (x > 3) {
  System.out.println("x is greater than 3");
} else {
  System.out.println("x is not greater than 3");
}
```

The `else` block is optional, so you can also use the following:

```
if (x > 3) {
  y = 2;
}
z += 8;
a = y + x;
```

The preceding code will assign 2 to `y` if the test succeeds (meaning `x` really is greater than 3), but the other two lines will execute regardless. Even the curly braces are optional if you have only one statement to execute within the body of the conditional block. The following code example is legal (although not recommended for readability):

```
if (x > 3)     // bad practice, but seen on the exam
  y = 2;
z += 8;
a = y + x;
```

Most developers consider it good practice to enclose blocks within curly braces, even if there's only one statement in the block. Be careful with code like the preceding, because you might think it should read as

"If `x` is greater than 3, then set `y` to 2, `z` to `z` + 8, and `a` to `y` + `x`."

But the last two lines are going to execute no matter what! They aren't part of the conditional flow. You might find it even more misleading if the code were indented as follows:

```
if (x > 3)
  y = 2;
  z += 8;
  a = y + x;
```

You might have a need to nest `if-else` statements (although, again, it's not recommended for readability, so nested `if` tests should be kept to a minimum). You can set up an `if-else` statement to test for multiple conditions. The following example uses two conditions so that if the first test fails, we want to perform a second test before deciding what to do:

```
if (price < 300) {
  buyProduct();
} else {
  if (price < 400) {
    getApproval();
  }
  else {
    dontBuyProduct();
  }
}
```

This brings up the other `if-else` construct, the `if`, `else if`, `else`. The preceding code could (and should) be rewritten like this:

```
if (price < 300) {
  buyProduct();
} else if (price < 400) {
    getApproval();
} else {
    dontBuyProduct();
}
```

There are a couple of rules for using `else` and `else if`:

- You can have zero or one `else` for a given `if`, and it must come after any `else ifs`.
- You can have zero to many `else ifs` for a given `if` and they must come before the (optional) `else`.
- Once an `else if` succeeds, none of the remaining `else ifs` nor the `else` will be tested.

The following example shows code that is horribly formatted for the real world. As you've probably guessed, it's fairly likely that you'll encounter formatting like this on the exam. In any case, the code demonstrates the use of multiple `else ifs`:

```
int x = 1;
if ( x == 3 ) { }
else if (x < 4) {System.out.println("<4"); }
else if (x < 2) {System.out.println("<2"); }
else { System.out.println("else"); }
```

It produces this output:

```
<4
```

(Notice that even though the second `else if` is true, it is never reached.)

Sometimes you can have a problem figuring out which `if` your `else` should pair with, as follows:

```
if (exam.done())
if (exam.getScore() < 0.61)
System.out.println("Try again.");
// Which if does this belong to?
else System.out.println("Java master!");
```

We intentionally left out the indenting in this piece of code so it doesn't give clues as to which `if` statement the `else` belongs to. Did you figure it out? Java law decrees that an `else` clause belongs to the innermost `if` statement to which it might possibly belong (in other words, the closest preceding `if` that doesn't have an `else`). In the case of the preceding example, the `else` belongs to the second `if` statement in the listing. With proper indenting, it would look like this:

```
if (exam.done())
  if (exam.getScore() < 0.61)
    System.out.println("Try again.");
  // Which if does this belong to?
  else
    System.out.println("Java master!");
```

Following our coding conventions by using curly braces, it would be even easier to read:

```
if (exam.done()) {
  if (exam.getScore() < 0.61) {
    System.out.println("Try again.");
  // Which if does this belong to?
  } else {
    System.out.println("Java master!");
  }
}
```

Don't get your hopes up about the exam questions being all nice and indented properly. Some exam takers even have a slogan for the way questions are presented on the exam: Anything that can be made more confusing, will be.

Be prepared for questions that not only fail to indent nicely, but intentionally indent in a misleading way. Pay close attention for misdirection like the following:

```
if (exam.done())
  if (exam.getScore() < 0.61)
    System.out.println("Try again.");
else
  System.out.println("Java master!"); // Hmmmmm... now where does
                                      // it belong?
```

Of course, the preceding code is exactly the same as the previous two examples, except for the way it looks.

Legal Expressions for if Statements

The expression in an `if` statement must be a `boolean` expression. Any expression that resolves to a `boolean` is fine, and some of the expressions can be complex. Assume `doStuff()` returns `true`,

```
int y = 5;
int x = 2;
if (((x > 3) && (y < 2)) | doStuff()) {
  System.out.println("true");
}
```

which prints

```
true
```

You can read the preceding code as, "If both `(x > 3)` and `(y < 2)` are `true`, or if the result of `doStuff()` is `true`, then print `true`." So, basically, if just `doStuff()` alone is `true`, we'll still get `true`. If `doStuff()` is `false`, though, then both `(x > 3)` and `(y < 2)` will have to be `true` in order to print `true`. The preceding code is even more complex if you leave off one set of parentheses as follows:

```
int y = 5;
int x = 2;
if ((x > 3) && (y < 2) | doStuff()) {
  System.out.println("true");
}
```

This now prints...nothing! Because the preceding code (with one less set of parentheses) evaluates as though you were saying, "If `(x > 3)` is `true`, and either `(y < 2)` or the result of `doStuff()` is `true`, then print `true`. So if `(x > 3)` is not `true`, no point in looking at the rest of the expression." Because of the short-circuit `&&`, the expression is evaluated as though there were parentheses around `(y < 2) | doStuff()`. In other words, it is evaluated as a single expression before the `&&` and a single expression after the `&&`.

Remember that the only legal expression in an `if` test is a `boolean`. In some languages, 0 == false, and 1 == true. Not so in Java! The following code shows `if` statements that might look tempting but are illegal, followed by legal substitutions:

```
int trueInt = 1;
int falseInt = 0;
if (trueInt)              // illegal
if (trueInt == true)      // illegal
if (1)                    // illegal
if (falseInt == false)    // illegal
if (trueInt == 1)         // legal
if (falseInt == 0)        // legal
```

exam watch

One common mistake programmers make (and that can be difficult to spot), is assigning a `boolean` variable when you meant to test a `boolean` variable. Look out for code like the following:

```
boolean boo = false;
if (boo = true) { }
```

You might think one of three things:

1. ***The code compiles and runs fine, and the `if` test fails because `boo` is `false`.***
2. ***The code won't compile because you're using an assignment (=) rather than an equality test (==).***
3. ***The code compiles and runs fine, and the `if` test succeeds because `boo` is SET to `true` (rather than TESTED for `true`) in the `if` argument!***

Well, number 3 is correct—pointless, but correct. Given that the result of any assignment is the value of the variable after the assignment, the expression `(boo = true)` has a result of `true`. Hence, the `if` test succeeds. But the only variables that can be assigned (rather than tested against something else) are a `boolean` or a `Boolean`; all other assignments will result in something non-`boolean`, so they're not legal, as in the following:

```
int x = 3;
if (x = 5) { }  // Won't compile because x is not a boolean!
```

Because `if` tests require `boolean` expressions, you need to be really solid on both logical operators and `if` test syntax and semantics.

switch Statements (OCA, OCP, and Upgrade Topic)

You've seen how `if` and `else-if` statements can be used to support both simple and complex decision logic. In many cases, the `switch` statement provides a cleaner way to handle complex decision logic. Let's compare the following `if-else if` statement to the equivalently performing `switch` statement:

```
int x = 3;
if(x == 1) {
  System.out.println("x equals 1");
}
else if(x == 2) {
  System.out.println("x equals 2");
}
else {
  System.out.println("No idea what x is");
}
```

Now let's see the same functionality represented in a switch construct:

```
int x = 3;
switch (x) {
  case 1:
    System.out.println("x equals 1");
    break;
  case 2:
    System.out.println("x equals 2");
    break;
  default:
    System.out.println("No idea what x is");
}
```

Note: The reason this switch statement emulates the if is because of the break statements that were placed inside of the switch. In general, break statements are optional, and as you will see in a few pages, their inclusion or exclusion causes huge changes in how a switch statement will execute.

Legal Expressions for switch and case

The general form of the switch statement is

```
switch (expression) {
  case constant1: code block
  case constant2: code block
  default: code block
}
```

A switch's expression must evaluate to a char, byte, short, int, an enum (as of Java 5), and a String (as of Java 7). That means if you're not using an enum or a String, only variables and values that can be automatically promoted (in other words, implicitly cast) to an int are acceptable. You won't be able to compile if you use anything else, including the remaining numeric types of long, float, and double.

Note: For OCA candidates, enums are not covered on your exam, and you won't encounter any questions related to switch statements that use enums.

A case constant must evaluate to the same type that the switch expression can use, with one additional—and big—constraint: the case constant must be a compile-time constant! Since the case argument has to be resolved at compile time, you can use only a constant or final variable that is immediately initialized with a literal value. It is not enough to be final; it must be a compile time *constant*. Here's an example:

```
final int a = 1;
final int b;
b = 2;
int x = 0;
switch (x) {
  case a:       // ok
  case b:       // compiler error
```

Also, the `switch` can only check for equality. This means that the other relational operators such as greater than are rendered unusable in a `case`. The following is an example of a valid expression using a method invocation in a `switch` statement. Note that for this code to be legal, the method being invoked on the object reference must return a value compatible with an `int`.

```
String s = "xyz";
switch (s.length()) {
  case 1:
    System.out.println("length is one");
    break;
  case 2:
    System.out.println("length is two");
    break;
  case 3:
    System.out.println("length is three");
    break;
  default:
    System.out.println("no match");
}
```

One other rule you might not expect involves the question, "What happens if I `switch` on a variable smaller than an `int`?" Look at the following `switch`:

```
byte g = 2;
switch(g) {
  case 23:
  case 128:
}
```

This code won't compile. Although the `switch` argument is legal—a byte is implicitly cast to an `int`—the second `case` argument (128) is too large for a `byte`, and the compiler knows it! Attempting to compile the preceding example gives you an error something like this:

```
Test.java:6: possible loss of precision
found   : int
required: byte
    case 128:
         ^
```

It's also illegal to have more than one `case` label using the same value. For example, the following block of code won't compile because it uses two `cases` with the same value of 80:

```
int temp = 90;
switch(temp) {
  case 80 :  System.out.println("80");
  case 80 :  System.out.println("80");    // won't compile!
  case 90 :  System.out.println("90");
  default :  System.out.println("default");
}
```

It *is* legal to leverage the power of boxing in a `switch` expression. For instance, the following is legal:

```
switch(new Integer(4)) {
  case 4: System.out.println("boxing is OK");
}
```

exam watch

Look for any violation of the rules for `switch` and `case` arguments. For example, you might find illegal examples like the following snippets:

```
switch(x) {
  case 0 {
    y = 7;
  }
}

switch(x) {
  0: { }
  1: { }
}
```

In the first example, the `case` uses a curly brace and omits the colon. The second example omits the keyword `case`.

An Intro to String "equality"

As we've been discussing, the operation of `switch` statements depends on the expression "matching" or being "equal" to one of the cases. We've talked about how we know when primitives are equal, but what does it mean for objects to be equal? This is another one of those surprisingly tricky topics, and for those of you who intend to take the OCP exam, we'll spend a lot of time discussing "object equality" in Part II. For you OCA candidates, all you have to know is that for a switch statement, two Strings will be considered "equal" if they have the same case-sensitive sequence of characters. For example, in the following partial switch statement, the expression would match the case:

```
String s = "Monday";
switch(s) {
  case "Monday":   // matches!
```

But the following would NOT match:

```
String s = "MONDAY";
switch(s) {
  case "Monday":   // Strings are case-sensitive, DOES NOT match
```

Break and Fall-Through in switch Blocks

We're finally ready to discuss the break statement and offer more details about flow control within a switch statement. The most important thing to remember about the flow of execution through a switch statement is this:

> case constants are evaluated from the top down, and the first case constant that matches the switch's expression is the execution *entry point.*

In other words, once a case constant is matched, the Java Virtual Machine (JVM) will execute the associated code block and ALL subsequent code blocks (barring a break statement) too! The following example uses a String in a case statement:

```
class SwitchString {
  public static void main(String [] args) {
    String s = "green";
    switch(s) {
      case "red": System.out.print("red ");
      case "green": System.out.print("green ");
      case "blue": System.out.print("blue ");
      default: System.out.println("done");
    }
  }
}
```

In this example case "green": matched, so the JVM executed that code block and all subsequent code blocks to produce the output:

```
green blue done
```

Again, when the program encounters the keyword break during the execution of a switch statement, execution will immediately move out of the switch block to the next statement after the `switch`. If `break` is omitted, the program just keeps executing the remaining `case` blocks until either a `break` is found or the `switch` statement ends. Examine the following code:

```
int x = 1;
switch(x) {
  case 1:  System.out.println("x is one");
  case 2:  System.out.println("x is two");
  case 3:  System.out.println("x is three");
}
System.out.println("out of the switch");
```

The code will print the following:

```
x is one
x is two
x is three
out of the switch
```

This combination occurs because the code didn't hit a `break` statement; execution just kept dropping down through each `case` until the end. This dropping down is actually called "fall-through," because of the way execution falls from one `case` to the next. Remember, the matching `case` is simply your entry point into the `switch` block! In other words, you must *not* think of it as, "Find the matching `case`, execute just that code, and get out." That's *not* how it works. If you do want that "just the matching code" behavior, you'll insert a `break` into each `case` as follows:

```
int x = 1;
switch(x) {
  case 1:  {
    System.out.println("x is one");  break;
  }
  case 2:  {
    System.out.println("x is two");  break;
  }
  case 3:  {
    System.out.println("x is two");  break;
  }
}
System.out.println("out of the switch");
```

Running the preceding code, now that we've added the `break` statements, will print this:

```
x is one
out of the switch
```

And that's it. We entered into the `switch` block at `case 1`. Because it matched the `switch()` argument, we got the `println` statement and then hit the `break` and jumped to the end of the `switch`.

An interesting example of this fall-through logic is shown in the following code:

```
int x = someNumberBetweenOneAndTen;

switch (x) {
  case 2:
  case 4:
  case 6:
  case 8:
  case 10: {
    System.out.println("x is an even number");  break;
  }
}
```

This switch statement will print x is an even number or nothing, depending on whether the number is between one and ten and is odd or even. For example, if x is 4, execution will begin at case 4, but then fall down through 6, 8, and 10, where it prints and then breaks. The break at case 10, by the way, is not needed; we're already at the end of the switch anyway.

Note: Because fall-through is less than intuitive, Oracle recommends that you add a comment such as // fall through when you use fall-through logic.

The Default Case

What if, using the preceding code, you wanted to print x is an odd number if none of the cases (the even numbers) matched? You couldn't put it after the switch statement, or even as the last case in the switch, because in both of those situations it would always print x is an odd number. To get this behavior, you'd use the default keyword. (By the way, if you've wondered why there is a default keyword even though we don't use a modifier for default access control, now you'll see that the default keyword is used for a completely different purpose.) The only change we need to make is to add the default case to the preceding code:

```
int x = someNumberBetweenOneAndTen;

switch (x) {
  case 2:
  case 4:
  case 6:
  case 8:
  case 10: {
    System.out.println("x is an even number");
    break;
  }
  default: System.out.println("x is an odd number");
}
```

exam watch

The `default case` doesn't have to come at the end of the `switch`. Look for it in strange places such as the following:

```
int x = 2;
switch (x) {
  case 2:  System.out.println("2");
  default: System.out.println("default");
  case 3: System.out.println("3");
  case 4: System.out.println("4");
}
```

Running the preceding code prints this:

```
2
default
3
4
```

And if we modify it so that the only match is the `default case`, like this,

```
int x = 7;
switch (x) {
  case 2:  System.out.println("2");
  default: System.out.println("default");
  case 3: System.out.println("3");
  case 4: System.out.println("4");
}
```

then running the preceding code prints this:

```
default
3
4
```

The rule to remember is that `default` works just like any other `case` for fall-through!

EXERCISE 6-1

Creating a switch-case Statement

Try creating a `switch` statement using a `char` value as the `case`. Include a default behavior if none of the `char` values match.

- Make sure a `char` variable is declared before the `switch` statement.
- Each `case` statement should be followed by a `break`.
- The `default case` can be located at the end, middle, or top.

CERTIFICATION OBJECTIVE

Creating Loops Constructs (OCA Objectives 5.1, 5.2, 5.3, 5.4, and 5.5)

5.1 *Create and use while loops.*

5.2 *Create and use for loops including the enhanced for loop.*

5.3 *Create and use do/while loops.*

5.4 *Compare loop constructs.*

5.5 *Use break and continue.*

Java loops come in three flavors: `while`, `do`, and `for` (and as of Java 5, the `for` loop has two variations). All three let you repeat a block of code as long as some condition is true, or for a specific number of iterations. You're probably familiar with loops from other languages, so even if you're somewhat new to Java, these won't be a problem to learn.

Using while Loops

The `while` loop is good when you don't know how many times a block or statement should repeat, but you want to continue looping as long as some condition is true. A `while` statement looks like this:

```
while (expression) {
  // do stuff
}
```

Or this:

```
int x = 2;
while(x == 2) {
  System.out.println(x);
  ++x;
}
```

In this case, as in all loops, the expression (test) must evaluate to a `boolean` result. The body of the `while` loop will execute only if the expression (sometimes called the "condition") results in a value of `true`. Once inside the loop, the loop body will repeat until the condition is no longer met because it evaluates to `false`. In the previous example, program control will enter the loop body because `x` is equal to 2. However, `x` is incremented in the loop, so when the condition is checked again it will evaluate to `false` and exit the loop.

Any variables used in the expression of a `while` loop must be declared before the expression is evaluated. In other words, you can't say this:

```
while (int x = 2) { }    // not legal
```

Then again, why would you? Instead of testing the variable, you'd be declaring and initializing it, so it would always have the exact same value. Not much of a test condition!

The key point to remember about a `while` loop is that it might not ever run. If the test expression is `false` the first time the `while` expression is checked, the loop body will be skipped and the program will begin executing at the first statement *after* the `while` loop. Look at the following example:

```
int x = 8;
while (x > 8) {
  System.out.println("in the loop");
  x = 10;
}
System.out.println("past the loop");
```

Running this code produces

```
past the loop
```

Because the expression `(x > 8)` evaluates to `false`, none of the code within the `while` loop ever executes.

Using do Loops

The do loop is similar to the `while` loop, except that the expression is not evaluated until after the do loop's code is executed. Therefore, the code in a do loop is guaranteed to execute at least once. The following shows a do loop in action:

```
do {
  System.out.println("Inside loop");
} while(false);
```

The `System.out.println()` statement will print once, even though the expression evaluates to `false`. Remember, the do loop will always run the code in the loop body at least once. Be sure to note the use of the semicolon at the end of the `while` expression.

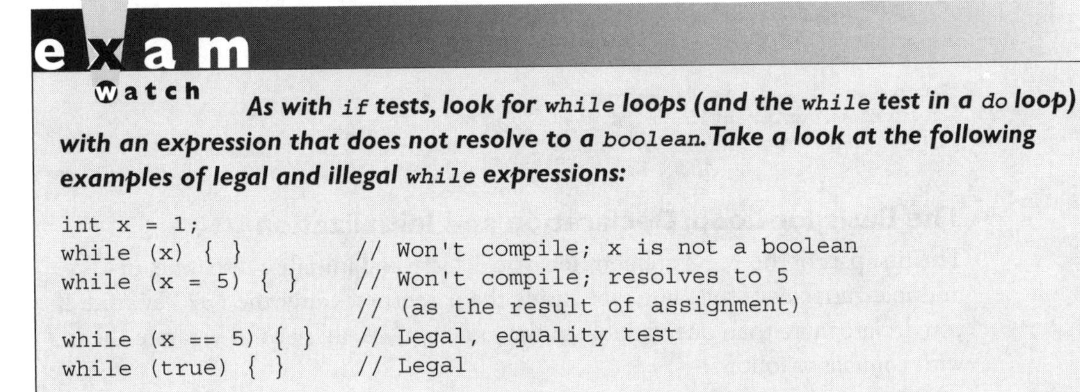

exam watch

As with `if` tests, look for `while` loops (and the `while` test in a `do` loop) with an expression that does not resolve to a `boolean`. Take a look at the following examples of legal and illegal `while` expressions:

```
int x = 1;
while (x) { }          // Won't compile; x is not a boolean
while (x = 5) { }      // Won't compile; resolves to 5
                       // (as the result of assignment)
while (x == 5) { }     // Legal, equality test
while (true) { }       // Legal
```

Using for Loops

As of Java 5, the `for` loop took on a second structure. We'll call the old style of `for` loop the "basic `for` loop," and we'll call the new style of `for` loop the "enhanced `for` loop" (it's also sometimes called the `for-each`). Depending on what documentation you use, you'll see both terms, along with `for-in`. The terms `for-in`, `for-each`, and "enhanced `for`" all refer to the same Java construct.

The basic `for` loop is more flexible than the enhanced `for` loop, but the enhanced `for` loop was designed to make iterating through arrays and collections easier to code.

The Basic for Loop

The `for` loop is especially useful for flow control when you already know how many times you need to execute the statements in the loop's block. The `for` loop declaration has three main parts, besides the body of the loop:

- Declaration and initialization of variables
- The `boolean` expression (conditional test)
- The iteration expression

The three `for` declaration parts are separated by semicolons. The following two examples demonstrate the `for` loop. The first example shows the parts of a `for` loop in a pseudocode form, and the second shows a typical example of a `for` loop:

```
for (/*Initialization*/ ; /*Condition*/ ;  /* Iteration */) {
  /* loop body */
}

for (int i = 0; i<10; i++) {
  System.out.println("i is " + i);
}
```

The Basic for Loop: Declaration and Initialization

The first part of the `for` statement lets you declare and initialize zero, one, or multiple variables of the same type inside the parentheses after the `for` keyword. If you declare more than one variable of the same type, you'll need to separate them with commas as follows:

```
for (int x = 10, y = 3; y > 3; y++) { }
```

The declaration and initialization happens before anything else in a `for` loop. And whereas the other two parts—the `boolean` test and the iteration expression—will run with each iteration of the loop, the declaration and initialization happens just once, at the very beginning. You also must know that the scope of variables declared in the `for` loop ends with the `for` loop! The following demonstrates this:

```
for (int x = 1; x < 2; x++) {
  System.out.println(x);  // Legal
}
System.out.println(x);    // Not Legal! x is now out of scope
                          // and can't be accessed.
```

If you try to compile this, you'll get something like this:

```
Test.java:19: cannot resolve symbol
symbol  : variable x
location: class Test
  System.out.println(x);
                     ^
```

Basic for Loop: Conditional (boolean) Expression

The next section that executes is the conditional expression, which (like all other conditional tests) must evaluate to a `boolean` value. You can have only one logical expression, but it can be very complex. Look out for code that uses logical expressions like this:

```
for (int x = 0; ((((x < 10) && (y-- > 2)) | x == 3)); x++) { }
```

The preceding code is legal, but the following is not:

```
for (int x = 0; (x > 5), (y < 2); x++) { } // too many
                                            // expressions
```

The compiler will let you know the problem:

```
TestLong.java:20: ';' expected
for (int x = 0; (x > 5), (y < 2); x++) { }
                        ^
```

The rule to remember is this: *You can have only one test expression.*

In other words, you can't use multiple tests separated by commas, even though the other two parts of a `for` statement can have multiple parts.

Basic for Loop: Iteration Expression

After each execution of the body of the `for` loop, the iteration expression is executed. This is where you get to say what you want to happen with each iteration of the loop. Remember that it always happens after the loop body runs! Look at the following:

```
for (int x = 0; x < 1; x++) {
  // body code that doesn't change the value of x
}
```

This loop executes just once. The first time into the loop, `x` is set to 0, then `x` is tested to see if it's less than 1 (which it is), and then the body of the loop executes. After the body of the loop runs, the iteration expression runs, incrementing `x` by 1.

Next, the conditional test is checked, and since the result is now `false`, execution jumps to below the `for` loop and continues on.

Keep in mind that barring a forced exit, evaluating the iteration expression and then evaluating the conditional expression are always the last two things that happen in a `for` loop!

Examples of forced exits include a `break`, a return, a `System.exit()`, and an exception, which will all cause a loop to terminate abruptly, without running the iteration expression. Look at the following code:

```
static boolean doStuff() {
  for (int x = 0; x < 3; x++) {
    System.out.println("in for loop");
    return true;
  }
  return true;
}
```

Running this code produces

```
in for loop
```

The statement prints only once, because a `return` causes execution to leave not just the current iteration of a loop, but the entire method. So the iteration expression never runs in that case. Table 6-1 lists the causes and results of abrupt loop termination.

Basic for Loop: for Loop Issues

None of the three sections of the `for` declaration are required! The following example is perfectly legal (although not necessarily good practice):

```
for( ; ; ) {
  System.out.println("Inside an endless loop");
}
```

In this example, all the declaration parts are left out, so the `for` loop will act like an endless loop.

TABLE 6-1 Causes of Early Loop Termination

Code in Loop	What Happens
`break`	Execution jumps immediately to the first statement after the `for` loop.
`return`	Execution jumps immediately back to the calling method.
`System.exit()`	All program execution stops; the VM shuts down.

For the exam, it's important to know that with the absence of the initialization and increment sections, the loop will act like a `while` loop. The following example demonstrates how this is accomplished:

```
int i = 0;

for (;i<10;) {
  i++;
  // do some other work
}
```

The next example demonstrates a `for` loop with multiple variables in play. A comma separates the variables, and they must be of the same type. Remember that the variables declared in the `for` statement are all local to the `for` loop and can't be used outside the scope of the loop.

```
for (int i = 0,j = 0; (i<10) && (j<10); i++, j++) {
  System.out.println("i is " + i + " j is " +j);
}
```

exam watch

Variable scope plays a large role in the exam. You need to know that a variable declared in the `for` loop can't be used beyond the `for` loop. But a variable only initialized in the `for` statement (but declared earlier) can be used beyond the loop. For example, the following is legal:

```
int x = 3;
for (x = 12; x < 20; x++) { }
System.out.println(x);
```

But this is not:

```
for (int x = 3; x < 20; x++) { } System.out.println(x);
```

The last thing to note is that all three sections of the `for` loop are independent of each other. The three expressions in the `for` statement don't need to operate on the same variables, although they typically do. But even the iterator expression, which many mistakenly call the "increment expression," doesn't need to increment or set anything; you can put in virtually any arbitrary code statements that you want to happen with each iteration of the loop. Look at the following:

```
int b = 3;
for (int a = 1;  b != 1; System.out.println("iterate")) {
  b = b - a;
}
```

The preceding code prints

```
iterate
iterate
```

exam watch

Many questions in the Java 7 exams list "Compilation fails" and "An exception occurs at runtime" as possible answers. This makes them more difficult, because you can't simply work through the behavior of the code. You must first make sure the code isn't violating any fundamental rules that will lead to a compiler error, and then look for possible exceptions. Only after you've satisfied those two should you dig into the logic and flow of the code in the question.

The Enhanced for Loop (for Arrays)

The enhanced `for` loop, new as of Java 5, is a specialized `for` loop that simplifies looping through an array or a collection. In this chapter we're going to focus on using the enhanced `for` to loop through arrays. In Chapter 11 we'll revisit the enhanced `for` as we discuss collections—where the enhanced `for` really comes into its own.

Instead of having *three* components, the enhanced `for` has *two*. Let's loop through an array the basic (old) way, and then using the enhanced `for`:

```
int [] a = {1,2,3,4};
for(int x = 0; x < a.length; x++)    // basic for loop
  System.out.print(a[x]);
for(int n : a)                       // enhanced for loop
  System.out.print(n);
```

This produces the following output:

```
12341234
```

More formally, let's describe the enhanced `for` as follows:

```
for(declaration : expression)
```

The two pieces of the `for` statement are

- **`declaration`** The *newly declared* block variable, of a type compatible with the elements of the array you are accessing. This variable will be available within the `for` block, and its value will be the same as the current array element.
- **`expression`** This must evaluate to the array you want to loop through. This could be an array variable or a method call that returns an array. The array can be any type: primitives, objects, or even arrays of arrays.

Using the preceding definitions, let's look at some legal and illegal enhanced `for` declarations:

```
int x;
long x2;
long [] la = {7L, 8L, 9L};
int [][] twoDee = {{1,2,3}, {4,5,6}, {7,8,9}};
String [] sNums = {"one", "two", "three"};
Animal [] animals = {new Dog(), new Cat()};

// legal 'for' declarations
for(long y : la ) ;          // loop thru an array of longs
for(int[] n : twoDee) ;      // loop thru the array of arrays
for(int n2 : twoDee[2]) ;    // loop thru the 3rd sub-array
for(String s : sNums) ;      // loop thru the array of Strings
for(Object o : sNums) ;      // set an Object reference to
                             // each String
for(Animal a : animals) ;    // set an Animal reference to each
                             // element

// ILLEGAL 'for' declarations
for(x2 : la) ;               // x2 is already declared
for(int x2 : twoDee) ;       // can't stuff an array into an int
for(int x3 : la) ;           // can't stuff a long into an int
for(Dog d : animals) ;       // you might get a Cat!
```

The enhanced `for` loop assumes that, barring an early exit from the loop, you'll always loop through every element of the array. The following discussions of `break` and `continue` apply to both the basic and enhanced `for` loops.

Using break and continue

The break and continue keywords are used to stop either the entire loop (break) or just the current iteration (continue). Typically, if you're using break or continue, you'll do an if test within the loop, and if some condition becomes true (or false depending on the program), you want to get out immediately. The difference between them is whether or not you continue with a new iteration or jump to the first statement below the loop and continue from there.

exam watch

Remember, continue statements must be inside a loop; otherwise, you'll get a compiler error. break statements must be used inside either a loop or a switch statement.

The break statement causes the program to stop execution of the innermost loop and start processing the next line of code after the block.

The continue statement causes only the current iteration of the innermost loop to cease and the next iteration of the same loop to start if the condition of the loop is met. When using a continue statement with a for loop, you need to consider the effects that continue has on the loop iteration. Examine the following code:

```
for (int i = 0; i < 10; i++) {
  System.out.println("Inside loop");
  continue;
}
```

The question is, is this an endless loop? The answer is no. When the continue statement is hit, the iteration expression still runs! It runs just as though the current iteration ended "in the natural way." So in the preceding example, i will still increment before the condition (i < 10) is checked again.

Most of the time, a continue is used within an if test as follows:

```
for (int i = 0; i < 10; i++) {
  System.out.println("Inside loop");
  if (foo.doStuff() == 5) {
    continue;
  }
  // more loop code, that won't be reached when the above if
  // test is true
}
```

Unlabeled Statements

Both the `break` statement and the `continue` statement can be unlabeled or labeled. Although it's far more common to use `break` and `continue` unlabeled, the exam expects you to know how labeled `break` and `continue` statements work. As stated before, a `break` statement (unlabeled) will exit out of the innermost looping construct and proceed with the next line of code beyond the loop block. The following example demonstrates a `break` statement:

```
boolean problem = true;
while (true) {
  if (problem) {
    System.out.println("There was a problem");
    break;
  }
}
// next line of code
```

In the previous example, the `break` statement is unlabeled. The following is an example of an unlabeled `continue` statement:

```
while (!EOF) {
                          // read a field from a file
  if (wrongField) {
    continue;             // move to the next field in the file
  }
                          // otherwise do other stuff with the field
}
```

In this example, a file is being read one field at a time. When an error is encountered, the program moves to the next field in the file and uses the `continue` statement to go back into the loop (if it is not at the end of the file) and keeps reading the various fields. If the `break` command were used instead, the code would stop reading the file once the error occurred and move on to the next line of code after the loop. The `continue` statement gives you a way to say, "This particular iteration of the loop needs to stop, but not the whole loop itself. I just don't want the rest of the code in this iteration to finish, so do the iteration expression and then start over with the test, and don't worry about what was below the `continue` statement."

Labeled Statements

Although many statements in a Java program can be labeled, it's most common to use labels with loop statements like `for` or `while`, in conjunction with `break` and `continue` statements. A label statement must be placed just before the statement being labeled, and it consists of a valid identifier that ends with a colon (`:`).

You need to understand the difference between labeled and unlabeled `break` and `continue`. The labeled varieties are needed only in situations where you have a nested loop, and they need to indicate which of the nested loops you want to break from, or from which of the nested loops you want to continue with the next iteration. A `break` statement will exit out of the labeled loop, as opposed to the innermost loop, if the `break` keyword is combined with a label.

Here's an example of what a label looks like:

```
foo:
  for (int x = 3; x < 20; x++) {
    while(y > 7) {
      y--;
    }
  }
```

The label must adhere to the rules for a valid variable name and should adhere to the Java naming convention. The syntax for the use of a label name in conjunction with a `break` statement is the `break` keyword, then the label name, followed by a semicolon. A more complete example of the use of a labeled `break` statement is as follows:

```
boolean isTrue = true;
outer:
  for(int i=0; i<5; i++) {
    while (isTrue) {
      System.out.println("Hello");
      break outer;
    }     // end of inner while loop
    System.out.println("Outer loop."); // Won't print
  }       // end of outer for loop
System.out.println("Good-Bye");
```

Running this code produces

```
Hello
Good-Bye
```

In this example, the word `Hello` will be printed one time. Then, the labeled `break` statement will be executed, and the flow will exit out of the loop labeled `outer`. The next line of code will then print out `Good-Bye`.

Let's see what will happen if the `continue` statement is used instead of the `break` statement. The following code example is similar to the preceding one, with the exception of substituting `continue` for `break`:

```
outer:
  for (int i=0; i<5; i++) {
    for (int j=0; j<5; j++) {
      System.out.println("Hello");
      continue outer;
    }    // end of inner loop
    System.out.println("outer"); // Never prints
  }
System.out.println("Good-Bye");
```

Running this code produces

```
Hello
Hello
Hello
Hello
Hello
Good-Bye
```

In this example, `Hello` will be printed five times. After the `continue` statement is executed, the flow continues with the next iteration of the loop identified with the label. Finally, when the condition in the outer loop evaluates to `false`, this loop will finish and `Good-Bye` will be printed.

EXERCISE 6-2

Creating a Labeled while Loop

Try creating a labeled `while` loop. Make the label `outer` and provide a condition to check whether a variable `age` is less than or equal to 21. Within the loop, increment `age` by 1. Every time the program goes through the loop, check whether `age` is 16. If it is, print the message "get your driver's license" and continue to the outer loop. If not, print "Another year."

- The `outer` label should appear just before the `while` loop begins.
- Make sure `age` is declared outside of the `while` loop.

exam watch

Labeled `continue` and `break` statements must be inside the loop that has the same label name; otherwise, the code will not compile.

CERTIFICATION OBJECTIVE

Handling Exceptions (OCA Objectives 8.1, 8.2, 8.3, and 8.4)

8.1 *Differentiate among checked exceptions, RuntimeExceptions, and errors.*

8.2 *Create a try-catch block and determine how exceptions alter normal program flow.*

8.3 *Describe what exceptions are used for in Java.*

8.4 *Invoke a method that throws an exception.*

An old maxim in software development says that 80 percent of the work is used 20 percent of the time. The 80 percent refers to the effort required to check and handle errors. In many languages, writing program code that checks for and deals with errors is tedious and bloats the application source into confusing spaghetti. Still, error detection and handling may be the most important ingredient of any robust application. Java arms developers with an elegant mechanism for handling errors that produces efficient and organized error-handling code: exception handling.

Exception handling allows developers to detect errors easily without writing special code to test return values. Even better, it lets us keep exception-*handling* code cleanly separated from exception-*generating* code. It also lets us use the same exception-handling code to deal with a range of possible exceptions.

Java 7 added several new exception-handling capabilities to the language. For our purposes, Oracle split the various exception-handling topics into two main parts:

1. The OCA exam covers the Java 6 version of exception handling.
2. The OCP exam adds the new exception features added in Java 7.

In order to mirror Oracle's objectives, we split exception handling into two chapters. This chapter will give you the basics—plenty to handle the OCA exam. Chapter 7 (which also marks the beginning of the OCP part of the book) will pick up where we left off by discussing the new Java 7 exception handling features.

Catching an Exception Using try and catch

Before we begin, let's introduce some terminology. The term "exception" means "exceptional condition" and is an occurrence that alters the normal program flow. A bunch of things can lead to exceptions, including hardware failures, resource exhaustion, and good old bugs. When an exceptional event occurs in Java, an exception is said to be "thrown." The code that's responsible for doing something about the exception is called an "exception handler," and it "catches" the thrown exception.

Exception handling works by transferring the execution of a program to an appropriate exception handler when an exception occurs. For example, if you call a method that opens a file but the file cannot be opened, execution of that method will stop, and code that you wrote to deal with this situation will be run. Therefore, we need a way to tell the JVM what code to execute when a certain exception happens. To do this, we use the `try` and `catch` keywords. The `try` is used to define a block of code in which exceptions may occur. This block of code is called a "guarded region" (which really means "risky code goes here"). One or more `catch` clauses match a specific exception (or group of exceptions—more on that later) to a block of code that handles it. Here's how it looks in pseudocode:

```
 1. try {
 2.   // This is the first line of the "guarded region"
 3.   // that is governed by the try keyword.
 4.   // Put code here that might cause some kind of exception.
 5.   // We may have many code lines here or just one.
 6. }
 7. catch(MyFirstException) {
 8.   // Put code here that handles this exception.
 9.   // This is the next line of the exception handler.
10.   // This is the last line of the exception handler.
11. }
12. catch(MySecondException) {
13.   // Put code here that handles this exception
14. }
15.
16.   // Some other unguarded (normal, non-risky) code begins here
```

In this pseudocode example, lines 2 through 5 constitute the guarded region that is governed by the `try` clause. Line 7 is an exception handler for an exception of type `MyFirstException`. Line 12 is an exception handler for an exception of type `MySecondException`. Notice that the `catch` blocks immediately follow the `try` block. This is a requirement; if you have one or more `catch` blocks, they must immediately follow the `try` block. Additionally, the `catch` blocks must all follow each other, without any other statements or blocks in between. Also, the order in which the `catch` blocks appear matters, as we'll see a little later.

Execution of the guarded region starts at line 2. If the program executes all the way past line 5 with no exceptions being thrown, execution will transfer to line 15 and continue downward. However, if at any time in lines 2 through 5 (the `try` block) an exception of type `MyFirstException` is thrown, execution will immediately transfer to line 7. Lines 8 through 10 will then be executed so that the entire `catch` block runs, and then execution will transfer to line 15 and continue.

Note that if an exception occurred on, say, line 3 of the `try` block, the rest of the lines in the `try` block (4 and 5) would never be executed. Once control jumps to the `catch` block, it never returns to complete the balance of the `try` block. This is exactly what you want, though. Imagine that your code looks something like this pseudocode:

```
try {
  getTheFileFromOverNetwork
  readFromTheFileAndPopulateTable
}
catch(CantGetFileFromNetwork) {
  displayNetworkErrorMessage
}
```

This pseudocode demonstrates how you typically work with exceptions. Code that's dependent on a risky operation (as populating a table with file data is dependent on getting the file from the network) is grouped into a `try` block in such a way that if, say, the first operation fails, you won't continue trying to run other code that's also guaranteed to fail. In the pseudocode example, you won't be able to read from the file if you can't get the file off the network in the first place.

One of the benefits of using exception handling is that code to handle any particular exception that may occur in the governed region needs to be written only once. Returning to our earlier code example, there may be three different places in our `try` block that can generate a `MyFirstException`, but wherever it occurs it will be handled by the same `catch` block (on line 7). We'll discuss more benefits of exception handling near the end of this chapter.

Using finally

Although `try` and `catch` provide a terrific mechanism for trapping and handling exceptions, we are left with the problem of how to clean up after ourselves if an exception occurs. Because execution transfers out of the `try` block as soon as an exception is thrown, we can't put our cleanup code at the bottom of the `try` block and expect it to be executed if an exception occurs. Almost as bad an idea would be placing our cleanup code in each of the `catch` blocks—let's see why.

Exception handlers are a poor place to clean up after the code in the `try` block because each handler then requires its own copy of the cleanup code. If, for example, you allocated a network socket or opened a file somewhere in the guarded region, each exception handler would have to close the file or release the socket. That would make it too easy to forget to do cleanup and also lead to a lot of redundant code. To address this problem, Java offers the `finally` block.

A `finally` block encloses code that is always executed at some point after the `try` block, whether an exception was thrown or not. Even if there is a `return` statement in the `try` block, the `finally` block executes right after the `return` statement is encountered and before the `return` executes!

This is the right place to close your files, release your network sockets, and perform any other cleanup your code requires. If the `try` block executes with no exceptions, the `finally` block is executed immediately after the `try` block completes. If there was an exception thrown, the `finally` block executes immediately after the proper `catch` block completes. Let's look at another pseudocode example:

```
 1: try {
 2:   // This is the first line of the "guarded region".
 3: }
 4: catch(MyFirstException) {
 5:   // Put code here that handles this exception
 6: }
 7: catch(MySecondException) {
 8:   // Put code here that handles this exception
 9: }
10: finally {
11:   // Put code here to release any resource we
12:   // allocated in the try clause
13: }
14:
15:   // More code here
```

As before, execution starts at the first line of the `try` block, line 2. If there are no exceptions thrown in the `try` block, execution transfers to line 11, the first line of the `finally` block. On the other hand, if a `MySecondException` is thrown while the code in the `try` block is executing, execution transfers to the first line of that exception handler, line 8 in the `catch` clause. After all the code in the `catch` clause is executed, the program moves to line 11, the first line of the `finally` clause. Repeat after me: `finally` always runs! Okay, we'll have to refine that a little, but for now, start burning in the idea that `finally` always runs. If an exception is thrown, `finally` runs. If an exception is not thrown, `finally` runs. If the exception is caught, `finally` runs. If the exception is not caught, `finally` runs. Later we'll look at the few scenarios in which `finally` might not run or complete.

Remember, `finally` clauses are not required. If you don't write one, your code will compile and run just fine. In fact, if you have no resources to clean up after your `try` block completes, you probably don't need a `finally` clause. Also, because the compiler doesn't even require `catch` clauses, sometimes you'll run across code that has a `try` block immediately followed by a `finally` block. Such code is useful when the exception is going to be passed back to the calling method, as explained in the next section. Using a `finally` block allows the cleanup code to execute even when there isn't a `catch` clause.

The following legal code demonstrates a `try` with a `finally` but no `catch`:

```
try {
  // do stuff
} finally {
  // clean up
}
```

The following legal code demonstrates a `try`, `catch`, and `finally`:

```
try {
  // do stuff
} catch (SomeException ex) {
  // do exception handling
} finally {
  // clean up
}
```

The following ILLEGAL code demonstrates a `try` without a `catch` or `finally`:

```
try {
  // do stuff
}
  // need a catch or finally here
System.out.println("out of try block");
```

The following ILLEGAL code demonstrates a misplaced `catch` block:

```
try {
  // do stuff
}
  // can't have code between try/catch
System.out.println("out of try block");
catch(Exception ex) { }
```

exam watch

It is illegal to use a `try` clause without either a `catch` clause or a `finally` clause. A `try` clause by itself will result in a compiler error. Any `catch` clauses must immediately follow the `try` block. Any `finally` clause must immediately follow the last `catch` clause (or it must immediately follow the `try` block if there is no `catch`). It is legal to omit either the `catch` clause or the `finally` clause, but not both.

Propagating Uncaught Exceptions

Why aren't `catch` clauses required? What happens to an exception that's thrown in a `try` block when there is no `catch` clause waiting for it? Actually, there's no requirement that you code a `catch` clause for every possible exception that could be thrown from the corresponding `try` block. In fact, it's doubtful that you could accomplish such a feat! If a method doesn't provide a `catch` clause for a particular exception, that method is said to be "ducking" the exception (or "passing the buck").

So what happens to a ducked exception? Before we discuss that, we need to briefly review the concept of the call stack. Most languages have the concept of a method stack or a call stack. Simply put, the call stack is the chain of methods that your program executes to get to the current method. If your program starts in method `main()` and `main()` calls method `a()`, which calls method `b()`, which in turn calls method `c()`, the call stack consists of the following:

```
c
b
a
main
```

We will represent the stack as growing upward (although it can also be visualized as growing downward). As you can see, the last method called is at the top of the stack, while the first calling method is at the bottom. The method at the very top of the stack trace would be the method you were currently executing. If we move back down the call stack, we're moving from the current method to the previously called method. Figure 6-1 illustrates a way to think about how the call stack in Java works.

Now let's examine what happens to ducked exceptions. Imagine a building, say, five stories high, and at each floor there is a deck or balcony. Now imagine that on each deck, one person is standing holding a baseball mitt. Exceptions are like balls dropped from person to person, starting from the roof. An exception is first thrown

FIGURE 6-1

The Java method call stack

1) The call stack while `method3()` is running.

4	method3()	method2 invokes method3
3	method2()	method1 invokes method2
2	method1()	main invokes method1
1	main()	main begins

The order in which methods are put on the call stack

2) The call stack after `method3()` completes
Execution returns to `method2()`

1	method2()	method2() will complete
2	method1()	method1() will complete
3	main()	main() will complete and the JVM will exit

The order in which methods complete

from the top of the stack (in other words, the person on the roof), and if it isn't caught by the same person who threw it (the person on the roof), it drops down the call stack to the previous method, which is the person standing on the deck one floor down. If not caught there by the person one floor down, the exception/ball again drops down to the previous method (person on the next floor down), and so on until it is caught or until it reaches the very bottom of the call stack. This is called "exception propagation."

If an exception reaches the bottom of the call stack, it's like reaching the bottom of a very long drop; the ball explodes, and so does your program. An exception that's never caught will cause your application to stop running. A description (if one is available) of the exception will be displayed, and the call stack will be "dumped." This helps you debug your application by telling you what exception was thrown, from what method it was thrown, and what the stack looked like at the time.

exam watch

You can keep throwing an exception down through the methods on the stack. But what happens when you get to the `main()` method at the bottom? You can throw the exception out of `main()` as well. This results in the JVM halting, and the stack trace will be printed to the output. The following code throws an exception:

```
class TestEx {
  public static void main (String [] args) {
    doStuff();
  }
  static void doStuff() {
    doMoreStuff();
  }
  static void doMoreStuff() {
    int x = 5/0;   // Can't divide by zero!
                   // ArithmeticException is thrown here
  }
}
```

It prints out a stack trace something like this:

```
 %java TestEx
Exception in thread "main" java.lang.ArithmeticException: / by zero
at TestEx.doMoreStuff(TestEx.java:10)
at TestEx.doStuff(TestEx.java:7)
at TestEx.main(TestEx.java:3)
```

EXERCISE 6-3

Propagating and Catching an Exception

In this exercise you're going to create two methods that deal with exceptions. One of the methods is the `main()` method, which will call another method. If an exception is thrown in the other method, `main()` must deal with it. A `finally` statement will be included to indicate that the program has completed. The method that `main()` will call will be named `reverse`, and it will reverse the order of the characters in a `String`. If the `String` contains no characters, `reverse` will propagate an exception up to the `main()` method.

1. Create a class called `Propagate` and a `main()` method, which will remain empty for now.
2. Create a method called `reverse`. It takes an argument of a `String` and returns a `String`.
3. In `reverse`, check whether the `String` has a length of 0 by using the `String.length()` method. If the length is 0, the `reverse` method will throw an exception.

4. Now include the code to reverse the order of the `String`. Because this isn't the main topic of this chapter, the reversal code has been provided, but feel free to try it on your own.

```
String reverseStr = "";
for(int i=s.length()-1;i>=0;--i) {
  reverseStr += s.charAt(i);
}
return reverseStr;
```

5. Now in the `main()` method you will attempt to call this method and deal with any potential exceptions. Additionally, you will include a `finally` statement that displays when `main()` has finished.

Defining Exceptions

We have been discussing exceptions as a concept. We know that they are thrown when a problem of some type happens, and we know what effect they have on the flow of our program. In this section we will develop the concepts further and use exceptions in functional Java code.

Earlier we said that an exception is an occurrence that alters the normal program flow. But because this is Java, anything that's not a primitive must be...an object. Exceptions are no exception to this rule. Every exception is an instance of a class that has class `Exception` in its inheritance hierarchy. In other words, exceptions are always some subclass of `java.lang.Exception`.

When an exception is thrown, an object of a particular `Exception` subtype is instantiated and handed to the exception handler as an argument to the `catch` clause. An actual `catch` clause looks like this:

```
try {
  // some code here
}
catch (ArrayIndexOutOfBoundsException e) {
  e.printStackTrace();
}
```

In this example, `e` is an instance of the `ArrayIndexOutOfBoundsException` class. As with any other object, you can call its methods.

Exception Hierarchy

All exception classes are subtypes of class `Exception`. This class derives from the class `Throwable` (which derives from the class `Object`). Figure 6-2 shows the hierarchy for the exception classes.

As you can see, there are two subclasses that derive from `Throwable`: `Exception` and `Error`. Classes that derive from `Error` represent unusual situations that are not caused by program errors and indicate things that would not normally happen during program execution, such as the JVM running out of memory. Generally, your application won't be able to recover from an `Error`, so you're not required to handle them. If your code does not handle them (and it usually won't), it will still compile with no trouble. Although often thought of as exceptional conditions, `Errors` are technically not exceptions because they do not derive from class `Exception`.

In general, an exception represents something that happens not as a result of a programming error, but rather because some resource is not available or some other condition required for correct execution is not present. For example, if your application is supposed to communicate with another application or computer that is not answering, this is an exception that is not caused by a bug. Figure 6-2 also shows a subtype of `Exception` called `RuntimeException`. These exceptions are a special case because they sometimes do indicate program errors. They can also represent rare, difficult-to-handle exceptional conditions. Runtime exceptions are discussed in greater detail later in this chapter.

FIGURE 6-2

Exception class hierarchy

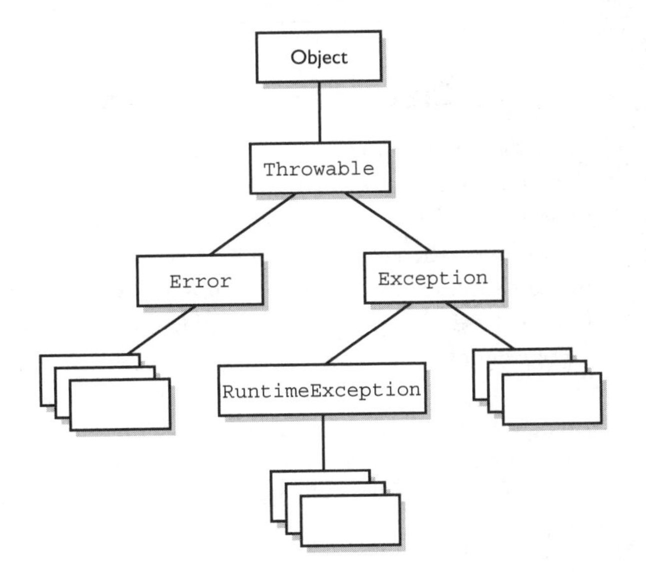

Java provides many exception classes, most of which have quite descriptive names. There are two ways to get information about an exception. The first is from the type of the exception itself. The next is from information that you can get from the exception object. Class `Throwable` (at the top of the inheritance tree for exceptions) provides its descendants with some methods that are useful in exception handlers. One of these is `printStackTrace()`. As you would expect, if you call an exception object's `printStackTrace()` method, as in the earlier example, a stack trace from where the exception occurred will be printed.

We discussed that a call stack builds upward with the most recently called method at the top. You will notice that the `printStackTrace()` method prints the most recently entered method first and continues down, printing the name of each method as it works its way down the call stack (this is called "unwinding the stack") from the top.

exam Watch

For the exam, you don't need to know any of the methods contained in the `Throwable` classes, including `Exception` and `Error`. You are expected to know that `Exception`, `Error`, `RuntimeException`, and `Throwable` types can all be thrown using the `throw` keyword and can all be caught (although you rarely will catch anything other than `Exception` subtypes).

Handling an Entire Class Hierarchy of Exceptions

We've discussed that the `catch` keyword allows you to specify a particular type of exception to catch. You can actually catch more than one type of exception in a single `catch` clause. If the exception class that you specify in the `catch` clause has no subclasses, then only the specified class of exception will be caught. However, if the class specified in the `catch` clause does have subclasses, any exception object that subclasses the specified class will be caught as well.

For example, class `IndexOutOfBoundsException` has two subclasses, `ArrayIndexOutOfBoundsException` and `StringIndexOutOfBoundsException`. You may want to write one exception handler that deals with exceptions produced by either type of boundary error, but you might not be concerned with which exception you actually have. In this case, you could write a `catch` clause like the following:

```
try {
  // Some code here that can throw a boundary exception
}
catch (IndexOutOfBoundsException e) {
  e.printStackTrace();
}
```

If any code in the `try` block throws `ArrayIndexOutOfBoundsException` or `StringIndexOutOfBoundsException`, the exception will be caught and handled. This can be convenient, but it should be used sparingly. By specifying an exception class's superclass in your `catch` clause, you're discarding valuable information about the exception. You can, of course, find out exactly what exception class you have, but if you're going to do that, you're better off writing a separate `catch` clause for each exception type of interest.

on the job

Resist the temptation to write a single catchall exception handler such as the following:

```
try {
  // some code
}
catch (Exception e) {
  e.printStackTrace();
}
```

This code will catch every exception generated. Of course, no single exception handler can properly handle every exception, and programming in this way defeats the design objective. Exception handlers that trap many errors at once will probably reduce the reliability of your program, because it's likely that an exception will be caught that the handler does not know how to handle.

Exception Matching

If you have an exception hierarchy composed of a superclass exception and a number of subtypes, and you're interested in handling one of the subtypes in a special way but want to handle all the rest together, you need write only two `catch` clauses.

When an exception is thrown, Java will try to find (by looking at the available `catch` clauses from the top down) a `catch` clause for the exception type. If it doesn't find one, it will search for a handler for a supertype of the exception. If it does not find a `catch` clause that matches a supertype for the exception, then the exception is propagated down the call stack. This process is called "exception matching." Let's look at an example.

```
 1: import java.io.*;
 2: public class ReadData {
 3:   public static void main(String args[]) {
 4:     try {
 5:       RandomAccessFile raf =
 6:         new RandomAccessFile("myfile.txt", "r");
 7:       byte b[] = new byte[1000];
 8:       raf.readFully(b, 0, 1000);
 9:     }
10:     catch(FileNotFoundException e) {
11:       System.err.println("File not found");
12:       System.err.println(e.getMessage());
13:       e.printStackTrace();
14:     }
15:     catch(IOException e) {
16:       System.err.println("IO Error");
17:       System.err.println(e.toString());
18:       e.printStackTrace();
19:     }
20:   }
21: }
```

This short program attempts to open a file and to read some data from it. Opening and reading files can generate many exceptions, most of which are some type of `IOException`. Imagine that in this program we're interested in knowing only whether the exact exception is a `FileNotFoundException`. Otherwise, we don't care exactly what the problem is.

`FileNotFoundException` is a subclass of `IOException`. Therefore, we could handle it in the `catch` clause that catches all subtypes of `IOException`, but then we would have to test the exception to determine whether it was a `FileNotFoundException`. Instead, we coded a special exception handler for the `FileNotFoundException` and a separate exception handler for all other `IOException` subtypes.

If this code generates a `FileNotFoundException`, it will be handled by the `catch` clause that begins at line 10. If it generates another `IOException`—perhaps `EOFException`, which is a subclass of `IOException`—it will be handled by the `catch` clause that begins at line 15. If some other exception is generated, such as a runtime exception of some type, neither `catch` clause will be executed and the exception will be propagated down the call stack.

Notice that the `catch` clause for the `FileNotFoundException` was placed above the handler for the `IOException`. This is really important! If we do it the opposite way, the program will not compile. The handlers for the most specific exceptions must always be placed above those for more general exceptions. The following will not compile:

```
try {
  // do risky IO things
} catch (IOException e) {
  // handle general IOExceptions
} catch (FileNotFoundException ex) {
  // handle just FileNotFoundException
}
```

You'll get a compiler error something like this:

```
TestEx.java:15: exception java.io.FileNotFoundException has
 already been caught
} catch (FileNotFoundException ex) {
  ^
```

If you think back to the people with baseball mitts (in the section "Propagating Uncaught Exceptions"), imagine that the most general mitts are the largest and can thus catch many different kinds of balls. An `IOException` mitt is large enough and flexible enough to catch any type of `IOException`. So if the person on the fifth floor (say, Fred) has a big ol' `IOException` mitt, he can't help but catch a `FileNotFoundException` ball with it. And if the guy (say, Jimmy) on the second floor is holding a `FileNotFoundException` mitt, that `FileNotFoundException` ball will never get to him, since it will always be stopped by Fred on the fifth floor, standing there with his big-enough-for-any-`IOException` mitt.

So what do you do with exceptions that are siblings in the class hierarchy? If one `Exception` class is not a subtype or supertype of the other, then the order in which the `catch` clauses are placed doesn't matter.

Exception Declaration and the Public Interface

So, how do we know that some method throws an exception that we have to catch? Just as a method must specify what type and how many arguments it accepts and what is returned, the exceptions that a method can throw must be *declared* (unless the exceptions are subclasses of `RuntimeException`). The list of thrown exceptions is part of a method's public interface. The `throws` keyword is used as follows to list the exceptions that a method can throw:

```
void myFunction() throws MyException1, MyException2 {
  // code for the method here
}
```

This method has a `void` return type, accepts no arguments, and declares that it can throw one of two types of exceptions: either type `MyException1` or type `MyException2`.

(Just because the method declares that it throws an exception doesn't mean it always will. It just tells the world that it might.)

Suppose your method doesn't directly throw an exception, but calls a method that does. You can choose not to handle the exception yourself and instead just declare it, as though it were your method that actually throws the exception. If you do declare the exception that your method might get from another method, and you don't provide a `try/catch` for it, then the method will propagate back to the method that called your method and will either be caught there or continue on to be handled by a method further down the stack.

Any method that might throw an exception (unless it's a subclass of `RuntimeException`) must declare the exception. That includes methods that aren't actually throwing it directly, but are "ducking" and letting the exception pass down to the next method in the stack. If you "duck" an exception, it is just as if you were the one actually throwing the exception. `RuntimeException` subclasses are exempt, so the compiler won't check to see if you've declared them. But all non-`RuntimeExceptions` are considered "checked" exceptions, because the compiler checks to be certain you've acknowledged that "bad things could happen here."

Remember this:

> Each method must either handle all checked exceptions by supplying a `catch` clause or list each unhandled checked exception as a thrown exception.

This rule is referred to as Java's "handle or declare" requirement (sometimes called "catch or declare").

exam watch

Look for code that invokes a method declaring an exception, where the calling method doesn't handle or declare the checked exception. The following code (which uses the `throw` keyword to throw an exception manually—more on this next) has two big problems that the compiler will prevent:

```
void doStuff() {
  doMore();
}
void doMore() {
  throw new IOException();
}
```

First, the `doMore()` method throws a checked exception but does not declare it! But suppose we fix the `doMore()` method as follows:

```
void doMore() throws IOException { … }
```

The `doStuff()` method is still in trouble because it, too, must declare the `IOException`, unless it handles it by providing a `try/catch`, with a `catch` clause that can take an `IOException`.

Again, some exceptions are exempt from this rule. An object of type `RuntimeException` may be thrown from any method without being specified as part of the method's public interface (and a handler need not be present). And even if a method does declare a `RuntimeException`, the calling method is under no obligation to handle or declare it. `RuntimeException`, `Error`, and all of their subtypes are unchecked exceptions, and unchecked exceptions do not have to be specified or handled. Here is an example:

```
import java.io.*;
class Test {
  public int myMethod1() throws EOFException {
    return myMethod2();
  }
  public int myMethod2() throws EOFException {
    // code that actually could throw the exception goes here
    return 1;
  }
}
```

Let's look at `myMethod1()`. Because `EOFException` subclasses `IOException`, and `IOException` subclasses `Exception`, it is a checked exception and must be declared as an exception that may be thrown by this method. But where will the exception actually come from? The public interface for method `myMethod2()` called here declares that an exception of this type can be thrown. Whether that method actually throws the exception itself or calls another method that throws it is unimportant to us; we simply know that we either have to catch the exception or declare that we threw it. The method `myMethod1()` does not catch the exception, so it declares that it throws it. Now let's look at another legal example, `myMethod3()`:

```
public void myMethod3() {
  // code that could throw a NullPointerException goes here
}
```

According to the comment, this method can throw a `NullPointerException`. Because `RuntimeException` is the superclass of `NullPointerException`, it is an unchecked exception and need not be declared. We can see that `myMethod3()` does not declare any exceptions.

Runtime exceptions are referred to as *unchecked* exceptions. All other exceptions are *checked* exceptions, and they don't derive from `java.lang.RuntimeException`. A checked exception must be caught somewhere in your code. If you invoke a method that throws a checked exception but you don't catch the checked exception somewhere, your code will not compile. That's why they're called checked exceptions: the compiler checks to make sure that they're handled or declared. A number of the methods in the Java API throw checked exceptions, so you will often write exception handlers to cope with exceptions generated by methods you didn't write.

You can also throw an exception yourself, and that exception can be either an existing exception from the Java API or one of your own. To create your own exception, you simply subclass `Exception` (or one of its subclasses) as follows:

```
class MyException extends Exception { }
```

And if you throw the exception, the compiler will guarantee that you declare it as follows:

```
class TestEx {
  void doStuff() {
    throw new MyException();   // Throw a checked exception
  }
}
```

The preceding code upsets the compiler:

```
TestEx.java:6: unreported exception MyException; must be caught or
declared to be thrown
  throw new MyException();
  ^
```

You need to know how an `Error` compares with checked and unchecked exceptions. Objects of type `Error` are not `Exception` objects, although they do represent exceptional conditions. Both `Exception` and `Error` share a common superclass, `Throwable`; thus both can be thrown using the `throw` keyword. When an `Error` or a subclass of `Error` (like `RuntimeException`) is thrown, it's unchecked. You are not required to catch `Error` objects or `Error` subtypes. You can also throw

exam watch

When an object of a subtype of `Exception` is thrown, it must be handled or declared. These objects are called checked exceptions and include all exceptions except those that are subtypes of `RuntimeException`, which are unchecked exceptions. Be ready to spot methods that don't follow the "handle or declare" rule, such as this:

```
class MyException extends Exception {
  void someMethod () {
    doStuff();
  }
  void doStuff() throws MyException {
    try {
      throw new MyException();
    }
    catch(MyException me) {
      throw me;
    }
  }
}
```

You need to recognize that this code won't compile. If you try, you'll get this:

```
MyException.java:3: unreported exception MyException;
must be caught or declared to be thrown
doStuff();
      ^
```

Notice that `someMethod()` fails either to handle or declare the exception that can be thrown by `doStuff()`.

an `Error` yourself (although, other than `AssertionError`, you probably won't ever want to), and you can catch one, but again, you probably won't. What, for example, would you actually do if you got an `OutOfMemoryError`? It's not like you can tell the garbage collector to run; you can bet the JVM fought desperately to save itself (and reclaimed all the memory it could) by the time you got the error. In other words, don't expect the JVM at that point to say, "Run the garbage collector? Oh, thanks so much for telling me. That just never occurred to me. Sure, I'll get right on it." Even better, what would you do if a `VirtualMachineError` arose? Your program is toast by the time you'd catch the error, so there's really no point in trying to catch one of these babies. Just remember, though, that you can! The following compiles just fine:

```
class TestEx {
  public static void main (String [] args) {
    badMethod();
  }
  static void badMethod() {  // No need to declare an Error
    doStuff();
  }
  static void doStuff() {    // No need to declare an Error
    try {
      throw new Error();
    }
    catch(Error me) {
      throw me;              // We catch it, but then rethrow it
    }
  }
}
```

If we were throwing a checked exception rather than `Error`, then the `doStuff()` method would need to declare the exception. But remember, since `Error` is not a subtype of `Exception`, it doesn't need to be declared. You're free to declare it if you like, but the compiler just doesn't care one way or another when or how the `Error` is thrown, or by whom.

on the Job

Because Java has checked exceptions, it's commonly said that Java forces developers to handle exceptions. Yes, Java forces us to write exception handlers for each exception that can occur during normal operation, but it's up to us to make the exception handlers actually do something useful. We know software managers who melt down when they see a programmer write something like this:

```
try {
  callBadMethod();
} catch (Exception ex) { }
```

Notice anything missing? Don't "eat" the exception by catching it without actually handling it. You won't even be able to tell that the exception occurred, because you'll never see the stack trace.

Rethrowing the Same Exception

Just as you can throw a new exception from a `catch` clause, you can also throw the same exception you just caught. Here's a `catch` clause that does this:

```
catch(IOException e) {
  // Do things, then if you decide you can't handle it…
  throw e;
}
```

All other `catch` clauses associated with the same `try` are ignored; if a `finally` block exists, it runs, and the exception is thrown back to the calling method (the next method down the call stack). If you throw a checked exception from a `catch` clause, you must also declare that exception! In other words, you must handle *and* declare, as opposed to handle *or* declare. The following example is illegal:

```
public void doStuff() {
  try {
    // risky IO things
  } catch(IOException ex) {
    // can't handle it
     throw ex;  // Can't throw it unless you declare it
  }
}
```

In the preceding code, the `doStuff()` method is clearly able to throw a checked exception—in this case an `IOException`—so the compiler says, "Well, that's just peachy that you have a `try/catch` in there, but it's not good enough. If you might rethrow the `IOException` you catch, then you must declare it (in the method signature)!"

EXERCISE 6-4

Creating an Exception

In this exercise we attempt to create a custom exception. We won't put in any new methods (it will have only those inherited from `Exception`), and because it extends `Exception`, the compiler considers it a checked exception. The goal of the program is to determine whether a command-line argument representing a particular food (as a string) is considered bad or okay.

1. Let's first create our exception. We will call it `BadFoodException`. This exception will be thrown when a bad food is encountered.

2. Create an enclosing class called `MyException` and a `main()` method, which will remain empty for now.
3. Create a method called `checkFood()`. It takes a `String` argument and throws our exception if it doesn't like the food it was given. Otherwise, it tells us it likes the food. You can add any foods you aren't particularly fond of to the list.
4. Now in the `main()` method, you'll get the command-line argument out of the `String` array and then pass that `String` on to the `checkFood()` method. Because it's a checked exception, the `checkFood()` method must declare it, and the `main()` method must handle it (using a `try/catch`). Do not have `main()` declare the exception, because if `main()` ducks the exception, who else is back there to catch it? (Actually, `main()` can legally declare exceptions, but don't do that in this exercise.)

As nifty as exception handling is, it's still up to the developer to make proper use of it. Exception handling makes organizing our code and signaling problems easy, but the exception handlers still have to be written. You'll find that even the most complex situations can be handled, and your code will be reusable, readable, and maintainable.

CERTIFICATION OBJECTIVE

Common Exceptions and Errors (OCA Objective 8.5)

8.5 *Recognize common exception classes and categories.*

Exception handling is another area that the exam creation team decided to expand for the OCJP 5, OCJP 6, and both Java 7 exams. The intention of this objective is to make sure that you are familiar with some of the most common exceptions and errors you'll encounter as a Java programmer.

exam watch

The questions from this section are likely to be along the lines of, "Here's some code that just did something bad, which exception will be thrown?" Throughout the exam, questions will present some code and ask you to determine whether the code will run, or whether an exception will be thrown. Since these questions are so common, understanding the causes for these exceptions is critical to your success.

This is another one of those objectives that will turn up all through the real exam (does "An exception is thrown at runtime" ring a bell?), so make sure this section gets a lot of your attention.

Where Exceptions Come From

Jump back a page and take a look at the last sentence. It's important that you understand what causes exceptions and errors, and where they come from. For the purposes of exam preparation, let's define two broad categories of exceptions and errors:

- **JVM exceptions** Those exceptions or errors that are either exclusively or most logically thrown by the JVM
- **Programmatic exceptions** Those exceptions that are thrown explicitly by application and/or API programmers

JVM Thrown Exceptions

Let's start with a very common exception, the `NullPointerException`. As we saw in earlier chapters, this exception occurs when you attempt to access an object using a reference variable with a current value of `null`. There's no way that the compiler can hope to find these problems before runtime. Take a look at the following:

```
class NPE {
  static String s;
  public static void main(String [] args) {
    System.out.println(s.length());
  }
}
```

Surely, the compiler can find the problem with that tiny little program! Nope, you're on your own. The code will compile just fine, and the JVM will throw a `NullPointerException` when it tries to invoke the `length()` method.

Earlier in this chapter we discussed the call stack. As you recall, we used the convention that `main()` would be at the bottom of the call stack, and that as `main()` invokes another method, and that method invokes another, and so on, the stack grows upward. Of course the stack resides in memory, and even if your OS gives you a gigabyte of RAM for your program, it's still a finite amount. It's possible to grow the stack so large that the OS runs out of space to store the call stack. When this happens, you get (wait for it...) a `StackOverflowError`. The most common way for this to occur is to create a recursive method. A recursive method invokes itself in the method body. Although that may sound weird, it's a very common and useful technique for such things as searching and sorting algorithms. Take a look at this code:

```
void go() {     // recursion gone bad
   go();
}
```

As you can see, if you ever make the mistake of invoking the `go()` method, your program will fall into a black hole—`go()` invoking `go()` invoking `go()`, until, no matter how much memory you have, you'll get a `StackOverflowError`. Again, only the JVM knows when this moment occurs, and the JVM will be the source of this error.

Programmatically Thrown Exceptions

Now let's look at programmatically thrown exceptions. Remember we defined "programmatically" as meaning something like this:

Created by an application and/or API developer.

For instance, many classes in the Java API have methods that take `String` arguments and convert these `Strings` into numeric primitives. A good example of these classes are the so-called "wrapper classes" that OCP candidates will study in Chapter 8. Even though we haven't talked about wrapper classes yet, the following example should make sense.

At some point long ago, some programmer wrote the `java.lang.Integer` class and created methods like `parseInt()` and `valueOf()`. That programmer wisely decided that if one of these methods was passed a `String` that could not be converted into a number, the method should throw a `NumberFormatException`. The partially implemented code might look something like this:

```
int parseInt(String s) throws NumberFormatException {
  boolean parseSuccess = false;
  int result = 0;
  // do complicated parsing
  if (!parseSuccess)    // if the parsing failed
    throw new NumberFormatException();
  return result;
}
```

Other examples of programmatic exceptions include an `AssertionError` (okay, it's not an exception, but it IS thrown programmatically), and throwing an `IllegalArgumentException`. In fact, our mythical API developer could have used `IllegalArgumentException` for her `parseInt()` method. But it turns out that `NumberFormatException` extends `IllegalArgumentException` and is a little more precise, so in this case, using `NumberFormatException` supports the notion we discussed earlier: that when you have an exception hierarchy, you should use the most precise exception that you can.

Of course, as we discussed earlier, you can also make up your very own special custom exceptions and throw them whenever you want to. These homemade exceptions also fall into the category of "programmatically thrown exceptions."

A Summary of the Exam's Exceptions and Errors

OCA Objective 8.5 does not list specific exceptions and errors; it says "recognize common exceptions...." Table 6-2 summarizes the ten exceptions and errors that are a part of the SCJP 6 exam; it will cover OCA Objective 8.5, too.

End of Part I—OCA

Barring our standard end-of-chapter stuff, such as mock exam questions, you've reached the end of the OCA part of the book. If you've studied these six chapters carefully, and then taken and reviewed the end-of-chapter mock exams and the OCA master exams and done well on them, we're confident that you're a little bit over-prepared for the official Oracle OCA exam. (Not "way" over-prepared—just a little.) Good luck, and we hope to see you back here for Part II, Chapter 7, in which we'll explore the exception handling features added in Java 7.

TABLE 6-2 Descriptions and Sources of Common Exceptions

Exception	Description	Typically Thrown
`ArrayIndexOutOfBoundsException` (Chapter 5)	Thrown when attempting to access an array with an invalid index value (either negative or beyond the length of the array).	By the JVM
`ClassCastException` (Chapter 2)	Thrown when attempting to cast a reference variable to a type that fails the IS-A test.	By the JVM
`IllegalArgumentException`	Thrown when a method receives an argument formatted differently than the method expects.	Programmatically
`IllegalStateException`	Thrown when the state of the environment doesn't match the operation being attempted—for example, using a scanner that's been closed.	Programmatically
`NullPointerException` (Chapter 3)	Thrown when attempting to invoke a method on, or access a property from, a reference variable whose current value is `null`.	By the JVM
`NumberFormatException` (this chapter)	Thrown when a method that converts a `String` to a number receives a `String` that it cannot convert.	Programmatically
`AssertionError`	Thrown when an `assert` statement's `boolean` test returns `false`.	Programmatically
`ExceptionInInitializerError` (Chapter 2)	Thrown when attempting to initialize a static variable or an initialization block.	By the JVM
`StackOverflowError` (this chapter)	Typically thrown when a method recurses too deeply. (Each invocation is added to the stack.)	By the JVM
`NoClassDefFoundError`	Thrown when the JVM can't find a class it needs, because of a command-line error, a classpath issue, or a missing `.class` file.	By the JVM

CERTIFICATION SUMMARY

This chapter covered a lot of ground, all of which involved ways of controlling your program flow, based on a conditional test. First you learned about `if` and `switch` statements. The `if` statement evaluates one or more expressions to a `boolean` result. If the result is `true`, the program will execute the code in the block that is encompassed by the `if`. If an `else` statement is used and the `if` expression evaluates to `false`, then the code following the `else` will be performed. If no `else` block is defined, then none of the code associated with the `if` statement will execute.

You also learned that the `switch` statement can be used to replace multiple `if-else` statements. The `switch` statement can evaluate integer primitive types that can be implicitly cast to an `int` (those types are `byte`, `short`, `int`, and `char`), or it can evaluate `enums`, and as of Java 7, it can evaluate `Strings`. At runtime, the JVM will try to find a match between the expression in the `switch` statement and a constant in a corresponding `case` statement. If a match is found, execution will begin at the matching case and continue on from there, executing code in all the remaining `case` statements until a `break` statement is found or the end of the `switch` statement occurs. If there is no match, then the `default` case will execute, if there is one.

You've learned about the three looping constructs available in the Java language. These constructs are the `for` loop (including the basic `for` and the enhanced `for`, which was new to Java 5), the `while` loop, and the `do` loop. In general, the `for` loop is used when you know how many times you need to go through the loop. The `while` loop is used when you do not know how many times you want to go through, whereas the `do` loop is used when you need to go through at least once. In the `for` loop and the `while` loop, the expression will have to evaluate to `true` to get inside the block and will check after every iteration of the loop. The `do` loop does not check the condition until after it has gone through the loop once. The major benefit of the `for` loop is the ability to initialize one or more variables and increment or decrement those variables in the `for` loop definition.

The `break` and `continue` statements can be used in either a labeled or unlabeled fashion. When unlabeled, the `break` statement will force the program to stop processing the innermost looping construct and start with the line of code following the loop. Using an unlabeled `continue` command will cause the program to stop execution of the current iteration of the innermost loop and proceed with the next iteration. When a `break` or a `continue` statement is used in a labeled manner, it will perform in the same way, with one exception: the statement will not apply to the innermost loop; instead, it will apply to the loop with the label. The `break` statement is used most often in conjunction with the `switch` statement. When there is a match between the `switch` expression and the `case` constant, the code following the `case` constant will be performed. To stop execution, a `break` is needed.

You've seen how Java provides an elegant mechanism in exception handling. Exception handling allows you to isolate your error-correction code into separate blocks so that the main code doesn't become cluttered by error-checking code. Another elegant feature allows you to handle similar errors with a single error-handling block, without code duplication. Also, the error handling can be deferred to methods further back on the call stack.

You learned that Java's `try` keyword is used to specify a guarded region—a block of code in which problems might be detected. An exception handler is the code that is executed when an exception occurs. The handler is defined by using Java's `catch` keyword. All `catch` clauses must immediately follow the related `try` block.

Java also provides the `finally` keyword. This is used to define a block of code that is always executed, either immediately after a `catch` clause completes or immediately after the associated `try` block in the case that no exception was thrown (or there was a `try` but no `catch`). Use `finally` blocks to release system resources and to perform any cleanup required by the code in the `try` block. A `finally` block is not required, but if there is one, it must immediately follow the last `catch`. (If there is no `catch` block, the `finally` block must immediately follow the `try` block.) It's guaranteed to be called except when the `try` or `catch` issues a `System.exit()`.

An exception object is an instance of class `Exception` or one of its subclasses. The `catch` clause takes, as a parameter, an instance of an object of a type derived from the `Exception` class. Java requires that each method either catches any checked exception it can throw or else declares that it throws the exception. The exception declaration is part of the method's signature. To declare that an exception may be thrown, the `throws` keyword is used in a method definition, along with a list of all checked exceptions that might be thrown.

Runtime exceptions are of type `RuntimeException` (or one of its subclasses). These exceptions are a special case because they do not need to be handled or declared, and thus are known as "unchecked" exceptions. Errors are of type `java.lang.Error` or its subclasses, and like runtime exceptions, they do not need to be handled or declared. Checked exceptions include any exception types that are not of type `RuntimeException` or `Error`. If your code fails either to handle a checked exception or declare that it is thrown, your code won't compile. But with unchecked exceptions or objects of type `Error`, it doesn't matter to the compiler whether you declare them or handle them, do nothing about them, or do some combination of declaring and handling. In other words, you're free to declare them and handle them, but the compiler won't care one way or the other. It's not good practice to handle an `Error`, though, because you can rarely recover from one.

Finally, remember that exceptions can be generated by the JVM, or by a programmer.

✓ TWO-MINUTE DRILL

Here are some of the key points from each certification objective in this chapter. You might want to loop through them several times.

Writing Code Using if and switch Statements (OCA Objectives 3.4 and 3.5)

- The only legal expression in an `if` statement is a `boolean` expression—in other words, an expression that resolves to a `boolean` or a `Boolean` reference.
- Watch out for `boolean` assignments (=) that can be mistaken for `boolean` equality (==) tests:

```
boolean x = false;
if (x = true) { } // an assignment, so x will always be true!
```

- Curly braces are optional for `if` blocks that have only one conditional statement. But watch out for misleading indentations.
- `switch` statements can evaluate only to `enums` or the `byte`, `short`, `int`, `char`, and, as of Java 7, `String` data types. You can't say this:

```
long s = 30;
switch(s) { }
```

- The `case` constant must be a literal or `final` variable, or a constant expression, including an `enum` or a `String`. You cannot have a case that includes a non-final variable or a range of values.
- If the condition in a `switch` statement matches a `case` constant, execution will run through all code in the `switch` following the matching `case` statement until a `break` statement or the end of the `switch` statement is encountered. In other words, the matching `case` is just the entry point into the `case` block, but unless there's a `break` statement, the matching `case` is not the only `case` code that runs.
- The `default` keyword should be used in a `switch` statement if you want to run some code when none of the `case` values match the conditional value.
- The `default` block can be located anywhere in the `switch` block, so if no preceding `case` matches, the `default` block will be entered, and if the `default` does not contain a `break`, then code will continue to execute (fall-through) to the end of the `switch` or until the `break` statement is encountered.

Writing Code Using Loops (OCA Objectives 5.1, 5.2, 5.3, and 5.4)

- ❑ A basic `for` statement has three parts: declaration and/or initialization, boolean evaluation, and the iteration expression.
- ❑ If a variable is incremented or evaluated within a basic `for` loop, it must be declared before the loop or within the `for` loop declaration.
- ❑ A variable declared (not just initialized) within the basic `for` loop declaration cannot be accessed outside the `for` loop—in other words, code below the `for` loop won't be able to use the variable.
- ❑ You can initialize more than one variable of the same type in the first part of the basic `for` loop declaration; each initialization must be separated by a comma.
- ❑ An enhanced `for` statement (new as of Java 5) has two parts: the *declaration* and the *expression*. It is used only to loop through arrays or collections.
- ❑ With an enhanced `for`, the *expression* is the array or collection through which you want to loop.
- ❑ With an enhanced `for`, the *declaration* is the block variable, whose type is compatible with the elements of the array or collection, and that variable contains the value of the element for the given iteration.
- ❑ You cannot use a number (old C-style language construct) or anything that does not evaluate to a `boolean` value as a condition for an `if` statement or looping construct. You can't, for example, say `if(x)`, unless `x` is a `boolean` variable.
- ❑ The `do` loop will enter the body of the loop at least once, even if the test condition is not met.

Using break and continue (OCA Objective 5.5)

- ❑ An unlabeled `break` statement will cause the current iteration of the innermost looping construct to stop and the line of code following the loop to run.
- ❑ An unlabeled `continue` statement will cause the current iteration of the innermost loop to stop, the condition of that loop to be checked, and if the condition is met, the loop to run again.
- ❑ If the `break` statement or the `continue` statement is labeled, it will cause similar action to occur on the labeled loop, not the innermost loop.

Handling Exceptions (OCA Objectives 8.1, 8.2, 8.3, and 8.4)

- ❑ Exceptions come in two flavors: checked and unchecked.
- ❑ Checked exceptions include all subtypes of `Exception`, excluding classes that extend `RuntimeException`.
- ❑ Checked exceptions are subject to the handle or declare rule; any method that might throw a checked exception (including methods that invoke methods that can throw a checked exception) must either declare the exception using `throws`, or handle the exception with an appropriate `try/catch`.
- ❑ Subtypes of `Error` or `RuntimeException` are unchecked, so the compiler doesn't enforce the handle or declare rule. You're free to handle them or to declare them, but the compiler doesn't care one way or the other.
- ❑ If you use an optional `finally` block, it will always be invoked, regardless of whether an exception in the corresponding `try` is thrown or not, and regardless of whether a thrown exception is caught or not.
- ❑ The only exception to the `finally`-will-always-be-called rule is that a `finally` will not be invoked if the JVM shuts down. That could happen if code from the `try` or `catch` blocks calls `System.exit()`.
- ❑ Just because `finally` is invoked does not mean it will complete. Code in the `finally` block could itself raise an exception or issue a `System.exit()`.
- ❑ Uncaught exceptions propagate back through the call stack, starting from the method where the exception is thrown and ending with either the first method that has a corresponding catch for that exception type or a JVM shutdown (which happens if the exception gets to `main()`, and `main()` is "ducking" the exception by declaring it).
- ❑ You can create your own exceptions, normally by extending `Exception` or one of its subtypes. Your exception will then be considered a checked exception (unless you are extending from `RuntimeException`), and the compiler will enforce the handle or declare rule for that exception.
- ❑ All `catch` blocks must be ordered from most specific to most general. If you have a `catch` clause for both `IOException` and `Exception`, you must put the `catch` for `IOException` first in your code. Otherwise, the `IOException` would be caught by `catch(Exception e)`, because a `catch` argument can catch the specified exception or any of its subtypes! The compiler will stop you from defining `catch` clauses that can never be reached.
- ❑ Some exceptions are created by programmers, and some by the JVM.

SELF TEST

1. (Also an Upgrade topic) Given:

```
public class Flipper {
  public static void main(String[] args) {
    String o = "-";
    switch("FRED".toLowerCase().substring(1,3)) {
      case "yellow":
        o += "y";
      case "red":
        o += "r";
      case "green":
        o += "g";
    }
    System.out.println(o);
  }
}
```

What is the result?

A. `-`

B. `-r`

C. `-rg`

D. Compilation fails

E. An exception is thrown at runtime

2. Given:

```
class Plane {
  static String s = "-";
  public static void main(String[] args) {
    new Plane().s1();
    System.out.println(s);
  }
  void s1() {
    try { s2(); }
    catch (Exception e) { s += "c"; }
  }
  void s2() throws Exception  {
    s3();  s += "2";
    s3();  s += "2b";
  }
  void s3() throws Exception {
    throw new Exception();
  }
}
```

What is the result?

A. `-`

B. `-c`

C. `-c2`

D. `-2c`

E. `-c22b`

F. `-2c2b`

G. `-2c2bc`

H. Compilation fails

3. Given:

```
try { int x = Integer.parseInt("two"); }
```

Which could be used to create an appropriate `catch` block? (Choose all that apply.)

A. `ClassCastException`

B. `IllegalStateException`

C. `NumberFormatException`

D. `IllegalArgumentException`

E. `ExceptionInInitializerError`

F. `ArrayIndexOutOfBoundsException`

4. Given:

```
public class Flip2 {
  public static void main(String[] args) {
    String o = "-";
    String[] sa = new String[4];
    for(int i = 0; i < args.length; i++)
      sa[i] = args[i];
    for(String n: sa) {
      switch(n.toLowerCase()) {
        case "yellow": o += "y";
        case "red":    o += "r";
        case "green":  o += "g";
      }
    }
    System.out.print(o);
  }
}
```

And given the command-line invocation:

```
Java Flip2 RED Green YeLLow
```

Which are true? (Choose all that apply.)

A. The string `rgy` will appear somewhere in the output

B. The string `rgg` will appear somewhere in the output

C. The string `gyr` will appear somewhere in the output

D. Compilation fails

E. An exception is thrown at runtime

5. Given:

```
1. class Loopy {
2.   public static void main(String[] args) {
3.     int[] x = {7,6,5,4,3,2,1};
4.     // insert code here
5.       System.out.print(y + " ");
6.     }
7.   }
8. }
```

Which, inserted independently at line 4, compiles? (Choose all that apply.)

A. `for(int y : x) {`

B. `for(x : int y) {`

C. `int y = 0; for(y : x) {`

D. `for(int y=0, z=0; z<x.length; z++) { y = x[z];`

E. `for(int y=0, int z=0; z<x.length; z++) { y = x[z];`

F. `int y = 0; for(int z=0; z<x.length; z++) { y = x[z];`

6. Given:

```
class Emu {
  static String s = "-";
  public static void main(String[] args) {
    try {
      throw new Exception();
    } catch (Exception e) {
        try {
          try { throw new Exception();
          } catch (Exception ex) { s += "ic "; }
          throw new Exception(); }
        catch (Exception x) { s += "mc "; }
        finally { s += "mf "; }
    } finally { s += "of "; }
    System.out.println(s);
} }
```

What is the result?

A. `-ic of`

B. `-mf of`

C. `-mc mf`

D. `-ic mf of`

E. `-ic mc mf of`

F. `-ic mc of mf`

G. Compilation fails

7. Given:

```
 3. class SubException extends Exception { }
 4. class SubSubException extends SubException { }
 5.
 6. public class CC { void doStuff() throws SubException { } }
 7.
 8. class CC2 extends CC { void doStuff() throws SubSubException { } }
 9.
10. class CC3 extends CC { void doStuff() throws Exception { } }
11.
12. class CC4 extends CC { void doStuff(int x) throws Exception { } }
13.
14. class CC5 extends CC {  void doStuff()  { } }
```

What is the result? (Choose all that apply.)

A. Compilation succeeds

B. Compilation fails due to an error on line 8

C. Compilation fails due to an error on line 10

D. Compilation fails due to an error on line 12

E. Compilation fails due to an error on line 14

8. (OCP only) Given:

```
 3. public class Ebb {
 4.   static int x = 7;
 5.   public static void main(String[] args) {
 6.     String s = "";
 7.     for(int y = 0; y < 3; y++) {
 8.       x++;
 9.       switch(x) {
10.         case 8: s += "8 ";
11.         case 9: s += "9 ";
12.         case 10: { s+= "10 "; break; }
13.         default: s += "d ";
14.         case 13: s+= "13 ";
15.       }
```

```
16.        }
17.        System.out.println(s);
18.     }
19.     static { x++; }
20. }
```

What is the result?

A. `9 10 d`

B. `8 9 10 d`

C. `9 10 10 d`

D. `9 10 10 d 13`

E. `8 9 10 10 d 13`

F. `8 9 10 9 10 10 d 13`

G. Compilation fails

9. Given:

```
 3. class Infinity { }
 4. public class Beyond extends Infinity {
 5.   static Integer i;
 6.   public static void main(String[] args) {
 7.     int sw = (int)(Math.random() * 3);
 8.     switch(sw) {
 9.       case 0: {  for(int x = 10; x > 5; x++)
10.                    if(x > 10000000) x = 10;
11.                  break; }
12.       case 1: {  int y = 7 * i;  break;  }
13.       case 2: {  Infinity inf = new Beyond();
14.                  Beyond b = (Beyond)inf;  }
15.     }
16.   }
17. }
```

And given that line 7 will assign the value 0, 1, or 2 to `sw`, which are true? (Choose all that apply.)

A. Compilation fails

B. A `ClassCastException` might be thrown

C. A `StackOverflowError` might be thrown

D. A `NullPointerException` might be thrown

E. An `IllegalStateException` might be thrown

F. The program might hang without ever completing

G. The program will always complete without exception

10. Given:

```
 3. public class Circles {
 4.   public static void main(String[] args) {
 5.     int[] ia = {1,3,5,7,9};
 6.     for(int x : ia) {
 7.       for(int j = 0; j < 3; j++) {
 8.         if(x > 4 && x < 8) continue;
 9.         System.out.print(" " + x);
10.         if(j == 1) break;
11.         continue;
12.       }
13.       continue;
14.     }
15.   }
16. }
```

What is the result?

A. `1 3 9`

B. `5 5 7 7`

C. `1 3 3 9 9`

D. `1 1 3 3 9 9`

E. `1 1 1 3 3 3 9 9 9`

F. Compilation fails

11. Given:

```
 3. public class OverAndOver {
 4.   static String s = "";
 5.   public static void main(String[] args) {
 6.     try {
 7.       s += "1";
 8.       throw new Exception();
 9.     } catch (Exception e) { s += "2";
10.     } finally { s += "3"; doStuff(); s += "4";
11.     }
12.     System.out.println(s);
13.   }
14.   static void doStuff() { int x = 0; int y = 7/x; }
15. }
```

What is the result?

A. `12`

B. `13`

C. `123`

D. `1234`

E. Compilation fails

F. 123 followed by an exception

G. 1234 followed by an exception

H. An exception is thrown with no other output

12. Given:

```
 3. public class Wind {
 4.   public static void main(String[] args) {
 5.     foreach:
 6.     for(int j=0; j<5; j++) {
 7.       for(int k=0; k< 3; k++) {
 8.         System.out.print(" " + j);
 9.         if(j==3 && k==1) break foreach;
10.         if(j==0 || j==2) break;
11.       }
12.     }
13.   }
14. }
```

What is the result?

A. 0 1 2 3

B.1 1 1 3 3

C. 0 1 1 1 2 3 3

D. 1 1 1 3 3 4 4 4

E. 0 1 1 1 2 3 3 4 4 4

F. Compilation fails

13. Given:

```
 3. public class Gotcha {
 4.   public static void main(String[] args) {
 5.     // insert code here
 6.
 7.   }
 8.   void go() {
 9.     go();
10.   }
11. }
```

And given the following three code fragments:

```
I.   new Gotcha().go();

II.  try { new Gotcha().go(); }
     catch (Error e) { System.out.println("ouch"); }

III. try { new Gotcha().go(); }
     catch (Exception e) { System.out.println("ouch"); }
```

When fragments I–III are added, independently, at line 5, which are true? (Choose all that apply.)

A. Some will not compile

B. They will all compile

C. All will complete normally

D. None will complete normally

E. Only one will complete normally

F. Two of them will complete normally

14. Given the code snippet:

```
String s = "bob";
String[] sa = {"a", "bob"};
final String s2 = "bob";
StringBuilder sb = new StringBuilder("bob");

// switch(sa[1]) {           // line 1
// switch("b" + "ob") {      // line 2
// switch(sb.toString()) {   // line 3

// case "ann":   ;           // line 4
// case s:       ;           // line 5
// case s2:      ;           // line 6
}
```

And given that the numbered lines will all be tested by un-commenting one `switch` statement and one `case` statement together, which line(s) will FAIL to compile? (Choose all that apply.)

A. line 1

B. line 2

C. line 3

D. line 4

E. line 5

F. line 6

G. All six lines of code will compile

15. Given:

```
1. public class Frisbee {
2.   // insert code here
3.     int x = 0;
4.     System.out.println(7/x);
5.   }
6. }
```

And given the following four code fragments:

```
I.   public static void main(String[] args) {
II.  public static void main(String[] args) throws Exception {
III. public static void main(String[] args) throws IOException {
IV.  public static void main(String[] args) throws RuntimeException {
```

If the four fragments are inserted independently at line 2, which are true? (Choose all that apply.)

A. All four will compile and execute without exception

B. All four will compile and execute and throw an exception

C. Some, but not all, will compile and execute without exception

D. Some, but not all, will compile and execute and throw an exception

E. When considering fragments II, III, and IV, of those that will compile, adding a `try/catch` block around line 4 will cause compilation to fail

16. Given:

```
 2. class MyException extends Exception { }
 3. class Tire {
 4.   void doStuff() {  }
 5. }
 6. public class Retread extends Tire {
 7.   public static void main(String[] args) {
 8.     new Retread().doStuff();
 9.   }
10.   // insert code here
11.     System.out.println(7/0);
12.   }
13. }
```

And given the following four code fragments:

```
I.   void doStuff() {
II.  void doStuff() throws MyException {
III. void doStuff() throws RuntimeException {
IV.  void doStuff() throws ArithmeticException {
```

When fragments I–IV are added, independently, at line 10, which are true? (Choose all that apply.)

A. None will compile

B. They will all compile

C. Some, but not all, will compile

D. All of those that compile will throw an exception at runtime

E. None of those that compile will throw an exception at runtime

F. Only some of those that compile will throw an exception at runtime

SELF TEST ANSWERS

1. ☑ **A** is correct. As of Java 7 the code is legal, but the `substring()` method's second argument is exclusive. If the invocation had been `substring(1,4)`, the output would have been `-rg`. Note: We hope you won't have too many exam questions that focus on API trivia like this one. If you knew the switch was legal, give yourself "almost full credit."
   ☒ **B, C, D,** and **E** are incorrect based on the above. (OCA Objectives 2.7 and 3.5, and Upgrade Objective 1.1)

2. ☑ **B** is correct. Once `s3()` throws the exception to `s2()`, `s2()` throws it to `s1()`, and no more of `s2()`'s code will be executed.
   ☒ **A, C, D, E, F, G,** and **H** are incorrect based on the above. (OCA Objectives 8.2 and 8.4)

3. ☑ **C** and **D** are correct. `Integer.parseInt` can throw a `NumberFormatException`, and `IllegalArgumentException` is its superclass (that is, a broader exception).
   ☒ **A, B, E,** and **F** are not in `NumberFormatException`'s class hierarchy. (OCA Objective 8.5)

4. ☑ **E** is correct. As of Java 7 the syntax is legal. The `sa[]` array receives only three arguments from the command line, so on the last iteration through `sa[]`, a `NullPointerException` is thrown.
   ☒ **A, B, C,** and **D** are incorrect based on the above. (OCA Objectives 3.5, 5.2, and 8.5, and Upgrade Objective 1.1)

5. ☑ **A, D,** and **F** are correct. **A** is an example of the enhanced `for` loop. **D** and **F** are examples of the basic `for` loop.
   ☒ **B, C,** and **E** are incorrect. **B** is incorrect because its operands are swapped. **C** is incorrect because the enhanced `for` must declare its first operand. **E** is incorrect syntax to declare two variables in a `for` statement. (OCA Objective 5.2)

6. ☑ **E** is correct. There is no problem nesting `try/catch` blocks. As is normal, when an exception is thrown, the code in the `catch` block runs, and then the code in the `finally` block runs.
   ☒ **A, B, C, D,** and **F** are incorrect based on the above. (OCA Objectives 8.2 and 8.4)

7. ☑ **C** is correct. An overriding method cannot throw a broader exception than the method it's overriding. Class CC4's method is an overload, not an override.
   ☒ **A, B, D,** and **E** are incorrect based on the above. (OCA Objectives 8.2 and 8.4)

8. ☑ **D** is correct. Did you catch the static initializer block? Remember that switches work on "fall-through" logic, and that fall-through logic also applies to the default case, which is used when no other case matches.
   ☒ **A, B, C, E, F,** and **G** are incorrect based on the above. (OCA Objective 3.5)

9. ☑ **D** and **F** are correct. Because `i` was not initialized, case 1 will throw a `NullPointerException`. Case 0 will initiate an endless loop, not a stack overflow. Case 2's downcast will *not* cause an exception.

☒ **A, B, C, E,** and **G** are incorrect based on the above. (OCA Objectives 3.5 and 8.4)

10. ☑ **D** is correct. The basic rule for unlabeled `continue` statements is that the current iteration stops early and execution jumps to the next iteration. The last two `continue` statements are redundant!

☒ **A, B, C, E,** and **F** are incorrect based on the above. (OCA Objectives 5.2 and 5.5)

11. ☑ **H** is correct. It's true that the value of `String s` is `123` at the time that the divide-by-zero exception is thrown, but `finally()` is *not* guaranteed to complete, and in this case `finally()` never completes, so the `System.out.println` (S.O.P) never executes.

☒ **A, B, C, D, E, F,** and **G** are incorrect based on the above. (OCA Objective 8.2)

12. ☑ **C** is correct. A `break` breaks out of the current innermost loop and carries on. A labeled `break` breaks out of and terminates the labeled loops.

☒ **A, B, D, E,** and **F** are incorrect based on the above. (OCA Objectives 5.2 and 5.5)

13. ☑ **B** and **E** are correct. First off, `go()` is a badly designed recursive method, guaranteed to cause a `StackOverflowError`. Since `Exception` is not a superclass of `Error`, catching an `Exception` will not help handle an `Error`, so fragment III will not complete normally. Only fragment II will catch the `Error`.

☒ **A, C, D,** and **F** are incorrect based on the above. (OCA Objectives 8.1, 8.2, and 8.4)

14. ☑ **E** is correct. A `switch`'s `cases` must be compile-time constants or `enum` values.

☒ **A, B, C, D, F,** and **G** are incorrect based on the above. (OCA Objective 3.5 and Upgrade Objective 1.1)

15. ☑ **D** is correct. This is kind of sneaky, but remember that we're trying to toughen you up for the real exam. If you're going to throw an `IOException`, you have to import the java.io package or declare the exception with a fully qualified name.

☒ **A, B, C,** and **E** are incorrect. **A, B,** and **C** are incorrect based on the above. **E** is incorrect because it's okay both to handle and declare an exception. (OCA Objectives 8.2 and 8.5)

16. ☑ **C** and **D** are correct. An overriding method cannot throw checked exceptions that are broader than those thrown by the overridden method. However, an overriding method *can* throw `RuntimeExceptions` not thrown by the overridden method.

☒ **A, B, E,** and **F** are incorrect based on the above. (OCA Objective 8.1)

CHAPTERS

7

Assertions and Java 7 Exceptions

CERTIFICATION OBJECTIVES

- Test Invariants by Using Assertions
- Develop Code That Handles Multiple Exception Types in a Single catch Block
- Develop Code That Uses try-with-resources Statements (Including Using Classes That Implement the AutoCloseable Interface)

✓ Two-Minute Drill

Q&A Self Test

If you are coming back after having sat the OCA, congratulations! You are now ready to progress to the OCP. The assertion mechanism, added to the language with version 1.4, gives you a way to do testing and debugging checks on conditions you expect to smoke out while developing, when you don't necessarily need or want the runtime overhead associated with exception handling.

If you do need or want exception handling, you'll be learning about two new features added to exception handling in Java 7. Multi-`catch` gives you a way of dealing with two or more exception types at once. `try`-with-resources lets you close your resources very easily.

CERTIFICATION OBJECTIVE

Working with the Assertion Mechanism (OCP Objective 6.5)

6.5 *Test invariants by using assertions.*

You know you're not supposed to make assumptions, but you can't help it when you're writing code. You put them in comments:

```
if (x > 2) {
  // do something
} else if (x < 2) {
  // do something
} else {
  // x must be 2
  // do something else
}
```

You write `print` statements with them:

```
while (true) {
  if (x > 2) {
    break;
  }
  System.out.print("If we got here " +
                   "something went horribly wrong");
}
```

Added to the Java language beginning with version 1.4, assertions let you test your assumptions during development, without the expense (in both your time and program overhead) of writing exception handlers for exceptions that you assume will never happen once the program is out of development and fully deployed.

Starting with exam 310-035 (version 1.4 of the Sun Certified Java Programmer exam) and continuing through to the current exam 1Z0-804 (OCPJP 7), you're expected to know the basics of how assertions work, including how to enable them, how to use them, and how *not* to use them.

Assertions Overview

Suppose you assume that a number passed into a method (say, `methodA()`) will never be negative. While testing and debugging, you want to validate your assumption, but you don't want to have to strip out `print` statements, runtime exception handlers, or if/else tests when you're done with development. But leaving any of those in is, at the least, a performance hit. Assertions to the rescue! Check out the following code:

```
private void methodA(int num) {
  if (num >= 0) {
    useNum(num + x);
  } else {  // num < 0 (this should never happen!)
    System.out.println("Yikes! num is a negative number! "
                        + num);
  }
}
```

Because you're so certain of your assumption, you don't want to take the time (or program performance hit) to write exception-handling code. And at runtime, you don't want the `if/else` either because if you do reach the `else` condition, it means your earlier logic (whatever was running prior to this method being called) is flawed.

Assertions let you test your assumptions during development, but the assertion code basically evaporates when the program is deployed, leaving behind no overhead or debugging code to track down and remove. Let's rewrite `methodA()` to validate that the argument was not negative:

```
private void methodA(int num) {
  assert (num>=0);    // throws an AssertionError
                      // if this test isn't true
  useNum(num + x);
}
```

Not only do assertions let your code stay cleaner and tighter, but because assertions are inactive unless specifically "turned on" (enabled), the code will run as though it were written like this:

```
private void methodA(int num) {
  useNum(num + x);  // we've tested this;
                    // we now know we're good here
}
```

Assertions work quite simply. You always assert that something is `true`. If it is, no problem. Code keeps running. But if your assertion turns out to be wrong (`false`), then a stop-the-world `AssertionError` is thrown (which you should never, ever handle!) right then and there, so you can fix whatever logic flaw led to the problem.

Assertions come in two flavors: *really simple* and *simple*, as follows:

Really simple:

```
private void doStuff() {
  assert (y > x);
  // more code assuming y is greater than x
}
```

Simple:

```
private void doStuff() {
  assert (y > x): "y is " + y + " x is " + x;
  // more code assuming y is greater than x
}
```

The difference between the two is that the simple version adds a second expression separated from the first (boolean expression) by a colon—this expression's string value is added to the stack trace. Both versions throw an immediate `AssertionError`, but the simple version gives you a little more debugging help, while the really simple version tells you only that your assumption was false.

on the job

Assertions are typically enabled when an application is being tested and debugged, but disabled when the application is deployed. The assertions are still in the code, although ignored by the JVM, so if you do have a deployed application that starts misbehaving, you can always choose to enable assertions in the field for additional testing.

Assertion Expression Rules

Assertions can have either one or two expressions, depending on whether you're using the "simple" or the "really simple." The first expression must always result in a `boolean` value! Follow the same rules you use for `if` and `while` tests. The whole point is to assert `aTest`, which means you're asserting that `aTest` is `true`. If it is `true`, no problem. If it's not `true`, however, then your assumption was wrong and you get an `AssertionError`.

The second expression, used only with the simple version of an `assert` statement, can be anything that results in a value. Remember, the second expression is used to generate a `String` message that displays in the stack trace to give you a little more debugging information. It works much like `System.out.println()` in that you can pass it a primitive or an object, and it will convert it into a `String` representation. It must resolve to a value!

The following code lists legal and illegal expressions for both parts of an `assert` statement. Remember, expression2 is used only with the simple `assert` statement, whereas the second expression exists solely to give you a little more debugging detail:

```
void noReturn() { }
int aReturn() { return 1; }
void go() {
  int x = 1;
  boolean b = true;

  // the following six are legal assert statements
  assert(x == 1);
  assert(b);
  assert true;
  assert(x == 1) : x;
  assert(x == 1) : aReturn();
  assert(x == 1) : new ValidAssert();

  // the following six are ILLEGAL assert statements
  assert(x = 1);              // none of these are booleans
  assert(x);
  assert 0;
  assert(x == 1) : ;          // none of these return a value
  assert(x == 1) : noReturn();
  assert(x == 1) : ValidAssert va;
}
```

exam watch

If you see the word "expression" in a question about assertions and the question doesn't specify whether it means expression1 (the boolean test) or expression2 (the value to print in the stack trace), always assume the word "expression" refers to expression1, the boolean test. For example, consider the following question:

Exam Question: An `assert` expression must result in a `boolean` value, true or false?

Assume that the word "expression" refers to expression1 of an `assert`, so the question statement is correct. If the statement were referring to expression2, however, the statement would not be correct since expression2 can have a result of any value, not just a `boolean`.

Enabling Assertions

If you want to use assertions, you have to think first about how to compile with assertions in your code and then about how to run with assertions enabled. Both require version 1.4 or greater, and that brings us to the first issue: how to compile with assertions in your code.

Identifier vs. Keyword

Prior to version 1.4, you might very well have written code like this:

```
int assert = getInitialValue();
if (assert == getActualResult()) {
  // do something
}
```

Notice that in the preceding code, `assert` is used as an identifier. That's not a problem prior to 1.4. But you cannot use a keyword/reserved word as an identifier, and beginning with version 1.4, `assert` is a keyword. The bottom line is this:

You can use `assert` as a keyword or as an identifier, but not both.

on the job

If, for some reason, you're using a Java 1.4 compiler and you're using `assert` as a keyword (in other words, you're actually trying to `assert` something in your code), then you must explicitly enable assertion-awareness at compile time, as follows:

```
javac -source 1.4 com/geeksanonymous/TestClass.java
```

You can read that as "compile the class `TestClass`, in the directory `com/geeksanonymous`, and do it in the 1.4 way, where `assert` is a keyword."

Use Version 7 of java and javac

As far as the exam is concerned, you'll ALWAYS be using version 7 of the Java compiler (`javac`) and version 7 of the Java application launcher (`java`). You might see questions about older versions of source code, but those questions will always be in the context of compiling and launching old code with the current versions of `javac` and `java`.

Compiling Assertion-Aware Code

The Java 7 compiler will use the `assert` keyword by default. Unless you tell it otherwise, the compiler will generate an error message if it finds the word `assert` used as an identifier. However, you can tell the compiler that you're giving it an old piece of code to compile and that it should pretend to be an old compiler! Let's say you've got to make a quick fix to an old piece of 1.3 code that uses `assert` as an identifier. At the command line, you can type

```
javac -source 1.3 OldCode.java
```

The compiler will issue warnings when it discovers the word `assert` used as an identifier, but the code will compile and execute. Suppose you tell the compiler that your code is version 1.4 or later; for instance:

```
javac -source 1.4 NotQuiteSoOldCode.java
```

In this case, the compiler will issue errors when it discovers the word `assert` used as an identifier.

If you want to tell the compiler to use Java 7 rules, you can do one of three things: omit the `-source` option, which is the default, or add one of two source options:

```
-source 1.7 or -source 7
```

If you want to use `assert` as an identifier in your code, you MUST compile using the `-source 1.3` option. Table 7-1 summarizes how the Java 7 compiler will react to `assert` as either an identifier or a keyword.

TABLE 7-1 Using Various Java Versions to Compile Code That Uses `assert` as an Identifier or a Keyword

Command Line	If assert Is an Identifier	If assert Is a Keyword
`javac -source 1.3 TestAsserts.java`	Code compiles with warnings	Compilation fails
`javac -source 1.4 TestAsserts.java`	Compilation fails	Code compiles
`javac -source 1.5 TestAsserts.java` `javac -source 5 TestAsserts.java`	Compilation fails	Code compiles
`javac -source 1.6 TestAsserts.java` `javac -source 6 TestAsserts.java`	Compilation fails	Code compiles
`javac -source 1.7 TestAsserts.java` `javac -source 7 TestAsserts.java`	Compilation fails	Code compiles
`javac TestAsserts.java`	Compilation fails	Code compiles

Running with Assertions

Here's where it gets cool. Once you've written your assertion-aware code (in other words, code that uses `assert` as a keyword, to actually perform assertions at runtime), you can choose to enable or disable your assertions at runtime! Remember, assertions are disabled by default.

Enabling Assertions at Runtime

You enable assertions at runtime with

```
java -ea com.geeksanonymous.TestClass
```

or

```
java -enableassertions com.geeksanonymous.TestClass
```

The preceding command-line switches tell the JVM to run with assertions enabled.

Disabling Assertions at Runtime

You must also know the command-line switches for disabling assertions:

```
java -da com.geeksanonymous.TestClass
```

or

```
java -disableassertions com.geeksanonymous.TestClass
```

Because assertions are disabled by default, using the disable switches might seem unnecessary. Indeed, using the switches the way we do in the preceding example just gives you the default behavior (in other words, you get the same result, regardless of whether you use the disabling switches). But... you can also selectively enable and disable assertions in such a way that they're enabled for some classes and/or packages and disabled for others while a particular program is running.

Selective Enabling and Disabling

The command-line switches for assertions can be used in various ways:

- **With no arguments (as in the preceding examples)** Enables or disables assertions in all classes, except for the system classes.
- **With a package name** Enables or disables assertions in the package specified and in any packages below this package in the same directory hierarchy (more on that in a moment).
- **With a class name** Enables or disables assertions in the class specified.

You can combine switches to, say, disable assertions in a single class but keep them enabled for all others as follows:

```
java -ea  -da:com.geeksanonymous.Foo
```

The preceding command line tells the JVM to enable assertions in general, but disable them in the class `com.geeksanonymous.Foo`. You can do the same selectivity for a package as follows:

```
java -ea -da:com.geeksanonymous...
```

The preceding command line tells the JVM to enable assertions in general, but disable them in the package `com.geeksanonymous` and all of its subpackages! You may not be familiar with the term subpackages, since there wasn't much use of that term prior to assertions. A subpackage is any package in a subdirectory of the named package. For example, look at the following directory tree:

```
com
   |_geeksanonymous
                  |_Foo.class
                  |_twelvesteps
                             |_StepOne.class
                             |_StepTwo.class
```

This tree lists three directories:

```
com
geeksanonymous
twelvesteps
and three classes:
com.geeksanonymous.Foo
com.geeksanonymous.twelvesteps.StepOne
com.geeksanonymous.twelvesteps.StepTwo
```

The subpackage of `com.geeksanonymous` is the `twelvesteps` package. Remember that in Java, the `com.geeksanonymous.twelvesteps` package is treated as a completely distinct package that has no relationship with the packages above it (in this example, the `com.geeksanonymous` package), except they just happen to share a couple of directories. Table 7-2 lists examples of command-line switches for enabling and disabling assertions.

Using Assertions Appropriately

Not all legal uses of assertions are considered appropriate. As with so much of Java, you can abuse the intended use of assertions, despite the best efforts of Oracle's Java engineers to discourage you from doing so. For example, you're never supposed to handle an assertion failure. That means you shouldn't catch it with a `catch` clause and attempt to recover. Legally, however, `AssertionError` is a subclass of `Throwable`, so it can be caught. But just don't do it! If you're going to try to recover from something, it should be an exception. To discourage you from trying to substitute an assertion for an exception, the `AssertionError` doesn't provide access to the object that generated it. All you get is the `String` message.

So who gets to decide what's appropriate? Oracle. The exam uses Oracle's "official" assertion documentation to define appropriate and inappropriate uses.

Don't Use Assertions to Validate Arguments to a public Method

The following is an inappropriate use of assertions:

```
public void doStuff(int x) {
  assert (x > 0);              // inappropriate !
  // do things with x
}
```

TABLE 7-2 Assertion Command-Line Switches

Command-Line Example	What It Means
`java -ea` `java -enableassertions`	Enable assertions.
`java -da` `java -disableassertions`	Disable assertions (the default behavior).
`java -ea:com.foo.Bar`	Enable assertions in class `com.foo.Bar`.
`java -ea:com.foo...`	Enable assertions in package `com.foo` and any of its subpackages.
`java -ea -dsa`	Enable assertions in general, but disable assertions in system classes.
`java -ea -da:com.foo...`	Enable assertions in general, but disable assertions in package `com.foo` and any of its subpackages.

exam watch

If you see the word "appropriate" on the exam, do not mistake that for "legal." "Appropriate" always refers to the way in which something is supposed to be used, according to either the developers of the mechanism or best practices officially embraced by Oracle. If you see the word "correct" in the context of assertions, as in, "Line 3 is a correct use of assertions," you should also assume that correct is referring to how assertions SHOULD be used rather than how they legally COULD be used.

A `public` method might be called from code that you don't control (or from code you have never seen). Because `public` methods are part of your interface to the outside world, you're supposed to guarantee that any constraints on the arguments will be enforced by the method itself. But since assertions aren't guaranteed to actually run (they're typically disabled in a deployed application), the enforcement won't happen if assertions aren't enabled. You don't want publicly accessible code that works only conditionally, depending on whether assertions are enabled.

If you need to validate `public` method arguments, you'll probably use exceptions to throw, say, an `IllegalArgumentException` if the values passed to the `public` method are invalid.

Do Use Assertions to Validate Arguments to a private Method

If you write a `private` method, you almost certainly wrote (or control) any code that calls it. When you assume that the logic in code calling your `private` method is correct, you can test that assumption with an assertion as follows:

```
private void doMore(int x) {
  assert (x > 0);
  // do things with x
}
```

The only difference that matters between the preceding example and the one before it is the access modifier. So, do enforce constraints on `private` methods' arguments, but do not enforce constraints on `public` methods. You're certainly free to compile assertion code with an inappropriate validation of `public` arguments, but for the exam (and real life), you need to know that you shouldn't do it.

Don't Use Assertions to Validate Command-Line Arguments

This is really just a special case of the "Do not use assertions to validate arguments to a `public` method" rule. If your program requires command-line arguments, you'll probably use the exception mechanism to enforce them.

Do Use Assertions, Even in public Methods, to Check for Cases That You Know Are Never, Ever Supposed to Happen

This can include code blocks that should never be reached, including the default of a `switch` statement as follows:

```
switch(x) {
  case 1: y = 3; break;
  case 2: y = 9; break;
  case 3: y = 27; break;
  default: assert false; // we're never supposed to get here!
}
```

If you assume that a particular code block won't be reached, as in the preceding example where you assert that `x` must be 1, 2, or 3, then you can use `assert false` to cause an `AssertionError` to be thrown immediately if you ever do reach that code. So in the `switch` example, we're not performing a boolean test—we've already asserted that we should never be there, so just getting to that point is an automatic failure of our assertion/assumption.

Don't Use assert Expressions That Can Cause Side Effects!

The following would be a very bad idea:

```
public void doStuff() {
  assert (modifyThings());
  // continues on
}
public boolean modifyThings() {
  y = x++;
  return true;
}
```

The rule is that an `assert` expression should leave the program in the same state it was in before the expression! Think about it. `assert` expressions aren't guaranteed to always run, so you don't want your code to behave differently depending on whether assertions are enabled. Assertions must not cause any side effects. If assertions are enabled, the only change to the way your program runs is that an `AssertionError` can be thrown if one of your assertions (think *assumptions*) turns out to be false.

Using assertions that cause side effects can cause some of the most maddening and hard-to-find bugs known to man! When a hot-tempered QA analyst is screaming at you that your code doesn't work, trotting out the old "well, it works on MY machine" excuse won't get you very far.

CERTIFICATION OBJECTIVE

Working with Java 7 Exception Handling (OCP Objectives 6.2 and 6.3)

6.2 *Develop code that handles multiple exception types in a single catch block.*

6.3 *Develop code that uses try-with-resources statements (including using classes that implement the AutoCloseable interface).*

Use the try Statement with multi-catch and finally Clauses

Sometimes we want to handle different types of exceptions the same way. Especially when all we can do is log the exception and declare defeat. But we don't want to repeat code. So what to do? In the previous chapter's section "Handling an Entire Class Hierarchy of Exceptions," we've already seen that having a single catch-all exception handler is a bad idea. Prior to Java 7, the best we could do was:

```
try {
  // access the database and write to a file
} catch (SQLException e) {
  handleErrorCase(e);
} catch (IOException e) {
  handleErrorCase(e);
}
```

You may be thinking that it is only one line of duplicate code. But what happens when you are catching six different exception types? That's a lot of duplication. Luckily, Java 7 made this nice and easy with a feature called multi-`catch`:

```
try {
  // access the database and write to a file
} catch (SQLException | IOException e) {
  handleErrorCase(e);
}
```

No more duplication. This is great. As you might imagine, multi-`catch` is short for "multiple `catch`." You just list out the types you want the multi-`catch` to handle separated by pipe (|) characters. This is easy to remember because | is the "or" operator in Java. Which means the `catch` can be read as "`SQLException` or `IOException e`."

exam watch

You can't use the variable name multiple times in a `multi`-catch. The following won't compile:

```
catch(Exception1 e1 | Exception2 e2)
```

It makes sense that this example doesn't compile. After all, the code in the exception handler needs to know which variable name to refer to.

```
catch(Exception1 e | Exception2 e)
```

This one is tempting. When we declare variables, we normally put the variable name right after the type. Try to think of it as a list of types. We are declaring variable `e` to be caught and it must be one of `Exception1` or `Exception2` types.

With multi-catch, order doesn't matter. The following two snippets are equivalent to each other:

```
catch(SQLException | IOException e)    // these two statements are equivalent
catch(IOException | SQLException e)
```

Just like with exception matching in a regular catch block, you can't just throw any two exceptions together. With multi-catch, you have to make sure a given exception can only match one type. The following will not compile:

```
catch(FileNotFoundException | IOException e)
catch(IOException | FileNotFoundException e)
```

You'll get a compiler error that looks something like:

```
The exception FileNotFoundException is already caught by the
alternative IOException
```

Since FileNotFoundException is a subclass of IOException, we could have just written that in the first place! There was no need to use multi-catch. The simplified and working version simply says:

```
catch(IOException e)
```

Remember, multi-catch is only for exceptions in different inheritance hierarchies. To make sure this is clear, what do you think happens with the following code:

```
catch(IOException | Exception e)
```

That's right. It won't compile because IOException is a subclass of Exception. Which means it is redundant and the compiler won't accept it.

To summarize, we use multi-catch when we want to reuse an exception handler. We can list as many types as we want so long as none of them have a superclass/subclass relationship with each other.

Multi-catch and catch Parameter Assignment

There is one tricky thing with multi-catch. And we know the exam creators like tricky things!

The following LEGAL code demonstrates assigning a new value to the single catch parameter:

```
try {
  // access the database and write to a file
} catch (IOException e) {
  e = new IOException();
}
```

on the Job

Don't assign a new value to the catch parameter. It isn't good practice and creates confusing, hard-to-maintain code. But it is legal Java code to assign a new value to the `catch` block's parameter when there is only one type listed, and it will compile.

The following ILLEGAL code demonstrates trying to assign a value to the final multi-`catch` parameter:

```
try {
  // access the database and write to a file
} catch (SQLException | IOException e) {
  e = new IOException();
}
```

At least you get a clear compiler error if you try to do this. The compiler tells you:

```
The parameter e of a multi-catch block cannot be assigned
```

Since multi-`catch` uses multiple types, there isn't a clearly defined type for the variable that you can set. Java solves this by making the catch parameter `final` when that happens. And then the code doesn't compile because you can't assign to a `final` variable.

Rethrowing Exceptions

Sometimes, we want to do something with the thrown exceptions before we rethrow them:

```
public void couldThrowAnException() throws IOException, SQLException {}

public void rethrow() throws SQLException, IOException {
  try {
     couldThrowAnException();
  } catch (SQLException | IOException e) {
    log(e);
    throw e;
  }
}
```

This is a common pattern called "handle and declare." We want to do something with the exception—log it. We also want to acknowledge we couldn't completely handle it, so we declare it and let the caller deal with it. (As an aside, many programmers believe that logging an exception and rethrowing it is a bad practice, but you never know—you might see this kind of code on the exam.)

You may have noticed that `couldThrowAnException()` doesn't actually throw an exception. The compiler doesn't know this. The method signature is key to the compiler. It can't assume that no exception gets thrown, as a subclass could override the method and throw an exception.

There is a bit of duplicate code here. We have the list of exception types thrown by the methods we call typed twice. Multi-`catch` was introduced to avoid having duplicate code, yet here we are with duplicate code.

Lucky for us, Java 7 helps us out here as well with a new feature. This example is a nicer way of writing the previous code:

```
1. public void rethrow() throws SQLException, IOException {
2.   try {
3.      couldThrowAnException();
4.   } catch (Exception e) {      // watch out: this isn't really
5.                                // catching all exception subclasses
6.     log(e);
7.     throw e;                   // note: won't compile in Java 6
8.   }
9. }
```

Notice the multi-`catch` is gone and replaced with `catch(Exception e)`. It's not bad practice here, though, because we aren't really catching all exceptions. The compiler is treating `Exception` as "any exceptions that the called methods happen to throw." (You'll see this idea of code shorthand again with the diamond operator when you get to generics.)

This is very different from Java 6 code that catches `Exception`. In Java 6, we'd need the `rethrow()` method signature to be `throws Exception` in order to make this code compile.

In Java 7, `} catch (Exception e) {` doesn't really catch ANY `Exception` subclass. The code may say that, but the compiler is translating for you. The compiler says, "Well, I know it can't be just any exception because the throws clause won't let me. I'll pretend the developer meant to only catch `SQLException` and `IOException`. After all, if any others show up, I'll just fail compilation on `throw e;` —just like I used to in Java 6." Tricky, isn't it?

At the risk of being too repetitive, remember that `catch (Exception e)` doesn't necessarily catch all `Exception` subclasses. In Java 7, it means catch all `Exception` subclasses that would allow the method to compile.

Got that? Now why on earth would Oracle do this to us? It sounds more complicated than it used to be! Turns out they were trying to solve another problem at the same time they were changing this stuff. Suppose the API developer of `couldThrowAnException()` decided the method will never throw a `SQLException` and removes `SQLException` from the signature to reflect that.

Imagine we were using the Java 6 style of having one `catch` block per exception or even the multi-`catch` style of:

```
} catch (SQLException | IOException e) {
```

Our code would stop compiling with an error like:

```
Unreachable catch block for SQLException
```

It is reasonable for code to stop compiling if we add exceptions to a method. But we don't want our code to break if a method's implementation gets LESS brittle. And that's the advantage of using:

```
} catch (Exception e) {
```

Java infers what we mean here and doesn't say a peep when the API we are calling removes an exception.

Don't go changing your API signatures on a whim. Most code was written before Java 7 and will break if you change signatures. Your callers won't thank you when their code suddenly fails compilation because they tried to use your new, shiny, "cleaner" API.

You've probably noticed by now that Oracle values backward compatibility and doesn't change the behavior or "compiler worthiness" of code from older versions of Java. That still stands. In Java 6, we can't write `catch (Exception e)` and merely throw specific exceptions. If we tried, it would still complain about:

```
Unhandled exception type Exception.
```

Backward compatibility only needs to work for code that compiles! It's OK for the compiler to get less strict over time.

To make sure you understand what is going on here, think about what happens in this example:

```
public class A extends Exception{}
public class B extends Exception{}
public void rain() throws A, B {}
```

Table 7.3 summarizes handling changes to the exception-related parts of method signatures in Java 6 and Java 7.

TABLE 7-3 Exceptions and Signatures

<table>
<tr><th></th><th>What happens if rain() adds a new checked exception?</th><th>What happens if rain() removes a checked exception from the signature?</th></tr>
<tr><td>Java 6 style:

<code>public void ahhh() throws A, B {</code>
<code> try {</code>
<code>   rain();</code>
<code> } catch (A e) {</code>
<code>   throw e;</code>
<code> } catch (B e) {</code>
<code>   throw e;</code>
<code> }</code>
<code> }</code></td><td>Add another <code>catch</code> block to handle the new exception.</td><td>Remove a <code>catch</code> block to avoid compiler error about unreachable code.</td></tr>
<tr><td>Java 7 with duplication:

<code>public void ahhh() throws A, B {</code>
<code> try {</code>
<code>   rain();</code>
<code> } catch (A | B e) {</code>
<code>   throw e;</code>
<code> }</code>
<code> }</code></td><td>Add another exception to the multi-<code>catch</code> block to handle the new exception.</td><td>Remove an expression from the multi-<code>catch</code> block to avoid compiler error about unreachable code.</td></tr>
<tr><td>Java 7 without duplication:

<code>public void ahhh() throws A, B {</code>
<code> try {</code>
<code>   rain();</code>
<code> } catch (Exception e) {</code>
<code>   throw e;</code>
<code> }</code>
<code> }</code></td><td>Add another exception to the method signature to handle the new exception that can be thrown.</td><td>No code changes needed.</td></tr>
</table>

There is one more trick. If you assign a value to the catch parameter, the code no longer compiles:

```
public void rethrow() throws SQLException, IOException {
  try {
     couldThrowAnException();
  } catch (Exception e) {
    e = new IOException();
    throw e;
  }
}
```

As with multi-catch, you shouldn't be assigning a new value to the catch parameter in real life anyway. The difference between this and multi-catch is where the compiler error occurs. For multi-catch, the compiler error occurs on the line where we attempt to assign a new value to the parameter, whereas here, the compiler error occurs on the line where we `throw e`. It is different because code written prior to Java 7 still needs to compile. Since the multi-catch syntax is brand new, there is no legacy code to worry about.

Autocloseable Resources with a try-with-resources Statement

When we learned about using `finally` in Chapter 6, we saw that the `finally` block is a good place for closing files and assorted other resources. The examples made this clean-up code in the `finally` block look nice and short by writing `// clean up`. Unfortunately, real-world clean-up code is easy to get wrong. And when correct, it is verbose. Let's look at the code to close our one resource when closing a file:

```
 1: Reader reader = null;
 2: try {
 3:   // read from file
 4: } catch(IOException e) {
 5:   log(); throw e;
 6: } finally {
 7:   if (reader != null) {
 8:     try {
 9:       reader.close();
10:   } catch (IOException e) {
11:     // ignore exceptions on closing file
12:     }
13:   }
14: }
```

That's a lot of code just to close a single file! But it's all necessary. First, we need to check if the reader is null on line 7. It is possible the `try` block threw an exception before creating the reader, or while trying to create the reader if the file we are trying to read doesn't exist. It isn't until line 9 that we get to the one line in the whole `finally` block that does what we care about—closing the file. Lines 8 and 10 show a bit more housekeeping. We can get an `IOException` on attempting to close the file. While we could try to handle that exception, there isn't much we can do, thus making it common to just ignore the exception. This gives us nine lines of code (lines 6–14) just to close a file.

Developers typically write a helper class to close resources or they use the open-source, Apache Commons helper to get this mess down to three lines:

```
6:  } finally {
7:      HelperClass.close(reader);
8:  }
```

Which is still three lines too many.

Lucky for us, Java 7 introduced a new feature called *Automatic Resource Management* using "`try`-with-resources" to get rid of even these three lines. The following code is equivalent to the previous example:

```
1:  try (Reader reader =
2:    new BufferedReader(new FileReader(file))) {    // note the new syntax
3:    // read from file
4:  } catch (IOException e) { log(); throw e;}
```

No `finally` left at all! We don't even mention closing the reader. Automatic Resource Management takes care of it for us. Let's take a look at what happens here. **We start out by declaring the reader inside the `try` declaration. The parentheses are new. Think of them as a `for` loop in which we declare a loop index variable that is scoped to just the loop. Here, the reader is scoped to just the `try` block. Not the `catch` block; just the `try` block.**

The actual `try` block does the same thing as before. It reads from the file. Or, at least, it comments that it would read from the file. The `catch` block also does the same thing as before. And just like in our traditional `try` statement, `catch` is optional.

Remembering back to the section "Using `finally`" in Chapter 6, we learned that a `try` must have `catch` or `finally`. Time to learn something new about that rule.

We remember this is ILLEGAL code because it demonstrates a `try` without a `catch` or `finally`:

```
1: try {
2:    // do stuff
3: } // need a catch or finally here
```

The following LEGAL code demonstrates a `try`-with-resources with no `catch` or `finally`:

```
1:  try (Reader reader =
2:    new BufferedReader(new FileReader(file))) {
3:    // do stuff
4:  }
```

What's the difference? The legal example does have a `finally` block; you just don't see it. **The `try`-with-resources statement is logically calling a `finally` block to close the reader.** And just to make this even trickier, you can add your own `finally` block to `try`-with-resources as well. Both will get called. We'll take a look at how this works shortly.

Since the syntax is inspired from the `for` loop, we get to use a semicolon when declaring multiple resources in the `try`. For example:

```
try (MyResource mr = MyResource.createResource();     // first resource
     MyThingy mt = mr.createThingy()) {               // second resource
  // do stuff
}
```

There is something new here. Our declaration calls methods. Remember that the `try`-with-resources is just Java code. It is just restricted to only be declarations. This means if you want to do anything more than one statement long, you'll need to put it into a method.

To review, Table 7-4 lists the big differences that are new for `try`-with-resources.

AutoCloseable and Closeable

Because Java is a statically typed language, it doesn't let you declare just any type in a `try`-with-resources statement. The following code will not compile:

```
try (String s = "hi") {}
```

You'll get a compiler error that looks something like:

```
The resource type String does not implement java.lang.AutoCloseable
```

`AutoCloseable` only has one method to implement. Let's take a look at the simplest code we can write using this interface:

```
public class MyResource implements AutoCloseable {
  public void close() {
    // take care of closing the resource
  }
}
```

There's also an interface called `Closeable`, which is similar to `AutoCloseable` but with some key differences. Why are there two similar interfaces, you may wonder? The `Closeable` interface was introduced in Java 5. When `try`-with-resources was invented in Java 7, the language designers wanted to change some

TABLE 7-4 Comparing Traditional `try` Statement to `try`-with-resources

	try-catch-finally	try-with-resources
Resource declared	Before `try` keyword	In parentheses within `try` declaration
Resource initialized	In `try` block	In parentheses within `try` declaration
Resource closed	In `finally` block	Nowhere—happens automatically
Required keywords	`try` One of `catch` or `finally`	`try`

things but needed backward compatibility with all existing code. So they created a superinterface with the rules they wanted.

One thing the language designers wanted to do was make the signature more generic. `Closeable` allows implementors to throw only an `IOException` or a `RuntimeException`. `AutoCloseable` allows any `Exception` at all to be thrown. Look at some examples:

```
// ok because AutoCloseable allows throwing any Exception
class A implements AutoCloseable { public void close() throws Exception{}}

// ok because subclasses or implementing methods can throw
// a subclass of Exception or none at all
class B implements AutoCloseable { public void close() {}}
class C implements AutoCloseable { public void close() throws IOException {}}

// ILLEGAL - Closeable only allows IOExceptions or subclasses
class D implements Closeable { public void close() throws Exception{}}

// ok because Closeable allows throwing IOException
class E implements Closeable { public void close() throws IOException{}}
```

In your code, Oracle recommends throwing the narrowest `Exception` subclass that will compile. However, they do limit `Closeable` to `IOException`, and you must use `AutoCloseable` for anything more.

The next difference is even trickier. What happens if we call the `close()` multiple times? It depends. For classes that implement `AutoCloseable`, the implementation is required to be idempotent. Which means you can call `close()` all day and nothing will happen the second time and beyond. It will not attempt to close the resource again and it will not blow up. For classes that implement `Closeable`, there is no such guarantee.

If you look at the JavaDoc, you'll notice many classes implement both `AutoCloseable` and `Closeable`. These classes use the stricter signature rules and are idempotent. They still need to implement `Closeable` for backward compatibility, but added `AutoCloseable` for the new contract.

To review, Table 7-5 shows the differences between `AutoCloseable` and `Closeable`. Remember the exam creators like to ask about "similar but not quite the same" things!

A Complex try-with-resources Example The following example is as complicated as `try`-with-resources gets:

```
1:  class One implements AutoCloseable {
2:   public void close() {
3:     System.out.println("Close - One");
4:   } }
5: class Two implements AutoCloseable {
6:   public void close() {
7:     System.out.println("Close - Two");
8:   } }
9: class TryWithResources {
10:   public static void main(String[] args) {
11:     try (One one = new One(); Two two = new Two()) {
12:       System.out.println("Try");
13:       throw new RuntimeException();
14:     } catch (Exception e) {
15:       System.out.println("Catch");
16:     } finally {
17:       System.out.println("Finally");
18:     } } }
```

Running the preceding code will print:

```
Try
Close - Two
Close - One
Catch
Finally
```

TABLE 7-5 Comparing `AutoCloseable` and `Closeable`

	AutoCloseable	Closeable
Extends	None	`AutoCloseable`
`close` method throws	`Exception`	`IOException`
Must be idempotent (can call more than once without side effects)	Yes	No, but encouraged

It's actually more logical than it looks at first glance. We first enter the `try` block on line 11, and Java creates our two resources. Line 12 prints `Try`. When we throw an exception on line 13, the first interesting thing happens. The `try` block "ends" and Automatic Resource Management automatically cleans up the resources before moving on to the `catch` or `finally`. The resources get cleaned up, "backwards" printing `Close - Two` and then `Close - One`. The `close()` method gets called in the reverse order in which resources are declared to allow for the fact that resources might depend on each other. Then we are back to the regular `try` block order, printing `Catch` and `Finally` on lines 15 and 17.

If you only remember two things from this example, remember that `try`-with-resources is part of the `try` block, and resources are cleaned up in the reverse order they were created.

Suppressed Exceptions

We're almost done with exceptions. There's only one more wrinkle to cover in Java 7 exception handling. Now that we have an extra step of closing resources in the `try`, it is possible for multiple exceptions to get thrown. Each `close()` method can throw an exception in addition to the `try` block itself.

```
1: public class Suppressed {
2:   public static void main(String[] args) {
3:     try (One one = new One()) {
4:       throw new Exception("Try");
5:     } catch (Exception e) {
6:       System.err.println(e.getMessage());
7:       for (Throwable t : e.getSuppressed()) {
8.         System.err.println("suppressed:" + t);
9. } } } }

class One implements AutoCloseable {
  public void close() throws IOException {
    throw new IOException("Closing");
} }
```

We know that after the exception in the `try` block gets thrown on line 4, the `try`-with-resources still calls `close()` on line 3 and the `catch` block on line 5 catches one of the exceptions. Running the code prints:

```
Try
suppressed:java.io.IOException: Closing
```

This tells us the exception we thought we were throwing still gets treated as most important. Java also adds any exceptions thrown by the `close()` methods to a suppressed array in that main exception. The `catch` block or caller can deal with any or all of these. If we remove line 4, the code just prints `Closing`.

In other words, the exception thrown in `close()` doesn't always get suppressed. It becomes the main exception if there isn't already one existing. As one more example, think about what the following prints:

```
class Bad implements AutoCloseable {
  String name;
  Bad(String n) { name = n; }
  public void close() throws IOException {
    throw new IOException("Closing - "  + name);
  } }

public class Suppressed {
  public static void main(String[] args) {
    try (Bad b1 = new Bad("1"); Bad b2 = new Bad("2")) {
      // do stuff
    } catch (Exception e) {
      System.err.println(e.getMessage());
      for (Throwable t : e.getSuppressed()) {
        System.err.println("suppressed:" + t);
      } } } }
```

The answer is:

```
Closing - 2
suppressed:java.io.IOException: Closing - 1
```

Up until `try`-with-resources calls `close()`, everything is going just dandy. When Automatic Resource Management calls `b2.close()`, we get our first exception. This becomes the main exception. Then, Automatic Resource Management calls `b1.close()` and throws another exception. Since there was already an exception thrown, this second exception gets added as a second exception.

If the `catch` or `finally` block throws an exception, no suppressions happen. The last exception thrown gets sent to the caller rather than the one from the `try`—just like before `try`-with-resources was created.

CERTIFICATION SUMMARY

Assertions, added to the language in version 1.4, are a useful debugging tool. You learned how you can use them for testing by enabling them, but keep them disabled when the application is deployed. If you have older Java code that uses the word `assert` as an identifier, then you won't be able to use assertions, and you must recompile your older code using the `-source 1.3` flag. Remember that for Java 7, assertions are compiled as a keyword by default, but must be enabled explicitly at runtime.

You learned how `assert` statements always include a boolean expression, and if the expression is `true`, the code continues on, but if the expression is false, an AssertionError is thrown. If you use the two-expression `assert` statement, then the second expression is evaluated, converted to a String representation, and inserted into the stack trace to give you a little more debugging info. Finally, you saw why assertions should not be used to enforce arguments to public methods, and why `assert` expressions must not contain side effects!

Exception handling was enhanced in version 7, making exceptions easier to use. First you learned that you can specify multiple exception types to share a `catch` block using the new multi-`catch` syntax. The major benefit is in reducing code duplication by having multiple exception types share the same exception handler. The variable name is listed only once, even though multiple types are listed. You can't assign a new exception to that variable in the `catch` block. Then you saw the "handle and declare" pattern where the exception types in the multi-`catch` are listed in the method signature and Java translates "`catch Exception e`" into that exception type list.

Next, you learned about the `try`-with-resources syntax where Java will take care of calling `close()` for you. The objects are scoped to the `try` block. Java treats them as a `finally` block and closes these resources for you in the opposite order to which they were opened. If you have your own `finally` block, it is executed after `try`-with-resources closes the objects. You also learned the difference between `AutoCloseable` and `Closeable`. `Closable` was introduced in Java 5, allowing only `IOException` (and `RuntimeException`) to be thrown. `AutoCloseable` was added in Java 7, allowing any type of `Exception`.

✓ TWO-MINUTE DRILL

Here are some of the key points from the certification objectives in this chapter.

Test Invariants Using Assertions (OCP Objective 6.5)

- ❑ Assertions give you a way to test your assumptions during development and debugging.
- ❑ Assertions are typically enabled during testing but disabled during deployment.
- ❑ You can use `assert` as a keyword (as of version 1.4) or an identifier, but not both together. To compile older code that uses `assert` as an identifier (for example, a method name), use the `-source 1.3` command-line flag to `javac`.
- ❑ Assertions are disabled at runtime by default. To enable them, use a command-line flag: `-ea` or `-enableassertions`.
- ❑ Selectively disable assertions by using the `-da` or `-disableassertions` flag.
- ❑ If you enable or disable assertions using the flag without any arguments, you're enabling or disabling assertions in general. You can combine enabling and disabling switches to have assertions enabled for some classes and/or packages, but not others.
- ❑ You can enable and disable assertions on a class-by-class basis, using the following syntax:

  ```
  java -ea -da:MyClass TestClass
  ```
- ❑ You can enable and disable assertions on a package-by-package basis, and any package you specify also includes any subpackages (packages further down the directory hierarchy).
- ❑ Do not use assertions to validate arguments to `public` methods.
- ❑ Do not use `assert` expressions that cause side effects. Assertions aren't guaranteed to always run, and you don't want behavior that changes depending on whether assertions are enabled.
- ❑ Do use assertions—even in `public` methods—to validate that a particular code block will never be reached. You can use `assert false;` for code that should never be reached so that an assertion error is thrown immediately if the `assert` statement is executed.

Use the try Statement with Multi-catch and finally Clauses (OCP Objective 6.2)

- ❑ If two `catch` blocks have the same exception handler code, you can merge them with multi-`catch` using `catch (Exception1 | Exception2 e)`.
- ❑ The types in a multi-`catch` list must not extend one another.
- ❑ When using multi-`catch`, the `catch` block parameter is final and cannot have a new value assigned in the `catch` block.
- ❑ If you catch a general exception as shorthand for specific subclass exceptions and rethrow the caught exception, you can still list the specific subclasses in the method signature. The compiler will treat it as if you had listed them out in the catch.

Autocloseable Resources with a try-with-resources Statement (OCP Objective 6.3)

- ❑ `try`-with-resources automatically calls `close()` on any resources declared in the `try` as `try(Resource r = new Foo())`.
- ❑ A `try` must have at least a `catch` or `finally` unless it is a `try`-with-resources. For `try`-with-resources, it can have neither, one, or both of the keywords.
- ❑ `AutoCloseable`'s `close()` method throws `Exception` and must be idempotent. `Closeable`'s `close()` throws `IOException` and is not required to be idempotent.
- ❑ `try`-with-resources are closed in reverse order of creation and before going on to `catch` or `finally`.
- ❑ If more than one exception is thrown in a `try`-with-resources block, it gets added as a suppressed exception.
- ❑ The type used in a `try`-with-resources statement must implement `AutoCloseable`.

SELF TEST

The following questions will help you measure your understanding of the material presented in this chapter. Read all of the choices carefully, as there may be more than one correct answer. Choose all correct answers for each question. Stay focused.

1. Given two files:

```
1. class One {
2.   public static void main(String[] args) {
3.     int assert = 0;
4.   }
5. }

1. class Two {
2.   public static void main(String[] args) {
3.     assert(false);
4.   }
5. }
```

And the four command-line invocations:

```
javac -source 1.3 One.java
javac -source 1.4 One.java
javac -source 1.3 Two.java
javac -source 1.4 Two.java
```

What is the result? (Choose all that apply.)

A. Only one compilation will succeed

B. Exactly two compilations will succeed

C. Exactly three compilations will succeed

D. All four compilations will succeed

E. No compiler warnings will be produced

F. At least one compiler warning will be produced

2. Which are true? (Choose all that apply.)

A. It is appropriate to use assertions to validate arguments to methods marked `public`

B. It is appropriate to catch and handle assertion errors

C. It is NOT appropriate to use assertions to validate command-line arguments

D. It is appropriate to use assertions to generate alerts when you reach code that should not be reachable

E. It is NOT appropriate for assertions to change a program's state

3. Given:

```
 3. public class Clumsy {
 4.   public static void main(String[] args) {
 5.     int j = 7;
 6.     assert(++j > 7);
 7.     assert(++j > 8): "hi";
 8.     assert(j > 10): j=12;
 9.     assert(j==12): doStuff();
10.     assert(j==12): new Clumsy();
11.   }
12.   static void doStuff() { }
13. }
```

Which are true? (Choose all that apply.)

A. Compilation succeeds

B. Compilation fails due to an error on line 6

C. Compilation fails due to an error on line 7

D. Compilation fails due to an error on line 8

E. Compilation fails due to an error on line 9

F. Compilation fails due to an error on line 10

4. Given:

```
class AllGoesWrong {
  public static void main(String[] args) {
    AllGoesWrong a = new AllGoesWrong();
    try {
      a.blowUp();
      System.out.println("a");
    } catch (IOException e | SQLException e) {
      System.out.println("c");
    } finally {
      System.out.println("d");
    }
  }
  void blowUp() throws IOException, SQLException {
    throw new SQLException();
  }
}
```

What is the result?

A. `ad`

B. `acd`

C. `cd`

D. `d`

E. Compilation fails

F. An exception is thrown at runtime

5. Given:

```
class BadIO {
  public static void main(String[] args) {
    BadIO a = new BadIO();
    try {
      a.fileBlowUp();
      a.databaseBlowUp();
      System.out.println("a");
    } // insert code here
      System.out.println("b");
    } catch (Exception e) {
      System.out.println("c");
    } }
  void databaseBlowUp() throws SQLException {
    throw new SQLException();
  }
  void fileBlowUp() throws IOException {
    throw new IOException();
  }}
```

Which inserted independently at `// insert code here` will compile and produce the output: `b`? (Choose all that apply.)

A. `catch(Exception e) {`

B. `catch(FileNotFoundException e) {`

C. `catch(IOException e) {`

D. `catch(IOException | SQLException e) {`

E. `catch(IOException e | SQLException e) {`

F. `catch(SQLException e) {`

G. `catch(SQLException | IOException e) {`

H. `catch(SQLException e | IOException e) {`

6. Given:

```
class Train {
  class RanOutOfTrack extends Exception { }
  class AnotherTrainComing extends Exception { }

  public static void main(String[] args) throws RanOutOfTrack,
      AnotherTrainComing {
    Train a = new Train();
    try {
      a.drive();
      System.out.println("honk! honk!");
    } // insert code here
      System.out.println("error driving");
      throw e;
    }
  }
  void drive() throws RanOutOfTrack, AnotherTrainComing {
    throw new RanOutOfTrack();
  } }
```

Which inserted independently at `// insert code here` will compile and produce the output `error driving` before throwing an exception? (Choose all that apply.)

A. `catch(AnotherTrainComing e) {`

B. `catch(AnotherTrainComing | RanOutOfTrack e) {`

C. `catch(AnotherTrainComing e | RanOutOfTrack e) {`

D. `catch(Exception e) {`

E. `catch(IllegalArgumentException e) {`

F. `catch(RanOutOfTrack e) {`

G. None of the above—code fails to compile for another reason

7. Given:

```
class Conductor {
  static String s = "-";
  class Whistle implements AutoCloseable {
    public void toot() {     s += "t";    }
    public void close() {    s += "c";    }
  }
  public static void main(String[] args) {
    new Conductor().run();
    System.out.println(s);
  }
```

```
public void run() {
   try (Whistle w = new Whistle()) {
      w.toot();
      s += "1";
      throw new Exception();
   } catch (Exception e) { s += "2";
   } finally { s += "3"; } } }
```

What is the result?

A. `-t123t`

B. `-t12c3`

C. `-t123`

D. `-t1c3`

E. `-t1c23`

F. None of the above; `main()` throws an exception

G. Compilation fails

8. Given:

```
public class MultipleResources {
  class Lamb implements AutoCloseable {
    public void close() throws Exception {
        System.out.print("l");
    } }
  class Goat implements AutoCloseable {
    public void close() throws Exception {
        System.out.print("g");
    } }
  public static void main(String[] args) throws Exception {
    new MultipleResources().run();
  }
  public void run() throws Exception {
    try (Lamb l = new Lamb();
         System.out.print("t");
         Goat g = new Goat();) {
      System.out.print("2");
    } finally {
      System.out.print("f");
    } } }
```

What is the result?

A. `2glf`

B. `21gf`

C. `tglf`

D. `t2lgf`

E. `t21gf`

F. None of the above; `main()` throws an exception

G. Compilation fails

9. Given:

```
 1: public class Animals {
 2:   class Lamb {
 3:   public void close() throws Exception { }
 4:   }
 5:   public static void main(String[] args) throws Exception {
 6:     new Animals().run();
 7:   }
 8:
 9:   public void run() throws Exception {
10:    try (Lamb l = new Lamb();) {
11:    }
12:   }
13: }
```

And the following possible changes:

C1. Replace line 2 with class `Lamb` implements `AutoCloseable {`

C2. Replace line 2 with class `Lamb` implements `Closeable {`

C3. Replace line 11 with `} finally {}`

What change(s) allow the code to compile? (Choose all that apply.)

A. Just C1 is sufficient

B. Just C2 is sufficient

C. Just C3 is sufficient

D. Both C1 and C3

E. Both C2 and C3

F. The code compiles without any changes

10. Given:

```
public class Animals {
  class Lamb implements Closeable {
    public void close() {
      throw new RuntimeException("a");
    } }
  public static void main(String[] args)  {
    new Animals().run();
  }
  public void run()  {
    try (Lamb l = new Lamb();) {
      throw new IOException();
    } catch(Exception e) {
      throw new RuntimeException("c");
    } } }
```

Which exceptions will the code throw?

A. `IOException` with suppressed `RuntimeException a`

B. `IOException` with suppressed `RuntimeException c`

C. `RuntimeException a` with no suppressed exception

D. `RuntimeException c` with no suppressed exception

E. `RuntimeException a` with suppressed `RuntimeException c`

F. `RuntimeException c` with suppressed `RuntimeException a`

G. Compilation fails

11. Given:

```
public class Animals {
  class Lamb implements AutoCloseable {
    public void close() {
      throw new RuntimeException("a");
    } }
  public static void main(String[] args) throws IOException {
    new Animals().run();
  }
  public void run() throws IOException {
    try (Lamb l = new Lamb();) {
      throw new IOException();
    } catch(Exception e) {
      throw e;

    } } }
```

Which exceptions will the code throw?

A. `IOException` with suppressed `RuntimeException a`

B. `IOException` with suppressed `RuntimeException c`

C. `RuntimeException a` with no suppressed exception

D. `RuntimeException c` with no suppressed exception

E. `RuntimeException a` with suppressed `RuntimeException c`

F. `RuntimeException c` with suppressed `RuntimeException a`

G. Compilation fails

12. Given:

```
public class Concert {
  static class PowerOutage extends Exception {}
  static class Thunderstorm extends Exception {}
  public static void main(String[] args) {
    try {
    new Concert().listen();
    System.out.println("a");
    } catch(PowerOutage | Thunderstorm e) {
      e = new PowerOutage();
      System.out.println("b");
    } finally { System.out.println("c"); }
  }
  public void listen() throws PowerOutage, Thunderstorm{ }
}
```

What will this code print?

A. `a`

B. `ab`

C. `ac`

D. `abc`

E. `bc`

F. Compilation fails

SELF TEST ANSWERS

1. ☑ **B** and **F** are correct. `class One` will compile (and issue a warning) using the 1.3 flag, and `class Two` will compile using the 1.4 flag.
☒ **A, C, D,** and **E** are incorrect based on the above. (OCP Objective 6.5)

2. ☑ **C, D,** and **E** are correct statements.
☒ **A** is incorrect. It is acceptable to use assertions to test the arguments of `private` methods. **B** is incorrect. While assertion errors can be caught, Oracle discourages you from doing so. (OCP Objective 6.5)

3. ☑ **E** is correct. When an `assert` statement has two expressions, the second expression must return a value. The only two-expression `assert` statement that doesn't return a value is on line 9.
☒ **A, B, C, D,** and **F** are incorrect based on the above. (OCP Objective 6.5)

4. ☑ **E** is correct. `catch (IOException e | SQLException e)` doesn't compile. While multiple exception types can be specified in the multi-`catch`, only one variable name is allowed. The correct syntax is `catch (IOException | SQLException e)`. Other than this, the code is valid. Note that it is legal for `blowUp()` to have `IOException` in its signature even though that `Exception` can't be thrown.
☒ **A, B, C, D,** and **F** are incorrect based on the above. If the `catch` block's syntax error were corrected, the code would output `cd`. The multi-`catch` would catch the `SQLException` from `blowUp()` since it is one of the exception types listed. And, of course, the `finally` block runs at the end of the `try/catch`. (OCP Objective 6.2)

5. ☑ **C, D,** and **G** are correct. Since order doesn't matter, both **D** and **G** show correct use of the multi-`catch` block. And **C** catches the `IOException` from `fileBlowUp()` directly. Note that `databaseBlowUp()` is never called at runtime. However, if you remove the call, the compiler won't let you catch the `SQLException` since it would be impossible to be thrown.
☒ **A** is incorrect because it will not compile. Since there is already a `catch` block for `Exception`, adding another will make the compiler think there is unreachable code. **B** is incorrect because it will print `c` rather than `b`. Since `FileNotFoundException` is a subclass of `IOException`, the thrown `IOException` will not match the `catch` block for `FileNotFoundException`. **E** and **H** are incorrect because they are invalid syntax for multi-`catch`. The catch parameter `e` can only appear once. **F** is incorrect because it will print `c` rather than `b`. Since the `IOException` thrown by `fileBlowUp()` is never caught, the thrown exception will match the `catch` block for `Exception`. (OCP Objective 6.2)

6. ☑ **B, D,** and **F** are correct. **B** uses multi-`catch` to identify both exceptions `drive()` may throw. **D** still compiles since it uses the new enhanced exception typing to recognize that `Exception` may only refer to `AnotherTrainComing` and `RanOutOfTrack`. **F** is the simple case that catches a single exception. Since `main` throws `AnotherTrainComing`, the `catch` block doesn't need to handle it.

☒ A and E are incorrect because the `catch` block will not handle `RanOutOfTrack` when `drive()` throws it. The `main` method will still throw the exception, but the `println()` will not run. **C** is incorrect because it is invalid syntax for multi-`catch`. The `catch` parameter `e` can only appear once. **G** is incorrect because of the above. (OCP Objective 6.2)

7. ☑ **E** is correct. After the exception is thrown, Automatic Resource Management calls `close()` before completing the `try` block. From that point, `catch` and `finally` execute in the normal order.

☒ **F** is incorrect because the `catch` block catches the exception and does not rethrow it. **A, B, C, D,** and **G** are incorrect because of the above. (OCP Objective 6.3)

8. ☑ **G** is correct. `System.out.println` cannot be in the declaration clause of a `try`-with-resources block because it does not declare a variable. If the `println` was removed, the answer would be **A** because resources are closed in the opposite order they are created.

☒ **A, B, C, D, E,** and **F** are incorrect because of the above. (OCP Objective 6.3)

9. ☑ **A** and **D** are correct. If the code is left with no changes, it will not compile because `try`-with-resources requires `Lamb` to implement `AutoCloseable` or a subinterface. If C2 is implemented, the code will not compile because `close()` throws `Exception` instead of `IOException`. Unlike the traditional `try`, `try`-with-resources does not require `catch` or `finally` to present. So the code works equally well with or without C3.

☒ **B, C, E,** and **F** are incorrect because of the above. (OCP Objective 6.3)

10. ☑ **D** is correct. While the exception caught by the `catch` block matches choice **A**, it is ignored by the `catch` block. The `catch` block just throws `RuntimeException c` without any suppressed exceptions.

☒ **A, B, C, E, F,** and **G** are incorrect because of the above. (OCP Objective 6.3)

11. ☑ **A** is correct. After the `try` block throws an `IOException`, Automatic Resource Management calls `close()` to clean up the resources. Since an exception was already thrown in the `try` block, `RuntimeException a` gets added to it as a suppressed exception. The `catch` block merely rethrows the caught exception. The code does compile even though the `catch` block catches an `Exception` and the method merely throws an `IOException`. In Java 7, the compiler is able to pick up on this.

☒ **B, C, D, E, F,** and **G** are incorrect because of the above. (OCP Objective 6.3)

12. ☑ **F** is correct. The exception variable in a `catch` block may not be reassigned when using multi-`catch`. It CAN be reassigned if we are only catching one exception.

☒ **C** would have been correct if `e = new PowerOutage();` were removed. **A, B, D,** and **E** are incorrect because of the above. (OCP Objectives 6.2 and 6.4)

8

String Processing, Data Formatting, Resource Bundles

CERTIFICATION OBJECTIVES

- Search, Parse, and Build Strings (Including Scanner, StringTokenizer, StringBuilder, String, and Formatter)
- Search, Parse, and Replace Strings by Using Regular Expressions, Using Expression Patterns for Matching Limited to . (dot), * (star), + (plus), ?, \d, \D, \s, \S, \w, \W, \b, \B, [], and ()
- Format Strings Using the Formatting Parameters %b, %c, %d, %f, and %s in Format Strings
- Read and Set the Locale Using the Locale Object
- Build a Resource Bundle for Each Locale
- Call a Resource Bundle from an Application
- Format Dates, Numbers, and Currency Values for Localization with the NumberFormat and DateFormat Classes (Including Number Format Patterns)
- Describe the Advantages of Localizing an Application
- Define a Locale Using Language and Country Codes

✓ Two-Minute Drill

Q&A Self Test

This chapter focuses on the exam objectives related to searching, formatting, and parsing strings; formatting dates, numbers, and currency values; and using resource bundles for localization and internationalization tasks. Many of these topics could fill an entire book. Fortunately, you won't have to become a total regex guru to do well on the exam. The intention of the exam team was to include just the basic aspects of these technologies, and in this chapter, we cover *more* than you'll need to get through the related objectives on the exam.

CERTIFICATION OBJECTIVE

String, StringBuilder, and StringBuffer (OCP Objective 5.1)

5.1 Search, parse, and build strings (including Scanner, StringTokenizer, StringBuilder, String, and Formatter).

The OCA 7 exam covers the basics of building and using `Strings` and `StringBuilders`. While most of the OCP 7 `String` and `StringBuilder` questions will focus on searching and parsing, you might also get more basic questions, similar to those found on the OCA 7 exam. We recommend that you refresh your `String` and `StringBuilder` knowledge (the stuff we covered in Chapter 5), before taking the OCP 7 exam.

We're going to start this chapter with date and number formatting and such, and we'll return to parsing and tokenizing later in the chapter.

CERTIFICATION OBJECTIVE

Dates, Numbers, Currencies, and Locales (OCP Objectives 12.1, 12.4, 12.5, and 12.6)

12.1 Read and set the locale using the Locale object.

12.4 *Format dates, numbers, and currency values for localization with the NumberFormat and DateFormat classes (including number format patterns).*

12.5 *Describe the advantages of localizing an application.*

12.6 *Define a locale using language and country codes.*

The Java API provides an extensive (perhaps a little *too* extensive) set of classes to help you work with dates, numbers, and currency. The exam will test your knowledge of the basic classes and methods you'll use to work with dates and such. When you've finished this section, you should have a solid foundation in tasks such as creating new `Date` and `DateFormat` objects, converting `Strings` to `Dates` and back again, performing Calendaring functions, printing properly formatted currency values, and doing all of this for locations around the globe. In fact, a large part of why this section was added to the exam was to test whether you can do some basic internationalization (often shortened to "i18n").

Note: In this section, we'll introduce the `Locale` class. Later in the chapter, we'll be discussing resource bundles, and you'll learn more about `Locale` then.

Working with Dates, Numbers, and Currencies

If you want to work with dates from around the world (and who doesn't?), you'll need to be familiar with at least four classes from the `java.text` and `java.util` packages. In fact, we'll admit it right up front: You might encounter questions on the exam that use classes that aren't specifically mentioned in the Oracle objective. Here are the five date-related classes you'll need to understand:

- **`java.util.Date`** Most of this class's methods have been deprecated, but you can use this class to bridge between the `Calendar` and `DateFormat` class. An instance of `Date` represents a mutable date and time, to a millisecond.
- **`java.util.Calendar`** This class provides a huge variety of methods that help you convert and manipulate dates and times. For instance, if you want to add a month to a given date or find out what day of the week January 1, 3000, falls on, the methods in the `Calendar` class will save your bacon.
- **`java.text.DateFormat`** This class is used to format dates, not only providing various styles such as "01/01/70" or "January 1, 1970," but also dates for numerous locales around the world.

- **java.text.NumberFormat** This class is used to format numbers and currencies for locales around the world.
- **java.util.Locale** This class is used in conjunction with `DateFormat` and `NumberFormat` to format dates, numbers, and currency for specific locales. With the help of the `Locale` class, you'll be able to convert a date like "10/10/2005" to "Segunda-feira, 10 de Outubro de 2005" in no time. If you want to manipulate dates without producing formatted output, you can use the `Locale` class directly with the `Calendar` class.

Orchestrating Date- and Number-Related Classes

When you work with dates and numbers, you'll often use several classes together. It's important to understand how the classes we described earlier relate to each other and when to use which classes in combination. For instance, you'll need to know that if you want to do date formatting for a specific locale, you need to create your `Locale` object before your `DateFormat` object, because you'll need your `Locale` object as an argument to your `DateFormat` factory method. Table 8-1 provides a quick overview of common date- and number-related use cases and solutions using these classes. Table 8-1 will undoubtedly bring up specific questions about individual classes, and we will dive into specifics for each class next. Once you've gone through the class-level discussions, you should find that Table 8-1 provides a good summary.

The Date Class

The `Date` class has a checkered past. Its API design didn't do a good job of handling internationalization and localization situations. In its current state, most of its methods have been deprecated, and for most purposes, you'll want to use the `Calendar` class instead of the `Date` class. The `Date` class is on the exam for several reasons: You might find it used in legacy code; it's really easy if all you want is a quick and dirty way to get the current date and time; it's good when you want a universal time that is not affected by time zones; and finally, you'll use it as a temporary bridge to format a `Calendar` object using the `DateFormat` class.

As we mentioned briefly earlier, an instance of the `Date` class represents a single date and time. Internally, the date and time are stored as a primitive `long`. Specifically, the `long` holds the number of milliseconds (you know, 1000 of these per second) between the date being represented and January 1, 1970.

TABLE 8-1 Common Use Cases When Working with Dates and Numbers

Use Case	Steps
Get the current date and time.	1. Create a `Date`: `Date d = new Date();` 2. Get its value: `String s = d.toString();`
Get an object that lets you perform date and time calculations in your locale.	1. Create a `Calendar`: `Calendar c = Calendar.getInstance();` 2. Use `c.add(...)` and `c.roll(...)` to perform date and time manipulations.

Get an object that lets you perform date and time calculations in a different locale.	1. Create a `Locale`:
	`Locale loc = new Locale(language);` or
	`Locale loc = Locale(language, country);new`
	2. Create a `Calendar` for that locale:
	`Calendar c = Calendar.getInstance(loc);`
	3. Use `c.add(...)` and `c.roll(...)` to perform date and time manipulations.

Get an object that lets you perform date and time calculations, and then format it for output in different locales with different date styles.	1. Create a `Calendar`:
	`Calendar c = Calendar.getInstance();`
	2. Create a `Locale` for each location:
	`Locale loc = new Locale(...);`
	3. Convert your `Calendar` to a `Date`:
	`Date d = c.getTime();`
	4. Create a `DateFormat` for each `Locale`:
	`DateFormat df = DateFormat.getDateInstance (style, loc);`
	5. Use the `format()` method to create formatted dates:
	`String s = df.format(d);`

Get an object that lets you format numbers or currencies across many different locales.	1. Create a `Locale` for each location:
	`Locale loc = new Locale(...);`
	2. Create a `NumberFormat`:
	`NumberFormat nf = NumberFormat.getInstance(loc);`
	-or- `NumberFormat nf = NumberFormat. getCurrencyInstance(loc);`
	3. Use the `format()` method to create formatted output:
	`String s = nf.format(someNumber);`

Have you ever tried to grasp how big really big numbers are? Let's use the `Date` class to find out how long it took for a trillion milliseconds to pass, starting at January 1, 1970:

```
import java.util.*;
class TestDates {
  public static void main(String[] args) {
    Date d1 = new Date(1_000_000_000_000L);       // a trillion, Java 7 style
    System.out.println("1st date " + d1.toString());
  }
}
```

On our JVM, which has a U.S. locale, the output is

```
1st date Sat Sep 08 19:46:40 MDT 2001
```

Okay, for future reference, remember that there are a trillion milliseconds for every 31 and 2/3 years.

Although most of `Date`'s methods have been deprecated, it's still acceptable to use the `getTime` and `setTime` methods, although, as we'll soon see, it's a bit painful. Let's add an hour to our `Date` instance, `d1`, from the previous example:

```
import java.util.*;
class TestDates {
  public static void main(String[] args) {
    Date d1 = new Date(1_000_000_000_000L);      // a trillion!
    System.out.println("1st date " + d1.toString());
    d1.setTime(d1.getTime() + 3_600_000);        // 3_600_000 millis / hour
    System.out.println("new time " + d1.toString());
  }
}
```

which produces (again, on our JVM):

```
1st date Sat Sep 08 19:46:40 MDT 2001
new time Sat Sep 08 20:46:40 MDT 2001
```

Notice that both `setTime()` and `getTime()` used the handy millisecond scale... if you want to manipulate dates using the `Date` class, that's your only choice. While that wasn't too painful, imagine how much fun it would be to add, say, a year to a given date.

We'll revisit the `Date` class later on, but for now, the only other thing you need to know is that if you want to create an instance of `Date` to represent "now," you use `Date`'s no-argument constructor:

```
Date now = new Date();
```

(We're guessing that if you call `now.getTime()`, you'll get a number somewhere between one trillion and two trillion.)

The Calendar Class

We've just seen that manipulating dates using the `Date` class is tricky. The `Calendar` class is designed to make date manipulation easy! (Well, easier.) While the `Calendar` class has about a million fields and methods, once you get the hang of a few of them, the rest tend to work in a similar fashion.

When you first try to use the `Calendar` class, you might notice that it's an abstract class. You can't say

```
Calendar c = new Calendar();    // illegal, Calendar is abstract
```

In order to create a `Calendar` instance, you have to use one of the overloaded `getInstance()` static factory methods:

```
Calendar cal = Calendar.getInstance();
```

When you get a `Calendar` reference like `cal`, from earlier, your `Calendar` reference variable is actually referring to an instance of a concrete subclass of `Calendar`. You can't know for sure what subclass you'll get (`java.util.GregorianCalendar` is what you'll almost certainly get), but it won't matter to you. You'll be using `Calendar`'s API. (As Java continues to spread around the world, in order to maintain cohesion, you might find additional, locale-specific subclasses of `Calendar`.)

Okay, so now we've got an instance of `Calendar`, let's go back to our earlier example and find out what day of the week our trillionth millisecond falls on, and then let's add a month to that date:

```
import java.util.*;
class Dates2 {
  public static void main(String[] args) {
    Date d1 = new Date(1_000_000_000_000L);
    System.out.println("1st date " + d1.toString());

    Calendar c = Calendar.getInstance();
    c.setTime(d1);                                  // #1

    if(Calendar.SUNDAY == c.getFirstDayOfWeek())    // #2
      System.out.println("Sunday is the first day of the week");
    System.out.println("trillionth milli day of week is "
                + c.get(Calendar.DAY_OF_WEEK));     // #3

    c.add(Calendar.MONTH, 1);                       // #4
    Date d2 = c.getTime();                          // #5
    System.out.println("new date " + d2.toString() );
  }
}
```

This produces something like

```
1st date Sat Sep 08 19:46:40 MDT 2001
Sunday is the first day of the week
trillionth milli day of week is 7
new date Mon Oct 08 19:46:40 MDT 2001
```

Let's take a look at this program, focusing on the five highlighted lines:

1. We assign the `Date d1` to the `Calendar` instance `c`.

2. We use `Calendar`'s `SUNDAY` field to determine whether, for our JVM, `SUNDAY` is considered to be the first day of the week. (In some locales, `MONDAY` is the first day of the week.) The `Calendar` class provides similar fields for days of the week, months, the day of the month, the day of the year, and so on.
3. We use the `DAY_OF_WEEK` field to find out the day of the week that the trillionth millisecond falls on.
4. So far, we've used "setter" and "getter" methods that should be intuitive to figure out. Now we're going to use `Calendar`'s `add()` method. This very powerful method lets you add or subtract units of time appropriate for whichever `Calendar` field you specify. For instance:

```
c.add(Calendar.HOUR, -4);              // subtract 4 hours from c's
                                       // value
c.add(Calendar.YEAR, 2);               // add 2 years to c's value
c.add(Calendar.DAY_OF_WEEK, -2);       // subtract two days from
                                       // c's  value
```

5. Convert c's value back to an instance of `Date`.

The other `Calendar` method you should know for the exam is the `roll()` method. The `roll()` method acts like the `add()` method, except that when a part of a `Date` gets incremented or decremented, larger parts of the `Date` will not get incremented or decremented. Hmmm... for instance:

```
// assume c is October 8, 2001
c.roll(Calendar.MONTH, 9);           // notice the year in the output
Date d4 = c.getTime();
System.out.println("new date " + d4.toString() );
```

The output would be something like this:

```
new date Fri Jul 08 19:46:40 MDT 2001
```

Notice that the year did not change, even though we added nine months to an October date. In a similar fashion, invoking `roll()` with `HOUR` won't change the date, the month, or the year.

For the exam, you won't have to memorize the `Calendar` class's fields. If you need them to help answer a question, they will be provided as part of the question.

The DateFormat Class

Having learned how to create dates and manipulate them, let's find out how to format them. So that we're all on the same page, here's an example of how a date can be formatted in different ways:

```
import java.text.*;
import java.util.*;
class Dates3 {
  public static void main(String[] args) {
    Date d1 = new Date(1_000_000_000_000L);     // project Coin at work!
    DateFormat[] dfa = new DateFormat[6];
    dfa[0] = DateFormat.getInstance();
    dfa[1] = DateFormat.getDateInstance();
    dfa[2] = DateFormat.getDateInstance(DateFormat.SHORT);
    dfa[3] = DateFormat.getDateInstance(DateFormat.MEDIUM);
    dfa[4] = DateFormat.getDateInstance(DateFormat.LONG);
    dfa[5] = DateFormat.getDateInstance(DateFormat.FULL);

    for(DateFormat df : dfa)
      System.out.println(df.format(d1));
  }
}
```

which on our JVM produces

```
9/8/01 7:46 PM
Sep 8, 2001
9/8/01
Sep 8, 2001
September 8, 2001
Saturday, September 8, 2001
```

Examining this code, we see a couple of things right away. First off, it looks like `DateFormat` is another abstract class, so we can't use `new` to create instances of `DateFormat`. In this case, we used two factory methods: `getInstance()` and `getDateInstance()`. Notice that `getDateInstance()` is overloaded; when we discuss locales, we'll look at the other version of `getDateInstance()` that you'll need to understand for the exam.

Next, we used static fields from the `DateFormat` class to customize our various instances of `DateFormat`. Each of these static fields represents a formatting *style*. In this case, it looks like the no-arg version of `getDateInstance()` gives us the same style as the `MEDIUM` version of the method, but that's not a hard-and-fast rule. (More on this when we discuss locales.) Finally, we used the `format()` method to create strings representing the properly formatted versions of the `Date` we're working with.

The last method you should be familiar with is the `parse()` method. The `parse()` method takes a string formatted in the style of the `DateFormat` instance being used and converts the string into a `Date` object. As you might imagine, this is a risky operation because the `parse()` method could easily receive a badly formatted string. Because of this, `parse()` can throw a `ParseException`. The following code creates a `Date` instance, uses `DateFormat.format()` to convert it into a string, and then uses `DateFormat.parse()` to change it back into a `Date`:

```
Date d1 = new Date(1000000000000L);
System.out.println("d1 = " + d1.toString());

DateFormat df = DateFormat.getDateInstance(
                                   DateFormat.SHORT);
String s = df.format(d1);
System.out.println(s);

try {
  Date d2 = df.parse(s);
  System.out.println("parsed = " + d2.toString());
} catch (ParseException pe) {
  System.out.println("parse exc"); }
```

which on our JVM produces

```
d1 = Sat Sep 08 19:46:40 MDT 2001
9/8/01
parsed = Sat Sep 08 00:00:00 MDT 2001
```

Note: If we'd wanted to retain the time along with the date, we could have used the `getDateTimeInstance()` method, but it's not on the exam.

The API for `DateFormat.parse()` explains that, by default, the `parse()` method is lenient when parsing dates. Our experience is that `parse()` isn't very lenient about the formatting of strings it will successfully parse into dates; take care when you use this method!

The Locale Class

Earlier, we said that a big part of why this objective exists is to test your ability to do some basic internationalization tasks. Your wait is over; the `Locale` class is your ticket to worldwide domination. Both the `DateFormat` class and the `NumberFormat` class (which we'll cover next) can use an instance of `Locale` to customize formatted output to be specific to a locale. You might ask how Java defines a locale. The API says a locale is "a specific geographical, political, or cultural region." The two `Locale` constructors you'll need to understand for the exam are

```
Locale(String language)
Locale(String language, String country)
```

The language argument represents an ISO 639 Language code, so, for instance, if you want to format your dates or numbers in Walloon (the language sometimes used in southern Belgium), you'd use "wa" as your language string. There are over 500 ISO Language codes, including one for Klingon ("tlh"), although, unfortunately, Java doesn't yet support the Klingon locale. We thought about telling you that you'd have to memorize all these codes for the exam… but we didn't want to cause any heart attacks. So rest assured, you won't have to memorize any ISO Language codes or ISO Country codes (of which there are about 240) for the exam.

Let's get back to how you might use these codes. If you want to represent basic Italian in your application, all you need is the language code. If, on the other hand, you want to represent the Italian used in Switzerland, you'd want to indicate that the country is Switzerland (yes, the country code for Switzerland is "CH"), but that the language is Italian:

```
Locale locIT = new Locale("it");          // Italian
Locale locCH = new Locale("it", "CH");    // Switzerland
```

Using these two locales on a date could give us output like this:

```
sabato 1 ottobre 2005
sabato, 1. ottobre 2005
```

Now let's put this all together in some code that creates a Calendar object, sets its date, and then converts it to a Date. After that, we'll take that Date object and print it out using locales from around the world:

```
Calendar c = Calendar.getInstance();
c.set(2010, 11, 14);                      // December 14, 2010
                                          // (month is 0-based)
Date d2 = c.getTime();

Locale locIT = new Locale("it", "IT");    // Italy
Locale locPT = new Locale("pt");          // Portugal
Locale locBR = new Locale("pt", "BR");    // Brazil
Locale locIN = new Locale("hi", "IN");    // India
Locale locJA = new Locale("ja");          // Japan

DateFormat dfUS = DateFormat.getInstance();
System.out.println("US         " + dfUS.format(d2));

DateFormat dfUSfull = DateFormat.getDateInstance(
                                          DateFormat.FULL);
System.out.println("US full    " + dfUSfull.format(d2));

DateFormat dfIT = DateFormat.getDateInstance(
                                          DateFormat.FULL, locIT);
System.out.println("Italy      " + dfIT.format(d2));
```

```
DateFormat dfPT = DateFormat.getDateInstance(
                                  DateFormat.FULL, locPT);
System.out.println("Portugal " + dfPT.format(d2));

DateFormat dfBR = DateFormat.getDateInstance(
                                  DateFormat.FULL, locBR);
System.out.println("Brazil   " + dfBR.format(d2));

DateFormat dfIN = DateFormat.getDateInstance(
                                  DateFormat.FULL, locIN);
System.out.println("India    " + dfIN.format(d2));

DateFormat dfJA = DateFormat.getDateInstance(
                                  DateFormat.FULL, locJA);
System.out.println("Japan    " + dfJA.format(d2));
```

This, on our JVM, produces

```
US       12/14/10 3:32 PM
US full  Sunday, December 14, 2010
Italy    domenica 14 dicembre 2010
Portugal Domingo, 14 de Dezembro de 2010
Brazil   Domingo, 14 de Dezembro de 2010
India    ??????, ?? ??????, ????
Japan    2010?12?14?
```

Oops! Our machine isn't configured to support locales for India or Japan, but you can see how a single `Date` object can be formatted to work for many locales.

exam watch

Remember that both `DateFormat` and `NumberFormat` objects can have their locales set only at the time of instantiation. Watch for code that attempts to change the locale of an existing instance—no such methods exist!

There are a couple more methods in `Locale` (`getDisplayCountry()` and `getDisplayLanguage()`) that you'll have to know for the exam. These methods let you create strings that represent a given locale's country and language in terms of both the default locale and any other locale:

```
Locale locBR = new Locale("pt", "BR");  // Brazil
Locale locDK = new Locale("da", "DK");  // Denmark
Locale locIT = new Locale("it", "IT");  // Italy

System.out.println("def " + locBR.getDisplayCountry());
```

```
System.out.println("loc " + locBR.getDisplayCountry(locBR));

System.out.println("def " + locDK.getDisplayLanguage());
System.out.println("loc " + locDK.getDisplayLanguage(locDK));
System.out.println("D>I " + locDK.getDisplayLanguage(locIT));
```

This, on our JVM, produces

```
def Brazil
loc Brasil
def Danish
loc dansk
D>I danese
```

Given that our JVM's locale (the default for us) is `US`, the default for the country Brazil is `Brazil`, and the default for the Danish language is `Danish`. In Brazil, the country is called `Brasil`, and in Denmark, the language is called `dansk`. Finally, just for fun, we discovered that in Italy, the Danish language is called `danese`.

The NumberFormat Class

We'll wrap up this objective by discussing the `NumberFormat` class. Like the `DateFormat` class, `NumberFormat` is abstract, so you'll typically use some version of either `getInstance()` or `getCurrencyInstance()` to create a `NumberFormat` object. Not surprisingly, you use this class to format numbers or currency values:

```
float f1 = 123.4567f;
Locale locFR = new Locale("fr");          // France
NumberFormat[] nfa = new NumberFormat[4];

nfa[0] = NumberFormat.getInstance();
nfa[1] = NumberFormat.getInstance(locFR);
nfa[2] = NumberFormat.getCurrencyInstance();
nfa[3] = NumberFormat.getCurrencyInstance(locFR);

for(NumberFormat nf : nfa)
  System.out.println(nf.format(f1));
```

This, on our JVM, produces

```
123.457
123,457
$123.46
123,46 ?
```

Don't be worried if, like us, you're not set up to display the symbols for francs, pounds, rupees, yen, baht, or drachmas. You won't be expected to know the symbols used for currency: If you need one, it will be specified in the question. You might encounter methods other than the `format()` method on the exam. Here's a little code that uses `getMaximumFractionDigits()`, `setMaximumFractionDigits()`, `parse()`, and `setParseIntegerOnly()`:

```
float f1 = 123.45678f;
NumberFormat nf = NumberFormat.getInstance();
System.out.print(nf.getMaximumFractionDigits() + " ");
System.out.print(nf.format(f1) + "  ");

nf.setMaximumFractionDigits(5);
System.out.println(nf.format(f1) + "  ");

try {
  System.out.println(nf.parse("1234.567"));
  nf.setParseIntegerOnly(true);
  System.out.println(nf.parse("1234.567"));
} catch (ParseException pe) {
  System.out.println("parse exc");
}
```

This, on our JVM, produces

```
3  123.457  123.45678
1234.567
1234
```

Notice that in this case, the initial number of fractional digits for the default `NumberFormat` is three, and that the `format()` method rounds `f1`'s value—it doesn't truncate it. After changing `nf`'s fractional digits, the entire value of `f1` is displayed. Next, notice that the `parse()` method must run in a try/catch block and that the `setParseIntegerOnly()` method takes a `boolean` and, in this case, causes subsequent calls to `parse()` to return only the integer part of strings formatted as floating-point numbers.

As we've seen, several of the classes covered in this objective are `abstract`. In addition, for all of these classes, key functionality for every instance is established at the time of creation. Table 8-2 summarizes the constructors or methods used to create instances of all the classes we've discussed in this section.

TABLE 8-2 Instance Creation for Key `java.text` and `java.util` Classes

Class	Key Instance Creation Options
`util.Date`	`new Date();` `new Date(long millisecondsSince010170);`
`util.Calendar`	`Calendar.getInstance();` `Calendar.getInstance(Locale);`

`util.Locale`	`Locale.getDefault();`
	`new Locale(String language);`
	`new Locale(String language, String country);`

`text.DateFormat`	`DateFormat.getInstance();`
	`DateFormat.getDateInstance();`
	`DateFormat.getDateInstance(style);`
	`DateFormat.getDateInstance(style, Locale);`

`text.NumberFormat`	`NumberFormat.getInstance()`
	`NumberFormat.getInstance(Locale)`
	`NumberFormat.getNumberInstance()`
	`NumberFormat.getNumberInstance(Locale)`
	`NumberFormat.getCurrencyInstance()`
	`NumberFormat.getCurrencyInstance(Locale)`

CERTIFICATION OBJECTIVE

Parsing, Tokenizing, and Formatting (OCP Objectives 5.1, 5.2, and 5.3)

5.1 Search, parse, and build strings (including Scanner, StringTokenizer, StringBuilder, String, and Formatter).

*5.2 Search, parse, and replace strings by using regular expressions, using expression patterns for matching limited to . (dot), * (star), + (plus), ?, \d, \D, \s, \S, \w, \W, \b, \B, [], and ().*

5.3 Format strings using the formatting parameters %b, %c, %d, %f, and %s in format strings.

We're going to start with yet another disclaimer: This small section isn't going to morph you from regex newbie to regex guru. In this section, we'll cover three basic ideas:

- **Finding stuff** You've got big heaps of text to look through. Maybe you're doing some screen scraping; maybe you're reading from a file. In any case, you need easy ways to find textual needles in textual haystacks. We'll use the `java.util.regex.Pattern`, `java.util.regex.Matcher`, and `java.util.Scanner` classes to help us find stuff.

- **Tokenizing stuff** You've got a delimited file that you want to get useful data out of. You want to transform a piece of a text file that looks like "1500.00,343.77,123.4" into some individual float variables. We'll show you the basics of using the `String.split()` method and the `java.util.Scanner` class to tokenize your data.
- **Formatting stuff** You've got a report to create and you need to take a float variable with a value of 32500.000f and transform it into a string with a value of "$32,500.00". We'll introduce you to the `java.util.Formatter` class and to the `printf()` and `format()` methods.

A Search Tutorial

Whether you're looking for stuff or tokenizing stuff, a lot of the concepts are the same, so let's start with some basics. No matter what language you're using, sooner or later you'll probably be faced with the need to search through large amounts of textual data, looking for some specific stuff.

Regular expressions (regex for short) are a kind of language within a language, designed to help programmers with these searching tasks. Every language that provides regex capabilities uses one or more regex *engines*. Regex engines search through textual data using instructions that are coded into *expressions*. A regex expression is like a very short program or script. When you invoke a regex engine, you'll pass it the chunk of textual data you want it to process (in Java, this is usually a string or a stream), and you pass it the expression you want it to use to search through the data.

It's fair to think of regex as a language, and we will refer to it that way throughout this section. The regex language is used to create expressions, and as we work through this section, whenever we talk about expressions or expression syntax, we're talking about syntax for the regex "language." Oh, one more disclaimer... we know that you regex mavens out there can come up with better expressions than what we're about to present. Keep in mind that for the most part, we're creating these expressions using only a portion of the total regex instruction set, thanks.

Simple Searches

For our first example, we'd like to search through the following *source* `String`

```
abaaaba
```

for all occurrences (or *matches*) of the *expression*

```
ab
```

In all of these discussions, we'll assume that our data sources use zero-based indexes, so if we display an index under our source `String`, we get

```
source: abaaaba
index:  0123456
```

We can see that we have two occurrences of the expression `ab`: one starting at position 0 and the second starting at position 4. If we sent the previous source data and expression to a regex engine, it would reply by telling us that it found matches at positions 0 and 4. Below is a program (which we'll explain in a few pages) that you can use to perform as many regex experiments as you want to get the feel for how regex works. We'll use this program to show you some of the basics that are covered in the exam:

```
import java.util.regex.*;
class RegTest {
  public static void main(String [] args) {
    Pattern p = Pattern.compile(args[0]);
    Matcher m = p.matcher(args[1]);                  // string to search
    System.out.println("\nsource: " + args[1]);
    System.out.println(" index: 01234567890123456\n"); // the index
    System.out.println("expression: " + m.pattern());  // the search expression
    System.out.print("match positions: ");             // matches positions
    while(m.find()) {
      System.out.print(m.start() + " ");
    }
    System.out.println("");
  }
}
```

So this invocation:

```
java RegTest "ab" "abaaaba"
```

produces

```
source: abaaaba
 index: 01234567890123456

expression: ab
match positions: 0 4
```

In a few pages, we're going to show you a lot more regex code, but first we want to go over some more regex syntax. Once you understand a little more regex, the code samples will make a lot more sense. Here's a more complicated example of a source and an expression:

```
source: abababa
index:  0123456
expression: aba
```

How many occurrences do we get in this case? Well, there is clearly an occurrence starting at position 0 and another starting at position 4. But how about starting at position 2? In general in the world of regex, the `aba` string that starts at position 2 will not be considered a valid occurrence. The first general regex search rule is

In general, a regex search runs from left to right, and once a source's character has been used in a match, it cannot be reused.

So in our previous example, the first match used positions 0, 1, and 2 to match the expression. (Another common term for this is that the first three characters of the source were *consumed*.) Because the character in position 2 was consumed in the first match, it couldn't be used again. So the engine moved on and didn't find another occurrence of `aba` until it reached position 4. This is the typical way that a regex matching engine works. However, in a few pages, we'll look at an exception to the first rule we stated earlier.

So we've matched a couple of exact strings, but what would we do if we wanted to find something a little more dynamic? For instance, what if we wanted to find all of the occurrences of hex numbers or phone numbers or ZIP codes?

Searches Using Metacharacters

As luck would have it, regex has a powerful mechanism for dealing with the cases we described earlier. At the heart of this mechanism is the idea of a *metacharacter*. As an easy example, let's say that we want to search through some source data looking for all occurrences of numeric digits. In regex, the following expression is used to look for numeric digits:

```
\d
```

If we change the previous program to apply the expression `\d` to the following source string, we'd see:

```
java RegTest "\\d" "a12c3e456f"

source: a12c3e456f
index: 01234567890123456

expression: \d
match positions: 1 2 4 6 7 8
```

regex will tell us that it found digits at positions 1, 2, 4, 6, 7, and 8. (If you want to try this at home, you'll need to "escape" the `compile` method's `\d` argument by making it `"\\d"`; more on this a little later.)

Regex provides a rich set of metacharacters that you can find described in the API documentation for `java.util.regex.Pattern`. We won't discuss them all here, but we will describe the ones you'll need for the exam:

- **`\d`** A digit (0–9)
  `\D` A non-digit (anything BUT 0–9)
- **`\s`** A whitespace character (e.g. space, `\t`, `\n`, `\f`, `\r`)
  `\S` A non-whitespace character
- **`\w`** A word character (letters (a–z and A–Z), digits, or the "_" [underscore])
  `\W` A non-word character (everything else)
- **`\b`** A word "boundary" (ends of the string and between `\w` and not `\w`—more soon)
  `\B` A non-word "boundary" (between two `\w`'s or two not `\w`'s)

So, for example, given

```
source: "a 1 56 _Z"
index:   012345678
pattern: \w
```

regex will return positions 0, 2, 4, 5, 7, and 8. The only characters in this source that don't match the definition of a word character are the whitespaces. (Note: In this example, we enclosed the source data in quotes to clearly indicate that there was no whitespace at either end.)

Character Matching The first six (`\d`, `\D`, `\s`, `\S`, `\w`, `\W`), are fairly straightforward. Regex returns the positions where occurrences of those types of characters (or their opposites occur). Here's an example of an "opposites" match:

```
java RegTest "\\S" "w1w w$ &#w1"

source: w1w w$ &#w1
 index: 01234567890123456

expression: \S
match positions: 0 1 2 4 5 7 8 9 10
```

Here you can see that regex matched on everything BUT whitespace.

Boundary Matching The last two (`\b` and `\B`) are a bit different. In these cases, regex is looking for a specific relationship between two adjacent characters. When it finds a match, it returns the position of the second character. Also note that the ends of the strings are considered to be "non-word" characters. Let's look at a few examples:

```
java RegTest "\\b" "w2w w$ &#w2"

source: w2w w$ &#w2
 index: 01234567890123456

expression: \b
match positions: 0 3 4 5 9 11
```

First, let's recall that "word characters" are A–Z, a–z, and 0–9. It's not too tricky to understand the matches at positions 3, 4, 5, and 9. Regex is telling us that characters 2 and 3 are a boundary between a word character and a non-word character. Remembering that order doesn't matter, it's easy to see that positions 4, 5, and 9 are similar "boundaries" between the two classes of characters—the character specified and the one preceding it.

But the matches on positions 0 and 11 are a bit confusing. For the sake of the exam, just imagine that for `\b` and `\B`, there is a hidden, non-word character at each end of the string that you can see. Let's look at an example of using `\b` and then `\B` against the same string:

```
source: #ab de#
 index: 01234567890123456

expression: \b
match positions: 1 3 4 6
```

In this case, the matches should be intuitive; they mark the second character in a pair of characters that represent a boundary (word versus non-word). But here:

```
source: #ab de#
 index: 01234567890123456

expression: \B
match positions: 0 2 5 7
```

in this case, assuming invisible, non-word characters at each end of the string, we see places where there are NOT word boundaries (i.e., where two-word characters abut or where two non-word characters abut).

Searches Using Ranges

You can also specify sets of characters to search for using square brackets and ranges of characters to search for using square brackets and a dash:

- `[abc]` Searches only for a's, b's, or c's
- `[a-f]` Searches only for a, b, c, d, e, or f characters

In addition, you can search across several ranges at once. The following expression is looking for occurrences of the letters `a-f` or `A-F`; it's NOT looking for an `fA` combination:

- `[a-fA-F]` Searches for the first six letters of the alphabet, both cases.

So, for instance,

```
source: "cafeBABE"
index:   01234567
pattern: [a-cA-C]
```

returns positions 0, 1, 4, 5, 6.

on the job

In addition to the capabilities described for the exam, you can apply the following attributes to sets and ranges within square brackets: "^" to negate the characters specified, nested brackets to create a union of sets, and "&&" to specify the intersection of sets. While these constructs are not on the exam, they are quite useful, and good examples can be found in the API for the `java.util.regex.Pattern` class.

Searches Using Quantifiers

Let's say that we want to create a regex pattern to search for hexadecimal literals. As a first step, let's solve the problem for one-digit hexadecimal numbers:

```
0[xX][0-9a-fA-F]
```

The preceding expression could be stated:

Find a set of characters in which the first character is a "`0`", the second character is either an "`x`" or an "`X`", and the third character is a digit from "`0`" to "`9`", a letter from "`a`" to "`f`", or an uppercase letter from "`A`" to "`F`".

Using the preceding expression and the following data:

```
source: 12 0x 0x12 0Xf 0xg
 index: 012345678901234567
```

regex would return 6 and 11. (Note: `0x` and `0xg` are not valid hex numbers.)

As a second step, let's think about an easier problem. What if we just wanted regex to find occurrences of integers? Integers can be one or more digits long, so it would be great if we could say "one or more" in an expression. There is a set of regex constructs called quantifiers that let us specify concepts such as "one or more." In fact, the quantifier that represents "one or more" is the "+" character. We'll see the others shortly.

The other issue this raises is that when we're searching for something whose length is variable, getting only a starting position as a return value is of limited use. So, in addition to returning starting positions, another bit of information that a regex engine can return is the entire match, or *group*, that it finds. We're going to change the way we talk about what regex returns by specifying each return on its own line, remembering that now for each return we're going to get back the starting position AND then the group. Here's the revised code:

```
import java.util.regex.*;
class GroupTest {
  public static void main(String [] args) {
    Pattern p = Pattern.compile(args[0]);
    Matcher m = p.matcher(args[1]);
    System.out.println("\nsource: " + args[1]);
    System.out.println(" index: 01234567890123456\n");
    System.out.println("pattern: " + m.pattern());
    while(m.find()) {
      System.out.println(m.start() + " " + m.group());
    }
    System.out.println("");
  }
}
```

So, if we invoke `GroupTest` like this:

```
java GroupTest "\d+" "1 a12 234b"
```

you can read this expression as saying: "Find one or more digits in a row." This expression produces this regex output:

```
source: 1 a12 234b
 index: 01234567890123456

pattern: \d+
0 1
3 12
6 234
```

You can read this as "At position 0, there's an integer with a value of 1; then at position 3, there's an integer with a value of 12; then at position 6, there's an integer with a value of 234." Returning now to our hexadecimal problem, the last thing we need to know is how to specify the use of a quantifier for only part of an expression. In this case, we must have exactly one occurrence of `0x` or `0X`, but we can have from one to many occurrences of the hex "digits" that follow. The following expression adds parentheses to limit the "+" quantifier to only the hex digits:

```
0[xX]([0-9a-fA-F])+
```

The parentheses and "+" augment the previous find-the-hex expression by saying in effect: "Once we've found our `0x` or `0X`, you can find from one to many occurrences of hex digits." Notice that we put the "+" quantifier at the end of the expression. It's useful to think of quantifiers as always quantifying the part of the expression that precedes them.

The other two quantifiers we're going to look at are

- `*` Zero or more occurrences
- `?` Zero or one occurrence

Let's say you have a text file containing a comma-delimited list of all the filenames in a directory that contains several very important projects. (BTW, this isn't how we'd arrange our directories. :)) You want to create a list of all the files whose names start with `proj1`. You might discover .txt files, .java files, .pdf files—who knows? What kind of regex expression could we create to find these various `proj1` files? First, let's take a look at what a part of this text might look like:

```
..."proj3.txt,proj1sched.pdf,proj1,proj2,proj1.java"...
```

To solve this problem, we're going to use the regex ^ (carat) operator, which we mentioned earlier. The regex ^ operator isn't on the exam, but it will help us create a fairly clean solution to our problem. The ^ is the negation symbol in regex. For instance, if you want to find anything but a's, b's, or c's in a file, you could say

```
[^abc]
```

So, armed with the ^ operator and the `*` (zero or more) quantifier, we can create the following:

```
proj1([^,])*
```

If we apply this expression to just the portion of the text file we listed earlier, regex returns

```
10 proj1sched.pdf
25 proj1
37 proj1.java
```

The key part of this expression is the "give me zero or more characters that aren't a comma."

The last quantifier example we'll look at is the ? (zero or one) quantifier. Let's say that our job this time is to search a text file and find anything that might be a local seven-digit phone number. We're going to say, arbitrarily, that if we find seven digits in a row, or three digits followed by a dash, or a space followed by four digits, that we have a candidate. Here are examples of "valid" phone numbers:

```
1234567
123 4567
123-4567
```

The key to creating this expression is to see that we need "zero or one instance of either a space or a dash" in the middle of our digits:

```
\d\d\d([-\s])?\d\d\d\d
```

The Predefined Dot

In addition to the `\s`, `\d`, and `\w` metacharacters that we discussed, you have to understand the "`.`" (dot) metacharacter. When you see this character in a regex expression, it means "any character can serve here." For instance, the following source and pattern:

```
source: "ac abc a c"
pattern: a.c
```

will produce the output

```
3 abc
7 a c
```

The "`.`" was able to match both the "`b`" and the "` `" in the source data.

Greedy Quantifiers

When you use the `*`, `+`, and `?` quantifiers, you can fine-tune them a bit to produce behavior that's known as "greedy," "reluctant," or "possessive." Although you need to understand only the greedy quantifier for the exam, we're also going to discuss the reluctant quantifier to serve as a basis for comparison. First, the syntax:

- `?` is greedy, `??` is reluctant, for zero or once
- `*`is greedy, `*?` is reluctant, for zero or more
- `+` is greedy, `+?` is reluctant, for one or more

What happens when we have the following source and pattern:

```
source:   yyxxxyxx
pattern:   .*xx
```

First off, we're doing something a bit different here by looking for characters that prefix the static (xx) portion of the expression. We think we're saying something like: "Find sets of characters that end with xx". Before we tell what happens, we at least want you to consider that there are two plausible results… can you find them? Remember we said earlier that in general, regex engines worked from left to right and consumed characters as they went. So, working from left to right, we might predict that the engine would search the first four characters (`0-3`), find `xx` starting in position 2, and have its first match. Then it would proceed and find the second `xx` starting in position 6. This would lead us to a result like this:

```
0 yyxx
4 xyxx
```

A plausible second argument is that since we asked for a set of characters that ends with `xx`, we might get a result like this:

```
0 yyxxxyxx
```

The way to think about this is to consider the name *greedy*. In order for the second answer to be correct, the regex engine would have to look (greedily) at the *entire* source data before it could determine that there was an `xx` at the end. So, in fact, the second result is the correct result because in the original example we used the greedy quantifier `*`. The result that finds two different sets can be generated by using the reluctant quantifier `*?`. Let's review:

```
source:   yyxxxyxx
pattern:   .*xx
```

is using the greedy quantifier `*` and produces

```
0 yyxxxyxx
```

If we change the pattern to

```
source:   yyxxxyxx
pattern:   .*?xx
```

we're now using the reluctant qualifier `*?`, and we get the following:

```
0 yyxx
4 xyxx
```

The greedy quantifier does, in fact, read the entire source data and then it works backward (from the right) until it finds the rightmost match. At that point, it includes everything from earlier in the source data, up to and including the data that is part of the rightmost match.

on the Job

There are a lot more aspects to regex quantifiers than we've discussed here, but we've covered more than enough for the exam. Oracle has several tutorials that will help you learn more about quantifiers and turn you into the go-to person at your job.

When Metacharacters and Strings Collide

So far, we've been talking about regex from a theoretical perspective. Before we can put regex to work, we have to discuss one more gotcha. When it's time to implement regex in our code, it will be quite common that our source data and/or our expressions will be stored in strings. The problem is that metacharacters and strings don't mix too well. For instance, let's say we just want to do a simple regex pattern that looks for digits. We might try something like

```
String pattern = "\d";     // compiler error!
```

This line of code won't compile! The compiler sees the \ and thinks, "Okay, here comes an escape sequence; maybe it'll be a new line!" But no, next comes the `d` and the compiler says, "I've never heard of the `\d` escape sequence." The way to satisfy the compiler is to add another backslash in front of the `\d`:

```
String pattern = "\\d";     // a compilable metacharacter
```

The first backslash tells the compiler that whatever comes next should be taken literally, not as an escape sequence. How about the dot (`.`) metacharacter? If we want a dot in our expression to be used as a metacharacter, no problem, but what if we're reading some source data that happens to use dots as delimiters? Here's another way to look at our options:

```
String p = ".";        // regex sees this as the "." metacharacter
String p = "\.";       // the compiler sees this as an illegal
                       // Java escape sequence
String p = "\\.";      // the compiler is happy, and regex sees a
                       // dot, not a metacharacter
```

A similar problem can occur when you hand metacharacters to a Java program via command-line arguments. If we want to pass the `\d` metacharacter into our Java program, our JVM does the right thing if we say

```
% java DoRegex "\d"
```

But your JVM might not. If you have problems running the following examples, you might try adding a backslash (i.e., \\d) to your command-line metacharacters. Don't worry—you won't see any command-line metacharacters on the exam!

on the job

The Java language defines several escape sequences, including

`\n` ***= linefeed (which you might see on the exam)***
`\b` ***= backspace***
`\t` ***= tab***

And others, which you can find in the Java Language Specification. Other than perhaps seeing a `\n` ***inside a string, you won't have to worry about Java's escape sequences on the exam.***

At this point, we've learned enough of the regex language to start using it in our Java programs. We'll start by looking at using regex expressions to find stuff, and then we'll move to the closely related topic of tokenizing stuff.

Locating Data via Pattern Matching

Over the last few pages, we've used a few small Java programs to explore some regex basics. Now we're going to take a more detailed look at the two classes we've been using: `java.util.regex.Pattarn` and `java.util.regex.Matcher`. Once you know a little regex, using the `java.util.regex.Pattern` (`Pattern`) and `java.util.regex.Matcher` (`Matcher`) classes is pretty straightforward. The `Pattern` class is used to hold a representation of a regex expression so that it can be used and reused by instances of the `Matcher` class. The `Matcher` class is used to invoke the regex engine, with the intention of performing match operations. The following program shows `Pattern` and `Matcher` in action, and, as we've seen, it's not a bad way for you to do your own regex experiments. Note, once you've read about the `Console` class in Chapter 9, you might want to modify the following class by adding some functionality from the `Console` class. That way, you'll get some practice with the `Console` class, and it'll be easier to run multiple regex experiments.

```
import java.util.regex.*;
class Regex {
  public static void main(String [] args) {
    Pattern p = Pattern.compile(args[0]);
    Matcher m = p.matcher(args[1]);
    System.out.println("Pattern is " + m.pattern());
    while(m.find()) {
      System.out.println(m.start() + " " + m.group());
    }
  }
}
```

As with our earlier programs, this program uses the first command-line argument (`args[0]`) to represent the regex expression you want to use, and it uses the second argument (`args[1]`) to represent the source data you want to search. Here's a test run:

```
% java Regex "\d\w" "ab4 56_7ab"
```

produces the output

```
Pattern is \d\w
4 56
7 7a
```

(Remember, if you want this expression to be represented in a string, you'd use `\\d\\w`.) Because you'll often have special characters or whitespace as part of your arguments, you'll probably want to get in the habit of always enclosing your argument in quotes. Let's take a look at this code in more detail. First off, notice that we aren't using `new` to create a `Pattern`; if you check the API, you'll find no constructors are listed. You'll use the overloaded, static `compile()` method (which takes `String expression`) to create an instance of `Pattern`. For the exam, all you'll need to know to create a `Matcher` is to use the `Pattern.matcher()` method (which takes `String sourceData`).

The important method in this program is the `find()` method. This is the method that actually cranks up the regex engine and does some searching. The `find()` method returns `true` if it gets a match and remembers the start position of the match. If `find()` returns `true`, you can call the `start()` method to get the starting position of the match, and you can call the `group()` method to get the string that represents the actual bit of source data that was matched.

To provide the most flexibility, `Matcher.find()`, when coupled with the greedy quantifiers `?` or `*`, allows for (somewhat unintuitively) the idea of a zero-length match. As an experiment, modify the previous `Regex` class and add an invocation of `m.end()` to the `System.out.print` (S.O.P.) in the `while` loop. With that modification in place, the invocation

```
java Regex "a?" "aba"
```

should produce something very similar to this:

```
Pattern is a?
0 1 a
1 1
2 3 a
3 3
```

The lines of output `1 1` and `3 3` are examples of zero-length matches. Zero-length matches can occur in several places:

- ***After the last character of source data (the `3 3` example)***
- ***In between characters after a match has been found (the `1 1` example)***
- ***At the beginning of source data (try `java Regex "a?" "baba"`)***
- ***At the beginning of zero-length source data***

on the job

A common reason to use regex is to perform search-and-replace operations. Although replace operations are not on the exam, you should know that the `Matcher` class provides several methods that perform search-and-replace operations. See the `appendReplacement()`, `appendTail()`, and `replaceAll()` methods in the `Matcher` API for more details.

The `Matcher` class allows you to look at subsets of your source data by using a concept called *regions*. In real life, regions can greatly improve performance, but you won't need to know anything about them for the exam.

Searching Using the Scanner Class Although the `java.util.Scanner` class is primarily intended for tokenizing data (which we'll cover next), it can also be used to find stuff, just like the `Pattern` and `Matcher` classes. While `Scanner` doesn't provide location information or search-and-replace functionality, you can use it to apply regex expressions to source data to tell you how many instances of an expression exist in a given piece of source data. The following program uses the first command-line argument as a regex expression and then asks for input using `System.in`. It outputs a message every time a match is found:

```
import java.util.*;
class ScanIn {
  public static void main(String[] args) {
    System.out.print("input: ");
    System.out.flush();
    try {
      Scanner s = new Scanner(System.in);
      String token;
      do {
        token = s.findInLine(args[0]);
        System.out.println("found " + token);
      } while (token != null);
    } catch (Exception e) { System.out.println("scan exc"); }
  }
}
```

The invocation and input

```
java ScanIn "\d\d"
input: 1b2c335f456
```

produce the following:

```
found 33
found 45
found null
```

Tokenizing

Tokenizing is the process of taking big pieces of source data, breaking them into little pieces, and storing the little pieces in variables. Probably the most common tokenizing situation is reading a delimited file in order to get the contents of the file moved into useful places, like objects, arrays, or collections. We'll look at two classes in the API that provide tokenizing capabilities: `String` (using the `split()` method) and `Scanner`, which has many methods that are useful for tokenizing.

Tokens and Delimiters

When we talk about tokenizing, we're talking about data that starts out composed of two things: tokens and delimiters. Tokens are the actual pieces of data, and delimiters are the expressions that *separate* the tokens from each other. When most people think of delimiters, they think of single characters, like commas or backslashes or maybe a single whitespace. These are indeed very common delimiters, but strictly speaking, delimiters can be much more dynamic. In fact, as we hinted at a few sentences ago, delimiters can be anything that qualifies as a regex expression. Let's take a single piece of source data and tokenize it using a couple of different delimiters:

```
source: "ab,cd5b,6x,z4"
```

If we say that our delimiter is a comma, then our four tokens would be

```
ab
cd5b
6x
z4
```

If we use the same source but declare our delimiter to be `\d`, we get three tokens:

```
ab,cd
b,
x,z
```

In general, when we tokenize source data, the delimiters themselves are discarded and all that we are left with are the tokens. So in the second example, we defined digits to be delimiters, so the 5, 6, and 4 do not appear in the final tokens.

Tokenizing with String.split()

The `String` class's `split()` method takes a regex expression as its argument and returns a `String` array populated with the tokens produced by the split (or tokenizing) process. This is a handy way to tokenize relatively small pieces of data. The following program uses `args[0]` to hold a source string, and `args[1]` to hold the regex pattern to use as a delimiter:

```
import java.util.*;
class SplitTest {
  public static void main(String[] args) {
    String[] tokens = args[0].split(args[1]);
    System.out.println("count " + tokens.length);
    for(String s : tokens)
      System.out.println(">" + s + "<");
  }
}
```

Everything happens all at once when the `split()` method is invoked. The source string is split into pieces, and the pieces are all loaded into the `tokens String` array. All the code after that is just there to verify what the split operation generated. The following invocation

```
% java SplitTest "ab5 ccc 45 @" "\d"
```

produces

```
count 4
>ab<
> ccc <
><
> @<
```

(Note: Remember that to represent "\" in a string, you may need to use the escape sequence "\\". Because of this, and depending on your OS, your second argument might have to be "\\d" or even "\\\\d".)

We put the tokens inside > < characters to show whitespace. Notice that every digit was used as a delimiter and that contiguous digits created an empty token.

One drawback to using the `String.split()` method is that often you'll want to look at tokens as they are produced, and possibly quit a tokenization operation early when you've created the tokens you need. For instance, you might be searching a large file for a phone number. If the phone number occurs early in the file, you'd like to quit the tokenization process as soon as you've got your number. The `Scanner` class provides a rich API for doing just such on-the-fly tokenization operations.

exam watch

Because `System.out.println()` is so heavily used on the exam, you might see examples of escape sequences tucked in with questions on most any topic, including regex. Remember that if you need to create a string that contains a double quote (") or a backslash (\), you need to add an escape character first:

```
System.out.println("\" \\");
```

This prints

```
" \
```

But what if you need to search for periods (.) in your source data? If you just put a period in the regex expression, you get the "any character" behavior. But what if you try "\."? Now the Java compiler thinks you're trying to create an escape sequence that doesn't exist. The correct syntax is

```
String s = "ab.cde.fg";
String[] tokens = s.split("\\.");
```

Tokenizing with Scanner

The `java.util.Scanner` class is the Cadillac of tokenizing. When you need to do some serious tokenizing, look no further than `Scanner`—this beauty has it all. In addition to the basic tokenizing capabilities provided by `String.split()`, the `Scanner` class offers the following features:

- Scanners can be constructed using files, streams, or strings as a source.
- Tokenizing is performed within a loop so that you can exit the process at any point.
- Tokens can be converted to their appropriate primitive types automatically.

Let's look at a program that demonstrates several of `Scanner's` methods and capabilities. `Scanner`'s default delimiter is whitespace, which this program uses. The program makes two `Scanner` objects: `s1` is iterated over with the more generic `next()` method, which returns every token as a `String`, while `s2` is analyzed with several of the specialized `nextXxx()` methods (where `Xxx` is a primitive type):

```
import java.util.Scanner;
class ScanNext {
  public static void main(String [] args) {
    boolean b2, b;
    int i;
    String s, hits = " ";
    Scanner s1 = new Scanner(args[0]);
    Scanner s2 = new Scanner(args[0]);
    while(b = s1.hasNext()) {
      s = s1.next();  hits += "s";
    }
    while(b = s2.hasNext()) {
      if (s2.hasNextInt()) {
        i = s2.nextInt();  hits += "i";
      } else if (s2.hasNextBoolean()) {
        b2 = s2.nextBoolean();  hits += "b";
      } else {
        s2.next();  hits += "s2";
      }
    }
    System.out.println("hits " + hits);
  }
}
```

If this program is invoked with

```
% java ScanNext "1 true 34 hi"
```

it produces

```
hits  ssssibis2
```

Of course, we're not doing anything with the tokens once we've got them, but you can see that s2's tokens are converted to their respective primitives. A key point here is that the methods named hasNextXxx() test the value of the next token but do not actually get the token, nor do they move to the next token in the source data. The nextXxx() methods all perform two functions: They get the next token, and then they move to the next token.

The Scanner class has nextXxx() (for instance, nextLong()) and hasNextXxx() (for instance, hasNextDouble()) methods for every primitive type except char. In addition, the Scanner class has a useDelimiter() method that allows you to set the delimiter to be any valid regex expression.

Tokenizing with java.util.StringTokenizer

The java.util.StringTokenizer class is the rusty old Buick of tokenizing. These days, when you want to do tokenizing, the Scanner class and String.split() are the preferred approaches. In fact, in the API docs, the StringTokenizer class is not recommended. The reason it's on the exam is because you'll often find it in older code, and when you do, you'll want to understand how it works. The following list of features summarizes the capabilities of StringTokenizer and relates them to the Scanner class:

- StringTokenizer objects are constructed using strings as a source.
- StringTokenizer objects use whitespace characters by default as delimiters, but they can be constructed with a custom set of delimiters (which are listed as a string).
- Tokenizing is performed within a loop so that you can exit the process at any point.
- The loop used for tokenizing uses the Enumerator interface, and typically uses the hasMoreTokens() and nextToken() methods, which are very similar to Scanner's next() and hasNext() methods. (Note: These days, the Iterator interface is recommended instead of Enumerator.)

Let's look at a program that demonstrates several of StringTokenizer's methods and capabilities:

```
import java.util.*;

public class STtest {
  public static void main(String[] args) {
    StringTokenizer st = new StringTokenizer("a bc d e");
```

```
      System.out.println("\n " + st.countTokens());
      while(st.hasMoreTokens()) {
        System.out.print(">" + st.nextToken() + "<  ");
      }
      System.out.println("\n " + st.countTokens());

      // Second argument "a" is this StringTokenizer's delimiter

      StringTokenizer st2 = new StringTokenizer("a b cab a ba d", "a");
      System.out.println("\n " + st2.countTokens());
      while(st2.hasMoreTokens()) {
        System.out.print(">" + st2.nextToken() + "<  ");
      }
      System.out.println("\n " + st2.countTokens());
    }
  }
```

which produces the output:

```
 4
>a<  >bc<  >d<  >e<
 0

 4
> b c<  >b <  > b<  > d<
 0
```

To recap, the first `StringTokenizer`, `st`, uses whitespace as its delimiter, and the second `StringTokenizer`, `st2`, uses `"a"` as its delimiter. In both cases, we surrounded the tokens with "> <" characters to show any whitespace included in tokens. We also used the `countTokens()` method to display how many tokens were `Enumerator`-able before and after each enumeration loop.

There are a few more details in the `StringTokenizer` class, but this is all you'll need for the exam.

Formatting with printf() and format()

What fun would accounts receivable reports be if the decimal points didn't line up? Where would you be if you couldn't put negative numbers inside of parentheses? Burning questions like these caused the exam creation team to include formatting as a part of the exam. The `format()` and `printf()` methods were added to `java.io.PrintStream` in Java 5. These two methods behave exactly the same way, so anything we say about one of these methods applies to both of them. (The rumor is that `printf()` was added just to make old C programmers happy.)

Behind the scenes, the `format()` method uses the `java.util.Formatter` class to do the heavy formatting work. You can use the `Formatter` class directly if you choose, but for the exam, all you have to know is the basic syntax of the arguments you pass to the `format()` method. The documentation for these formatting arguments can be found in the `Formatter` API. We're going to take the "nickel tour" of the formatting `String` syntax, which will be more than enough to allow you to do a lot of basic formatting work AND ace all the formatting questions on the exam.

Let's start by paraphrasing the API documentation for format strings (for more complete, way-past-what-you-need-for-the-exam coverage, check out the `java.util.Formatter` API):

```
printf("format string", argument(s));<F255D>
```

The format string can contain both normal string-literal information that isn't associated with any arguments and argument-specific formatting data. The clue to determining whether you're looking at formatting data is that formatting data will always start with a percent sign (`%`). Let's look at an example, and don't panic, we'll cover everything that comes after the `%` next:

```
System.out.printf("%2$d  +  %1$d", 123, 456);
```

This produces

```
456 + 123
```

Let's look at what just happened. Inside the double quotes there is a format string, then a `+`, and then a second format string. Notice that we mixed literals in with the format strings. Now let's dive in a little deeper and look at the construction of format strings:

```
%[arg_index$][flags][width][.precision]conversion char
```

The values within `[ ]` are optional. In other words, the only required elements of a format string are the `%` and a conversion character. In the previous example, the only optional values we used were for argument indexing. The `2$` represents the second argument, and the `1$` represents the first argument. (Notice that there's no problem switching the order of arguments.) The `d` after the arguments is a conversion character (more or less the type of the argument). Here's a rundown of the format string elements you'll need to know for the exam:

- **arg_index** An integer followed directly by a `$`, this indicates which argument should be printed in this position.

- **flags** While many flags are available, for the exam, you'll need to know:
  - `-` Left-justify this argument
  - `+` Include a sign (+ or -) with this argument
  - `0` Pad this argument with zeroes
  - `,` Use locale-specific grouping separators (i.e., the comma in 123,456)
  - `(` Enclose negative numbers in parentheses
- **width** This value indicates the minimum number of characters to print. (If you want nice, even columns, you'll use this value extensively.)
- **precision** For the exam, you'll only need this when formatting a floating-point number, and in the case of floating-point numbers, precision indicates the number of digits to print after the decimal point.
  - **conversion** The type of argument you'll be formatting. You'll need to know:
  - `b` boolean
  - `c` char
  - `d` integer
  - `f` floating point
  - `s` string

Let's see some of these formatting strings in action:

```
int i1 = -123;
int i2 = 12345;
System.out.printf(">%1$(7d< \n", i1);
System.out.printf(">%0,7d< \n", i2);
System.out.format(">%+-7d< \n", i2);
System.out.printf(">%2$b + %1$5d< \n", i1, false);
```

This produces:

```
>  (123)<
>012,345<
>+12345 <
>false +  -123<
```

(We added the > and < literals to help show how minimum widths, zero padding, and alignments work.) Finally, it's important to remember that—barring the use of booleans—if you have a mismatch between the type specified in your conversion character and your argument, you'll get a runtime exception:

```
System.out.format("%d", 12.3);
```

This produces something like

```
Exception in thread "main" java.util.IllegalFormatConversionException: d !=
java.lang.Double
```

CERTIFICATION OBJECTIVE

Resource Bundles (OCP Objectives 12.2, 12.3, and 12.5)

12.2 *Build a resource bundle for each object.*

12.3 *Call a resource bundle from an application.*

12.5 *Describe the advantages of localizing an application.*

Resource Bundles

Earlier, we used the `Locale` class to display numbers and dates for basic localization. For full-fledged localization, we also need to provide language and country-specific strings for display. There are only two parts to building an application with resource bundles:

- **`Locale`** You can use the same `Locale` we used for `DateFormat` and `NumberFormat` to identify which resource bundle to choose.
- **`ResourceBundle`** Think of a `ResourceBundle` as a map. You can use property files or Java classes to specify the mappings.

Let's build up a simple application to be used in Canada. Since Canada has two official languages, we want to let the user choose her favorite language. Designing our application, we decided to have it just output "Hello Java" to show off how cool it is. We can always add more text later.

We are going to externalize everything language specific to special files called resource bundles. They're just property files that contain keys and string values to display. Here are two simple resource bundle files:

A file named `Labels_en.properties` that contains a single line of data:

```
hello=Hello Java!
```

A second file named `Labels_fr.properties` that contains a single line of data:

```
hello=Bonjour Java!
```

Using a resource bundle has three steps: obtaining the `Locale`, getting the `ResourceBundle`, and looking up a value from the resource bundle. First, we create a `Locale` object. To review, this means one of the following:

```
new Locale("en")            // language - English
new Locale("en", "CA")      // language and country - Canadian English
Locale.CANADA               // constant for common locales - Canadian
English
```

Next, we need to create the resource bundle. We need to know the "title" of the resource bundle and the locale. Then we pass those values to a factory, which creates the resource bundle. The `getBundle()` method looks in the classpath for bundles that match the bundle name (`"Labels"`) and the provided `locale`.

```
ResourceBundle rb = ResourceBundle.getBundle("Labels", locale);
```

Finally, we use the resource bundle like a map and get a value based on the key:

```
rb.getString("hello");
```

Putting this together and adding `java.util` imports, we have everything we need in order to read from a resource bundle:

```
import java.util.Locale;
import java.util.ResourceBundle;

public class WhichLanguage {
  public static void main(String[] args) {
    Locale locale = new Locale(args[0]);
    ResourceBundle rb = ResourceBundle.getBundle("Labels", locale);
    System.out.println(rb.getString("hello"));
  }
}
```

Running the code twice, we get:

```
> java WhichLanguage en
Hello Java!
> java WhichLanguage fr
Bonjour Java!
```

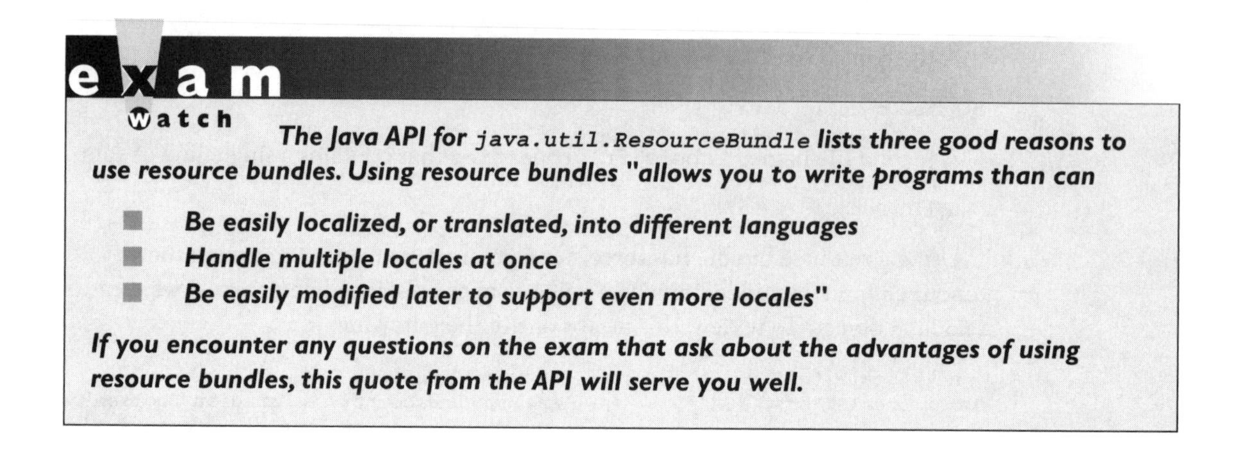

The Java API for `java.util.ResourceBundle` lists three good reasons to use resource bundles. Using resource bundles "allows you to write programs than can

- ***Be easily localized, or translated, into different languages***
- ***Handle multiple locales at once***
- ***Be easily modified later to support even more locales"***

If you encounter any questions on the exam that ask about the advantages of using resource bundles, this quote from the API will serve you well.

The most common use of localization in Java is web applications. You can get the user's locale from information passed in the request rather than hard-coding it.

Property Resource Bundles

Let's take a closer look at the property file. Aside from comments, a property file contains key/value pairs:

```
# this file contains a single key/value
hello=Hello Java
```

As you can see, comments are lines beginning with #. A key is the first string on a line. Keys and values are separated by an equal sign. If you want to break up a single line into multiple lines, you use a backslash:

```
hello1 = Hello \
  World!
System.out.println(rb.getString("hello1"));
Hello World!
```

If you actually want a line break, you use the standard Java \n escape sequence:

```
hello2 = Hello \nWorld  !
System.out.println(rb.getString("hello2"));
Hello
World  !
```

You can mix and match these to your heart's content. Java helpfully ignores any whitespace before subsequent lines of a multiline property. This is so you can use indentation for clarity:

```
hello3 =     123\
  45
System.out.println(rb.getString("hello3"));
12345
```

Almost everyone uses # for comments and = to separate key/value pairs. There are alternative syntax choices, though, which you should understand if you come across them.

Property files can use two styles of commenting:

```
! comment
```

or

```
# comment
```

Property files can define key/value pairs in any of the following formats:

```
key=value
key:value
key value
```

These few rules are all you need to know about the `PropertyResourceBundle`. While property files are the most common format for resource bundles, what happens if we want to represent types of values other than `String`? Or if we want to load the resource bundles from a database?

Java Resource Bundles

When we need to move beyond simple property file key to string value mappings, we can use resource bundles that are Java classes. We write Java classes that extend `ListResourceBundle`. The class name is similar to the one for property files. Only the extension is different.

```
import java.util.ListResourceBundle;
public class Labels_en_CA extends ListResourceBundle {
  protected Object[][] getContents() {
    return new Object[][] {
       { "hello", new StringBuilder("from Java") }
     };
  }
}
```

We implement `ListResourceBundle`'s one required method that returns an array of arrays. The inner array is key/value pairs. The outer array accumulates such pairs. Notice that now we aren't limited to `String` values. We can call `getObject()` to get a non-`String` value:

```
Locale locale = new Locale(args[0], "CA");
ResourceBundle rb = ResourceBundle.getBundle("Labels", locale);
System. out.println(rb.getObject("hello"));
```

Which prints `"from Java"`.

Default Locale

What do you think happens if we call `ResourceBundle.getBundle("Labels")` without any locale? It depends. Java will pick the resource bundle that matches the locale the JVM is using. Typically, this matches the locale of the machine running the program, but it doesn't have to. You can even change the default locale at runtime. Which might be useful if you are working with people in different locales so you can get the same behavior on all machines.

Exploring the API to get and set the default locale:

```
// store locale so can put it back at end
Locale initial  = Locale.getDefault();
System.out.println(initial);

// set locale to Germany
Locale.setDefault(Locale.GERMANY);
System.out.println(Locale.getDefault());

// put original locale back
Locale.setDefault(initial);
System.out.println(Locale.getDefault());
```

which on our computer prints:

```
en_US
de_DE
en_US
```

For the first and last line, you may get different output depending on where you live. The key is that the middle of the program executes as if it were in Germany, regardless of where it is actually being run. It is good practice to restore the default unless your program is ending right away. That way, the rest of your code works normally—it probably doesn't expect to be in Germany.

Choosing the Right Resource Bundle

There are two main ways to get a resource bundle:

```
ResourceBundle.getBundle(baseName)
ResourceBundle.getBundle(baseName, locale)
```

Luckily, `ResourceBundle.getBundle(baseName)` is just shorthand for `ResourceBundle.getBundle(baseName, Locale.getDefault())` and you only have to remember one set of rules. There are a few other overloaded signatures for `getBundle()`, such as taking a `ClassLoader`. But don't worry—these aren't on the exam.

Now on to the rules. How does Java choose the right resource bundle to use? In a nutshell, Java chooses the most specific resource bundle it can while giving preference to Java `ListResourceBundle`.

Going back to our Canadian application, we decide to request the Canadian French resource bundle:

```
Locale locale = new Locale("fr", "CA");
ResourceBundle rb = ResourceBundle.getBundle("RB", locale);
```

Java will look for the following files in the classpath in this order:

```
RB_fr_CA.java          // exactly what we asked for
RB_fr_CA.properties

RB_fr.java             // couldn't find exactly what we asked for
RB_fr.properties       // now trying just requested language
RB_en_US.java          // couldn't find French
RB_en_US.properties    // now trying default Locale
RB_en.java             // couldn't find full default Locale country
RB_en.properties       // now trying default Locale language
RB.java                // couldn't find anything any matching Locale,
RB.properties          // now trying default bundle
```

If none of these files exist, Java gives up and throws a `MissingResourceException`. While this is a lot of things for Java to try, it is pretty easy to remember. Start with the full `Locale` requested. Then fall back to just language. Then fall back to the default `Locale`. Then fall back to the default bundle. Then cry.

Make sure you understand this because it is about to get more complicated.

You don't have to specify all the keys in all the property files. They can inherit from each other. This is a good thing, as it reduces duplication.

```
RB_en.properties
  ride.in=Take a ride in the

RB_en_US.properties
  elevator=elevator

RB_en_UK.properties
  elevator=lift

Locale locale = new Locale("en", "UK");
ResourceBundle rb = ResourceBundle.getBundle("RB", locale);
System.out.println(rb.getString("ride.in") +
                   rb.getString("elevator"));
```

Outputs:

```
Take a ride in the lift
```

The common `"ride.in"` property comes from the parent noncountry-specific bundle "`RB_en.properties`." The `"elevator"` property is different by country and comes from the UK version that we specifically requested.

The parent hierarchy is more specific than the search order. A bundle's parent always has a shorter name than the child bundle. If a parent is missing, Java just skips along that hierarchy. `ListResourceBundles` and `PropertyResourcesBundles` do not share a hierarchy. Similarly, the default locale's resource bundles do not share a hierarchy with the requested locale's resource bundles. Table 8-3 shows examples of bundles that do share a hierarchy.

TABLE 8-3 Resource Bundle Lookups

Name of Resource Bundle	Hierarchy
RB_fr_CA.java	RB.java RB_fr.java RB_fr_CA.java
RB_fr_CA.properties	RB.properties RB_fr.properties RB_fr_CA.properties
RB_en_US.java	RB.java RB_en.java RB_en_US.java
RB_en_US.properties	RB.properties RB_en.properties RB_en_US.properties

Remember that searching for a property file uses a linear list. However, once a matching resource bundle is found, keys can only come from that resource bundle's hierarchy.

One more example to make this clear. Think about which resource bundles will be used from the previous code if I use the following code to request a resource bundle:

```
Locale locale = new Locale("fr", "FR");
ResourceBundle  rb = ResourceBundle.getBundle("RB", locale);
```

First, Java looks for `RB_fr_FR.java` and `RB_fr_FR.properties`. Since neither is found, Java falls back to using `RB_fr.java`. Then as we request keys from `rb`, Java starts looking in `RB_fr.java` and additionally looks in `RB.java`. Java started out looking for a matching file and then switched to searching the hierarchy of that file.

CERTIFICATION SUMMARY

Dates, Numbers, and Currency Remember that the objective is a bit misleading and that you'll have to understand the basics of five related classes: `java.util.Date`, `java.util.Calendar`, `java.util.Locale`, `java.text.DateFormat`, and `java.text.NumberFormat`. A `Date` is the number of milliseconds since January 1, 1970, stored in a `long`. Most of `Date`'s methods have been deprecated, so use the `Calendar` class for your date-manipulation tasks. Remember that in order to create instances of `Calendar`, `DateFormat`, and `NumberFormat`, you have to use static factory methods like `getInstance()`. The `Locale` class is used with `DateFormat` and `NumberFormat` to generate a variety of output styles that are language and/or country specific.

Parsing, Tokenizing, and Formatting To find specific pieces of data in large data sources, Java provides several mechanisms that use the concepts of regular expressions (regex). Regex expressions can be used with the `java.util.regex` package's `Pattern` and `Matcher` classes, as well as with `java.util.Scanner` and with the `String.split()` method. When creating regex patterns, you can use literal characters for matching or you can use metacharacters that allow you to match on concepts like "find digits" or "find whitespace." Regex provides quantifiers that allow you to say things like "find one or more of these things in a row." You won't have to understand the `Matcher` methods that facilitate replacing strings in data.

Tokenizing is splitting delimited data into pieces. Delimiters are usually as simple as a comma, but they can be as complex as any other regex pattern. The `java.util.Scanner` class provides full tokenizing capabilities using regex and allows you to tokenize in a loop so that you can stop the tokenizing process at any point. `String.split()` allows full regex patterns for tokenizing, but tokenizing is done in one step; hence, large data sources can take a long time to process. The `java.util.StringTokenizer` class is almost deprecated, but you might find it in old code. It's similar to `Scanner`.

Formatting data for output can be handled by using the `Formatter` class, or more commonly, by using the new `PrintStream` methods `format()` and `printf()`. Remember `format()` and `printf()` behave identically. To use these methods, you create a format string that is associated with every piece of data you want to format.

Resource Bundles Finally, resource bundles allow you to move locale-specific information (usually strings) out of your code and into external files where they can easily be amended. This provides an easy way for you to localize your applications across many locales.

✓ TWO-MINUTE DRILL

Here are some of the key points from the certification objectives in this chapter.

Dates, Numbers, and Currency (OCP Objectives 12.1, 12.4, and 12.5)

- ❑ The classes you need to understand are `java.util.Date`, `java.util.Calendar`, `java.text.DateFormat`, `java.text.NumberFormat`, and `java.util.Locale`.
- ❑ Most of the `Date` class's methods have been deprecated.
- ❑ A `Date` is stored as a `long`, the number of milliseconds since January 1, 1970.
- ❑ Date objects are go-betweens for the `Calendar` and `DateFormat` classes.
- ❑ The `Calendar` provides a powerful set of methods to manipulate dates, performing tasks such as getting days of the week or adding some number of months or years (or other increments) to a date.
- ❑ Create `Calendar` instances using static factory methods (`getInstance()`).
- ❑ The `Calendar` methods you should understand are `add()`, which allows you to add or subtract various pieces (minutes, days, years, and so on) of dates, and `roll()`, which works like `add()` but doesn't increment a date's bigger pieces. (For example, adding ten months to an October date changes the month to August, but doesn't increment the `Calendar`'s year value.)
- ❑ `DateFormat` instances are created using static factory methods (`getInstance()` and `getDateInstance()`).
- ❑ There are several format "styles" available in the `DateFormat` class.
- ❑ `DateFormat` styles can be applied against various `Locales` to create a wide array of outputs for any given date.
- ❑ The `DateFormat.format()` method is used to create strings containing properly formatted dates.
- ❑ The `Locale` class is used in conjunction with `DateFormat` and `NumberFormat`.
- ❑ Both `DateFormat` and `NumberFormat` objects can be constructed with a specific, immutable `Locale`.
- ❑ For the exam, you should understand creating `Locales` using either language or a combination of language and country.

Parsing, Tokenizing, and Formatting (OCP Objectives 5.1, 5.2, 5.3, 12.4)

- ❑ Regex is short for regular expressions, which are the patterns used to search for data within large data sources.
- ❑ Regex is a sublanguage that exists in Java and other languages (such as Perl).
- ❑ Regex lets you create search patterns using literal characters or metacharacters. Metacharacters allow you to search for slightly more abstract data like "digits" or "whitespace."
- ❑ Study the `\d`, `\s`, `\w`, and `.` metacharacters.
- ❑ Regex provides for quantifiers, which allow you to specify concepts like "look for one or more digits in a row."
- ❑ Study the `?`, `*`, and `+` greedy quantifiers.
- ❑ Remember that metacharacters and strings don't mix well unless you remember to "escape" them properly. For instance, `String s = "\\d";`.
- ❑ The `Pattern` and `Matcher` classes have Java's most powerful regex capabilities.
- ❑ You should understand the `Pattern compile()` method and the `Matcher matches()`, `pattern()`, `find()`, `start()`, and `group()` methods.
- ❑ You WON'T need to understand `Matcher`'s replacement-oriented methods.
- ❑ You can use `java.util.Scanner` to do simple regex searches, but it is primarily intended for tokenizing.
- ❑ Tokenizing is the process of splitting delimited data into small pieces.
- ❑ In tokenizing, the data you want is called tokens, and the strings that separate the tokens are called delimiters.
- ❑ Tokenizing should be done with the `Scanner` class or with `String.split()`.
- ❑ Delimiters are either single characters like commas or complex regex expressions.
- ❑ The `Scanner` class allows you to tokenize data from within a loop, which allows you to stop whenever you want to.

- The `Scanner` class allows you to tokenize strings or streams or files.
- The old `StringTokenizer` class allows you to tokenize strings.
- The `String.split()` method tokenizes the entire source data all at once, so large amounts of data can be quite slow to process.
- As of Java 5 there are two methods used to format data for output. These methods are `format()` and `printf()`. These methods are found in the `PrintStream` class, an instance of which is the `out` in `System.out`.
- The `format()` and `printf()` methods have identical functionality.
- Formatting data with `printf()` (or `format()`) is accomplished using formatting strings that are associated with primitive or string arguments.
- The `format()` method allows you to mix literals in with your format strings.
- The format string values you should know are
  - Flags: `-`, `+`, `0`, `","` , and `(`
  - Conversions: `b`, `c`, `d`, `f`, and `s`
- Barring booleans, if your conversion character doesn't match your argument type, an exception will be thrown.

Resource Bundles

- A `ListResourceBundle` comes from Java classes, and a `PropertyResourceBundle` comes from .property files.
- `ResourceBundle.getBundle(name)` uses the default `Locale`.
- `Locale.getDefault()` returns the JVM's default `Locale` . `Locale.setDefault(locale)` can change the JVM's `locale`.
- Java searches for resource bundles in this order: requested language/country, requested language, default locale language/country, default locale language, default bundle. Within each item, Java `ListResourceBundle` is favored over `PropertyResourceBundle`.
- Once a `ResourceBundle` is found, only parents of that bundle can be used to look up keys.

SELF TEST

Note: Both the OCA 7 and OCP 7 exams have objectives concerning `Strings` and `StringBuilders`. In Chapter 5, we discussed these two classes. This chapter's self test includes questions about `Strings` and `StringBuilders` for the sake of preparing you for the OCP exam. If you need a refresher on `Strings` and `Stringbuilders`, head back to Chapter 5.

1. Given:

```
import java.util.regex.*;
class Regex2 {
  public static void main(String[] args) {
    Pattern p = Pattern.compile(args[0]);
    Matcher m = p.matcher(args[1]);
    boolean b = false;
    while(b = m.find()) {
      System.out.print(m.start() + m.group());
    }
  }
}
```

And the command line:

```
java Regex2 "\d*" ab34ef
```

What is the result?

A. `234`

B. `334`

C. `2334`

D. `0123456`

E. `01234456`

F. `12334567`

G. Compilation fails

2. Given:

```
public class Canada {
  public static void main(String[] args) {
    ResourceBundle rb = ResourceBundle.getBundle("Flag",
      new Locale("en_CA"));
    System.out.println(rb.getString("key"));
  }
}
```

Assume the default `Locale` is Italian. If each of the following is the only resource bundle on the classpath and contains key=value, which will be used? (Choose all that apply.)

A. `Flag.java`

B. `Flag_CA.properties`

C. `Flag_en.java`

D. `Flag_en.properties`

E. `Flag_en_CA.properties`

F. `Flag_fr_CA.properties`

3. Given:

```
import java.util.regex.*;
class Quetico {
  public static void main(String [] args) {
    Pattern p = Pattern.compile(args[0]);
    Matcher m = p.matcher(args[1]);
    System.out.print("match positions: ");
    while(m.find()) {
      System.out.print(m.start() + " ");
    }
    System.out.println("");
  }
}
```

Which invocation(s) will produce the output: `0 2 4 8` ? (Choose all that apply.)

A. `java Quetico "\b" "^23 *$76 bc"`

B. `java Quetico "\B" "^23 *$76 bc"`

C. `java Quetico "\S" "^23 *$76 bc"`

D. `java Quetico "\W" "^23 *$76 bc"`

E. None of the above

F. Compilation fails

G. An exception is thrown at runtime

4. Given:

```
public class Banana {
  public static void main(String[] args) {
    String in = "1 a2 b 3 c4d 5e";
    String[] chunks = in.split(args[0]);

    System.out.println("count " + chunks.length);
    for(String s : chunks)
      System.out.print(">" + s + "<  ");
  }
}
```

And two invocations:

```
java Banana " "
java Banana "\d"
```

What is the result? (Choose all that apply.)

A. In both cases, the count will be 5

B. In both cases, the count will be 6

C. In one case, the count will be 5, and in the other case, 6

D. Banana cannot be invoked because it will not compile

E. At least one of the invocations will throw an exception

5. Given three resource bundles and a Java class:

```
Train_en_US.properties: train=subway
Train_en_UK.properties: train=underground
Train_en.properties: ride = ride

1: public class ChooChoo {
2:   public static void main(String[] args) {
3:     Locale.setDefault(new Locale("en", "US"));
4:     ResourceBundle rb = ResourceBundle.getBundle("Train",
5:       new Locale("en", "US"));
6:     System.out.print(rb.getString("ride")
         + " " + rb.getString("train"));
7:   }
8: }
```

Which of the following, when made independently, will change the output to "ride underground"? (Choose all that apply.)

A. Add `train=underground` to `Train_en.properties`
B. Change line 1 to `Locale.setDefault(new Locale("en", "UK"));`
C. Change line 5 to `Locale.ENGLISH);`
D. Change line 5 to `new Locale("en", "UK"));`
E. Delete file `Train_en_US.properties`

6. Given that 1119280000000L is roughly the number of milliseconds from January 1, 1970, to June 20, 2005, and that you want to print that date in German, using the `LONG` style such that "`June`" will be displayed as "`Juni`," complete the code using the following fragments. Note: You can use each fragment either zero or one times, and you might not need to fill all of the slots.

Code:

```
import java.___________

import java.___________

class DateTwo {
  public static void main(String[] args) {
    Date d = new Date(1119280000000L);

    DateFormat df = ____________________________

                    ________________ , _________________ );

    System.out.println(________________
  }
}
```

Fragments:

```
io.*;      new DateFormat(                 Locale.LONG
nio.*;     DateFormat.getInstance(         Locale.GERMANY
util.*;    DateFormat.getDateInstance(     DateFormat.LONG
text.*;    util.regex;                     DateFormat.GERMANY
date.*;    df.format(d));                  d.format(df));
```

7. Given:

```
public class Legos {
  public static void main(String[] args) {
    StringBuilder sb = new StringBuilder(8);
    System.out.print(sb.length() + " " + sb + " ");
    sb.insert(0, "abcdef");
    sb.append("789");
    System.out.println(sb.length() + " " + sb);
  }
}
```

What is the result?

A. `0 8 abcdef78`

B. `0 8 789abcde`

C. `0 9 abcdef789`

D. `0 9 789abcdef`

E. Compilations fails

F. `0`, followed by an exception

8. Given two files:

```
package rb;
public class Bundle extends java.util.ListResourceBundle {
  protected Object[][] getContents() {
    return new Object[][] { { "123", 456 } };
  }
}
```

```
package rb;
import java.util.*;
public class KeyValue {
  public static void main(String[] args) {
    ResourceBundle rb = ResourceBundle.getBundle("rb.Bundle",
      Locale.getDefault());
    // insert code here
  }
}
```

Which, inserted independently, will compile? (Choose all that apply.)

A. `Object obj = rb.getInteger("123");`

B. `Object obj = rb.getInteger(123);`

C. `Object obj = rb.getObject("123");`

D. `Object obj = rb.getObject(123);`

E. `Object obj = rb.getString("123");`

F. `Object obj = rb.getString(123);`

9. Given:

```
 3. public class Theory {
 4.   public static void main(String[] args) {
 5.     String s1 = "abc";
 6.     String s2 = s1;
 7.     s1 += "d";
 8.     System.out.println(s1 + " " + s2 + " " + (s1==s2));
 9.
10.     StringBuffer sb1 = new StringBuffer("abc");
11.     StringBuffer sb2 = sb1;
12.     sb1.append("d");
13.     System.out.println(sb1 + " " + sb2 + " " + (sb1==sb2));
14.   }
15. }
```

Which are true? (Choose all that apply.)

A. Compilation fails

B. The first line of output is `abc abc true`

C. The first line of output is `abc abc false`

D. The first line of output is `abcd abc false`

E. The second line of output is `abcd abc false`

F. The second line of output is `abcd abcd true`

G. The second line of output is `abcd abcd false`

10. Given:

```
public class Stone {
  public static void main(String[] args) {
    String s = "abc";
    System.out.println(">" + doStuff(s) + "<");
  }
  static String doStuff(String s) {
    s = s.concat(" ef h ");
    return s.trim();
  }
}
```

What is the result?

A. `>abcefh<`

B. `>efhabc<`

C. `>abc ef h<`

D. `\>>ef h abc<`

E. `>abc ef h <`

11. Given:

```
 3. import java.text.*;
 4. public class Slice {
 5.   public static void main(String[] args) {
 6.     String s = "987.123456";
 7.     double d  = 987.123456d;
 8.     NumberFormat nf = NumberFormat.getInstance();
 9.     nf.setMaximumFractionDigits(5);
10.     System.out.println(nf.format(d) + " ");
11.     try {
12.       System.out.println(nf.parse(s));
13.     } catch (Exception e) { System.out.println("got exc"); }
14.   }
15. }
```

Which are true? (Choose all that apply.)

A. The output is `987.12345 987.12345`

B. The output is `987.12346 987.12345`

C. The output is `987.12345 987.123456`

D. The output is `987.12346 987.123456`

E. The try/catch block is unnecessary

F. The code compiles and runs without exception

G. The invocation of `parse()` must be placed within a try/catch block

12. Given:

```
 3. import java.util.regex.*;
 4. public class Archie {
 5.   public static void main(String[] args) {
 6.     Pattern p = Pattern.compile(args[0]);
 7.     Matcher m = p.matcher(args[1]);
 8.     int count = 0;
 9.     while(m.find())
10.       count++;
11.     System.out.print(count);
12.   }
13. }
```

And given the command-line invocation:

```
java Archie "\d+" ab2c4d67
```

What is the result?

A. `0`

B. `3`

C. `4`

D. `8`

E. `9`

F. Compilation fails

13. Given:

```
 3. import java.util.*;
 4. public class Looking {
 5.   public static void main(String[] args) {
 6.     String input = "1 2 a 3 45 6";
 7.     Scanner sc = new Scanner(input);
 8.     int x = 0;
 9.     do {
10.       x = sc.nextInt();
11.       System.out.print(x + " ");
12.     } while (x!=0);
13.   }
14. }
```

What is the result?

A. `1 2`

B. `1 2 3 45 6`

C. `1 2 3 4 5 6`

D. `1 2 a 3 45 6`

E. Compilation fails

F. `1 2` followed by an exception

SELF TEST ANSWERS

1. ☑ **E** is correct. The `\d` is looking for digits. The `*` is a quantifier that looks for `0` to many occurrences of the pattern that precedes it. Because we specified `*`, the `group()` method returns empty strings until consecutive digits are found, so the only time `group()` returns a value is when it returns `34`, when the matcher finds digits starting in position 2. The `start()` method returns the starting position of the previous match because, again, we said find `0` to many occurrences.
☒ **A, B, C, D, F,** and **G** are incorrect based on the above. (OCP Objective 5.2)

2. ☑ **A, C, D,** and **E** are correct. The default `Locale` is irrelevant here since none of the choices use Italian. **A** is the default resource bundle. **C** and **D** use the language but not the country from the requested locale. **E** uses the exact match of the requested locale.
☒ **B** is incorrect because the language code of `CA` does not match `en`. And `CA` isn't a valid language code. **F** is incorrect because the language code `"fr"` does not match `en`. Even though the country code of `CA` does match, the language code is more important. (OCP Objectives 12.2 and 12.3)

3. ☑ **B** is correct. Remember that the boundary metacharacters (`\b` and `\B`), act as though the string being searched is bounded with invisible, non-word characters. Then remember that `\B` reports on boundaries between word to word or non-word to non-word characters.
☒ **A, C, D, E, F,** and **G** are incorrect based on the above. (OCP Objective 5.2)

4. ☑ **B** is correct. In the second case, the first token is empty. Remember that in the first case, the delimiter is a space, and in the second case, the delimiter is any numeric digit.
☒ **A, C, D,** and **E** are incorrect based on the above. (OCP Objectives 5.1 and 5.2)

5. ☑ **D** is correct. As is, the code finds resource bundle `Train_en_US.properties`, which uses `Train_en.properties` as a parent. Choice **D** finds resource bundle `Train_en_UK.properties`, which uses `Train_en.properties` as a parent.
☒ **A** is incorrect because both the parent and child have the same property. In this scenario, the more specific one (child) gets used. **B** is incorrect because the default locale only gets used if the requested resource bundle can't be found. **C** is incorrect because it finds the resource bundle `Train_en.properties`, which does not have any "train" key. **E** is incorrect because there is no "ride" key once we delete the parent. **F** is incorrect based on the above. (OCP Objectives 12.2 and 12.3)

6. ☑ Answer:

```
import java.util.*;
import java.text.*;
class DateTwo {
```

```
    public static void main(String[] args) {
      Date d = new Date(1119280000000L);
      DateFormat df = DateFormat.getDateInstance(
                      DateFormat.LONG, Locale.GERMANY);
      System.out.println(df.format(d));
    }
  }
```

Notes: Remember that you must build `DateFormat` objects using static methods. Also, remember that you must specify a `Locale` for a `DateFormat` object at the time of instantiation. The `getInstance()` method does not take a `Locale`. (OCP Objective 12.4)

7. ☑ **C** is correct. The `append()` method appends to the end of the `StringBuilder`'s current value, and if you append past the current capacity, the capacity is automatically increased. Note: Invoking `insert()` past the current capacity will cause an exception to be thrown.
☒ **A, B, D, E,** and **F** are incorrect based on the above. (OCP Objective 5.1)

8. ☑ **C** and **E** are correct. When getting a key from a resource bundle, the key must be a string. The returned result must be a string or an object. While that object may happen to be an integer, the API is still `getObject()`. **E** will throw a ClassCastException since 456 is not a string, but it will compile.
☒ **A, B, D,** and **F** are incorrect because of the above. (OCP Objectives 12.2 and 12.3)

9. ☑ **D** and **F** are correct. While `String` objects are immutable, references to `Strings` are mutable. The code `s1 += "d";` creates a new `String` object. `StringBuffer` objects are mutable, so the `append()` is changing the single `StringBuffer` object to which both `StringBuffer` references refer.
☒ **A, B, C, E,** and **G** are incorrect based on the above. (OCP Objective 5.1)

10. ☑ **C** is correct. The `concat()` method adds to the end of the `String`, not the front. The trickier part is the `return` statement. Remember that `Strings` are immutable. The `String` referred to by "s" in `doStuff()` is not changed by the `trim()` method. Instead, a new `String` object is created via the `trim()` method, and a reference to that new `String` is returned to `main()`.
☒ **A, B, D,** and **E** are incorrect based on the above. (OCP Objective 5.1)

11. ☑ **D, F,** and **G** are correct. The `setMaximumFractionDigits()` applies to the formatting, but not the parsing. The try/catch block is placed appropriately. This one might scare you into thinking that you'll need to memorize more than you really do. If you can remember that you're formatting the number and parsing the string, you should be fine for the exam.
☒ **A, B, C,** and **E** are incorrect based on the above. (OCP Objective 12.4)

12. ☑ **B** is correct. The "`\d`" metacharacter looks for digits, and the `+` quantifier says look for "one or more" occurrences. The `find()` method will find three sets of one or more consecutive digits: 2, 4, and 67.

☒ **A, C, D, E,** and **F** are incorrect based on the above. (OCP Objective 5.2)

13. ☑ **F** is correct. The `nextXxx()` methods are typically invoked after a call to a `hasNextXxx()`, which determines whether the next token is of the correct type.

☒ **A, B, C, D,** and **E** are incorrect based on the above. (OCP Objective 5.1)

9

I/O and NIO

CERTIFICATION OBJECTIVES

- Read and Write Data from the Console
- Use Streams to Read From and Write To Files by Using Classes in the java .io Package, Including BufferedReader, BufferedWriter, File, FileReader, FileWriter, DataInputStream, DataOutputStream, ObjectOutputStream, ObjectInputStream, and PrintWriter
- Operate on File and Directory Paths with the Path Class (sic)
- Check, Delete, Copy, or Move a File or Directory with the Files Class
- Read and Change File and Directory Attributes, Focusing on the BasicFileAttributes, DosFileAttributes, and PosixFileAttributes Interfaces
- Recursively Access a Directory Tree Using the DirectoryStream and FileVisitor Interfaces
- Find a File with the PathMatcher Interface
- Watch a Directory for Changes with the WatchService Interface

 Two-Minute Drill

Q&A Self Test

I/O (input/output) has been around since the beginning of Java. You could read and write files along with some other common operations. Then with Java 1.4, Java added more I/O functionality and cleverly named it NIO. That stands for "new I/O." Don't worry—you won't be asked about those Java 1.4 additions on the exam.

The APIs prior to Java 7 still had a few limitations when you had to write applications that focused heavily on files and file manipulation. Trying to write a little routine listing all the files created in the past day within a directory tree would give you some headaches. There was no support for navigating directory trees, and just reading attributes of a file was also quite hard. In Java 7, this whole routine is less than 15 lines of code!

Now what to name yet another I/O API? The name "new I/O" was taken, and "new new I/O" would just sound silly. Since the Java 7 functionality was added to package names that begin with `java.nio`, the new name was NIO.2. For the purposes of this chapter and the exam, NIO is shorthand for NIO.2.

Since NIO (or NIO.2 if you like) builds upon the original I/O, some of those concepts are still tested on the exam in addition to the new parts. Fortunately, you won't have to become a total I/O or NIO guru to do well on the exam. The intention of the exam team was to include just the basic aspects of these technologies, and in this chapter, we cover *more* than you'll need to get through these objectives on the exam.

CERTIFICATION OBJECTIVE

File Navigation and I/O (OCP Objectives 7.1 and 7.2)

7.1 Read and write data from the console.

7.2 Use streams to read from and write to files by using classes in the java.io package, including BufferedReader, BufferedWriter, File, FileReader, FileWriter, DataInputStream, DataOutputStream, ObjectOutputStream, ObjectInputStream, and PrintWriter.

I/O has had a strange history with the OCP certification. It was included in all the versions of the exam, up to and including 1.2, then removed from the 1.4 exam, reintroduced for Java 5, extended for Java 6, and extended still more for Java 7.

I/O is a huge topic in general, and the Java APIs that deal with I/O in one fashion or another are correspondingly huge. A general discussion of I/O could include topics such as file I/O, console I/O, thread I/O, high-performance I/O, byte-oriented I/O, character-oriented I/O, I/O filtering and wrapping, serialization, and more. Luckily for us, the I/O topics included in the Java 7 exam are fairly well restricted to file I/O for characters and Serialization. Due to a late change in the Oracle objectives, you WILL NOT find Serialization discussed in this chapter. Instead, we created a complete "Serialization mini-chapter" (along with a Self Test) on the CD-ROM.

Here's a summary of the I/O classes you'll need to understand for the exam:

- **`File`** The API says that the `File` class is "an abstract representation of file and directory pathnames." The `File` class isn't used to actually read or write data; it's used to work at a higher level, making new empty files, searching for files, deleting files, making directories, and working with paths.
- **`FileReader`** This class is used to read character files. Its `read()` methods are fairly low-level, allowing you to read single characters, the whole stream of characters, or a fixed number of characters. `FileReaders` are usually *wrapped* by higher-level objects such as `BufferedReaders`, which improve performance and provide more convenient ways to work with the data.
- **`BufferedReader`** This class is used to make lower-level `Reader` classes like `FileReader` more efficient and easier to use. Compared to `FileReaders`, `BufferedReaders` read relatively large chunks of data from a file at once and keep this data in a buffer. When you ask for the next character or line of data, it is retrieved from the buffer, which minimizes the number of times that time-intensive, file-read operations are performed. In addition, `BufferedReader` provides more convenient methods, such as `readLine()`, that allow you to get the next line of characters from a file.
- **`FileWriter`** This class is used to write to character files. Its `write()` methods allow you to write character(s) or strings to a file. `FileWriters` are usually *wrapped* by higher-level `Writer` objects, such as `BufferedWriters` or `PrintWriters`, which provide better performance and higher-level, more flexible methods to write data.
- **`BufferedWriter`** This class is used to make lower-level classes like `FileWriters` more efficient and easier to use. Compared to `FileWriters`, `BufferedWriters` write relatively large chunks of data to a file at once,

minimizing the number of times that slow, file-writing operations are performed. The `BufferedWriter` class also provides a `newLine()` method to create platform-specific line separators automatically.

- **`PrintWriter`** This class has been enhanced significantly in Java 5. Because of newly created methods and constructors (like building a `PrintWriter` with a `File` or a `String`), you might find that you can use `PrintWriter` in places where you previously needed a `Writer` to be wrapped with a `FileWriter` and/or a `BufferedWriter`. New methods like `format()`, `printf()`, and `append()` make `PrintWriters` very flexible and powerful.
- **`Console`** This new Java 6 convenience class provides methods to read input from the console and write formatted output to the console.

exam watch

Stream classes are used to read and write bytes, and `Readers` and `Writers` are used to read and write characters. Since all of the file I/O on the exam is related to characters, if you see API class names containing the word "Stream"—for instance, `DataOutputStream`—then the question is probably about serialization or something unrelated to the actual I/O objective.

Creating Files Using the File Class

Objects of type `File` are used to represent the actual files (but not the data in the files) or directories that exist on a computer's physical disk. Just to make sure we're clear, when we talk about an object of type `File`, we'll say `File`, with a capital *F*. When we're talking about what exists on a hard drive, we'll call it a file with a lowercase *f* (unless it's a variable name in some code). Let's start with a few basic examples of creating files, writing to them, and reading from them. First, let's create a new file and write a few lines of data to it:

```
import java.io.*;                            // The section 7 objectives
                                             // focus on classes from
                                             // java.io
class Writer1 {
  public static void main(String [] args) {
    File file = new File("fileWrite1.txt");  // There's no
                                             // file yet!
  }
}
```

If you compile and run this program, when you look at the contents of your current directory, you'll discover absolutely no indication of a file called `fileWrite1.txt`. When you make a new instance of the class `File`, *you're not yet making an actual file; you're just creating a filename*. Once you have a `File` *object*, there are several ways to make an actual file. Let's see what we can do with the `File` object we just made:

```
import java.io.*;

class Writer1 {
 public static void main(String [] args) {
   try {                                    // warning: exceptions possible
     boolean newFile = false;
     File file = new File                   // it's only an object
                 ("fileWrite1.txt");
     System.out.println(file.exists());     // look for a real file
     newFile = file.createNewFile();        // maybe create a file!
     System.out.println(newFile);           // already there?
     System.out.println(file.exists());     // look again
   } catch(IOException e) { }
 }
}
```

This produces the output

```
false
true
true
```

And also produces an empty file in your current directory. If you run the code a *second* time, you get the output

```
true
false
true
```

Let's examine these sets of output:

- **First execution** The first call to `exists()` returned `false`, which we expected... remember, `new File()` doesn't create a file on the disk! The `createNewFile()` method created an actual file and returned `true`, indicating that a new file was created and that one didn't already exist. Finally, we called `exists()` again, and this time it returned `true`, indicating that the file existed on the disk.
- **Second execution** The first call to `exists()` returns `true` because we built the file during the first run. Then the call to `createNewFile()` returns

`false` since the method didn't create a file this time through. Of course, the last call to `exists()` returns `true`.

A couple of other new things happened in this code. First, notice that we had to put our file creation code in a try/catch. This is true for almost all of the file I/O code you'll ever write. I/O is one of those inherently risky things. We're keeping it simple for now and ignoring the exceptions, but we still need to follow the handle-or-declare rule, since most I/O methods declare checked exceptions. We'll talk more about I/O exceptions later. We used a couple of `File`'s methods in this code:

- **`boolean exists()`** This method returns `true` if it can find the actual file.
- **`boolean createNewFile()`** This method creates a new file if it doesn't already exist.

Remember, the exam creators are trying to jam as much code as they can into a small space, so in the previous example, instead of these three lines of code:

```
boolean newFile = false;
...
newFile = file.createNewFile();
System.out.println(newFile);
```

you might see something like the following single line of code, which is a bit harder to read, but accomplishes the same thing:

```
System.out.println(file.createNewFile());
```

Using FileWriter and FileReader

In practice, you probably won't use the `FileWriter` and `FileReader` classes without wrapping them (more about "wrapping" very soon). That said, let's go ahead and do a little "naked" file I/O:

```
import java.io.*;

class Writer2 {
  public static void main(String [] args) {
    char[] in = new char[50];           // to store input
    int size = 0;
```

```
    try {
      File file = new File(              // just an object
                 "fileWrite2.txt");
      FileWriter fw =
                new FileWriter(file);   // create an actual file
                                        // & a FileWriter obj
      fw.write("howdy\nfolks\n");       // write characters to
                                        // the file
      fw.flush();                       // flush before closing
      fw.close();                       // close file when done

      FileReader fr =
                new FileReader(file);   // create a FileReader
                                        // object
      size = fr.read(in);               // read the whole file!
      System.out.print(size + " ");     // how many bytes read
      for(char c : in)                  // print the array
        System.out.print(c);
      fr.close();                       // again, always close
    } catch(IOException e) { }
  }
}
```

which produces the output:

```
12 howdy
folks
```

Here's what just happened:

1. `FileWriter fw = new FileWriter(file)` did three things:
   a. It created a `FileWriter` reference variable, `fw`.
   b. It created a `FileWriter` object and assigned it to `fw`.
   c. It created an actual empty file out on the disk (and you can prove it).
2. We wrote 12 characters to the file with the `write()` method, and we did a `flush()` and a `close()`.
3. We made a new `FileReader` object, which also opened the file on disk for reading.
4. The `read()` method read the whole file, a character at a time, and put it into the `char[] in`.
5. We printed out the number of characters we read in `size`, and we looped through the `in` array, printing out each character we read, and then we closed the file.

Before we go any further, let's talk about `flush()` and `close()`. When you write data out to a stream, some amount of buffering will occur, and you never know for sure exactly when the last of the data will actually be sent. You might perform many write operations on a stream before closing it, and invoking the `flush()` method guarantees that the last of the data you thought you had already written actually gets out to the file. Whenever you're done using a file, either reading it or writing to it, you should invoke the `close()` method. When you are doing file I/O, you're using expensive and limited operating system resources, and so when you're done, invoking `close()` will free up those resources.

Now, back to our last example. This program certainly works, but it's painful in a couple of different ways:

1. When we were writing data to the file, we manually inserted line separators (in this case `\n`) into our data.
2. When we were reading data back in, we put it into a character array. It being an array and all, we had to declare its size beforehand, so we'd have been in trouble if we hadn't made it big enough! We could have read the data in one character at a time, looking for the end of the file after each `read()`, but that's pretty painful too.

Because of these limitations, we'll typically want to use higher-level I/O classes like `BufferedWriter` or `BufferedReader` in combination with `FileWriter` or `FileReader`.

Combining I/O Classes

Java's entire I/O system was designed around the idea of using several classes in combination. Combining I/O classes is sometimes called *wrapping* and sometimes called *chaining*. The `java.io` package contains about 50 classes, 10 interfaces, and 15 exceptions. Each class in the package has a specific purpose (creating high cohesion), and the classes are designed to be combined with each other in countless ways to handle a wide variety of situations.

When it's time to do some I/O in real life, you'll undoubtedly find yourself poring over the `java.io` API, trying to figure out which classes you'll need and how to hook them together. For the exam, you'll need to do the same thing, but Oracle artificially reduced the API (phew!). In terms of studying for Exam Objective 7.2, we can imagine that the entire `java.io` package—consisting of the classes listed in Exam Objective 7.2 and summarized in Table 9-1—is our mini I/O API.

TABLE 9-1 `java.io` Mini API

java.io Class	Extends From	Key Constructor(s) Arguments	Key Methods

`File`	`Object`	`File, String`
		`String`
		`String, String`
			`createNewFile()`
			`delete()`
			`exists()`
			`isDirectory()`
			`isFile()`
			`list()`
			`mkdir()`
			`renameTo()`

`FileWriter`	`Writer`	`File`
		`String`
			`close()`
			`flush()`
			`write()`

`BufferedWriter`	`Writer`	`Writer`	`close()`
			`flush()`
			`newLine()`
			`write()`

`PrintWriter`	`Writer`	`File (as of Java 5)`
		`String (as of Java 5)`
		`OutputStream`
		`Writer`
			`close()`
			`flush()`
			`format(), printf()`
			`print(), println()`
			`write()`

`FileReader`	`Reader`	`File` `String`	`read()`
`BufferedReader`	`Reader`	`Reader`	`read()` `readLine()`

Now let's say that we want to find a less painful way to write data to a file and read the file's contents back into memory. Starting with the task of writing data to a file, here's a process for determining what classes we'll need and how we'll hook them together:

1. We know that ultimately we want to hook to a `File` object. So whatever other class or classes we use, one of them must have a constructor that takes an object of type `File`.
2. Find a method that sounds like the most powerful, easiest way to accomplish the task. When we look at Table 9-1 we can see that `BufferedWriter` has a `newLine()` method. That sounds a little better than having to manually embed a separator after each line, but if we look further, we see that `PrintWriter` has a method called `println()`. That sounds like the easiest approach of all, so we'll go with it.

3. When we look at `PrintWriter`'s constructors, we see that we can build a `PrintWriter` object if we have an object of type `File`, so all we need to do to create a `PrintWriter` object is the following:

```
File file = new File("fileWrite2.txt");     // create a File
PrintWriter pw = new PrintWriter(file);     // pass file to
                                            // the PrintWriter
                                            // constructor
```

Okay, time for a pop quiz. Prior to Java 5, `PrintWriter` did not have constructors that took either a `String` or a `File`. If you were writing some I/O code in Java 1.4, how would you get a `PrintWriter` to write data to a file? Hint: You can figure this out by studying the mini I/O API in Table 9-1.

Here's one way to go about solving this puzzle: First, we know that we'll create a `File` object on one end of the chain, and that we want a `PrintWriter` object on the other end. We can see in Table 9-1 that a `PrintWriter` can also be built using a `Writer` object. Although `Writer` isn't a *class* we see in the table, we can see that several other classes extend `Writer`, which for our purposes is just as good; any class that extends `Writer` is a candidate. Looking further, we can see that `FileWriter` has the two attributes we're looking for:

- It can be constructed using a `File`.
- It extends `Writer`.

Given all of this information, we can put together the following code (remember, this is a Java 1.4 example):

```
File file = new File("fileWrite2.txt");  // create a File object
FileWriter fw = new FileWriter(file);    // create a FileWriter
                                         // that will send its
                                         // output to a File

PrintWriter pw = new PrintWriter(fw);    // create a PrintWriter
                                         // that will send its
                                         // output to a Writer

pw.println("howdy");                     // write the data
pw.println("folks");
```

At this point, it should be fairly easy to put together the code to more easily read data from the file back into memory. Again, looking through the table, we see a method called `readLine()` that sounds like a much better way to read data. Going through a similar process, we get the following code:

```
File file =
      new File("fileWrite2.txt");  // create a File object AND
                                   // open "fileWrite2.txt"
FileReader fr =
          new FileReader(file);    // create a FileReader to get
                                   // data from 'file'
BufferedReader br =
         new BufferedReader(fr);   // create a BufferReader to
                                   // get its data from a Reader
String data = br.readLine();       // read some data
```

exam watch

You're almost certain to encounter exam questions that test your knowledge of how I/O classes can be chained. If you're not totally clear on this last section, we recommend that you use Table 9-1 as a reference and write code to experiment with which chaining combinations are legal and which are illegal.

Working with Files and Directories

Earlier, we touched on the fact that the `File` class is used to create files and directories. In addition, `File`'s methods can be used to delete files, rename files, determine whether files exist, create temporary files, change a file's attributes, and differentiate between files and directories. A point that is often confusing is that an object of type `File` is used to represent *either a file or a directory*. We'll talk about both cases next.

We saw earlier that the statement

```
File file = new File("foo");
```

always creates a `File` object and then does one of two things:

1. If `"foo"` does NOT exist, no actual file is created.
2. If `"foo"` *does* exist, the new `File` object refers to the existing file.

Notice that `File file = new File("foo");` NEVER creates an actual file. There are two ways to create a file:

1. Invoke the `createNewFile()` method on a `File` object. For example:

```
File file = new File("foo");    // no file yet
file.createNewFile();           // make a file, "foo" which
                                // is assigned to 'file'
```

2. Create a `Writer` or a `Stream`. Specifically, create a `FileWriter`, a `PrintWriter`, or a `FileOutputStream`. Whenever you create an instance of one of these classes, you automatically create a file, unless one already exists; for instance

```
File file = new File("foo");        // no file yet
PrintWriter pw =
       new PrintWriter(file);       // make a PrintWriter object AND
                                    // make a file, "foo" to which
                                    // 'file' is assigned, AND assign
                                    // 'pw' to the PrintWriter
```

Creating a directory is similar to creating a file. Again, we'll use the convention of referring to an object of type `File` that represents an actual directory as a `Directory` object, with a capital *D* (even though it's of type `File`). We'll call an actual directory on a computer a directory, with a small *d*. Phew! As with creating a file, creating a directory is a two-step process; first we create a `Directory` (`File`) object; then we create an actual directory using the following `mkdir()` method:

```
File myDir = new File("mydir");    // create an object
myDir.mkdir();                     // create an actual directory
```

Once you've got a directory, you put files into it and work with those files:

```
File myFile = new File(myDir, "myFile.txt");
myFile.createNewFile();
```

This code is making a new file in a subdirectory. Since you provide the subdirectory to the constructor, from then on, you just refer to the file by its reference variable. In this case, here's a way that you could write some data to the file `myFile`:

```
PrintWriter pw = new PrintWriter(myFile);
pw.println("new stuff");
pw.flush();
pw.close();
```

Be careful when you're creating new directories! As we've seen, constructing a `Writer` or a `Stream` will often create a file for you automatically if one doesn't exist, but that's not true for a directory.

```
File myDir = new File("mydir");
// myDir.mkdir();                      // call to mkdir() omitted!
File myFile = new File(
              myDir, "myFile.txt");
myFile.createNewFile();                // exception if no mkdir!
```

This will generate an exception that looks something like

```
java.io.IOException: No such file or directory
```

You can refer a `File` object to an existing file or directory. For example, assume that we already have a subdirectory called `existingDir` in which resides an existing file `existingDirFile.txt`, which contains several lines of text. When you run the following code:

```
File existingDir = new File("existingDir");      // assign a dir
System.out.println(existingDir.isDirectory());

File existingDirFile = new File(
          existingDir, "existingDirFile.txt");  // assign a file
System.out.println (existingDirFile.isFile());

FileReader fr = new FileReader(existingDirFile);
BufferedReader br = new BufferedReader(fr);      // make a Reader

String s;
while( (s = br.readLine()) != null)              // read data
  System.out.println(s);

br.close();
```

the following output will be generated:

```
true
true
existing sub-dir data
line 2 of text
line 3 of text
```

Take special note of what the `readLine()` method returns. When there is no more data to read, `readLine()` returns a `null`—this is our signal to stop reading the file. Also, notice that we didn't invoke a `flush()` method. When reading a file, no flushing is required, so you won't even find a `flush()` method in a `Reader` kind of class.

In addition to creating files, the `File` class lets you do things like renaming and deleting files. The following code demonstrates a few of the most common ins and outs of deleting files and directories (via `delete()`) and renaming files and directories (via `renameTo()`):

```
File delDir = new File("deldir");       // make a directory
delDir.mkdir();

File delFile1 = new File(
          delDir, "delFile1.txt");      // add file to directory
```

```
delFile1.createNewFile();

File delFile2 = new File(
          delDir, "delFile2.txt");      // add file to directory
delFile2.createNewFile();
delFile1.delete();                       // delete a file
System.out.println("delDir is "
                  + delDir.delete());   // attempt to delete
                                         // the directory
File newName = new File(
          delDir, "newName.txt");       // a new object
delFile2.renameTo(newName);              // rename file

File newDir = new File("newDir");       // rename directory
delDir.renameTo(newDir);
```

This outputs

```
delDir is false
```

and leaves us with a directory called `newDir` that contains a file called `newName.txt`. Here are some rules that we can deduce from this result:

- **`delete()`** You can't delete a directory if it's not empty, which is why the invocation `delDir.delete()` failed.
- **`renameTo()`** You must give the existing `File` object a valid new `File` object with the new name that you want. (If `newName` had been `null`, we would have gotten a `NullPointerException`.)
- **`renameTo()`** It's okay to rename a directory, even if it isn't empty.

There's a lot more to learn about using the `java.io` package, but as far as the exam goes, we only have one more thing to discuss, and that is how to search for a file. Assuming that we have a directory named `searchThis` that we want to search through, the following code uses the `File.list()` method to create a `String` array of files and directories. We then use the enhanced `for` loop to iterate through and print.

```
String[] files = new String[100];
File search = new File("searchThis");
files = search.list();                  // create the list

for(String fn : files)                  // iterate through it
  System.out.println("found " + fn);
```

On our system, we got the following output:

```
found dir1
found dir2
found dir3
found file1.txt
found file2.txt
```

Your results will almost certainly vary :)

In this section, we've scratched the surface of what's available in the `java.io` package. Entire books have been written about this package, so we're obviously covering only a very small (but frequently used) portion of the API. On the other hand, if you understand everything we've covered in this section, you will be in great shape to handle any `java.io` questions you encounter on the exam, except for the `Console` class, which we'll cover next. (Note: Serialization is covered in the Serialization chapter on the CD-ROM.)

The java.io.Console Class

New to Java 6 is the `java.io.Console` class. In this context, the *console* is the physical device with a keyboard and a display (like your Mac or PC). If you're running Java SE 6 from the command line, you'll typically have access to a console object, to which you can get a reference by invoking `System.console()`. Keep in mind that it's possible for your Java program to be running in an environment that doesn't have access to a console object, so be sure that your invocation of `System.console()` actually returns a valid console reference and not null.

The `Console` class makes it easy to accept input from the command line, both echoed and nonechoed (such as a password), and makes it easy to write formatted output to the command line. It's a handy way to write test engines for unit testing or if you want to support a simple but secure user interaction and you don't need a GUI.

On the input side, the methods you'll have to understand are `readLine` and `readPassword`. The `readLine` method returns a string containing whatever the user keyed in—that's pretty intuitive. However, the `readPassword` method doesn't return a string; it returns a character array. Here's the reason for this: Once you've got the password, you can verify it and then absolutely remove it from memory. If a string was returned, it could exist in a pool somewhere in memory, and perhaps some nefarious hacker could find it.

Let's take a look at a small program that uses a console to support testing another class:

```
import java.io.Console;

public class NewConsole {
  public static void main(String[] args) {
    String name = "";
    Console c = System.console();              // #1: get a Console
    char[] pw;
    pw = c.readPassword("%s", "pw: ");         // #2: return a char[]
    for(char ch: pw)
      c.format("%c ", ch);                     // #3: format output
    c.format("\n");

    MyUtility mu = new MyUtility();
    while(true) {
      name = c.readLine("%s", "input?: ");    // #4: return a String

      c.format("output: %s \n", mu.doStuff(name));
    }
  }
}

class MyUtility {                              // #5: class to test
  String doStuff(String arg1) {
    // stub code
    return "result is " + arg1;
  }
}
```

Let's review this code:

- At line 1, we get a new `Console` object. Remember that we can't say this:

```
Console c = new Console();
```

- At line 2, we invoke `readPassword`, which returns a `char[]`, not a string. You'll notice when you test this code that the password you enter isn't echoed on the screen.
- At line 3, we're just manually displaying the password you keyed in, separating each character with a space. Later on in this chapter, you'll read about the `format()` method, so stay tuned.
- At line 4, we invoke `readLine`, which returns a string.

- At line 5 is the class that we want to test. Later in this chapter, when you're studying regex and formatting, we recommend that you use something like `NewConsole` to test the concepts that you're learning.

The `Console` class has more capabilities than are covered here, but if you understand everything discussed so far, you'll be in good shape for the exam.

CERTIFICATION OBJECTIVE

Files, Path, and Paths (OCP Objectives 8.1 and 8.2)

8.1 *Operate on file and directory paths with the Path class.*

8.2 *Check, delete, copy, or move a file or directory with the Files class.*

Note: For coverage of Serialization, please go to the CD-ROM provided with the book.

The OCP 7 exam has two sections devoted to I/O. The previous section Oracle refers to as "Java I/O Fundamentals" (which we've referred to as the 7.*x* objectives), and it was focused on the `java.io` package. Now we're going to look at the set of objectives Oracle calls "Java File I/O (NIO.2)," whose specific objectives we'll refer to as 8.*x*. The term *NIO.2* is a bit loosely defined, but most people (and the exam creators) define NIO.2 as being the key new features introduced in Java 7 that reside in two packages:

- `java.nio.file`
- `java.nio.file.attribute`

We'll start by looking at the important classes and interfaces in the `java.nio.file` package, and then we'll move to the `java.nio.file.attribute` package later in the chapter.

As you read earlier in the chapter, the `File` class represents a file or directory at a high level. NIO.2 adds three new central classes that you'll need to understand well for the exam:

- **`Path`** This interface replaces `File` as the representation of a file or a directory when working in NIO.2. It is a lot more powerful than a `File` though.

- **`Paths`** This class contains static methods that create `Path` objects. (In the next chapter, you'll learn this is called a factory.)
- **`Files`** This class contains static methods that work with `Path` objects. You'll find basic operations in here like copying or deleting files.

The interface `java.nio.file.Path` is one of the key classes of file-based I/O under NIO.2. Just like the good old `java.io.File`, a `Path` represents only a location in the file system, like `C:\java\workspace\ocpjp7` (a Windows directory) or `/home/nblack/docs` (the `docs` directory of user `nblack` on UNIX). When you create a `Path` to a new file, that file does not exist until you actually create the file using `Files.createFile(Path target)`. The `Files` utility class will be covered in depth in the next section.

Let's take a look at these relationships another way. The `Paths` class is used to create a class implementing the `Path` interface. The `Files` class uses `Path` objects as parameters. All three of these are new to Java 7. Then there is the `File` class. It's been around for a long time. `File` and `Path` objects know how to convert to the other. This lets any older code interact with the new APIs in `Files`. But notice what is missing. In the figure, there is no line between `File` and `Files`. Despite the similarity in name, these two classes do not know about each other.

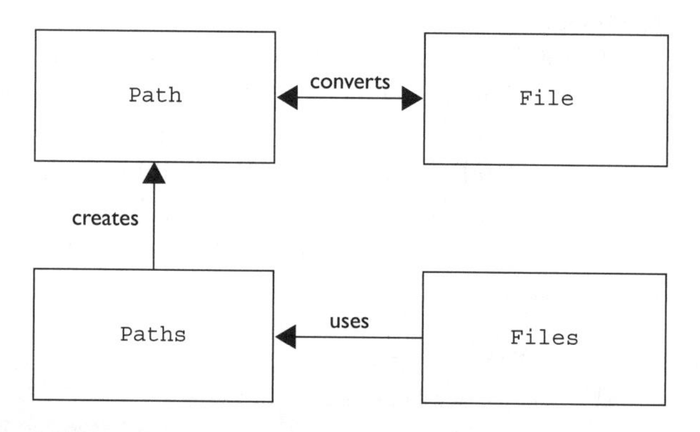

exam watch

The difference between `File`, `Files`, `Path`, and `Paths` is really important. Read carefully on the exam. A one-letter difference can mean a big difference in what the class does.

To make sure you know the difference between these key classes backward and forward, make sure you can fill in the four rightmost columns in Table 9-2.

TABLE 9-2 Comparing the Core Classes

	File	Files	Path	Paths
Existed in Java 6?	Yes	No	No	No
Concrete class or interface?	Concrete class	Concrete class	Interface	Concrete class
Create using "new"	Yes	No	No	No
Contains only static methods	No	Yes	No	Yes

Creating a Path

A `Path` object can be easily created by using the `get` methods from the `Paths` helper class. Remember you are calling `Paths.get()` and not `Path.get()`. If you don't remember why, study the last section some more. It's important to have this down cold.

Taking a look at two simple examples, we have:

```
Path p1 = Paths.get("/tmp/file1.txt");     // on UNIX
Path p2 = Paths.get("c:\\temp\\test");     // On Windows
```

The actual method we just called is `Paths.get(String first, String... more)`. This means we can write it out by separating the parts of the path.

```
Path p3 = Paths.get("/tmp", "file1.txt");    // same as p1
Path p4 = Paths.get("c:", "temp", "test");   // same as p2
Path p5 = Paths.get("c:\\temp", "test") ;    // also same as p2
```

As you can see, you can separate out folder and filenames as much or as little as you want when calling `Paths.get()`. For Windows, that is particularly cool because you can make the code easier to read by getting rid of the backslash and escape character.

Be careful when creating paths. The previous examples are absolute paths since they begin with the root (/ on UNIX or c: on Windows). When you don't begin with the root, the `Path` is considered a relative path, which means Java looks from the current directory. Which `file1.txt` do you think `p6` has in mind?

```
Path  p6 = Paths.get("tmp", "file1.txt");  // relative path - NOT same as p1
/ (root)
   |-- tmp
          | - file1.txt
          | - tmp
                 | - file1.txt
```

It depends. If the program is run from the root, it is the one in `/tmp/file1.txt`. If the program is run from `/tmp`, it is the one in `/tmp/tmp/file1.txt`. If the program is run from anywhere else, `p6` refers to a file that does not exist.

One more thing to watch for. If you are on Windows, you might deal with a URL that looks like `file:///c:/temp`. The `file://` is a protocol just like `http://` is. This syntax allows you to browse to a folder in Internet Explorer. Your program might have to deal with such a `String` that a user copied/pasted from the browser. No problem, right? We learned to code:

```
Path  p = Paths.get("file:///c:/temp/test");
```

Unfortunately, this doesn't work and you get an Exception about the colon being invalid that looks something like this:

```
Exception in thread "main" java.nio.file.InvalidPathException:
Illegal char <:>
at index 4: file:///c:/temp
```

`Paths` provides another method that solves this problem. `Paths.get(URI uri)` lets you (indirectly),convert the `String` to a `URI` (Uniform Resource Identifier) before trying to create a `Path`.

```
Path   p = Paths.get(URI.create("file:///C:/temp"));
```

The last thing you should know is that the `Paths.get()` method we've been discussing is really a shortcut. You won't need to code the longer version, but it is good to understand what is going on under the hood. First, Java finds out what the default file system is. For example, it might be `WindowsFileSystemProvider`. Then Java gets the path using custom logic for that file system. Luckily, this all goes on without us having to write any special code or even think about it.

```
Path short = Paths.get("c:", "temp");
Path longer = FileSystems.getDefault()        // get default file system
      .getPath("c:", "temp");                 // then get the Path
```

Now that you know how to create a `Path` instance, you can manipulate it in various ways. We'll get back to that in a bit.

on the job

As far as the exam is concerned, `Paths.get()` is how to create a `Path` initially. There is another way that is useful when working with code that was written before Java 7:

```
Path  convertedPath = file.toPath();
File  convertedFile = path.toFile();
```

If you are updating older code that uses `File`, you can convert it to a `Path` and start calling the new classes. And if your newer code needs to call older code, it can convert back to a `File`.

Creating Files and Directories

With I/O, we saw that a `File` doesn't exist just because you have a `File` object. You have to call `createNewFile()` to bring the file into existence and `exists()` to check if it exists. Rewriting the example from earlier in the chapter to use NIO.2 methods, we now have:

```
Path path = Paths.get("fileWrite1.txt");     // it's only an object
System.out.println(Files.exists(path));      // look for a real file
Files.createFile(path);                      // create a file!
System.out.println(Files.exists(path));      // look again
```

NIO.2 has equivalent methods with two differences:

- You call static methods on `Files` rather than instance methods on `File`.
- Method names are slightly different.

See Table 9-3 for the mapping between old class/method names and new ones. You can still continue to use the older I/O approach if you happen to be dealing with `File` objects.

on the job

There is a new method `Files.notExists()` to supplement `Files.exists()`. In some incredibly rare situations, Java won't have enough permissions to know whether the file exists. When this happens, both methods return false.

You can also create directories in Java. Suppose we have a directory named `/java` and we want to create the file `/java/source/directory/Program.java`. We could do this one at a time:

```
Path  path1 = Paths.get("/java/source");
Path  path2 = Paths.get("/java/source/directory");
Path   file = Paths.get("/java/source/directory/Program.java");
Files.createDirectory(path1);       // create first level of directory
Files.createDirectory(path2);       // create second level of directory
Files.createFile(file);             // create file
```

Or we could create all the directories in one go:

```
Files.createDirectories(path2);    // create all levels of directories
Files.createFile(file);            // create file
```

While both work, the second is clearly better if you have a lot of directories to create. And remember that the directory needs to exist by the time the file is created.

TABLE 9-3 I/O vs. NIO.2

Description	I/O Approach	NIO.2 Approach
Create an empty file	`File file = new File("test");` `file.createNewFile():`	`Path path = Paths.get("test");` `Files.createFile(path);`
Create an empty directory	`File file = new File("dir");` `file.mkdir()`	`Path path = Paths.get("dir");` `Files.createDirectory(path);`
Create a directory, including any missing parent directories	`File file = new File("/a/b/c");` `file.mkdirs():`	`Path path = Paths.get("/a/b/c");` `Files.createDirectories(path);`
Check if a file or directory exists	`File file = new File("test");` `file.exists();`	`Path path = Paths.get("test");` `Files.exists(path);`

Copying, Moving, and Deleting Files

We often copy, move, or delete files when working with the file system. Up until Java 7, this was hard to do. In Java 7, however, each is one line. Let's look at some examples:

```
Path source = Paths.get("/temp/test1");      // exists
Path target = Paths.get("/temp/test2.txt");  // doesn't yet exist
Files.copy(source, target);                  // now two copies of the file
Files.delete(target);                        // back to one copy
Files.move(source, target);                  // still one copy
```

This is all pretty self-explanatory. We copy a file, delete the copy, and then move the file. Now, let's try another example:

```
Path one = Paths.get("/temp/test1");        // exists
Path two = Paths.get("/temp/test2.txt");    // exists
Path targ = Paths.get("/temp/test23.txt");  // doesn't yet exist
Files.copy(one, targ);                      // now two copies of the file
Files.copy(two, targ);                      // oops,
                                            // FileAlreadyExistsException
```

Java sees it is about to overwrite a file that already exists. Java doesn't want us to lose the file, so it "asks" if we are sure by throwing an Exception. `copy()` and `move()` actually take an optional third parameter—zero or more `CopyOptions`. The most useful option you can pass is `StandardCopyOption.REPLACE_EXISTING`.

```
Files.copy(two,  target,                      // ok. You know what
  StandardCopyOption.REPLACE_EXISTING);       // you are doing
```

We have to think about whether a file exists when deleting the file too. Let's say we wrote this test code:

```
Path path = Paths.get("/java/out.txt");
try {
   methodUnderTest();              // might throw an exception
   Files.createFile(path);         // file only gets created
                                   // if methodUnderTest() succeeds
} finally {
  Files.delete(path);              // NoSuchFileException if no file
}
```

We don't know whether `methodUnderTest` works properly yet. If it does, the code works fine. If it throws an Exception, we never create the file and `Files.delete()` throws a `NoSuchFileException`. This is a problem, as we only want to delete the file if it was created so we aren't leaving stray files around. There is an alternative. `Files.deleteIfExists(path)` returns true and deletes the file only if it exists. If not, it just quietly returns false. Most of the time, you can ignore this return value. You just want the file to not be there. If it never existed, mission accomplished.

If you have to work on pre-Java 7 code, you can use the `FileUtils` class in Apache Commons IO (http://commons.apache.org/io.) It has methods similar to many of the copy, move, and delete methods that are now built into Java 7.

To review, Table 9-4 lists the methods on `Files` that you are likely to come across on the exam. Luckily, the exam doesn't expect you to know all 30 methods in the API. The important thing to remember is to check the Files `JavaDoc` when you find yourself dealing with files.

TABLE 9-4 `Files` Methods

Method	Description
`Path copy(Path source, Path target, CopyOption... options)`	Copy the file from source to target and return target
`Path move(Path source, Path target, CopyOption... options)`	Move the file from source to target and return target
`void delete(Path path)`	Delete the file and throw an Exception if it does not exist
`boolean deleteIfExists(Path path)`	Delete the file if it exists and return whether file was deleted
`boolean exists(Path path, LinkOption... options)`	Return true if file exists
`boolean notExists(Path path, LinkOption... options)`	Return true if file does not exist

Retrieving Information about a Path

The `Path` interface defines a bunch of methods that return useful information about the path that you're dealing with. In the following code listing, a `Path` is created referring to a directory and then we output information about the `Path` instance:

```
Path  path = Paths.get("C:/home/java/workspace");
System.out.println("getFileName: "   + path.getFileName());
System.out.println("getName(1): " +  path.getName(1));
System.out.println("getNameCount: "   + path.getNameCount());
System.out.println("getParent: " +  path.getParent());
System.out.println("getRoot: " +  path.getRoot());
System.out.println("subpath(0, 2): " + path.subpath(0, 2));
System.out.println("toString: " +  path.toString());
```

When you execute this code snippet on Windows, the following output is printed:

```
getFileName: workspace
getName(1): java
getNameCount: 3
getParent: C:\home\java
getRoot: C:\
subpath(0, 2): home\java
toString: C:\home\java\workspace
```

Based on this output, it is fairly simple to describe what each method does. Table 9-5 does just that.

TABLE 9-5 `Path` Methods

Method	Description
`String getFileName()`	Returns the filename or the last element of the sequence of name elements.
`Path getName(int index)`	Returns the path element corresponding to the specified index. The 0th element is the one closest to the root. (On Windows, the root is usually C:\ and on UNIX, the root is /.)
`int getNameCount()`	Returns the number of elements in this path, excluding the root.
`Path getParent()`	Returns the parent path, or `null` if this path does not have a parent.
`Path getRoot()`	Returns the root of this path, or `null` if this path does not have a root.
`Path subpath(int beginIndex, int endIndex)`	Returns a subsequence of this path (not including a root element) as specified by the beginning (included) and ending (not included) indexes.
`String toString()`	Returns the string representation of this path.

Here is yet another interesting fact about the `Path` interface: It extends from `Iterable<Path>`. At first sight, this seems anything but interesting. But every class that (correctly) implements the `Iterable<?>` interface can be used as an expression in the enhanced `for` loop. So you know you can iterate through an array or a `List`, but you can iterate through a `Path` as well. That's pretty cool!

Using this functionality, it's easy to print the hierarchical tree structure of a file (or directory), as the following example shows:

```
int spaces = 1;
Path myPath = Paths.get("tmp", "dir1", "dir2", "dir3", "file.txt");
for (Path subPath : myPath) {
  System.out.format("%" + spaces + "s%s%n", "", subPath);
  spaces += 2; }
```

When you run this example, a (simplistic) tree is printed. Thanks to the variable `spaces` (which is increased with each iteration by 2), the different subpaths are printed like a directory tree.

```
 tmp
   dir1
     dir2
       dir3
         file.txt
```

Normalizing a Path

Normally (no pun intended), when you create a `Path`, you create it in a direct way. However, all three of these return the same logical `Path`:

```
Path p1 = Paths.get("myDirectory");
Path p2 = Paths.get("./myDirectory");              // one dot means
                                                   // current directory
Path p3 = Paths.get("anotherDirectory", "..",      // two dots means go up
                    "myDirectory");                // one directory
```

`p1` is probably what you would type if you were coding. `p2` is just plain redundant. `p3` is more interesting. The two directories—`anotherDirectory` and `myDirectory`—are on the same level, but we have to go up one level to get there:

```
/ (root)
   |-- anotherDirectory
   |-- myDirectory
```

You might be wondering why on earth we wouldn't just type `myDirectory` in the first place. And you would if you could. Sometimes, that doesn't work out. Let's look at a real example of why this might be.

```
/ (root)
   |-- Build_Project
      |-- scripts
         |-- buildScript.sh
   |-- My_Project
      |-- source
         |-- MyClass.java
```

If you wanted to compile `MyClass`, you would `cd` to `/My_Project/source` and run `javac MyClass.java`. Once your program gets bigger, it could be thousands of classes and have hundreds of jar files. You don't want to type in all of those just to compile, so someone writes a script to build your program. `buildScript.sh` now finds everything that is needed to compile and runs the `javac` command for you. The problem is that the current directory is now `/Build_Project/scripts` and not `/My_Project/source`. The build script helpfully builds a path for you by doing something like this:

```
String buildProject                          // build scripts like to express
    = "/Build_Project/scripts";              // paths in relation to themselves

String upTwoDirectories = "../..";           // remember what .. means?

String myProject = "/My_Project/source";
Path path = Paths.get(buildProject,
            upTwoDirectories, myProject);   // build path from variables
System.out.println("Original: " + path);
System.out.println("Normalized: " + path.normalize());
```

which outputs:

```
Original:/Build_Project/scripts/../../My_Project/source
Normalized:/My_Project/source
```

Whew. The second one is much easier to read. The `normalize()` method knows that a single dot can be ignored. It also knows that any directory followed by two dots can be removed from a path.

Be careful when using this `normalize()`! It just looks at the `String` equivalent of the path and doesn't check the file system to see whether the directories or files actually exist.

Let's practice and see what `normalize` returns for these paths. This time, we aren't providing a directory structure to show that the directories and files don't need to be present on the computer. What do you think the following prints out?

```
System.out.println(Paths.get("/a/./b/./c").normalize());
System.out.println(Paths.get(".classpath").normalize());
System.out.println(Paths.get("/a/b/c/..").normalize());
System.out.println(Paths.get("../a/b/c").normalize());
```

The output is:

```
/a/b/c
.classpath
/a/b
../a/b/c
```

The first one removes all the single dots since they just point to the current directory. The second doesn't change anything since the dot is part of a filename and not a directory. The third sees one set of double dots, so it only goes up one directory. The last one is a little tricky. The two dots do say to go up one directory. But since there isn't a directory before it, `Path` can't simplify it.

To review, `normalize()` removes unneeded parts of the `Path`, making it more like you'd normally type it. (That's not where the word "normalize" comes from, but it is a nice way to remember it.)

Resolving a Path

So far, you have an overview of all methods that can be invoked on a single `Path` object, but what if you need to combine two paths? You might want to do this if you have one `Path` representing your home directory and another containing the `Path` within that directory.

```
Path dir = Paths.get("/home/java");
Path file = Paths.get("models/Model.pdf");
Path result = dir.resolve(file);
System.out.println("result = " + result);
```

This produces the absolute path by merging the two paths:

```
result = /home/java/models/Model.pdf
```

`path1.resolve(path2)` should be read as "resolve `path2` within `path1`'s directory." In this example, we resolved the path of the `file` within the directory provided by `dir`.

Keeping this definition in mind, let's look at some more complex examples:

```
Path absolute = Paths.get("/home/java");
Path relative = Paths.get("dir");
Path file = Paths.get("Model.pdf");
System.out.println("1: " + absolute.resolve(relative));
System.out.println("2: " + absolute.resolve(file));
System.out.println("3: " + relative.resolve(file));
System.out.println("4: " + relative.resolve(absolute));   // BAD
System.out.println("5: " + file.resolve(absolute));       // BAD
System.out.println("6: " + file.resolve(relative));       // BAD
```

The output is:

```
1:  /home/java/dir
2:  /home/java/Model.pdf
3:  dir/Model.pdf
4:  /home/java
5:  /home/java
6:  Model.pdf/dir
```

The first three do what you'd expect. They add the parameter to resolve to the provided path object. The fourth and fifth ones try to resolve an absolute path within the context of something else. The problem is that an absolute path doesn't depend on other directories. It is absolute. Therefore, resolve just returns that absolute path. The sixth one tries to resolve a directory within the context of a file. Since that doesn't make any sense, Java just tries its best and gives you nonsense.

Just like `normalize()`, keep in mind that `resolve()` will not check that the directory or file actually exists. To review, `resolve()` tells you how to resolve one path within another.

exam watch

Be careful with methods that come in two flavors: one with a `Path` parameter and the other with a `String` parameter such as `resolve()`. The tricky part here is that `null` is a valid value for both a `Path` and a `String`. What will happen if you pass just `null` as a parameter? Which method will be invoked?

```
Path path = Paths.get("/usr/bin/zip");
path.resolve(null);
```

The compiler can't decide which method to invoke: the one with the `Path` parameter or the other one with the `String` parameter. That's why this code won't compile, and if you see such code in an exam question, you'll know what to do.

The following examples will compile without any problem, because the compiler knows which method to invoke thanks to the type of the variable `other` and the explicit cast to `String`.

```
Path path = Paths.get("/usr/bin/zip");
Path other = null;
path.resolve(other);
path.resolve ((String) null);
```

Relativizing a Path

Now suppose we want to do the opposite of resolve. We have the absolute path of our home directory and the absolute path of the music file in our home directory. We want to know just the music file directory and name.

```
Path dir = Paths.get("/home/java");
Path music = Paths.get("/home/java/country/Swift.mp3");
Path mp3 = dir.relativize(music);
System.out.println(mp3);
```

The output is: `country/Swift.mp3`. Java recognized that the `/home/java` part is the same and returned a path of just the remainder.

`path1.relativize(path2)` should be read as "give me a path that shows how to get from `path1` to `path2`." In this example, we determined that `music` is a file in a directory named country within `dir`.

Keeping this definition in mind, let's look at some more complex examples:

```
Path absolute1 = Paths.get("/home/java");
Path absolute2 = Paths.get("/usr/local");
Path absolute3 = Paths.get("/home/java/temp/music.mp3");
Path relative1 = Paths.get("temp");
Path relative2 = Paths.get("temp/music.pdf");
System.out.println("1: " + absolute1.relativize(absolute3));
System.out.println("2: " + absolute3.relativize(absolute1));
System.out.println("3: " + absolute1.relativize(absolute2));
System.out.println("4: " + relative1.relativize(relative2));
System.out.println("5: " + absolute1.relativize(relative1));//BAD
```

The output is

```
1: temp/music.mp3
2: ../..
3: ../../usr/local
4: music.pdf
Exception in thread "main" java.lang.IllegalArgumentException: 'other'
is different type of Path
```

Before you scratch your head, let's look at the logical directory structure here. Keep in mind the directory doesn't actually need to exist; this is just to visualize it.

```
/root
  | - usr
          | - local
  | - home
          | -- java
            | - temp
                    | - music.mp3
```

Now we can trace it through. The first example is straightforward. It tells us how to get to `absolute3` from `absolute1` by going down two directories. The second is similar. We get to `absolute1` from `absolute3` by doing the opposite—going up two directories. Remember from `normalize()` that a double dot means to go up a directory.

The third output statement says that we have to go up two directories and then down two directories to get from `absolute1` to `absolute2`. Java knows this since we provided absolute paths. The worst possible case is to have to go all the way up to the root like we did here.

The fourth output statement is okay. Even though they are both relative paths, there is enough in common for Java to tell what the difference in path is.

The fifth example throws an exception. Java can't figure out how to make a relative path out of one absolute path and one relative path.

Remember, `relativize()` and `resolve()` are opposites. And just like `resolve()`, `relativize()` does not check that the path actually exists. To review, `relativize()` tells you how to get a relative path between two paths.

CERTIFICATION OBJECTIVE

File and Directory Attributes (OCP Objective 8.3)

8.3 *Read and change file and directory attributes, focusing on the BasicFileAttributes, DosFileAttributes, and PosixFileAttributes interfaces.*

Reading and Writing Attributes the Easy Way

In this section, we'll add classes and interfaces from the `java.nio.file.attribute` package to the discussion. Prior to NIO.2, you could read and write just a handful of attributes. Just like we saw when creating files, there is a new way to do this using `Files` instead of `File`. Oracle also took the opportunity to clean up the method signatures a bit. The following example creates a file, changes the last modified date, prints it out, and deletes the file using both the old and new method names. We might do this if we want to make a file look as if it were created in the past. (As you can see, there is a lesson about not relying on file timestamps here!)

```
Date januaryFirst = new GregorianCalendar(      // create a date
      2013, Calendar.JANUARY, 1).getTime();
// old way
File file = new File("c:/temp/file");
            file.createNewFile();               // create the file
file.setLastModified(januaryFirst.getTime());  // set time
System.out.println(file.lastModified());       // get time
file.delete();                                  // delete the file

// new way
Path path = Paths.get("c:/temp/file2");
Files.createFile(path);                                // create another file
FileTime fileTime = FileTime.fromMillis(               // convert to the new
                    januaryFirst.getTime());            // FileTime object
Files.setLastModifiedTime(path, fileTime);             // set time
System.out.println(Files.getLastModifiedTime(path));   // get time
Files.delete(path);                                    // delete the file
```

As you can see from the output, the only change in functionality is that the new `Files.getLastModifiedTime()` uses a human-friendly date format.

```
1357016400000
2013-01-01T05:00:00Z
```

The other common type of attribute you can set are file permissions. Both Windows and UNIX have the concept of three types of permissions. Here's what they mean:

- **Read** You can open the file or list what is in that directory.
- **Write** You can make a change to the file or add a file to that directory.
- **Execute** You can run the file if it is a runnable program or go into that directory.

Printing out the file permissions is easy. Note that these permissions are just for the user who is running the program—you! There are other types of permissions as well, but these can't be set in one line.

```
System.out.println(Files.isExecutable(path));
System.out.println(Files.isReadable(path));
System.out.println(Files.isWritable(path));
```

Table 9-6 shows how to get and set these attributes that can be set in one line, both using the older I/O way and the new `Files` class. You may have noticed that setting file permissions isn't in the table. That's more code, so we will talk about it later.

TABLE 9-6 I/O vs. NIO.2 Permissions

Description	I/O Approach	Approach
Get the last modified date/time	`File file = new File("test");` `file.lastModified();`	`Path path = Paths.get("test");` `Files.getLastModifiedTime(path);`
Is read permission set	`File file = new File("test");` `file.canRead();`	`Path path = Paths.get("test");` `Files.isReadable(path);`
Is write permission set	`File file = new File("test");` `file.canWrite();`	`Path path = Paths.get("test");` `Files.isWritable(path);`
Is executable permission set	`File file = new File("test");` `file.canExecute();`	`Path path = Paths.get("test");` `Files.isExecutable(path);`

Set the last modified date/time (Note: `timeInMillis` is an appropriate `long`.)	`File file = new File("test");`
	`file.setLastModified(timeInMillis);`
		`Path path = Paths.get("test");`
		`FileTime fileTime = FileTime.fromMillis(timeInMillis);`
		`Files.setLastModifiedTime(path, fileTime);`

Types of Attribute Interfaces

The attributes you set by calling methods on `Files` are the most straightforward ones. Beyond that, Java NIO.2 added attribute interfaces so that you could read attributes that might not be on every operating system.

- **`BasicFileAttributes`** In the JavaDoc, Oracle says these are "attributes common to many file systems." What they mean is that you can rely on these attributes being available to you unless you are writing Java code for some funky new operating system. Basic attributes include things like creation date.
- **`PosixFileAttributes`** POSIX stands for Portable Operating System Interface. This interface is implemented by both UNIX- and Linux-based operating systems. You can remember this because POSIX ends in "x," as do UNIX and Linux.
- **`DosFileAttributes`** DOS stands for Disk Operating System. It is part of all Windows operating systems. Even Windows 8 has a DOS prompt available.

There are also separate interfaces for setting or updating attributes. While the details aren't in scope for the exam, you should be familiar with the purpose of each one.

- **`BasicFileAttributeView`** Used to set the last updated, last accessed, and creation dates.

- **`PosixFileAttributeView`** Used to set the groups or permissions on UNIX/ Linux systems. There is an easier way to set these permissions though, so you won't be using the attribute view.
- **`DosFileAttributeView`** Used to set file permissions on DOS/Windows systems. Again, there is an easier way to set these, so you won't be using the attribute view.
- **`FileOwnerAttributeView`** Used to set the primary owner of a file or directory.
- **`AclFileAttributeView`** Sets more advanced permissions on a file or directory.

Working with BasicFileAttributes

The `BasicFileAttributes` interface provides methods to get information about a file or directory.

```
BasicFileAttributes basic =  Files.readAttributes(path,  // assume a valid path
      BasicFileAttributes.class);
System.out.println("create: " + basic.creationTime());
System.out.println("access: " + basic.lastAccessTime());
System.out.println("modify: " + basic.lastModifiedTime());
System.out.println("directory: " + basic.isDirectory());
```

The sample output shows that all three date/time values can be different. A file is created once. It can be modified many times. And it can be last accessed for reading after that. The `isDirectory` method is the same as `Files.isDirectory(path)`. It is just an alternative way of getting the same information.

```
create: 2013-01-01T18:06:01Z
access: 2013-01-29T14:44:218
modify: 2014-01-13T16:13:21Z
directory: false
```

There are some more attributes on `BasicFileAttributes`, but they aren't on the exam and you aren't likely to need them when coding. Just remember to check the JavaDoc if you need more information about a file.

So far, you've noticed that all the attributes are read only. That is because Java provides a different interface for updating attributes. Let's write code to update the last accessed time:

```
BasicFileAttributes basic = Files.readAttributes(
      path, BasicFileAttributes.class);                    // attributes
FileTime lastUpdated = basic.lastModifiedTime();           // get current
FileTime created = basic.creationTime();                   // values
FileTime now = FileTime.fromMillis(System.currentTimeMillis());
BasicFileAttributeView basicView = Files.getFileAttributeView(
      path, BasicFileAttributeView.class);                 // "view" this time
basicView.setTimes(lastUpdated, now, created);             // set all three
```

In this example, we demonstrated getting all three times. In practice, when calling `setTimes()`, you should pass null values for any of the times you don't want to change, and only pass `Filetimes` for the times you want to change.

The key takeaways here are that the "`XxxFileAttributes`" classes are read only and the "`XxxFileAttributeView`" classes allow updates.

exam watch

The `BasicFileAttributes` and `BasicFileAttributeView` interfaces are a bit confusing. They have similar names but different functionality, and you get them in different ways. Try to remember these three things:

- ***`BasicFileAttributeView` is singular, but `BasicFileAttributes` is not.***
- ***You get `BasicFileAttributeView` using `Files.getFileAttributeView`, and you get `BasicFileAttributes` using `Files.readAttributes`.***
- ***You can ONLY update attributes in `BasicFileAttributeView`, not in `BasicFileAttributes`. Remember that the view is for updating.***

`PosixFileAttributes` and `DosFileAttributes` inherit from `BasicFileAttributes`. This means that you can call Basic methods on a POSIX or DOS subinterface.

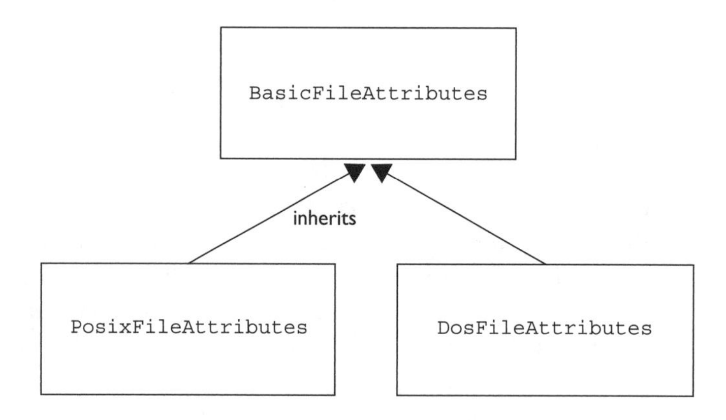

Try to use the more general type if you can. For example, if you are only going to use basic attributes, just get `BasicFileAttributes`. This lets your code remain operating system independent. If you are using a mix of basic and POSIX attributes, you can use `PosixFileAttributes` directly rather than calling `readAttributes()` twice to get two different ones.

Working with DosFileAttributes

`DosFileAttributes` adds four more attributes to the basics. We'll look at the most common ones here—hidden files and read-only files. Hidden files typically begin with a dot and don't show up when you type **dir** to list the contents of a directory. Read-only files are what they sound like—files that can't be updated. (The other two attributes are "archive" and "system," which you are quite unlikely to ever use.)

```
Path path= Paths.get("C:/test");
Files.createFile(path);                                  // create file
Files.setAttribute(path, "dos:hidden", true);            // set attribute
Files.setAttribute(path, "dos:readonly", true);          // another one
DosFileAttributes dos = Files.readAttributes(path,
      DosFileAttributes.class);                          // dos attributes
System.out.println(dos.isHidden());
System.out.println(dos.isReadOnly());
Files.setAttribute(path, "dos:hidden", false);
Files.setAttribute(path, "dos:readonly", false);
dos = Files.readAttributes(path,
      DosFileAttributes.class);                         // get attributes again
System.out.println(dos.isHidden());
System.out.println(dos.isReadOnly());
Files.delete(path);
```

The output is:

```
true
true
false
false
```

The first tricky thing in this code is that the `String` "`readonly`" is lowercase even though the method name is mixed case. If you forget and use the `String` "`readOnly`," Java will silently ignore the statement and the file will still allow anyone to write to it.

The other tricky thing is that you cannot delete a read-only file. That's why the code calls `setAttribute` a second time with `false` as a parameter, to make it no longer "read only" so the code can clean up after itself. And you can see that we had to call `readAttributes` again to see those updated values.

on the job

There is an alternative way to set these attributes where you don't have to worry about the `String` values. However, the exam wants you to know how to use `Files`. It is good to know both ways, though.

```
DosFileAttributeView view = Files.getFileAttributeView(path,
                              DosFileAttributeView.class);
view.setHidden(true);
view.setReadOnly(true);
```

Working with PosixFileAttributes

`PosixFileAttributes` adds two more attributes to the basics—groups and permissions. On UNIX, every file or directory has both an owner and group name.

UNIX permissions are also more elaborate than the basic ones. Each file or directory has nine permissions set in a `String`. A sample is "rwxrw-r--." Breaking this into groups of three, we have "rwx", "rw-," and "r--." These sets of permissions correspond to who gets them. In this example, the "user" (owner) of the file has read, write, and execute permissions. The "group" only has read and write permissions. UNIX calls everyone who is not the owner or in the group "other." "Other" only has read access in this example.

Now let's look at some code to set the permissions and output them in human-readable form:

```
Path path = Paths.get("/tmp/file2");
Files.createFile(path);
PosixFileAttributes posix = Files.readAttributes(path,
PosixFileAttributes.class);                          // get the Posix type
Set<PosixFilePermission> perms =
      PosixFilePermissions.fromString("rw-r--r--");  // UNIX style
Files.setPosixFilePermissions(path, perms);          // set permissions
System.out.println(posix.permissions());             // get permissions
```

The output looks like this:

```
[OWNER_WRITE, GROUP_READ, OTHERS_READ, OWNER_READ]
```

It's not symmetric. We gave Java the permissions in cryptic UNIX format and got them back in plain English. You can also output the group name:

```
System.out.println(posix.group());              // get group
```

which outputs something like this:

```
horse
```

Reviewing Attributes

Let's review the most common attributes information in Table 9-7.

TABLE 9-7 Common Attributes

<table>
<tr><th>Type</th><th>Read and Write an Attribute</th></tr>
<tr><td>Basic</td><td><pre>// read

BasicFileAttributes basic = Files.readAttributes(path,
     BasicFileAttributes.class);
FileTime lastUpdated = basic.lastModifiedTime();
FileTime created = basic.creationTime();
FileTime now = FileTime.fromMillis(System.currentTimeMillis());

// write
BasicFileAttributeView basicView =
Files.getFileAttributeView(path,
BasicFileAttributeView.class);
basicView.setTimes(lastUpdated, now, created);</pre></td></tr>
<tr><td>Posix
(UNIX/Linux)</td><td><pre>PosixFileAttributes posix = Files.readAttributes(path, PosixFileAttributes.class);
Set<PosixFilePermission> perms = PosixFilePermissions.fromString("rw-r--r--");
Files.setPosixFilePermissions(path, perms);
System.out.println(posix.group());
System.out.println(posix.permissions());</pre></td></tr>
<tr><td>Dos
(Windows)</td><td><pre>DosFileAttributes dos = Files.readAttributes(path,
 DosFileAttributes.class);
System.out.println(dos.isHidden());
System.out.println(dos.isReadOnly());
Files.setAttribute(path, "dos:hidden", false);
Files.setAttribute(path, "dos:readonly", false);</pre></td></tr>
</table>

CERTIFICATION OBJECTIVE

DirectoryStream (OCP Objective 8.4)

8.4 Recursively access a directory tree using the DirectoryStream and FileVisitor interfaces.

Now let's return to more NIO.2 capabilities that you'll find in the `java.nio.file` package... You might need to loop through a directory. Let's say you were asked to list out all the users with a home directory on this computer.

```
/home
  | - users
          | - vafi
          | - eyra
```

```
Path dir = Paths.get("/home/users");
try (DirectoryStream<Path> stream =                 // use try with resources
      Files.newDirectoryStream(dir)) {              // so we don't have close()
  for (Path path : stream)                          // loop through the stream
      System.out.println(path.getFileName());
}
```

As expected, this outputs

```
vafi
eyra
```

The `DirectoryStream` interface lets you iterate through a directory. But this is just the tip of the iceberg. Let's say we have hundreds of users and each day we want to only report on a few of them. The first day, we only want the home directories of users whose names begin with either the letter *v* or the letter *w*.

```
Path dir = Paths.get("/home/users");
try (DirectoryStream<Path> stream = Files.newDirectoryStream(
  dir, "[vw]*")) {                              // "v" or "w" followed by anything
for (Path path : stream)
      System.out.println(path.getFileName());
}
```

This time, the output is

```
vafi
```

Let's examine the expression `[vw]*`. `[vw]` means either of the characters `v` or `w`. The `*` is a wildcard that means zero or more of any character. Notice this is not a regular expression. (If it were, the syntax would be `[vw].*`—see the dot in there.)

DirectoryStream uses something new called a glob. We will see more on globs later in the chapter.

There is one limitation with DirectoryStream. It can only look at one directory. One way to remember this is that it works like the dir command in DOS or the ls command in UNIX. Or you can remember that DirectoryStream streams one directory.

CERTIFICATION OBJECTIVE

FileVisitor (OCP Objective 8.4)

8.4 Recursively access a directory tree using the DirectoryStream and FileVisitor interfaces.

Luckily, there is another class that does, in fact, look at subdirectories. Let's say you want to get rid of all the .class files before zipping up and submitting your assignment. You could go through each directory manually, but that would get tedious really fast. You could write a complicated command in Windows and another in UNIX, but then you'd have two programs that do the same thing. Luckily, you can use Java and only write the code once.

Java provides a SimpleFileVisitor. You extend it and override one or more methods. Then you can call Files.*walkFileTree*, which knows how to recursively look through a directory structure and call methods on a visitor subclass. Let's try our example:

```
/home
  | - src
          | - Test.java
          | - Test.class
          | - dir
                 | - AnotherTest.java
                 | - AnotherTest.class

public class RemoveClassFiles
      extends SimpleFileVisitor<Path> {           // need to extend visitor
      public FileVisitResult visitFile(           // called "automatically"
         Path file, BasicFileAttributes attrs)
                  throws IOException {
            if ( file.getFileName().endsWith(".class"))
              Files.delete(file);                 // delete the file
            return FileVisitResult.CONTINUE;      // go on to next file
      }
      public static void main(String[] args) throws Exception {
```

```
            RemoveClassFiles dirs = new RemoveClassFiles();
            Files.walkFileTree(                    // kick off recursive check
                     Paths.get("/home/src"),       // starting point
                     dirs);                        // the visitor
      }
}
```

This is a simple file visitor. It only implements one method: `visitFile`. This method is called for every file in the directory structure. It checks the extension of the file and deletes it if appropriate. In our case, two .class files are deleted.

There are two parameters to `visitFile()`. The first one is the `Path` object representing the current file. The other is a `BasicFileAttributes` interface. Do you remember what this does? That's right—it lets you find out if the current file is a directory, when it was created, and many other similar pieces of data.

Finally, `visitFile()` returns `FileVisitResult.CONTINUE`. This tells `walkFileTree()` that it should keep looking through the directory structure for more files.

Now that we have a feel for the power of this class, let's take a look at all the methods available to us with another example:

```
/home
  | - a.txt
  | - emptyChild
  | - child
          | - b.txt
          | - grandchild
                | - c.txt
```

```
public class PrintDirs extends SimpleFileVisitor<Path> {
  public FileVisitResult preVisitDirectory(Path dir, BasicFileAttributes attrs) {
    System.out.println("pre: " + dir);
    return FileVisitResult.CONTINUE; }
  public FileVisitResult visitFile(Path file, BasicFileAttributes attrs) {
    System.out.println("file: " + file);
    return FileVisitResult.CONTINUE; }
  public FileVisitResult visitFileFailed(Path file, IOException exc) {
    return FileVisitResult.CONTINUE; }
  public FileVisitResult postVisitDirectory(Path dir, IOException exc) {
    System.out.println("post: " + dir);
    return FileVisitResult.CONTINUE; }
  public static void main(String[] args) throws Exception {
    PrintDirs dirs = new PrintDirs();
    Files.walkFileTree(Paths.get("/home"), dirs); } }
```

You might get the following output:

```
pre: /home
file: /home/a.txt
pre: /home/child
file: /home/child/b.txt
pre: /home/child/grandchild
file: /home/child/grandchild/c.txt
```

```
post: /home/child/grandchild
post: /home/child
pre: /home/emptyChild
post: /home/emptyChild
post: /home
```

Note that Java goes down as deep as it can before returning back up the tree. This is called a *depth-first search*. We said "might" because files and directories at the same level can get visited in either order.

You can override as few or many of the four methods as you'd like. Note that the second half of the methods have IOException as a parameter. This allows those methods to handle problems that came earlier when walking through the tree. Table 9-8 summarizes the methods.

You actually do have some control, though, through those `FileVisitResult` constants. Suppose we changed the `preVisitDirectory` method to the following:

```
public FileVisitResult preVisitDirectory(
  Path dir, BasicFileAttributes attrs) {
  System.out.println("pre: " + dir);
  String name = dir.getFileName().toString();
  if (name.equals("child"))
    return FileVisitResult.SKIP_SUBTREE;
  return FileVisitResult.CONTINUE;
}
```

Now the output is:

```
pre: /home
file: /home/a.txt
pre: /home/child
pre: /home/emptyChild
post: /home/emptyChild
post: /home
```

TABLE 9-8 `FileVisitor` Methods

Method	Description	IOException Parameter?
`preVisitDirectory`	Called before drilling down into the directory	No
`visitFile`	Called once for each file (but not for directories)	No
`visitFileFailed`	Called only if there was an error accessing a file, usually a permissions issue	Yes
`postVisitDirectory`	Called when finished with the directory on the way back up	Yes

Since we instructed the program to skip the entire `child` subtree—i.e., we don't see the file: `b.txt` or the sub-directory: `grandchild`—we also don't see the post visit call.

Now what do you think would happen if we changed `FileVisitResult.SKIP_SIBLINGS` to `FileVisitResult.TERMINATE`? The output might be:

```
pre: /home
file: /home/a.txt
pre: /home/child
```

We see that as soon as the "child" directory came up, the program stopped walking the tree. And again, we are using "might" in terms of the output. It's also possible for `emptyChild` to come up first, in which case, the last line of the output would be `/home/emptyChild`.

There's one more result type. What do you think would happen if we changed `FileVisitResult.TERMINATE` to `FileVisitResult.SKIP_SIBLINGS`? The output happens to be the same as the previous example:

```
pre: /home
file: /home/a.txt
pre: /home/child
```

`SKIP_SIBLINGS` is a combination of `SKIP_SUBTREE` and "don't look in any folders at the same level." This means we skip everything under `child` and also skip `emptyChild`.

One more example to make sure you really understand what is going on. What do you think gets output if we use this method?

```
public FileVisitResult preVisitDirectory(Path dir,
  BasicFileAttributes attrs) {
  System.out.println("pre: " + dir);
  String name = dir.getFileName().toString();
  if (name.equals("grandchild"))
    return FileVisitResult.SKIP_SUBTREE;
  if ( name.equals("emptyChild"))
    return FileVisitResult.SKIP_SIBLINGS;
  return FileVisitResult.CONTINUE;
}
```

Assuming child is encountered before `emptyChild`, the output is:

```
pre: /home
file: /home/a.txt
pre: /home/child
file: /home/child/b.txt
pre: /home/child/grandchild
post: /home/child
pre: /home/emptyChild
post: /home
```

We don't see `file: c.txt` or `post: /home/child/grandchild` because we skip `grandchild` the subtree. We don't see "`post: /home/emptyChild`" because we skip siblings of `emptyChild`. But wait. Isn't `/home/child` a sibling? It is. But the visitor goes in order. Since `child` was seen before `emptyChild`, it is too late to skip it. Just like when you print a document, it is too late to prevent pages from printing that have already printed. File visitor can only skip subtrees that it has not encountered yet.

CERTIFICATION OBJECTIVE

PathMatcher (OCP Objective 8.5)

8.5 *Find a file with PathMatcher interface.*

`DirectoryStream` and `FileVisitor` allowed us to go through the files that exist. Things can get complicated fast, though. Imagine you had a requirement to print out the names of all text files in any subdirectory of "password." You might be wondering why anyone would want to do this. Maybe a teammate foolishly stored passwords for everyone to see and you want to make sure nobody else did that. You could write logic to keep track of the directory structure, but that makes the code harder to read and understand. By the end of this section, you'll know a better way.

Let's start out with a simpler example to see what a `PathMatcher` can do:

```
Path path1 = Paths.get("/home/One.txt");
Path path2 = Paths.get("One.txt");
PathMatcher matcher = FileSystems.getDefault()  // get the PathMatcher
            .getPathMatcher(                    // for the right file system
            "glob:*.txt");                      // wait. What's a glob?
System.out.println(matcher.matches(path1));
System.out.println(matcher.matches(path2));
```

which outputs:

```
false
true
```

We can see that the code checks if a `Path` consists of any characters followed by ".txt." To get a `PathMatcher`, you have to call `FileSystems.getDefault()
.getPathMatcher` because matching works differently on different operating systems. `PathMatchers` use a new type that you probably haven't seen before called

a glob. Globs are not regular expressions, although they might look similar at first. Let's look at some more examples of globs using a common method so we don't have to keep reading the same "boilerplate" code. (Boilerplate code is the part of the code that is always the same.)

```
public void matches(Path path, String glob) {
  PathMatcher matcher = FileSystems.getDefault().getPathMatcher(glob);
  System.out.println(matcher.matches(path));
}
```

In the world of globs, one asterisk means "match any character except for a directory boundary." Two asterisks means "match any character, including a directory boundary."

```
Path path = Paths.get("/com/java/One.java");
matches(path, "glob:*.java");        // false
matches(path, "glob:**/*.java");     // true
matches(path, "glob:*");             // false
matches(path, "glob:**");            // true
```

on the Job

Remember that we are using a file system–specific `PathMatcher`. This means slashes and backslashes can be treated differently, depending on what operating system you happen to be running. The previous example does print the same output on both Windows and UNIX because it uses forward slashes. However, if you change just one line of code, the output changes:

```
Path path = Paths.get("com\\java\\One.java");
```

Now Windows still prints:

```
false
true
false
true
```

However, UNIX prints:

```
true
false
true
true
```

Why? Because UNIX doesn't see the backslash as a directory boundary. The lesson here is to use / instead of \\ so your code behaves more predictably across operating systems.

Now let's match files with a four-character extension. A question mark matches any character. A character could be a letter or a number or anything else.

```
Path path1 = Paths.get("One.java");
Path path2 = Paths.get("One.ja^a");
matches(path1, "glob:*.????");      // true
matches(path1, "glob:*.???");       // false
matches(path2, "glob:*.????");      // true
matches(path2, "glob:*.???");       // false
```

Globs also provide a nice way to match multiple patterns. Suppose we want to match anything that begins with the names Kathy or Bert:

```
Path path1 = Paths.get("Bert-book");
Path path2 = Paths.get("Kathy-horse");
matches(path1, "glob:{Bert*,Kathy*}");     // true
matches(path2, "glob:{Bert,Kathy}*");      // true
matches(path1, "glob:{Bert,Kathy}");       // false
```

The first glob shows we can put wildcards inside braces to have multiple glob expressions. The second glob shows that we can put common wildcards outside the braces to share them. The third glob shows that without the wildcard, we will only match the literal strings "Bert" and "Kathy."

You can also use sets of characters like `[a-z]` or `[#$%]` in globs just like in regular expressions. You can also escape special characters with a backslash. Let's put this all together with a tricky example:

```
Path path1 = Paths.get("0*b/test/1");
Path path2 = Paths.get("9\\*b/test/1");
Path path3 = Paths.get("01b/test/1");
Path path4 = Paths.get("0*b/1");
String glob = "glob:[0-9]\\*{A*,b}/**/1";
matches(path1, glob);                        // true
matches(path2, glob);                        // false
matches(path3, glob);                        // false
matches(path4, glob);                        // false
```

Spelling out what the glob does, we have the following:

- **`[0-9]`** One single digit. Can also be read as any one character from 0 to 9.
- **`\\*`** The literal character asterisk rather than the asterisk that means to match anything. A single backslash before `*` escapes it. However, Java won't let you type a single backslash, so you have to escape the backslash itself with another backslash.
- **`{A*,b}`** Either a capital A followed by anything or the single character *b*.
- **`/**/`** One or more directories with any name.
- **`1`** The single character 1.

The second path doesn't match because it has the literal backslash followed by the literal asterisk. The glob was looking for the literal asterisk by itself. The third path also doesn't match because there is no literal asterisk. The fourth path doesn't match because there is no directory between "b" and "1" for the `**` to match. Luckily, nobody would write such a crazy, meaningless glob. But if you can understand this one, you are all set. Globs tend to be simple expressions like `{*.txt,*.html}` when used for real.

Since globs are just similar enough to regular expressions to be tricky, Table 9-10 reviews the similarities and differences in common expressions. Regular expressions are more powerful, but globs focus on what you are likely to need when matching filenames.

By now, you've probably noticed that we are dealing with `Path` objects, which means they don't actually need to exist on the file system. But we wanted to print out all the text files that actually exist in a subdirectory of password. Luckily, we can combine the power of `PathMatchers` with what we already know about walking the file tree to accomplish this.

```
public class MyPathMatcher extends SimpleFileVisitor<Path> {
  private PathMatcher matcher =
    FileSystems.getDefault().getPathMatcher(
    "glob:**/password/**.txt");                  // ** means any subdirectory
  public FileVisitResult visitFile(Path file, BasicFileAttributes attrs)
     throws IOException {
    if (matcher.matches(file)) {
      System.out.println(file);

    }
    return FileVisitResult.CONTINUE;
  }
  public static void main(String[] args) throws Exception {
    MyPathMatcher dirs = new MyPathMatcher();
    Files.walkFileTree(Paths.get("/"),   dirs);  // start with root
  }
}
```

The code looks similar, regardless of what you want to do. You just change the glob pattern to what you actually want to match.

TABLE 9-10 Glob vs. Regular Expression

What to Match	In a Glob	In a Regular Expression
Zero or more of any character, including a directory boundary	`**`	`.*`
Zero or more of any character, not including a directory boundary	`*`	N/A – no special syntax
Exactly one character	`?`	`.`
Any digit	`[0-9]`	`[0-9]`
Begins with cat or dog	`{cat, dog}*`	`(cat|dog).*`

CERTIFICATION OBJECTIVE

WatchService (OCP Objective 8.6)

8.6 *Watch a directory for changes with the* `WatchService` *interface.*

The last thing you need to know about in NIO.2 is `WatchService`. Suppose you are writing an installer program. You check that the directory you are about to install into is empty. If not, you want to wait until the user manually deletes that directory before continuing. Luckily, you won't have to write this code from scratch, but you should be familiar with the concepts. Here's the directory tree:

```
/dir
  | - directoryToDelete
  | - other
```

Here's the code snippet:

```
Path dir = Paths.get("/dir");                    // get directory containing
                                                 // file/directory we care
                                                 // about
WatchService watcher = FileSystems.getDefault() // file system specific code
      .newWatchService();                        // create empty watch service
dir.register(watcher, ENTRY_DELETE);             // needs a static import!
                                                 // start watching for
                                                 // deletions
while (true) {                                   // loop until say to stop
  WatchKey key;
  try {
    key = watcher.take();                        // wait for a deletion
  } catch (InterruptedException x) {
      return;                                    // give up if something goes
                                                 // wrong
  }
  for (WatchEvent<?> event : key.pollEvents()) {
    WatchEvent.Kind<?> kind = event.kind();
    System.out.println(kind.name());             // create/delete/modify
    System.out.println(kind.type());             // always a Path for us
    System.out.println(event.context());         // name of the file
    String name = event.context().toString();
    if (name.equals("directoryToDelete")) {      // only delete right directory
       System.out.format("Directory deleted, now we can proceed");
       return;                                   // end program, we found what
                                                 // we were waiting for
    }
  }
  key.reset();                                   // keep looking for events
}
```

Supposing we delete directory "other" followed by directory `directoryToDelete`, this outputs:

```
ENTRY_DELETE
interface java.nio.file.Path
other
ENTRY_DELETE
interface java.nio.file.Path
directoryToDelete
Directory deleted, now we can proceed
```

Notice that we had to watch the directory that contains the files or directories we are interested in. This is why we watched `/dir` instead of `/dir/directoryToDelete`. This is also why we had to check the context to make sure the directory we were actually interested in is that one that was deleted.

The basic flow of `WatchService` stays the same, regardless of what you want to do:

1. Create a new `WatchService`
2. Register it on a `Path` listening to one or more event types
3. Loop until you are no longer interested in these events
4. Get a `WatchKey` from the `WatchService`
5. Call `key.pollEvents` and do something with the events
6. Call `key.reset` to look for more events

Let's look at some of these in more detail. You register the `WatchService` on a `Path` using statements like the following:

```
dir1.register(watcher, ENTRY_DELETE);
dir2.register(watcher, ENTRY_DELETE, ENTRY_CREATE);
dir3.register(watcher, ENTRY_DELETE, ENTRY_CREATE, ENTRY_MODIFY);
```

(Note: These `ENTRY_XXX` constants can be found in the `StandardWatchEventsKinds` class. Here and in later code, you'll probably want to create static imports for these constants.) You can register one, two, or three of the event types. `ENTRY_DELETE` means you want your program to be informed when a file or directory has been deleted. Similarly, `ENTRY_CREATE` means a new file or directory has been created. `ENTRY_MODIFY` means a file has been edited in the directory. These changes can be made manually by a human or by another program on the computer.

Renaming a file or directory is interesting, as it does not show up as `ENTRY_MODIFY`. From Java's point of view, a rename is equivalent to creating a new file and deleting the original. This means that two events will trigger for a rename—both `ENTRY_CREATE` and `ENTRY_DELETE`. Actually editing a file will show up as `ENTRY_MODIFY`.

To loop through the events, we use `while(true)`. It might seem a little odd to write a loop that never ends. Normally, there is a `break` or `return` statement in the loop so you stop looping once whatever event you were waiting for has occurred. It's also possible you want the program to run until you kill or terminate it at the command line.

Within the loop, you need to get a `WatchKey`. There are two ways to do this. The most common is to call `take()`, which waits until an event is available. It throws an `InterruptedException` if it gets interrupted without finding a key. This allows you to end the program. The other way is to call `poll()`, which returns `null` if an event is not available. You can provide optional timeout parameters to wait up to a specific period of time for an event to show up.

```
watcher.take();                        // wait "forever" for an event
watcher.poll();                        // get event if present right NOW
watcher.poll(10, TimeUnit.SECONDS);    // wait up to 10 seconds for an event
watcher.poll(1, TimeUnit.MINUTES);     // wait up to 1 minute for an event
```

Next, you loop through any events on that key. In the case of rename, you'll get one key with two events—the `EVENT_CREATE` and `EVENT_DELETE`. Remember that you get all the events that happened since the last time you called `poll()` or `take()`. This means you can get multiple seemingly unrelated events out of the same key. They can be from different files but are for the same `WatchService`.

```
for (WatchEvent<?> event : key.pollEvents()) {
```

Finally, you call `key.reset()`. This is very important. If you forget to call reset, the program will work for the first event, but then you will not be notified of any other events.

on the Job

There are a few limitations you should be aware of with `WatchService`. To begin with, it is slow. You could easily wait five seconds for the event to register. It also isn't 100 percent reliable. You can add code to check if `kind == OVERFLOW`, but that just tells you something went wrong. You don't know what events you lost. In practice, you are unlikely to use `WatchService`.

WatchService only watches the files and directories immediately beneath it. What if we want to watch to see if either p.txt or c.txt is modified?

```
/dir
  | - parent
         | - p.txt
         | - child
             | - c.txt
```

One way is to register both directories:

```
WatchService watcher =
  FileSystems.getDefault().newWatchService();
Path dir = Paths.get("/dir/parent");
dir.register(watcher, ENTRY_MODIFY);
Path child = Paths.get("dir/parent/child");
child.register(watcher, ENTRY_MODIFY);
```

This works. You can type in all the directories you want to watch. If we had a lot of child directories, this would quickly get to be too much work. Instead, we can have Java do it for us:

```
Path myDir = Paths.get("/dir/parent");
final WatchService watcher =                    // final so visitor can use it
  FileSystems.getDefault().newWatchService();
Files.walkFileTree(myDir, new SimpleFileVisitor<Path>() {
  public FileVisitResult preVisitDirectory(Path dir,
      BasicFileAttributes attrs) throws IOException {
      dir.register(watcher, ENTRY_MODIFY);      // watch each directory
     return FileVisitResult.CONTINUE;
  }
});
```

This code goes through the file tree recursively registering each directory with the watcher. The NIO.2 classes are designed to work together. For example, we could add PathMatcher to the previous example to only watch directories that have a specific pattern in their path.

CERTIFICATION OBJECTIVE

Serialization (Objective 7.2)

7.2 Use streams to read from and write to files by using classes in the java.io package, including BufferedReader, BufferedWriter, File, FileReader, FileWriter, DataInputStream, DataOutputStream, ObjectOutputStream, ObjectInputStream, and PrintWriter.

Over time, Oracle has fine-tuned the objectives of the OCP 7 exam. Serialization was a topic on the old SCJP 5 and SCJP 6 exams, and recently (as of the summer of 2014), Oracle reintroduced serialization for the OCP 7 exam. Please see the CD-ROM included with this book for in-depth, complete chapter coverage of serialization, right down to a self-test.

CERTIFICATION SUMMARY

File I/O Remember that objects of type File can represent either files or directories but that until you call `createNewFile()` or `mkdir()` you haven't actually created anything on your hard drive. Classes in the `java.io` package are designed to be chained together. It will be rare that you'll use a `FileReader` or a `FileWriter` without "wrapping" them with a `BufferedReader` or `BufferedWriter` object, which gives you access to more powerful, higher-level methods. As of Java 5, the `PrintWriter` class has been enhanced with advanced `append()`, `format()`, and `printf()` methods, and when you couple that with new constructors that allow you to create `PrintWriters` directly from a `String` name or a `File` object, you may use `BufferedWriters` a lot less. The `Console` class allows you to read nonechoed input (returned in a `char[?]`), and is instantiated using `System.console()`.

NIO.2 Objects of type `Path` can be files or directories and are a replacement of type `File`. `Paths` are created with `Paths.get()`. Utility methods in `Files` allow you to create, delete, move, copy, or check information about a `Path`. In addition, `BasicFileAttributes`, `DosFileAttributes` (Windows), and `PosixFileAttributes` (UNIX/Linux/Mac) allow you to check more advanced information about a `Path`. `BasicFileAttributeView`, `DosFileAttributeView`, and `PosixFileAttributeView` allow you to update advanced `Path` attributes.

Using a `DirectoryStream` allows you to iterate through a directory. Extending `SimpleFileVisitor` lets you walk a directory tree recursively looking at files and/or directories. With a `PathMatcher`, you can search directories for files using regex-esqu expressions called globs.

Finally, registering a `WatchService` provides notifications for new/changed/removed files or directories.

✓ TWO-MINUTE DRILL

Here are some of the key points from the certification objectives in this chapter.

File I/O (OCP Objectives 7.1 and 7.2)

- ❑ The classes you need to understand in `java.io` are `File`, `FileReader`, `BufferedReader`, `FileWriter`, `BufferedWriter`, `PrintWriter`, and `Console`.
- ❑ A new `File` object doesn't mean there's a new file on your hard drive.
- ❑ `File` objects can represent either a file or a directory.
- ❑ The `File` class lets you manage (add, rename, and delete) files and directories.
- ❑ The methods `createNewFile()` and `mkdir()` add entries to your file system.
- ❑ `FileWriter` and `FileReader` are low-level I/O classes. You can use them to write and read files, but they should usually be wrapped.
- ❑ Classes in `java.io` are designed to be "chained" or "wrapped." (This is a common use of the decorator design pattern.)
- ❑ It's very common to "wrap" a `BufferedReader` around a `FileReader` or a `BufferedWriter` around a `FileWriter` to get access to higher-level (more convenient) methods.
- ❑ `PrintWriters` can be used to wrap other `Writers`, but as of Java 5, they can be built directly from `Files` or `Strings`.
- ❑ As of Java 5, `PrintWriters` have new `append()`, `format()`, and `printf()` methods.
- ❑ `Console` objects can read nonechoed input and are instantiated using `System.console()`.

Path, Paths, and File (OCP Objectives 8.1 and 8.2)

- ❑ NIO.2 was introduced in Java 7.
- ❑ `Path` replaces `File` for a representation of a file or directory.
- ❑ `Paths.get()` lets you create a `Path` object.
- ❑ Static methods in `Files` let you work with `Path` objects.
- ❑ A `Path` object doesn't mean the file or directory exists on your hard drive.
- ❑ The methods `Files.createFile()` and `Files.createDirectory()` add entries to your file system.

- The `Files` class provides methods to move, copy, and delete `Path` objects.
- `Files.delete()` throws an Exception if the file does not exist and `Files.deleteIfExists()` returns false.
- On `Path`, `normalize()` simplifies the path representation.
- On `Path`, `resolve()` and `relativize()` work with the relationship between two path objects.

File Attributes (OCP Objective 8.3)

- The `Files` class provides methods for common attributes such as whether the file is executable and when it was last modified.
- For less common attributes the classes: `BasicFileAttributes`, `DosFileAttributes`, and `PosixFileAttributes` read the attributes.
- `DosFileAttributes` works on Windows operating systems.
- `PosixFileAttributes` works on UNIX, Linux, and Mac operating systems.
- Attributes that can't be updated via the `Files` class are set using the classes: `BasicFileAttributeView`, `DosFileAttributeView`, `PosixFileAttributeView`, `FileOwnerAttributeView`, and `AclFileAttributeView`.

Directory Trees, Matching, and Watching for Changes (OCP Objectives 8.4, 8.5, and 8.6)

- `DirectoryStream` iterates through immediate children of a directory using glob patterns.
- `FileVisitor` walks recursively through a directory tree.
- You can override one or all of the methods of `SimpleFileVisitor`—`preVisitDirectory`, `visitFile`, `visitFileFailed`, and `postVisitDirectory`.
- You can change the flow of a file visitor by returning one of the `FileVisitResult` constants: CONTINUE, SKIP_SUBTREE, SKIP_SIBLINGS, or TERMINATE.
- `PathMatcher` checks if a path matches a glob pattern.
- Know what the following expressions mean for globs: `*`, `**`, `?`, and `{a,b}`.
- Directories register with `WatchService` to be notified about creation, deletion, and modification of files or immediate subdirectories.
- `PathMatcher` and `WatchService` use `FileSystem`-specific implementations.

SELF TEST

The following questions will help you measure your understanding of the material presented in this chapter. Read all of the choices carefully, as there may be more than one correct answer. Choose all correct answers for each question. Stay focused.

1. Note: The use of "drag-and-drop" questions has come and gone over the years. In case Oracle brings them back into fashion, we threw a couple of them in the book.

Using the fewest fragments possible (and filling the fewest slots possible), complete the following code so that the class builds a directory named "dir3" and creates a file named "file3" inside "dir3." Note you can use each fragment either zero or one times.

Code:

```
import java.io.____________

class Maker {
  public static void main(String[] args) {

    __________  __________  __________

    __________  __________  __________

    __________  __________  __________

    __________  __________  __________

    __________  __________  __________

    __________  __________  __________

    __________  __________  __________
} }
```

Fragments:

```
File;       FileDescriptor;         FileWriter;     Directory;
try {       .createNewDir();        File dir        File
{ }         (Exception x)           ("dir3");       file
file        .createNewFile();       = new File      = new File
dir         (dir, "file3");         (dir, file);    .createFile();
} catch     ("dir3", "file3");      .mkdir();       File file
```

2. Given:

```
import java.io.*;

class Directories {
  static String [] dirs = {"dir1", "dir2"};
  public static void main(String [] args) {
    for (String d : dirs) {

      // insert code 1 here

      File file = new File(path, args[0]);

      // insert code 2 here
    }
  }
}
```

and that the invocation

```
java Directories file2.txt
```

is issued from a directory that has two subdirectories, "dir1" and "dir2," and that "dir1" has a file "file1.txt" and "dir2" has a file "file2.txt," and the output is "false true," which set(s) of code fragments must be inserted? (Choose all that apply.)

A.
```
String path = d;
System.out.print(file.exists() + " ");
```

B.
```
String path = d;
System.out.print(file.isFile() + " ");
```

C.
```
String path = File.separator + d;
System.out.print(file.exists() + " ");
```

D.
```
String path = File.separator + d;
System.out.print(file.isFile() + " ");
```

3. Given:

```
 3. import java.io.*;
 4. public class ReadingFor {
 5.   public static void main(String[] args) {
 6.     String s;
 7.     try {
 8.       FileReader fr = new FileReader("myfile.txt");
 9.       BufferedReader br = new BufferedReader(fr);
10.       while((s = br.readLine()) != null)
```

```
11.         System.out.println(s);
12.       br.flush();
13.     } catch (IOException e) { System.out.println("io error"); }
16.   }
17. }
```

And given that `myfile.txt` contains the following two lines of data:

```
ab
cd
```

What is the result?

A. `ab`

B. `abcd`

C. `ab`
`cd`

D. `a`
`b`
`c`
`d`

E. Compilation fails

4. Given:

```
3. import java.io.*;
4. public class Talker {
5.   public static void main(String[] args) {
6.     Console c = System.console();
7.     String u = c.readLine("%s", "username: ");
8.     System.out.println("hello " + u);
9.     String pw;
10.    if(c != null && (pw = c.readPassword("%s", "password: ")) != null)
11.      // check for valid password
12.  }
13. }
```

If line 6 creates a valid `Console` object and if the user enters *fred* as a username and *1234* as a password, what is the result? (Choose all that apply.)

A. `username:`
`password:`

B. `username: fred`
`password:`

C. `username: fred`
`password: 1234`

D. Compilation fails

E. An Exception is thrown at runtime

5. This question is about serialization, which Oracle reintroduced to the OCP 7 exam and a topic covered in the Serialization chapter on the CD-ROM.

Given:

```
 3. import java.io.*;
 4. class Vehicle { }
 5. class Wheels { }
 6. class Car extends Vehicle implements Serializable {  }
 7. class Ford extends Car { }
 8. class Dodge extends Car {
 9.   Wheels w = new Wheels();
10. }
```

Instances of which class(es) can be serialized? (Choose all that apply.)

A. `Car`

B. `Ford`

C. `Dodge`

D. `Wheels`

E. `Vehicle`

6. Which of the following creates a `Path` object pointing to `c:/temp/exam`? (Choose all that apply.)

A. `new Path("c:/temp/exam")`

B. `new Path("c:/temp", "exam")`

C. `Files.get("c:/temp/exam")`

D. `Files.get("c:/temp", "exam")`

E. `Paths.get("c:/temp/exam")`

F. `Paths.get("c:/temp", "exam")`

7. Given a directory tree at the root of the C: drive and the fact that no other files exist:

```
dir x - |
..........| - dir y
..........| - file a
```

and these two paths:

```
Path one = Paths.get("c:/x");
Path two = Paths.get("c:/x/y/a");
```

Which of the following statements prints out: `y/a` ?

A. `System.out.println(one.relativize(two));`

B. `System.out.println(two.relativize(one));`

C. `System.out.println(one.resolve(two));`

D. `System.out.println(two.resolve(one));`

E. `System.out.println(two.resolve(two));`

F. None of the above

8. Given the following statements:

I. A nonempty directory can usually be deleted using `Files.delete`

II. A nonempty directory can usually be moved using `Files.move`

III. A nonempty directory can usually be copied using `Files.copy`

Which of the following is true?

A. I only

B. II only

C. III only

D. I and II only

E. II and III only

F. I and III only

G. I, II, and III

9. Given:

```
new File("c:/temp/test.txt").delete();
```

How would you write this line of code using Java 7 APIs?

A. `Files.delete(Paths.get("c:/temp/test.txt"));`

B. `Files.deleteIfExists(Paths.get("c:/temp/test.txt"));`

C. `Files.deleteOnExit(Paths.get("c:/temp/test.txt"));`

D. `Paths.get("c:/temp/test.txt").delete();`

E. `Paths.get("c:/temp/test.txt").deleteIfExists();`

F. `Paths.get("c:/temp/test.txt").deleteOnExit();`

10. Given:

```
public void read(Path dir) throws IOException {
  // CODE HERE
  System.out.println(attr.creationTime());
}
```

Which code inserted at `// CODE HERE` will compile and run without error on Windows? (Choose all that apply.)

A. `BasicFileAttributes attr = Files.readAttributes(dir, BasicFileAttributes.class);`

B. `BasicFileAttributes attr = Files.readAttributes(dir, DosFileAttributes.class);`

C. `DosFileAttributes attr = Files.readAttributes(dir, BasicFileAttributes.class);`

D. `DosFileAttributes attr = Files.readAttributes(dir, DosFileAttributes.class);`

E. `PosixFileAttributes attr = Files.readAttributes(dir, PosixFileAttributes.class);`

F. `BasicFileAttributes attr = new BasicFileAttributes(dir);`

G. `BasicFileAttributes attr =dir.getBasicFileAttributes();`

11. Which of the following are true? (Choose all that apply.)

A. The class `AbstractFileAttributes` applies to all operating systems

B. The class `BasicFileAttributes` applies to all operating systems

C. The class `DosFileAttributes` applies to Windows-based operating systems

D. The class `WindowsFileAttributes` applies to Windows-based operating systems

E. The class `PosixFileAttributes` applies to all Linux/UNIX-based operating systems

F. The class `UnixFileAttributes` applies to all Linux/UNIX-based operating systems

12. Given a partial directory tree:

```
dir x - |
..........| - dir y
..........| - file a
```

In what order can the following methods be called if walking the directory tree from `x`? (Choose all that apply.)

I: `preVisitDirectory x`

II: `preVisitDirectory x/y`

III: `postVisitDirectory x/y`

IV: `postVisitDirectory x`

V: `visitFile x/a`

A. I, II, III, IV, V

B. I, II, III, V, IV

C. I, V, II, III, IV

D. I, V, II, IV, III

E. V, I, II, III, IV

F. V, I, II, VI, III

13. Given:

```
public class MyFileVisitor extends SimpleFileVisitor<Path> {
  // more code here
  public FileVisitResult visitFile(Path file, BasicFileAttributes attrs)
    throws IOException {
    System.out.println("File " + file);
    if ( file.getFileName().endsWith("Test.java")) {
      // CODE HERE
    }
    return FileVisitResult.CONTINUE;
  }
  // more code here
}
```

Which code inserted at `// CODE HERE` would cause the `FileVisitor` to stop visiting files after it sees the file `Test.java`?

A. `return FileVisitResult.CONTINUE;`

B. `return FileVisitResult.END;`

C. `return FileVisitResult.SKIP_SIBLINGS;`

D. `return FileVisitResult.SKIP_SUBTREE;`

E. `return FileVisitResult.TERMINATE;`

F. `return null;`

14. Assume all the files referenced by these paths exist:

```
Path a = Paths.get("c:/temp/dir/a.txt");
Path b = Paths.get("c:/temp/dir/subdir/b.txt");
```

What is the correct string to pass to `PathMatcher` to match both these files?

A. `"glob:*/*.txt"`

B. `"glob:**.txt"`

C. `"glob:*.txt"`

D. `"glob:/*/*.txt"`

E. `"glob:/**.txt"`

F. `"glob:/*.txt"`

G. None of the above

15. Given a partial directory tree at the root of the drive:

```
dir x - |
..........| = file a.txt
..........| - dir y
....................| - file b.txt
....................| - dir y
..............................| - file c.txt
```

And the following snippet:

```
Path dir = Paths.get("c:/x");
try (DirectoryStream<Path> stream = Files.newDirectoryStream(dir, "**/*.txt")) {
for (Path path : stream) {
  System.out.println(path);
} }
```

What is the result?

A. `c:/x/a.txt`

B. `c:/x/a.txt`
`c:/x/y/b.txt`
`c:/x/y/z/c.txt`

C. Code compiles but does not output anything

D. Does not compile because `DirectoryStream` comes from `FileSystems`, not `Files`

E. Does not compile for another reason

16. Given a partial directory tree:

```
dir x - |
..........| - dir y
..........| -file a
```

and given that a valid `Path` object, `dir`, points to `x`, and given this snippet:

```
WatchKey key = dir.register(watcher, ENTRY_CREATE);
```

If a `WatchService` is set using the given `WatchKey`, what would be the result if a file is added to `dir y`?

A. No notice is given

B. A notice related to `dir x` is issued

C. A notice related to `dir y` is issued

D. Notices for both `dir x` and `dir y` are given

E. An Exception is thrown

F. The behavior depends on the underlying operating system

SELF TEST ANSWERS

1. ☑ **Answer:**

```
import java.io.File;
class Maker {
  public static void main(String[] args) {
    try {
      File dir = new File("dir3");
      dir.mkdir();
      File file = new File(dir, "file3");
      file.createNewFile();
    } catch (Exception x) { }
} }
```

Notes: The `new File` statements don't make actual files or directories, just objects. You need the `mkdir()` and `createNewFile()` methods to actually create the directory and the file. While drag-and-drop questions are no longer on the exam, it is still good to be able to complete them. (OCP Objective 7.2)

2. ☑ **A** and **B** are correct. Because you are invoking the program from the directory whose direct subdirectories are to be searched, you don't start your path with a `File.separator` character. The `exists()` method tests for either files or directories; the `isFile()` method tests only for files. Since we're looking for a file, both methods work.
☒ **C** and **D** are incorrect based on the above. (OCP Objective 7.2)

3. ☑ **E** is correct. You need to call `flush()` only when you're writing data. Readers don't have `flush()` methods. If not for the call to `flush()`, answer **C** would be correct.
☒ **A, B, C,** and **D** are incorrect based on the above. (OCP Objective 7.2)

4. ☑ **D** is correct. The `readPassword()` method returns a `char[]`. If a `char[]` were used, answer **B** would be correct.
☒ **A, B, C,** and **E** are incorrect based on the above. (OCP Objective 7.1)

5. ☑ **A** and **B** are correct. `Dodge` instances cannot be serialized because they "have" an instance of `Wheels`, which is not serializable. `Vehicle` instances cannot be serialized even though the subclass `Car` can be.
☒ **C, D,** and **E** are incorrect based on the above. (Pre-OCPJP 7 only)

6. ☑ **E** and **F** are correct since `Paths` must be created using the `Paths.get()` method. This method takes a varargs `String` parameter, so you can pass as many path segments to it as you like.
☒ **A** and **B** are incorrect because you cannot construct a `Path` directly. **C** and **D** are incorrect because the `Files` class works with `Path` objects but does not create them from Strings. (Objective 8.1)

7. ☑ **A** is correct because it prints the path to get to `two` from `one`.
☒ **B** is incorrect because it prints out `../..` which is the path to navigate to one from two. This is the reverse of what we want. **C**, **D**, and **E** are incorrect because it does not make sense to call resolve with absolute paths. They **might** print out `c:/x/c:/x/y/a`, `c:/x/y/a/c:/x`, and `c:/x/y/a/c:/x/y/a`, respectively. **F** is incorrect because of the above. Note that the directory structure provided is redundant. Neither `relativize()` nor `resolve()` requires either path to actually exist. (OCP Objective 8.1)

8. ☑ **E** is correct because a directory containing files or subdirectories is copied or moved in its entirety. Directories can only be deleted if they are empty. Trying to delete a nonempty directory will throw a `DirectoryNotEmptyException`. The question says "usually" because copy and move success depends on file permissions. Think about the most common cases when encountering words such as "usually" on the exam.
☒ **A**, **B**, **C**, **D**, **F**, and **G** are incorrect because of the above. (OCP Objective 8.2)

9. ☑ **B** is correct because, like the Java 7 code, it returns `false` if the file does not exist.
☒ **A** is incorrect because this code throws an Exception if the file does not exist.
C, **D**, **E**, and **F** are incorrect because they do not compile. There is no `deleteOnExit()` method, and file operations such as delete occur using the `Files` class rather than the path object directly. (OCP Objective 8.2)

10. ☑ **A**, **B**, and **D** are correct. Creation time is a basic attribute, which means you can read `BasicFileAttributes` or any of its subclasses to read it. `DosFileAttributes` is one such subclass.
☒ **C** is incorrect because you cannot cast a more general type to a more specific type. **E** is incorrect because this example specifies it is being run on Windows. While it would work on UNIX, it throws an `UnsupportedOperationException` on Windows due to requesting the `WindowsFileSystemProvider` to get a POSIX class. **F** and **G** are incorrect because those methods do not exist. You must use the `Files` class to get the attributes. (OCP Objective 8.3)

11. ☑ **B**, **C**, and **E** are correct. `BasicFileAttributes` is the general superclass. `DosFileAttributes` subclasses `BasicFileAttributes` for Windows operating systems. `PosixFileAttributes` subclasses `BasicFileAttributes` for UNIX/Linux/Mac operating systems.
☒ **A**, **D**, and **F** are incorrect because no such classes exist. (Objective 8.3)

12. ☑ **B** and **C** are correct because file visitor does a depth-first search. When files and directories are at the same level of the file tree, they can be visited in either order. Therefore, "`y`" and "`a`" could be reversed. All of the subdirectories and files are visited before `postVisit` is called on the directory.
☒ **A**, **D**, and **E** are incorrect because of the above. (Objective 8.4)

13. ☑ **E** is correct because it is the correct constant to end the `FileVisitor`.
☒ **B** is incorrect because `END` is not defined as a result constant. **A**, **C**, and **D** are incorrect. While they are valid constants, they do not end file visiting. `CONTINUE` proceeds as if nothing special has happened. `SKIP_SUBTREE` skips the subdirectory, which doesn't even make sense for a Java file. `SKIP_SIBLINGS` would skip any files in the same directory. Since we weren't told what the file structure is, we can't assume there aren't other directories or subdirectories. Therefore, we have to choose the most general answer of `TERMINATE`. **F** is incorrect because file visitor throws a `NullPointerException` if null is returned as the result. (OCP Objective 8.4)

14. ☑ **B** is correct. `**` matches zero or more characters, including multiple directories.
☒ **A** is incorrect because `*/` only matches one directory. It will match "`temp`" but not "`c:/temp`," let alone "`c:/temp/dir`." **C** is incorrect because `*.txt` only matches filenames and not directory paths. **D**, **E**, and **F** are incorrect because the paths we want to match do not begin with a slash. **G** is incorrect because of the above. (Objective 8.5)

15. ☑ **C** is correct because `DirectoryStream` only looks at files in the immediate directory. `**/*.txt` means zero or more directories followed by a slash, followed by zero or more characters followed by `.txt`. Since the slash is in there, it is required to match, which makes it mean one or more directories. However, this is impossible because `DirectoryStream` only looks at one directory. If the expression were simply `*.txt`, answer **A** would be correct.
☒ **A**, **B**, **D**, and **E** are incorrect because of the above. (OCP Objective 8.5)

16. ☑ **A** is correct because watch service only looks at a single directory. If you want to look at subdirectories, you need to set recursive watch keys. This is usually done using a `FileVisitor`.
☒ **B**, **C**, **D**, **E**, and **F** are incorrect because of the above. (OCP Objective 8.6)

10

Advanced OO and Design Patterns

CERTIFICATION OBJECTIVES

- Write Code that Declares, Implements, and/or Extends Interfaces
- Choose Between Interface Inheritance and Class Inheritance
- Apply Cohesion, Low-Coupling, IS-A, and HAS-A Principles
- Apply Object Composition Principles (Including HAS-A Relationships)
- Design a Class Using the Singleton Design Pattern
- Write Code to Implement the DAO Pattern
- Design and Create Objects Using a Factory and Use Factories from the API

✓ Two-Minute Drill

Q&A Self Test

You were introduced to object-oriented (OO) principles in Chapter 2. We will be looking at some more advanced principles here, including coupling and cohesion. You'll also learn what a design pattern is and dip your toe into the world of patterns by exploring three of them. As a bit of a teaser, a design pattern is a reusable solution to problems. Which will come in handy so you aren't reinventing new ways to solve common problems.

CERTIFICATION OBJECTIVE

IS-A and HAS-A (OCP Objectives 3.3 and 3.4)

3.3 *Apply cohesion, low-coupling, IS-A, and HAS-A principles.*

3.4 *Apply object composition principles (including HAS-A relationships).*

You learned the difference between IS-A and HAS-A in Chapter 2. As a brief review, how many IS-A/HAS-A statements can you write about `BeachUmbrella`?

```
class BeachUmbrella extends Umbrella implements SunProtector {
  Stand stand;
}
class Umbrella{}
interface SunProtector {};
class Stand{}
```

We can make four statements about `BeachUmbrella`:

- `BeachUmbrella` IS-A `Umbrella`
- `BeachUmbrella` IS-A `SunProtector`
- `BeachUmbrella` HAS-A `Stand`
- And, of course, as always, `BeachUmbrella` IS-A `Object`

In a nutshell, IS-A happens when a class uses inheritance—e.g., when a class extends another class or implements an interface. HAS-A happens when a class has instance variables of a class.

Coupling and Cohesion

We're going to admit it up front: The Oracle exam's definitions for cohesion and coupling are somewhat subjective, so what we discuss in this chapter is from the perspective of the exam and is by no means The One True Word on these two OO design principles. It may not be exactly the way that you've learned it, but it's what you need to understand to answer the questions. You'll have very few questions about coupling and cohesion on the real exam.

These two topics, coupling and cohesion, have to do with the quality of an OO design. In general, good OO design calls for *loose coupling* and shuns tight coupling, and good OO design calls for *high cohesion* and shuns low cohesion. As with most OO design discussions, the goals for an application are

- Ease of creation
- Ease of maintenance
- Ease of enhancement

Coupling

Let's start by attempting to define coupling. Coupling is the degree to which one class knows about another class. If the only knowledge that class A has about class B is what class B has exposed through its interface, then class A and class B are said to be loosely coupled… that's a good thing. If, on the other hand, class A relies on parts of class B that are not part of class B's interface, then the coupling between the classes is tighter… *not* a good thing. In other words, if A knows more than it should about the way in which B was implemented, then A and B are tightly coupled.

Using this second scenario, imagine what happens when class B is enhanced. It's quite possible that the developer enhancing class B has no knowledge of class A—why would she? Class B's developer ought to feel that any enhancements that don't break the class's interface should be safe, so she might change some noninterface part of the class, which then causes class A to break.

At the far end of the coupling spectrum is the horrible situation in which class A knows non-API stuff about class B, and class B knows non-API stuff about class A—this is REALLY BAD. If either class is ever changed, there's a chance that the other class will break. Let's look at an obvious example of tight coupling that has been enabled by poor encapsulation.

```
class DoTaxes {
  float rate;
  float doColorado() {
    SalesTaxRates str = new SalesTaxRates();
    rate = str.salesRate;            // ouch this should be a method call like:
                                     // rate = str.getSalesRate("CO");
    // do stuff with rate
  }
}

class SalesTaxRates {
  public float salesRate;                       // should be private
  public float adjustedSalesRate;               // should be private

  public float getSalesRate(String region) {
    salesRate = new DoTaxes().doColorado();     // ouch again!
    // do region-based calculations
    return adjustedSalesRate;
  }
}
```

All nontrivial OO applications are a mix of many classes and interfaces working together. Ideally, all interactions between objects in an OO system should use the APIs—in other words, the contracts of the objects' respective classes. Theoretically, if all of the classes in an application have well-designed APIs, then it should be possible for all interclass interactions to use those APIs exclusively. As we discussed in Chapter 2, an aspect of good class and API design is that classes should be well encapsulated.

The bottom line is that coupling is a somewhat subjective concept. Because of this, the exam will test you on really obvious examples of tight coupling; you won't be asked to make subtle judgment calls.

Cohesion

While coupling has to do with how classes interact with each other, cohesion is all about how a single class is designed. The term *cohesion* is used to indicate the degree to which a class has a single, well-focused purpose. Keep in mind that cohesion is a subjective concept. The more focused a class is, the higher its cohesiveness—a good thing. The key benefit of high cohesion is that such classes are typically much easier to maintain (and less frequently changed) than classes with low cohesion. Another benefit of high cohesion is that classes with a well-focused purpose tend to be more reusable than other classes. Let's look at a pseudo-code example:

```
class BudgetReport {
  void connectToRDBMS(){ }
  void generateBudgetReport() { }
  void saveToFile() { }
  void print() { }
}
```

Now imagine your manager comes along and says, "Hey, you know that accounting application we're working on? The clients just decided that they're also going to want to generate a revenue projection report, oh and they want to do some inventory reporting also. They do like our reporting features, however, so make sure that all of these reports will let them choose a database, choose a printer, and save generated reports to data files…." Ouch!

Rather than putting all the printing code into one report class, we probably would have been better off with the following design right from the start:

```
class BudgetReport {
  Options getReportingOptions() { }
  void generateBudgetReport(Options o) { }
}

class RDBMSmanager {
  DBconnection getRDBMS() { }
}

class PrintStuff {
  PrintOptions getPrintOptions() { }
}

class FileSaver {
  SaveOptions getFileSaveOptions() { }
}
```

This design is much more cohesive. Instead of one class that does everything, we've broken the system into four main classes, each with a very specific, or *cohesive*, role. Because we've built these specialized, reusable classes, it'll be much easier to write a new report since we already have the database connection class, the printing class, and the file saver class, and that means they can be reused by other classes that might want to print a report.

CERTIFICATION OBJECTIVE

Object Composition Principles (OCP Objective 3.4)

3.4 *Apply object composition principles.*

Object composition principles build on IS-A and HAS-A. If you aren't 100 percent comfortable with the differences between IS-A and HAS-A, go back and reread Chapter 2 before continuing on.

Object composition refers to one object having another as an instance variable (HAS-A). Sometimes, that instance variable might be the same type as the object we are writing. Think about when you get that package from Amazon that is a box containing some bubble wrap, a receipt, and yet another box. That is composition at work. The outer (containing class) box contains an inner (instance) box.

Let's build out this box example. We want to reuse as much code as possible. After all, the procedure for sealing a box with some tape doesn't change from box to box. Let's start with the concept of a `Box`:

```
public interface Box {
  void pack();
  void seal();
}
```

Wait. Boxes are simple. Why do we need an interface? We realize there are many types of boxes. There are gift boxes, jewelry boxes, small boxes, large boxes, etc. Now we create a concrete type of `Box`:

```
public class GiftBox implements Box {
  public void pack() {                        // from
    System.out.println("pack box");           // interface
  }
  public void seal() {                        // from
    System.out.println("seal box");           // interface
  }
}
```

`GiftBox` implements `Box` by implementing the two methods `Box` requires. Providing an interface lets us keep the `Box` logic where it belongs—in the relevant subclasses. And to review, `GiftBox` IS-A `Box`.

Now that we've figured out `Box`, it's time to build a `MailerBox`:

```
public class MailerBox implements Box {
  public void pack() {
    System.out.println("pack box");
  }
  public void seal() {
    System.out.println("seal box");
  }
  public void addPostage() {
    System.out.println("affix stamps");
  }
  public void ship() {
    System.out.println("put in mailbox");
  }
}
```

See any problems? That's right, we've duplicated the logic to pack and seal the `Box`. All two lines of it. Our real `Box` logic would be a lot longer, though. And when we start manufacturing different types of boxes, we'd have that `Box` logic all over the place.

One thought is to solve this by having `MailerBox` extend `GiftBox`. It doesn't take long to see the problem here. We would need `MailerGiftBox`, `MailerSmallBox`, `MailerMediumBox`, etc. That's a lot of classes! And this technique would repeat for other types of functionality we create. Which means we would also need `WrappedGiftBox`, `MailerWrappedGiftBox`. Uh oh. We can only extend one class in Java. We can't inherit both `Mailer` and `GiftBox` functionality. Clearly, IS-A isn't going to work for us here.

Instead, we can use HAS-A. First, we create the interface for our desired functionality:

```
public interface Mailer {
  void addPostage();
  void ship();
}
```

Then we can create the object that is both a `Box` and `Mailer`:

```
public class MailerBox implements Box, Mailer {
  private Box box;
  public MailerBox(Box box) {                     // pass in a Box
    this.box = box;
  }
  public void pack() {                            // from Box
    box.pack();                                   // delegate to box
  }
  public void seal() {                            // from Box
    box.seal();                                   // delegate to box
  }
  public void addPostage() {                      // from Mailer
    System.out.println("affix stamps");
  }
  public void ship() {                            // from Mailer
    System.out.println("put in mailbox");
  }
}
```

The first thing to notice is that the logic to pack and seal a box is only in one place—in the `Box` hierarchy where it belongs. In fact, the `MailerBox` doesn't even know what kind of `Box` it has. This allows us to be very flexible.

Next, notice the implementation of `pack()` and `seal()`. That's right—each is one line. We delegate to `Box` to actually do the work. This is called method forwarding or method delegation. These two terms mean the same thing.

Finally, notice that `MailerBox` is both a `Box` and a `Mailer`. This allows us to pass it to any method that needs a `Box` or a `Mailer`.

Polymorphism

Looking at these classes graphically, we have the following:

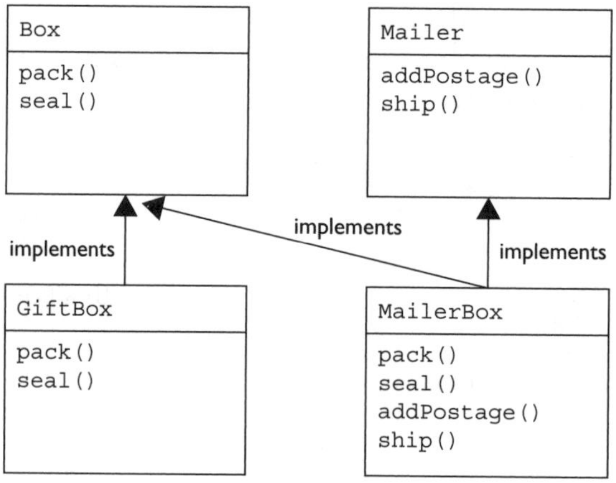

Box
pack()
seal()

Mailer
addPostage()
ship()

implements
implements
implements

GiftBox
pack()
seal()

MailerBox
pack()
seal()
addPostage()
ship()

Think about which of the objects can be passed to this method:

```
public void load(Box b) {
  b.pack();
}
```

`GiftBox` can because it implements `Box`. So can `MailerBox` for the same reason. `MailerBox` knows how to pack—by delegating to the `Box` instance. This is why it is important for the composing class to both contain and implement the same interface. Repeating the relevant parts here, we have:

```
public class MailerBox implements Box, Mailer {
  private Box box;
```

You can see the composition part. `MailerBox` both IS-A `Box` and HAS-A `Box`. `MailerBox` is composed of a `Box` and delegates to `Box` for logic. That's the terminology for object composition.

Benefits of Composition

Benefits of composition include

- **Reuse** An object can delegate to another object rather than repeating the same code.
- **Preventing a proliferation of subclasses** We can have one class per functionality rather than needing one for every combination of functionalities.

CERTIFICATION OBJECTIVE

Singleton Design Pattern (OCP Objective 3.5)

3.5 Design a class using the singleton design pattern.

In a nutshell, the singleton design pattern ensures we only have one instance of a class of an object within the application. It's called a creational design pattern because it deals with creating objects. But wait, what's this "design pattern"?

What Is a Design Pattern?

Wikipedia currently defines a design pattern as "a general reusable solution to a commonly occurring problem within a given context." What does that mean? As programmers, we frequently need to solve the same problem repeatedly. Such as how to only have one of a class of an object in the application. Rather than have everyone come up with their own solution, we use a "best practice" type solution that has been documented and proven to work. The word "general" is important. We can't just copy and paste a design pattern into our code. It's just an idea. We can write an implementation for it and put that in our code.

Using a design pattern has a few advantages. We get to use a solution that is known to work. The tradeoffs, if any, are well documented so we don't stumble over problems that have already been solved. Design patterns also serve as a communication aid. Your boss can say, "We will use a singleton," and that one word is enough to tell you what is expected.

When books or web pages document patterns, they do so using consistent sections. In this book, we have sections for the "Problem," "Solution," and "Benefits." The "Problem" section explains why we need the pattern—what problem we are trying to solve. The "Solution" section explains how to implement the pattern. The "Benefits" section reviews why we need the pattern and how it has helped us solve the problem. Some of the benefits are hinted at in the "Problem" section. Others are additional benefits that come from the pattern.

on the job

While the exam only covers three patterns, this is just to get your feet wet. Whole books are written on the topic of design patterns. *Head First Design Patterns* ***(O'Reilly Media, 2004) covers more patterns. And the most famous book on patterns,*** *Design Patterns: Elements of Reusable Object-Oriented Software* ***(Addison-Wesley Professional, 1994)—also known as "Gang of Four"—covers 23 design patterns. You may notice that these books are over 10 years old. That's because the classic patterns haven't changed.***

While each book does use a consistent set of sections, there isn't one common set of names. You will see synonyms used such as "Problem" versus "Motivation." You will also see additional sections such as "Consequences." The exam picks simpler patterns so you can use the simpler sections.

When talking about patterns, they are usually presented in a problem/solution format. Then, depending on the level of detail, other sections are added. In this book, each pattern will cover the problem, solution, and benefits.

Problem

Let's suppose we are going to put on a show. We have one performance of this show and we only have a few seats in the theater.

```
import java.util.*;

public class Show {

  private Set<String> availableSeats;

  public Show() {
    availableSeats = new HashSet<String>();
    availableSeats.add("1A");
    availableSeats.add("1B");
  }
  public boolean bookSeat(String seat) {
    return availableSeats.remove(seat);
  }
```

```
    public static void main(String[] args) {
      ticketAgentBooks("1A");
      ticketAgentBooks("1A");
    }
      private static void ticketAgentBooks(String seat) {
      Show show = new Show();                 // a new Show gets created
                                              // each time we call the method
      System.out.println(show.bookSeat(seat));
    }
  }
```

This code prints out `true` twice. That's a problem. We just put two people in the same seat. Why? We created a new `Show` object every time we needed it. Even though we want to use the same theater and seats, `Show` deals with a new set of seats each time. Which causes us to double-book seats.

Solution

There are a few ways to implement the singleton pattern. The simplest is

```
import java.util.*;

public class Show {
  private static final Show INSTANCE  // store one instance
          = new Show();               // (this is the singleton)
  private Set<String> availableSeats;

  public static Show getInstance() { // callers can get to
    return INSTANCE;                 // the instance
  }
  private Show() {                   // callers can't create
                                     // directly anymore.
                                     // Must use getInstance()
  availableSeats = new HashSet<String>();
  availableSeats.add("1A");
  availableSeats.add("1B");
    }
  public boolean bookSeat(String seat) {
    return availableSeats.remove(seat);
    }
  public static void main(String[] args) {
    ticketAgentBooks("1A");
    ticketAgentBooks("1A");
  }
  private static void ticketAgentBooks(String seat) {
    Show show = Show.getInstance();
    System.out.println(show.bookSeat(seat));
  }
}
```

Now the code prints `true` and `false`. Much better! We are no longer going to have two people in the same seat. The bolded bits in the code call attention to the implementation of the singleton pattern.

The key parts of the singleton pattern are

- A private static variable to store the single instance called the singleton. This variable is usually final to keep developers from accidentally changing it.
- A public static method for callers to get a reference to the instance.
- A private constructor so no callers can instantiate the object directly.

Remember, the code doesn't create a new `Show` each time, but merely returns the singleton instance of `Show` each time `getInstance()` is called.

To understand this a little better, consider what happens if we change parts of the code.

If the constructor weren't private, we wouldn't have a singleton. Callers would be free to ignore `getInstance()` and instantiate their own instances. Which would leave us with multiple instances in the program and defeat the purpose entirely.

If `getInstance()` weren't public, we would still have a singleton. However, it wouldn't be as useful because only static methods of the class `Show` would be able to use the singleton.

If `getInstance()` weren't static, we'd have a bigger problem. Callers couldn't instantiate the class directly, which means they wouldn't be able to call `getInstance()` at all.

If `INSTANCE` weren't static and final, we could have multiple instances at different points in time. These keywords signal that we assign the field once and it stays that way for the life of the program.

When talking about design patterns, it is common to also communicate the pattern in diagram form. The singleton pattern diagram looks like this:

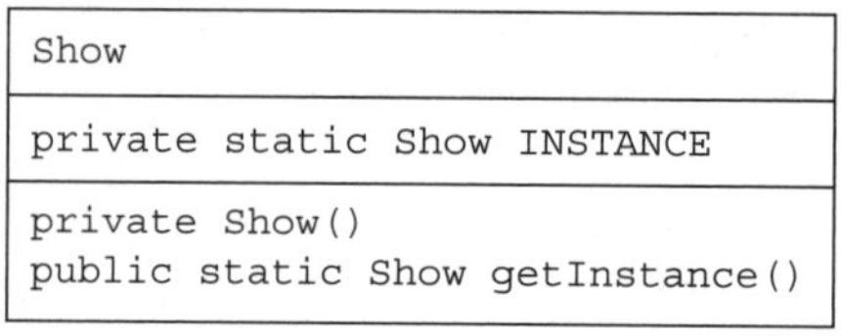

Show
private static Show INSTANCE
private Show() public static Show getInstance()

on the Job

A format called UML (Unified Modeling Language) is used. The diagrams in this book use some aspects of UML, such as a box with three sections representing each class. Actual UML uses more notation, such as showing public versus private visibility. You can think of this as faux-UML.

As long as the method in the diagram keeps the same signature, we can change our logic to other implementations of the singleton pattern. One "feature" of the above implementation is that it creates the `Show` object before we need it. This is called eager initialization, which is good if the object isn't expensive to create or we know it will be needed for every run of the program. Sometimes, however, we want to create the object only on the first use. This is called lazy initialization.

```
  private static Show INSTANCE;
private Set<String> availableSeats;
public static Show getInstance() {
  if (INSTANCE == null) {
    INSTANCE = new Show();
  }
  return INSTANCE;
}
```

In this case, `INSTANCE` isn't set to be a `Show` until the first time `getInstance()` is called. Walking through what happens, the first time `getInstance()` is called, Java sees `INSTANCE` is still null and creates the singleton. The second time `getInstance()` is called, Java sees `INSTANCE` has already been set and simply returns it. In this example, `INSTANCE` isn't final because that would prevent the code from compiling.

on the Job

The singleton code here assumes you are only running one thread at a time. It is NOT thread-safe. Think about if this were a web site and two users managed to be booking a seat at the exact same time. If `getInstance()` were running at the exact same time, it would be possible for both of them to see that INSTANCE was null and create a new `Show` at the same time. There are a few ways to solve this. One is to add `synchronized` to the `getInstance()` method. This works, but comes with a small performance hit. We're getting way beyond the scope of the exam, but you can Google "double checked locked pattern" for more information.

You might have noticed that the code for `getInstance()` can get a bit complicated. In Java 5, there became a much shorter way of creating a singleton:

```
public enum ShowEnum {                    // this is an enum
  INSTANCE;                               // instead of a class

  private Set<String> availableSeats;
  private ShowEnum() {
    availableSeats = new HashSet<String>();
    availableSeats.add("1A");
    availableSeats.add("1B");
  }
  public boolean bookSeat(String seat) {
    return availableSeats.remove(seat);
  }
  public static void main(String[] args) {
    ticketAgentBooks("1A");
    ticketAgentBooks("1A");
  }

  private static void ticketAgentBooks(String seat) {
    ShowEnum show = ShowEnum.INSTANCE;    // we don't even
                                          // need a method to
                                          // get the instance
    System.out.println(show.bookSeat(seat));
  }

}
```

Short and sweet. By definition, there is only one instance of an enum constant. You are probably wondering why we've had this whole discussion of the singleton pattern when it can be written so easily. The main reason is that enums were introduced with Java 5 and there is a ton of older code out there that you need to be able to understand. Another reason is that sometimes the older versions of the pattern are still needed.

Benefits

Benefits of the singleton pattern include the following:

- The primary benefit is that there is only one instance of the object in the program. When an object's instance variables are keeping track of information that is used across the program, this becomes useful. For example, consider a web site visitor counter. You only want one count that is shared.
- Another benefit is performance. Some objects are expensive to create. For example, maybe we need to make a database call to look up the state for the object.

CERTIFICATION OBJECTIVE

DAO Design Pattern (OCP Objective 3.6)

3.6 *Write code to implement the DAO pattern.*

DAO stands for "Data Access Object." A DAO is only responsible for storing data. Nothing else. Why can't we do this in the object with everything else, you ask?

Suppose we have three objects in our program as shown in Table 10-1.

Already there is a problem. These classes aren't cohesive. Remember cohesion? We want each class to have a single purpose. Storing and searching objects in the database is NOT that purpose. Having that database code all over makes it hard to focus on the classes' core purpose for existing, which is clearly for our entertainment. Since dealing with a database is very common, separating out that responsibility is a pattern—the DAO.

Problem

Let's drill down into just the `Book` class. This is the poorly written, noncohesive version. Pay particular attention to the two responsibilities.

```
import java.util.*;
public class Book {
  private static Map<String, Book> bookstore // storage: extra
     = new HashMap<String, Book>();          // responsibility

  private String isbn;                       // core responsibility:
  private String title;                      // book instance
  private String author;                     // variables

  public Collection<Book> findAllBooks() {   // more storage
    return bookstore.values();               // extra responsibility
  }
  public Book findBookByIsbn(String isbn) {  // more storage
    return bookstore.get(isbn);
  }
  public void create() {
    bookstore.put(isbn, this);
  }
  public void delete() {                     // still more storage
    bookstore.remove(isbn);
  }
  public void update() {                     // yet still more storage
    // no operation - for an in-memory database,
    // we update automatically in real time
  }
  // omitted getters and setters
}
```

TABLE 10-1 Object Responsibilities

Object	Responsibilities	Still More Responsibilities
Book	Store book information, be read	Store and search in database
CD	Store CD information, be listened to	Store and search in database
DVD	Store DVD information, be watched	Store and search in database

Counting the getters and setters we didn't want to bore you with, the `Book` class is over 50 lines. And it hardly does anything! A real `Book` class would have a lot more fields. A bookstore needs to tell you when the book was written, the edition, the price, and all sorts of other information. A bookstore also needs to be able to keep track of books somewhere other than a map. After all, we don't want our bookstore to forget everything when we reboot.

The problem is that our class is responsible for two things. The first is keeping track of being a book. This seems like a good responsibility for a class to have that is named `Book`. The other is keeping track of storage responsibilities.

A datastore is the name of—wait for it—where data is stored. In the real world, we'd use a database or possibly a file containing the books. For testing, we might use an in-memory database. The map in `Book` is actually a bare-bones in-memory datastore. As you'll see in Chapter 15, using a real database would make the `Book` class MUCH longer.

This is a problem. We want our code to be easy to read and focused on one responsibility.

Solution

The DAO pattern has us split up these two responsibilities. We start by letting our `Book` class focus on being a book:

```
public class Book {
  private String isbn;          // core responsibility:
  private String title;         // book instance
  private String author;        // variables

  // omitted getters and setters
}
```

There can be other methods in `Book` such as `toString()`, `hashCode()`, and `equals()`. These methods have to do with the `Book` object. Methods that have to do with a bookstore or database are now gone. Much better. Now we can go on to the data access code:

```
import java.util.*;

public class InMemoryBookDao {

  private static Map<String, Book> bookstore  // storage:
          = new HashMap<String, Book>();      // core responsibility

  public Collection<Book> findAllBooks() {
    return bookstore.values();
  }
  public Book findBookByIsbn(Book book) {
    return bookstore.get(book.getIsbn());
  }
  public void create(Book book) {
    bookstore.put(book.getIsbn(), book);
  }
  public void delete(Book book) {
    bookstore.remove(book.getIsbn());
  }
  public void update(Book book) {
                                  // no operation - for an in-memory
                                  // database,
                                  // we update automatically in real time
  } }
```

The new `InMemoryBookDao` class only knows how to do one thing—deal with the datastore. This is such a common technique that it has a name: the single responsibility principle. The method names in the DAO are actually standard. You'll see them again when you get to Chapter 15.

When everything was in the `Book` object, we just created a `Book` and started calling methods. Now that `Book` and DAO are separate objects, the caller deals with two objects:

```
public class Student {
  public static void main(String[] args) {
    BookDao dao = new BookDao();        // dao
    Book book = new Book();
    // call setters
    dao.create(book);                   // dao - storage
    book.setTitle("Updated");
    dao.update(book);                   // dao - storage
    dao.delete(book);                   // dao - storage
  } }
```

The new DAO object gets all the calls that have to do with the datastore. Table 10-2 shows why each method call is associated with each class.

TABLE 10-2 DAO Method Call Associations

	Book	DAO
`dao.create(book)`		Deals with datastore
`book.setTitle("updated")`	Changes a Book instance variable	
`dao.update(book)`		Deals with datastore
`dao.delete(book)`		Deals with datastore

Good so far? The DAO pattern only has one more part. Our datastore is pretty wimpy right now. Every time we restart the program, it forgets what books we have. At some point, we are going to want to change that. But when we do, we want to make it easier for callers to change.

It's time to add an interface!

```
import java.util.*;

public interface BookDao {
  Collection<Book> findAllBooks();
  Book findBookByIsbn(Book book);
  void create(Book book);
  void delete(Book book);
  void update(Book book);
}
```

Since all the method names in the interface match our existing DAO, all we have to do is have it implement the new interface:

```
public class InMemoryBookDao implements BookDao {
```

And we can use the interface type when declaring the DAO:

```
BookDao dao = new InMemoryBookDao();
```

Wait a minute. We still have `InMemoryBookDao` in the line of code that instantiates the DAO. It is a bit like writing `Collection c = new ArrayList();`. It just so happens to be an `ArrayList` right now, but we could change it at any time. It is a bit like signifying that the surrounding code shouldn't get too cozy with any particular implementation. We can always change the specific DAO implementation later without changing the interface. And we will learn in the next section how to get rid of even the one reference to `InMemoryBookDao`.

To review the classes involved in the DAO pattern, we have the following illustration:

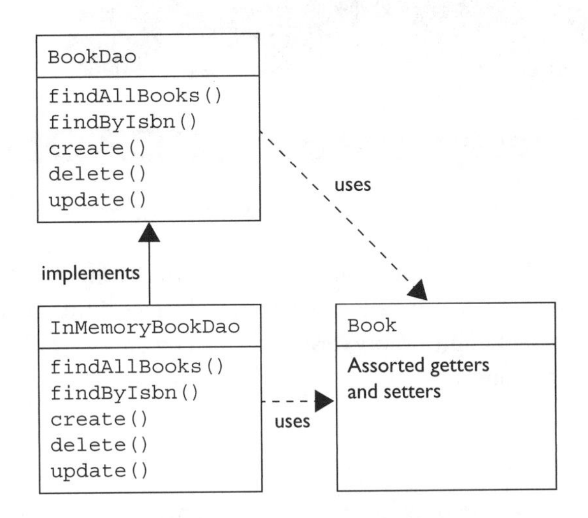

Now we have three objects, each responsible for one thing. We have the public interface `BookDao`, which specifies the contract. Next, we have the implementation of that interface, `InMemoryBookDao`. Finally, we have the `Book` class itself, which focuses on the object state and any methods related to `Book`.

on the job

In addition to making the code easier to read, this pattern makes it easy for us to organize code. We could put all the JavaBeans in one package, the interfaces in another package, and the implementations in still another package. This approach allows us to have one package for in-memory implementations and another for JDBC implementations.

Benefits

To review, the benefits of the DAO pattern are as follows:

- The main object (`Book` in this case) is cohesive and doesn't have database code cluttering it up.
- All the database code is in one part of the program, making it easy to find.
- We can change the database implementation without changing the business object.
- Reuse is easier. As the database code grows, we can create helper classes and even helper superclasses.

CERTIFICATION OBJECTIVE

Factory Design Pattern (OCP Objective 3.7)

3.7 Design and create objects using a factory and use factories from the API.

Like the singleton design pattern, the factory design pattern is a creational design pattern. Unlike the singleton, it doesn't limit you to only having one copy of an object. The factory design pattern creates new objects of whatever implementation it chooses.

Problem

So far, we only have one implementation of our `BookDAO` called `InMemoryBookDao`. It isn't very robust since it only stores objects in memory. We will need to create a version of it that uses JDBC or writes to a file or does something else where we can remember state. We want to be able to change the DAO implementation without having to change the caller code (`Student`). Remember coupling? This is loose coupling. Interfaces are part of loose coupling, but we want to go a step further.

Solution

The simplest factory we can write while still implementing the pattern is an abstract class and implementation with one method:

```
public abstract class Factory {
  public abstract BookDao createDao();
}
public class FactoryImpl extends Factory {
  public BookDao createDao() {           // right now, we only
    return new InMemoryBookDao();        // have one DAO
  }
}
public class Student {
  public static void main(String[] args) {
    Factory factory = new FactoryImpl();
    BookDao dao = factory.createDao();   // create the DAO
    // work with dao
  }
}
```

This is very simple. The `Factory` is an abstract class with one method. Its implementation simply returns an in-memory DAO. From `Student`'s point of view, this is all that exists—the `Factory` class and the `BookDao` interface. Note that `Student` no longer has the code `new InMemoryBookDao`.

In diagram form, here is how our classes fit together:

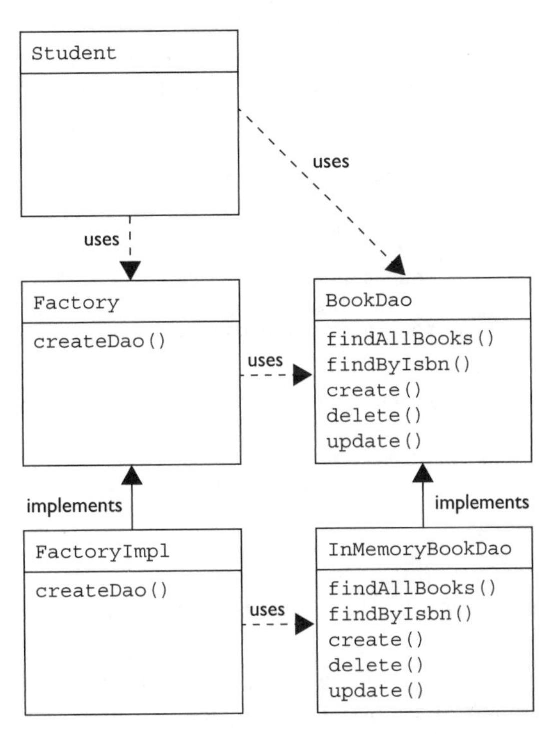

To review, `Student` only interacts with the two abstract classes `Factory` and `BookDao`. All implementation is in the concrete subclasses.

This setup frees us up to change the implementation of `FactoryImpl` without affecting the caller.

Let's try an example to show how we can change the factory. Suppose we write a DAO implementation `OracleBookDao` that uses a real database. We might change `FactoryImpl` to:

```
public class FactoryImpl extends Factory {     // factory subclass
  public BookDao createDao() {
    if (Util.isTestMode()) {
      return new InMemoryBookDao();            // for test
    } else {
      return new OracleBookDao();              // for real
    }
  }
}
```

Just like that—nothing changes in `Student`. Yet it starts using the real database implementation. This is good design. A change only needs to be made in one place.

You might be wondering why `Factory` is an abstract class rather than an interface. It is common with the factory method pattern to work "around" the creation logic, or at least recognize that it might happen later.

As an example here, we could decide that we want to include the test logic check in the superclass so any future subclasses use it:

```
public abstract class Factory {

  public BookDao createDao() {
    if (Util.isTestMode()) {
      return new InMemoryBookDao();
    } else {
      return createDatabaseBookDao();        // for subclass
    }                                        // to implement
  }
  protected abstract BookDao createDatabaseBookDao();
}
public class FactoryImpl extends Factory {
  protected BookDao createDatabaseBookDao() {    // fills in the
    return new OracleBookDao();                  // missing part
  }
}
```

In this case, the superclass `Factory` has all the common logic, and the subclass `FactoryImpl` merely creates the relevant object. Notice how the API `createDao()` hasn't changed its signature at all despite our extensive changes to the method implementation. That is why we are using the factory pattern. So the caller `Student` isn't affected by any changes to our factory and DAO.

on the job

There are three patterns with factory in their name:

- ***`Factory`* method** ***This is the pattern we are talking about in this chapter and is on the exam.***
- **Abstract factory** ***This takes the factory method pattern a bit further and is used to create families of related classes.***
- **Factory** ***It's debatable whether this is even a pattern. It's not in the "Gang of Four" book. However, on the job, when developers say "factory," they are often referring to a method like***
  `public Foo createFoo() {return new Foo(); }`
  rather than a full-fledged factory method pattern. The method may return* *`Foo`* or *`SubclassOfFoo`*, *but it doesn't have the superclass/subclass relationship for the creator object that the factory method pattern has.

You might have noticed we didn't say anything about making the DAO constructors private. In the singleton pattern, we needed to force callers to use `getInstance()` to prevent multiple copies. The factory pattern is merely a convenience. At times, it is a pretty big convenience. However, callers can still instantiate the DAO directly without breaking our logic, so we let them.

In fact, Oracle uses the factory pattern in the Java API in many places. When we learned how to create a `DateFormat`, we used `DateFormat.getInstance()`, `DateFormat.getDateInstance()`, and other similar factory methods. If you wanted more control over the format string, you could still write `new SimpleDateFormat("yyyy MM")`. Oracle leaves the constructor available for when you need it.

Similarly, when we learned how to create a `Calendar`, we wrote `Calendar.getInstance()` or `Calendar.getInstance(Locale)`. You will see many more examples of the factory pattern as you explore the Java API.

Benefits

Benefits of the factory design pattern include the following

- The caller doesn't change when the factory returns different subclasses. This is useful when the final implementation isn't ready yet. For example, maybe the database isn't yet available. It's also useful when we want to use different implementations for unit testing and production code. For example, you want to write code that behaves the same way, regardless of what happens to be in the database.
- Centralizes creation logic outside the calling class. This prevents duplication and makes the code more cohesive.
- Allows for extra logic in the object creation process. For example, an object is time-consuming to create, and you want to reuse the same one each time.

CERTIFICATION SUMMARY

We started the chapter by reviewing the difference between IS-A and HAS-A. To review the review, IS-A is implemented using inheritance, and HAS-A is implemented using instance variables that refer to other objects.

We discussed the OO concepts of coupling and cohesion. Loose coupling is the desirable state of two or more classes that interact with each other only through their respective APIs. Tight coupling is the undesirable state of two or more classes that know inside details about another class, details not revealed in the class's API. High cohesion is the desirable state of a single class whose purpose and responsibilities are limited and well focused.

Then we built on those concepts and learned about object composition principles. In particular, we learned how to build objects out of other objects. We saw how method delegation and method forwarding prevent the need to duplicate code. For example:

```
public class MailerBox implements Box {
  private Box box;
      ...
  public void pack() { box.pack(); }
```

Next, we moved on to design patterns. We learned that design patterns are reusable solutions to common problems.

We saw the singleton pattern used to ensure we only have one instance of a given class within the application. We created a private static variable to store the single instance, which we called the singleton. We then created a public static method for callers to get a reference to the instance. Finally, we made the constructor private so no callers can instantiate the object directly.

We also looked at the DAO design pattern. DAO stands for Data Access Object and provides a way to separate database functionality from the main business object. We saw how using an interface allows us to easily change the data access implementation. A DAO interface typically looks like this:

```
public interface BookDao {
  void create(Book book);
  void delete(Book book);
  ...
}
```

Finally, we looked at the factory design pattern as another way of creating objects. We learned how to create an abstract and concrete factory object. We also saw that we could have common logic in the abstract class. For example:

```
public abstract class Factory {
  public BookDao createDao() {
     BookDao dao = createDatabaseBookDao();
           // more setup on DAO
           return dao;
  }
  public abstract BookDao createDatabaseBookDao();
}
public class FactoryImpl extends Factory {
  public BookDao createDatabaseBookDao() {
    return new OracleBookDao();
  }
}
```

✓ TWO-MINUTE DRILL

Here are some of the key points from each certification objective in this chapter.

IS-A/HAS-A (OCP Objective 3.3)

- ❑ IS-A refers to inheritance.
- ❑ IS-A is expressed with either the keyword `extends` or `implements`.
- ❑ IS-A, "inherits from," and "is a subtype of" are all equivalent expressions.
- ❑ HAS-A means an instance of one class "has a" reference to an instance of another class or another instance of the same class.

Coupling and Cohesion (OCP Objective 3.3)

- ❑ Coupling refers to the degree to which one class knows about or uses members of another class.
- ❑ Loose coupling is the desirable state of having classes that are well encapsulated, minimize references to each other, and limit the breadth of API usage.
- ❑ Tight coupling is the undesirable state of having classes that break the rules of loose coupling.
- ❑ Cohesion refers to the degree to which a class has a single well-defined role or responsibility.
- ❑ High cohesion is the desirable state of a class whose members support a single well-focused role or responsibility.
- ❑ Low cohesion is the undesirable state of a class whose members support multiple unfocused roles or responsibilities.

Object Composition Principles (OCP Objective 3.4)

- ❑ Object composition takes advantage of IS-A, HAS-A, and polymorphism.
- ❑ Object composition prevents proliferation of subclasses by having each class responsible for one thing.

- Object composition delegates to objects to which it "has" to implement functionality.
- The terms *method forwarding* and *method delegation* are used interchangeably.

Singleton Design Pattern (OCP Objective 3.5)

- Design pattern is "a general reusable solution to a commonly occurring problem within a given context."
- Having only one instance of the object allows a program to share its state.
- This pattern might improve performance by not repeating the same work.
- This pattern often stores a single instance as a static variable.
- We can instantiate right away (eager) or when needed (lazy).

DAO Design Pattern (OCP Objective 3.6)

- DAO stands for Data Access Object.
- DAO separates datastore responsibilities from the core responsibilities of the object.
- DAO uses an interface so we can change the implementation.
- DAO is only responsible for database operations. The main object remains cohesive.
- DAO facilitates reuse.

Factory Design Pattern (OCP Objective 3.7)

- Factory is a creational design pattern.
- Factory can create any subclass of an interface or abstract class.
- `Factory` is an abstract class.
- Factory subclassing allows for multiple factories.
- The factory method return type is an interface or abstract class.
- Factory method implementation returns subclasses of the target object.
- There may be common logic in the abstract class that all factory subclasses share.

SELF TEST

The following questions will help you measure your understanding of the material presented in this chapter. Read all of the choices carefully, as there may be more than one correct answer. Choose all correct answers for each question. Stay focused.

1. Given:

```
class A extends B {
  C tail;
}
```

Which is true?

A. A HAS-A B and A HAS-A C

B. A HAS-A B and A IS-A C

C. A IS-A B and A HAS-A C

D. A IS-A B and A IS-A C

E. B IS-A A and A-HAS-A C

F. B IS-A A and A IS-A C

2. Which statements are true? (Choose all that apply.)

A. Method delegation relies on IS-A relationships

B. Method forwarding relies on HAS-A relationships

C. The DAO pattern limits you to one instance of the DAO object

D. The singleton pattern relies on IS-A relationships

E. To use object composition, classes must be final

3. Given:

```
public class F {
  private static final F f = new F();
  public static F c() {
    return f;
  }
  public void update(F a) { }

  public void delete(F a) { }
}
```

Which design pattern or principle is implemented?

A. Coupling

B. DAO

C. Factory
D. IS-A
E. Object composition
F. Singleton

4. Given:

```
public class E {
  private D d;
  public void m() {
    d.m();
  }
     public static E getInstance() {
    return new E();
  }
}
class D {
  public void m() {}
}
```

Which design pattern or principle is implemented?

A. DAO
B. Factory
C. IS-A
D. Object composition
E. Singleton

5. Given:

```
class A {}

abstract class G {
 A m() { return n(); }
 abstract A n() ;
}
```

Which design pattern or principle is implemented?

A. DAO
B. Factory
C. IS-A
D. Object composition
E. Singleton

6. Which design patterns are classified as creational design patterns? (Choose all that apply.)
   A. Coupling
   B. DAO
   C. Factory
   D. IS-A
   E. Object composition
   F. Singleton

7. Which statements indicate the need to use the factory pattern? (Choose all that apply.)
   A. You don't want the caller to depend on a specific implementation
   B. You have two classes that do the same thing
   C. You only want one instance of the object to exist
   D. You want one class to be responsible for database operations
   E. You want to build a chain of objects

8. Given:

```
public class Dao {
  Collection<String> findAll() { return null;}
  void create(String a) {}
  void delete(String a) {}
  void update(String a){}
}
```

   And the following statements:

   I – This is a good use of the DAO pattern

   II – The DAO needs an interface

   III – The DAO is missing a method

   IV – The DAO must use a type other than `String`

   Which of these statements are true?
   A. Statement I only
   B. Statement II only
   C. Statement III only
   D. Statement IV only
   E. Statements II and III
   F. Statements III and IV

9. Which is a benefit of the DAO pattern? (Choose all that apply.)

- A. Reuse is easier
- B. The database code is automatically generated
- C. We can change the database implementation independently
- D. Your business object extends the DAO pattern to reduce coding
- E. You are limited to one DAO object

10. Which are true of design patterns? (Choose all that apply.)

- A. Design patterns are chunks of code you can copy into your application unchanged
- B. Design patterns are conceptual reusable solutions
- C. Design patterns are shortcuts to talking about code
- D. There are three design patterns defined for Java
- E. You can only use each design pattern once per application
- F. Design patterns are libraries you can call from your code

11. Which statement is true? (Choose all that apply.)

- A. Cohesion is the OO principle most closely associated with hiding implementation details
- B. Cohesion is the OO principle most closely associated with making sure that classes know about other classes only through their APIs
- C. Cohesion is the OO principle most closely associated with making sure that a class is designed with a single well-focused purpose
- D. Cohesion is the OO principle most closely associated with allowing a single object to be seen as having many types

12. Given:

1) `ClassA` has a `ClassD`
2) Methods in `ClassA` use public methods in `ClassB`
3) Methods in `ClassC` use public methods in `ClassA`
4) Methods in `ClassA` use public variables in `ClassB`

Which is most likely true? (Choose only one.)

- A. `ClassD` has low cohesion.
- B. `ClassA` has weak encapsulation.
- C. `ClassB` has weak encapsulation.
- D. `ClassB` has strong encapsulation.
- E. `ClassC` is tightly coupled to `ClassA`.

SELF TEST ANSWERS

1. ☑ **C** is correct. Since `A` extends `B`, it IS-A `B`. Since `C` is an instance variable in `A`, `A` HAS-A `C`.
   ☒ **A, B, D, E,** and **F** are incorrect because of the above. (OCP Objective 3.3)

2. ☑ **B** is correct. Method forwarding is an object composition principle and calls methods on an instance variable of an object.
   ☒ **A** is incorrect because method delegation and method forwarding are the same thing. **C** is incorrect because it is the singleton pattern that limits you to one object. **D** is incorrect because singleton classes typically don't have a superclass (other than `Object`). **E** is incorrect because there is no such requirement. (OCP Objective 3.4)

3. ☑ **F** is correct. The singleton pattern is identifiable by the static variable for the single instance and the accessor returning it.
   ☒ **B** is incorrect because there is no interface. The class just happens to have methods `update()` and `delete()`, which are similar to those found in a DAO. **A, C, D,** and **E** are incorrect because of the above. (OCP Objective 3.5)

4. ☑ **D** is correct. The object composition principle of method forwarding is shown.
   ☒ **E** is tricky, but incorrect. Although `getInstance()` is a common name for a method in a singleton, the method doesn't return a static object. While it does create an object, it isn't a factory either, since there is no superclass. **A, B,** and **C** are incorrect because of the above. (OCP Objective 3.4)

5. ☑ **B** is correct. Class A is the object we are creating using the factory method. Class G is the abstract superclass for the factory. Not shown is a class implementing class G that actually creates the object.
   ☒ **A, C, D,** and **E** are incorrect because of the above. (OCP Objective 3.7)

6. ☑ **C** and **F** are correct. The factory design pattern creates new objects for each call, and the singleton design pattern creates one object, returning it each time.
   ☒ **A, B, D,** and **E** are incorrect because of the above. (OCP Objectives 3.5 and 3.7)

7. ☑ **A** is correct. The factory design pattern decouples the caller from the implementation class name.
   ☒ **B** is incorrect because that would be poor design. **C** is incorrect because it describes the singleton pattern. **D** is incorrect because it describes the DAO pattern. **E** is incorrect because of the above. (OCP Objective 3.7)

8. ☑ **B** is correct. The Data Access Object pattern uses an interface so callers aren't dependent on a specific implementation class.
   ☒ **A, C, D, E,** and **F** are incorrect because of the above. (OCP Objective 3.6)

9. ☑ **A** and **C** are correct. The DAO pattern centralizes logic for the data access code, making reuse easier and allowing you to switch out implementations.
☒ **B** is incorrect because you still have to code the DAO. **D** is incorrect because you call a DAO from your business object; you do not inherit from it. **E** is incorrect because you can have many DAO objects. (OCP Objective 3.6)

10. ☑ **B** and **C** are correct. Design patterns are conceptual and design level. You have to code the implementation for each use.
☒ **D** is incorrect because there are dozens of patterns defined for Java. Only three of them are tested on the exam, but you should be aware that more exist. **E** is incorrect because it makes sense to reuse the same pattern. For example, you might have multiple DAO objects. **A** and **F** are incorrect because of the above. (OCP Objectives 3.5, 3.6, and 3.7)

11. ☑ **C** is correct.
☒ **A, B,** and **D** are incorrect. **A** refers to encapsulation, **B** refers to coupling, and **D** refers to polymorphism. (OCP Objective 3.3)

12. ☑ **C** is correct. Generally speaking, public variables are a sign of weak encapsulation.
☒ **A, B, D,** and **E** are incorrect because based on the information given, none of these statements can be supported. (OCP Objective 3.3)

11

Generics and Collections

CERTIFICATION OBJECTIVES

- Create a Generic Class
- Use the Diamond Syntax to Create a Collection
- Analyze the Interoperability of Collections that Use Raw and Generic Types
- Use Wrapper Classes and Autoboxing
- Create and Use a List, a Set, and a Deque
- Create and Use a Map
- Use java.util.Comparator and java.lang.Comparable
- Sort and Search Arrays and Lists

✓ Two-Minute Drill

Q&A Self Test

Generics were the most talked about feature of Java 5. Some people love 'em, some people hate 'em, but they're here to stay. At their simplest, they can help make code easier to write and more robust. At their most complex, they can be very, very hard to create and maintain. Luckily, the exam creators stuck to the simple end of generics, covering the most common and useful features and leaving out most of the especially tricky bits.

CERTIFICATION OBJECTIVE

toString(), hashCode(), and equals() (OCP Objectives 4.7 and 4.8)

4.X *toString() will show up in numerous places throughout the exam.*

4.7 *Use java.util.Comparator and java.lang.Comparable.*

4.8 *Sort and search arrays and lists.*

It might not be immediately obvious, but understanding `hashCode()` and `equals()` is essential to working with Java collections, especially when using Maps and when searching and sorting in general.

You're an object. Get used to it. You have state, you have behavior, you have a job. (Or at least your chances of getting one will go up after passing the exam.) If you exclude primitives, everything in Java is an object. Not just an *object*, but an Object with a capital O. Every exception, every event, every array extends from `java.lang.Object`. For the exam, you don't need to know every method in class `Object`, but you will need to know about the methods listed in Table 11-1.

Chapter 13 covers `wait()`, `notify()`, and `notifyAll()`. The `finalize()` method was covered in Chapter 3. In this section, we'll look at the `hashCode()` and `equals()` methods because they are so often critical when using collections. Oh, that leaves `toString()`, doesn't it? Okay, we'll cover that right now because it takes two seconds.

TABLE 11-1 Methods of Class Object Covered on the Exam

Method	Description
`boolean equals (Object obj)`	Decides whether two objects are meaningfully equivalent
`void finalize()`	Called by the garbage collector when the garbage collector sees that the object cannot be referenced
`int hashCode()`	Returns a hashcode `int` value for an object so that the object can be used in Collection classes that use hashing, including `Hashtable`, `HashMap`, and `HashSet`
`final void notify()`	Wakes up a thread that is waiting for this object's lock
`final void notifyAll()`	Wakes up *all* threads that are waiting for this object's lock
`final void wait()`	Causes the current thread to wait until another thread calls `notify()` or `notifyAll()` on this object
`String toString()`	Returns a "text representation" of the object

The toString() Method

Override `toString()` when you want a mere mortal to be able to read something meaningful about the objects of your class. Code can call `toString()` on your object when it wants to read useful details about your object. When you pass an object reference to the `System.out.println()` method, for example, the object's `toString()` method is called, and the return of `toString()` is shown in the following example:

```
public class HardToRead {
  public static void main (String [] args) {
    HardToRead h = new HardToRead();
    System.out.println(h);
  }
}
```

Running the `HardToRead` class gives us the lovely and meaningful

```
% java HardToRead
HardToRead@a47e0
```

The preceding output is what you get when you don't override the `toString()` method of class `Object`. It gives you the class name (at least that's meaningful) followed by the `@` symbol, followed by the unsigned hexadecimal representation of the object's hashcode.

Trying to read this output might motivate you to override the `toString()` method in your classes, for example:

```
public class BobTest {
  public static void main (String[] args) {
   Bob f = new Bob("GoBobGo", 19);
   System.out.println(f);
  }
}
class Bob {
  int shoeSize;
  String nickName;
  Bob(String nickName, int shoeSize) {
    this.shoeSize = shoeSize;
    this.nickName = nickName;
  }
  public String toString() {
    return ("I am a Bob, but you can call me " + nickName +
            ". My shoe size is " + shoeSize);
  }
}
```

This ought to be a bit more readable:

```
% java BobTest
I am a Bob, but you can call me GoBobGo. My shoe size is 19
```

Some people affectionately refer to `toString()` as the "spill-your-guts method" because the most common implementations of `toString()` simply spit out the object's state (in other words, the current values of the important instance variables). That's it for `toString()`. Now we'll tackle `equals()` and `hashCode()`.

Overriding equals()

As we mentioned earlier, you might be wondering why we decided to talk about `Object.equals()` near the beginning of the chapter on collections. We'll be spending a lot of time answering that question over the next pages, but for now, it's enough to know that whenever you need to sort or search through a collection of objects, the `equals()` and `hashCode()` methods are essential. But before we go there, let's look at the more common uses of the `equals()` method.

You learned a bit about the `equals()` method in Chapter 4. We discussed how comparing two object references using the `==` operator evaluates to `true` only when both references refer to the same object because `==` simply looks at the bits in the variable, and they're either identical or they're not. You saw that the `String` class has overridden the `equals()` method (inherited from the class `Object`), so you could compare two different `String` objects to see if their contents are meaningfully equivalent. Later in this chapter, we'll be discussing the so-called wrapper classes when it's time to put primitive values into collections. For now, remember that there is a wrapper class for every kind of primitive. The folks who created the `Integer` class (to support `int` primitives) decided that if two different `Integer` instances both hold the `int` value `5`, as far as you're concerned, they are equal. The fact that the value `5` lives in two separate objects doesn't matter.

When you really need to know if two references are identical, use `==`. But when you need to know if the objects themselves (not the references) are equal, use the `equals()` method. For each class you write, you must decide if it makes sense to consider two different instances equal. For some classes, you might decide that two objects can never be equal. For example, imagine a `class Car` that has instance variables for things like make, model, year, configuration—you certainly don't want your car suddenly to be treated as the very same car as someone with a car that has identical attributes. Your car is your car and you don't want your neighbor Billy driving off in it just because "hey, it's really the same car; the `equals()` method said so." So no two cars should ever be considered exactly equal. If two references refer to one car, then you know that both are talking about one car, not two cars that have the same attributes. So in the case of `class Car` you might not ever need, or want, to override the `equals()` method. Of course, you know that isn't the end of the story.

What It Means If You Don't Override equals()

There's a potential limitation lurking here: If you don't override a class's `equals()` method, you won't be able to use those objects as a key in a hashtable and you probably won't get accurate Sets such that there are no conceptual duplicates.

The `equals()` method in class `Object` uses only the == operator for comparisons, so unless you override `equals()`, two objects are considered equal only if the two references refer to the same object.

Let's look at what it means to not be able to use an object as a hashtable key. Imagine you have a car, a very specific car (say, John's red Subaru Outback as opposed to Mary's purple Mini) that you want to put in a `HashMap` (a type of hashtable we'll look at later in this chapter) so that you can search on a particular car and retrieve the corresponding `Person` object that represents the owner. So you add the car instance as the key to the `HashMap` (along with a corresponding `Person` object as the value). But now what happens when you want to do a search? You want to say to the `HashMap` collection, "Here's the car; now give me the `Person` object that goes with this car." But now you're in trouble unless you still have a reference to the exact object you used as the key when you added it to the Collection. *In other words, you can't make an identical `Car` object and use it for the search.*

The bottom line is this: If you want objects of your class to be used as keys for a hashtable (or as elements in any data structure that uses equivalency for searching for—and/or retrieving—an object), then you must override `equals()` so that two different instances can be considered the same. So how would we fix the car? You might override the `equals()` method so that it compares the unique VIN (Vehicle Identification Number) as the basis of comparison. That way, you can use one instance when you add it to a Collection and essentially re-create an identical instance when you want to do a search based on that object as the key. Of course, overriding the `equals()` method for `Car` also allows the potential for more than one object representing a single unique car to exist, which might not be safe in your design. Fortunately, the `String` and wrapper classes work well as keys in hashtables—they override the `equals()` method. So rather than using the actual car instance as the key into the car/owner pair, you could simply use a `String` that represents the unique identifier for the car. That way, you'll never have more than one instance representing a specific car, but you can still use the car—or rather, one of the car's attributes—as the search key.

Implementing an equals() Method

Let's say you decide to override `equals()` in your class. It might look like this:

```
public class EqualsTest {
  public static void main (String [] args) {
    Moof one = new Moof(8);
    Moof two = new Moof(8);
    if (one.equals(two)) {
      System.out.println("one and two are equal");
    }
  }
}
class Moof {
  private int moofValue;
  Moof(int val) {
    moofValue = val;
  }
  public int getMoofValue() {
    return moofValue;
  }
  public boolean equals(Object o) {
    if ((o instanceof Moof) && (((Moof)o).getMoofValue()
          == this.moofValue)) {
      return true;
    } else {
       return false;
    }
  }
}
```

Let's look at this code in detail. In the `main()` method of `EqualsTest`, we create two `Moof` instances, passing the same value `8` to the `Moof` constructor. Now look at the `Moof` class and let's see what it does with that constructor argument—it assigns the value to the `moofValue` instance variable. Now imagine that you've decided two `Moof` objects are the same if their `moofValue` is identical. So you override the `equals()` method and compare the two `moofValues`. It is that simple. But let's break down what's happening in the `equals()` method:

```
1. public boolean equals(Object o) {
2.   if ((o instanceof Moof) && (((Moof)o).getMoofValue()
           == this.moofValue)) {
3.       return true;
4.     } else {
5.       return false;
6.     }
7.  }
```

First of all, you must observe all the rules of overriding, and in line 1 we are indeed declaring a valid override of the `equals()` method we inherited from `Object`.

Line 2 is where all the action is. Logically, we have to do two things in order to make a valid equality comparison.

First, be sure that the object being tested is of the correct type! It comes in polymorphically as type `Object`, so you need to do an `instanceof` test on it. Having two objects of different class types be considered equal is usually not a good idea, but that's a design issue we won't go into here. Besides, you'd still have to do the `instanceof` test just to be sure that you could cast the object argument to the correct type so that you can access its methods or variables in order to actually do the comparison. Remember, if the object doesn't pass the `instanceof` test, then you'll get a runtime ClassCastException. For example:

```
public boolean equals(Object o) {
  if (((Moof)o).getMoofValue() == this.moofValue){
    // the preceding line compiles, but it's BAD!
    return true;
  } else {
    return false;
  }
}
```

The `(Moof)o` cast will fail if `o` doesn't refer to something that IS-A `Moof`.

Second, compare the attributes we care about (in this case, just `moofValue`). Only the developer can decide what makes two instances equal. (For best performance, you're going to want to check the fewest number of attributes.)

In case you were a little surprised by the whole `((Moof)o).getMoofValue()` syntax, we're simply casting the object reference, `o`, just-in-time as we try to call a method that's in the `Moof` class but not in `Object`. Remember, without the cast, you can't compile because the compiler would see the object referenced by `o` as simply, well, an `Object`. And since the `Object` class doesn't have a `getMoofValue()` method, the compiler would squawk (technical term). But then, as we said earlier, even with the cast, the code fails at runtime if the object referenced by `o` isn't something that's castable to a `Moof`. So don't ever forget to use the `instanceof` test first. Here's another reason to appreciate the short-circuit `&&` operator—if the `instanceof` test fails, we'll never get to the code that does the cast, so we're always safe at runtime with the following:

```
if ((o instanceof Moof) && (((Moof)o).getMoofValue()
      == this.moofValue)) {
    return true;
} else {
    return false;
}
```

So that takes care of `equals()`...

Whoa... not so fast. If you look at the `Object` class in the Java API spec, you'll find what we call a contract specified in the `equals()` method. A Java contract is a set of rules that should be followed, or rather must be followed, if you want to provide a "correct" implementation as others will expect it to be. Or to put it another way: If you don't follow the contract, your code may still compile and run, but your code (or someone else's) may break at runtime in some unexpected way.

exam watch

Remember that the `equals()`, `hashCode()`, and `toString()` methods are all `public`. The following would not be a valid override of the `equals()` method, although it might appear to be if you don't look closely enough during the exam:

```
class Foo { boolean equals(Object o) { } }
```

And watch out for the argument types as well. The following method is an overload, but not an override of the `equals()` ***method:***

```
class Boo { public boolean equals(Boo b) { } }
```

Be sure you're very comfortable with the rules of overriding so that you can identify whether a method from `Object` is being overridden, overloaded, or illegally redeclared in a class. The `equals()` method in class `Boo` changes the argument from `Object` to `Boo`, so it becomes an overloaded method and won't be called unless it's from your own code that knows about this new, different method that happens to also be named `equals()`.

The equals() Contract

Pulled straight from the Java docs, the `equals()` contract says

- It is **reflexive**. For any reference value `x`, `x.equals(x)` should return `true`.
- It is **symmetric**. For any reference values `x` and `y`, `x.equals(y)` should return `true` if and only if `y.equals(x)` returns `true`.
- It is **transitive**. For any reference values `x`, `y`, and `z`, if `x.equals(y)` returns `true` and `y.equals(z)` returns `true`, then `x.equals(z)` must return `true`.
- It is **consistent**. For any reference values `x` and `y`, multiple invocations of `x.equals(y)` consistently return `true` or consistently return `false`, provided no information used in `equals()` comparisons on the object is modified.
- For any non-`null` reference value `x`, `x.equals(null)` should return `false`.

And you're so not off the hook yet. We haven't looked at the `hashCode()` method, but `equals()` and `hashCode()` are bound together by a joint contract that specifies if two objects are considered equal using the `equals()` method, then they must have identical hashcode values. So to be truly safe, your rule of thumb should be if you override `equals()`, override `hashCode()` as well. So let's switch over to `hashCode()` and see how that method ties in to `equals()`.

Overriding hashCode()

Hashcodes are typically used to increase the performance of large collections of data. The hashcode value of an object is used by some collection classes (we'll look at the collections later in this chapter). Although you can think of it as kind of an object ID number, it isn't necessarily unique. Collections such as `HashMap` and `HashSet` use the hashcode value of an object to determine how the object should be *stored* in the collection, and the hashcode is used again to help *locate* the object in the collection. For the exam, you do not need to understand the deep details of how the collection classes that use hashing are implemented, but you do need to know which collections use them (but, um, they all have "hash" in the name, so you should be good there). You must also be able to recognize an appropriate or correct implementation of `hashCode()`. This does not mean legal and does not even mean efficient. It's perfectly legal to have a terribly inefficient hashcode method in your class, as long as it doesn't violate the contract specified in the `Object` class documentation (we'll look at that contract in a moment). So for the exam, if you're asked to pick out an appropriate or correct use of hashcode, don't mistake appropriate for legal or efficient.

Understanding Hashcodes

In order to understand what's appropriate and correct, we have to look at how some of the collections use hashcodes.

Imagine a set of buckets lined up on the floor. Someone hands you a piece of paper with a name on it. You take the name and calculate an integer code from it by using A is 1, B is 2, and so on, adding the numeric values of all the letters in the name together. A given name will always result in the same code; see Figure 11-1.

We don't introduce anything random; we simply have an algorithm that will always run the same way given a specific input, so the output will always be identical for any two identical inputs. So far, so good? Now the way you use that code (and we'll call it a hashcode now) is to determine which bucket to place the piece of paper into (imagine that each bucket represents a different code number you might get). Now imagine that someone comes up and shows you a name and says, "Please retrieve the piece of paper that matches this name." So you look at the name they show you and run the same hashcode-generating algorithm. The hashcode tells you in which bucket you should look to find the name.

You might have noticed a little flaw in our system, though. Two different names might result in the same value. For example, the names `Amy` and `May` have the same letters, so the hashcode will be identical for both names. That's acceptable, but it does mean that when someone asks you (the bucket clerk) for the `Amy` piece of paper, you'll still have to search through the target bucket, reading each name until we find `Amy` rather than `May`. The hashcode tells you only which bucket to go into and not how to locate the name once we're in that bucket.

FIGURE 11-1 A simplified hashcode example

Key	Hashcode Algorithm	Hashcode
Alex	A(1) + L(12) + E(5) + X(24)	= 42
Bob	B(2) + O(15) + B(2)	= 19
Dirk	D(4) + I(9) + R(18) + K(11)	= 42
Fred	F(6) + R(18) + E(5) + D(4)	= 33

HashMap Collection

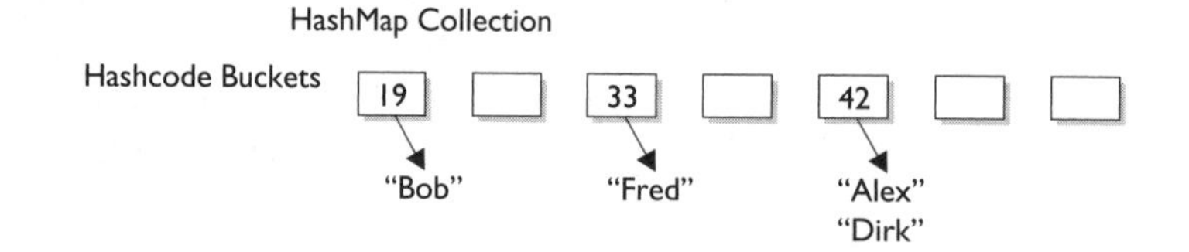

exam watch

In real-life hashing, it's not uncommon to have more than one entry in a bucket. Hashing retrieval is a two-step process.

1. ***Find the right bucket (using `hashCode()`).***
2. ***Search the bucket for the right element (using `equals()`).***

So, for efficiency, your goal is to have the papers distributed as evenly as possible across all buckets. Ideally, you might have just one name per bucket so that when someone asked for a paper, you could simply calculate the hashcode and just grab the one paper from the correct bucket, without having to flip through different papers in that bucket until you locate the exact one you're looking for. The least efficient (but still functional) hashcode generator would return the same hashcode (say, 42), regardless of the name, so that all the papers landed in the same bucket while the others stood empty. The bucket clerk would have to keep going to that one bucket and flipping painfully through each one of the names in the bucket until the right one was found. And if that's how it works, they might as well not use the hashcodes at all, but just go to the one big bucket and start from one end and look through each paper until they find the one they want.

This distributed-across-the-buckets example is similar to the way hashcodes are used in collections. When you put an object in a collection that uses hashcodes, the collection uses the hashcode of the object to decide in which bucket/slot the object should land. Then when you want to fetch that object (or, for a hashtable, retrieve the associated value for that object), you have to give the collection a reference to an object, which it then compares to the objects it holds in the collection. As long as the object stored in the collection, like a paper in the bucket, you're trying to search for has the same hashcode as the object you're using for the search (the name you show to the person working the buckets), then the object will be found. But—and this is a Big One—imagine what would happen if, going back to our name example, you showed the bucket worker a name and they calculated the code based on only half the letters in the name instead of all of them. They'd never find the name in the bucket because they wouldn't be looking in the correct bucket!

Now can you see why if two objects are considered equal, their hashcodes must also be equal? Otherwise, you'd never be able to find the object, since the default hashcode method in class `Object` virtually always comes up with a unique number for each object, even if the `equals()` method is overridden in such a way that two or more objects are considered equal. It doesn't matter how equal the objects are if their hashcodes don't reflect that. So one more time: If two objects are equal, their hashcodes must be equal as well.

Implementing hashCode()

What the heck does a real hashcode algorithm look like? People get their PhDs on hashing algorithms, so from a computer science viewpoint, it's beyond the scope of the exam. The part we care about here is the issue of whether you follow the contract. And to follow the contract, think about what you do in the `equals()` method. You compare attributes because that comparison almost always involves instance variable values (remember when we looked at two `Moof` objects and considered them equal if their `int moofValues` were the same?). Your `hashCode()` implementation should use the same instance variables. Here's an example:

```
class HasHash {
  public int x;
  HasHash(int xVal) { x = xVal; }

  public boolean equals(Object o) {
    HasHash h = (HasHash) o;      // Don't try at home without
                                  // instanceof test
    if (h.x == this.x) {
      return true;
    } else {
      return false;
    }
  }
  public int hashCode() { return (x * 17); }
}
```

This `equals()` method says two objects are equal if they have the same x value, so objects with the same x value will have to return identical hashcodes.

exam watch

A `hashCode()` that returns the same value for all instances, whether they're equal or not, is still a legal—even appropriate—`hashCode()` method! For example:

```
public int hashCode() { return 1492; }
```

This does not violate the contract. Two objects with an `x` value of `8` will have the same hashcode. But then again, so will two unequal objects, one with an `x` value of `12` and the

other with a value of `-920`. This `hashCode()` method is horribly inefficient, remember, because it makes all objects land in the same bucket. Even so, the object can still be found as the collection cranks through the one and only bucket—using `equals()`—trying desperately to finally, painstakingly, locate the correct object. In other words, the hashcode was really no help at all in speeding up the search, even though improving search speed is hashcode's intended purpose! Nonetheless, this one-hash-fits-all method would be considered appropriate and even correct because it doesn't violate the contract. Once more, correct does not necessarily mean good.

Typically, you'll see `hashCode()` methods that do some combination of ^-ing (XOR-ing) a class's instance variables (in other words, twiddling their bits), along with perhaps multiplying them by a prime number. In any case, while the goal is to get a wide and random distribution of objects across buckets, the contract (and whether or not an object can be found) requires only that two equal objects have equal hashcodes. The exam does not expect you to rate the efficiency of a `hashCode()` method, but you must be able to recognize which ones will and will not work ("work" meaning "will cause the object to be found in the collection").

Now that we know that two equal objects must have identical hashcodes, is the reverse true? Do two objects with identical hashcodes have to be considered equal? Think about it—you might have lots of objects land in the same bucket because their hashcodes are identical, but unless they also pass the `equals()` test, they won't come up as a match in a search through the collection. This is exactly what you'd get with our very inefficient, everybody-gets-the-same-hashcode method. It's legal and correct, just slooooow.

So in order for an object to be located, the search object and the object in the collection must both have identical hashcode values and return `true` for the `equals()` method. So there's just no way out of overriding both methods to be absolutely certain that your objects can be used in Collections that use hashing.

The hashCode() Contract

Now coming to you straight from the fabulous Java API documentation for class `Object`, may we present (drumroll) the `hashCode()` contract:

- Whenever it is invoked on the same object more than once during an execution of a Java application, the `hashCode()` method must consistently return the same integer, provided that no information used in `equals()`

comparisons on the object is modified. This integer need not remain consistent from one execution of an application to another execution of the same application.

- If two objects are equal according to the `equals(Object)` method, then calling the `hashCode()` method on each of the two objects must produce the same integer result.
- It is NOT required that if two objects are unequal according to the `equals(java.lang.Object)` method, then calling the `hashCode()` method on each of the two objects must produce distinct integer results. However, the programmer should be aware that producing distinct integer results for unequal objects may improve the performance of hashtables.

And what this means to you is...

Condition	Required	Not Required (But Allowed)
`x.equals(y) == true`	`x.hashCode() == y.hashCode()`	
`x.hashCode() == y.hashCode()`		`x.equals(y) == true`
`x.equals(y) == false`		No `hashCode()` requirements
`x.hashCode() != y.hashCode()`	`x.equals(y) == false`	

So let's look at what else might cause a `hashCode()` method to fail. What happens if you include a transient variable in your `hashCode()` method? While that's legal (the compiler won't complain), under some circumstances, an object you put in a collection won't be found. As you might know, serialization saves an object so that it can be reanimated later by deserializing it back to full objectness. But danger, Will Robinson—**transient variables are not saved when an object is serialized.** A bad scenario might look like this:

```
class SaveMe implements Serializable{
  transient int x;
  int y;
   SaveMe(int xVal, int yVal) {
      x = xVal;
      y = yVal;
   }
```

```
    public int hashCode() {
        return (x ^ y);                  // Legal, but not correct to
                                         // use a transient variable
    }
    public boolean equals(Object o) {
        SaveMe test = (SaveMe)o;
        if (test.y == y && test.x == x) { // Legal, not correct
          return true;
        } else {
          return false;
        }
    }
}
```

Here's what could happen using code like the preceding example:

1. Give an object some state (assign values to its instance variables).
2. Put the object in a `HashMap`, using the object as a key.
3. Save the object to a file using serialization without altering any of its state.
4. Retrieve the object from the file through deserialization.
5. Use the deserialized (brought back to life on the heap) object to get the object out of the `HashMap`.

Oops. The object in the collection and the supposedly same object brought back to life are no longer identical. The object's transient variable will come back with a default value rather than the value the variable had at the time it was saved (or put into the `HashMap`). So using the preceding SaveMe code, if the value of `x` is `9` when the instance is put in the `HashMap`, then since `x` is used in the calculation of the hashcode, when the value of `x` changes, the hashcode changes too. And when that same instance of SaveMe is brought back from deserialization, `x == 0`, regardless of the value of `x` at the time the object was serialized. So the new hashcode calculation will give a different hashcode and the `equals()` method fails as well since `x` is used to determine object equality.

Bottom line: `transient` variables can really mess with your `equals()` and `hashCode()` implementations. Keep variables non-`transient` or, if they must be marked `transient`, don't use them to determine hashcodes or equality.

CERTIFICATION OBJECTIVE

Collections Overview (OCP Objectives 4.5 and 4.6)

4.5 Create and use a List, a Set, and a Deque.

4.6 Create and use a Map.

In this section, we're going to present a relatively high-level discussion of the major categories of collections covered on the exam. We'll be looking at their characteristics and uses from an abstract level. In the section after this one, we'll dive into each category of collection and show concrete examples of using each.

Can you imagine trying to write object-oriented applications without using data structures like hashtables or linked lists? What would you do when you needed to maintain a sorted list of, say, all the members in your *Simpsons* fan club? Obviously, you can do it yourself; Amazon.com must have thousands of algorithm books you can buy. But with the kind of schedules programmers are under today, it's almost too painful to consider.

The Collections Framework in Java, which took shape with the release of JDK 1.2 and was expanded in 1.4 and again in Java 5, and yet again in Java 6 and Java 7, gives you lists, sets, maps, and queues to satisfy most of your coding needs. They've been tried, tested, and tweaked. Pick the best one for your job, and you'll get reasonable performance. And when you need something a little more custom, the Collections Framework in the `java.util` package is loaded with interfaces and utilities.

So What Do You Do with a Collection?

There are a few basic operations you'll normally use with collections:

- Add objects to the collection.
- Remove objects from the collection.
- Find out if an object (or group of objects) is in the collection.
- Retrieve an object from the collection without removing it.
- Iterate through the collection, looking at each element (object) one after another.

Key Interfaces and Classes of the Collections Framework

The Collections API begins with a group of interfaces, but also gives you a truckload of concrete classes. The core interfaces you need to know for the exam (and life in general) are the following nine:

`Collection`	`Set`	`SortedSet`
`List`	`Map`	`SortedMap`
`Queue`	`NavigableSet`	`NavigableMap`

In Chapter 14, which deals with concurrency, we will discuss several classes related to the `Deque` interface. Other than those, the concrete implementation classes you need to know for the exam are the following 13 (there are others, but the exam doesn't specifically cover them).

Maps	Sets	Lists	Queues	Utilities
`HashMap`	`HashSet`	`ArrayList`	`PriorityQueue`	`Collections`
`Hashtable`	`LinkedHashSet`	`Vector`		`Arrays`
`TreeMap`	`TreeSet`	`LinkedList`		
`LinkedHashMap`				

Not all collections in the Collections Framework actually implement the Collection interface. In other words, not all collections pass the IS-A test for Collection. Specifically, none of the Map-related classes and interfaces extend from Collection. So while `SortedMap`, `Hashtable`, `HashMap`, `TreeMap`, and `LinkedHashMap` are all thought of as collections, none are actually extended from Collection-with-a-capital-C (see Figure 11-2). To make things a little more confusing, there are really three overloaded uses of the word "collection":

- collection (lowercase *c*), which represents any of the data structures in which objects are stored and iterated over.
- Collection (capital C), which is actually the `java.util.Collection` interface from which `Set`, `List`, and `Queue` extend. (That's right, extend, not implement. There are no direct implementations of `Collection`.)
- Collections (capital C and ends with *s*) is the `java.util.Collections` class that holds a pile of `static` utility methods for use with collections.

FIGURE 11-2 The interface and class hierarchy for collections

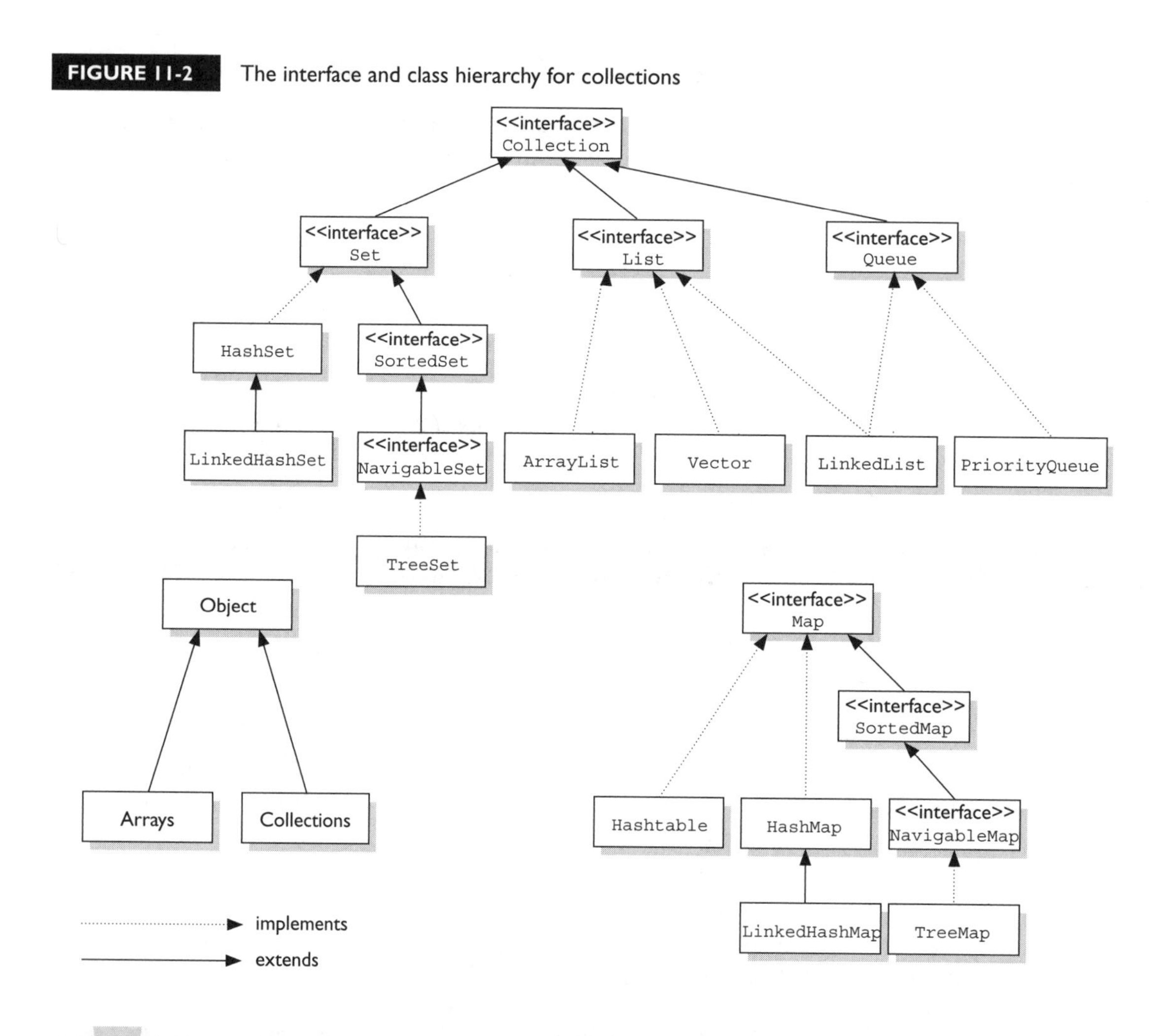

exam watch

You can so easily mistake "Collections" for "Collection"—be careful. Keep in mind that Collections is a class, with static utility methods, while Collection is an interface with declarations of the methods common to most collections, including `add()`, `remove()`, `contains()`, `size()`, and `iterator()`.

Collections come in four basic flavors:

- **Lists** *Lists* of things (classes that implement `List`)
- **Sets** *Unique* things (classes that implement `Set`)
- **Maps** Things with a *unique* ID (classes that implement `Map`)
- **Queues** Things arranged by the order in which they are to be processed

Figure 11-3 illustrates the relative structures of a `List`, a `Set`, and a `Map`. But there are subflavors within those four flavors of collections:

Sorted	Unsorted	Ordered	Unordered

An implementation class can be unsorted and unordered, ordered but unsorted, or both ordered and sorted. But an implementation can never be sorted but unordered, because sorting is a specific type of ordering, as you'll see in a moment. For example, a `HashSet` is an unordered, unsorted set, while a `LinkedHashSet` is an ordered (but not sorted) set that maintains the order in which objects were inserted.

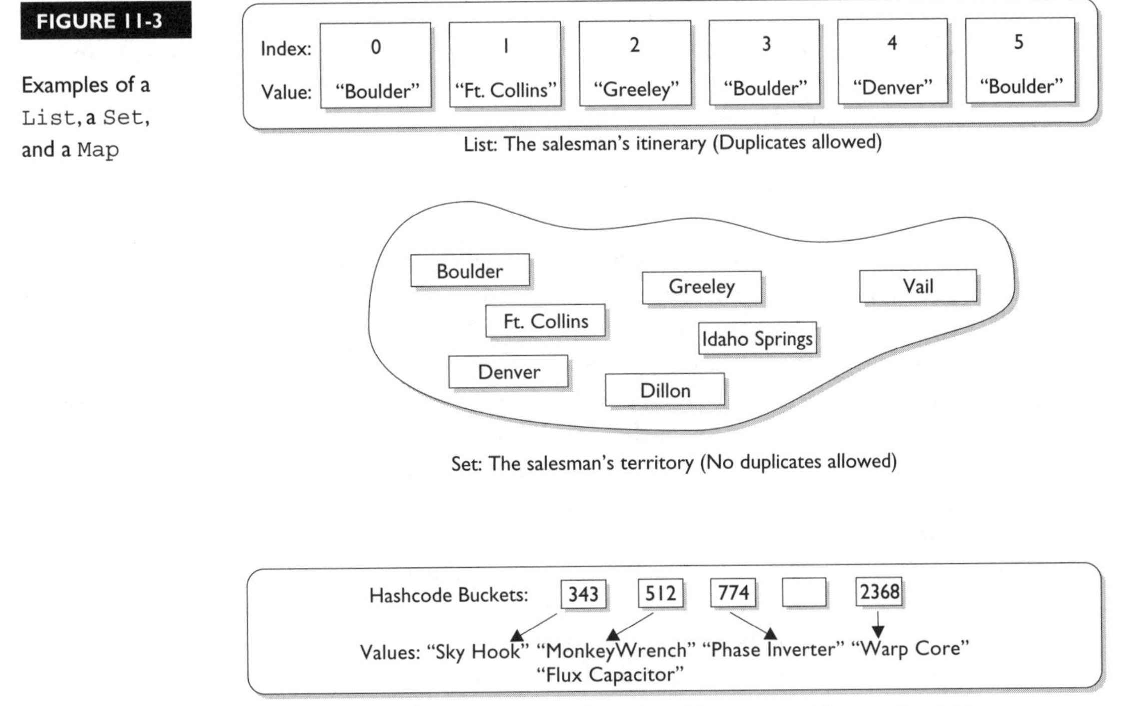

FIGURE 11-3 Examples of a `List`, a `Set`, and a `Map`

Maybe we should be explicit about the difference between sorted and ordered, but first we have to discuss the idea of iteration. When you think of iteration, you may think of iterating over an array using, say, a `for` loop to access each element in the array in order ([0], [1], [2], and so on). Iterating through a collection usually means walking through the elements one after another, starting from the first element. Sometimes, though, even the concept of *first* is a little strange—in a `Hashtable`, there really isn't a notion of first, second, third, and so on. In a `Hashtable`, the elements are placed in a (seemingly) chaotic order based on the hashcode of the key. But something has to go first when you iterate; thus, when you iterate over a `Hashtable`, there will indeed be an order. But as far as you can tell, it's completely arbitrary and can change in apparently random ways as the collection changes.

Ordered When a collection is ordered, it means you can iterate through the collection in a specific (not random) order. A `Hashtable` collection is not ordered. Although the `Hashtable` itself has internal logic to determine the order (based on hashcodes and the implementation of the collection itself), you won't find any order when you iterate through the `Hashtable`. An `ArrayList`, however, keeps the order established by the elements' index position (just like an array). `LinkedHashSet` keeps the order established by insertion, so the last element inserted is the last element in the `LinkedHashSet` (as opposed to an `ArrayList`, where you can insert an element at a specific index position). Finally, there are some collections that keep an order referred to as the natural order of the elements, and those collections are then not just ordered, but also sorted. Let's look at how natural order works for sorted collections.

Sorted A sorted collection means that the order in the collection is determined according to some rule or rules, known as the sort order. A sort order has nothing to do with when an object was added to the collection or when was the last time it was accessed, or what "position" it was added at. Sorting is done based on properties of the objects themselves. You put objects into the collection, and the collection will figure out what order to put them in, based on the sort order. A collection that keeps an order (such as any List, which uses insertion order) is not really considered sorted unless it sorts using some kind of sort order. Most commonly, the sort order used is something called the natural order. What does that mean?

You know how to sort alphabetically—A comes before B, F comes before G, and so on. For a collection of `String` objects, then, the natural order is alphabetical. For `Integer` objects, the natural order is by numeric value—1 before 2, and so on. And for `Foo` objects, the natural order is... um... we don't know. There is no natural order for `Foo` unless or until the `Foo` developer provides one through an interface (*`Comparable`*) that defines how instances of a class can be compared to one another (does instance `a` come before `b`, or does instance `b` come before `a`?). If the developer decides that `Foo` objects should be compared using the value of some instance variable (let's say there's one called `bar`), then a sorted collection will order the `Foo` objects according to the rules in the `Foo` class for how to use the `bar` instance variable to determine the order. Of course, the `Foo` class might also inherit a natural order from a superclass rather than define its own order in some cases.

Aside from natural order as specified by the `Comparable` interface, it's also possible to define other, different sort orders using another interface: *`Comparator`*. We will discuss how to use both `Comparable` and `Comparator` to define sort orders later in this chapter. But for now, just keep in mind that sort order (including natural order) is not the same as ordering by insertion, access, or index.

Now that we know about ordering and sorting, we'll look at each of the four interfaces, and we'll dive into the concrete implementations of those interfaces.

List Interface

A `List` cares about the index. The one thing that `List` has that non-lists don't is a set of methods related to the index. Those key methods include things like `get(int index)`, `indexOf(Object o)`, `add(int index, Object obj)`, and so on. All three `List` implementations are ordered by index position—a position that you determine either by setting an object at a specific index or by adding it without specifying position, in which case the object is added to the end. The three `List` implementations are described in the following sections.

ArrayList Think of this as a growable array. It gives you fast iteration and fast random access. To state the obvious: It is an ordered collection (by index), but not sorted. You might want to know that as of version 1.4, `ArrayList` now implements the new `RandomAccess` interface—a marker interface (meaning it has no methods) that says, "This list supports fast (generally constant time) random access." Choose this over a `LinkedList` when you need fast iteration but aren't as likely to be doing a lot of insertion and deletion.

Vector `Vector` is a holdover from the earliest days of Java; `Vector` and `Hashtable` were the two original collections—the rest were added with Java 2 versions 1.2 and 1.4. A `Vector` is basically the same as an `ArrayList`, but `Vector` methods are synchronized for thread safety. You'll normally want to use `ArrayList` instead of

`Vector` because the synchronized methods add a performance hit you might not need. And if you do need thread safety, there are utility methods in class `Collections` that can help. `Vector` is the only class other than `ArrayList` to implement `RandomAccess`.

LinkedList A `LinkedList` is ordered by index position, like `ArrayList`, except that the elements are doubly linked to one another. This linkage gives you new methods (beyond what you get from the `List` interface) for adding and removing from the beginning or end, which makes it an easy choice for implementing a stack or queue. Keep in mind that a `LinkedList` may iterate more slowly than an `ArrayList`, but it's a good choice when you need fast insertion and deletion. As of Java 5, the `LinkedList` class has been enhanced to implement the `java.util.Queue` interface. As such, it now supports the common queue methods `peek()`, `poll()`, and `offer()`.

Set Interface

A `Set` cares about uniqueness—it doesn't allow duplicates. Your good friend the `equals()` method determines whether two objects are identical (in which case, only one can be in the set). The three `Set` implementations are described in the following sections.

HashSet A `HashSet` is an unsorted, unordered `Set`. It uses the hashcode of the object being inserted, so the more efficient your `hashCode()` implementation, the better access performance you'll get. Use this class when you want a collection with no duplicates and you don't care about order when you iterate through it.

LinkedHashSet A `LinkedHashSet` is an ordered version of `HashSet` that maintains a doubly linked `List` across all elements. Use this class instead of `HashSet` when you care about the iteration order. When you iterate through a `HashSet`, the order is unpredictable, while a `LinkedHashSet` lets you iterate through the elements in the order in which they were inserted.

exam watch

When using `HashSet` or `LinkedHashSet`, the objects you add to them must override `hashCode()`. If they don't override `hashCode()`, the default `Object.hashCode()` method will allow multiple objects that you might consider "meaningfully equal" to be added to your "no duplicates allowed" set.

TreeSet The TreeSet is one of two sorted collections (the other being TreeMap). It uses a Red-Black tree structure (but you knew that), and guarantees that the elements will be in ascending order, according to natural order. Optionally, you can construct a TreeSet with a constructor that lets you give the collection your own rules for what the order should be (rather than relying on the ordering defined by the elements' class) by using a Comparator. As of Java 6, TreeSet implements NavigableSet.

Map Interface

A Map cares about unique identifiers. You map a unique key (the ID) to a specific value, where both the key and the value are, of course, objects. You're probably quite familiar with Maps since many languages support data structures that use a key/value or name/value pair. The Map implementations let you do things like search for a value based on the key, ask for a collection of just the values, or ask for a collection of just the keys. Like Sets, Maps rely on the equals() method to determine whether two keys are the same or different.

HashMap The HashMap gives you an unsorted, unordered Map. When you need a Map and you don't care about the order when you iterate through it, then HashMap is the way to go; the other maps add a little more overhead. Where the keys land in the Map is based on the key's hashcode, so, like HashSet, the more efficient your hashCode() implementation, the better access performance you'll get. HashMap allows one null key and multiple null values in a collection.

Hashtable Like Vector, Hashtable has existed from prehistoric Java times. For fun, don't forget to note the naming inconsistency: HashMap vs. Hashtable. Where's the capitalization of *t*? Oh well, you won't be expected to spell it. Anyway, just as Vector is a synchronized counterpart to the sleeker, more modern ArrayList, Hashtable is the synchronized counterpart to HashMap. Remember that you don't synchronize a class, so when we say that Vector and Hashtable are synchronized, we just mean that the key methods of the class are synchronized. Another difference, though, is that while HashMap lets you have null values as well as one null key, a Hashtable doesn't let you have anything that's null.

LinkedHashMap Like its Set counterpart, LinkedHashSet, the LinkedHashMap collection maintains insertion order (or, optionally, access order). Although it will be somewhat slower than `HashMap` for adding and removing elements, you can expect faster iteration with a `LinkedHashMap`.

TreeMap You can probably guess by now that a `TreeMap` is a sorted `Map`. And you already know that, by default, this means "sorted by the natural order of the elements." Like `TreeSet`, `TreeMap` lets you define a custom sort order (via a `Comparator`) when you construct a `TreeMap` that specifies how the elements should be compared to one another when they're being ordered. As of Java 6, `TreeMap` implements `NavigableMap`.

Queue Interface

A `Queue` is designed to hold a list of "to-dos," or things to be processed in some way. Although other orders are possible, queues are typically thought of as FIFO (first-in, first-out). `Queues` support all of the standard Collection methods and they also have methods to add and subtract elements and review queue elements.

PriorityQueue This class is new as of Java 5. Since the `LinkedList` class has been enhanced to implement the `Queue` interface, basic queues can be handled with a `LinkedList`. The purpose of a `PriorityQueue` is to create a "priority-in, priority out" queue as opposed to a typical FIFO queue. A `PriorityQueue`'s elements are ordered either by natural ordering (in which case the elements that are sorted first will be accessed first) or according to a `Comparator`. In either case, the elements' ordering represents their relative priority.

exam watch

You can easily eliminate some answers right away if you recognize that, for example, a `Map` can't be the class to choose when you need a name/value pair collection, since `Map` is an interface and not a concrete implementation class. The wording on the exam is explicit when it matters, so if you're asked to choose an interface, choose an interface rather than a class that implements that interface. The reverse is also true—if you're asked to choose a class, don't choose an interface type.

Table 11-2 summarizes 11 of the 13 concrete collection-oriented classes you'll need to understand for the exam. (Arrays and Collections are coming right up!)

TABLE 11-2 Collection Interface Concrete Implementation Classes

Class	Map	Set	List	Ordered	Sorted
`HashMap`	X			No	No
`Hashtable`	X			No	No
`TreeMap`	X			Sorted	By *natural order* or custom comparison rules
`LinkedHashMap`	X			By insertion order or last access order	No
`HashSet`		X		No	No
`TreeSet`		X		Sorted	By *natural order* or custom comparison rules
`LinkedHashSet`		X		By insertion order	No
`ArrayList`			X	By index	No
`Vector`			X	By index	No
`LinkedList`			X	By index	No
`PriorityQueue`				Sorted	By to-do order

exam watch

Be sure you know how to interpret Table 11-2 in a practical way. For the exam, you might be expected to choose a collection based on a particular requirement, where that need is expressed as a scenario. For example, which collection would you use if you needed to maintain and search on a list of parts identified by their unique alphanumeric serial number where the part would be of type `Part`? Would you change your answer at all if we modified the requirement such that you also need to be able to print out the parts in order by their serial number? For the first question, you can see that since you have a `Part` class but need to search for the objects based on a serial number, you need a `Map`. The key will be the serial number as a `String`, and the value will be the `Part` instance. The default choice should be `HashMap`, the quickest `Map` for access. But now when we amend the requirement to include getting the parts in order of their serial number, then we need a `TreeMap`—which maintains the natural order of the keys. Since the key is a `String`, the natural order for a `String` will be a standard alphabetical sort. If the requirement had been to keep track of which part was last accessed, then we'd probably need a `LinkedHashMap`. But since a `LinkedHashMap` loses the natural order (replacing it with last-accessed order), if we need to list the parts by serial number, we'll have to explicitly sort the collection using a utility method.

CERTIFICATION OBJECTIVE

Using Collections (OCP Objectives 4.2, 4.4, 4.5, 4.6, 4.7, and 4.8)

4.3 *Use the diamond syntax to create a collection.*

4.4 *Use wrapper classes and autoboxing.*

4.5 *Create and use a* `List`*, a Set, and a Deque.*

4.6 *Create and use a Map.*

4.7 *Use java.util.Comparator and java.lang.Comparable.*

4.8 *Sort and search arrays and lists.*

We've taken a high-level theoretical look at the key interfaces and classes in the Collections Framework; now let's see how they work in practice.

ArrayList Basics

Let's start with a quick review of what we learned about `ArrayLists` from Chapter 5. The `java.util.ArrayList` class is one of the most commonly used classes in the Collections Framework. It's like an array on vitamins. Some of the advantages `ArrayList` has over arrays are

- It can grow dynamically.
- It provides more powerful insertion and search mechanisms than arrays.

Let's take a look at using an `ArrayList` that contains strings. A key design goal of the Collections Framework was to provide rich functionality at the level of the main interfaces: `List`, `Set`, and `Map`. In practice, you'll typically want to instantiate an `ArrayList` polymorphically, like this:

```
List myList = new ArrayList();
```

As of Java 5, you'll want to say

```
List<String> myList = new ArrayList<String>();
```

This kind of declaration follows the object-oriented programming principle of "coding to an interface," and it makes use of generics. We'll say lots more about generics later in this chapter, but for now, just know that, as of Java 5, the `<String>` syntax is the way that you declare a collection's type. (Prior to Java 5, there was no way to specify the type of a collection, and when we cover generics, we'll talk about the implications of mixing Java 5 [typed] and pre-Java 5 [untyped] collections.)

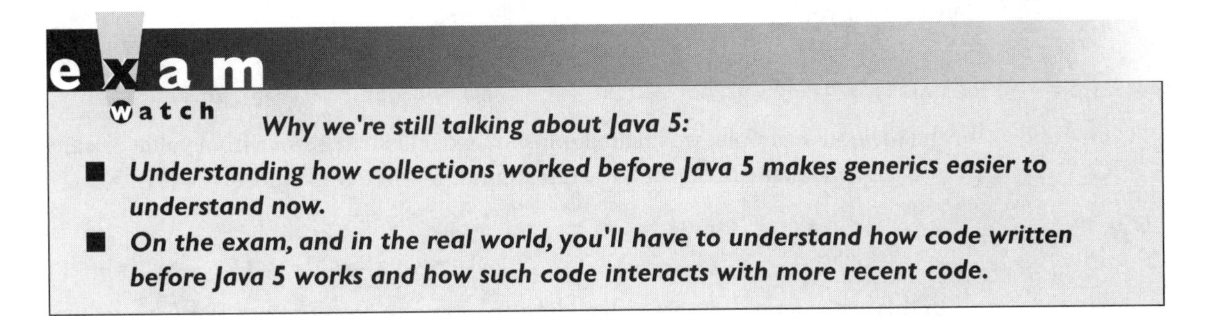

Why we're still talking about Java 5:

- ***Understanding how collections worked before Java 5 makes generics easier to understand now.***
- ***On the exam, and in the real world, you'll have to understand how code written before Java 5 works and how such code interacts with more recent code.***

In many ways, `ArrayList<String>` is similar to a `String[]` in that it declares a container that can hold only strings, but it's more powerful than a `String[]`. Let's look at some of the capabilities that an `ArrayList` has:

```
List<String> test = new ArrayList<String>();    // declare the ArrayList
String s = "hi";
test.add("string");                             // add some strings
test.add(s);
test.add(s+s);
System.out.println(test.size());                // use ArrayList methods
System.out.println(test.contains(42));
System.out.println(test.contains("hihi"));
test.remove("hi");
System.out.println(test.size());
```

which produces

```
3
false
true
2
```

There's a lot going on in this small program. Notice that when we declared the `ArrayList` we didn't give it a size. Then we were able to ask the `ArrayList` for its size, we were able to ask whether it contained specific objects, we removed an object right out from the middle of it, and then we rechecked its size.

Autoboxing with Collections

In general, collections can hold Objects but not primitives. Prior to Java 5, a common use for the so-called "wrapper classes" (e.g., `Integer`, `Float`, `Boolean`, and so on) was to provide a way to get primitives into and out of collections. Prior to Java 5, you had to "wrap" a primitive manually before you could put it into a collection. With Java 5, primitives still have to be wrapped, but autoboxing takes care of it for you.

```
List myInts = new ArrayList();    // pre Java 5 declaration
myInts.add(new Integer(42));      // Use Integer to "wrap" an int
```

In the previous example, we create an instance of class `Integer` with a value of `42`. We've created an entire object to "wrap around" a primitive value. As of Java 5, we can say:

```
myInts.add(42);                   // autoboxing handles it!
```

In this last example, we are still adding an `Integer` object to `myInts` (not an `int` primitive); it's just that autoboxing handles the wrapping for us. There are some sneaky implications when we need to use wrapper objects; let's take a closer look...

In the old, pre–Java 5 days, if you wanted to make a wrapper, unwrap it, use it, and then rewrap it, you might do something like this:

```
Integer y = new Integer(567);     // make it
int x = y.intValue();             // unwrap it
x++;                              // use it
y = new Integer(x);               // rewrap it
System.out.println("y = " + y);   // print it
```

Now, with new and improved Java 5, you can say

```
Integer y = new Integer(567);     // make it
y++;                              // unwrap it, increment it,
                                  // rewrap it
System.out.println("y = " + y);   // print it
```

Both examples produce the following output:

```
y = 568
```

And yes, you read that correctly. The code appears to be using the postincrement operator on an object reference variable! But it's simply a convenience. Behind the scenes, the compiler does the unboxing and reassignment for you. Earlier, we mentioned that wrapper objects are immutable... this example appears to contradict that statement. It sure looks like `y`'s value changed from `567` to `568`. What actually happened, however, is that a second wrapper object was created and its value was set to `568`. If only we could access that first wrapper object, we could prove it...

Let's try this:

```
Integer y = 567;                   // make a wrapper
Integer x = y;                     // assign a second ref
                                   // var to THE wrapper

System.out.println(y==x);          // verify that they refer
                                   // to the same object
y++;                               // unwrap, use, "rewrap"
System.out.println(x + " " + y);   // print values

System.out.println(y==x);          // verify that they refer
                                   // to different objects
```

Which produces the output:

```
true
  567 568
  false
```

So, under the covers, when the compiler got to the line `y++;` it had to substitute something like this:

```
int x2 = y.intValue();           // unwrap it
x2++;                            // use it
y = new Integer(x2);             // rewrap it
```

Just as we suspected, there's gotta be a call to `new` in there somewhere.

Boxing, ==, and equals()

We just used `==` to do a little exploration of wrappers. Let's take a more thorough look at how wrappers work with `==`, `!=`, and `equals()`. The API developers decided that for all the wrapper classes, two objects are equal if they are of the same type and have the same value. It shouldn't be surprising that

```
Integer i1 = 1000;
Integer i2 = 1000;
if(i1 != i2) System.out.println("different objects");
if(i1.equals(i2)) System.out.println("meaningfully equal");
```

produces the output

```
different objects
meaningfully equal
```

It's just two wrapper objects that happen to have the same value. Because they have the same `int` value, the `equals()` method considers them to be "meaningfully equivalent," and therefore returns `true`. How about this one:

```
Integer i3 = 10;
Integer i4 = 10;
if(i3 == i4) System.out.println("same object");
if(i3.equals(i4)) System.out.println("meaningfully equal");
```

This example produces the output:

```
same object
meaningfully equal
```

Yikes! The `equals()` method seems to be working, but what happened with `==` and `!=`? Why is `!=` telling us that `i1` and `i2` are different objects, when `==` is saying that `i3` and `i4` are the same object? In order to save memory, two instances of the following wrapper objects (created through boxing) will always be `==` when their primitive values are the same:

- `Boolean`
- `Byte`
- `Character` from `\u0000` to `\u007f` (`7f` is `127` in decimal)
- `Short` and `Integer` from `-128` to `127`

When `==` is used to compare a primitive to a wrapper, the wrapper will be unwrapped and the comparison will be primitive to primitive.

Where Boxing Can Be Used

As we discussed earlier, it's common to use wrappers in conjunction with collections. Any time you want your collection to hold objects and primitives, you'll want to use wrappers to make those primitives collection-compatible. The general rule is that boxing and unboxing work wherever you can normally use a primitive or a wrapped object. The following code demonstrates some legal ways to use boxing:

```
class UseBoxing {
  public static void main(String [] args) {
    UseBoxing u = new UseBoxing();
    u.go(5);
  }
  boolean go(Integer i) {        // boxes the int it was passed
    Boolean ifSo = true;         // boxes the literal
    Short s = 300;               // boxes the primitive
```

```
    if(ifSo) {                    // unboxing
      System.out.println(++s);  // unboxes, increments, reboxes
    }
    return !ifSo;                 // unboxes, returns the inverse
  }
}
```

exam watch

Remember, wrapper reference variables can be null. That means you have to watch out for code that appears to be doing safe primitive operations but that could throw a `NullPointerException`:

```
class Boxing2 {
  static Integer x;
  public static void main(String [] args) {
    doStuff(x);
  }
  static void doStuff(int z) {
    int z2 = 5;
    System.out.println(z2 + z);
} }
```

This code compiles fine, but the JVM throws a `NullPointerException` when it attempts to invoke `doStuff(x)` because `x` doesn't refer to an `Integer` object, so there's no value to unbox.

The Java 7 "Diamond" Syntax

In the OCA part of the book, we discussed several small additions/improvements to the language that were added under the name "Project Coin." The last Project Coin improvement we'll discuss in this book is the "diamond syntax." We've already seen several examples of declaring type-safe collections, and as we go deeper into collections, we'll see lots more like this:

```
ArrayList<String> stuff = new ArrayList<String>();
List<Dog> myDogs = new ArrayList<Dog>();
Map<String, Dog> dogMap = new HashMap<String, Dog>();
```

Notice that the type parameters are duplicated in these declarations. As of Java 7, these declarations could be simplified to:

```
ArrayList<String> stuff = new ArrayList<>();
List<Dog> myDogs = new ArrayList<>();
Map<String, Dog> dogMap = new HashMap<>();
```

Notice that in the simpler Java 7 declarations, the right side of the declaration included the two characters "<>," which together make a diamond shape—doh!

You cannot swap these; for example, the following declaration is NOT legal:

```
List<> stuff = new ArrayList<String>();     // NOT a legal diamond syntax
```

For the purposes of the exam, that's all you'll need to know about the diamond operator. For the remainder of the book, we'll use the pre-diamond syntax and the Java 7 diamond syntax somewhat randomly—just like the real world!

Sorting Collections and Arrays

Sorting and searching topics were added to the exam as of Java 5. Both collections and arrays can be sorted and searched using methods in the API.

Sorting Collections

Let's start with something simple, like sorting an `ArrayList` of strings alphabetically. What could be easier? Okay, we'll wait while you go find `ArrayList`'s `sort()` method... got it? Of course, `ArrayList` doesn't give you any way to sort its contents, but the `java.util.Collections` class does

```
import java.util.*;
class TestSort1 {
  public static void main(String[] args) {
    ArrayList<String> stuff = new ArrayList<String>(); // #1
    stuff.add("Denver");
    stuff.add("Boulder");
    stuff.add("Vail");
    stuff.add("Aspen");
    stuff.add("Telluride");
    System.out.println("unsorted " + stuff);
    Collections.sort(stuff);                            // #2
    System.out.println("sorted   " + stuff);
  }
}
```

This produces something like this:

```
unsorted [Denver, Boulder, Vail, Aspen, Telluride]
sorted   [Aspen, Boulder, Denver, Telluride, Vail]
```

Line 1 is declaring an `ArrayList` of `Strings`, and line 2 is sorting the `ArrayList` alphabetically. We'll talk more about the `Collections` class, along with the `Arrays` class, in a later section; for now, let's keep sorting stuff.

Let's imagine we're building the ultimate home-automation application. Today we're focused on the home entertainment center, and more specifically, the DVD control center. We've already got the file I/O software in place to read and write data between the `dvdInfo.txt` file and instances of class `DVDInfo`. Here are the key aspects of the class:

```
class DVDInfo {
  String title;
  String genre;
  String leadActor;
  DVDInfo(String t, String g, String a) {
    title = t;  genre = g;  leadActor = a;
  }
  public String toString() {
    return title + " " + genre + " " + leadActor + "\n";
  }
  // getters and setter go here
}
```

Here's the DVD data that's in the `dvdinfo.txt` file:

```
Donnie Darko/sci-fi/Gyllenhall, Jake
Raiders of the Lost Ark/action/Ford, Harrison
2001/sci-fi/??
Caddyshack/comedy/Murray, Bill
Star Wars/sci-fi/Ford, Harrison
Lost in Translation/comedy/Murray, Bill
Patriot Games/action/Ford, Harrison
```

In our home-automation application, we want to create an instance of `DVDInfo` for each line of data we read in from the `dvdInfo.txt` file. For each instance, we will parse the line of data (remember `String.split()`?) and populate `DVDInfo`'s three instance variables. Finally, we want to put all of the `DVDInfo` instances into an ArrayList. Imagine that the `populateList()` method (shown next) does all of this. Here is a small piece of code from our application:

```
ArrayList<DVDInfo> dvdList = new ArrayList<DVDInfo>();
populateList();   // adds the file data to the ArrayList
System.out.println(dvdList);
```

You might get output like this:

```
[Donnie Darko sci-fi Gyllenhall, Jake
, Raiders of the Lost Ark action Ford, Harrison
, 2001 sci-fi ??
, Caddyshack comedy Murray, Bill
, Star Wars sci-fi Ford, Harrison
, Lost in Translation comedy Murray, Bill
, Patriot Games action Ford, Harrison
]
```

(Note: We overrode `DVDInfo`'s `toString()` method, so when we invoked `println()` on the `ArrayList`, it invoked `toString()` for each instance.)

Now that we've got a populated `ArrayList`, let's sort it:

```
Collections.sort(dvdlist);
```

Oops! You get something like this:

```
TestDVD.java:13: cannot find symbol
symbol  : method sort(java.util.ArrayList<DVDInfo>)
location: class java.util.Collections
    Collections.sort(dvdlist);
```

What's going on here? We know that the `Collections` class has a `sort()` method, yet this error implies that `Collections` does NOT have a `sort()` method that can take a `dvdlist`. That means there must be something wrong with the argument we're passing (`dvdlist`).

If you've already figured out the problem, our guess is that you did it without the help of the obscure error message shown earlier… How the heck do you sort instances of `DVDInfo`? Why were we able to sort instances of `String`? When you look up `Collections.sort()` in the API, your first reaction might be to panic. Hang tight—once again, the generics section will help you read that weird-looking method signature. If you read the description of the one-arg `sort()` method, you'll see that the `sort()` method takes a `List` argument, and that the objects in the `List` must implement an interface called `Comparable`. It turns out that `String` implements `Comparable`, and that's why we were able to sort a list of `String`s using the `Collections.sort()` method.

The Comparable Interface

The `Comparable` interface is used by the `Collections.sort()` method and the `java.util.Arrays.sort()` method to sort `List`s and arrays of objects, respectively. To implement `Comparable`, a class must implement a single method, `compareTo()`. Here's an invocation of `compareTo()`:

```
int x = thisObject.compareTo(anotherObject);
```

The `compareTo()` method returns an `int` with the following characteristics:

- **Negative** If `thisObject < anotherObject`
- **Zero** If `thisObject == anotherObject`
- **Positive** If `thisObject > anotherObject`

The `sort()` method uses `compareTo()` to determine how the `List` or object array should be sorted. Since you get to implement `compareTo()` for your own classes, you can use whatever weird criteria you prefer to sort instances of your classes. Returning to our earlier example for class `DVDInfo`, we can take the easy way out and use the `String` class's implementation of `compareTo()`:

```
class DVDInfo implements Comparable<DVDInfo> {    // #1
  // existing code
  public int compareTo(DVDInfo d) {
    return title.compareTo(d.getTitle());          // #2
} }
```

In line 1, we declare that class `DVDInfo` implements `Comparable` in such a way that `DVDInfo` objects can be compared to other `DVDInfo` objects. In line 2, we implement `compareTo()` by comparing the two `DVDInfo` object's titles. Since we know that the titles are strings and that `String` implements `Comparable`, this is an easy way to sort our `DVDInfo` objects by title. Before generics came along in Java 5, you would have had to implement `Comparable` using something like this:

```
class DVDInfo implements Comparable {
  // existing code
  public int compareTo(Object o) {   // takes an Object rather
                                     // than a specific type
    DVDInfo d = (DVDInfo)o;
    return title.compareTo(d.getTitle());
} }
```

This is still legal, but you can see that it's both painful and risky because you have to do a cast, and you need to verify that the cast will not fail before you try it.

exam watch

It's important to remember that when you override `equals()`, you MUST take an argument of type `Object`, but that when you override `compareTo()`, you should take an argument of the type you're sorting.

Putting it all together, our `DVDInfo` class should now look like this:

```
class DVDInfo implements Comparable<DVDInfo> {
  String title;
  String genre;
  String leadActor;
  DVDInfo(String t, String g, String a) {
    title = t;  genre = g;  leadActor = a;
  }
  public String toString() {
    return title + " " + genre + " " + leadActor + "\n";
  }
  public int compareTo(DVDInfo d) {
    return title.compareTo(d.getTitle());
  }
  public String getTitle() {
    return title;
  }
  // other getters and setters
}
```

Now, when we invoke `Collections.sort(dvdList)`, we get

```
[2001 sci-fi ??
, Caddyshack comedy Murray, Bill
, Donnie Darko sci-fi Gyllenhall, Jake
, Lost in Translation comedy Murray, Bill
, Patriot Games action Ford, Harrison
, Raiders of the Lost Ark action Ford, Harrison
, Star Wars sci-fi Ford, Harrison
]
```

Hooray! Our `ArrayList` has been sorted by title. Of course, if we want our home-automation system to really rock, we'll probably want to sort DVD collections in lots of different ways. Since we sorted our `ArrayList` by implementing the `compareTo()` method, we seem to be stuck. We can only implement `compareTo()` once in a class, so how do we go about sorting our classes in an order different from what we specify in our `compareTo()` method? Good question. As luck would have it, the answer is coming up next.

Sorting with Comparator

While you were looking up the `Collections.sort()` method, you might have noticed that there is an overloaded version of `sort()` that takes both a `List` AND something called a *`Comparator`*. The `Comparator` interface gives you the capability to sort a given collection any number of different ways. The other handy thing about the `Comparator` interface is that you can use it to sort instances of any class—even classes you can't modify—unlike the `Comparable` interface, which forces you to change the class whose instances you want to sort. The `Comparator` interface is also very easy to implement, having only one method, `compare()`. Here's a small class that can be used to sort a `List` of `DVDInfo` instances by `genre`:

```
import java.util.*;
class GenreSort implements Comparator<DVDInfo> {
  public int compare(DVDInfo one, DVDInfo two) {
    return one.getGenre().compareTo(two.getGenre());
  }
}
```

The `Comparator.compare()` method returns an `int` whose meaning is the same as the `Comparable.compareTo()` method's return value. In this case, we're taking advantage of that by asking `compareTo()` to do the actual comparison work for us. Here's a test program that lets us test both our `Comparable` code and our new `Comparator` code:

```
import java.util.*;
import java.io.*;                    // populateList() needs this
public class TestDVD {
  ArrayList<DVDInfo> dvdlist = new ArrayList<DVDInfo>();
  public static void main(String[] args) {
    new TestDVD().go();
  }
  public void go() {
    populateList();
    System.out.println(dvdlist);      // output as read from file
    Collections.sort(dvdlist);
    System.out.println(dvdlist);      // output sorted by title

    GenreSort gs = new GenreSort();
    Collections.sort(dvdlist, gs);
    System.out.println(dvdlist);      // output sorted by genre
  }
  public void populateList() {
     // read the file, create DVDInfo instances, and
     // populate the ArrayList dvdlist with these instances
  }
}
```

You've already seen the first two output lists; here's the third:

```
[Patriot Games action Ford, Harrison
, Raiders of the Lost Ark action Ford, Harrison
, Caddyshack comedy Murray, Bill
, Lost in Translation comedy Murray, Bill
, 2001 sci-fi ??
, Donnie Darko sci-fi Gyllenhall, Jake
, Star Wars sci-fi Ford, Harrison
]
```

Because the `Comparable` and `Comparator` interfaces are so similar, expect the exam to try to confuse you. For instance, you might be asked to implement the `compareTo()` method in the `Comparator` interface. Study Table 11-3 to burn into your mind the differences between these two interfaces.

Sorting with the Arrays Class

We've been using the `java.util.Collections` class to sort collections; now let's look at using the `java.util.Arrays` class to sort arrays. The good news is that sorting arrays of objects is just like sorting collections of objects. The `Arrays.sort()` method is overloaded in the same way the `Collections.sort()` method is:

- `Arrays.sort(arrayToSort)`
- `Arrays.sort(arrayToSort, Comparator)`

In addition, the `Arrays.sort()` method (the one argument version), is overloaded about a million times to provide a couple of sort methods for every type of primitive. The `Arrays.sort(myArray)` methods that sort primitives always sort based on natural order. Don't be fooled by an exam question that tries to sort a primitive array using a `Comparator`.

Finally, remember that the `sort()` methods for both the `Collections` class and the `Arrays` class are `static` methods, and that they alter the objects they are sorting instead of returning a different sorted object.

TABLE 11-3 Comparing `Comparable` to `Comparator`

java.lang.Comparable	java.util.Comparator
`int objOne.compareTo(objTwo)`	`int compare(objOne, objTwo)`
Returns negative if `objOne < objTwo` zero if `objOne == objTwo` positive if `objOne > objTwo`	Same as `Comparable`
You must modify the class whose instances you want to sort.	You build a class separate from the class whose instances you want to sort.
Only **one** sort sequence can be created.	**Many** sort sequences can be created.
Implemented frequently in the API by: `String`, Wrapper classes, `Date`, `Calendar`...	Meant to be implemented to sort instances of third-party classes.

exam watch

We've talked a lot about sorting by natural order and using `Comparators` to sort. The last rule you'll need to burn in your mind is that whenever you want to sort an array or a collection, the elements inside must all be mutually comparable. In other words, if you have an `Object[]` and you put `Cat` and `Dog` objects into it, you won't be able to sort it. In general, objects of different types should be considered NOT mutually comparable unless specifically stated otherwise.

Searching Arrays and Collections

The `Collections` class and the `Arrays` class both provide methods that allow you to search for a specific element. When searching through collections or arrays, the following rules apply:

- Searches are performed using the `binarySearch()` method.
- Successful searches return the `int` index of the element being searched.
- Unsuccessful searches return an `int` index that represents the *insertion point*. The insertion point is the place in the collection/array where the element would be inserted to keep the collection/array properly sorted. Because positive return values and `0` indicate successful searches, the `binarySearch()` method uses negative numbers to indicate insertion points. Since `0` is a valid result for a successful search, the first available insertion point is `-1`. Therefore, the actual insertion point is represented as (`-`(insertion point) `-1`). For instance, if the insertion point of a search is at element `2`, the actual insertion point returned will be `-3`.
- The collection/array being searched must be sorted before you can search it.
- If you attempt to search an array or collection that has not already been sorted, the results of the search will not be predictable.
- If the collection/array you want to search was sorted in natural order, it *must* be searched in natural order. (Usually, this is accomplished by NOT sending a `Comparator` as an argument to the `binarySearch()` method.)
- If the collection/array you want to search was sorted using a `Comparator`, it *must* be searched using the same `Comparator`, which is passed as the second argument to the `binarySearch()` method. Remember that `Comparators` cannot be used when searching arrays of primitives.

Let's take a look at a code sample that exercises the `binarySearch()` method:

```
import java.util.*;
class SearchObjArray {
  public static void main(String [] args) {
    String [] sa = {"one", "two", "three", "four"};

    Arrays.sort(sa);                                          // #1
    for(String s : sa)
      System.out.print(s + " ");
    System.out.println("\none = "
                       + Arrays.binarySearch(sa,"one"));      // #2

    System.out.println("now reverse sort");
    ReSortComparator rs = new ReSortComparator();             // #3
    Arrays.sort(sa,rs);
    for(String s : sa)
      System.out.print(s + " ");
    System.out.println("\none = "
                       + Arrays.binarySearch(sa,"one"));      // #4
    System.out.println("one = "
                    + Arrays.binarySearch(sa,"one",rs));      // #5
  }
  static class ReSortComparator
                implements Comparator<String> {               // #6
    public int compare(String a, String b) {
      return b.compareTo(a);                                  // #7
    }
  }
}
```

which produces something like this:

```
four one three two
one = 1
now reverse sort
two three one four
one = -1
one = 2
```

Here's what happened:

- **#1** Sort the `sa` array, alphabetically (the natural order).
- **#2** Search for the location of element `"one"`, which is 1.
- **#3** Make a `Comparator` instance. On the next line, we re-sort the array using the `Comparator`.

- #4 Attempt to search the array. We didn't pass the `binarySearch()` method the `Comparator` we used to sort the array, so we got an incorrect (undefined) answer.
- #5 Search again, passing the `Comparator` to `binarySearch()`. This time, we get the correct answer, 2.
- #6 We define the `Comparator`; it's okay for this to be an inner class. (We'll be discussing inner classes in Chapter 12.)
- #7 By switching the use of the arguments in the invocation of `compareTo()`, we get an inverted sort.

exam watch

When solving, searching, and sorting questions, two big gotchas are

1. ***Searching an array or collection that hasn't been sorted.***
2. ***Using a `Comparator` in either the sort or the search, but not both.***

Converting Arrays to Lists to Arrays

A couple of methods allow you to convert arrays to `List`s and `List`s to arrays. The `List` and `Set` classes have `toArray()` methods, and the `Arrays` class has a method called `asList()`.

The `Arrays.asList()` method copies an array into a `List`. The API says, "Returns a fixed-size list backed by the specified array. (Changes to the returned list 'write through' to the array.)" When you use the `asList()` method, the array and the `List` become joined at the hip. When you update one of them, the other is updated automatically. Let's take a look:

```
String[] sa = {"one", "two", "three", "four"};
List sList = Arrays.asList(sa);                  // make a List
System.out.println("size " + sList.size());
System.out.println("idx2 " + sList.get(2));

sList.set(3,"six");                              // change List
sa[1] = "five";                                  // change array
for(String s : sa)
  System.out.print(s + " ");
System.out.println("\nsl[1] " + sList.get(1));
```

This produces

```
size 4
idx2 three
one five three six
sl[1] five
```

Notice that when we print the final state of the array and the `List`, they have both been updated with each other's changes. Wouldn't something like this behavior make a great exam question?

Now let's take a look at the `toArray()` method. There's nothing too fancy going on with the `toArray()` method; it comes in two flavors: one that returns a new `Object` array, and one that uses the array you send it as the destination array:

```
List<Integer> iL = new ArrayList<Integer>();
for(int x=0; x<3; x++)
  iL.add(x);
Object[] oa = iL.toArray();          // create an Object array
Integer[] ia2 = new Integer[3];
ia2 = iL.toArray(ia2);               // create an Integer array
```

Using Lists

Remember that `Lists` are usually used to keep things in some kind of order. You can use a `LinkedList` to create a first-in, first-out queue. You can use an `ArrayList` to keep track of what locations were visited and in what order. Notice that in both of these examples, it's perfectly reasonable to assume that duplicates might occur. In addition, `Lists` allow you to manually override the ordering of elements by adding or removing elements via the element's index. Before Java 5 and the enhanced `for` loop, the most common way to examine a List "element by element" was through the use of an `Iterator`. You'll still find `Iterators` in use in the Java code you encounter, and you might just find an Iterator or two on the exam. An `Iterator` is an object that's associated with a specific collection. It lets you loop through the collection step by step. The two `Iterator` methods you need to understand for the exam are

- **`boolean hasNext()`** Returns `true` if there is at least one more element in the collection being traversed. Invoking `hasNext()` does NOT move you to the next element of the collection.
- **`Object next()`** This method returns the next object in the collection AND moves you forward to the element after the element just returned.

Let's look at a little code that uses a `List` and an `Iterator`:

```
import java.util.*;
class Dog {
  public String name;
  Dog(String n) { name = n; }
}
class ItTest {
  public static void main(String[] args) {
    List<Dog> d = new ArrayList<Dog>();
    Dog dog = new Dog("aiko");
    d.add(dog);
    d.add(new Dog("clover"));
    d.add(new Dog("magnolia"));
    Iterator<Dog> i3 = d.iterator();  // make an iterator
    while (i3.hasNext()) {
      Dog d2 = i3.next();             // cast not required
      System.out.println(d2.name);
    }
    System.out.println("size " + d.size());
    System.out.println("get1 " + d.get(1).name);
    System.out.println("aiko " + d.indexOf(dog));
    d.remove(2);
    Object[] oa = d.toArray();
    for(Object o : oa) {
      Dog d2 = (Dog)o;
      System.out.println("oa " + d2.name);
    }
  }
}
```

This produces

```
aiko
clover
magnolia
size 3
get1 clover
aiko 0
oa aiko
oa clover
```

First off, we used generics syntax to create the `Iterator` (an `Iterator` of type `Dog`). Because of this, when we used the `next()` method, we didn't have to cast the `Object` returned by `next()` to a `Dog`. We could have declared the `Iterator` like this:

```
Iterator i3 = d.iterator();  // make an iterator
```

But then we would have had to cast the returned value:

```
Dog d2 = (Dog)i3.next();
```

The rest of the code demonstrates using the size(), get(), indexOf(), and toArray() methods. There shouldn't be any surprises with these methods. Later in the chapter, Table 11-7 will list all of the List, Set, and Map methods you should be familiar with for the exam. As a last warning, remember that List is an interface!

Using Sets

Remember that Sets are used when you don't want any duplicates in your collection. If you attempt to add an element to a set that already exists in the set, the duplicate element will not be added, and the add() method will return false. Remember, HashSets tend to be very fast because, as we discussed earlier, they use hashcodes.

You can also create a TreeSet, which is a Set whose elements are sorted. You must use caution when using a TreeSet (we're about to explain why):

```
import java.util.*;
class SetTest {
  public static void main(String[] args) {
    boolean[] ba = new boolean[5];
    // insert code here

    ba[0] = s.add("a");
    ba[1] = s.add(new Integer(42));
    ba[2] = s.add("b");
    ba[3] = s.add("a");
    ba[4] = s.add(new Object());
    for(int x=0; x<ba.length; x++)
      System.out.print(ba[x] + " ");
    System.out.println();
    for(Object o : s)
      System.out.print(o + " ");
  }
}
```

If you insert the following line of code, you'll get output that looks something like this:

```
Set s = new HashSet();        // insert this code

true true true false true
a java.lang.Object@e09713 42 b
```

It's important to know that the order of objects printed in the second for loop is not predictable: HashSets do not guarantee any ordering. Also, notice that the fourth invocation of add() failed because it attempted to insert a duplicate entry (a String with the value a) into the Set.

If you insert this line of code, you'll get something like this:

```
Set s = new TreeSet();          // insert this code

Exception in thread "main" java.lang.ClassCastException: java.lang.
String
        at java.lang.Integer.compareTo(Integer.java:35)
        at java.util.TreeMap.compare(TreeMap.java:1093)
        at java.util.TreeMap.put(TreeMap.java:465)
        at java.util.TreeSet.add(TreeSet.java:210)
```

The issue is that whenever you want a collection to be sorted, its elements must be mutually comparable. Remember that unless otherwise specified, objects of different types are not mutually comparable.

Using Maps

Remember that when you use a class that implements `Map`, any classes that you use as a part of the keys for that map must override the `hashCode()` and `equals()` methods. (Well, you only have to override them if you're interested in retrieving stuff from your `Map`. Seriously, it's legal to use a class that doesn't override `equals()` and `hashCode()` as a key in a `Map`; your code will compile and run, you just won't find your stuff.) Here's some crude code demonstrating the use of a `HashMap`:

```
import java.util.*;
class Dog {
  public Dog(String n) { name = n; }
  public String name;
  public boolean equals(Object o) {
    if((o instanceof Dog) &&
       (((Dog)o).name == name)) {
      return true;
    } else {
      return false;
    }
  }
  public int hashCode() {return name.length(); }
}
class Cat { }

enum Pets {DOG, CAT, HORSE }

class MapTest {
  public static void main(String[] args) {
    Map<Object, Object> m = new HashMap<Object, Object>();

    m.put("k1", new Dog("aiko"));   // add some key/value pairs
    m.put("k2", Pets.DOG);
```

```
        m.put(Pets.CAT, "CAT key");
        Dog d1 = new Dog("clover");      // let's keep this reference
        m.put(d1, "Dog key");
        m.put(new Cat(), "Cat key");

        System.out.println(m.get("k1"));                  // #1
        String k2 = "k2";
        System.out.println(m.get(k2));                    // #2
        Pets p = Pets.CAT;
        System.out.println(m.get(p));                     // #3
        System.out.println(m.get(d1));                    // #4
        System.out.println(m.get(new Cat()));             // #5
        System.out.println(m.size());                     // #6
    }
}
```

which produces something like this:

```
Dog@1c
DOG
CAT key
Dog key
null
5
```

Let's review the output. The first value retrieved is a Dog object (your value will vary). The second value retrieved is an enum value (DOG). The third value retrieved is a String; note that the key was an enum value. Pop quiz: What's the implication of the fact that we were able to successfully use an enum as a key?

The implication of this is that enums override equals() and hashCode(). And, if you look at the java.lang.Enum class in the API, you will see that, in fact, these methods have been overridden.

The fourth output is a String. The important point about this output is that the key used to retrieve the String was made of a Dog object. The fifth output is null. The important point here is that the get() method failed to find the Cat object that was inserted earlier. (The last line of output confirms that, indeed, 5 key/value pairs exist in the Map.) Why didn't we find the Cat key String? Why did it work to use an instance of Dog as a key, when using an instance of Cat as a key failed?

It's easy to see that Dog overrode equals() and hashCode() while Cat didn't.

Let's take a quick look at hashcodes. We used an incredibly simplistic hashcode formula in the Dog class—the hashcode of a Dog object is the length of the instance's name. So in this example, the hashcode = 6. Let's compare the following two hashCode() methods:

```
public int hashCode() {return name.length(); }    // #1
public int hashCode() {return 4; }                // #2
```

Time for another pop quiz: Are the preceding two hashcodes legal? Will they successfully retrieve objects from a Map? Which will be faster?

The answer to the first two questions is Yes and Yes. Neither of these hashcodes will be very efficient (in fact, they would both be incredibly inefficient), but they are both legal, and they will both work. The answer to the last question is that the first hashcode will be a little bit faster than the second hashcode. In general, the more *unique* hashcodes a formula creates, the faster the retrieval will be. The first hashcode formula will generate a different code for each name length (for instance, the name Robert will generate one hashcode and the name Benchley will generate a different hashcode). The second hashcode formula will always produce the same result, 4, so it will be slower than the first.

Our last Map topic is what happens when an object used as a key has its values changed? If we add two lines of code to the end of the earlier MapTest.main(),

```
d1.name = "magnolia";
System.out.println(m.get(d1));
```

we get something like this:

```
Dog@4
DOG
CAT key
Dog key
null
5
null
```

The Dog that was previously found now cannot be found. Because the Dog.name variable is used to create the hashcode, changing the name changed the value of the hashcode. As a final quiz for hashcodes, determine the output for the following lines of code if they're added to the end of MapTest.main():

```
d1.name = "magnolia";
System.out.println(m.get(d1));                    // #1
d1.name = "clover";
System.out.println(m.get(new Dog("clover")));     // #2
d1.name = "arthur";
System.out.println(m.get(new Dog("clover")));     // #3
```

Remember that the hashcode is equal to the length of the name variable. When you study a problem like this, it can be useful to think of the two stages of retrieval:

1. Use the hashCode() method to find the correct bucket.
2. Use the equals() method to find the object in the bucket.

In the first call to `get()`, the hashcode is 8 (`magnolia`) and it should be 6 (`clover`), so the retrieval fails at step 1 and we get `null`. In the second call to `get()`, the hashcodes are both 6, so step 1 succeeds. Once in the correct bucket (the "length of name = 6" bucket), the `equals()` method is invoked, and since `Dog`'s `equals()` method compares names, `equals()` succeeds, and the output is `Dog key`. In the third invocation of `get()`, the hashcode test succeeds, but the `equals()` test fails because `arthur` is NOT equal to `clover`.

Navigating (Searching) TreeSets and TreeMaps

Note: This section and the next ("Backed Collections") are fairly complex, and there is a good chance that OCP 7 candidates will NOT get any questions on these topics. On the other hand, OCPJP 6 candidates are likely to be tested on these topics.

We've talked about searching lists and arrays. Let's turn our attention to searching `TreeSets` and `TreeMaps`. Java 6 introduced (among other things) two new interfaces: `java.util.NavigableSet` and `java.util.NavigableMap`. For the purposes of the exam, you're interested in how `TreeSet` and `TreeMap` implement these interfaces.

Imagine that the Santa Cruz–Monterey ferry has an irregular schedule. Let's say that we have the daily Santa Cruz departure times stored in military time in a `TreeSet`. Let's look at some code that determines two things:

1. The last ferry that leaves before 4 PM (1600 hours)
2. The first ferry that leaves after 8 PM (2000 hours)

```
import java.util.*;
public class Ferry {
  public static void main(String[] args) {
    TreeSet<Integer> times = new TreeSet<Integer>();
    times.add(1205);    // add some departure times
    times.add(1505);
    times.add(1545);
    times.add(1830);
    times.add(2010);
    times.add(2100);

    // Java 5 version

    TreeSet<Integer> subset = new TreeSet<Integer>();
    subset = (TreeSet)times.headSet(1600);
    System.out.println("J5 - last before 4pm is: " + subset.last());

    TreeSet<Integer> sub2 = new TreeSet<Integer>();
```

```
            sub2 = (TreeSet)times.tailSet(2000);
            System.out.println("J5 - first after 8pm is: " + sub2.first());

            // Java 6 version using the new lower() and higher() methods

            System.out.println("J6 - last before 4pm is: " + times.lower(1600));
            System.out.println("J6 - first after 8pm is: " + times.higher(2000));
        }
    }
```

This should produce the following:

```
J5 - last before 4pm is: 1545
J5 - first after 8pm is: 2010
J6 - last before 4pm is: 1545
J6 - first after 8pm is: 2010
```

As you can see in the preceding code, before the addition of the `NavigableSet` interface, zeroing in on an arbitrary spot in a `Set`—using the methods available in Java 5—was a compute-expensive and clunky proposition. On the other hand, using the new Java 6 methods `lower()` and `higher()`, the code becomes a lot cleaner.

For the purpose of the exam, the `NavigableSet` methods related to this type of navigation are `lower()`, `floor()`, `higher()`, and `ceiling()`, and the mostly parallel `NavigableMap` methods are `lowerKey()`, `floorKey()`, `ceilingKey()`, and `higherKey()`. The difference between `lower()` and `floor()` is that `lower()` returns the element less than the given element, and `floor()` returns the element less than *or equal to* the given element. Similarly, `higher()` returns the element greater than the given element, and `ceiling()` returns the element greater than *or equal to* the given element. Table 11-4 summarizes the methods you should know for the exam.

Other Navigation Methods

In addition to the methods we just discussed, there are a few more new Java 6 methods that could be considered "navigation" methods. (Okay, it's a little bit of a stretch to call these "navigation" methods, but just play along.)

Polling

Although the idea of polling isn't new to Java 6 (as you'll see in a minute, `PriorityQueue` had a `poll()` method before Java 6), it *is* new to `TreeSet` and `TreeMap`. The idea of polling is that we want *both* to retrieve *and* remove an element from either the beginning or the end of a collection. In the case of `TreeSet`, `pollFirst()` returns and removes the first entry in the set, and `pollLast()`

returns and removes the last. Similarly, `TreeMap` now provides `pollFirstEntry()` and `pollLastEntry()` to retrieve and remove key/value pairs.

Descending Order

Also new to Java 6 for `TreeSet` and `TreeMap` are methods that return a collection in the reverse order of the collection on which the method was invoked. The important methods for the exam are `TreeSet.descendingSet()` and `TreeMap.descendingMap()`.

Table 11-4 summarizes the "navigation" methods you'll need to know for the exam.

Backed Collections

Some of the classes in the `java.util` package support the concept of "backed collections." We'll use a little code to help explain the idea:

```
TreeMap<String, String> map = new TreeMap<String, String>();
map.put("a", "ant"); map.put("d", "dog"); map.put("h", "horse");

SortedMap<String, String> submap;
submap = map.subMap("b", "g");              // #1 create a backed collection

System.out.println(map + " " + submap);     // #2 show contents

map.put("b", "bat");                        // #3 add to original
submap.put("f", "fish");                    // #4 add to copy

map.put("r", "raccoon");                    // #5 add to original - out of range
// submap.put("p", "pig");                  // #6 add to copy - out of range

System.out.println(map + " " + submap);     // #7 show final contents
```

This should produce something like this:

```
{a=ant, d=dog, h=horse} {d=dog}
{a=ant, b=bat, d=dog, f=fish, h=horse, r=raccoon} {b=bat, d=dog, f=fish}
```

The important method in this code is the `TreeMap.subMap()` method. It's easy to guess (and it's correct) that the `subMap()` method is making a copy of a portion of the `TreeMap` named `map`. The first line of output verifies the conclusions we've just drawn.

What happens next is powerful, and a little bit unexpected (now we're getting to why they're called *backed* collections). When we add key/value pairs to either the original `TreeMap` or the partial-copy `SortedMap`, the new entries were automatically added to the other collection—sometimes. When `submap` was created, we provided

TABLE 11-4 Important "Navigation"-Related Methods

Method	Description
`TreeSet.ceiling(e)`	Returns the lowest element >= `e`
`TreeMap.ceilingKey(key)`	Returns the lowest key >= `key`
`TreeSet.higher(e)`	Returns the lowest element > `e`
`TreeMap.higherKey(key)`	Returns the lowest key > `key`
`TreeSet.floor(e)`	Returns the highest element <= `e`
`TreeMap.floorKey(key)`	Returns the highest key <= `key`
`TreeSet.lower(e)`	Returns the highest element < `e`
`TreeMap.lowerKey(key)`	Returns the highest key < `key`
`TreeSet.pollFirst()`	Returns and removes the first entry
`TreeMap.pollFirstEntry()`	Returns and removes the first key/value pair
`TreeSet.pollLast()`	Returns and removes the last entry
`TreeMap.pollLastEntry()`	Returns and removes the last key/value pair
`TreeSet.descendingSet()`	Returns a `NavigableSet` in reverse order
`TreeMap.descendingMap()`	Returns a `NavigableMap` in reverse order

a value range for the new collection. This range defines not only what should be included when the partial copy is created, but also defines the range of values that can be added to the copy. As we can verify by looking at the second line of output, we can add new entries to either collection within the range of the copy, and the new entries will show up in both collections. In addition, we can add a new entry to the original collection, even if it's outside the range of the copy. In this case, the new entry will show up only in the original—it won't be added to the copy because it's outside the copy's range. Notice that we commented out line 6. If you attempt to add an out-of-range entry to the copied collection, an exception will be thrown.

For the exam, you'll need to understand the basics just explained, plus a few more details about three methods from `TreeSet`—`headSet()`, `subSet()`, and `tailSet()`—and three methods from `TreeMap`—`headMap()`, `subMap()`, and `tailMap()`. As with the navigation-oriented methods we just discussed, we can see a lot of parallels between the `TreeSet` and the `TreeMap` methods. The `headSet()`/`headMap()` methods create a subset that starts at the beginning of the original collection and ends at the point specified by the method's argument. The `tailSet()`/`tailMap()` methods create a subset that starts at the point specified by the method's argument and goes to the end of the original collection. Finally, the `subSet()`/`subMap()`

methods allow you to specify both the start and end points for the subset collection you're creating.

As you might expect, the question of whether the subsetted collection's end points are inclusive or exclusive is a little tricky. The good news is that for the exam you have to remember only that when these methods are invoked with end point *and* boolean arguments, the boolean always means "is inclusive". A little more good news is that all you have to know for the exam is that, unless specifically indicated by a boolean argument, a subset's starting point will always be inclusive. Finally, you'll notice when you study the API that all of the methods we've been discussing here have an overloaded version that's new to Java 6. The older methods return either a `SortedSet` or a `SortedMap`; the new Java 6 methods return either a `NavigableSet` or a `NavigableMap`. Table 11-5 summarizes these methods.

exam watch

Let's say that you've created a backed collection using either a `tailXxx()` or `subXxx()` method. Typically in these cases, the original and copy collections have different "first" elements. For the exam, it's important that you remember that the `pollFirstXxx()` methods will always remove the first entry from the collection on which they're invoked, but they will remove an element from the other collection only if it has the same value. So it's most likely that invoking `pollFirstXxx()` on the copy will remove an entry from both collections, but invoking `pollFirstXxx()` on the original will remove only the entry from the original.

TABLE 11-5 Important "Backed Collection" Methods for `TreeSet` and `TreeMap`

Method	Description
`headSet(e, b*)`	Returns a subset ending at element `e` and *exclusive* of `e`
`headMap(k, b*)`	Returns a submap ending at key `k` and *exclusive* of key `k`
`tailSet(e, b*)`	Returns a subset starting at and *inclusive* of element `e`
`tailMap(k, b*)`	Returns a submap starting at and *inclusive* of key `k`
`subSet(s, b*, e, b*)`	Returns a subset starting at element `s` and ending just before element `e`
`subMap(s, b*, e, b*)`	Returns a submap starting at key `s` and ending just before key `e`

* Note: These boolean arguments are optional. If they exist, it's a Java 6 method that lets you specify whether the start point and/or end point are exclusive, and these methods return a `NavigableXxx`. If the boolean argument(s) don't exist, the method returns either a `SortedSet` or a `SortedMap`.

Using the PriorityQueue Class and the Deque Interface

Note: Having completed the Navigable Collections and Backed Collections discussions, we're now back to topics that all candidates (OCPJP 5 and 6 and OCP 7), are likely to be tested on.

For the exam, you'll need to understand several of the classes that implement the `Deque` interface. These classes will be discussed in Chapter 14, the concurrency chapter.

Other than those concurrency-related classes, the last collection class you'll need to understand for the exam is the `PriorityQueue`. Unlike basic queue structures that are first-in, first-out by default, a `PriorityQueue` orders its elements using a user-defined priority. The priority can be as simple as natural ordering (in which, for instance, an entry of `1` would be a higher priority than an entry of `2`). In addition, a `PriorityQueue` can be ordered using a `Comparator`, which lets you define any ordering you want. `Queues` have a few methods not found in other collection interfaces: `peek()`, `poll()`, and `offer()`.

```
import java.util.*;
class PQ {
  static class PQsort
          implements Comparator<Integer> {  // inverse sort
    public int compare(Integer one, Integer two) {
      return two - one;                     // unboxing
    }
  }
  public static void main(String[] args) {
    int[] ia = {1,5,3,7,6,9,8 };           // unordered data
    PriorityQueue<Integer> pq1 =
      new PriorityQueue<Integer>();         // use natural order

    for(int x : ia)                         // load queue
      pq1.offer(x);
    for(int x : ia)                         // review queue
      System.out.print(pq1.poll() + " ");
    System.out.println("");

    PQsort pqs = new PQsort();              // get a Comparator
    PriorityQueue<Integer> pq2 =
      new PriorityQueue<Integer>(10,pqs);   // use Comparator

    for(int x : ia)                         // load queue
      pq2.offer(x);
    System.out.println("size " + pq2.size());
    System.out.println("peek " + pq2.peek());
    System.out.println("size " + pq2.size());
    System.out.println("poll " + pq2.poll());
    System.out.println("size " + pq2.size());
    for(int x : ia)                         // review queue
      System.out.print(pq2.poll() + " ");
  }
}
```

This code produces something like this:

```
1 3 5 6 7 8 9
size 7
peek 9
size 7
poll 9
size 6
8 7 6 5 3 1 null
```

Let's look at this in detail. The first `for` loop iterates through the `ia` array and uses the `offer()` method to add elements to the `PriorityQueue` named `pq1`. The second `for` loop iterates through `pq1` using the `poll()` method, which returns the highest-priority entry in `pq1` AND removes the entry from the queue. Notice that the elements are returned in priority order (in this case, natural order). Next, we create a `Comparator`—in this case, a `Comparator` that orders elements in the opposite of natural order. We use this `Comparator` to build a second `PriorityQueue`, `pq2`, and we load it with the same array we used earlier. Finally, we check the size of `pq2` before and after calls to `peek()` and `poll()`. This confirms that `peek()` returns the highest-priority element in the queue without removing it, and `poll()` returns the highest-priority element AND removes it from the queue. Finally, we review the remaining elements in the queue.

Method Overview for Arrays and Collections

For these two classes, we've already covered the trickier methods you might encounter on the exam. Table 11-6 lists a summary of the methods you should be aware of. (Note: The `T[]` syntax will be explained later in this chapter; for now, think of it as meaning "any array that's NOT an array of primitives.")

Method Overview for List, Set, Map, and Queue

For these four interfaces, we've already covered the trickier methods you might encounter on the exam. Table 11-7 lists a summary of the `List`, `Set`, and `Map` methods you should be aware of, **and—if you're an OCPJP 6 candidate—don't forget the new "Navigable" methods floor, lower, ceiling, and higher that we discussed a few pages back.**

TABLE 11-6 Key Methods in Arrays and Collections

Key Methods in java.util.Arrays	Descriptions
`static List asList(T[])`	Convert an array to a `List` (and bind them).
`static int binarySearch(Object[], key)` `static int binarySearch(primitive[], key)`	Search a sorted array for a given value; return an index or insertion point.
`static int binarySearch(T[], key, Comparator)`	Search a `Comparator`-sorted array for a value.
`static boolean equals(Object[], Object[])` `static boolean equals(primitive[], primitive[])`	Compare two arrays to determine if their contents are equal.
`static void sort(Object[ ] )` `static void sort(primitive[ ] )`	Sort the elements of an array by natural order.
`static void sort(T[], Comparator)`	Sort the elements of an array using a `Comparator`.
`static String toString(Object[])` `static String toString(primitive[])`	Create a `String` containing the contents of an array.
Key Methods in java.util.Collections	**Descriptions**
`static int binarySearch(List, key)` `static int binarySearch(List, key, Comparator)`	Search a "sorted" `List` for a given value; return an index or insertion point.
`static void reverse(List)`	Reverse the order of elements in a `List`.
`static Comparator reverseOrder()` `static Comparator reverseOrder(Comparator)`	Return a `Comparator` that sorts the reverse of the collection's current sort sequence.
`static void sort(List)` `static void sort(List, Comparator)`	Sort a `List` either by natural order or by a `Comparator`.

For the exam, the `PriorityQueue` methods that are important to understand are `offer()` (which is similar to `add()`), `peek()` (which retrieves the element at the head of the queue but doesn't delete it), and `poll()` (which retrieves the head element and removes it from the queue).

TABLE 11-7 Key Methods in `List`, `Set`, and `Map`

Key Interface Methods	List	Set	Map	Descriptions
`boolean add(element)` `boolean add(index, element)`	X X	X		Add an element. For `Lists`, optionally add the element at an index point.

`boolean contains(object)`
`boolean containsKey(object key)`
`boolean containsValue(object value)`
	X	X	
			X
			X
				Search a collection for an object (or, optionally for `Maps`, a key); return the result as a `boolean`.

`object get(index)` `object get(key)`	X		 X	Get an object from a collection via an index or a key.
`int indexOf(object)`	X			Get the location of an object in a `List`.
`Iterator iterator()`	X	X		Get an `Iterator` for a `List` or a `Set`.
`Set keySet()`			X	Return a `Set` containing a `Map`'s keys.
`put(key, value)`			X	Add a key/value pair to a `Map`.

`element remove(index)`
`element remove(object)`
`element remove(key)`
	X
	X
		
		X
			
			X
				Remove an element via an index, or via the element's value, or via a key.

`int size()`	X	X	X	Return the number of elements in a collection.
`Object[] toArray()` `T[] toArray(T[])`	X	X		Return an array containing the elements of the collection.

exam watch

It's important to know some of the details of natural ordering. The following code will help you understand the relative positions of uppercase characters, lowercase characters, and spaces in a natural ordering:

```
String[] sa = {">ff<", "> f<", ">f <", ">FF<" }; // ordered?
PriorityQueue<String> pq3 = new PriorityQueue<String>();
for(String s : sa)
  pq3.offer(s);
for(String s : sa)
  System.out.print(pq3.poll() + " ");
```

This produces

```
> f< >FF< >f < >ff<
```

If you remember that spaces sort before characters and that uppercase letters sort before lowercase characters, you should be good to go for the exam.

CERTIFICATION OBJECTIVE

Generic Types (OCP Objectives 4.1 and 4.3)

4.1 Create a generic class.

4.3 Analyze the interoperability of collections that use raw and generic types.

Now would be a great time to take a break. Those two innocent-sounding objectives unpack into a world of complexity. When you're well rested, come on back and strap yourself in—the next several pages might get bumpy.

Arrays in Java have always been type-safe—an array declared as type `String` (`String []`) can't accept `Integers` (or `ints`), `Dogs`, or anything other than `Strings`. But remember that before Java 5 there was no syntax for declaring a type-safe collection. To make an `ArrayList` of `Strings`, you said,

```
ArrayList myList = new ArrayList();
```

or the polymorphic equivalent

```
List myList = new ArrayList();
```

There was no syntax that let you specify that `myList` will take `Strings` and only `Strings`. And with no way to specify a type for the `ArrayList`, the compiler couldn't enforce that you put only things of the specified type into the list. As of Java 5, we can use generics, and while they aren't only for making type-safe collections, that's just about all most developers use generics for. So, while generics aren't just for collections, think of collections as the overwhelming reason and motivation for adding generics to the language.

And it was not an easy decision, nor has it been an entirely welcome addition. Because along with all the nice, happy type-safety, generics come with a lot of baggage—most of which you'll never see or care about—but there are some gotchas that come up surprisingly quickly. We'll cover the ones most likely to show up in your own code, and those are also the issues that you'll need to know for the exam.

The biggest challenge for the Java engineers in adding generics to the language (and the main reason it took them so long) was how to deal with legacy code built without generics. The Java engineers obviously didn't want to break everyone's existing Java code, so they had to find a way for Java classes with both type-safe (generic) and nontype-safe (nongeneric/pre–Java 5) collections to still work together. Their solution isn't the friendliest, but it does let you use older nongeneric code, as well as use generic code that plays with nongeneric code. But notice we said "plays" and not "plays WELL."

While you can integrate Java 5 and later generic code with legacy, nongeneric code, the consequences can be disastrous, and unfortunately, most of the disasters happen at runtime, not compile time. Fortunately, though, most compilers will generate warnings to tell you when you're using unsafe (meaning nongeneric) collections.

The Java 7 exam covers both pre–Java 5 (nongeneric) and generic-style collections, and you'll see questions that expect you to understand the tricky problems that can come from mixing nongeneric and generic code together. And like some of the other topics in this book, you could fill an entire book if you really wanted to cover every detail about generics, but the exam (and this book) covers more than most developers will ever need to use.

The Legacy Way to Do Collections

Here's a review of a pre–Java 5 `ArrayList` intended to hold `Strings`. (We say "intended" because that's about all you had—good intentions—to make sure that the `ArrayList` would hold only `Strings`.)

```
List myList = new ArrayList();  // can't declare a type

myList.add("Fred");             // OK, it will hold Strings

myList.add(new Dog());          // and it will hold Dogs too

myList.add(new Integer(42));    // and Integers...
```

A nongeneric collection can hold any kind of object! A nongeneric collection is quite happy to hold anything that is NOT a primitive.

This meant it was entirely up to the programmer to be... careful. Having no way to guarantee collection type wasn't very programmer-friendly for such a strongly typed language. We're so used to the compiler stopping us from, say, assigning an `int` to a `boolean` or a `String` to a `Dog` reference, but with collections, it was, "Come on in! The door is always open! All objects are welcome here any time!"

And since a collection could hold anything, the methods that get objects out of the collection could have only one kind of return type—`java.lang.Object`. That meant that getting a `String` back out of our only-`Strings`-intended list required a cast:

```
String s = (String) myList.get(0);
```

And since you couldn't guarantee that what was coming out really was a `String` (since you were allowed to put anything in the list), the cast could fail at runtime.

So generics takes care of both ends (the putting in and getting out) by enforcing the type of your collections. Let's update the `String` list:

```
List<String> myList = new ArrayList<String>();
myList.add("Fred");          // OK, it will hold Strings
myList.add(new Dog());       // compiler error!!
```

Perfect. That's exactly what we want. By using generics syntax—which means putting the type in angle brackets `<String>`—we're telling the compiler that this collection can hold only `String` objects. The type in angle brackets is referred to as the "parameterized type," "type parameter," or, of course, just old-fashioned "type." In this chapter, we'll refer to it both new ways.

So now that what you put IN is guaranteed, you can also guarantee what comes OUT, and that means you can get rid of the cast when you get something from the collection. Instead of

```
String s = (String)myList.get(0);  // pre-generics, when a
                                   // String wasn't guaranteed
```

we can now just say

```
String s = myList.get(0);
```

The compiler already knows that `myList` contains only things that can be assigned to a `String` reference, so now there's no need for a cast. So far, it seems pretty simple. And with the new `for` loop, you can, of course, iterate over the guaranteed-to-be-`String` list:

```
for (String s : myList) {
  int x = s.length();
  // no need for a cast before calling a String method! The
  // compiler already knew "s" was a String coming from myList
}
```

And, of course, you can declare a type parameter for a method argument, which then makes the argument a type-safe reference:

```
void takeListOfStrings(List<String> strings) {
  strings.add("foo");  // no problem adding a String
}
```

The previous method would NOT compile if we changed it to

```
void takeListOfStrings(List<String> strings) {
  strings.add(new Integer(42)); // NO!! strings is type safe
}
```

Return types can obviously be declared type-safe as well:

```
public List<Dog> getDogList() {
  List<Dog> dogs = new ArrayList<Dog>();
  // more code to insert dogs
  return dogs;
}
```

The compiler will stop you from returning anything not compatible with a `List<Dog>` (although what is and is not compatible is going to get very interesting in a minute). And since the compiler guarantees that only a type-safe `Dog List` is returned, those calling the method won't need a cast to take `Dogs` from the `List`:

```
Dog d = getDogList().get(0);  // we KNOW a Dog is coming out
```

With pre–Java 5 nongeneric code, the `getDogList()` method would be

```
public List getDogList() {
  List dogs = new ArrayList();
  // code to add only Dogs... fingers crossed...
  return dogs; // a List of ANYTHING will work here
}
```

and the caller would need a cast:

```
Dog d = (Dog) getDogList().get(0);
```

(The cast in this example applies to what comes from the `List`'s `get()` method; we aren't casting what is returned from the `getDogList()` method, which is a `List`.)

But what about the benefit of a completely heterogeneous collection? In other words, what if you liked the fact that before generics you could make an `ArrayList` that could hold any kind of object?

```
List myList = new ArrayList();  // old-style, non-generic
```

is almost identical to

```
List<Object> myList = new
                 ArrayList<Object>(); // holds ANY object type
```

Declaring a `List` with a type parameter of `<Object>` makes a collection that works in almost the same way as the original pre–Java 5 nongeneric collection—you can put ANY Object type into the collection. You'll see a little later that nongeneric collections and collections of type `<Object>` aren't entirely the same, but most of the time, the differences do not matter.

Oh, if only this were the end of the story… but there are still a few tricky issues with methods, arguments, polymorphism, and integrating generic and nongeneric code, so we're just getting warmed up here.

Generics and Legacy Code

The easiest thing about generics you'll need to know for the exam is how to update nongeneric code to make it generic. You just add a type in angle brackets (<>) immediately following the collection type in BOTH the variable declaration and the constructor call (or you use the Java 7 diamond syntax), including any place you declare a variable (so that means arguments and return types too). A pre–Java 5 `List` meant to hold only Integers:

```
List myList = new ArrayList();
```

becomes

```
List<Integer> myList = new ArrayList<Integer>();  // (or the J7 diamond!)
```

and a list meant to hold only `Strings` goes from

```
public List changeStrings(ArrayList s) { }
```

to this:

```
public List<String> changeStrings(ArrayList<String> s) { }
```

Easy. And if there's code that used the earlier nongeneric version and performed a cast to get things out, that won't break anyone's code:

```
Integer i = (Integer) list.get(0); // cast no longer needed,
                                   // but it won't hurt
```

Mixing Generic and Nongeneric Collections

Now here's where it starts to get interesting... imagine we have an `ArrayList` of type `Integer` and we're passing it into a method from a class whose source code we don't have access to. Will this work?

```
// a Java 5 or later class using a generic collection
import java.util.*;
public class TestLegacy {
  public static void main(String[] args) {
    List<Integer> myList = new ArrayList<Integer>();
                                  // type safe collection
    myList.add(4);
    myList.add(6);
    Adder adder = new Adder();
    int total = adder.addAll(myList);
                                 // pass it to an untyped argument
    System.out.println(total);
  }
}
```

The older nongenerics class we want to use:

```
import java.util.*;
class Adder {
  int addAll(List list) {
    // method with a non-generic List argument,
    // but assumes (with no guarantee) that it will be Integers
    Iterator it = list.iterator();
    int total = 0;
    while (it.hasNext()) {
      int i = ((Integer)it.next()).intValue();
      total += i;
    }
    return total;
  }
}
```

Yes, this works just fine. You can mix correct generic code with older nongeneric code, and everyone is happy.

In the previous example, the `addAll()` legacy method assumed (trusted? hoped?) that the list passed in was indeed restricted to `Integers`, even though when the code was written, there was no guarantee. It was up to the programmers to be careful.

Since the `addAll()` method wasn't doing anything except getting the `Integer` (using a cast) from the list and accessing its value, there were no problems. In that example, there was no risk to the caller's code, but the legacy method might have blown up if the list passed in contained anything but `Integers` (which would cause a ClassCastException).

But now imagine that you call a legacy method that doesn't just *read* a value, but *adds* something to the `ArrayList`. Will this work?

```
import java.util.*;
public class TestBadLegacy {
  public static void main(String[] args) {
    List<Integer> myList = new ArrayList<Integer>();
    myList.add(4);
    myList.add(6);
    Inserter in  = new Inserter();
    in.insert(myList);          // pass List<Integer> to legacy code
  }
}
class Inserter {
  // method with a non-generic List argument
  void insert(List list) {
    list.add(new Integer(42));  // adds to the incoming list
  }
}
```

Sure, this code works. It compiles, and it runs. The `insert()` method puts an `Integer` into the list that was originally typed as `<Integer>`, so no problem.

But... what if we modify the `insert()` method like this:

```
void insert(List list) {
  list.add(new String("42"));  // put a String in the list
                               // passed in
}
```

Will that work? Yes, sadly, it does! It both compiles and runs. No runtime exception. Yet, someone just stuffed a `String` into a *supposedly* type-safe `ArrayList` of type `<Integer>`. How can that be?

Remember, the older legacy code was allowed to put anything at all (except primitives) into a collection. And in order to support legacy code, Java 5 and Java 6 allow your newer type-safe code to make use of older code (the last thing Sun wanted to do was ask several million Java developers to modify all their existing code).

So, the Java 5 or later compiler (from now on "the Java 5 compiler") is *forced* into letting you compile your new type-safe code even though your code invokes a method of an older class that takes a nontype-safe argument and does who knows what with it.

However, just because **the Java 5 compiler** (remember this means Java 5 and later), allows this code to compile doesn't mean it has to be HAPPY about it. In fact, the compiler will warn you that you're taking a big, big risk sending your nice, protected `ArrayList<Integer>` into a dangerous method that can have its way with your list and put in `Floats`, `Strings`, or even `Dogs`.

When you called the `addAll()` method in the earlier example, it didn't insert anything to the list (it simply added up the values within the collection), so there was no risk to the caller that his list would be modified in some horrible way. It compiled and ran just fine. But in the second version, with the legacy `insert()` method that adds a `String`, the compiler generated a warning:

```
javac TestBadLegacy.java
Note: TestBadLegacy.java uses unchecked or unsafe operations.
Note: Recompile with -Xlint:unchecked for details.
```

Remember that *compiler warnings are NOT considered a compiler failure*. The compiler generated a perfectly valid class file from the compilation, but it was kind enough to tell you by saying, in so many words, "I seriously hope you know what you are doing because this old code has NO respect (or even knowledge) of your `<Integer>` typing and can do whatever the heck it wants to your precious `ArrayList<Integer>`."

exam watch

Be sure you know the difference between "compilation fails" and "compiles without error" and "compiles without warnings" and "compiles with warnings." In most questions on the exam, you care only about compiles versus compilation fails—compiler warnings don't matter for most of the exam. But when you are using generics and mixing both typed and untyped code, warnings matter.

Back to our example with the legacy code that does an insert. Keep in mind that for BOTH versions of the `insert()` method (one that adds an `Integer` and one that adds a `String`), the compiler issues warnings. The compiler does NOT know whether the `insert()` method is adding the right thing (`Integer`) or the wrong thing (`String`). The reason the compiler produces a warning is because the method is ADDING something to the collection! In other words, the compiler knows there's a chance the method might add the wrong thing to a collection the caller thinks is type-safe.

exam watch

For the purposes of the exam, unless the question includes an answer that mentions warnings, even if you know the compilation will produce warnings, that is still a successful compile! Compiling with warnings is NEVER considered a compilation failure.

One more time—if you see code that you know will compile with warnings, you must NOT choose "Compilation fails" as an answer. The bottom line is this: Code that compiles with warnings is still a successful compile. If the exam question wants to test your knowledge of whether code will produce a warning (or what you can do to the code to ELIMINATE warnings), the question (or answer) will explicitly include the word "warnings."

So far, we've looked at how the compiler will generate warnings if it sees that there's a chance your type-safe collection could be harmed by older, nontype-safe code. But one of the questions developers often ask is, "Okay, sure, it compiles, but why does it RUN? Why does the code that inserts the wrong thing into my list work at runtime?" In other words, why does the JVM let old code stuff a `String` into your `ArrayList<Integer>` without any problems at all? No exceptions, nothing. Just a quiet, behind-the-scenes, total violation of your type safety that you might not discover until the worst possible moment.

There's one Big Truth you need to know to understand why it runs without problems—the JVM has no idea that your `ArrayList` was supposed to hold only `Integers`. The typing information does not exist at runtime! All your generic code is strictly for the compiler. Through a process called "type erasure," the compiler does all of its verifications on your generic code and then strips the type information out of the class bytecode. At runtime, ALL collection code—both legacy and new Java 5 code you write using generics—looks exactly like the pregeneric version of collections. None of your typing information exists at runtime. In other words, even though you WROTE

```
List<Integer> myList = new ArrayList<Integer>();
```

by the time the compiler is done with it, the JVM sees what it always saw before Java 5 and generics:

```
List myList = new ArrayList();
```

The compiler even inserts the casts for you—the casts you had to do to get things out of a pre–Java 5 collection.

Think of generics as strictly a compile-time protection. The compiler uses generic type information (the `<type>` in the angle brackets) to make sure that your code doesn't put the wrong things into a collection and that you do not assign what you get from a collection to the wrong reference type. But NONE of this protection exists at runtime.

This is a little different from arrays, which give you BOTH compile-time protection and runtime protection. Why did they do generics this way? Why is there no type information at runtime? To support legacy code. At runtime, collections are collections just like the old days. What you gain from using generics is compile-time protection that guarantees you won't put the wrong thing into a typed collection, and it also eliminates the need for a cast when you get something out, since the compiler already knows that only an `Integer` is coming out of an `Integer` list.

The fact is, you don't NEED runtime protection... until you start mixing up generic and nongeneric code, as we did in the previous example. Then you can have disasters at runtime. The only advice we have is to pay very close attention to those compiler warnings:

```
javac TestBadLegacy.java
Note: TestBadLegacy.java uses unchecked or unsafe operations.
Note: Recompile with -Xlint:unchecked for details.
```

This compiler warning isn't very descriptive, but the second note suggests that you recompile with `-Xlint:unchecked`. If you do, you'll get something like this:

```
javac -Xlint:unchecked TestBadLegacy.java
TestBadLegacy.java:17: warning: [unchecked] unchecked call to add(E)
as a member of the raw type java.util.List
       list.add(new String("42"));
               ^
1 warning
```

When you compile with the `-Xlint:unchecked` flag, the compiler shows you exactly which method(s) might be doing something dangerous. In this example, since the list argument was not declared with a type, the compiler treats it as legacy code and assumes no risk for what the method puts into the "raw" list.

On the exam, you must be able to recognize when you are compiling code that will produce warnings but still compile. And any code that compiles (even with warnings) will run! No type violations will be caught at runtime by the JVM, *until* those type violations mess with your code in some other way. In other words, the act of adding a `String` to an `<Integer>` list won't fail at runtime *until* you try to treat that `String`-you-think-is-an-`Integer` as an `Integer`.

For example, imagine you want your code to pull something out of your *supposedly* type-safe `ArrayList<Integer>` that older code put a `String` into. It compiles (with warnings). It runs... or at least the code that actually adds the `String` to the list runs. But when you take the `String` that wasn't supposed to be there out of the list and try to assign it to an `Integer` reference or invoke an `Integer` method, you're dead.

Keep in mind, then, that the problem of putting the wrong thing into a typed (generic) collection does not show up at the time you actually do the `add()` to the collection. It only shows up later, when you try to use something in the list and it doesn't match what you were expecting. In the old (pre–Java 5) days, you always assumed that you might get the wrong thing out of a collection (since they were all nontype-safe), so you took appropriate defensive steps in your code. The problem with mixing generic and nongeneric code is that you won't be expecting those problems if you have been lulled into a false sense of security by having written type-safe code. Just remember that the moment you turn that type-safe collection over to older, nontype-safe code, your protection vanishes.

Again, pay very close attention to compiler warnings and be prepared to see issues like this come up on the exam.

exam watch

When using legacy (nontype-safe) collections, watch out for unboxing problems! If you declare a nongeneric collection, the `get()` method ALWAYS returns a reference of type `java.lang.Object`. Remember that unboxing can't convert a plain old `Object` to a primitive, even if that `Object` reference refers to an `Integer` (or some other wrapped primitive) on the heap. Unboxing converts only from a wrapper class reference (like an `Integer` or a `Long`) to a primitive.

Unboxing gotcha, continued:

```
List test = new ArrayList();
test.add(43);
int x = (Integer)test.get(0);     // you must cast !!

List<Integer> test2 = new ArrayList<Integer>();
test2.add(343);
int x2 = test2.get(0);            // cast not necessary
```

Watch out for missing casts associated with pre–Java 5 nongeneric collections.

Polymorphism and Generics

Generic collections give you the same benefits of type safety that you've always had with arrays, but there are some crucial differences that can bite you if you aren't prepared. Most of these have to do with polymorphism.

You've already seen that polymorphism applies to the "base" type of the collection:

```
List<Integer> myList = new ArrayList<Integer>();
```

In other words, we were able to assign an `ArrayList` to a `List` reference because `List` is a supertype of `ArrayList`. Nothing special there—this polymorphic assignment works the way it always works in Java, regardless of the generic typing.

But what about this?

```
class Parent { }
class Child extends Parent { }
List<Parent> myList = new ArrayList<Child>();
```

Think about it for a minute.

Keep thinking…

No, it doesn't work. There's a very simple rule here—the type of the variable declaration must match the type you pass to the actual object type. If you declare `List<Foo>` foo, then whatever you assign to the foo reference MUST be of the generic type `<Foo>`. Not a subtype of `<Foo>`. Not a supertype of `<Foo>`. Just `<Foo>`.

These are wrong:

```
List<Object> myList = new ArrayList<JButton>();        // NO!
List<Number> numbers = new ArrayList<Integer>();       // NO!
// remember that Integer is a subtype of Number
```

But these are fine:

```
List<JButton> bList = new ArrayList<JButton>(); // yes
List<Object> oList = new ArrayList<Object>();   // yes
List<Integer> iList = new ArrayList<Integer>(); // yes
```

So far, so good. Just keep the generic type of the reference and the generic type of the object to which it refers identical. In other words, polymorphism applies here to only the "base" type. And by "base," we mean the type of the collection class itself—the class that can be customized with a type. In this code,

```
List<JButton> myList = new ArrayList<JButton>();
```

`List` and `ArrayList` are the *base* type and `JButton` is the *generic* type. So an `ArrayList` can be assigned to a `List`, but a collection of `<JButton>` cannot be assigned to a reference of `<Object>`, even though `JButton` is a subtype of `Object`.

The part that feels wrong for most developers is that this is NOT how it works with arrays, where you *are* allowed to do this:

```
import java.util.*;
class Parent { }
class Child extends Parent { }
public class TestPoly {
  public static void main(String[] args) {
    Parent[] myArray = new Child[3];           // yes
  }
}
```

which means you're also allowed to do this:

```
Object[] myArray = new JButton[3];             // yes
```

but not this:

```
List<Object> list = new ArrayList<JButton>();  // NO!
```

Why are the rules for typing of arrays different from the rules for generic typing? We'll get to that in a minute. For now, just burn it into your brain that polymorphism does not work the same way for generics as it does with arrays.

Generic Methods

If you weren't already familiar with generics, you might be feeling very uncomfortable with the implications of the previous no-polymorphic-assignment-for-generic-types thing. And why shouldn't you be uncomfortable? One of the biggest benefits of polymorphism is that you can declare, say, a method argument of a particular type and at runtime be able to have that argument refer to any subtype—including those you'd never known about at the time you wrote the method with the supertype argument.

For example, imagine a classic (simplified) polymorphism example of a veterinarian (`AnimalDoctor`) class with a method `checkup()`. And right now, you have three `Animal` subtypes—`Dog`, `Cat`, and `Bird`—each implementing the `abstract checkup()` method from `Animal`:

```
abstract class Animal {
  public abstract void checkup();
}
class Dog extends Animal {
  public void checkup() {    // implement Dog-specific code
    System.out.println("Dog checkup");
  }
}
class Cat extends Animal {
  public void checkup() {    // implement Cat-specific code
    System.out.println("Cat checkup");
  }
}
class Bird extends Animal {
  public void checkup() {    // implement Bird-specific code
    System.out.println("Bird checkup");
} }
```

Forgetting collections/arrays for a moment, just imagine what the `AnimalDoctor` class needs to look like in order to have code that takes any kind of `Animal` and invokes the `Animal checkup()` method. Trying to overload the `AnimalDoctor` class with `checkup()` methods for every possible kind of animal is ridiculous, and obviously not extensible. You'd have to change the `AnimalDoctor` class every time someone added a new subtype of `Animal`.

So in the `AnimalDoctor` class, you'd probably have a polymorphic method:

```
public void checkAnimal(Animal a) {
  a.checkup(); // does not matter which animal subtype each
               // Animal's overridden checkup() method runs
}
```

And, of course, we do want the `AnimalDoctor` to also have code that can take arrays of `Dogs`, `Cats`, or `Birds` for when the vet comes to the dog, cat, or bird kennel. Again, we don't want overloaded methods with arrays for each potential `Animal` subtype, so we use polymorphism in the `AnimalDoctor` class:

```
public void checkAnimals(Animal[] animals) {
  for(Animal a : animals) {
    a.checkup();
    }
  }
```

Here is the entire example, complete with a test of the array polymorphism that takes any type of animal array (`Dog[], Cat[], Bird[]`):

```
import java.util.*;
abstract class Animal {
  public abstract void checkup();
}
class Dog extends Animal {
  public void checkup() {   // implement Dog-specific code
    System.out.println("Dog checkup");
  }
}
class Cat extends Animal {
  public void checkup() {    // implement Cat-specific code
    System.out.println("Cat checkup");
  }
}
class Bird extends Animal {
  public void checkup() {     // implement Bird-specific code
    System.out.println("Bird checkup");
  }
}
public class AnimalDoctor  {
  // method takes an array of any animal subtype
  public void checkAnimals(Animal[] animals) {
    for(Animal a : animals) {
      a.checkup();
    }
  }
  public static void main(String[] args) {
      // test it
    Dog[] dogs = {new Dog(), new Dog()};
    Cat[] cats = {new Cat(), new Cat(), new Cat()};
    Bird[] birds = {new Bird()};

    AnimalDoctor doc = new AnimalDoctor();
    doc.checkAnimals(dogs);  // pass the Dog[]
    doc.checkAnimals(cats);  // pass the Cat[]
    doc.checkAnimals(birds); // pass the Bird[]
  }
}
```

This works fine, of course (we know, we know, this is old news). But here's why we brought this up as a refresher—this approach does NOT work the same way with type-safe collections!

In other words, a method that takes, say, an `ArrayList<Animal>` will NOT be able to accept a collection of any `Animal` subtype! That means `ArrayList<Dog>` cannot be passed into a method with an argument of `ArrayList<Animal>`, even though we already know that this works just fine with plain old arrays.

Obviously, this difference between arrays and `ArrayList` is consistent with the polymorphism assignment rules we already looked at—the fact that you cannot assign an object of type `ArrayList<JButton>` to a `List<Object>`. But this is where you really start to feel the pain of the distinction between typed arrays and typed collections.

We know it won't work correctly, but let's try changing the `AnimalDoctor` code to use generics instead of arrays:

```
public class AnimalDoctorGeneric  {
  // change the argument from Animal[] to ArrayList<Animal>
  public void checkAnimals(ArrayList<Animal> animals) {
    for(Animal a : animals) {
      a.checkup();
    }
  }
  public static void main(String[] args) {
    // make ArrayLists instead of arrays for Dog, Cat, Bird
    List<Dog> dogs = new ArrayList<Dog>();
    dogs.add(new Dog());
    dogs.add(new Dog());
    List<Cat> cats = new ArrayList<Cat>();
    cats.add(new Cat());
    cats.add(new Cat());
    List<Bird> birds = new ArrayList<Bird>();
    birds.add(new Bird());
    // this code is the same as the Array version
    AnimalDoctorGeneric doc = new AnimalDoctorGeneric();
    // this worked when we used arrays instead of ArrayLists
    doc.checkAnimals(dogs);  // send a List<Dog>
    doc.checkAnimals(cats);  // send a List<Cat>
    doc.checkAnimals(birds); // send a List<Bird>
  }
}
```

So what does happen?

```
javac AnimalDoctorGeneric.java
AnimalDoctorGeneric.java:51: checkAnimals(java.util.ArrayList<Animal>)
in AnimalDoctorGeneric cannot be applied to (java.util.List<Dog>)
       doc.checkAnimals(dogs);
          ^
```

```
AnimalDoctorGeneric.java:52: checkAnimals(java.util.ArrayList<Animal>)
in AnimalDoctorGeneric cannot be applied to (java.util.List<Cat>)
       doc.checkAnimals(cats);
          ^
AnimalDoctorGeneric.java:53: checkAnimals(java.util.ArrayList<Animal>)
in AnimalDoctorGeneric cannot be applied to (java.util.List<Bird>)
       doc.checkAnimals(birds);
          ^
3 errors
```

The compiler stops us with errors, not warnings. You simply CANNOT assign the individual `ArrayLists` of `Animal` subtypes (`<Dog>`, `<Cat>`, or `<Bird>`) to an `ArrayList` of the supertype `<Animal>`, which is the declared type of the argument.

This is one of the biggest gotchas for Java programmers who are so familiar with using polymorphism with arrays, where the same scenario (`Animal[]` can refer to `Dog[]`, `Cat[]`, or `Bird[]`) works as you would expect. So we have two real issues:

1. Why doesn't this work?
2. How do you get around it?

You'd hate us and all of the Java engineers if we told you that there wasn't a way around it—that you had to accept it and write horribly inflexible code that tried to anticipate and code overloaded methods for each specific `<type>`. Fortunately, there is a way around it.

But first, why can't you do it if it works for arrays? Why can't you pass an `ArrayList<Dog>` into a method with an argument of `ArrayList<Animal>`?

We'll get there, but first, let's step way back for a minute and consider this perfectly legal scenario:

```
Animal[] animals = new Animal[3];
animals[0] = new Cat();
animals[1] = new Dog();
```

Part of the benefit of declaring an array using a more abstract supertype is that the array itself can hold objects of multiple subtypes of the supertype, and then you can manipulate the array, assuming everything in it can respond to the `Animal` interface (in other words, everything in the array can respond to method calls defined in the `Animal` class). So here, we're using polymorphism not for the object that the array reference points to, but rather what the array can actually HOLD—in this case, any subtype of `Animal`. You can do the same thing with generics:

```
List<Animal> animals = new ArrayList<Animal>();
animals.add(new Cat());  // OK
animals.add(new Dog());  // OK
```

So this part works with both arrays and generic collections—we can add an instance of a subtype into an array or collection declared with a supertype. You can add `Dogs` and `Cats` to an `Animal` array (`Animal[]`) or an `Animal` collection (`ArrayList<Animal>`).

And with arrays, this applies to what happens within a method:

```
public void addAnimal(Animal[] animals) {
  animals[0] = new Dog();  // no problem, any Animal works
                           // in Animal[]
}
```

So if this is true and you can put `Dogs` into an `ArrayList<Animal>`, then why can't you use that same kind of method scenario? Why can't you do this?

```
public void addAnimal(ArrayList<Animal> animals) {
  animals.add(new Dog()); // sometimes allowed...
}
```

Actually, you CAN do this under certain conditions. The previous code WILL compile just fine IF what you pass into the method is also an `ArrayList<Animal>`. This is the part where it differs from arrays, because in the array version, you COULD pass a `Dog[]` into the method that takes an `Animal[]`.

The ONLY thing you can pass to a method argument of `ArrayList<Animal>` is an `ArrayList<Animal>`! (Assuming you aren't trying to pass a subtype of `ArrayList`, since, remember, the "base" type can be polymorphic.)

The question is still out there—why is this bad? And why is it bad for `ArrayList` but not arrays? Why can't you pass an `ArrayList<Dog>` to an argument of `ArrayList<Animal>`? Actually, the problem IS just as dangerous whether you're using arrays or a generic collection. It's just that the compiler and JVM behave differently for arrays versus generic collections.

The reason it is dangerous to pass a collection (array or `ArrayList`) of a subtype into a method that takes a collection of a supertype is because you might add something. And that means you might add the WRONG thing! This is probably really obvious, but just in case (and to reinforce), let's walk through some scenarios. The first one is simple:

```
public void foo() {
  Dog[] dogs = {new Dog(), new Dog()};
  addAnimal(dogs);            // no problem, send the Dog[] to the method
}
public void addAnimal(Animal[] animals) {
  animals[0] = new Dog();   // ok, any Animal subtype works
}
```

This is no problem. We passed a `Dog[]` into the method and added a `Dog` to the array (which was allowed since the method parameter was type `Animal[]`, which can hold any `Animal` subtype). But what if we changed the calling code to

```
public void foo() {
  Cat[] cats = {new Cat(), new Cat()};
  addAnimal(cats);          // no problem, send the Cat[] to the method
}
```

and the original method stays the same:

```
public void addAnimal(Animal[] animals) {
  animals[0] = new Dog();  // Eeek! We just put a Dog
                           // in a Cat array!
}
```

The compiler thinks it is perfectly fine to add a `Dog` to an `Animal[]` array, since a `Dog` can be assigned to an `Animal` reference. The problem is that if you passed in an array of an `Animal` subtype (`Cat`, `Dog`, or `Bird`), the compiler does not know. The compiler does not realize that out on the heap somewhere is an array of type `Cat[]`, not `Animal[]`, and you're about to try to add a `Dog` to it. To the compiler, you have passed in an array of type `Animal`, so it has no way to recognize the problem.

THIS is the scenario we're trying to prevent, regardless of whether it's an array or an `ArrayList`. The difference is that the compiler lets you get away with it for arrays, but not for generic collections.

The reason the compiler won't let you pass an `ArrayList<Dog>` into a method that takes an `ArrayList<Animal>` is because within the method, that parameter is of type `ArrayList<Animal>`, and that means you could put *any* kind of `Animal` into it. There would be no way for the compiler to stop you from putting a `Dog` into a `List` that was originally declared as `<Cat>` but is now referenced from the `<Animal>` parameter.

We still have two questions… how do you get around it and why the heck does the compiler allow you to take that risk for arrays but not for `ArrayList` (or any other generic collection)?

The reason you can get away with compiling this for arrays is that there is a runtime exception (`ArrayStoreException`) that will prevent you from putting the wrong type of object into an array. If you send a `Dog` array into the method that takes an `Animal` array and you add only `Dogs` (including `Dog` subtypes, of course) into the array now referenced by `Animal`, no problem. But if you DO try to add a `Cat` to the object that is actually a `Dog` array, you'll get the exception.

But there IS no equivalent exception for generics because of type erasure! In other words, at runtime, the JVM KNOWS the type of arrays, but does NOT know the type of a collection. All the generic type information is removed during compilation, so by the time it gets to the JVM, there is simply no way to recognize the disaster of putting a Cat into an ArrayList<Dog> and vice versa (and it becomes exactly like the problems you have when you use legacy, nontype-safe code).

So this actually IS legal code:

```
public void addAnimal(List<Animal> animals) {
  animals.add(new Dog());  // this is always legal,
                           // since Dog can
                           // be assigned to an Animal
                           // reference
  }
  public static void main(String[] args) {
    List<Animal> animals = new ArrayList<Animal>();
    animals.add(new Dog());
    animals.add(new Dog());
    AnimalDoctorGeneric doc = new AnimalDoctorGeneric();
    doc.addAnimal(animals); // OK, since animals matches
                            // the method arg
  }
```

As long as the only thing you pass to the addAnimals(List<Animal>) is an ArrayList<Animal>, the compiler is pleased—knowing that any Animal subtype you add will be valid (you can always add a Dog to an Animal collection, yada, yada, yada). But if you try to invoke addAnimal() with an argument of any OTHER ArrayList type, the compiler will stop you, since at runtime the JVM would have no way to stop you from adding a Dog to what was created as a Cat collection.

For example, this code that changes the generic type to <Dog> without changing the addAnimal() method will NOT compile:

```
public void addAnimal(List<Animal> animals) {
  animals.add(new Dog());  // still OK as always
}
public static void main(String[] args) {
  List<Dog> animals = new ArrayList<Dog>();
  animals.add(new Dog());
  animals.add(new Dog());
  AnimalDoctorGeneric doc = new AnimalDoctorGeneric();
  doc.addAnimal(animals); // THIS is where it breaks!
}
```

The compiler says something like:

```
javac AnimalDoctorGeneric.java
AnimalDoctorGeneric.java:49: addAnimal(java.util.List<Animal>) in
AnimalDoctorGeneric cannot be applied to (java.util.List<Dog>)
       doc.addAnimal(animals);
          ^
1 error
```

Notice that this message is virtually the same one you'd get trying to invoke any method with the wrong argument. It's saying that you simply cannot invoke `addAnimal(List<Animal>)` using something whose reference was declared as `List<Dog>`. (It's the reference type, not the actual object type, that matters—but remember: The generic type of an object is ALWAYS the same as the generic type declared on the reference. `List<Dog>` can refer ONLY to collections that are subtypes of `List` but which were instantiated as generic type `<Dog>`.)

Once again, remember that once inside the `addAnimals()` method, all that matters is the type of the parameter—in this case, `List<Animal>`. (We changed it from `ArrayList` to `List` to keep our "base" type polymorphism cleaner.)

Back to the key question—how do we get around this? If the problem is related only to the danger of adding the wrong thing to the collection, what about the `checkup()` method that used the collection passed in as read-only? In other words, what about methods that invoke `Animal` methods on each thing in the collection, which will work regardless of which kind of `ArrayList` subtype is passed in?

And that's a clue! It's the `add()` method that is the problem, so what we need is a way to tell the compiler, "Hey, I'm using the collection passed in just to invoke methods on the elements—and I promise not to ADD anything into the collection." And there IS a mechanism to tell the compiler that you can take any generic subtype of the declared argument type because you won't be putting anything in the collection. And that mechanism is the wildcard `<?>`.

The method signature would change from

```
public void addAnimal(List<Animal> animals)
```

to

```
public void addAnimal(List<? extends Animal> animals)
```

By saying `<? extends Animal>`, we're saying, "I can be assigned a collection that is a subtype of `List` and typed for `<Animal>` or anything that *extends* `Animal`. And, oh yes, I SWEAR that I will not ADD anything into the collection." (There's a little more to the story, but we'll get there.)

So, of course, the `addAnimal()` method shown previously won't actually compile, even with the wildcard notation, because that method DOES add something.

```
public void addAnimal(List<? extends Animal> animals) {
  animals.add(new Dog());   // NO! Can't add if we
                            // use <? extends Animal>
}
```

You'll get a very strange error that might look something like this:

```
javac AnimalDoctorGeneric.java
AnimalDoctorGeneric.java:38: cannot find symbol
symbol  : method add(Dog)
location: interface java.util.List<capture of ? extends Animal>
      animals.add(new Dog());
             ^
1 error
```

which basically says, "you can't add a `Dog` here." If we change the method so that it doesn't add anything, it works.

But wait—there's more. (And by the way, everything we've covered in this generics section is likely to be tested for on the exam, with the exception of "type erasure," which you aren't required to know any details of.)

First, the `<? extends Animal>` means that you can take any subtype of `Animal`; however, that subtype can be EITHER a subclass of a class (abstract or concrete) OR a type that implements the interface after the word `extends`. In other words, the keyword `extends` in the context of a wildcard represents BOTH subclasses and interface implementations. There is no `<? implements Serializable>` syntax. If you want to declare a method that takes anything that is of a type that implements `Serializable`, you'd still use `extends` like this:

```
void foo(List<? extends Serializable> list) // odd, but correct
                                            // to use "extends"
```

This looks strange since you would never say this in a class declaration because `Serializable` is an interface, not a class. But that's the syntax, so burn it in your brain!

One more time—there is only ONE wildcard keyword that represents *both* interface implementations and subclasses. And that keyword is `extends`. But when you see it, think "IS-A," as in something that passes the `instanceof` test.

However, there is another scenario where you can use a wildcard AND still add to the collection, but in a safe way—the keyword `super`.

Imagine, for example, that you declared the method this way:

```
public void addAnimal(List<? super Dog> animals) {
  animals.add(new Dog());       // adding is sometimes OK with super
}
public static void main(String[] args) {
  List<Animal> animals = new ArrayList<Animal>();
  animals.add(new Dog());
  animals.add(new Dog());
  AnimalDoctorGeneric doc = new AnimalDoctorGeneric();
  doc.addAnimal(animals);      // passing an Animal List
}
```

Now what you've said in this line

```
public void addAnimal(List<? super Dog> animals)
```

is essentially, "Hey, compiler, please accept any List with a generic type that is of type Dog or a supertype of Dog. Nothing lower in the inheritance tree can come in, but anything higher than Dog is okay."

You probably already recognize why this works. If you pass in a list of type Animal, then it's perfectly fine to add a Dog to it. If you pass in a list of type Dog, it's perfectly fine to add a Dog to it. And if you pass in a list of type Object, it's STILL fine to add a Dog to it. When you use the <? super ...> syntax, you are telling the compiler that you can accept the type on the right side of super or any of its supertypes, since—and this is the key part that makes it work—a collection declared as any supertype of Dog will be able to accept a Dog as an element. List<Object> can take a Dog. List<Animal> can take a Dog. And List<Dog> can take a Dog. So passing any of those in will work. So the super keyword in wildcard notation lets you have a restricted, but still possible, way to add to a collection.

So, the wildcard gives you polymorphic assignments, but with certain restrictions that you don't have for arrays. Quick question: Are these two identical?

```
public void foo(List<?> list) { }
public void foo(List<Object> list) { }
```

If there IS a difference (and we're not yet saying there is), what is it?

There IS a huge difference. List<?>, which is the wildcard <?> without the keywords extends or super, simply means "any type." So that means any type of List can be assigned to the argument. That could be a List of <Dog>, <Integer>, <JButton>, <Socket>, whatever. And using the wildcard alone, without the keyword super (followed by a type), means that you cannot ADD anything to the list referred to as List<?>.

List<Object> is completely different from List<?>. List<Object> means that the method can take ONLY a List<Object>. Not a List<Dog> or a List<Cat>. It does, however, mean that you can add to the list, since the compiler has already made certain that you're passing only a valid List<Object> into the method.

Based on the previous explanations, figure out if the following will work:

```
import java.util.*;
public class TestWildcards {
  public static void main(String[] args) {
     List<Integer> myList = new ArrayList<Integer>();
     Bar bar = new Bar();
     bar.doInsert(myList);
  }
```

```
}
class Bar {
  void doInsert(List<?> list) {
     list.add(new Dog());
  }
}
```

If not, where is the problem?

The problem is in the `list.add()` method within `doInsert()`. The `<?>` wildcard allows a list of ANY type to be passed to the method, but the `add()` method is not valid, for the reasons we explored earlier (that you could put the wrong kind of thing into the collection). So this time, the `TestWildcards` class is fine, but the `Bar` class won't compile because it does an `add()` in a method that uses a wildcard (without `super`). What if we change the `doInsert()` method to this:

```
import java.util.*;
public class TestWildcards {
  public static void main(String[] args) {
     List<Integer> myList = new ArrayList<Integer>();
     Bar bar = new Bar();
     bar.doInsert(myList);
  }
}
class Bar {
   void doInsert(List<Object> list) {
     list.add(new Dog());
   }
}
```

Now will it work? If not, why not?

This time, class `Bar`, with the `doInsert()` method, compiles just fine. The problem is that the `TestWildcards` code is trying to pass a `List<Integer>` into a method that can take ONLY a `List<Object>`. And *nothing* else can be substituted for `<Object>`.

By the way, `List<? extends Object>` and `List<?>` are absolutely identical! They both say, "I can refer to any type of object." But as you can see, neither of them is the same as `List<Object>`. One way to remember this is that if you see the wildcard notation (a question mark `?`), this means "many possibilities." If you do NOT see the question mark, then it means the `<type>` in the brackets and absolutely NOTHING ELSE. `List<Dog>` means `List<Dog>` and not `List<Beagle>`, `List<Poodle>`, or any other subtype of `Dog`. But `List<? extends Dog>` could mean `List<Beagle>`, `List<Poodle>`, and so on. Of course `List<?>` could be... anything at all.

Keep in mind that the wildcards can be used only for reference declarations (including arguments, variables, return types, and so on). They can't be used as the type parameter when you create a new typed collection. Think about that—while a reference can be abstract and polymorphic, the actual object created must be of a specific type. You have to lock down the type when you make the object using `new`.

As a little review before we move on with generics, look at the following statements and figure out which will compile:

```
1) List<?> list = new ArrayList<Dog>();
2) List<? extends Animal> aList = new ArrayList<Dog>();
3) List<?> foo = new ArrayList<? extends Animal>();
4) List<? extends Dog> cList = new ArrayList<Integer>();
5) List<? super Dog> bList = new ArrayList<Animal>();
6) List<? super Animal> dList = new ArrayList<Dog>();
```

The correct answers (the statements that compile) are 1, 2, and 5.
The three that won't compile are

- **Statement** `List<?> foo = new ArrayList<? extends Animal>();`
- **Problem** You cannot use wildcard notation in the object creation. So the `new ArrayList<? extends Animal>()` will not compile.
- **Statement** `List<? extends Dog> cList = new ArrayList<Integer>();`
- **Problem** You cannot assign an `Integer` list to a reference that takes only a `Dog` (including any subtypes of `Dog`, of course).
- **Statement** `List<? super Animal> dList = new ArrayList<Dog>();`
- **Problem** You cannot assign a `Dog` to `<? super Animal>`. The `Dog` is too "low" in the class hierarchy. Only `<Animal>` or `<Object>` would have been legal.

Generic Declarations

Until now, we've talked about how to create type-safe collections and how to declare reference variables, including arguments and return types, using generic syntax. But here are a few questions: How do we even know that we're allowed/supposed to specify a type for these collection classes? And does generic typing work with any other classes in the API? And finally, can we declare our own classes as generic types? In other words, can we make a class that requires that someone pass a type in when they declare it and instantiate it?

First, the one you obviously know the answer to—the API tells you when a parameterized type is expected. For example, this is the API declaration for the `java.util.List` interface:

```
public interface List<E>
```

The `<E>` is a placeholder for the type you pass in. The `List` interface is behaving as a generic "template" (sort of like C++ templates), and when you write your code, you change it from a generic `List` to a `List<Dog>` or `List<Integer>`, and so on.

The `E`, by the way, is only a convention. Any valid Java identifier would work here, but `E` stands for "Element," and it's used when the template is a collection. The other main convention is `T` (stands for "type"), used for, well, things that are NOT collections.

Now that you've seen the interface declaration for `List`, what do you think the `add()` method looks like?

```
boolean add(E o)
```

In other words, whatever `E` is when you declare the `List`, *that's what you can add to it*. So imagine this code:

```
List<Animal> list = new ArrayList<Animal>();
```

The `E` in the List API suddenly has its waveform collapsed and goes from the abstract `<your type goes here>` to a `List` of `Animals`. And if it's a `List` of `Animals`, then the `add()` method of `List` must obviously behave like this:

```
boolean add(Animal a)
```

When you look at an API for a generics class or interface, pick a type parameter (`Dog`, `JButton`, even `Object`) and do a mental find and replace on each instance of `E` (or whatever identifier is used as the placeholder for the type parameter).

Making Your Own Generic Class

Let's try making our own generic class to get a feel for how it works, and then we'll look at a few remaining generics syntax details. Imagine someone created a class `Rental` that manages a pool of rentable items:

```
public class Rental {
  private List rentalPool;
  private int maxNum;
  public Rental(int maxNum, List rentalPool) {
    this.maxNum = maxNum;
    this.rentalPool = rentalPool;
```

```
  }
  public Object getRental() {
    // blocks until there's something available
    return rentalPool.get(0);
  }
  public void returnRental(Object o) {
    rentalPool.add(o);
  }
}
```

Now imagine you wanted to make a subclass of `Rental` that was just for renting cars. You might start with something like this:

```
import java.util.*;
public class CarRental extends Rental {
  public CarRental(int maxNum, List<Car> rentalPool) {
    super(maxNum, rentalPool);
  }
  public Car getRental() {
    return (Car) super.getRental();
  }
  public void returnRental(Car c) {
    super.returnRental(c);
  }
  public void returnRental(Object o) {
    if (o instanceof Car) {
      super.returnRental(o);
    } else {
       System.out.println("Cannot add a non-Car");
       // probably throw an exception
} } }
```

But then, the more you look at it, the more you realize

1. You are doing your own type checking in the `returnRental()` method. You can't change the argument type of `returnRental()` to take a `Car`, since it's an override (not an overload) of the method from class `Rental`. (Overloading would take away your polymorphic flexibility with `Rental`.)
2. You really don't want to make separate subclasses for every possible kind of rentable thing (cars, computers, bowling shoes, children, and so on).

But given your natural brilliance (heightened by this contrived scenario), you quickly realize that you can make the `Rental` class a generic type—a template for any kind of `Rentable` thing—and you're good to go.

(We did say contrived... since in reality, you might very well want to have different behaviors for different kinds of rentable things, but even that could be solved cleanly through some kind of behavior composition as opposed to inheritance (using the Strategy design pattern, for example). And no, the Strategy design pattern isn't on the exam, but we still think you should read our design patterns book. Think of the kittens.) So here's your new and improved generic `Rental` class:

```
import java.util.*;
public class RentalGeneric<T> {                 // "T" is for the type
                                                // parameter
  private List<T> rentalPool;                   // Use the class type for the
                                                // List type
  private int maxNum;
  public RentalGeneric(
    int maxNum, List<T> rentalPool) {          // constructor takes a
                                               // List of the class type
    this.maxNum = maxNum;
    this.rentalPool = rentalPool;
  }
  public T getRental() {                        // we rent out a T
    // blocks until there's something available
    return rentalPool.get(0);
  }
  public void returnRental(T returnedThing) { // and the renter
                                              // returns a T
    rentalPool.add(returnedThing);
  }
}
```

Let's put it to the test:

```
class TestRental {
  public static void main (String[] args) {
    //make some Cars for the pool
    Car c1 = new Car();
    Car c2 = new Car();
    List<Car> carList = new ArrayList<Car>();
    carList.add(c1);
    carList.add(c2);
    RentalGeneric<Car> carRental = new
                        RentalGeneric<Car>(2, carList);
    // now get a car out, and it won't need a cast
    Car carToRent = carRental.getRental();
    carRental.returnRental(carToRent);
    // can we stick something else in the original carList?
    carList.add(new Cat("Fluffy"));
  }
}
```

We get one error:

```
kathy% javac1.5 RentalGeneric.java
RentalGeneric.java:38: cannot find symbol
symbol  : method add(Cat)
location: interface java.util.List<Car>
     carList.add(new Cat("Fluffy"));
             ^
1 error
```

Now we have a `Rental` class that can be *typed* to whatever the programmer chooses, and the compiler will enforce it. In other words, it works just as the `Collections` classes do. Let's look at more examples of generic syntax you might find in the API or source code. Here's another simple class that uses the parameterized type of the class in several ways:

```
public class TestGenerics<T> {       // as the class type
  T anInstance;                      // as an instance variable type
  T [] anArrayOfTs;                  // as an array type

  TestGenerics(T anInstance) {       // as an argument type
     this.anInstance = anInstance;
  }
  T getT() {                         // as a return type
     return anInstance;
  }
}
```

Obviously, this is a ridiculous use of generics, and in fact, you'll see generics only rarely outside of collections. But you do need to understand the different kinds of generic syntax you might encounter, so we'll continue with these examples until we've covered them all.

You can use more than one parameterized type in a single class definition:

```
public class UseTwo<T, X> {
  T one;
  X two;
  UseTwo(T one, X two) {
    this.one = one;
    this.two = two;
  }
  T getT() { return one; }
  X getX() { return two; }

// test it by creating it with <String, Integer>

  public static void main (String[] args) {
    UseTwo<String, Integer> twos =
                    new UseTwo<String, Integer>("foo", 42);
```

```
      String theT = twos.getT(); // returns a String
      int theX = twos.getX();    // returns Integer, unboxes to int
    }
  }
```

And you can use a form of wildcard notation in a class definition to specify a range (called "bounds") for the type that can be used for the type parameter:

```
public class AnimalHolder<T extends Animal> {              // use "T" instead
                                                           // of "?"
 T animal;
 public static void main(String[] args) {
   AnimalHolder<Dog> dogHolder = new AnimalHolder<Dog>(); // OK
   AnimalHolder<Integer> x = new AnimalHolder<Integer>(); // NO!
 }
}
```

Creating Generic Methods

Until now, every example we've seen uses the class parameter type—the type declared with the class name. For example, in the `UseTwo<T,X>` declaration, we used the `T` and `X` placeholders throughout the code. But it's possible to define a parameterized type at a more granular level—a method.

Imagine you want to create a method that takes an instance of any type, instantiates an `ArrayList` of that type, and adds the instance to the `ArrayList`. The class itself doesn't need to be generic; basically, we just want a utility method that we can pass a type to and that can use that type to construct a type-safe collection. Using a generic method, we can declare the method without a specific type and then get the type information based on the type of the object passed to the method. For example:

```
import java.util.*;
public class CreateAnArrayList {
  public <T> void makeArrayList(T t) {   // take an object of an
                                         // unknown type and use a
                                         // "T" to represent the type
    List<T> list = new ArrayList<T>();   // now we can create the
                                         // list using "T"
    list.add(t);
  }
}
```

In the preceding code, if you invoke the `makeArrayList()` method with a `Dog` instance, the method will behave as though it looked like this all along:

```
public void makeArrayList(Dog t) {
  List<Dog> list = new ArrayList<Dog>();
  list.add(t);
}
```

And, of course, if you invoke the method with an `Integer`, then the `T` is replaced by `Integer` (not in the bytecode, remember—we're describing how it appears to behave, not how it actually gets it done).

The strangest thing about generic methods is that you must declare the type variable BEFORE the return type of the method:

```
public <T> void makeArrayList(T t)
```

The `<T>` before `void` simply defines what `T` is before you use it as a type in the argument. You MUST declare the type like that unless the type is specified for the class. In `CreateAnArrayList`, the class is not generic, so there's no type parameter placeholder we can use.

You're also free to put boundaries on the type you declare. For example, if you want to restrict the `makeArrayList()` method to only `Number` or its subtypes (`Integer`, `Float`, and so on), you would say

```
public <T extends Number> void makeArrayList(T t)
```

exam Watch

It's tempting to forget that the method argument is NOT where you declare the type parameter variable `T`. In order to use a type variable like `T`, you must have declared it either as the class parameter type or in the method, before the return type. The following might look right:

```
public void makeList(T t) { }
```

But the only way for this to be legal is if there is actually a class named `T`, in which case the argument is like any other type declaration for a variable. And what about constructor arguments? They, too, can be declared with a generic type, but then it looks even stranger, since constructors have no return type at all:

```
public class Radio {
  public <T> Radio(T t) { }  // legal constructor
}
```

exam watch

If you REALLY want to get ridiculous (or fired), you can declare a class with a name that is the same as the type parameter placeholder:

```
class X { public <X> X(X x) { } }
```

Yes, this works. The `X` that is the constructor name has no relationship to the `<X>` type declaration, which has no relationship to the constructor argument identifier, which is also, of course, `X`. The compiler is able to parse this and treat each of the different uses of `X` independently. So there is no naming conflict between class names, type parameter placeholders, and variable identifiers.

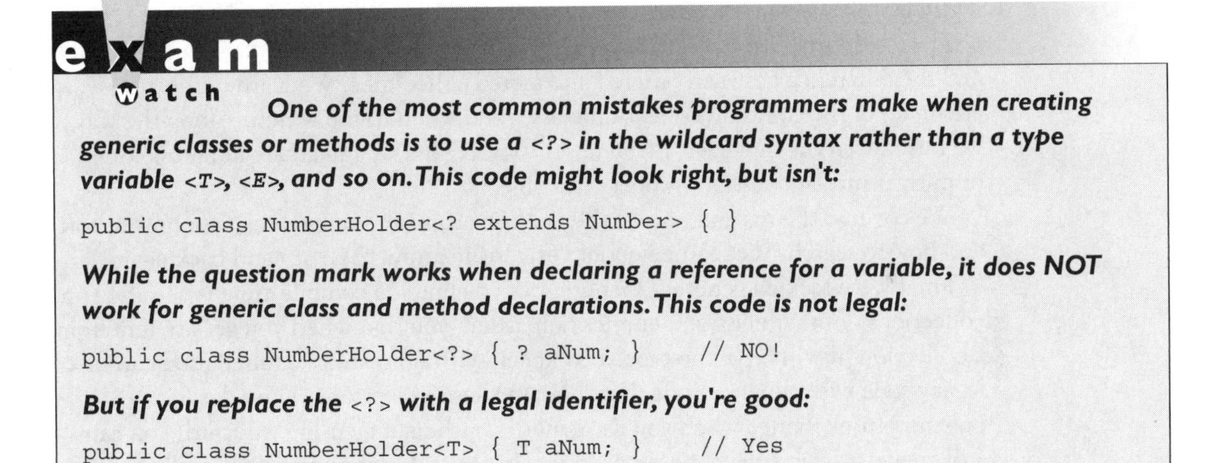

exam watch

One of the most common mistakes programmers make when creating generic classes or methods is to use a `<?>` in the wildcard syntax rather than a type variable `<T>`, `<E>`, and so on. This code might look right, but isn't:

```
public class NumberHolder<? extends Number> { }
```

While the question mark works when declaring a reference for a variable, it does NOT work for generic class and method declarations. This code is not legal:

```
public class NumberHolder<?> { ? aNum; }     // NO!
```

But if you replace the `<?>` with a legal identifier, you're good:

```
public class NumberHolder<T> { T aNum; }     // Yes
```

In practice, 98% of what you're likely to do with generics is simply declare and use type-safe collections, including using (and passing) them as arguments. But now you know much more (but by no means everything) about the way generics work.

If this was clear and easy for you, that's excellent. If it was… painful… just know that adding generics to the Java language very nearly caused a revolt among some of the most experienced Java developers. Most of the outspoken critics are simply unhappy with the complexity, or aren't convinced that gaining type-safe collections is worth the ten million little rules you have to learn now. It's true that with Java 5, learning Java just got harder. But trust us… we've never seen it take more than two days to "get" generics. That's 48 consecutive hours.

CERTIFICATION SUMMARY

We began with a quick review of the `toString()` method. The `toString()` method is automatically called when you ask `System.out.println()` to print an object—you override it to return a `String` of meaningful data about your objects.

Next, we reviewed the purpose of `==` (to see if two reference variables refer to the same object) and the `equals()` method (to see if two objects are meaningfully equivalent). You learned the downside of not overriding `equals()`—you may not be able to find the object in a collection. We discussed a little bit about how to write a good `equals()` method—don't forget to use `instanceof` and refer to the object's significant attributes. We reviewed the contracts for overriding `equals()` and `hashCode()`. We learned about the theory behind hashcodes, the difference between legal, appropriate, and efficient hashcoding. We also saw that even though wildly inefficient, it's legal for a `hashCode()` method to always return the same value.

Next, we turned to collections, where we learned about `Lists`, `Sets`, and `Maps` and the difference between ordered and sorted collections. We learned the key attributes of the common collection classes and when to use which. Along the way, we introduced the new Java 7 "diamond" syntax, and we talked about autoboxing primitives into and out of wrapper class objects.

We covered the ins and outs of the `Collections` and `Arrays` classes: how to sort and how to search. We learned about converting arrays to `Lists` and back again.

Finally, we tackled generics. Generics let you enforce compile-time type-safety on collections or other classes. Generics help assure you that when you get an item from a collection, it will be of the type you expect, with no casting required. You can mix legacy code with generics code, but this can cause exceptions. The rules for polymorphism change when you use generics, although by using wildcards you can still create polymorphic collections. Some generics declarations allow reading of a collection, but allow very limited updating of the collection.

All in all, one fascinating chapter.

✓ TWO-MINUTE DRILL

Here are some of the key points from this chapter.

Overriding hashCode() and equals() (OCP Objectives 4.7 and 4.8)

- `equals()`, `hashCode()`, and `toString()` are `public`.
- Override `toString()` so that `System.out.println()` or other methods can see something useful, like your object's state.
- Use `==` to determine if two reference variables refer to the same object.
- Use `equals()` to determine if two objects are meaningfully equivalent.
- If you don't override `equals()`, your objects won't be useful hashing keys.
- If you don't override `equals()`, different objects can't be considered equal.
- Strings and wrappers override `equals()` and make good hashing keys.
- When overriding `equals()`, use the `instanceof` operator to be sure you're evaluating an appropriate class.
- When overriding `equals()`, compare the objects' significant attributes.
- Highlights of the `equals()` contract:
  - Reflexive: `x.equals(x)` is `true`.
  - Symmetric: If `x.equals(y)` is `true`, then `y.equals(x)` must be `true`.
  - Transitive: If `x.equals(y)` is `true`, and `y.equals(z)` is `true`, then `z.equals(x)` is `true`.
  - Consistent: Multiple calls to `x.equals(y)` will return the same result.
  - Null: If `x` is not `null`, then `x.equals(null)` is `false`.
- If `x.equals(y)` is `true`, then `x.hashCode() == y.hashCode()` is `true`.
- If you override `equals()`, override `hashCode()`.
- `HashMap`, `HashSet`, `Hashtable`, `LinkedHashMap`, and `LinkedHashSet` use hashing.
- An appropriate `hashCode()` override sticks to the `hashCode()` contract.
- An efficient `hashCode()` override distributes keys evenly across its buckets.

- An overridden `equals()` must be at least as precise as its `hashCode()` mate.
- To reiterate: If two objects are equal, their hashcodes must be equal.
- It's legal for a `hashCode()` method to return the same value for all instances (although in practice it's very inefficient).
- Highlights of the `hashCode()` contract:
  - Consistent: Multiple calls to `x.hashCode()` return the same integer.
  - If `x.equals(y)` is `true`, `x.hashCode() == y.hashCode()` is `true`.
  - If `x.equals(y)` is `false`, then `x.hashCode() == y.hashCode()` can be either `true` or `false`, but `false` will tend to create better efficiency.
- Transient variables aren't appropriate for `equals()` and `hashCode()`.

Collections (OCP Objectives 4.5 and 4.6)

- Common collection activities include adding objects, removing objects, verifying object inclusion, retrieving objects, and iterating.
- Three meanings for "collection":
  - **collection** Represents the data structure in which objects are stored
  - **Collection** `java.util` interface from which `Set` and `List` extend
  - **Collections** A class that holds static collection utility methods
- Four basic flavors of collections include `Lists`, `Sets`, `Maps`, and `Queues`:
  - **Lists of things** Ordered, duplicates allowed, with an index
  - **Sets of things** May or may not be ordered and/or sorted; duplicates not allowed
  - **Maps of things with keys** May or may not be ordered and/or sorted; duplicate keys are not allowed
  - **Queues of things to process** Ordered by FIFO or by priority
- Four basic subflavors of collections: Sorted, Unsorted, Ordered, and Unordered:
  - **Ordered** Iterating through a collection in a specific, nonrandom order
  - **Sorted** Iterating through a collection in a sorted order
- Sorting can be alphabetic, numeric, or programmer-defined.

Key Attributes of Common Collection Classes (OCP Objectives 4.5 and 4.6)

- `ArrayList` Fast iteration and fast random access.
- `Vector` It's like a slower `ArrayList`, but it has synchronized methods.
- `LinkedList` Good for adding elements to the ends, i.e., stacks and queues.
- `HashSet` Fast access, assures no duplicates, provides no ordering.
- `LinkedHashSet` No duplicates; iterates by insertion order.
- `TreeSet` No duplicates; iterates in sorted order.
- `HashMap` Fastest updates (key/values); allows one `null` key, many `null` values.
- `Hashtable` Like a slower `HashMap` (as with `Vector`, due to its synchronized methods). No `null` values or `null` keys allowed.
- `LinkedHashMap` Faster iterations; iterates by insertion order or last accessed; allows one `null` key, many `null` values.
- `TreeMap` A sorted map.
- `PriorityQueue` A to-do list ordered by the elements' priority.

Using Collection Classes (OCP Objectives 4.2, 4.5, and 4.6)

- Collections hold only Objects, but primitives can be autoboxed.
- Java 7 allows "diamond" syntax: `List<Dog> d = new ArrayList<>();`.
- Iterate with the enhanced `for` or with an `Iterator` via `hasNext()` and `next()`.
- `hasNext()` determines if more elements exist; the `Iterator` does NOT move.
- `next()` returns the next element AND moves the `Iterator` forward.
- To work correctly, a `Map`'s keys must override `equals()` and `hashCode()`.
- `Queue`s use `offer()` to add an element, `poll()` to remove the head of the queue, and `peek()` to look at the head of a queue.
- For the OCJPJ 6: `TreeSet`s and `TreeMap`s have navigation methods like `floor()` and `higher()`.
- For the OCJPJ 6: You can create/extend "backed" subcopies of `TreeSet`s and `TreeMap`s.

Sorting and Searching Arrays and Lists (OCP Objectives 4.7 and 4.8)

- Sorting can be in natural order or via a `Comparable` or many `Comparators`.
- Implement `Comparable` using `compareTo()`; provides only one sort order.
- Create many `Comparators` to sort a class many ways; implement `compare()`.
- To be sorted and searched, an array's or `List`'s elements must be *comparable*.
- To be searched, an array or `List` must first be sorted.

Utility Classes: Collections and Arrays (OCP Objectives 4.7 and 4.8)

- These `java.util` classes provide
  - A `sort()` method. Sort using a `Comparator` or sort using natural order.
  - A `binarySearch()` method. Search a presorted array or `List`.
  - `Arrays.asList()` creates a `List` from an array and links them together.
  - `Collections.reverse()` reverses the order of elements in a `List`.
  - `Collections.reverseOrder()` returns a `Comparator` that sorts in reverse.
  - `Lists` and `Sets` have a `toArray()` method to create arrays.

Generics (OCP Objectives 4.1 and 4.3)

- Generics let you enforce compile-time type-safety on Collections (or other classes and methods declared using generic type parameters).
- An `ArrayList<Animal>` can accept references of type `Dog`, `Cat`, or any other subtype of `Animal` (subclass, or if `Animal` is an interface, implementation).
- When using generic collections, a cast is not needed to get (declared type) elements out of the collection. With nongeneric collections, a cast is required:

```
List<String> gList = new ArrayList<String>();
List list = new ArrayList();
// more code
String s = gList.get(0);          // no cast needed
String s = (String)list.get(0);   // cast required
```

- ❑ You can pass a generic collection into a method that takes a nongeneric collection, but the results may be disastrous. The compiler can't stop the method from inserting the wrong type into the previously type-safe collection.
- ❑ If the compiler can recognize that nontype-safe code is potentially endangering something you originally declared as type-safe, you will get a compiler warning. For instance, if you pass a `List<String>` into a method declared as

```
void foo(List aList) { aList.add(anInteger); }
```

  you'll get a warning because `add()` is potentially "unsafe."
- ❑ "Compiles without error" is not the same as "compiles without warnings." A compilation *warning* is not considered a compilation *error* or *failure*.
- ❑ Generic type information does not exist at runtime—it is for compile-time safety only. Mixing generics with legacy code can create compiled code that may throw an exception at runtime.
- ❑ Polymorphic assignments apply only to the base type, not the generic type parameter. You can say

```
List<Animal> aList = new ArrayList<Animal>();    // yes
```

  You can't say

```
List<Animal> aList = new ArrayList<Dog>();       // no
```

- ❑ The polymorphic assignment rule applies everywhere an assignment can be made. The following are NOT allowed:

```
void foo(List<Animal> aList) { }  // cannot take a List<Dog>
List<Animal> bar() { }            // cannot return a List<Dog>
```

- ❑ Wildcard syntax allows a generic method to accept subtypes (or supertypes) of the declared type of the method argument:

```
void addD(List<Dog> d) {}           // can take only <Dog>
void addD(List<? extends Dog>) {}  // take a <Dog> or <Beagle>
```

- ❑ The wildcard keyword `extends` is used to mean either "extends" or "implements." So in `<? extends Dog>`, `Dog` can be a class or an interface.

- When using a wildcard `List<? extends Dog>`, the collection can be accessed but not modified.
- When using a wildcard `List<?>`, any generic type can be assigned to the reference, but for access only—no modifications.
- `List<Object>` refers only to a `List<Object>`, while `List<?>` or `List<? extends Object>` can hold any type of object, but for access only.
- Declaration conventions for generics use `T` for type and `E` for element:

```
public interface List<E>  // API declaration for List
boolean add(E o)          // List.add() declaration
```

- The generics type identifier can be used in class, method, and variable declarations:

```
class Foo<t> { }          // a class
T anInstance;             // an instance variable
Foo(T aRef) {}            // a constructor argument
void bar(T aRef) {}       // a method argument
T baz() {}                // a return type
```

  The compiler will substitute the actual type.
- You can use more than one parameterized type in a declaration:

```
public class UseTwo<T, X> { }
```

- You can declare a generic method using a type not defined in the class:

```
public <T> void makeList(T t) { }
```

This is NOT using `T` as the return type. This method has a `void` return type, but to use `T` within the argument, you must declare the `<T>`, which happens before the return type.

SELF TEST

The following questions will help you measure your understanding of the material presented in this chapter. Read all of the choices carefully, as there may be more than one correct answer. Choose all correct answers for each question. Stay focused.

1. Given:

```
public static void main(String[] args) {

  // INSERT DECLARATION HERE
  for (int i = 0; i <= 10; i++) {
    List<Integer> row = new ArrayList<Integer>();
    for (int j = 0; j <= 10; j++)
      row.add(i * j);
    table.add(row);
  }
  for (List<Integer> row : table)
    System.out.println(row);
  }
```

Which statements could be inserted at `// INSERT DECLARATION HERE` to allow this code to compile and run? (Choose all that apply.)

A. `List<List<Integer>> table = new List<List<Integer>>();`

B. `List<List<Integer>> table = new ArrayList<List<Integer>>();`

C. `List<List<Integer>> table = new ArrayList<ArrayList<Integer>>();`

D. `List<List, Integer> table = new List<List, Integer>();`

E. `List<List, Integer> table = new ArrayList<List, Integer>();`

F. `List<List, Integer> table = new ArrayList<ArrayList, Integer>();`

G. None of the above

2. Which statements are true about comparing two instances of the same class, given that the `equals()` and `hashCode()` methods have been properly overridden? (Choose all that apply.)

A. If the `equals()` method returns `true`, the `hashCode()` comparison `==` might return `false`

B. If the `equals()` method returns `false`, the `hashCode()` comparison `==` might return `true`

C. If the `hashCode()` comparison `==` returns `true`, the `equals()` method must return `true`

D. If the `hashCode()` comparison `==` returns `true`, the `equals()` method might return `true`

E. If the `hashCode()` comparison `!=` returns `true`, the `equals()` method might return `true`

3. Given:

```
public static void before() {
  Set set = new TreeSet();
  set.add("2");
  set.add(3);
  set.add("1");
  Iterator it = set.iterator();
    while (it.hasNext())
  System.out.print(it.next() + " ");
}
```

Which statements are true?

A. The `before()` method will print `1 2`

B. The `before()` method will print `1 2 3`

C. The `before()` method will print three numbers, but the order cannot be determined

D. The `before()` method will not compile

E. The `before()` method will throw an exception at runtime

4. Given:

```
import java.util.*;
class MapEQ {
  public static void main(String[] args) {
    Map<ToDos, String> m = new HashMap<ToDos, String>();
    ToDos t1 = new ToDos("Monday");
    ToDos t2 = new ToDos("Monday");
    ToDos t3 = new ToDos("Tuesday");
    m.put(t1, "doLaundry");
    m.put(t2, "payBills");
    m.put(t3, "cleanAttic");
    System.out.println(m.size());
  }
}
class ToDos{
  String day;
  ToDos(String d) { day = d; }
  public boolean equals(Object o) {
    return ((ToDos)o).day.equals(this.day);
  }
  // public int hashCode() { return 9; }
}
```

Which is correct? (Choose all that apply.)

A. As the code stands, it will not compile

B. As the code stands, the output will be `2`

C. As the code stands, the output will be `3`

D. If the `hashCode()` method is uncommented, the output will be `2`

E. If the `hashCode()` method is uncommented, the output will be `3`

F. If the `hashCode()` method is uncommented, the code will not compile

5. Given:

```
12. public class AccountManager {
13.   private Map accountTotals = new HashMap();
14.   private int retirementFund;
15.
16.   public int getBalance(String accountName) {
17.     Integer total = (Integer) accountTotals.get(accountName);
18.     if (total == null)
19.       total = Integer.valueOf(0);
20.     return total.intValue();
21.   }
23.   public void setBalance(String accountName, int amount) {
24.     accountTotals.put(accountName, Integer.valueOf(amount));
25.   }
26. }
```

This class is to be updated to make use of appropriate generic types, with no changes in behavior (for better or worse). Which of these steps could be performed? (Choose three.)

A. Replace line 13 with

```
private Map<String, int> accountTotals = new HashMap<String, int>();
```

B. Replace line 13 with

```
private Map<String, Integer> accountTotals = new HashMap<String, Integer>();
```

C. Replace line 13 with

```
private Map<String<Integer>\> accountTotals = new HashMap<String<Integer>\>();
```

D. Replace lines 17–20 with

```
int total = accountTotals.get(accountName);
    if (total == null)
        total = 0;
    return total;
```

E. Replace lines 17–20 with

```
Integer total = accountTotals.get(accountName);
    if (total == null)
        total = 0;
    return total;
```

F. Replace lines 17–20 with

```
return accountTotals.get(accountName);
```

G. Replace line 24 with

```
accountTotals.put(accountName, amount);
```

H. Replace line 24 with

```
accountTotals.put(accountName, amount.intValue());
```

6. Given:

```
interface Hungry<E> { void munch(E x); }
interface Carnivore<E extends Animal> extends Hungry<E> {}
interface Herbivore<E extends Plant> extends Hungry<E> {}
abstract class Plant {}
class Grass extends Plant {}
abstract class Animal {}
class Sheep extends Animal implements Herbivore<Sheep> {
  public void munch(Sheep x) {}
}
class Wolf extends Animal implements Carnivore<Sheep> {
  public void munch(Sheep x) {}
}
```

Which of the following changes (taken separately) would allow this code to compile? (Choose all that apply.)

A. Change the `Carnivore` interface to

```
interface Carnivore<E extends Plant> extends Hungry<E> {}
```

B. Change the `Herbivore` interface to

```
interface Herbivore<E extends Animal> extends Hungry<E> {}
```

C. Change the `Sheep` class to

```
class Sheep extends Animal implements Herbivore<Plant> {
  public void munch(Grass x) {}
}
```

D. Change the `Sheep` class to

```
class Sheep extends Plant implements Carnivore<Wolf> {
   public void munch(Wolf x) {}
}
```

E. Change the `Wolf` class to

```
class Wolf extends Animal implements Herbivore<Grass> {
  public void munch(Grass x) {}
}
```

F. No changes are necessary

7. Which collection class(es) allows you to grow or shrink its size and provides indexed access to its elements, but whose methods are not synchronized? (Choose all that apply.)

A. `java.util.HashSet`

B. `java.util.LinkedHashSet`

C. `java.util.List`

D. `java.util.ArrayList`

E. `java.util.Vector`

F. `java.util.PriorityQueue`

8. Given a method declared as

```
public static <E extends Number> List<E> process(List<E> nums)
```

A programmer wants to use this method like this:

```
// INSERT DECLARATIONS HERE

output = process(input);
```

Which pairs of declarations could be placed at `// INSERT DECLARATIONS HERE` to allow the code to compile? (Choose all that apply.)

A.
```
ArrayList<Integer> input = null;
ArrayList<Integer> output = null;
```

B.
```
ArrayList<Integer> input = null;
List<Integer> output = null;
```

C.
```
ArrayList<Integer> input = null;
List<Number> output = null;
```

D.
```
List<Number> input = null;
ArrayList<Integer> output = null;
```

E.
```
List<Number> input = null;
List<Number> output = null;
```

F.
```
List<Integer> input = null;
List<Integer> output = null;
```

G. None of the above

9. Given the proper import statement(s) and

```
13.  PriorityQueue<String> pq = new PriorityQueue<String>();
14.  pq.add("2");
15.  pq.add("4");
16.  System.out.print(pq.peek() + " ");
17.  pq.offer("1");
18.  pq.add("3");
19.  pq.remove("1");
20.  System.out.print(pq.poll() + " ");
21.  if(pq.remove("2")) System.out.print(pq.poll() + " ");
22.  System.out.println(pq.poll() + " " + pq.peek());
```

What is the result?

A. `2 2 3 3`

B. `2 2 3 4`

C. `4 3 3 4`

D. `2 2 3 3 3`

E. `4 3 3 3 3`

F. `2 2 3 3 4`

G. Compilation fails

H. An exception is thrown at runtime

10. Given:

```
 3. import java.util.*;
 4. public class Mixup {
 5.   public static void main(String[] args) {
 6.     Object o = new Object();
 7.     // insert code here
 8.     s.add("o");
 9.     s.add(o);
10.   }
11. }
```

And these three fragments:

```
I.   Set s = new HashSet();
II.  TreeSet s = new TreeSet();
III. LinkedHashSet s = new LinkedHashSet();
```

When fragments I, II, or III are inserted independently at line 7, which are true? (Choose all that apply.)

A. Fragment I compiles

B. Fragment II compiles

C. Fragment III compiles

D. Fragment I executes without exception

E. Fragment II executes without exception

F. Fragment III executes without exception

11. Given:

```
 3. import java.util.*;
 4. class Turtle {
 5.   int size;
 6.   public Turtle(int s) { size = s; }
 7.   public boolean equals(Object o) { return (this.size == ((Turtle)o).size); }
 8.   // insert code here
 9. }
10. public class TurtleTest {
11.   public static void main(String[] args) {
12.     LinkedHashSet<Turtle> t = new LinkedHashSet<Turtle>();
13.     t.add(new Turtle(1));   t.add(new Turtle(2));   t.add(new Turtle(1));
14.     System.out.println(t.size());
15.   }
16. }
```

And these two fragments:

```
I.   public int hashCode() { return size/5; }
II.  // no hashCode method declared
```

If fragment I or II is inserted independently at line 8, which are true? (Choose all that apply.)

A. If fragment I is inserted, the output is `2`

B. If fragment I is inserted, the output is `3`

C. If fragment II is inserted, the output is `2`

D. If fragment II is inserted, the output is `3`

E. If fragment I is inserted, compilation fails

F. If fragment II is inserted, compilation fails

12. (OCJPJ 6 only) Given the proper import statement(s) and:

```
13.  TreeSet<String> s = new TreeSet<String>();
14.  TreeSet<String> subs = new TreeSet<String>();
15.  s.add("a"); s.add("b"); s.add("c"); s.add("d"); s.add("e");
16.
17.  subs = (TreeSet)s.subSet("b", true, "d", true);
18.  s.add("g");
19.  s.pollFirst();
20.  s.pollFirst();
21.  s.add("c2");
22.  System.out.println(s.size() +" "+ subs.size());
```

Which are true? (Choose all that apply.)

A. The size of `s` is `4`

B. The size of `s` is `5`

C. The size of `s` is `7`

D. The size of `subs` is `1`

E. The size of `subs` is `2`

F. The size of `subs` is `3`

G. The size of `subs` is `4`

H. An exception is thrown at runtime

13. (OCJPJ 6 only) Given:

```
 3. import java.util.*;
 4. public class Magellan {
 5.   public static void main(String[] args) {
 6.     TreeMap<String, String> myMap = new TreeMap<String, String>();
 7.     myMap.put("a", "apple"); myMap.put("d", "date");
 8.     myMap.put("f", "fig"); myMap.put("p", "pear");
 9.     System.out.println("1st after mango: " +   // sop 1
10.       myMap.higherKey("f"));
11.     System.out.println("1st after mango: " +   // sop 2
12.       myMap.ceilingKey("f"));
13.     System.out.println("1st after mango: " +   // sop 3
14.       myMap.floorKey("f"));
15.     SortedMap<String, String> sub = new TreeMap<String, String>();
16.     sub = myMap.tailMap("f");
17.     System.out.println("1st after mango: " +   // sop 4
18.       sub.firstKey());
19.   }
20. }
```

Which of the `System.out.println` statements will produce the output `1st after mango: p`? (Choose all that apply.)

A. `sop 1`

B. `sop 2`

C. `sop 3`

D. `sop 4`

E. None; compilation fails

F. None; an exception is thrown at runtime

14. Given:

```
 3. import java.util.*;
 4. class Business { }
 5. class Hotel extends Business { }
 6. class Inn extends Hotel { }
 7. public class Travel {
 8.   ArrayList<Hotel> go() {
 9.     // insert code here
10.   }
11. }
```

Which statement inserted independently at line 9 will compile? (Choose all that apply.)

A. `return new ArrayList<Inn>();`

B. `return new ArrayList<Hotel>();`

C. `return new ArrayList<Object>();`

D. `return new ArrayList<Business>();`

15. Given:

```
 3. import java.util.*;
 4. class Dog { int size; Dog(int s) { size = s; } }
 5. public class FirstGrade {
 6.   public static void main(String[] args) {
 7.     TreeSet<Integer> i = new TreeSet<Integer>();
 8.     TreeSet<Dog> d = new TreeSet<Dog>();
 9.
10.     d.add(new Dog(1));  d.add(new Dog(2));  d.add(new Dog(1));
11.     i.add(1);  i.add(2);  i.add(1);
12.     System.out.println(d.size() + " " + i.size());
13.   }
14. }
```

What is the result?

A. `1 2`

B. `2 2`

C. `2 3`

D. `3 2`

E. `3 3`

F. Compilation fails

G. An exception is thrown at runtime

16. Given:

```
 3. import java.util.*;
 4. public class GeoCache {
 5.   public static void main(String[] args) {
 6.     String[] s = {"map", "pen", "marble", "key"};
 7.     Othello o = new Othello();
 8.     Arrays.sort(s,o);
 9.     for(String s2: s) System.out.print(s2 + " ");
10.     System.out.println(Arrays.binarySearch(s, "map"));
11.   }
12.   static class Othello implements Comparator<String> {
13.     public int compare(String a, String b) { return b.compareTo(a); }
14.   }
15. }
```

Which are true? (Choose all that apply.)

A. Compilation fails

B. The output will contain a `1`

C. The output will contain a `2`

D. The output will contain a `-1`

E. An exception is thrown at runtime

F. The output will contain `"key map marble pen"`

G. The output will contain `"pen marble map key"`

SELF TEST ANSWERS

1. ☑ A is correct.
☒ B is incorrect because List is an interface, so you can't say new List(), regardless of any generic types. **D, E,** and **F** are incorrect because List only takes one type parameter (a Map would take two, not a List). **C** is tempting, but incorrect. The type argument <List<Integer>\> must be the same for both sides of the assignment, even though the constructor new ArrayList() on the right side is a subtype of the declared type List on the left. (OCP Objective 4.5)

2. ☑ **B** and **D. B** is true because often two dissimilar objects can return the same hashcode value. **D** is true because if the hashCode() comparison returns ==, the two objects might or might not be equal.
☒ **A, C,** and **E** are incorrect. **C** is incorrect because the hashCode() method is very flexible in its return values, and often two dissimilar objects can return the same hashcode value. **A** and **E** are a negation of the hashCode() and equals() contract. (OCP Objectives 4.7 and 4.8)

3. ☑ **E** is correct. You can't put both Strings and ints into the same TreeSet. Without generics, the compiler has no way of knowing what type is appropriate for this TreeSet, so it allows everything to compile. At runtime, the TreeSet will try to sort the elements as they're added, and when it tries to compare an Integer with a String, it will throw a ClassCastException. Note that although the before() method does not use generics, it does use autoboxing. Watch out for code that uses some new features and some old features mixed together.
☒ **A, B, C,** and **D** are incorrect based on the above. (OCP Objectives 4.3 and 4.5)

4. ☑ **C** and **D** are correct. If hashCode() is not overridden, then every entry will go into its own bucket, and the overridden equals() method will have no effect on determining equivalency. If hashCode() is overridden, then the overridden equals() method will view t1 and t2 as duplicates.
☒ **A, B, E,** and **F** are incorrect based on the above. (OCP Objectives 4.7 and 4.8)

5. ☑ **B, E,** and **G** are correct.
☒ **A** is incorrect because you can't use a primitive type as a type parameter. **C** is incorrect because a Map takes two type parameters separated by a comma. **D** is incorrect because an int can't autobox to a null, and **F** is incorrect because a null can't unbox to 0. **H** is incorrect because you can't autobox a primitive just by trying to invoke a method with it. (OCP Objectives 4.4 and 4.6)

6. ☑ **B** is correct. The problem with the original code is that `Sheep` tries to implement `Herbivore<Sheep>` and `Herbivore` declares that its type parameter `E` can be any type that extends `Plant`.
☒ Since a `Sheep` is not a `Plant`, `Herbivore<Sheep>` makes no sense—the type `Sheep` is outside the allowed range of `Herbivore`'s parameter `E`. Only solutions that either alter the definition of a `Sheep` or alter the definition of `Herbivore` will be able to fix this. So **A**, **E**, and **F** are eliminated. **B** works—changing the definition of an `Herbivore` to allow it to eat `Sheep` solves the problem. **C** doesn't work because an `Herbivore<Plant>` must have a `munch(Plant)` method, not `munch(Grass)`. And **D** doesn't work, because in **D** we made `Sheep` extend `Plant`—now the `Wolf` class breaks because its `munch(Sheep)` method no longer fulfills the contract of `Carnivore`. (OCP Objective 4.1)

7. ☑ **D** is correct. All of the collection classes allow you to grow or shrink the size of your collection. `ArrayList` provides an index to its elements. The newer collection classes tend not to have synchronized methods. `Vector` is an older implementation of `ArrayList` functionality and has synchronized methods; it is slower than `ArrayList`.
☒ **A**, **B**, **C**, **E**, and **F** are incorrect based on the logic described earlier. **C**, `List`, is an interface, and **F**, `PriorityQueue`, does not offer access by index. (OCP Objectives 4.5 and 4.6)

8. ☑ **B**, **E**, and **F** are correct.
☒ The return type of process is definitely declared as a `List`, not an `ArrayList`, so **A** and **D** are incorrect. **C** is incorrect because the return type evaluates to `List<Integer>`, and that can't be assigned to a variable of type `List<Number>`. Of course, all these would probably cause a NullPointerException since the variables are still null—but the question only asked us to get the code to compile. (OCP Objective 4.1)

9. ☑ **B** is correct. For the sake of the exam, `add()` and `offer()` both add to (in this case) naturally sorted queues. The calls to `poll()` both return and then remove the first item from the queue, so the test fails.
☒ **A**, **C**, **D**, **E**, **F**, **G**, and **H** are incorrect based on the above. (OCP Objective 4.5)

10. ☑ **A**, **B**, **C**, **D**, and **F** are all correct.
☒ Only **E** is incorrect. Elements of a `TreeSet` must in some way implement `Comparable`. (OCP Objective 4.7)

11. ☑ **A** and **D** are correct. While fragment II wouldn't fulfill the `hashCode()` contract (as you can see by the results), it is legal Java. For the purpose of the exam, if you don't override `hashCode()`, every object will have a unique hashcode.
☒ **B**, **C**, **E**, and **F** are incorrect based on the above. (OCP Objectives 4.7 and 4.8)

12. ☑ B and F are correct. After `"g"` is added, `TreeSet s` contains six elements and `TreeSet subs` contains three (`b, c, d`), because `"g"` is out of the range of `subs`. The first `pollFirst()` finds and removes only the `"a"`. The second `pollFirst()` finds and removes the `"b"` from *both* `TreeSets` (remember they are backed). The final `add()` is in range of both `TreeSets`. The final contents are `[c,c2,d,e,g]` and `[c,c2,d]`.

☒ **A, C, D, E, G,** and **H** are incorrect based on the above. (OCP Objective 4.5)

13. ☑ A is correct. The `ceilingKey()` method's argument is inclusive. The `floorKey()` method would be used to find keys before the specified key. The `firstKey()` method's argument is also inclusive.

☒ **B, C, D, E,** and **F** are incorrect based on the above. (OCP Objective 4.6)

14. ☑ B is correct.

☒ **A** is incorrect because polymorphic assignments don't apply to generic type parameters. **C** and **D** are incorrect because they don't follow basic polymorphism rules. (OCP Objective 4.1)

15. ☑ G is correct. Class `Dog` needs to implement `Comparable` in order for a `TreeSet` (which keeps its elements sorted) to be able to contain `Dog` objects.

☒ **A, B, C, D, E,** and **F** are incorrect based on the above. (OCP Objectives 4.5 and 4.7)

16. ☑ D and G are correct. First, the `compareTo()` method will reverse the normal sort. Second, the `sort()` is valid. Third, the `binarySearch()` gives `-1` because it needs to be invoked using the same `Comparator (o)` as was used to sort the array. Note that when the `binarySearch()` returns an "undefined result," it doesn't officially have to be a `-1`, but it usually is, so if you selected only **G**, you get full credit!

☒ **A, B, C, E,** and **F** are incorrect based on the above. (OCP Objectives 4.7 and 4.8)

12

Inner Classes

CERTIFICATION OBJECTIVES

- Create Top-Level and Nested Classes
- Inner Classes
- Method-Local Inner Classes
- Anonymous Inner Classes
- Static Nested Classes
- ✓ Two-Minute Drill
- Q&A Self Test

Inner classes (including static nested classes) appear throughout the exam. Although there are no official exam objectives **exclusively** about inner classes, OCP Objective 2.4 includes inner (aka nested) classes. More importantly, the code used to represent questions on virtually *any* topic on the exam can involve inner classes. Unless you deeply understand the rules and syntax for inner classes, you're likely to miss questions you'd otherwise be able to answer. *As if the exam weren't already tough enough.*

This chapter looks at the ins and outs (inners and outers?) of inner classes, and exposes you to the kinds of (often strange-looking) syntax examples you'll see scattered throughout the entire exam. So you've really got two goals for this chapter—to learn what you'll need to answer questions testing your inner class knowledge, and to learn how to read and understand inner class code so that you can handle questions testing your knowledge of *other* topics.

So what's all the hoopla about inner classes? Before we get into it, we have to warn you (if you don't already know) that inner classes have inspired passionate love 'em or hate 'em debates since first introduced in version 1.1 of the language. For once, we're going to try to keep our opinions to ourselves here and just present the facts as you'll need to know them for the exam. It's up to you to decide how—and to what extent—you should use inner classes in your own development. We mean it. We believe they have some powerful, efficient uses in very specific situations, including code that's easier to read and maintain, but they can also be abused and lead to code that's as clear as a cornfield maze and to the syndrome known as "reuseless": *code that's useless over and over again*.

Inner classes let you define one class within another. They provide a type of scoping for your classes, since you can make one class *a member of another class*. Just as classes have member *variables* and *methods*, a class can also have member *classes*. They come in several flavors, depending on how and where you define the inner class, including a special kind of inner class known as a "top-level nested class" (an inner class marked `static`), which technically isn't really an inner class. Because a static nested class is still a class defined within the scope of another class, we're still going to cover them in this chapter on inner classes.

Most of the questions on the exam that make use of inner classes are focused on other certification topics and only use inner classes along the way. So for this chapter, the Certification Objective headings in the following list represent the four inner class *topics* discussed in this chapter, rather than four official exam *objectives*:

- Inner classes
- Method-local inner classes

- Anonymous inner classes
- Static nested classes

CERTIFICATION OBJECTIVE

Nested Classes (OCP Objective 2.4)

2.4 Create top-level and nested classes.

Note: As we've mentioned, mapping Objective 2.4 to this chapter is somewhat accurate, but it's also a bit misleading. You'll find inner classes used for many different exam topics. For that reason, we're not going to keep saying that this chapter is for Objective 2.4.

Inner Classes

You're an OO programmer, so you know that for reuse and flexibility/extensibility, you need to keep your classes specialized. In other words, a class should have code *only* for the things an object of that particular type needs to do; any *other* behavior should be part of another class better suited for *that* job. Sometimes, though, you find yourself designing a class where you discover you need behavior that belongs in a separate, specialized class, but also needs to be intimately tied to the class you're designing.

Event handlers are perhaps the best example of this (and are, in fact, one of the main reasons inner classes were added to the language in the first place). If you have a GUI class that performs some job, like, say, a chat client, you might want the chat-client–specific methods (accept input, read new messages from server, send user input back to server, and so on) to be in the class. But how do those methods get invoked in the first place? A user clicks a button. Or types some text in the input field. Or a separate thread doing the I/O work of getting messages from the server has messages that need to be displayed in the GUI. So you have chat-client–specific methods, but you also need methods for handling the "events" (button presses, keyboard typing, I/O available, and so on) that drive the calls on those chat-client methods. The ideal scenario—from an OO perspective—is to keep the chat-client–specific methods in the `ChatClient` class and put the event-handling *code* in a separate event-handling *class*.

Nothing unusual about that so far; after all, that's how you're supposed to design OO classes. As *specialists*. But here's the problem with the chat-client scenario: The event-handling code is intimately tied to the chat-client–specific code! Think about it: When the user clicks a Send button (indicating that they want their typed-in message to be sent to the chat server), the chat-client code that sends the message needs to read from a *particular* text field. In other words, if the user clicks Button A, the program is supposed to extract the text from the TextField B *of a particular* `ChatClient` *instance*. Not from some *other* text field from some *other* object, but specifically the text field that a specific instance of the `ChatClient` class has a reference to. So the event-handling code needs access to the members of the `ChatClient` object to be useful as a "helper" to a particular `ChatClient` instance.

And what if the `ChatClient` class needs to inherit from one class, but the event-handling code is better off inheriting from some *other* class? You can't make a class extend more than one class, so putting all the code (the chat-client-specific code and the event-handling code) in one class won't work in that case. So what you'd really like to have is the benefit of putting your event code in a separate class (better OO, encapsulation, and the ability to extend a class other than the class the `ChatClient` extends), but still allow the event-handling code to have easy access to the members of the `ChatClient` (so the event-handling code can, for example, update the `ChatClient`'s private instance variables). You *could* manage it by making the members of the `ChatClient` accessible to the event-handling class by, for example, marking them `public`. But that's not a good solution either.

You already know where this is going—one of the key benefits of an inner class is the "special relationship" an *inner class instance* shares with *an instance of the outer class*. That "special relationship" gives code in the inner class access to members of the enclosing (outer) class, *as if the inner class were part of the outer class*. In fact, that's exactly what it means: The inner class *is* a part of the outer class. Not just a "part," but a full-fledged, card-carrying *member* of the outer class. Yes, an inner class instance has access to all members of the outer class, *even those marked private*. (Relax, that's the whole point, remember? We want this separate inner class instance to have an intimate relationship with the outer class instance, but we still want to keep everyone *else* out. And besides, if you wrote the outer class, then you also wrote the inner class! So you're not violating encapsulation; you *designed* it this way.)

Coding a "Regular" Inner Class

We use the term *regular* here to represent inner classes that are not

- Static
- Method-local
- Anonymous

For the rest of this section, though, we'll just use the term "inner class" and drop the "regular." (When we switch to one of the other three types in the preceding list, you'll know it.) You define an inner class within the curly braces of the outer class:

```
class MyOuter {
   class MyInner { }
}
```

Piece of cake. And if you compile it:

```
%javac MyOuter.java
```

you'll end up with *two* class files:

```
MyOuter.class
MyOuter$MyInner.class
```

The inner class is still, in the end, a separate class, so a separate class file is generated for it. But the inner class file isn't accessible to you in the usual way. You can't say

```
%java MyOuter$MyInner
```

in hopes of running the `main()` method of the inner class, **because a regular inner class cannot have static declarations of any kind. *The only way you can access the inner class is through a live instance of the outer class!*** In other words, only at runtime, when there's already an instance of the outer class to tie the inner class instance to. You'll see all this in a moment. First, let's beef up the classes a little:

```
class MyOuter {
   private int x = 7;

   // inner class definition
   class MyInner {
      public void seeOuter() {
         System.out.println("Outer x is " + x);
      }
   } // close inner class definition

} // close outer class
```

The preceding code is perfectly legal. Notice that the inner class is indeed accessing a private member of the outer class. That's fine, because the inner class is also a member of the outer class. So just as any member of the outer class (say, an instance method) can access any other member of the outer class, `private` or not, the inner class—also a member—can do the same.

Okay, so now that we know how to write the code giving an inner class access to members of the outer class, how do you actually use it?

Instantiating an Inner Class

To create an instance of an inner class, *you must have an instance of the outer class* to tie to the inner class. There are no exceptions to this rule: An inner class instance can never stand alone without a direct relationship to an instance of the outer class.

Instantiating an Inner Class from Within the Outer Class

Most often, it is the outer class that creates instances of the inner class, since it is usually the outer class wanting to use the inner instance as a helper for its own personal use. We'll modify the `MyOuter` class to create an instance of `MyInner`:

```
class MyOuter {
  private int x = 7;
  public void makeInner() {
    MyInner in = new MyInner();  // make an inner instance
    in.seeOuter();
  }

  class MyInner {
    public void seeOuter() {
      System.out.println("Outer x is " + x);
    }
  }
}
```

You can see in the preceding code that the `MyOuter` code treats `MyInner` just as though `MyInner` were any other accessible class—it instantiates it using the class name `(new MyInner())` and then invokes a method on the reference variable `(in.seeOuter())`. But the only reason this syntax works is because the outer class instance method code is doing the instantiating. In other words, *there's already an instance of the outer class—the instance running the* `makeInner()` *method*. So how do you instantiate a `MyInner` object from somewhere outside the `MyOuter` class? Is it even possible? (Well, since we're going to all the trouble of making a whole new subhead for it, as you'll see next, there's no big mystery here.)

Creating an Inner Class Object from Outside the Outer Class Instance Code Whew. Long subhead there, but it does explain what we're trying to do. If we want to create an instance of the inner class, we must have an instance of the outer class. You already know that, but think about the implications... it means that without a reference to an instance of the outer class, you can't instantiate the inner class from a `static` method of the outer class (because, don't forget, in static code, *there is no* `this` *reference*), or from any other code in any other class. Inner class instances are always handed an implicit reference to the outer class. The compiler takes care of it, so you'll never see anything but the end result—the ability of the inner class to access members of the outer class. The code to make an instance from anywhere outside nonstatic code of the outer class is simple, but you must memorize this for the exam!

```
public static void main(String[] args) {
  MyOuter mo = new MyOuter();     // gotta get an instance!
  MyOuter.MyInner inner = mo.new MyInner();
  inner.seeOuter();
}
```

The preceding code is the same, regardless of whether the `main()` method is within the `MyOuter` class or some *other* class (assuming the other class has access to `MyOuter`, and since `MyOuter` has default access, that means the code must be in a class within the same package as `MyOuter`).

If you're into one-liners, you can do it like this:

```
public static void main(String[] args) {
  MyOuter.MyInner inner = new MyOuter().new MyInner();
  inner.seeOuter();
}
```

You can think of this as though you're invoking a method on the outer instance, but the method happens to be a special inner class instantiation method, and it's invoked using the keyword `new`. Instantiating an inner class is the *only* scenario in which you'll invoke `new` *on* an instance as opposed to invoking `new` to *construct* an instance.

Here's a quick summary of the differences between inner class instantiation code that's *within* the outer class (but not `static`), and inner class instantiation code that's *outside* the outer class:

- From *inside* the outer class instance code, use the inner class name in the normal way:

  ```
  MyInner mi = new MyInner();
  ```

- From *outside* the outer class instance code (including static method code within the outer class), the inner class name must now include the outer class's name:

  `MyOuter.MyInner`

  To instantiate it, you must use a reference to the outer class:

  `new MyOuter().new MyInner(); or outerObjRef.new MyInner();`

  if you already have an instance of the outer class.

Referencing the Inner or Outer Instance from Within the Inner Class

How does an object refer to itself normally? By using the `this` reference. Here is a quick review of `this`:

- The keyword `this` can be used only from within instance code. In other words, not within static code.
- The `this` reference is a reference to the currently executing object. In other words, the object whose reference was used to invoke the currently running method.
- The `this` reference is the way an object can pass a reference to itself to some other code as a method argument:

```
public void myMethod() {
  MyClass mc = new MyClass();
  mc.doStuff(this);  // pass a ref to object running myMethod
}
```

Within an inner class code, the `this` reference refers to the instance of the inner class, as you'd probably expect, since `this` always refers to the currently executing object. But what if the inner class code wants an explicit reference to the outer class instance that the inner instance is tied to? In other words, *how do you reference the "outer `this`"*? Although normally, the inner class code doesn't need a reference to the outer class, since it already has an implicit one it's using to access the members of the outer class, it would need a reference to the outer class if it needed to pass that reference to some other code, as follows:

```
class MyInner {
  public void seeOuter() {
    System.out.println("Outer x is " + x);
    System.out.println("Inner class ref is " + this);
    System.out.println("Outer class ref is " + MyOuter.this);
  }
}
```

If we run the complete code as follows:

```
class MyOuter {
  private int x = 7;
  public void makeInner() {
    MyInner in = new MyInner();
    in.seeOuter();
  }
  class MyInner {
    public void seeOuter() {
      System.out.println("Outer x is " + x);
      System.out.println("Inner class ref is " + this);
      System.out.println("Outer class ref is " + MyOuter.this);
    }
  }
  public static void main (String[] args) {
    MyOuter.MyInner inner = new MyOuter().new MyInner();
    inner.seeOuter();
  }
}
```

the output is something like this:

```
Outer x is 7
Inner class ref is MyOuter$MyInner@113708
Outer class ref is MyOuter@33f1d7
```

So the rules for an inner class referencing itself or the outer instance are as follows:

- To reference the inner class instance itself from *within* the inner class code, use `this`.
- To reference the "*outer `this`*" (the outer class instance) from within the inner class code, use `NameOfOuterClass.this` (example, `MyOuter.this`).

Member Modifiers Applied to Inner Classes

A regular inner class is a member of the outer class just as instance variables and methods are, so the following modifiers can be applied to an inner class:

- `final`
- `abstract`
- `public`
- `private`
- `protected`
- `static`—*but static turns it into a* `static` *nested class, not an inner class*
- `strictfp`

CERTIFICATION OBJECTIVE

Method-Local Inner Classes

A regular inner class is scoped inside another class's curly braces, but outside any method code (in other words, at the same level that an instance variable is declared). But you can also define an inner class within a method:

```
class MyOuter2 {
  private String x = "Outer2";

  void doStuff() {
    class MyInner {
      public void seeOuter() {
      System.out.println("Outer x is " + x);
    } // close inner class method
    } // close inner class definition
  }   // close outer class method doStuff()

}     // close outer class
```

The preceding code declares a class, `MyOuter2`, with one method, `doStuff()`. But *inside* `doStuff()`, another class, `MyInner`, is declared, and it has a method of its own, `seeOuter()`. The previous code is completely useless, however, because *it never instantiates the inner class!* Just because you *declared* the class doesn't mean you created an *instance* of it. So to *use* the inner class, you must make an instance of it somewhere *within the method but below the inner class definition* (or the compiler won't be able to find the inner class). The following legal code shows how to instantiate and use a method-local inner class:

```
class MyOuter2 {
  private String x = "Outer2";
  void doStuff() {
    class MyInner {
      public void seeOuter() {
        System.out.println("Outer x is " + x);
      } // close inner class method
    }   // close inner class definition

    MyInner mi = new MyInner();  // This line must come
                                 // after the class
    mi.seeOuter();
  } // close outer class method doStuff()
}   // close outer class
```

What a Method-Local Inner Object Can and Can't Do

A method-local inner class can be instantiated only within the method where the inner class is defined. In other words, no other code running in any other method—inside or outside the outer class—can ever instantiate the method-local inner class. Like regular inner class objects, the method-local inner class object shares a special relationship with the enclosing (outer) class object and can access its `private` (or any other) members. However, *the inner class object cannot use the local variables of the method the inner class is in*. Why not?

Think about it. The local variables of the method live on the stack and exist only for the lifetime of the method. You already know that the scope of a local variable is limited to the method the variable is declared in. When the method ends, the stack frame is blown away and the variable is history. But even after the method completes, the inner class object created within it might still be alive on the heap if, for example, a reference to it was passed into some other code and then stored in an instance variable. Because the local variables aren't guaranteed to be alive as long as the method-local inner class object is, the inner class object can't use them. *Unless the local variables are marked* `final`*!* The following code attempts to access a local variable from within a method-local inner class:

```
class MyOuter2 {
  private String x = "Outer2";
  void doStuff() {
    String z = "local variable";
    class MyInner {
      public void seeOuter() {
        System.out.println("Outer x is " + x);
        System.out.println("Local var z is " + z);    // Won't Compile!
      } // close inner class method
    }   // close inner class definition
  }     // close outer class method doStuff()
}       // close outer class
```

Compiling the preceding code *really* upsets the compiler:

```
MyOuter2.java:8: local variable z is accessed from within inner class;

needs to be declared final
           System.out.println("Local var z is " + z);
                                                  ^
```

Marking the local variable `z` as `final` fixes the problem:

```
final String z = "local var";  // Now inner object can use it
```

And just a reminder about modifiers within a method: The same rules apply to method-local inner classes as to local variable declarations. You can't, for example, mark a method-local inner class `public`, `private`, `protected`, `static`, `transient`, and the like. For the purpose of the exam, the only modifiers you *can* apply to a method-local inner class are `abstract` and `final`, but, as always, never both at the same time.

exam watch

Remember that a local class declared in a `static` method has access to only `static` members of the enclosing class, since there is no associated instance of the enclosing class. If you're in a `static` method, there is no `this`, so an inner class in a `static` method is subject to the same restrictions as the `static` method. In other words, no access to instance variables.

CERTIFICATION OBJECTIVE

Anonymous Inner Classes

So far, we've looked at defining a class within an enclosing class (a regular inner class) and within a method (a method-local inner class). Finally, we're going to look at the most unusual syntax you might ever see in Java: inner classes declared without any class name at all (hence, the word *anonymous*). And if that's not weird enough, you can define these classes not just within a method, but even within an *argument* to a method. We'll look first at the *plain-old* (as if there is such a thing as a plain-old anonymous inner class) version (actually, even the plain-old version comes in two flavors), and then at the argument-declared anonymous inner class.

Perhaps your most important job here is to *learn to not be thrown when you see the syntax*. The exam is littered with anonymous inner class code—you might see it on questions about threads, wrappers, overriding, garbage collection, and… well, you get the idea.

Plain-Old Anonymous Inner Classes, Flavor One

Check out the following legal-but-strange-the-first-time-you-see-it code:

```
class Popcorn {
  public void pop() {
    System.out.println("popcorn");
  }
}
class Food {
  Popcorn p = new Popcorn() {
    public void pop() {
      System.out.println("anonymous popcorn");
    }
  };
}
```

Let's look at what's in the preceding code:

- We define two classes: `Popcorn` and `Food`.
- `Popcorn` has one method: `pop()`.
- `Food` has one instance variable, declared as type `Popcorn`. That's it for `Food`. `Food` has *no* methods.

And here's the big thing to get:

The `Popcorn` reference variable refers *not* to an instance of `Popcorn`, but to *an instance of an anonymous (unnamed) subclass of `Popcorn`*.

Let's look at just the anonymous class code:

```
2. Popcorn p = new Popcorn() {
3.   public void pop() {
4.     System.out.println("anonymous popcorn");
5.   }
6. };
```

Line 2 Line 2 starts out as an instance variable declaration of type `Popcorn`. But instead of looking like this:

```
Popcorn p = new Popcorn(); // notice the semicolon at the end
```

there's a curly brace at the end of line 2, where a semicolon would normally be.

```
Popcorn p = new Popcorn() { // a curly brace, not a semicolon
```

You can read line 2 as saying,

Declare a reference variable, `p`, of type `Popcorn`. Then declare a new class that has no name but that is a *subclass* of `Popcorn`. And here's the curly brace that opens the class definition…

Line 3 Line 3, then, is actually the first statement within the new class definition. And what is it doing? Overriding the `pop()` method of the superclass `Popcorn`. This is the whole point of making an anonymous inner class—to *override one or more methods of the superclass!* (Or to implement methods of an interface, but we'll save that for a little later.)

Line 4 Line 4 is the first (and in this case *only*) statement within the overriding `pop()` method. Nothing special there.

Line 5 Line 5 is the closing curly brace of the `pop()` method. Nothing special.

Line 6 Here's where you have to pay attention: Line 6 includes a *curly brace closing off the anonymous class definition* (it's the companion brace to the one on line 2), but there's more! Line 6 also has *the semicolon that ends the statement started on line 2*—the statement where it all began—the statement declaring and initializing the `Popcorn` reference variable. And what you're left with is a `Popcorn` reference to a brand-new *instance* of a brand-new, just-in-time, anonymous (no name) *subclass* of Popcorn.

exam watch

The closing semicolon is hard to spot. Watch for code like this:

```
2. Popcorn p = new Popcorn() {
3.   public void pop() {
4.     System.out.println("anonymous popcorn");
5.   }
6. }                    //  Missing the semicolon needed to end
                        //  the statement started on 2!
7. Foo f = new Foo();
```

You'll need to be especially careful about the syntax when inner classes are involved, because the code on line 6 looks perfectly natural. It's rare to see semicolons following curly braces.

Polymorphism is in play when anonymous inner classes are involved. Remember that, as in the preceding Popcorn example, we're using a superclass reference variable type to refer to a subclass object. What are the implications? You can only call methods on an anonymous inner class reference that are defined in the reference variable type! This is no different from any other polymorphic references—for example,

```
class Horse extends Animal{
  void buck() { }
}
class Animal {
  void eat() { }
}
class Test {
  public static void main (String[] args) {
    Animal h = new Horse();
    h.eat();  // Legal, class Animal has an eat() method
    h.buck();  // Not legal! Class Animal doesn't have buck()
  }
}
```

So on the exam, you must be able to spot an anonymous inner class that—rather than overriding a method of the superclass—defines its own new method. The method definition isn't the problem, though; the real issue is, how do you invoke that new method? The reference variable type (the superclass) won't know anything about that new method (defined in the anonymous subclass), so the compiler will complain if you try to invoke any method on an anonymous inner class reference that is not in the superclass class definition.

Check out the following **illegal** code:

```
class Popcorn {
  public void pop() {
    System.out.println("popcorn");
  }
}

class Food {
  Popcorn p = new Popcorn() {
    public void sizzle() {
      System.out.println("anonymous sizzling popcorn");
    }
    public void pop() {
      System.out.println("anonymous popcorn");
    }
  };

  public void popIt() {
    p.pop();     // OK, Popcorn has a pop() method
    p.sizzle();  // Not Legal! Popcorn does not have sizzle()
  }
}
```

Compiling the preceding code gives us something like this:

```
Anon.java:19: cannot resolve symbol
symbol  : method sizzle  ()
location: class Popcorn
      p.sizzle();
       ^
```

which is the compiler's way of saying, "I can't find method `sizzle()` in class `Popcorn`," followed by, "Get a clue."

Plain-Old Anonymous Inner Classes, Flavor Two

The only difference between flavor one and flavor two is that flavor one creates an anonymous *subclass* of the specified *class* type, whereas flavor two creates an anonymous *implementer* of the specified *interface* type. In the previous examples, we defined a new anonymous subclass of type `Popcorn` as follows:

```
Popcorn p = new Popcorn() {
```

But if `Popcorn` were an *interface* type instead of a *class* type, then the new anonymous class would be an *implementer* of the *interface* rather than a *subclass* of the *class*. Look at the following example:

```
interface Cookable {
  public void cook();
}
class Food {
  Cookable c = new Cookable() {
    public void cook() {
      System.out.println("anonymous cookable implementer");
    }
  };
}
```

The preceding code, like the Popcorn example, still creates an instance of an anonymous inner class, but this time, the new just-in-time class is an implementer of the `Cookable` interface. And note that this is the only time you will ever see the syntax:

```
new Cookable()
```

where `Cookable` is an *interface* rather than a non`abstract` class type. Think about it: *You can't instantiate an interface*, yet that's what the code *looks* like it's doing. But, of course, it's not instantiating a `Cookable` object—it's creating an instance of a new anonymous implementer of `Cookable`. You can read this line:

```
Cookable c = new Cookable() {
```

as, "Declare a reference variable of type `Cookable` that, obviously, will refer to an object from a class that implements the `Cookable` interface. But, oh yes, we don't yet *have* a class that implements `Cookable`, so we're going to make one right here, right now. We don't need a name for the class, but it will be a class that implements `Cookable`, and this curly brace starts the definition of the new implementing class." One more thing to keep in mind about anonymous interface implementers—*they can implement only one interface*. There simply isn't any mechanism to say that your anonymous inner class is going to implement multiple interfaces. In fact, an anonymous inner class can't even extend a class and implement an interface at the same time. The inner class has to choose either to be a subclass of a named class—and not directly implement any interfaces at all—*or* to implement a single interface. By directly, we mean actually using the keyword `implements` as part of the class declaration. If the anonymous inner class is a subclass of a class type, it automatically becomes an implementer of any interfaces implemented by the superclass.

exam watch

Don't be fooled by any attempts to instantiate an interface except in the case of an anonymous inner class. The following is not legal:

```
Runnable r = new Runnable();   // can't instantiate interface
```

whereas the following is legal, because it's instantiating an* implementer *of the* `Runnable` *interface (an anonymous implementation class):

```
Runnable r = new Runnable() {  // curly brace, not semicolon
  public void run() { }
};
```

Argument-Defined Anonymous Inner Classes

If you understood what we've covered so far in this chapter, then this last part will be simple. If you *are* still a little fuzzy on anonymous classes, however, then you should re-read the previous sections. If they're not completely clear, we'd like to take full responsibility for the confusion. But we'll be happy to share.

Okay, if you've made it to this sentence, then we're all going to assume you understood the preceding section, and now we're just going to add one new twist. Imagine the following scenario. You're typing along, creating the Perfect Class, when you write code calling a method on a `Bar` object, and that method takes an object of type `Foo` (an interface).

```
class MyWonderfulClass {
  void go() {
    Bar b = new Bar();
    b.doStuff(ackWeDoNotHaveAFoo!); // Don't try to compile this at home
  }
}
interface Foo {
  void foof();
}
class Bar {
  void doStuff(Foo f) { }
}
```

No problemo, except that you don't *have* an object from a class that implements `Foo`, and you can't instantiate one, either, because *you don't even have a class that implements* `Foo`, let alone an instance of one. So you first need a class that implements `Foo`, and then you need an instance of that class to pass to the `Bar` class's `doStuff()` method. Savvy Java programmer that you are, you simply define an anonymous inner class, *right inside the argument*. That's right, just where you least expect to find a class. And here's what it looks like:

```
 1. class MyWonderfulClass {
 2.   void go() {
 3.     Bar b = new Bar();
 4.     b.doStuff(new Foo() {
 5.       public void foof() {
 6.         System.out.println("foofy");
 7.       } // end foof method
 8.     }); // end inner class def, arg, and b.doStuff stmt.
 9.   }     // end go()
10. }       // end class
11.
12. interface Foo {
13.   void foof();
14. }
15. class Bar {
16.   void doStuff(Foo f) { }
17. }
```

All the action starts on line 4. We're calling `doStuff()` on a `Bar` object, but the method takes an instance that IS-A `Foo`, where `Foo` is an interface. So we must make both an *implementation* class and an *instance* of that class, all right here in the argument to `doStuff()`. So that's what we do. We write

```
new Foo() {
```

to start the new class definition for the anonymous class that implements the `Foo` interface. `Foo` has a single method to implement, `foof()`, so on lines 5, 6, and 7, we implement the `foof()` method. Then on line 8—whoa!—more strange syntax appears. The first curly brace closes off the new anonymous class definition. But don't forget that this all happened as part of a method argument, so the closing parenthesis,), finishes off the method invocation, and then we must still end the statement that began on line 4, so we end with a semicolon. Study this syntax! You will see anonymous inner classes on the exam, and you'll have to be very, very picky about the way they're closed. If they're *argument local*, they end like this:

```
});
```

but if they're just plain-old anonymous classes, then they end like this:

```
};
```

Regardless, the syntax is rare, so be careful. Any question from any part of the exam might involve anonymous inner classes as part of the code.

CERTIFICATION OBJECTIVE

Static Nested Classes

We saved the easiest for last, as a kind of treat. :)

You'll sometimes hear static nested classes referred to as *static inner classes*, but they really aren't inner classes at all based on the standard definition of an inner class. While an inner class (regardless of the flavor) enjoys that *special relationship* with the outer class (or rather, the *instances* of the two classes share a relationship), a static nested class does not. It is simply a non-inner (also called "top-level") class scoped within another. So with static classes, it's really more about name-space resolution than about an implicit relationship between the two classes.

A static nested class is simply a class that's a static member of the enclosing class:

```
class BigOuter {
  static class Nested { }
}
```

The class itself isn't really "static"; there's no such thing as a static class. The `static` modifier in this case says that the nested class is *a static member of the outer class*. That means it can be accessed, as with other static members, *without having an instance of the outer class*.

Instantiating and Using Static Nested Classes

You use standard syntax to access a static nested class from its enclosing class. The syntax for instantiating a static nested class from a nonenclosing class is a little different from a normal inner class, and looks like this:

```
class BigOuter {
  static class Nest {void go() { System.out.println("hi"); } }
}
class Broom {
  static class B2 {void goB2() { System.out.println("hi 2"); } }
  public static void main(String[] args) {
    BigOuter.Nest n = new BigOuter.Nest();   // both class names
    n.go();
    B2 b2 = new B2();                        // access the enclosed class
    b2.goB2();
  }
}
```

which produces

```
hi
hi 2
```

exam watch

Just as a static method does not have access to the instance variables and nonstatic methods of the class, a static nested class does not have access to the instance variables and nonstatic methods of the outer class. Look for static nested classes with code that behaves like a nonstatic (regular inner) class.

CERTIFICATION SUMMARY

Inner classes will show up throughout the exam, in any topic, and these are some of the exam's hardest questions. You should be comfortable with the sometimes bizarre syntax and know how to spot legal and illegal inner class definitions.

We looked first at "regular" inner classes, where one class is a member of another. You learned that coding an inner class means putting the class definition of the inner class inside the curly braces of the enclosing (outer) class, but outside of any method or other code block. You learned that an inner class *instance* shares a special relationship with a specific *instance* of the outer class, and that this special relationship lets the inner class access all members of the outer class, including those marked `private`. You learned that to instantiate an inner class, you *must* have a reference to an instance of the outer class.

Next, we looked at method-local inner classes—classes defined *inside* a method. The code for a method-local inner class looks virtually the same as the code for any other class definition, except that you can't apply an access modifier the way you can with a regular inner class. You learned why method-local inner classes cannot use non-`final` local variables declared within the method—the inner class instance may outlive the stack frame, so the local variable might vanish while the inner class object is still alive. You saw that to *use* the inner class you need to instantiate it and that the instantiation must come *after* the class declaration in the method.

We also explored the strangest inner class type of all—the *anonymous* inner class. You learned that they come in two forms: normal and argument-defined. Normal, ho-hum, anonymous inner classes are created as part of a variable assignment, while argument-defined inner classes are actually declared, defined, and automatically instantiated *all within the argument to a method!* We covered the way anonymous inner classes can be either a subclass of the named class type or an *implementer* of the named interface. Finally, we looked at how polymorphism applies to anonymous inner classes: You can invoke on the new instance only those methods defined in the named class or interface type. In other words, even if the anonymous inner class defines its own new method, no code from anywhere outside the inner class will be able to invoke that method.

As if we weren't already having enough fun for one day, we pushed on to static nested classes, which really aren't inner classes at all. Known as `static` nested classes, a nested class marked with the `static` modifier is quite similar to any other non-inner class, except that to access it, code must have access to both the nested and enclosing class. We saw that because the class is `static`, no instance of the enclosing class is needed, and thus the static nested class *does not share a special relationship with any instance of the enclosing class*. Remember, static inner classes can't access instance methods or variables.

✓ TWO-MINUTE DRILL

Here are some of the key points from this chapter.

Inner Classes

- ❑ A "regular" inner class is declared *inside* the curly braces of another class, but *outside* any method or other code block.
- ❑ An inner class is a full-fledged member of the enclosing (outer) class, so it can be marked with an access modifier as well as the `abstract` or `final` modifiers. (Never both `abstract` and `final` together— remember that `abstract` *must* be subclassed, whereas `final` *cannot* be subclassed.)
- ❑ An inner class instance shares a special relationship with an instance of the enclosing class. This relationship gives the inner class access to *all* of the outer class's members, including those marked `private`.
- ❑ To instantiate an inner class, you must have a reference to an instance of the outer class.
- ❑ From code within the enclosing class, you can instantiate the inner class using only the name of the inner class, as follows:

```
MyInner mi = new MyInner();
```

- ❑ From code outside the enclosing class's instance methods, you can instantiate the inner class only by using both the inner and outer class names and a reference to the outer class, as follows:

```
MyOuter mo = new MyOuter();
MyOuter.MyInner inner = mo.new MyInner();
```

- ❑ From code within the inner class, the keyword `this` holds a reference to the inner class instance. To reference the *outer* `this` (in other words, the instance of the outer class that this inner instance is tied to), precede the keyword `this` with the outer class name, as follows: `MyOuter.this;`

Method-Local Inner Classes

- ❑ A method-local inner class is defined within a method of the enclosing class.
- ❑ For the inner class to be used, you must instantiate it, and that instantiation must happen within the same method, but *after* the class definition code.
- ❑ A method-local inner class cannot use variables declared within the method (including parameters) unless those variables are marked `final`.

- The only modifiers you can apply to a method-local inner class are `abstract` and `final`. (Never both at the same time, though.)

Anonymous Inner Classes

- Anonymous inner classes have no name, and their type must be either a subclass of the named type or an implementer of the named interface.
- An anonymous inner class is always created as part of a statement; don't forget to close the statement after the class definition with a curly brace. This is a rare case in Java, a curly brace followed by a semicolon.
- Because of polymorphism, the only methods you can call on an anonymous inner class reference are those defined in the reference variable class (or interface), even though the anonymous class is really a subclass or implementer of the reference variable type.
- An anonymous inner class can extend one subclass *or* implement one interface. Unlike nonanonymous classes (inner or otherwise), an anonymous inner class cannot do both. In other words, it cannot both extend a class *and* implement an interface, nor can it implement more than one interface.
- An argument-defined inner class is declared, defined, and automatically instantiated as part of a method invocation. The key to remember is that the class is being defined within a method argument, so the syntax will end the class definition with a curly brace, followed by a closing parenthesis to end the method call, followed by a semicolon to end the statement: `});`

Static Nested Classes

- Static nested classes are inner classes marked with the `static` modifier.
- A `static` nested class is *not* an inner class; it's a top-level nested class.
- Because the nested class is `static`, it does not share any special relationship with an instance of the outer class. In fact, you don't need an instance of the outer class to instantiate a `static` nested class.
- For the purposes of the exam, instantiating a `static` nested class requires using both the outer and nested class names as follows:

  ```
  BigOuter.Nested n = new BigOuter.Nested();
  ```

- A `static` nested class cannot access non`static` members of the outer class, since it does not have an implicit reference to any outer instance (in other words, the nested class instance does not get an *outer* `this` reference).

SELF TEST

The following questions will help you measure your understanding of the dynamic and life-altering material presented in this chapter. Read all of the choices carefully. Take your time. Breathe.

1. Which are true about a `static` nested class? (Choose all that apply.)

A. You must have a reference to an instance of the enclosing class in order to instantiate it

B. It does not have access to nonstatic members of the enclosing class

C. Its variables and methods must be `static`

D. If the outer class is named `MyOuter` and the nested class is named `MyInner`, it can be instantiated using `new MyOuter.MyInner();`

E. It must extend the enclosing class

2. Given:

```
class Boo {
   Boo(String s) { }
   Boo() { }
}
class Bar extends Boo {
   Bar() { }
   Bar(String s) {super(s);}
   void zoo() {
   // insert code here
   }
}
```

Which statements create an anonymous inner class from within class `Bar`? (Choose all that apply.)

A. `Boo f = new Boo(24) { };`

B. `Boo f = new Bar() { };`

C. `Boo f = new Boo() {String s; };`

D. `Bar f = new Boo(String s) { };`

E. `Boo f = new Boo.Bar(String s) { };`

3. Which are true about a method-local inner class? (Choose all that apply.)

A. It must be marked `final`

B. It can be marked `abstract`

C. It can be marked `public`

D. It can be marked `static`

E. It can access private members of the enclosing class

4. Given:

```
 1. public class TestObj {
 2.   public static void main(String[] args) {
 3.     Object o = new Object() {
 4.       public boolean equals(Object obj) {
 5.         return true;
 6.       }
 7.     }
 8.     System.out.println(o.equals("Fred"));
 9.   }
10. }
```

What is the result?

A. An exception occurs at runtime

B. `true`

C. `Fred`

D. Compilation fails because of an error on line 3

E. Compilation fails because of an error on line 4

F. Compilation fails because of an error on line 8

G. Compilation fails because of an error on a line other than 3, 4, or 8

5. Given:

```
 1. public class HorseTest {
 2.   public static void main(String[] args) {
 3.     class Horse {
 4.       public String name;
 5.       public Horse(String s) {
 6.         name = s;
 7.       }
 8.     }
 9.     Object obj = new Horse("Zippo");
10.     System.out.println(obj.name);
11.   }
12. }
```

What is the result?

A. An exception occurs at runtime at line 10

B. `Zippo`

C. Compilation fails because of an error on line 3

D. Compilation fails because of an error on line 9

E. Compilation fails because of an error on line 10

6. Given:

```
public abstract class AbstractTest {
  public int getNum() {
    return 45;
  }
  public abstract class Bar {
    public int getNum() {
      return 38;
    }
  }
  public static void main(String[] args) {
    AbstractTest t = new AbstractTest() {
      public int getNum() {
        return 22;
      }
    };
    AbstractTest.Bar f = t.new Bar() {
       public int getNum() {
        return 57;
      }
    };
    System.out.println(f.getNum() + " " + t.getNum());
  }
}
```

What is the result?

A. `57 22`

B. `45 38`

C. `45 57`

D. An exception occurs at runtime

E. Compilation fails

7. Given:

```
 3. public class Tour {
 4.   public static void main(String[] args) {
 5.     Cathedral c = new Cathedral();
 6.     // insert code here
 7.     s.go();
 8.   }
 9. }
10. class Cathedral {
11.   class Sanctum {
12.     void go() { System.out.println("spooky"); }
13.   }
14. }
```

Which, inserted independently at line 6, compile and produce the output "spooky"? (Choose all that apply.)

A. `Sanctum s = c.new Sanctum();`

B. `c.Sanctum s = c.new Sanctum();`

C. `c.Sanctum s = Cathedral.new Sanctum();`

D. `Cathedral.Sanctum s = c.new Sanctum();`

E. `Cathedral.Sanctum s = Cathedral.new Sanctum();`

8. Given:

```
 5. class A { void m() { System.out.println("outer"); } }
 6.
 7. public class TestInners {
 8.   public static void main(String[] args) {
 9.     new TestInners().go();
10.   }
11.   void go() {
12.     new A().m();
13.     class A { void m() { System.out.println("inner"); } }
14.   }
15.   class A { void m() { System.out.println("middle"); } }
16. }
```

What is the result?

A. `inner`

B. `outer`

C. `middle`

D. Compilation fails

E. An exception is thrown at runtime

9. Given:

```
 3. public class Car {
 4.   class Engine {
 5.     // insert code here
 6.   }
 7.   public static void main(String[] args) {
 8.     new Car().go();
 9.   }
10.   void go() {
11.     new Engine();
12.   }
13.   void drive() { System.out.println("hi"); }
14. }
```

Which, inserted independently at line 5, produce the output "hi"? (Choose all that apply.)

A. `{ Car.drive(); }`

B. `{ this.drive(); }`

C. `{ Car.this.drive(); }`

D. `{ this.Car.this.drive(); }`

E. `Engine() { Car.drive(); }`

F. `Engine() { this.drive(); }`

G. `Engine() { Car.this.drive(); }`

10. Given:

```
 3. public class City {
 4.   class Manhattan {
 5.     void doStuff() throws Exception { System.out.print("x "); }
 6.   }
 7.   class TimesSquare extends Manhattan {
 8.     void doStuff() throws Exception { }
 9.   }
10.   public static void main(String[] args) throws Exception {
11.     new City().go();
12.   }
13.   void go() throws Exception { new TimesSquare().doStuff(); }
14. }
```

What is the result?

A. `x`

B. `x x`

C. No output is produced

D. Compilation fails due to multiple errors

E. Compilation fails due only to an error on line 4

F. Compilation fails due only to an error on line 7

G. Compilation fails due only to an error on line 10

H. Compilation fails due only to an error on line 13

11. Given:

```
 3. public class Navel {
 4.   private int size = 7;
 5.   private static int length = 3;
 6.   public static void main(String[] args) {
 7.     new Navel().go();
 8.   }
 9.   void go() {
10.     int size = 5;
11.     System.out.println(new Gazer().adder());
```

```
12.     }
13.     class Gazer {
14.       int adder() { return size * length; }
15.     }
16. }
```

What is the result?

A. `15`

B. `21`

C. An exception is thrown at runtime

D. Compilation fails due to multiple errors

E. Compilation fails due only to an error on line 4

F. Compilation fails due only to an error on line 5

12. Given:

```
 3. import java.util.*;
 4. public class Pockets {
 5.   public static void main(String[] args) {
 6.     String[] sa = {"nickel", "button", "key", "lint"};
 7.     Sorter s = new Sorter();
 8.     for(String s2: sa) System.out.print(s2 + " ");
 9.     Arrays.sort(sa,s);
10.     System.out.println();
11.     for(String s2: sa) System.out.print(s2 + " ");
12.   }
13.   class Sorter implements Comparator<String> {
14.     public int compare(String a, String b) {
15.       return b.compareTo(a);
16.     }
17.   }
18. }
```

What is the result?

A. Compilation fails

B. `button key lint nickel`
`nickel lint key button`

C. `nickel button key lint`
`button key lint nickel`

D. `nickel button key lint`
`nickel button key lint`

E. `nickel button key lint`
`nickel lint key button`

F. An exception is thrown at runtime

SELF TEST ANSWERS

Note: You could argue that all of the questions in this chapter relate to OCP Objective 2.4. We've talked about the actual mapping of inner class ideas to the exam, so we will NOT be citing Objective numbers in the answers to the questions in this chapter.

1. ☑ **B** and **D** are correct. **B** is correct because a static nested class is not tied to an instance of the enclosing class, and thus can't access the nonstatic members of the class (just as a `static` method can't access nonstatic members of a class). **D** uses the correct syntax for instantiating a static nested class.
   ☒ **A** is incorrect because static nested classes do not need (and can't use) a reference to an instance of the enclosing class. **C** is incorrect because static nested classes can declare and define nonstatic members. **E** is wrong because… it just is. There's no rule that says an inner or nested class has to extend anything.

2. ☑ **B** and **C** are correct. **B** is correct because anonymous inner classes are no different from any other class when it comes to polymorphism. That means you are always allowed to declare a reference variable of the superclass type and have that reference variable refer to an instance of a subclass type, which in this case is an anonymous subclass of `Bar`. Since `Bar` is a subclass of `Boo`, it all works. **C** uses correct syntax for creating an instance of `Boo`.
   ☒ **A** is incorrect because it passes an `int` to the `Boo` constructor, and there is no matching constructor in the `Boo` class. **D** is incorrect because it violates the rules of polymorphism; you cannot refer to a superclass type using a reference variable declared as the subclass type. The superclass doesn't have everything the subclass has. **E** uses incorrect syntax.

3. ☑ **B** and **E** are correct. **B** is correct because a method-local inner class can be `abstract`, although it means a subclass of the inner class must be created if the `abstract` class is to be used (so an `abstract` method-local inner class is probably not useful). **E** is correct because a method-local inner class works like any other inner class—it has a special relationship to an instance of the enclosing class, thus it can access all members of the enclosing class.
   ☒ **A** is incorrect because a method-local inner class does not have to be declared `final` (although it is legal to do so). **C** and **D** are incorrect because a method-local inner class cannot be made `public` (remember—local variables can't be `public`) or `static`.

4. ☑ **G** is correct. This code would be legal if line 7 ended with a semicolon. Remember that line 3 is a statement that doesn't end until line 7, and a statement needs a closing semicolon!
   ☒ **A, B, C, D, E,** and **F** are incorrect based on the program logic just described. If the semicolon were added at line 7, then answer **B** would be correct—the program would print `true`, the return from the `equals()` method overridden by the anonymous subclass of `Object`.

5. ☑ E is correct. If you use a reference variable of type `Object`, you can access only those members defined in class `Object`.
☒ **A, B, C,** and **D** are incorrect based on the program logic just described.

6. ☑ A is correct. You can define an inner class as `abstract`, which means you can instantiate only concrete subclasses of the `abstract` inner class. The object referenced by the variable `t` is an instance of an anonymous subclass of `AbstractTest`, and the anonymous class overrides the `getNum()` method to return `22`. The variable referenced by `f` is an instance of an anonymous subclass of `Bar`, and the anonymous `Bar` subclass also overrides the `getNum()` method to return `57`. Remember that to create a `Bar` instance, we need an instance of the enclosing `AbstractTest` class to tie to the new `Bar` inner class instance. `AbstractTest` can't be instantiated because it's `abstract`, so we created an anonymous subclass (non-`abstract`) and then used the instance of that anonymous subclass to tie to the new `Bar` subclass instance.
☒ **B, C, D,** and **E** are incorrect based on the program logic just described.

7. ☑ D is correct. It is the only code that uses the correct inner class instantiation syntax.
☒ **A, B, C,** and **E** are incorrect based on the above text.

8. ☑ C is correct. The `"inner"` version of `class A` isn't used because its declaration comes after the instance of `class A` is created in the `go()` method.
☒ **A, B, D,** and **E** are incorrect based on the above text.

9. ☑ C and G are correct. **C** is the correct syntax to access an inner class's outer instance method from an initialization block, and **G** is the correct syntax to access it from a constructor.
☒ **A, B, D, E,** and **F** are incorrect based on the above text.

10. ☑ C is correct. The inner classes are valid, and all the methods (including `main()`), correctly throw an exception, given that `doStuff()` throws an exception. The `doStuff()` in class `TimesSquare` overrides class `Manhattan`'s `doStuff()` and produces no output.
☒ **A, B, D, E, F, G,** and **H** are incorrect based on the above text.

11. ☑ B is correct. The inner class `Gazer` has access to `Navel`'s `private static` and private instance variables.
☒ **A, C, D, E,** and **F** are incorrect based on the above text.

12. ☑ A is correct. The inner class `Sorter` must be declared `static` to be called from the `static` method `main()`. If `Sorter` had been `static`, answer E would be correct.
☒ **B, C, D, E,** and **F** are incorrect based on the above text.

13 Threads

CERTIFICATION OBJECTIVES

- Create and Use the Thread Class and the Runnable Interface
- Manage and Control the Thread Lifecycle
- Synchronize Thread Access to Shared Data
- Identify Code that May Not Execute Correctly in a Multithreaded Environment

 Two-Minute Drill

Q&A Self Test

CERTIFICATION OBJECTIVE

Defining, Instantiating, and Starting Threads (OCP Objective 10.1)

10.1 Create and use the Thread class and the Runnable interface.

Imagine a stockbroker application with a lot of complex capabilities. One of its functions is "download last stock option prices," another is "check prices for warnings," and a third time-consuming operation is "analyze historical data for company XYZ."

In a single-threaded runtime environment, these actions execute one after another. The next action can happen *only* when the previous one is finished. If a historical analysis takes half an hour, and the user selects to perform a download and check afterward, the warning may come too late to, say, buy or sell stock as a result.

We just imagined the sort of application that cries out for multithreading. Ideally, the download should happen in the background (that is, in another thread). That way, other processes could happen at the same time so that, for example, a warning could be communicated instantly. All the while, the user is interacting with other parts of the application. The analysis, too, could happen in a separate thread so the user can work in the rest of the application while the results are being calculated.

So what exactly is a thread? In Java, "thread" means two different things:

- An instance of class `java.lang.Thread`
- A thread of execution

An instance of `Thread` is just… an object. Like any other object in Java, it has variables and methods, and lives and dies on the heap. But a *thread of execution* is an individual process (a "lightweight" process) that has its own call stack. In Java, there is *one thread per call stack*—or, to think of it in reverse, *one call stack per thread*. Even if you don't create any new threads in your program, threads are back there running.

The `main()` method, which starts the whole ball rolling, runs in one thread, called (surprisingly) the *main* thread. If you looked at the main call stack (and you can, any time you get a stack trace from something that happens after main begins, but not within another thread), you'd see that `main()` is the first method on the stack—the method at the bottom. But as soon as you create a *new* thread, a new stack materializes and methods called from *that* thread run in a call stack that's separate from the `main()` call stack. That second new call stack is said to run concurrently with the main thread, but we'll refine that notion as we go through this chapter.

You might find it confusing that we're talking about code running *concurrently*—what gives? The JVM, which gets its turn at the CPU by whatever scheduling mechanism the underlying OS uses, operates like a mini-OS and schedules *its* own threads, regardless of the underlying operating system. In some JVMs, the Java threads are actually mapped to native OS threads, but we won't discuss that here; native threads are not on the exam. Nor is it required to understand how threads behave in different JVM environments. In fact, the most important concept to understand from this entire chapter is this:

When it comes to threads, very little is guaranteed.

So be very cautious about interpreting the behavior you see on *one* machine as "the way threads work." The exam expects you to know what is and is not guaranteed behavior so that you can design your program in such a way that it will work, regardless of the underlying JVM. *That's part of the whole point of Java.*

on the Job

Don't make the mistake of designing your program to be dependent on a particular implementation of the JVM. As you'll learn a little later, different JVMs can run threads in profoundly different ways. For example, one JVM might be sure that all threads get their turn, with a fairly even amount of time allocated for each thread in a nice, happy, round-robin fashion. But in other JVMs, a thread might start running and then just hog the whole show, never stepping out so others can have a turn. If you test your application on the "nice turn-taking" JVM and you don't know what is and is not guaranteed in Java, then you might be in for a big shock when you run it under a JVM with a different thread-scheduling mechanism.

The thread questions are among the most difficult questions on the exam. In fact, for most people, they *are* the toughest questions on the exam, and with four objectives for threads, you'll be answering a *lot* of thread questions. If you're not already familiar with threads, you'll probably need to spend some time experimenting. Also, one final disclaimer: *This chapter makes almost no attempt to teach you how to design a good, safe, multithreaded application. We only scratch the surface of that huge topic in this chapter!* You're here to learn the basics of threading and what you need to get through the thread questions on the exam. Before you can write decent multithreaded code, however, you really need to do more study of the complexities and subtleties of multithreaded code.

(Note: The topic of daemon threads is NOT on the exam. All of the threads discussed in this chapter are "user" threads. You and the operating system can create a second kind of thread called a daemon thread. The difference between these two types of threads [user and daemon] is that the JVM exits an application only when all user threads are complete—the JVM doesn't care about letting daemon threads complete, so once all user threads are complete, the JVM will shut down, regardless of the state of any daemon threads. Once again, this topic is NOT on the exam.)

Making a Thread

A thread in Java begins as an instance of `java.lang.Thread`. You'll find methods in the `Thread` class for managing threads, including creating, starting, and pausing them. For the exam, you'll need to know, at a minimum, the following methods:

```
start()
yield()
sleep()
run()
```

The action happens in the `run()` method. Think of the code you want to execute in a separate thread as *the job to do*. In other words, you have some work that needs to be done—say, downloading stock prices in the background while other things are happening in the program—so what you really want is that *job* to be executed in its own thread. So if the *work* you want done is the *job*, the one *doing* the work (actually executing the job code) is the *thread*. And the *job always starts from a* `run()` *method*, as follows:

```
public void run() {
  // your job code goes here
}
```

You always write the code that needs to be run in a separate thread in a `run()` method. The `run()` method will call other methods, of course, but the thread of execution—the new call stack—always begins by invoking `run()`. So where does the `run()` method go? In one of the two classes you can use to define your thread job.

You can define and instantiate a thread in one of two ways:

- Extend the `java.lang.Thread` class.
- Implement the `Runnable` interface.

You need to know about both for the exam, although in the real world, you're much more likely to implement `Runnable` than extend `Thread`. Extending the

Thread class is the easiest, but it's usually not a good OO practice. Why? Because subclassing should be reserved for specialized versions of more general superclasses. So the only time it really makes sense (from an OO perspective) to extend Thread is when you have a more specialized version of a Thread class. In other words, because *you have more specialized thread-specific behavior*. Chances are, though, that the thread work you want is really just a job to be done *by* a thread. In that case, you should design a class that implements the Runnable interface, which also leaves your class free to extend some *other* class.

Defining a Thread

To define a thread, you need a place to put your run() method, and as we just discussed, you can do that by extending the Thread class or by implementing the Runnable interface. We'll look at both in this section.

Extending java.lang.Thread

The simplest way to define code to run in a separate thread is to

- Extend the java.lang.Thread class.
- Override the run() method.

It looks like this:

```
class MyThread extends Thread {
  public void run() {
    System.out.println("Important job running in MyThread");
  }
}
```

The limitation with this approach (besides being a poor design choice in most cases) is that if you extend Thread, *you can't extend anything else*. And it's not as if you really need that inherited Thread class behavior, because in order to use a thread, you'll need to instantiate one anyway.

Keep in mind that you're free to overload the run() method in your Thread subclass:

```
class MyThread extends Thread {
  public void run() {
    System.out.println("Important job running in MyThread");
  }
  public void run(String s) {
    System.out.println("String in run is " + s);
  }
}
```

But know this: The overloaded `run(String s)` method will be ignored by the `Thread` class unless you call it yourself. The `Thread` class expects a `run()` method with no arguments, and it will execute this method for you in a separate call stack after the thread has been started. With a `run(String s)` method, the `Thread` class won't call the method for you, and even if you call the method directly yourself, execution won't happen in a new thread of execution with a separate call stack. It will just happen in the same call stack as the code that you made the call from, just like any other normal method call.

Implementing java.lang.Runnable

Implementing the `Runnable` interface gives you a way to extend any class you like but still define behavior that will be run by a separate thread. It looks like this:

```
class MyRunnable implements Runnable {
  public void run() {
    System.out.println("Important job running in MyRunnable");
  }
}
```

Regardless of which mechanism you choose, you've now got yourself some code that can be run by a thread of execution. So now let's take a look at *instantiating* your thread-capable class, and then we'll figure out how to actually get the thing *running*.

Instantiating a Thread

Remember, every thread of execution begins as an instance of class `Thread`. Regardless of whether your `run()` method is in a `Thread` subclass or a `Runnable` implementation class, you still need a `Thread` object to do the work.

If you extended the `Thread` class, instantiation is dead simple (we'll look at some additional overloaded constructors in a moment):

```
MyThread t = new MyThread();
```

If you implement `Runnable`, instantiation is only slightly less simple. To have code run by a separate thread, *you still need a `Thread` instance*. But rather than combining both the *thread* and the *job* (the code in the `run()` method) into one class, you've split it into two classes—the `Thread` class for the *thread-specific* code and your `Runnable` implementation class for your *job-that-should-be-run-by-a-thread* code. (Another common way to think about this is that the `Thread` is the "worker," and the `Runnable` is the "job" to be done.)

First, you instantiate your `Runnable` class:

```
MyRunnable r = new MyRunnable();
```

Next, you get yourself an instance of `java.lang.Thread` (*somebody* has to run your job...), and you *give it your job*!

```
Thread t = new Thread(r);  // Pass your Runnable to the Thread
```

If you create a thread using the no-arg constructor, the thread will call its own `run()` method when it's time to start working. That's exactly what you want when you extend `Thread`, but when you use `Runnable`, you need to tell the new thread to use *your* `run()` method rather than its own. The `Runnable` you pass to the `Thread` constructor is called the *target* or the *target* `Runnable`.

You can pass a single `Runnable` instance to multiple `Thread` objects so that the same `Runnable` becomes the target of multiple threads, as follows:

```
public class TestThreads {
  public static void main (String [] args) {
    MyRunnable r = new MyRunnable();
    Thread foo = new Thread(r);
    Thread bar = new Thread(r);
    Thread bat = new Thread(r);
  }
}
```

Giving the same target to multiple threads means that several threads of execution will be running the very same job (and that the same job will be done multiple times).

exam watch

The `Thread` class itself implements `Runnable`. (After all, it has a `run()` method that we were overriding.) This means that you could pass a `Thread` to another `Thread`'s constructor:

```
Thread t = new Thread(new MyThread());
```

This is a bit silly, but it's legal. In this case, you really just need a `Runnnable`, and creating a whole other `Thread` is overkill.

Besides the no-arg constructor and the constructor that takes a `Runnable` (the target, i.e., the instance with the job to do), there are other overloaded constructors in class `Thread`. The constructors we care about are

- `Thread()`
- `Thread(Runnable target)`
- `Thread(Runnable target, String name)`
- `Thread(String name)`

You need to recognize all of them for the exam! A little later, we'll discuss some of the other constructors in the preceding list.

So now you've made yourself a `Thread` instance, and it knows which `run()` method to call. *But nothing is happening yet.* At this point, all we've got is a plain old Java object of type `Thread`. *It is not yet a thread of execution.* To get an actual thread—a new call stack—we still have to *start* the thread.

When a thread has been instantiated but not started (in other words, the `start()` method has not been invoked on the `Thread` instance), the thread is said to be in the *new* state. At this stage, the thread is not yet considered *alive*. Once the `start()` method is called, the thread is considered *alive* (even though the `run()` method may not have actually started executing yet). A thread is considered *dead* (no longer *alive*) after the `run()` method completes. The `isAlive()` method is the best way to determine if a thread has been started but has not yet completed its `run()` method. (Note: The `getState()` method is very useful for debugging, but you won't have to know it for the exam.)

Starting a Thread

You've created a `Thread` object and it knows its target (either the passed-in `Runnable` or itself if you extended class `Thread`). Now it's time to get the whole thread thing happening—to launch a new call stack. It's so simple, it hardly deserves its own subheading:

```
t.start();
```

Prior to calling `start()` on a `Thread` instance, the thread (when we use lowercase `t`, we're referring to the *thread of execution* rather than the `Thread` class) is said to be in the *new* state, as we said. The new state means you have a `Thread` *object* but you don't yet have a *true thread.* So what happens after you call `start()`? The good stuff:

- A new thread of execution starts (with a new call stack).
- The thread moves from the *new* state to the *runnable* state.
- When the thread gets a chance to execute, its target `run()` method will run.

Be *sure* you remember the following: You start a *`Thread`*, not a *`Runnable`*. You call `start()` on a `Thread` instance, not on a `Runnable` instance. The following example demonstrates what we've covered so far—defining, instantiating, and starting a thread:

```
class FooRunnable implements Runnable {
  public void run() {
    for(int x = 1; x < 6; x++) {
      System.out.println("Runnable running");
    }
  }
}

public class TestThreads {
  public static void main (String [] args) {
    FooRunnable r = new FooRunnable();
    Thread t = new Thread(r);
    t.start();
  }
}
```

Running the preceding code prints out exactly what you'd expect:

```
% java TestThreads
Runnable running
Runnable running
Runnable running
Runnable running
Runnable running
```

(If this isn't what you expected, go back and reread everything in this objective.)

exam watch

There's nothing special about the `run()` method as far as Java is concerned. Like `main()`, it just happens to be the name (and signature) of the method that the new thread knows to invoke. So if you see code that calls the `run()` method on a `Runnable` (or even on a `Thread` instance), that's perfectly legal. But it doesn't mean the `run()` method will run in a separate thread! Calling a `run()` method directly just means you're invoking a method from whatever thread is currently executing, and the `run()` method goes onto the current call stack rather than at the beginning of a new call stack. The following code does not start a new thread of execution:

```
Thread t = new Thread();
t.run();             // Legal, but does not start a new thread
```

So what happens if we start multiple threads? We'll run a simple example in a moment, but first we need to know how to print out which thread is executing. We can use the `getName()` method of class `Thread` and have each `Runnable` print out the name of the thread executing that `Runnable` object's `run()` method. The following example instantiates a thread and gives it a name, and then the name is printed out from the `run()` method:

```
class NameRunnable implements Runnable {
  public void run() {
    System.out.println("NameRunnable running");
    System.out.println("Run by "
      + Thread.currentThread().getName());
  }
}
public class NameThread {
  public static void main (String [] args) {
    NameRunnable nr = new NameRunnable();
    Thread t = new Thread(nr);
    t.setName("Fred");
    t.start();
  }
}
```

Running this code produces the following extra-special output:

```
% java NameThread
NameRunnable running
Run by Fred
```

To get the name of a thread, you call—who would have guessed—`getName()` on the `Thread` instance. But the target `Runnable` instance doesn't even *have* a reference to the `Thread` instance, so we first invoked the `static Thread.currentThread()` method, which returns a reference to the currently executing thread, and then we invoked `getName()` on that returned reference.

Even if you don't explicitly name a thread, it still has a name. Let's look at the previous code, commenting out the statement that sets the thread's name:

```
public class NameThread {
  public static void main (String [] args) {
    NameRunnable nr = new NameRunnable();
    Thread t = new Thread(nr);
    // t.setName("Fred");
    t.start();
  }
}
```

Running the preceding code now gives us

```
% java NameThread
NameRunnable running
Run by Thread-0
```

And since we're getting the name of the current thread by using the static `Thread.currentThread()` method, we can even get the name of the thread running our main code:

```
public class NameThreadTwo {
  public static void main (String [] args) {
    System.out.println("thread is "
      + Thread.currentThread().getName());
  }
}
```

which prints out

```
% java NameThreadTwo
thread is main
```

That's right, the main thread already has a name—*main*. (Once again, what are the odds?) Figure 13-1 shows the process of starting a thread.

FIGURE 13-1

Starting a thread

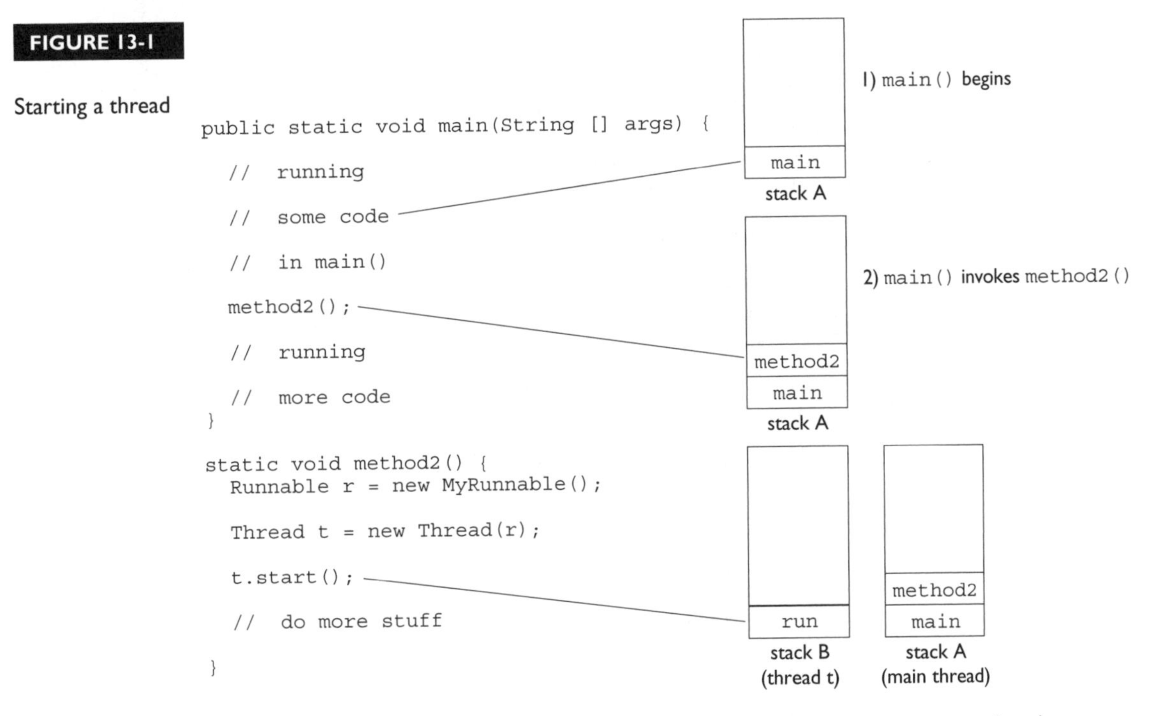

Starting and Running Multiple Threads

Enough playing around here; let's actually get multiple threads going (more than two, that is). We already had two threads, because the `main()` method starts in a thread of its own, and then `t.start()` started a *second* thread. Now we'll do more. The following code creates a single `Runnable` instance and three `Thread` instances. All three `Thread` instances get the same `Runnable` instance, and each thread is given a unique name. Finally, all three threads are started by invoking `start()` on the `Thread` instances.

```
class NameRunnable implements Runnable {
  public void run() {
    for (int x = 1; x <= 3; x++) {
      System.out.println("Run by "
        + Thread.currentThread().getName()
        + ", x is " + x);
    }
  }
}
public class ManyNames {
   public static void main(String [] args) {
    // Make one Runnable
    NameRunnable nr = new NameRunnable();
    Thread one = new Thread(nr);
    Thread two = new Thread(nr);
    Thread three = new Thread(nr);

      one.setName("Fred");
      two.setName("Lucy");
      three.setName("Ricky");
      one.start();
      two.start();
      three.start();
    }
}
```

Running this code **might** produce the following:

```
% java ManyNames
Run by Fred, x is 1
Run by Fred, x is 2
Run by Fred, x is 3
Run by Lucy, x is 1
Run by Lucy, x is 2
Run by Lucy, x is 3
Run by Ricky, x is 1
Run by Ricky, x is 2
Run by Ricky, x is 3
```

Well, at least that's what it printed when we ran it—this time, on our machine. But the behavior you see here is not guaranteed. This is so crucial that you need to stop right now, take a deep breath, and repeat after me, "The behavior is not guaranteed." You need to know, for your future as a Java programmer as well as for the exam, that there is nothing in the Java specification that says threads will start running in the order in which they were started (in other words, the order in which `start()` was invoked on each thread). And there is no guarantee that once a thread starts executing, it will keep executing until it's done. Or that a loop will complete before another thread begins. No siree, Bob.

Nothing is guaranteed in the preceding code except this:

Each thread will start, and each thread will run to completion.

Within each thread, things will happen in a predictable order. But the actions of different threads can mix in unpredictable ways. If you run the program multiple times or on multiple machines, you may see different output. Even if you don't see different output, you need to realize that the behavior you see is not guaranteed. Sometimes a little change in the way the program is run will cause a difference to emerge. Just for fun we bumped up the loop code so that each `run()` method ran the for loop 400 times rather than 3, and eventually we did start to see some wobbling:

```
public void run() {
  for (int x = 1; x <= 400; x++) {
    System.out.println("Run by "
      + Thread.currentThread().getName()
      + ", x is " + x);
  }
}
```

Running the preceding code, with each thread executing its run loop 400 times, started out fine but then became nonlinear. Here's just a snippet from the command-line output of running that code. To make it easier to distinguish each thread, we put Fred's output in italics and Lucy's in bold, and left Ricky's alone:

```
Run by Ricky, x is 313
Run by Lucy, x is 341
Run by Ricky, x is 314
Run by Lucy, x is 342
Run by Ricky, x is 315
Run by Fred, x is 346
Run by Lucy, x is 343
Run by Fred, x is 347
Run by Lucy, x is 344
```

... it continues on ...

Notice that there's not really any clear pattern here. If we look at only the output from Fred, we see the numbers increasing one at a time, as expected:

```
Run by Fred, x is 345
Run by Fred, x is 346
Run by Fred, x is 347
```

And similarly, if we look only at the output from Lucy or Ricky—each one individually is behaving in a nice, orderly manner. But together—chaos! In the previous fragment we see Fred, then Lucy, then Ricky (in the same order we originally started the threads), but then Lucy butts in when it was Fred's turn. What nerve! And then Ricky and Lucy trade back and forth for a while until finally Fred gets another chance. They jump around like this for a while after this. Eventually (after the part shown earlier), Fred finishes, then Ricky, and finally Lucy finishes with a long sequence of output. So even though Ricky was started third, he actually completed second. And if we run it again, we'll get a different result. Why? Because it's up to the scheduler, and we don't control the scheduler! Which brings up another key point to remember: Just because a series of threads are started in a particular order, this doesn't mean they'll run in that order. For any group of started threads, order is not guaranteed by the scheduler. And duration is not guaranteed. You don't know, for example, if one thread will run to completion before the others have a chance to get in, or whether they'll all take turns nicely, or whether they'll do a combination of both. There is a way, however, to start a thread but tell it not to run until some other thread has finished. You can do this with the `join()` method, which we'll look at a little later.

A thread is done being a thread when its target `run()` method completes.

When a thread completes its `run()` method, the thread ceases to be a thread of execution. The stack for that thread dissolves, and the thread is considered dead. (Technically, the API calls a dead thread "terminated," but we'll use "dead" in this chapter.) Not dead and gone, however—just dead. It's still a `Thread` *object*, just not a *thread of execution*. So if you've got a reference to a `Thread` instance, then even when that `Thread` instance is no longer a thread of execution, you can still call methods on the `Thread` instance, just like any other Java object. What you can't do, though, is call `start()` again.

Once a thread has been started, it can never be started again.

If you have a reference to a `Thread` and you call `start()`, it's started. If you call `start()` a second time, it will cause an exception (an `IllegalThreadStateException`, which is a kind of `RuntimeException`, but you don't need to worry about the exact type). This happens whether or not the `run()` method has completed from the first `start()` call. Only a new thread can be started, and then only once. A runnable thread or a dead thread cannot be restarted.

So far, we've seen three thread states: *new*, *runnable*, and *dead*. We'll look at more thread states before we're done with this chapter.

exam watch

In addition to using `setName()` and `getName` to identify threads, you might see `getId()`. The `getId()` method returns a positive, unique, long number, and that number will be that thread's only ID number for the thread's entire life.

The Thread Scheduler

The thread scheduler is the part of the JVM (although most JVMs map Java threads directly to native threads on the underlying OS) that decides which thread should run at any given moment, and also takes threads *out* of the run state. Assuming a single processor machine, only one thread can actually *run* at a time. Only one stack can ever be executing at one time. And it's the thread scheduler that decides *which* thread—of all that are eligible—will actually *run*. When we say *eligible*, we really mean *in the runnable state*.

Any thread in the *runnable* state can be chosen by the scheduler to be the one and only running thread. If a thread is not in a runnable state, then it cannot be chosen to be the *currently running* thread. And just so we're clear about how little is guaranteed here:

The order in which runnable threads are chosen to run is not guaranteed.

Although *queue* behavior is typical, it isn't guaranteed. Queue behavior means that when a thread has finished with its "turn," it moves to the end of the line of the runnable pool and waits until it eventually gets to the front of the line, where it can be chosen again. In fact, we call it a runnable *pool*, rather than a runnable *queue*, to help reinforce the fact that threads aren't all lined up in some guaranteed order.

Although we don't *control* the thread scheduler (we can't, for example, tell a specific thread to run), we can sometimes influence it. The following methods give us some tools for *influencing* the scheduler. Just don't ever mistake influence for control.

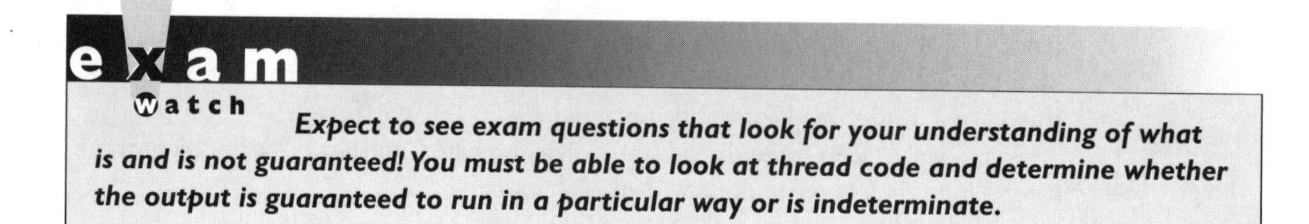

Expect to see exam questions that look for your understanding of what is and is not guaranteed! You must be able to look at thread code and determine whether the output is guaranteed to run in a particular way or is indeterminate.

from the java.lang.Thread Class Some of the methods that can help us influence thread scheduling are as follows:

```
public static void sleep(long millis) throws InterruptedException
public static void yield()
public final void join() throws InterruptedException
public final void setPriority(int newPriority)
```

Note that both `sleep()` and `join()` have overloaded versions not shown here.

Methods from the java.lang.Object Class Every class in Java inherits the following three thread-related methods:

```
public final void wait() throws InterruptedException
public final void notify()
public final void notifyAll()
```

The `wait()` method has three overloaded versions (including the one listed here).

We'll look at the behavior of each of these methods in this chapter. First, though, we're going to look at the different states a thread can be in.

CERTIFICATION OBJECTIVE

Thread States and Transitions (OCP Objective 10.2)

10.2 Manage and control thread lifecycle.

We've already seen three thread states—new, runnable, and *dead*—but wait! There's more! The thread scheduler's job is to move threads in and out of the *running* state.

While the thread scheduler can move a thread from the running state back to runnable, other factors can cause a thread to move out of running, but *not* back to runnable. One of these is when the thread's `run()` method completes, in which case, the thread moves from the running state directly to the dead state. Next, we'll look at some of the other ways in which a thread can leave the running state and where the thread goes.

Thread States

A thread can be only in one of five states (see Figure 13-2):

- **New** This is the state the thread is in after the `Thread` instance has been created but the `start()` method has not been invoked on the thread. It is a live `Thread` object, but not yet a thread of execution. At this point, the thread is considered *not alive*.
- **Runnable** This is the state a thread is in when it's eligible to run but the scheduler has not selected it to be the running thread. A thread first enters the runnable state when the `start()` method is invoked, but a thread can also return to the runnable state after either running or coming back from a blocked, waiting, or sleeping state. When the thread is in the runnable state, it is considered *alive*.
- **Running** This is it. The "big time." Where the action is. This is the state a thread is in when the thread scheduler selects it from the runnable pool to be the currently executing process. A thread can transition out of a running state for several reasons, including because "the thread scheduler felt like it." We'll look at those other reasons shortly. Note that in Figure 13-2, there are several ways to get to the runnable state, but only *one* way to get to the running state: The scheduler chooses a thread from the runnable pool.
- **Waiting/blocked/sleeping** This is the state a thread is in when it's not eligible to run. Okay, so this is really three states combined into one, but they all have one thing in common: The thread is still alive, but is currently not eligible to run. In other words, it is not *runnable*, but it might *return* to a runnable state later if a particular event occurs. A thread may be *blocked* waiting for a resource (like I/O or an object's lock), in which case the event that sends it back to runnable is the availability of the resource—for example, if data comes in through the input stream the thread code is reading from, or if the object's lock suddenly becomes available. A thread may be *sleeping*

FIGURE 13-2

Transitioning between thread states

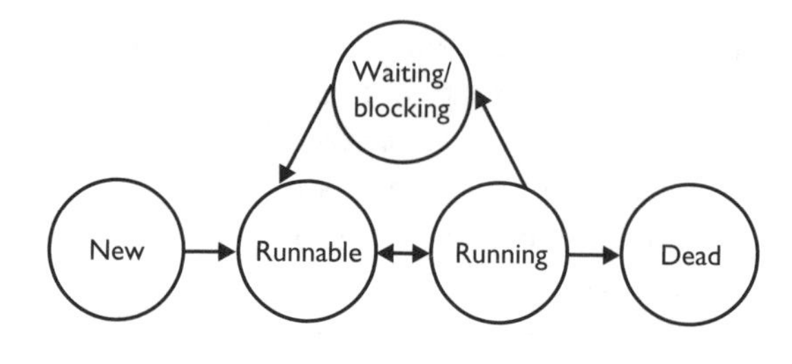

because the thread's run code *tells* it to sleep for some period of time, in which case, the event that sends it back to runnable causes it to wake up because its sleep time has expired. Or the thread may be *waiting* because the thread's run code *causes* it to wait, in which case, the event that sends it back to runnable causes another thread to send a notification that it may no longer be necessary for the thread to wait. The important point is that one thread does not *tell* another thread to block. Some methods may *look* like they tell another thread to block, but they don't. If you have a reference `t` to another thread, you can write something like this:

```
t.sleep();   or     t.yield();
```

But those are actually static methods of the `Thread` class—*they don't affect the instance* `t`; instead, they are defined to always affect the thread that's currently executing. (This is a good example of why it's a bad idea to use an instance variable to access a `static` method—it's misleading. There *is* a method, `suspend()`, in the `Thread` class that lets one thread tell another to suspend, but the `suspend()` method has been deprecated and won't be on the exam [nor will its counterpart `resume()`].) There is also a `stop()` method, but it, too, has been deprecated and we won't even go there. Both `suspend()` and `stop()` turned out to be very dangerous, so you shouldn't use them, and again, because they're deprecated, they won't appear on the exam. Don't study 'em; don't use 'em. Note also that a thread in a blocked state is still considered *alive*.

- **Dead** A thread is considered dead when its `run()` method completes. It may still be a viable `Thread` object, but it is no longer a separate thread of execution. Once a thread is dead, it can never be brought back to life! (The whole "I see dead threads" thing.) If you invoke `start()` on a dead `Thread` instance, you'll get a runtime (not compiler) exception. And it probably doesn't take a rocket scientist to tell you that if a thread is dead, it is no longer considered *alive*.

Preventing Thread Execution

A thread that's been stopped usually means a thread that's moved to the dead state. But Objective 4.2 is also looking for your ability to recognize when a thread will get kicked out of running but *not* be sent back to either runnable or dead.

For the purpose of the exam, we aren't concerned with a thread blocking on I/O (say, waiting for something to arrive from an input stream from the server). We *are* concerned with the following:

- Sleeping
- Waiting
- Blocked because it needs an object's lock

Sleeping

The `sleep()` method is a `static` method of class `Thread`. You use it in your code to "slow a thread down" by forcing it to go into a sleep mode before coming back to runnable (where it still has to beg to be the currently running thread). When a thread sleeps, it drifts off somewhere and doesn't return to runnable until it wakes up.

So why would you want a thread to sleep? Well, you might think the thread is moving too quickly through its code. Or you might need to force your threads to take turns, since reasonable turn taking isn't guaranteed in the Java specification. Or imagine a thread that runs in a loop, downloading the latest stock prices and analyzing them. Downloading prices one after another would be a waste of time, as most would be quite similar—and even more important, it would be an incredible waste of precious bandwidth. The simplest way to solve this is to cause a thread to pause (sleep) for five minutes after each download.

You do this by invoking the static `Thread.sleep()` method, giving it a time in milliseconds as follows:

```
try {
  Thread.sleep(5*60*1000);  // Sleep for 5 minutes
} catch (InterruptedException ex) { }
```

Notice that the `sleep()` method can throw a checked InterruptedException (you'll usually know if that is a possibility, since another thread has to explicitly do the interrupting), so you must acknowledge the exception with a handle or declare. Typically, you wrap calls to `sleep()` in a `try/catch`, as in the preceding code.

Let's modify our Fred, Lucy, Ricky code by using `sleep()` to *try* to force the threads to alternate rather than letting one thread dominate for any period of time. Where do you think the `sleep()` method should go?

```
class NameRunnable implements Runnable {
  public void run() {
    for (int x = 1; x < 4; x++) {
      System.out.println("Run by "
        + Thread.currentThread().getName());
      try {
        Thread.sleep(1000);
      } catch (InterruptedException ex) { }
    }
  }
}
public class ManyNames {
  public static void main (String [] args) {

    // Make one Runnable
    NameRunnable nr = new NameRunnable();

    Thread one = new Thread(nr);
    one.setName("Fred");
    Thread two = new Thread(nr);
    two.setName("Lucy");
    Thread three = new Thread(nr);
    three.setName("Ricky");

    one.start();
    two.start();
    three.start();
  }
}
```

Running this code shows Fred, Lucy, and Ricky alternating nicely:

```
% java ManyNames
Run by Fred
Run by Lucy
Run by Ricky
Run by Fred
Run by Lucy
Run by Ricky
Run by Fred
Run by Lucy
Run by Ricky
```

Just keep in mind that the behavior in the preceding output is still not guaranteed. You can't be certain how long a thread will actually run *before* it gets put to sleep, so you can't know with certainty that only one of the three threads will be in the runnable state when the running thread goes to sleep. In other words, if two threads are awake and in the runnable pool, you can't know with certainty that the least recently used thread will be the one selected to run. *Still, using `sleep()` is the best way to help all threads get a chance to run!* Or at least to guarantee that one thread doesn't get in and stay until it's done. When a thread encounters a sleep call, it *must* go to sleep for *at least* the specified number of milliseconds (unless it is interrupted before its wake-up time, in which case, it immediately throws the InterruptedException).

exam watch

Just because a thread's `sleep()` expires and it wakes up, this does not mean it will return to running! Remember, when a thread wakes up, it simply goes back to the runnable state. So the time specified in `sleep()` is the minimum duration in which the thread won't run, but it is not the exact duration in which the thread won't run. So you can't, for example, rely on the `sleep()` method to give you a perfectly accurate timer. Although in many applications using `sleep()` as a timer is certainly good enough, you must know that a `sleep()` time is not a guarantee that the thread will start running again as soon as the time expires and the thread wakes.

Remember that `sleep()` is a static method, so don't be fooled into thinking that one thread can put another thread to sleep. You can put `sleep()` code anywhere, since *all* code is being run by *some* thread. When the executing code (meaning the currently running thread's code) hits a `sleep()` call, it puts the currently running thread to sleep.

EXERCISE 13-1

Creating a Thread and Putting It to Sleep

In this exercise, we will create a simple counting thread. It will count to 100, pausing one second between each number. Also, in keeping with the counting theme, it will output a string every ten numbers.

1. Create a class and extend the `Thread` class. As an option, you can implement the `Runnable` interface.

2. Override the `run()` method of `Thread`. This is where the code will go that will output the numbers.
3. Create a `for` loop that will loop 100 times. Use the modulus operation to check whether there are any remainder numbers when divided by 10.
4. Use the static method `Thread.sleep()` to pause. (Remember, the one-arg version of `sleep()` specifies the amount of time of sleep in milliseconds.)

Thread Priorities and yield()

To understand `yield()`, you must understand the concept of thread *priorities*. Threads always run with some priority, usually represented as a number between 1 and 10 (although in some cases, the range is less than 10). The scheduler in most JVMs uses preemptive, priority-based scheduling (which implies some sort of time slicing). *This does not mean that all JVMs use time slicing.* The JVM specification does not require a VM to implement a time-slicing scheduler, where each thread is allocated a fair amount of time and then sent back to runnable to give another thread a chance. Although many JVMs do use time slicing, some may use a scheduler that lets one thread stay running until the thread completes its `run()` method.

In most JVMs, however, the scheduler does use thread priorities in one important way: If a thread enters the runnable state and it has a higher priority than any of the threads in the pool and a higher priority than the currently running thread, *the lower-priority running thread usually will be bumped back to runnable and the highest-priority thread will be chosen to run*. In other words, at any given time, the currently running thread usually will not have a priority that is lower than any of the threads in the pool. *In most cases, the running thread will be of equal or greater priority than the highest-priority threads in the pool*. This is as close to a guarantee about scheduling as you'll get from the JVM specification, so you must never rely on thread priorities to guarantee the correct behavior of your program.

on the Job

Don't rely on thread priorities when designing your multithreaded application. Because thread-scheduling priority behavior is not guaranteed, use thread priorities as a way to improve the efficiency of your program, but just be sure your program doesn't* depend *on that behavior for correctness.

What is also *not* guaranteed is the behavior when threads in the pool are of equal priority or when the currently running thread has the same priority as threads in the pool. All priorities being equal, a JVM implementation of the scheduler is free to do just about anything it likes. That means a scheduler might do one of the following (among other things):

- Pick a thread to run, and run it there until it blocks or completes.
- Time-slice the threads in the pool to give everyone an equal opportunity to run.

Setting a Thread's Priority

A thread gets a default priority that is *the priority of the thread of execution that creates it*. For example, in the code

```
public class TestThreads {
  public static void main (String [] args) {
    MyThread t = new MyThread();
  }
}
```

the thread referenced by `t` will have the same priority as the *main* thread, since the main thread is executing the code that creates the `MyThread` instance.

You can also set a thread's priority directly by calling the `setPriority()` method on a `Thread` instance as follows:

```
FooRunnable r = new FooRunnable();
Thread t = new Thread(r);
t.setPriority(8);
t.start();
```

Priorities are set using a positive integer, usually between 1 and 10, and the JVM will never change a thread's priority. However, values 1 through 10 are not guaranteed. Some JVMs might not recognize ten distinct values. Such a JVM might merge values from 1 to 10 down to maybe values from 1 to 5, so if you have, say, ten threads, each with a different priority, and the current application is running in a JVM that allocates a range of only five priorities, then two or more threads might be mapped to one priority.

Although *the default priority is* 5, the `Thread` class has the three following constants (`static final` variables) that define the range of thread priorities:

```
Thread.MIN_PRIORITY  (1)
Thread.NORM_PRIORITY  (5)
Thread.MAX_PRIORITY  (10)
```

The yield() Method

So what does the `static Thread.yield()` have to do with all this? Not that much, in practice. What `yield()` is *supposed* to do is make the currently running thread head back to runnable to allow other threads of the same priority to get their turn. So the intention is to use `yield()` to promote graceful turn-taking among equal-priority threads. In reality, though, the `yield()` method isn't guaranteed to do what it claims, and even if `yield()` does cause a thread to step out of running and back to runnable, *there's no guarantee the yielding thread won't just be chosen again over all the others!* So while `yield()` might—and often does—make a running thread give up its slot to another runnable thread of the same priority, there's no guarantee.

A `yield()` won't ever cause a thread to go to the waiting/sleeping/ blocking state. At most, a `yield()` will cause a thread to go from running to runnable, but again, it might have no effect at all.

The join() Method

The non-`static` `join()` method of class `Thread` lets one thread "join onto the end" of another thread. If you have a thread B that can't do its work until another thread A has completed *its* work, then you want thread B to "join" thread A. This means that thread B will not become runnable until A has finished (and entered the dead state).

```
Thread t = new Thread();
t.start();
t.join();
```

The preceding code takes the currently running thread (if this were in the `main()` method, then that would be the main thread) and *joins* it to the end of the thread referenced by `t`. This blocks the current thread from becoming runnable until after the thread referenced by `t` is no longer alive. In other words, the code `t.join()` means "Join me (the current thread) to the end of `t`, so that `t` must finish before I (the current thread) can run again." You can also call one of the overloaded versions of `join()` that takes a timeout duration so that you're saying, "wait until thread `t` is done, but if it takes longer than 5,000 milliseconds, then stop waiting and become runnable anyway." Figure 13-3 shows the effect of the `join()` method.

So far, we've looked at three ways a running thread could leave the running state:

- **A call to `sleep()`** Guaranteed to cause the current thread to stop executing for at least the specified sleep duration (although it might be *interrupted* before its specified time).

FIGURE 13-3

The `join()` method

Output
Key Events in the Threads' Code
A is running
A is running
A is running
A is running
A is running
Thread b = new Thread(aRunnable);
A is running
b.start();
A is running
// Threads bounce back and forth
B is running
B is running
A is running
B is running
A is running
A is running
B is running
B is running
A is running
B is running
A is running
b.join(); // A joins to the end
// of B
B is running
B is running
B is running
B is running
B is running
B is running
B is running
B is running
// Thread B completes !!
A is running
// Thread A starts again !
A is running
A is running
A is running
A is running
A is running
doStuff()
Stack A is running
doStuff()
doOther()
Stack A is running
Stack B is running
Stack B
doOther()
Stack A
doStuff()
Stack A joined to Stack B

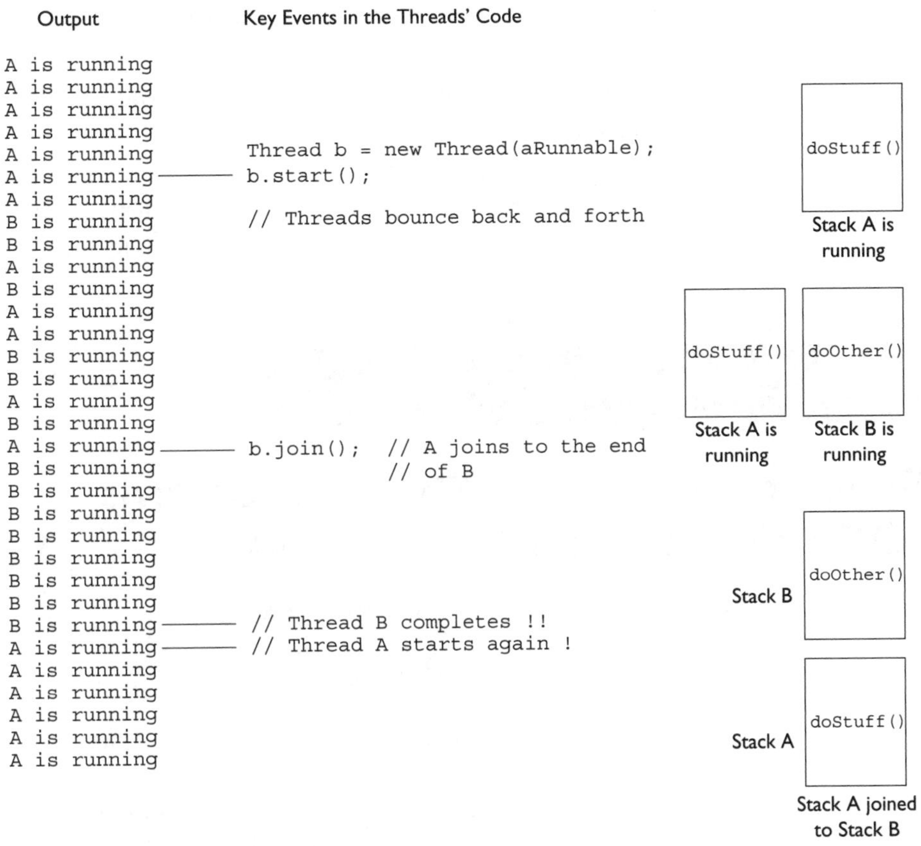

- **A call to `yield()`** Not guaranteed to do much of anything, although typically, it will cause the currently running thread to move back to runnable so that a thread of the same priority can have a chance.
- **A call to `join()`** Guaranteed to cause the current thread to stop executing until the thread it joins with (in other words, the thread it calls `join()` on) completes, or if the thread it's trying to join with is not alive, the current thread won't need to back out.

Besides those three, we also have the following scenarios in which a thread might leave the running state:

- The thread's `run()` method completes. Duh.

- A call to `wait()` on an object (we don't call `wait()` on a *thread*, as we'll see in a moment).
- A thread can't acquire the *lock* on the object whose method code it's attempting to run.
- The thread scheduler can decide to move the current thread from running to runnable in order to give another thread a chance to run. No reason is needed—the thread scheduler can trade threads in and out whenever it likes.

CERTIFICATION OBJECTIVE

Synchronizing Code, Thread Problems (OCP Objectives 10.3 and 10.4)

10.3 Synchronize thread access to shared data.

10.4 Identify potential threading problems.

Can you imagine the havoc that can occur when two different threads have access to a single instance of a class, and both threads invoke methods on that object... and those methods modify the state of the object? In other words, what might happen if *two* different threads call, say, a setter method on a *single* object? A scenario like that might corrupt an object's state by changing its instance variable values in an inconsistent way, and if that object's state is data shared by other parts of the program, well, it's too scary to even visualize.

But just because we enjoy horror, let's look at an example of what might happen. The following code demonstrates what happens when two different threads are accessing the same account data. Imagine that two people each have a checkbook for a single checking account (or two people each have ATM cards, but both cards are linked to only one account).

In this example, we have a class called Account that represents a bank account. To keep the code short, this account starts with a balance of 50 and can be used only for withdrawals. The withdrawal will be accepted even if there isn't enough money in the account to cover it. The account simply reduces the balance by the amount you want to withdraw:

```
class Account {
  private int balance = 50;
  public int getBalance() {
    return balance;
  }
  public void withdraw(int amount) {
    balance = balance - amount;
  }
}
```

Now here's where it starts to get fun. Imagine a couple, Fred and Lucy, who both have access to the account and want to make withdrawals. But they don't want the account to ever be overdrawn, so just before one of them makes a withdrawal, he or she will first check the balance to be certain there's enough to cover the withdrawal. Also, withdrawals are always limited to an amount of 10, so there must be at least 10 in the account balance in order to make a withdrawal. Sounds reasonable. But that's a two-step process:

1. Check the balance.
2. If there's enough in the account (in this example, at least 10), make the withdrawal.

What happens if something separates step 1 from step 2? For example, imagine what would happen if Lucy checks the balance and sees there's just exactly enough in the account, 10. *But before she makes the withdrawal, Fred checks the balance and also sees that there's enough for his withdrawal.* Since Lucy has verified the balance but not yet made her withdrawal, Fred is seeing "bad data." He is seeing the account balance *before* Lucy actually debits the account, but at this point, that debit is certain to occur. Now both Lucy and Fred believe there's enough to make their withdrawals. So now imagine that Lucy makes *her* withdrawal, and now there isn't enough in the account for Fred's withdrawal, but he thinks there is since when he checked, there was enough! Yikes. In a minute, we'll see the actual banking code, with Fred and Lucy, represented by two threads, each acting on the same `Runnable`, and that `Runnable` holds a reference to the one and only account instance—so, two threads, one account.

The logic in our code example is as follows:

1. The `Runnable` object holds a reference to a single account.
2. Two threads are started, representing Lucy and Fred, and each thread is given a reference to the same `Runnable` (which holds a reference to the actual account).

3. The initial balance on the account is 50, and each withdrawal is exactly 10.
4. In the `run()` method, we loop five times, and in each loop we
   - Make a withdrawal (if there's enough in the account).
   - Print a statement *if the account is overdrawn* (which it should never be since we check the balance *before* making a withdrawal).
5. The `makeWithdrawal()` method in the test class (representing the behavior of Fred or Lucy) will do the following:
   - Check the balance to see if there's enough for the withdrawal.
   - If there is enough, print out the name of the one making the withdrawal.
   - Go to sleep for 500 milliseconds—just long enough to give the other partner a chance to get in before you actually *make* the withdrawal.
   - Upon waking up, complete the withdrawal and print that fact.
   - If there wasn't enough in the first place, print a statement showing who you are and the fact that there wasn't enough.

So what we're really trying to discover is if the following is possible: for one partner to check the account and see that there's enough, but before making the actual withdrawal, the other partner checks the account and *also* sees that there's enough. When the account balance gets to 10, if both partners check it before making the withdrawal, both will think it's okay to withdraw, and the account will overdraw by 10!

Here's the code:

```
public class AccountDanger implements Runnable {
  private Account acct = new Account();
  public static void main (String [] args) {
    AccountDanger r = new AccountDanger();
    Thread one = new Thread(r);
    Thread two = new Thread(r);
    one.setName("Fred");
    two.setName("Lucy");
    one.start();
    two.start();
  }
  public void run() {
    for (int x = 0; x < 5; x++) {
      makeWithdrawal(10);
      if (acct.getBalance() < 0) {
        System.out.println("account is overdrawn!");
      }
    }
  }
```

```
    private void makeWithdrawal(int amt) {
      if (acct.getBalance() >= amt) {
        System.out.println(Thread.currentThread().getName()
                       + " is going to withdraw");
        try {
          Thread.sleep(500);
        } catch(InterruptedException ex) { }
        acct.withdraw(amt);
        System.out.println(Thread.currentThread().getName()
                       + " completes the withdrawal");
      } else {
        System.out.println("Not enough in account for "
                       + Thread.currentThread().getName()
                       + " to withdraw " + acct.getBalance());
      }
    }
  }
```

(Note: You might have to tweak this code a bit on your machine to the "account overdrawn" behavior. You might try much shorter sleep times; you might try adding a `sleep` to the `run()` method... In any case, experimenting will help you lock in the concepts.) So what happened? Is it possible that, say, Lucy checked the balance, fell asleep, Fred checked the balance, Lucy woke up and completed *her* withdrawal, then Fred completes *his* withdrawal, and in the end, they overdraw the account? Look at the (numbered) output:

```
% java AccountDanger
 1. Fred is going to withdraw
 2. Lucy is going to withdraw
 3. Fred completes the withdrawal
 4. Fred is going to withdraw
 5. Lucy completes the withdrawal
 6. Lucy is going to withdraw
 7. Fred completes the withdrawal
 8. Fred is going to withdraw
 9. Lucy completes the withdrawal
10. Lucy is going to withdraw
11. Fred completes the withdrawal
12. Not enough in account for Fred to withdraw 0
13. Not enough in account for Fred to withdraw 0
14. Lucy completes the withdrawal
15. account is overdrawn!
16. Not enough in account for Lucy to withdraw -10
17. account is overdrawn!
18. Not enough in account for Lucy to withdraw -10
19. account is overdrawn!
```

Although each time you run this code the output might be a little different, let's walk through this particular example using the numbered lines of output. For the first four attempts, everything is fine. Fred checks the balance on line 1 and finds it's okay. At line 2, Lucy checks the balance and finds it okay. At line 3, Fred makes his withdrawal. At this point, the balance Lucy checked for (and believes is still accurate) has actually changed since she last checked. And now Fred checks the balance *again*, before Lucy even completes her first withdrawal. By this point, even Fred is seeing a potentially inaccurate balance because we know Lucy is going to complete her withdrawal. It is possible, of course, that Fred will complete his before Lucy does, but that's not what happens here.

On line 5, Lucy completes her withdrawal and then, before Fred completes his, Lucy does another check on the account on line 6. And so it continues until we get to line 8, where Fred checks the balance and sees that it's 20. On line 9, Lucy completes a withdrawal that she had checked for earlier, and this takes the balance to 10. On line 10, Lucy checks again, sees that the balance is 10, so she knows she can do a withdrawal. *But she didn't know that Fred, too, has already checked the balance on line 8 so he thinks it's safe to do the withdrawal!* On line 11, Fred completes the withdrawal he approved on line 8. This takes the balance to zero. But Lucy still has a pending withdrawal that she got approval for on line 10! You know what's coming.

On lines 12 and 13, Fred checks the balance and finds that there's not enough in the account. But on line 14, Lucy completes her withdrawal and BOOM! The account is now overdrawn by 10—*something we thought we were preventing by doing a balance check prior to a withdrawal.*

Figure 13-4 shows the timeline of what can happen when two threads concurrently access the same object.

This problem is known as a "race condition," where multiple threads can access the same resource (typically an object's instance variables) and can produce corrupted data if one thread "races in" too quickly before an operation that should be "atomic" has completed.

Preventing the Account Overdraw So what can be done? The solution is actually quite simple. We must guarantee that the two steps of the withdrawal—*checking* the balance and *making* the withdrawal—are never split apart. We need them to always be performed as one operation, even when the thread falls asleep in between step 1 and step 2! We call this an "atomic operation" (although the physics is a little outdated—in this case, "atomic" means "indivisible") because the operation, regardless of the number of actual statements (or underlying bytecode instructions), is completed *before* any other thread code that acts on the same data.

You can't guarantee that a single thread will stay running throughout the entire atomic operation. But you can guarantee that even if the thread running the atomic operation moves in and out of the running state, no other running thread will be able to act on the same data. In other words, if Lucy falls asleep after checking the

FIGURE 13-4

Problems with concurrent access

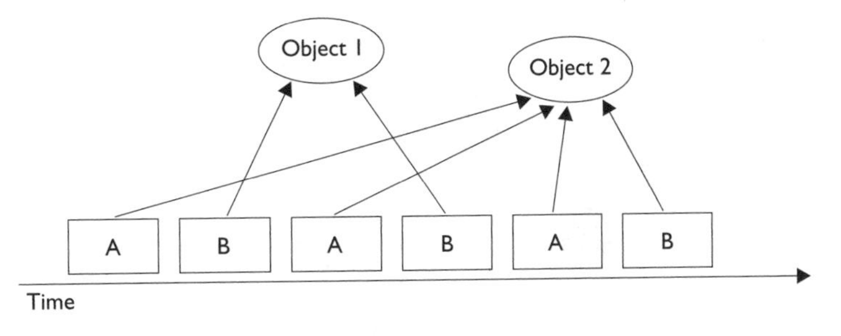

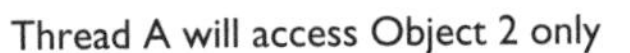

Thread B will access Object 1, and then Object 2

balance, we can stop Fred from checking the balance until after Lucy wakes up and completes her withdrawal.

So how do you protect the data? You must do two things:

- Mark the variables `private`.
- Synchronize the code that modifies the variables.

Remember, you protect the variables in the normal way—using an access control modifier. It's the method code that you must protect so that only one thread at a time can be executing that code. You do this with the `synchronized` keyword.

We can solve all of Fred and Lucy's problems by adding one word to the code. We mark the `makeWithdrawal()` method `synchronized` as follows:

```
private synchronized void makeWithdrawal(int amt) {
  if (acct.getBalance() >= amt) {
    System.out.println(Thread.currentThread().getName() +
                         " is going to withdraw");
    try {
      Thread.sleep(500);
    } catch(InterruptedException ex) { }
    acct.withdraw(amt);
    System.out.println(Thread.currentThread().getName() +
                          " completes the withdrawal");
  } else {
    System.out.println("Not enough in account for "
                         + Thread.currentThread().getName()
                         + " to withdraw " + acct.getBalance());
  }
}
```

Now we've guaranteed that once a thread (Lucy or Fred) starts the withdrawal process by invoking `makeWithdrawal()`, the other thread cannot enter that method until the first one completes the process by exiting the method. The new output shows the benefit of synchronizing the `makeWithdrawal()` method:

```
% java AccountDanger
Fred is going to withdraw
Fred completes the withdrawal
Lucy is going to withdraw
Lucy completes the withdrawal
Fred is going to withdraw
Fred completes the withdrawal
Lucy is going to withdraw
Lucy completes the withdrawal
Fred is going to withdraw
Fred completes the withdrawal
Not enough in account for Lucy to withdraw 0
Not enough in account for Fred to withdraw 0
Not enough in account for Lucy to withdraw 0
Not enough in account for Fred to withdraw 0
Not enough in account for Lucy to withdraw 0
```

Notice that now both threads, Lucy and Fred, always check the account balance *and* complete the withdrawal before the other thread can check the balance.

Synchronization and Locks

How does synchronization work? With locks. Every object in Java has a built-in lock that only comes into play when the object has synchronized method code. When we enter a synchronized non-`static` method, we automatically acquire the lock associated with the current instance of the class whose code we're executing (the `this` instance). Acquiring a lock for an object is also known as getting the lock, or locking the object, locking *on* the object, or synchronizing on the object. We may also use the term *monitor* to refer to the object whose lock we're acquiring. Technically, the lock and the monitor are two different things, but most people talk about the two interchangeably, and we will too.

Since there is only one lock per object, if one thread has picked up the lock, no other thread can pick up the lock until the first thread releases (or returns) the lock. This means no other thread can enter the synchronized code (which means it can't enter any `synchronized` method of that object) until the lock has been released. Typically, releasing a lock means the thread holding the lock (in other words, the thread currently in the `synchronized` method) exits the `synchronized` method. At that point, the lock is free until some other thread enters a `synchronized` method on that object. Remember the following key points about locking and synchronization:

- Only methods (or blocks) can be `synchronized`, not variables or classes.
- Each object has just one lock.
- Not all methods in a class need to be `synchronized`. A class can have both `synchronized` and non-`synchronized` methods.
- If two threads are about to execute a `synchronized` method in a class and both threads are using the same instance of the class to invoke the method, only one thread at a time will be able to execute the method. The other thread will need to wait until the first one finishes its method call. In other words, once a thread acquires the lock on an object, no other thread can enter any of the `synchronized` methods in that class (for that object).
- If a class has both `synchronized` and non-`synchronized` methods, multiple threads can still access the class's non-`synchronized` methods! If you have methods that don't access the data you're trying to protect, then you don't need to synchronize them. Synchronization can cause a hit in some cases (or even deadlock if used incorrectly), so you should be careful not to overuse it.
- If a thread goes to sleep, it holds any locks it has—it doesn't release them.
- A thread can acquire more than one lock. For example, a thread can enter a `synchronized` method, thus acquiring a lock, and then immediately invoke a `synchronized` method on a different object, thus acquiring that lock as well. As the stack unwinds, locks are released again. Also, if a thread acquires a lock and then attempts to call a `synchronized` method on that same object, no problem. The JVM knows that this thread already has the lock for this object, so the thread is free to call other `synchronized` methods on the same object, using the lock the thread already has.
- You can synchronize a block of code rather than a method.

Because synchronization does hurt concurrency, you don't want to synchronize any more code than is necessary to protect your data. So if the scope of a method is more than needed, you can reduce the scope of the synchronized part to something less than a full method—to just a block. We call this, strangely, a *synchronized block*, and it looks like this:

```
class SyncTest {
  public void doStuff() {
    System.out.println("not synchronized");
    synchronized(this) {
      System.out.println("synchronized");
    }
  }
}
```

When a thread is executing code from within a `synchronized` block, including any method code invoked from that `synchronized` block, the code is said to be executing in a synchronized context. The real question is, synchronized on what? Or, synchronized on which object's lock?

When you synchronize a method, the object used to invoke the method is the object whose lock must be acquired. But when you synchronize a block of code, you specify which object's lock you want to use as the lock, so you could, for example, use some third-party object as the lock for this piece of code. That gives you the ability to have more than one lock for code synchronization within a single object.

Or you can synchronize on the current instance (`this`) as in the previous code. Since that's the same instance that `synchronized` methods lock on, it means that you could always replace a `synchronized` method with a non-`synchronized` method containing a `synchronized` block. In other words, this:

```
public synchronized void doStuff() {
  System.out.println("synchronized");
}
```

is equivalent to this:

```
public void doStuff() {
  synchronized(this) {
    System.out.println("synchronized");
  }
}
```

These methods both have the exact same effect, in practical terms. The compiled bytecodes may not be exactly the same for the two methods, but they *could* be—and any differences are not really important. The first form is shorter and more familiar to most people, but the second can be more flexible.

Can Static Methods Be Synchronized?

`static` methods can be `synchronized`. There is only one copy of the static data you're trying to protect, so you only need one lock per class to synchronize `static` methods—a lock for the whole class. There is such a lock; every class loaded in Java has a corresponding instance of `java.lang.Class` representing that class. It's that `java.lang.Class` instance whose lock is used to protect the `static` methods of the class (if they're `synchronized`). There's nothing special you have to do to synchronize a `static` method:

```
public static synchronized int getCount() {
  return count;
}
```

Again, this could be replaced with code that uses a `synchronized` block. If the method is defined in a class called `MyClass`, the equivalent code is as follows:

```
public static int getCount() {
  synchronized(MyClass.class) {
    return count;
  }
}
```

Wait—what's that `MyClass.class` thing? That's called a *class literal*. It's a special feature in the Java language that tells the compiler (who tells the JVM): Go and find me the instance of `Class` that represents the class called `MyClass`. You can also do this with the following code:

```
public static void classMethod() throws ClassNotFoundException {
  Class cl = Class.forName("MyClass");
  synchronized (cl) {
    // do stuff
  }
}
```

However, that's longer, ickier, and most importantly, *not on the OCP exam*. But it's quick and easy to use a class literal—just write the name of the class and add `.class` at the end. No quotation marks needed. Now you've got an expression for the `Class` object you need to synchronize on.

EXERCISE 13-2

Synchronizing a Block of Code

In this exercise, we will attempt to synchronize a block of code. Within that block of code, we will get the lock on an object so that other threads cannot modify it while the block of code is executing. We will be creating three threads that will all attempt to manipulate the same object. Each thread will output a single letter 100 times and then increment that letter by one. The object we will be using is `StringBuffer`. We could synchronize on a `String` object, but strings cannot be modified once they are created, so we would not be able to increment the letter without generating a new `String` object. The final output should have 100 A's, 100 B's, and 100 C's, all in unbroken lines.

1. Create a class and extend the `Thread` class.
2. Override the `run()` method of `Thread`. This is where the `synchronized` block of code will go.

3. For our three thread objects to share the same object, we will need to create a constructor that accepts a `StringBuffer` object in the argument.
4. The `synchronized` block of code will obtain a lock on the `StringBuffer` object from step 3.
5. Within the block, output the `StringBuffer` 100 times and then increment the letter in the `StringBuffer`. You can check Chapter 5 for `StringBuffer` (`StringBuilder`) methods that will help with this.
6. Finally, in the `main()` method, create a single `StringBuffer` object using the letter A, then create three instances of our class and start all three of them.

What Happens If a Thread Can't Get the Lock?

If a thread tries to enter a `synchronized` method and the lock is already taken, the thread is said to be blocked on the object's lock. Essentially, the thread goes into a kind of pool for that particular object and has to sit there until the lock is released and the thread can again become runnable/running. Just because a lock is released doesn't mean any particular thread will get it. There might be three threads waiting for a single lock, for example, and there's no guarantee that the thread that has waited the longest will get the lock first.

When thinking about blocking, it's important to pay attention to which objects are being used for locking:

- Threads calling non-`static synchronized` methods in the same class will only block each other if they're invoked using the same instance. That's because they each lock on `this` instance, and if they're called using two different instances, they get two locks, which do not interfere with each other.
- Threads calling `static synchronized` methods in the same class will always block each other—they all lock on the same `Class` instance.
- A `static synchronized` method and a non-`static synchronized` method will not block each other, ever. The `static` method locks on a `Class` instance, while the non-`static` method locks on the `this` instance—these actions do not interfere with each other at all.
- For `synchronized` blocks, you have to look at exactly what object has been used for locking. (What's inside the parentheses after the word

synchronized?) Threads that synchronize on the same object will block each other. Threads that synchronize on different objects will not.

Table 13-1 lists the thread-related methods and whether the thread gives up its lock as a result of the call.

So When Do I Need to Synchronize?

Synchronization can get pretty complicated, and you may be wondering why you would want to do this at all if you can help it. But remember the earlier "race conditions" example with Lucy and Fred making withdrawals from their account. When we use threads, we usually need to use some synchronization somewhere to make sure our methods don't interrupt each other at the wrong time and mess up our data. Generally, any time more than one thread is accessing mutable (changeable) data, you synchronize to protect that data to make sure two threads aren't changing it at the same time (or that one isn't changing it at the same time the other is reading it, which is also confusing). You don't need to worry about local variables—each thread gets its own copy of a local variable. Two threads executing the same method at the same time will use different copies of the local variables, and they won't bother each other. However, you do need to worry about `static` and non-`static` fields if they contain data that can be changed.

For changeable data in a non-`static` field, you usually use a non-`static` method to access it. By synchronizing that method, you will ensure that any threads trying to run that method *using the same instance* will be prevented from simultaneous access. But a thread working with a *different* instance will not be affected because it's acquiring a lock on the other instance. That's what we want—threads working with the same data need to go one at a time, but threads working with different data can just ignore each other and run whenever they want to; it doesn't matter.

TABLE 13-1 Methods and Lock Status

Give Up Locks	Keep Locks	Class Defining the Method
`wait ()`	`notify()` (Although the thread will probably exit the synchronized code shortly after this call, and thus give up its locks.)	`java.lang.Object`
	`join()`	`java.lang.Thread`
	`sleep()`	`java.lang.Thread`
	`yield()`	`java.lang.Thread`

For changeable data in a `static` field, you usually use a `static` method to access it. And again, by synchronizing the method, you ensure that any two threads trying to access the data will be prevented from simultaneous access, because both threads will have to acquire locks on the `Class` object for the class the `static` method's defined in. Again, that's what we want.

However—what if you have a non-`static` method that accesses a `static` field? Or a `static` method that accesses a non-`static` field (using an instance)? In these cases, things start to get messy quickly, and there's a very good chance that things will not work the way you want. If you've got a `static` method accessing a non-`static` field and you synchronize the method, you acquire a lock on the Class object. But what if there's another method that also accesses the non-`static` field, this time using a non-`static` method? It probably synchronizes on the current instance (`this`) instead. Remember that a `static synchronized` method and a non-`static synchronized` method will not block each other—they can run at the same time. Similarly, if you access a `static` field using a non-`static` method, two threads might invoke that method using two different `this` instances. Which means they won't block each other because they use different locks. Which means two threads are simultaneously accessing the same `static` field—exactly the sort of thing we're trying to prevent.

It gets very confusing trying to imagine all the weird things that can happen here. To keep things simple, in order to make a class thread-safe, methods that access changeable fields need to be `synchronized`.

Access to `static` fields should be done using `static synchronized` methods. Access to non-`static` fields should be done using non-`static synchronized` methods. For example:

```
public class Thing {
  private static int staticField;
  private int nonstaticField;
  public static synchronized int getStaticField() {
    return staticField;
  }
  public static synchronized void setStaticField(
                                       int staticField) {
    Thing.staticField = staticField;
  }
  public synchronized int getNonstaticField() {
    return nonstaticField;
  }
  public synchronized void setNonstaticField(
                                       int nonstaticField) {
    this.nonstaticField = nonstaticField;
  }
}
```

What if you need to access both static and non-static fields in a method? Well, there are ways to do that, but it's beyond what you need for the exam. You will live a longer, happier life if you JUST DON'T DO IT. Really. Would we lie?

Thread-Safe Classes

When a class has been carefully synchronized to protect its data (using the rules just given or using more complicated alternatives), we say the class is "thread-safe." Many classes in the Java APIs already use synchronization internally in order to make the class "thread-safe." For example, StringBuffer and StringBuilder are nearly identical classes, except that all the methods in StringBuffer are synchronized when necessary, while those in StringBuilder are not. Generally, this makes StringBuffer safe to use in a multithreaded environment, while StringBuilder is not. (In return, StringBuilder is a little bit faster because it doesn't bother synchronizing.) However, even when a class is "thread-safe," it is often dangerous to rely on these classes to provide the thread protection you need. (C'mon, the repeated quotes used around "thread-safe" had to be a clue, right?) You still need to think carefully about how you use these classes. As an example, consider the following class:

```
import java.util.*;
public class NameList {
  private List names = Collections.synchronizedList(
                                          new LinkedList());
  public void add(String name) {
    names.add(name);
  }
  public String removeFirst() {
    if (names.size() > 0)
      return (String) names.remove(0);
    else
      return null;
  }
}
```

The method Collections.synchronizedList() returns a List whose methods are all synchronized and "thread-safe" according to the documentation (like a Vector—but since this is the 21st century, we're not going to use a Vector here). The question is, can the NameList class be used safely from multiple threads? It's tempting to think that yes, since the data in names is in a synchronized collection, the NameList class is "safe" too. However that's not the case—the removeFirst() may sometimes throw a IndexOutOfBoundsException. What's the problem? Doesn't it correctly check the size() of names before removing anything to make sure there's something there? How could this code fail? Let's try to use `NameList` like this:

```
public static void main(String[] args) {
  final NameList nl = new NameList();
  nl.add("Ozymandias");
  class NameDropper extends Thread {
    public void run() {
      String name = nl.removeFirst();
      System.out.println(name);
    }
  }
  Thread t1 = new NameDropper();
  Thread t2 = new NameDropper();
  t1.start();
  t2.start();
}
```

What might happen here is that one of the threads will remove the one name and print it, and then the other will try to remove a name and get `null`. If we think just about the calls to `names.size()` and `names.get(0)`, they occur in this order:

Thread `t1` executes `names.size()`, which returns `1`.
Thread `t1` executes `names.remove(0)`, which returns `Ozymandias`.
Thread `t2` executes `names.size()`, which returns `0`.
Thread `t2` does not call `remove(0)`.

The output here is

```
Ozymandias
null
```

However, if we run the program again, something different might happen:

Thread `t1` executes `names.size()`, which returns `1`.
Thread `t2` executes `names.size()`, which returns `1`.
Thread `t1` executes `names.remove(0)`, which returns `Ozymandias`.
Thread `t2` executes `names.remove(0)`, which throws an exception because the list is now empty.

The thing to realize here is that in a "thread-safe" class like the one returned by `synchronizedList()`, each *individual* method is synchronized. So `names.size()` is synchronized, and `names.remove(0)` is `synchronized`. But nothing prevents another thread from doing something else to the list *in between* those two calls. And that's where problems can happen.

There's a solution here: Don't rely on `Collections.synchronizedList()`. Instead, synchronize the code yourself:

```
import java.util.*;
public class NameList {
  private List names = new LinkedList();
  public synchronized void add(String name) {
    names.add(name);
  }
  public synchronized String removeFirst() {
    if (names.size() > 0)
      return (String) names.remove(0);
    else
      return null;
  }
}
```

Now the entire `removeFirst()` method is `synchronized`, and once one thread starts it and calls `names.size()`, there's no way the other thread can cut in and steal the last name. The other thread will just have to wait until the first thread completes the `removeFirst()` method.

The moral here is that just because a class is described as "thread-safe" doesn't mean it is *always* thread-safe. If individual methods are synchronized, that may not be enough—you may be better off putting in synchronization at a higher level (i.e., put it in the block or method that *calls* the other methods). Once you do that, the original synchronization (in this case, the synchronization inside the object returned by `Collections.synchronizedList()`) may well become redundant.

Thread Deadlock

Perhaps the scariest thing that can happen to a Java program is deadlock. Deadlock occurs when two threads are blocked, with each waiting for the other's lock. Neither can run until the other gives up its lock, so they'll sit there forever.

This can happen, for example, when thread A hits `synchronized` code, acquires a lock B, and then enters another method (still within the `synchronized` code it has the lock on) that's also `synchronized`. But thread A can't get the lock to enter this `synchronized` code—block C—because another thread D has the lock already. So thread A goes off to the waiting-for-the-C-lock pool, hoping that thread D will hurry up and release the lock (by completing the `synchronized` method). But thread A will wait a very long time indeed, because while thread D picked up lock C, it then entered a method `synchronized` on lock B. Obviously, thread D can't get the lock B because thread A has it. And thread A won't release it until thread D releases lock C. But thread D won't release lock C until after it can get lock B and continue. And there they sit. The following example demonstrates deadlock:

```
 1. public class DeadlockRisk {
 2.   private static class Resource {
 3.     public int value;
 4.   }
 5.   private Resource resourceA = new Resource();
 6.   private Resource resourceB = new Resource();
 7.   public int read() {
 8.     synchronized(resourceA) { // May deadlock here
 9.       synchronized(resourceB) {
10.         return resourceB.value + resourceA.value;
11.       }
12.     }
13.   }
14.
15.   public void write(int a, int b) {
16.     synchronized(resourceB) { // May deadlock here
17.       synchronized(resourceA) {
18.         resourceA.value = a;
19.         resourceB.value = b;
20.       }
21.     }
22.   }
23. }
```

Assume that `read()` is started by one thread and `write()` is started by another. If there are two different threads that may read and write independently, there is a risk of deadlock at line 8 or 16. The reader thread will have `resourceA`, the writer thread will have `resourceB`, and both will get stuck waiting for the other.

Code like this almost never results in deadlock because the CPU has to switch from the reader thread to the writer thread at a particular point in the code, and the chances of deadlock occurring are very small. The application may work fine 99.9 percent of the time.

The preceding simple example is easy to fix; just swap the order of locking for either the reader or the writer at lines 16 and 17 (or lines 8 and 9). More complex deadlock situations can take a long time to figure out.

Regardless of how little chance there is for your code to deadlock, the bottom line is that if you deadlock, you're dead. There are design approaches that can help avoid deadlock, including strategies for always acquiring locks in a predetermined order.

But that's for you to study and is beyond the scope of this book. We're just trying to get you through the exam. If you learn everything in this chapter, though, you'll still know more about threads than most experienced Java programmers.

CERTIFICATION OBJECTIVE

Thread Interaction (OCP Objectives 10.3 and 10.4)

10.3 Synchronize thread access to shared data.

10.4 Identify potential threading problems.

The last thing we need to look at is how threads can interact with one another to communicate about—among other things—their locking status. The `Object` class has three methods, `wait()`, `notify()`, and `notifyAll()`, that help threads communicate the status of an event that the threads care about. For example, if one thread is a mail-delivery thread and one thread is a mail-processor thread, the mail-processor thread has to keep checking to see if there's any mail to process. Using the wait and notify mechanism, the mail-processor thread could check for mail, and if it doesn't find any, it can say, "Hey, I'm not going to waste my time checking for mail every two seconds. I'm going to go hang out, and when the mail deliverer puts something in the mailbox, have him notify me so I can go back to runnable and do some work." In other words, using `wait()` and `notify()` lets one thread put itself into a "waiting room" until some *other* thread notifies it that there's a reason to come back out.

One key point to remember (and keep in mind for the exam) about wait/notify is this:

`wait()`, `notify()`, and `notifyAll()` must be called from within a synchronized context! A thread can't invoke a wait or notify method on an object unless it owns that object's lock.

Here we'll present an example of two threads that depend on each other to proceed with their execution, and we'll show how to use `wait()` and `notify()` to make them interact safely and at the proper moment.

Think of a computer-controlled machine that cuts pieces of fabric into different shapes and an application that allows users to specify the shape to cut. The current version of the application has one thread, which loops, first asking the user for instructions, and then directs the hardware to cut the requested shape:

```
public void run(){
  while(true){
    // Get shape from user
    // Calculate machine steps from shape
    // Send steps to hardware
  }
}
```

This design is not optimal because the user can't do anything while the machine is busy and while there are other shapes to define. We need to improve the situation.

A simple solution is to separate the processes into two different threads, one of them interacting with the user and another managing the hardware. The user thread sends the instructions to the hardware thread and then goes back to interacting with the user immediately. The hardware thread receives the instructions from the user thread and starts directing the machine immediately. Both threads use a common object to communicate, which holds the current design being processed.

The following pseudocode shows this design:

```
public void userLoop(){
  while(true){
    // Get shape from user
    // Calculate machine steps from shape
    // Modify common object with new machine steps
  }
}

public void hardwareLoop(){
  while(true){
    // Get steps from common object
    // Send steps to hardware
  }
}
```

The problem now is to get the hardware thread to process the machine steps as soon as they are available. Also, the user thread should not modify them until they have all been sent to the hardware. The solution is to use `wait()` and `notify()`, and also to synchronize some of the code.

The methods `wait()` and `notify()`, remember, are instance methods of `Object`. In the same way that every object has a lock, every object can have a list of threads that are waiting for a signal (a notification) from the object. A thread gets on this waiting list by executing the `wait()` method of the target object. From that moment, it doesn't execute any further instructions until the `notify()` method of the target object is called. If many threads are waiting on the same object, only one will be chosen (in no guaranteed order) to proceed with its execution. If there are no threads waiting, then no particular action is taken. Let's take a look at some real code that shows one object waiting for another object to notify it (take note, it is somewhat complex):

```
1. class ThreadA {
2.   public static void main(String [] args) {
3.     ThreadB b = new ThreadB();
4.     b.start();
5.
```

```
 6.     synchronized(b) {
 7.       try {
 8.         System.out.println("Waiting for b to complete...");
 9.         b.wait();
10.       } catch (InterruptedException e) {}
11.         System.out.println("Total is: " + b.total);
12.       }
13.     }
14.   }
15.
16. class ThreadB extends Thread {
17.   int total;
18.
19.   public void run() {
20.     synchronized(this) {
21.       for(int i=0;i<100;i++) {
22.         total += i;
23.       }
24.       notify();
25.     }
26.   }
27. }
```

This program contains two objects with threads: `ThreadA` contains the main thread, and `ThreadB` has a thread that calculates the sum of all numbers from 0 through 99. As soon as line 4 calls the `start()` method, `ThreadA` will continue with the next line of code in its own class, which means it could get to line 11 before `ThreadB` has finished the calculation. To prevent this, we use the `wait()` method in line 9.

Notice in line 6 the code synchronizes itself with the object `b`—this is because in order to call `wait()` on the object, `ThreadA` must own a lock on `b`. For a thread to call `wait()` or `notify()`, the thread has to be the owner of the lock for that object. When the thread waits, it temporarily releases the lock for other threads to use, but it will need it again to continue execution. It's common to find code like this:

```
synchronized(anotherObject) { // this has the lock on anotherObject
  try {
    anotherObject.wait();
      // the thread releases the lock and waits
      // To continue, the thread needs the lock,
      // so it may be blocked until it gets it.
  } catch(InterruptedException e){}
}
```

The preceding code waits until `notify()` is called on `anotherObject`.

```
synchronized(this) { notify(); }
```

This code notifies a single thread currently waiting on the `this` object. The lock can be acquired much earlier in the code, such as in the calling method. Note that if the thread calling `wait()` does not own the lock, it will throw an `IllegalMonitorStateException`. This exception is not a checked exception, so you don't have to *catch* it explicitly. You should always be clear whether a thread has the lock of an object in any given block of code.

Notice in lines 7–10 there is a `try/catch` block around the `wait()` method. A waiting thread can be interrupted in the same way as a sleeping thread, so you have to take care of the exception:

```
try {
  wait();
} catch(InterruptedException e) {
  // Do something about it
}
```

In the fabric example, the way to use these methods is to have the hardware thread wait on the shape to be available and the user thread to notify after it has written the steps. The machine steps may comprise global steps, such as moving the required fabric to the cutting area, and a number of substeps, such as the direction and length of a cut. As an example, they could be

```
int fabricRoll;
int cuttingSpeed;
Point startingPoint;
float[] directions;
float[] lengths;
etc..
```

It is important that the user thread does not modify the machine steps while the hardware thread is using them, so this reading and writing should be synchronized. The resulting code would look like this:

```
class Operator extends Thread {
  public void run(){
    while(true){
        // Get shape from user
      synchronized(this){
        // Calculate new machine steps from shape
      notify();
      }
    }
  }
}
class Machine extends Thread {
  Operator operator; // assume this gets initialized
  public void run(){
```

```
      while(true){
        synchronized(operator){
          try {
            operator.wait();
            } catch(InterruptedException ie) {}
            // Send machine steps to hardware
          }
        }
      }
    }
```

The machine thread, once started, will immediately go into the waiting state and will wait patiently until the operator sends the first notification. At that point, it is the operator thread that owns the lock for the object, so the hardware thread gets stuck for a while. It's only after the operator thread abandons the `synchronized` block that the hardware thread can really start processing the machine steps.

While one shape is being processed by the hardware, the user may interact with the system and specify another shape to be cut. When the user is finished with the shape and it is time to cut it, the operator thread attempts to enter the `synchronized` block, maybe blocking until the machine thread has finished with the previous machine steps. When the machine thread has finished, it repeats the loop, going again to the waiting state (and therefore releasing the lock). Only then can the operator thread enter the `synchronized` block and overwrite the machine steps with the new ones.

Having two threads is definitely an improvement over having one, although in this implementation, there is still a possibility of making the user wait. A further improvement would be to have many shapes in a queue, thereby reducing the possibility of requiring the user to wait for the hardware.

There is also a second form of `wait()` that accepts a number of milliseconds as a maximum time to wait. If the thread is not interrupted, it will continue normally whenever it is notified or the specified timeout has elapsed. This normal continuation consists of getting out of the waiting state, but to continue execution, it will have to get the lock for the object:

```
synchronized(a){  // The thread gets the lock on 'a'
  a.wait(2000);   // Thread releases the lock and waits for notify
                  // only for a maximum of two seconds, then goes back
                  // to Runnable
                  // The thread reacquires the lock
                  // More instructions here
}
```

exam watch

When the `wait()` method is invoked on an object, the thread executing that code gives up its lock on the object immediately. However, when `notify()` is called, that doesn't mean the thread gives up its lock at that moment. If the thread is still completing synchronized code, the lock is not released until the thread moves out of synchronized code. So just because `notify()` is called, this doesn't mean the lock becomes available at that moment.

Using notifyAll() When Many Threads May Be Waiting

In most scenarios, it's preferable to notify *all* of the threads that are waiting on a particular object. If so, you can use `notifyAll()` on the object to let all the threads rush out of the waiting area and back to runnable. This is especially important if you have several threads waiting on one object, but for different reasons, and you want to be sure that the *right* thread (along with all of the others) is notified.

```
notifyAll(); // Will notify all waiting threads
```

All of the threads will be notified and start competing to get the lock. As the lock is used and released by each thread, all of them will get into action without a need for further notification.

As we said earlier, an object can have many threads waiting on it, and using `notify()` will affect only one of them. Which one, exactly, is not specified and depends on the JVM implementation, so you should never rely on a particular thread being notified in preference to another.

In cases in which there might be a lot more waiting, the best way to do this is by using `notifyAll()`. Let's take a look at this in some code. In this example, there is one class that performs a calculation and many readers that are waiting to receive the completed calculation. At any given moment, many readers may be waiting.

```
 1. class Reader extends Thread {
 2.   Calculator c;
 3.
 4.   public Reader(Calculator calc) {
 5.     c = calc;
 6.   }
 7.
 8.   public void run() {
 9.     synchronized(c) {
10.       try {
11.         System.out.println("Waiting for calculation...");
12.           c.wait();
```

```
13.       } catch (InterruptedException e) {}
14.         System.out.println("Total is: " + c.total);
15.       }
16.     }
17.
18.   public static void main(String [] args) {
19.     Calculator calculator = new Calculator();
20.     new Reader(calculator).start();
21.     new Reader(calculator).start();
22.     new Reader(calculator).start();
23.     new Thread(calculator).start();
24.   }
25. }
26.
27. class Calculator implements Runnable {
28.   int total;
29.
30.   public void run() {
31.     synchronized(this) {
32.       for(int i = 0; i < 100; i++) {
33.         total += i;
34.       }
35.       notifyAll();
36.     }
37.   }
38. }
```

The program starts three threads that are all waiting to receive the finished calculation (lines 18–24) and then starts the calculator with its calculation. Note that if the `run()` method at line 30 used `notify()` instead of `notifyAll()`, only one reader would be notified instead of all the readers.

Using wait() in a Loop

Actually, both of the previous examples (Machine/Operator and Reader/Calculator) had a common problem. In each one, there was at least one thread calling `wait()` and another thread calling `notify()` or `notifyAll()`. This works well enough as long as the waiting threads have actually started waiting before the other thread executes the `notify()` or `notifyAll()`. But what happens if, for example, the `Calculator` runs first and calls `notify()` before the `Readers` have started waiting? This could happen, since we can't guarantee the order in which the different parts of the thread will execute. Unfortunately, when the `Readers` run, they just start waiting right away. They don't do anything to see if the event they're waiting for has already happened. So if the `Calculator` has already called `notifyAll()`, it's not going to call `notifyAll()` again—and the waiting `Readers` will keep waiting forever. This is probably *not* what the programmer wanted to happen. Almost always, when you want to wait for something, you also need to be able to check if it has already happened. Generally, the best way to solve this is to put in some sort of loop that checks on some sort of conditional expressions and only waits if the thing you're waiting for has not yet happened. Here's a modified, safer version of the earlier fabric-cutting machine example:

```
class Operator extends Thread {
  Machine machine; // assume this gets initialized
  public void run() {
    while (true) {
      Shape shape = getShapeFromUser();
      MachineInstructions job =
                          calculateNewInstructionsFor(shape);
      machine.addJob(job);
    }
  }
}
```

The operator will still keep on looping forever, getting more shapes from users, calculating new instructions for those shapes, and sending them to the machine. But now the logic for `notify()` has been moved into the `addJob()` method in the `Machine` class:

```
class Machine extends Thread {
  List<MachineInstructions> jobs =
                       new ArrayList<MachineInstructions>();

  public void addJob(MachineInstructions job) {
    synchronized (jobs) {
      jobs.add(job);
      jobs.notify();
    }
  }
  public void run() {
    while (true) {
      synchronized (jobs) {
        // wait until at least one job is available
        while (jobs.isEmpty()) {
          try {
            jobs.wait();
          } catch (InterruptedException ie) { }
        }
        // If we get here, we know that jobs is not empty
        MachineInstructions instructions = jobs.remove(0);
        // Send machine steps to hardware
      }
    }
  }
}
```

A machine keeps a list of the jobs it's scheduled to do. Whenever an operator adds a new job to the list, it calls the `addJob()` method and adds the new job to the list.

Meanwhile, the `run()` method just keeps looping, looking for any jobs on the list. If there are no jobs, it will start waiting. If it's notified, it will stop waiting and then recheck the loop condition: Is the list still empty? In practice, this double-check is probably not necessary, as the only time a `notify()` is ever sent is when a new job has been added to the list. However, it's a good idea to require the thread to recheck the `isEmpty()` condition whenever it's been woken up because it's possible that a thread has accidentally sent an extra `notify()` that was not intended. There's also a possible situation called *spontaneous wakeup* that may exist in some situations—a thread may wake up even though no code has called `notify()` or `notifyAll()`. (At least, no code you know about has called these methods. Sometimes, the JVM may call `notify()` for reasons of its own, or code in some other class calls it for reasons you just don't know.) What this means is that when your thread wakes up from a `wait()`, you don't know for sure why it was awakened. By putting the `wait()` method in a `while` loop and rechecking the condition that represents what we were waiting for, we ensure that *whatever* the reason we woke up, we will re-enter the `wait()` if (and only if) the thing we were waiting for has not happened yet. In the `Machine` class, the thing we were waiting for is for the jobs list to not be empty. If it's empty, we wait, and if it's not, we don't.

Note also that both the `run()` method and the `addJob()` method synchronize on the same object—the jobs list. This is for two reasons. One is because we're calling `wait()` and `notify()` on this instance, so we need to synchronize in order to avoid an `IllegalMonitorStateException`. The other reason is that the data in the jobs list is changeable data stored in a field that is accessed by two different threads. We need to synchronize in order to access that changeable data safely. Fortunately, the same `synchronized` blocks that allow us to `wait()` and `notify()` also provide the required thread safety for our other access to changeable data. In fact, this is a main reason why synchronization is required to use `wait()` and `notify()` in the first place—you almost always need to share some mutable data between threads at the same time, and that means you need synchronization. Notice that the `synchronized` block in `addJob()` is big enough to also include the call to `jobs.add(job)`—which modifies shared data. And the `synchronized` block in `run()` is large enough to include the whole `while` loop—which includes the call to `jobs.isEmpty()`, which accesses shared data.

The moral here is that when you use `wait()` and `notify()` or `notifyAll()`, you should almost always also have a `while` loop around the `wait()` that checks a condition and forces continued waiting until the condition is met. And you should also make use of the required synchronization for the `wait()` and `notify()` calls to also protect whatever other data you're sharing between threads. If you see code that fails to do this, there's usually something wrong with the code—even if you have a hard time seeing what exactly the problem is.

exam watch

The methods `wait()`, `notify()`, and `notifyAll()` are methods of only `java.lang.Object`, not of `java.lang.Thread` or `java.lang.Runnable`. Be sure you know which methods are defined in `Thread`, which in `Object`, and which in `Runnable` (just `run()`, so that's an easy one). Of the key methods in `Thread`, be sure you know which are `static`—`sleep()` and `yield()`, and which are* not *`static`—`join()` and `start()`. Table 13-2 lists the key methods you'll need to know for the exam, with the `static` methods shown in italics.

TABLE 13-2 Key `Thread` Methods

Class Object	Class Thread	Interface Runnable
`wait ()`	`start()`	`run()`
`notify()`	`yield()`	
`notifyAll()`	`sleep()`	
	`join()`	

CERTIFICATION SUMMARY

This chapter covered the required thread knowledge you'll need to apply on the certification exam. Threads can be created by either extending the `Thread` class or implementing the `Runnable` interface. The only method that must be overridden in the `Runnable` interface is the `run()` method, but the thread doesn't become a *thread of execution* until somebody calls the `Thread` object's `start()` method. We also looked at how the `sleep()` method can be used to pause a thread, and we saw that when an object goes to sleep, it holds onto any locks it acquired prior to sleeping.

We looked at five thread states: new, runnable, running, blocked/waiting/sleeping, and dead. You learned that when a thread is dead, it can never be restarted even if it's still a valid object on the heap. We saw that there is only one way a thread can transition to running, and that's from runnable. However, once running, a thread can become dead, go to sleep, wait for another thread to finish, block on an object's lock, wait for a notification, or return to runnable.

You saw how two threads acting on the same data can cause serious problems (remember Lucy and Fred's bank account?). We saw that to let one thread execute a method but prevent other threads from running the same object's method, we use the `synchronized` keyword. To coordinate activity between different threads, use the `wait()`, `notify()`, and `notifyAll()` methods.

TWO-MINUTE DRILL

Here are some of the key points from each certification objective in this chapter. Photocopy it and sleep with it under your pillow for complete absorption.

Defining, Instantiating, and Starting Threads (OCP Objective 10.1)

- ❑ Threads can be created by extending `Thread` and overriding the `public void run()` method.
- ❑ `Thread` objects can also be created by calling the `Thread` constructor that takes a `Runnable` argument. The `Runnable` object is said to be the *target* of the thread.
- ❑ You can call `start()` on a `Thread` object only once. If `start()` is called more than once on a `Thread` object, it will throw a `IllegalThreadStateException`.
- ❑ It is legal to create many `Thread` objects using the same `Runnable` object as the target.
- ❑ When a `Thread` object is created, it does not become a *thread of execution* until its `start()` method is invoked. When a `Thread` object exists but hasn't been started, it is in the *new* state and is not considered *alive*.

Transitioning Between Thread States (OCP Objective 10.2)

- ❑ Once a new thread is started, it will always enter the runnable state.
- ❑ The thread scheduler can move a thread back and forth between the runnable state and the running state.
- ❑ For a typical single-processor machine, only one thread can be running at a time, although many threads may be in the runnable state.
- ❑ There is no guarantee that the order in which threads were started determines the order in which they'll run.

- There's no guarantee that threads will take turns in any fair way. It's up to the thread scheduler, as determined by the particular virtual machine implementation. If you want a guarantee that your threads will take turns, regardless of the underlying JVM, you can use the `sleep()` method. This prevents one thread from hogging the running process while another thread starves. (In most cases, though, `yield()` works well enough to encourage your threads to play together nicely.)
- A running thread may enter a blocked/waiting state by a `wait()`, `sleep()`, or `join()` call.
- A running thread may enter a blocked/waiting state because it can't acquire the lock for a synchronized block of code.
- When the sleep or wait is over, or an object's lock becomes available, the thread can only reenter the runnable state. It will *go* directly from waiting to running (well, for all practical purposes anyway).
- A dead thread cannot be started again.

Sleep, Yield, and Join (OCP Objective 10.2)

- Sleeping is used to delay execution for a period of time, and no locks are released when a thread goes to sleep.
- A sleeping thread is guaranteed to sleep for at least the time specified in the argument to the `sleep()` method (unless it's interrupted), but there is no guarantee as to when the newly awakened thread will actually return to running.
- The `sleep()` method is a `static` method that sleeps the currently executing thread's state. One thread *cannot* tell another thread to sleep.
- The `setPriority()` method is used on `Thread` objects to give threads a priority of between 1 (low) and 10 (high), although priorities are not guaranteed, and not all JVMs recognize 10 distinct priority levels—some levels may be treated as effectively equal.
- If not explicitly set, a thread's priority will have the same priority as the thread that created it.

- The `yield()` method *may* cause a running thread to back out if there are runnable threads of the same priority. There is no guarantee that this will happen, and there is no guarantee that when the thread backs out there will be a *different* thread selected to run. A thread might yield and then immediately reenter the running state.
- The closest thing to a guarantee is that at any given time, when a thread is running, it will usually not have a lower priority than any thread in the runnable state. If a low-priority thread is running when a high-priority thread enters runnable, the JVM will usually preempt the running low-priority thread and put the high-priority thread in.
- When one thread calls the `join()` method of another thread, the currently running thread will wait until the thread it joins with has completed. Think of the `join()` method as saying, "Hey, thread, I want to join on to the end of you. Let me know when you're done, so I can enter the runnable state."

Concurrent Access Problems and Synchronized Threads (OCP Objectives 10.3 and 10.4)

- `synchronized` methods prevent more than one thread from accessing an object's critical method code simultaneously.
- You can use the `synchronized` keyword as a method modifier or to start a synchronized block of code.
- To synchronize a block of code (in other words, a scope smaller than the whole method), you must specify an argument that is the object whose lock you want to synchronize on.
- While only one thread can be accessing synchronized code of a particular instance, multiple threads can still access the same object's unsynchronized code.
- When a thread goes to sleep, its locks will be unavailable to other threads.
- `static` methods can be `synchronized` using the lock from the `java.lang.Class` instance representing that class.

Communicating with Objects by Waiting and Notifying (OCP Objectives 10.3 and 10.4)

- ❑ The `wait()` method lets a thread say, "There's nothing for me to do now, so put me in your waiting pool and notify me when something happens that I care about." Basically, a `wait()` call means "let me wait in your pool" or "add me to your waiting list."
- ❑ The `notify()` method is used to send a signal to one and only one of the threads that are waiting in that same object's waiting pool.
- ❑ The `notify()` method CANNOT specify which waiting thread to notify.
- ❑ The method `notifyAll()` works in the same way as `notify()`, only it sends the signal to *all* of the threads waiting on the object.
- ❑ All three methods—`wait()`, `notify()`, and `notifyAll()`—must be called from within a `synchronized` context! A thread invokes `wait()` or `notify()` on a particular object, and the thread must currently hold the lock on that object.

Deadlocked Threads (OCP Objective 10.4)

- ❑ Deadlocking is when thread execution grinds to a halt because the code is waiting for locks to be removed from objects.
- ❑ Deadlocking can occur when a locked object attempts to access another locked object that is trying to access the first locked object. In other words, both threads are waiting for each other's locks to be released; therefore, the locks will *never* be released!
- ❑ Deadlocking is bad. Don't do it.

SELF TEST

The following questions will help you measure your understanding of the material presented in this chapter. If you have a rough time with some of these at first, don't beat yourself up. Some of these questions are long and intricate. Expect long and intricate questions on the real exam too!

1. The following block of code creates a `Thread` using a `Runnable` target:

```
Runnable target = new MyRunnable();
Thread myThread = new Thread(target);
```

Which of the following classes can be used to create the target so that the preceding code compiles correctly?

A. `public class MyRunnable extends Runnable{public void run(){}}`

B. `public class MyRunnable extends Object{public void run(){}}`

C. `public class MyRunnable implements Runnable{public void run(){}}`

D. `public class MyRunnable implements Runnable{void run(){}}`

E. `public class MyRunnable implements Runnable{public void start(){}}`

2. Given:

```
 3. class MyThread extends Thread {
 4.    public static void main(String [] args) {
 5.       MyThread t = new MyThread();
 6.       Thread x = new Thread(t);
 7.       x.start();
 8.    }
 9.    public void run() {
10.       for(int i=0;i<3;++i) {
11.          System.out.print(i + "..");
12.       }
13.    }
14. }
```

What is the result of this code?

A. Compilation fails

B. `1..2..3..`

C. `0..1..2..3..`

D. `0..1..2..`

E. An exception occurs at runtime

3. Given:

```
 3. class Test {
 4.    public static void main(String [] args) {
 5.       printAll(args);
 6.    }
 7.    public static void printAll(String[] lines) {
 8.       for(int i=0;i<lines.length;i++){
 9.          System.out.println(lines[i]);
10.          Thread.currentThread().sleep(1000);
11.       }
12.    }
13. }
```

The `static` method `Thread.currentThread()` returns a reference to the currently executing `Thread` object. What is the result of this code?

A. Each `String` in the array `lines` will output, with a one-second pause between lines

B. Each `String` in the array `lines` will output, with no pause in between because this method is not executed in a `Thread`

C. Each `String` in the array `lines` will output, and there is no guarantee that there will be a pause because `currentThread()` may not retrieve this thread

D. This code will not compile

E. Each `String` in the `lines` array will print, with at least a one-second pause between lines

4. Assume you have a class that holds two `private` variables: `a` and `b`. Which of the following pairs can prevent concurrent access problems in that class? (Choose all that apply.)

A.
```
public int read(){return a+b;}
public void set(int a, int b){this.a=a;this.b=b;}
```

B.
```
public synchronized int read(){return a+b;}
public synchronized void set(int a, int b){this.a=a;this.b=b;}
```

C.
```
public int read(){synchronized(a){return a+b;}}
public void set(int a, int b){synchronized(a){this.a=a;this.b=b;}}
```

D.
```
public int read(){synchronized(a){return a+b;}}
public void set(int a, int b){synchronized(b){this.a=a;this.b=b;}}
```

E.
```
public synchronized(this) int read(){return a+b;}
public synchronized(this) void set(int a, int b){this.a=a;this.b=b;}
```

F.
```
public int read(){synchronized(this){return a+b;}}
public void set(int a, int b){synchronized(this){this.a=a;this.b=b;}}
```

5. Given:

```
 1. public class WaitTest {
 2.    public static void main(String [] args) {
 3.       System.out.print("1 ");
 4.       synchronized(args){
 5.          System.out.print("2 ");
 6.          try {
 7.             args.wait();
 8.          }
 9.          catch(InterruptedException e){}
10.       }
11.       System.out.print("3 ");
12.    }
13. }
```

What is the result of trying to compile and run this program?

A. It fails to compile because the `IllegalMonitorStateException` of `wait()` is not dealt with in line 7

B. `1 2 3`

C. `1 3`

D. `1 2`

E. At runtime, it throws an `IllegalMonitorStateException` when trying to wait

F. It will fail to compile because it has to be synchronized on the `this` object

6. Assume the following method is properly synchronized and called from a thread A on an object B:

```
wait(2000);
```

After calling this method, when will thread A become a candidate to get another turn at the CPU?

A. After object B is notified, or after two seconds

B. After the lock on B is released, or after two seconds

C. Two seconds after object B is notified

D. Two seconds after lock B is released

7. Which are true? (Choose all that apply.)

A. The `notifyAll()` method must be called from a synchronized context

B. To call `wait()`, an object must own the lock on the thread

C. The `notify()` method is defined in class `java.lang.Thread`

D. When a thread is waiting as a result of `wait()`, it releases its lock

E. The `notify()` method causes a thread to immediately release its lock

F. The difference between `notify()` and `notifyAll()` is that `notifyAll()` notifies all waiting threads, regardless of the object they're waiting on

8. Given this scenario: This class is intended to allow users to write a series of messages so that each message is identified with a timestamp and the name of the thread that wrote the message:

```
public class Logger {
  private StringBuilder contents = new StringBuilder();
  public void log(String message) {
      contents.append(System.currentTimeMillis());
      contents.append(": ");
      contents.append(Thread.currentThread().getName());
      contents.append(message);
      contents.append("\n");
  }
  public String getContents() { return contents.toString(); }
}
```

How can we ensure that instances of this class can be safely used by multiple threads?

A. This class is already thread-safe

B. Replacing `StringBuilder` with `StringBuffer` will make this class thread-safe

C. Synchronize the `log()` method only

D. Synchronize the `getContents()` method only

E. Synchronize both `log()` and `getContents()`

F. This class cannot be made thread-safe

9. Given:

```
public static synchronized void main(String[] args) throws InterruptedException {
  Thread t = new Thread();
  t.start();
  System.out.print("X");
  t.wait(10000);
  System.out.print("Y");
}
```

What is the result of this code?

A. It prints `X` and exits

B. It prints `X` and never exits

C. It prints `XY` and exits almost immediately

D. It prints `XY` with a 10-second delay between `X` and `Y`

E. It prints `XY` with a 10,000-second delay between `X` and `Y`

F. The code does not compile

G. An exception is thrown at runtime

10. Given:

```
class MyThread extends Thread {
  MyThread() {
    System.out.print("MyThread ");
  }
  public void run() {
    System.out.print("bar ");
  }
  public void run(String s) {
    System.out.print("baz ");
  }
}
public class TestThreads {
  public static void main (String [] args) {
    Thread t = new MyThread() {
      public void run() {
        System.out.print("foo ");
      }
    };
    t.start();
} }
```

What is the result?

A. `foo`

B. `MyThread foo`

C. `MyThread bar`

D. `foo bar`

E. `foo bar baz`

F. `bar foo`

G. Compilation fails

H. An exception is thrown at runtime

11. Given:

```
public class ThreadDemo {
  synchronized void a() { actBusy(); }
  static synchronized void b() { actBusy(); }
  static void actBusy() {
    try {
      Thread.sleep(1000);
    } catch (InterruptedException e) {}
  }
  public static void main(String[] args) {
    final ThreadDemo x = new ThreadDemo();
    final ThreadDemo y = new ThreadDemo();
    Runnable runnable = new Runnable() {
      public void run() {
        int option = (int) (Math.random() * 4);
        switch (option) {
          case 0: x.a(); break;
          case 1: x.b(); break;
          case 2: y.a(); break;
          case 3: y.b(); break;
          }
        }
      };
    Thread thread1 = new Thread(runnable);
    Thread thread2 = new Thread(runnable);
    thread1.start();
    thread2.start();
  }
}
```

Which of the following pairs of method invocations could NEVER be executing at the same time? (Choose all that apply.)

A. `x.a()` in `thread1`, and `x.a()` in `thread2`

B. `x.a()` in `thread1`, and `x.b()` in `thread2`

C. `x.a()` in `thread1`, and `y.a()` in `thread2`

D. `x.a()` in `thread1`, and `y.b()` in `thread2`

E. `x.b()` in `thread1`, and `x.a()` in `thread2`

F. `x.b()` in `thread1`, and `x.b()` in `thread2`

G. `x.b()` in `thread1`, and `y.a()` in `thread2`

H. `x.b()` in `thread1`, and `y.b()` in `thread2`

12. Given:

```
public class TwoThreads {
  static Thread laurel, hardy;
  public static void main(String[] args) {
    laurel = new Thread() {
      public void run() {
        System.out.println("A");
        try {
          hardy.sleep(1000);
          } catch (Exception e) {
            System.out.println("B");
          }
            System.out.println("C");
          }
      };
      hardy = new Thread() {
          public void run() {
            System.out.println("D");
            try {
              laurel.wait();
            } catch (Exception e) {
                System.out.println("E");
            }
            System.out.println("F");
        }
    };
    laurel.start();
    hardy.start();
  }
}
```

Which letters will eventually appear somewhere in the output? (Choose all that apply.)

A. A

B. B

C. C

D. D

E. E

F. F

G. The answer cannot be reliably determined

H. The code does not compile

13. Given:

```
 3. public class Starter implements Runnable {
 4.   void go(long id) {
 5.     System.out.println(id);
 6.   }
 7.   public static void main(String[] args) {
 8.     System.out.print(Thread.currentThread().getId() + " ");
 9.     // insert code here
10.   }
11.   public void run() { go(Thread.currentThread().getId()); }
12. }
```

And given the following five fragments:

```
I.   new Starter().run();
II.  new Starter().start();
III. new Thread(new Starter());
IV.  new Thread(new Starter()).run();
V.   new Thread(new Starter()).start();
```

When the five fragments are inserted, one at a time at line 9, which are true? (Choose all that apply.)

A. All five will compile

B. Only one might produce the output `4 4`

C. Only one might produce the output `4 2`

D. Exactly two might produce the output `4 4`

E. Exactly two might produce the output `4 2`

F. Exactly three might produce the output `4 4`

G. Exactly three might produce the output `4 2`

14. Given:

```
 3. public class Leader implements Runnable {
 4.   public static void main(String[] args) {
 5.     Thread t = new Thread(new Leader());
 6.     t.start();
 7.     System.out.print("m1 ");
 8.     t.join();
 9.     System.out.print("m2 ");
10.   }
11.   public void run() {
12.     System.out.print("r1 ");
13.     System.out.print("r2 ");
14.   }
15. }
```

Which are true? (Choose all that apply.)

A. Compilation fails

B. The output could be `r1 r2 m1 m2`

C. The output could be `m1 m2 r1 r2`

D. The output could be `m1 r1 r2 m2`

E. The output could be `m1 r1 m2 r2`

F. An exception is thrown at runtime

15. Given:

```
 3. class Dudes {
 4.   static long flag = 0;
 5.   // insert code here
 6.     if(flag == 0) flag = id;
 7.     for(int x = 1; x < 3; x++) {
 8.       if(flag == id) System.out.print("yo ");
 9.       else System.out.print("dude ");
10.     }
11.   }
12. }
13. public class DudesChat implements Runnable {
14.   static Dudes d;
15.   public static void main(String[] args) {
16.     new DudesChat().go();
17.   }
18.   void go() {
19.     d = new Dudes();
20.     new Thread(new DudesChat()).start();
21.     new Thread(new DudesChat()).start();
22.   }
23.   public void run() {
24.     d.chat(Thread.currentThread().getId());
25.   }
26. }
```

And given these two fragments:

```
I. synchronized void chat(long id) {
II. void chat(long id) {
```

When fragment I or fragment II is inserted at line 5, which are true? (Choose all that apply.)

A. An exception is thrown at runtime

B. With fragment I, compilation fails

C. With fragment II, compilation fails

D. With fragment I, the output could be `yo dude dude yo`

E. With fragment I, the output could be `dude dude yo yo`

F. With fragment II, the output could be `yo dude dude yo`

16. Given:

```
 3. class Chicks {
 4.   synchronized void yack(long id) {
 5.     for(int x = 1; x < 3; x++) {
 6.       System.out.print(id + " ");
 7.       Thread.yield();
 8.     }
 9.   }
10. }
11. public class ChicksYack implements Runnable {
12.   Chicks c;
13.   public static void main(String[] args) {
14.     new ChicksYack().go();
15.   }
16.   void go() {
17.     c = new Chicks();
18.     new Thread(new ChicksYack()).start();
19.     new Thread(new ChicksYack()).start();
20.   }
21.   public void run() {
22.     c.yack(Thread.currentThread().getId());
23.   }
24. }
```

Which are true? (Choose all that apply.)

A. Compilation fails

B. The output could be `4 4 2 3`

C. The output could be `4 4 2 2`

D. The output could be `4 4 4 2`

E. The output could be `2 2 4 4`

F. An exception is thrown at runtime

17. Given:

```
 3. public class Chess implements Runnable {
 4.   public void run() {
 5.     move(Thread.currentThread().getId());
 6.   }
 7.   // insert code here
 8.     System.out.print(id + " ");
 9.     System.out.print(id + " ");
10.   }
11.   public static void main(String[] args) {
12.     Chess ch = new Chess();
13.     new Thread(ch).start();
14.     new Thread(new Chess()).start();
15.   }
16. }
```

And given these two fragments:

```
I. synchronized void move(long id) {
II. void move(long id) {
```

When either fragment I or fragment II is inserted at line 7, which are true? (Choose all that apply.)

A. Compilation fails

B. With fragment I, an exception is thrown

C. With fragment I, the output could be `4 2 4 2`

D. With fragment I, the output could be `4 4 2 3`

E. With fragment II, the output could be `2 4 2 4`

SELF TEST ANSWERS

1. ☑ **C** is correct. The class implements the `Runnable` interface with a legal `run()` method.
☒ **A** is incorrect because interfaces are implemented, not extended. **B** is incorrect because even though the class has a valid `public void run()` method, it does not implement the `Runnable` interface. **D** is incorrect because the `run()` method must be public. **E** is incorrect because the method to implement is `run()`, not `start()`. (OCP Objective 10.1)

2. ☑ **D** is correct. The thread `MyThread` will start and loop three times (from 0 to 2).
☒ **A** is incorrect because the `Thread` class implements the `Runnable` interface; therefore, in line 6, `Thread` can take an object of type `Thread` as an argument in the constructor (this is NOT recommended). **B** and **C** are incorrect because the variable `i` in the `for` loop starts with a value of 0 and ends with a value of 2. **E** is incorrect based on the above. (OCP Objective 10.1)

3. ☑ **D** is correct. The `sleep()` method must be enclosed in a `try/catch` block, or the method `printAll()` must declare it throws the `InterruptedException`.
☒ **E** is incorrect, but it would be correct if the `InterruptedException` was dealt with (**A** is too precise). **B** is incorrect (even if the `InterruptedException` was dealt with) because all Java code, including the `main()` method, runs in threads. **C** is incorrect. The `sleep()` method is `static`; it always affects the currently executing thread. (OCP Objective 10.2)

4. ☑ **B** and **F** are correct. By marking the methods as `synchronized`, the threads will get the lock of the `this` object before proceeding. Only one thread will be setting or reading at any given moment, thereby assuring that `read()` always returns the addition of a valid pair.
☒ **A** is incorrect because it is not synchronized; therefore, there is no guarantee that the values added by the `read()` method belong to the same pair. **C** and **D** are incorrect; only objects can be used to synchronize on. **E** is incorrect because it fails—it is not possible to select other objects (even `this`) to synchronize on when declaring a method as `synchronized`. (OCP Objectives 10.3 and 10.4)

5. ☑ **D** is correct. 1 and 2 will be printed, but there will be no return from the `wait` call because no other thread will notify the main thread, so 3 will never be printed. It's frozen at line 7.
☒ **A** is incorrect; `IllegalMonitorStateException` is an unchecked exception. **B** and **C** are incorrect; 3 will never be printed, since this program will wait forever. **E** is incorrect because `IllegalMonitorStateException` will never be thrown because the `wait()` is done on `args` within a block of code synchronized on `args`. **F** is incorrect because any object can be used to synchronize on, and `this` and `static` don't mix. (OCP Objective 10.4)

6. ☑ **A** is correct. Either of the two events will make the thread a candidate for running again.
☒ **B** is incorrect because a waiting thread will not return to runnable when the lock is released unless a notification occurs. **C** is incorrect because the thread will become a candidate immediately after notification. **D** is also incorrect because a thread will not come out of a waiting pool just because a lock has been released. (OCP Objective 10.4)

7. ☑ A is correct because `notifyAll()` (and `wait()` and `notify()`) must be called from within a synchronized context. D is a correct statement.
☒ B is incorrect because to call `wait()`, the thread must own the lock on the object that `wait()` is being invoked on, not the other way around. C is incorrect because `notify()` is defined in `java.lang.Object`. E is incorrect because `notify()` will not cause a thread to release its locks. The thread can only release its locks by exiting the synchronized code. F is incorrect because `notifyAll()` notifies all the threads waiting on a particular locked object, not all threads waiting on *any* object. (OCP Objectives 10.3 and 10.4)

8. ☑ E is correct. Synchronizing the `public` methods is sufficient to make this safe, so F is incorrect. This class is not thread-safe unless some sort of synchronization protects the changing data.
☒ B is incorrect because although a `StringBuffer` is synchronized internally, we call `append()` multiple times, and nothing would prevent two simultaneous `log()` calls from mixing up their messages. C and D are incorrect because if one method remains unsynchronized, it can run while the other is executing, which could result in reading the contents while one of the messages is incomplete, or worse. (You don't want to call `toString()` on the `StringBuffer` as it's resizing its internal character array.) (OCP Objective 10.3)

9. ☑ G is correct. The code does not acquire a lock on `t` before calling `t.wait()`, so it throws an `IllegalMonitorStateException`. The method is `synchronized`, but it's not synchronized on `t` so the exception will be thrown. If the wait were placed inside a `synchronized(t)` block, then D would be correct.
☒ A, B, C, D, E, and F are incorrect based on the logic described above. (OCP Objective 10.2)

10. ☑ B is correct. In the first line of `main` we're constructing an instance of an anonymous inner class extending from `MyThread`. So the `MyThread` constructor runs and prints `MyThread`. Next, `main()` invokes `start()` on the new thread instance, which causes the overridden `run()` method (the `run()` method in the anonymous inner class) to be invoked.
☒ A, C, D, E, F, G, and H are incorrect based on the logic described above. (OCP Objective 10.1)

11. ☑ A, F, and H are correct. A is correct because when `synchronized` instance methods are called on the same *instance*, they block each other. F and H can't happen because `synchronized static` methods in the same class block each other, regardless of which instance was used to call the methods. (An instance is not required to call `static` methods; only the class.)

☒ C, although incorrect, could happen because `synchronized` instance methods called on different instances do not block each other. **B, D, E,** and **G** are incorrect but also could all happen because instance methods and `static` methods lock on different objects, and do not block each other. (OCP Objectives 10.3 and 10.4)

12. ☑ **A, C, D, E,** and **F** are correct. This may look like `laurel` and `hardy` are battling to cause the other to `sleep()` or `wait()`—but that's not the case. Since `sleep()` is a `static` method, it affects the current thread, which is `laurel` (even though the method is invoked using a reference to `hardy`). That's misleading, but perfectly legal, and the `Thread laurel` is able to sleep with no exception, printing **A** and **C** (after at least a one-second delay). Meanwhile, `hardy` tries to call `laurel.wait()`—but `hardy` has not `synchronized` on `laurel`, so calling `laurel.wait()` immediately causes an `IllegalMonitorStateException`, and so `hardy` prints **D, E,** and **F**. Although the *order* of the output is somewhat indeterminate (we have no way of knowing whether **A** is printed before **D**, for example), it is guaranteed that **A, C, D, E,** and **F** will all be printed in some order, eventually—so G is incorrect.
☒ **B, G,** and **H** are incorrect based on the above. (OCP Objective 10.4)

13. ☑ C and **D** are correct. Fragment I doesn't start a new thread. Fragment II doesn't compile. Fragment III creates a new thread but doesn't start it. Fragment IV creates a new thread and invokes `run()` directly, but it doesn't start the new thread. Fragment V creates and starts a new thread.
☒ **A, B, E, F,** and **G** are incorrect based on the above. (OCP Objective 10.1)

14. ☑ **A** is correct. The `join()` must be placed in a `try/catch` block. If it were, answers **B** and **D** would be correct. The `join()` causes the main thread to pause and join the end of the other thread, meaning `"m2"` must come last.
☒ **B, C, D, E,** and **F** are incorrect based on the above. (OCP Objective 10.2)

15. ☑ **F** is correct. With Fragment I, the `chat` method is `synchronized`, so the two threads can't swap back and forth. With either fragment, the first output must be `yo`.
☒ **A, B, C, D,** and **E** are incorrect based on the above. (OCP Objective 10.3)

16. ☑ **F** is correct. When `run()` is invoked, it is with a new instance of `ChicksYack` and `c` has not been assigned to an object. If `c` were static, then because `yack` is `synchronized`, answers **C** and **E** would have been correct.
☒ **A, B, C, D,** and **E** are incorrect based on the above. (OCP Objectives 10.1 and 10.3)

17. ☑ C and **E** are correct. **E** should be obvious. **C** is correct because even though `move()` is `synchronized`, it's being invoked on two different objects.
☒ **A, B,** and **D** are incorrect based on the above. (OCP Objective 10.3)

EXERCISE ANSWERS

Exercise 13-1: Creating a Thread and Putting It to Sleep

The final code should look something like this:

```
class TheCount extends Thread {
   public void run() {
      for(int i = 1;i<=100;++i) {
         System.out.print(i + "  ");
         if(i % 10 == 0)  System.out.println("Hahaha");
         try { Thread.sleep(1000); }
         catch(InterruptedException e) {}
      }
   }
   public static void main(String [] args) {
      new TheCount().start();
   }
}
```

Exercise 13-2: Synchronizing a Block of Code

Your code might look something like this when completed:

```
class InSync extends Thread {
  StringBuffer letter;
  public InSync(StringBuffer letter) { this.letter = letter; }
  public void run() {
    synchronized(letter) {      // #1
      for(int i = 1;i<=100;++i) System.out.print(letter);
      System.out.println();
      char temp = letter.charAt(0);
      ++temp;          // Increment the letter in StringBuffer:
      letter.setCharAt(0, temp);
    }     // #2
  }
  public static void main(String [] args) {
    StringBuffer sb = new StringBuffer("A");
    new InSync(sb).start();  new InSync(sb).start();
    new InSync(sb).start();
  }
}
```

Just for fun, try removing lines 1 and 2 and then run the program again. It will be unsynchronized—watch what happens.

14

Concurrency

CERTIFICATION OBJECTIVES

- Use Collections from the java.util .concurrent Package with a Focus on the Advantages over and Differences from the Traditional java.util Collections
- Use Lock, ReadWriteLock, and ReentrantLock Classes in the java.util .cuncurrent.locks Package to Support Lock-Free Thread-Safe Programming on Single Variables
- Use Executor, ExecutorService, Executors, Callable, and Future to Execute Tasks Using Thread Pools
- Use the Parallel Fork/Join Framework
- ✓ Two-Minute Drill
- Q&A Self Test

Concurrency with the java.util.concurrent Package

As you learned in the previous chapter on threads, the Java platform supports multithreaded programming. Supporting multithreaded programming is essential for any modern programming language because servers, desktop computers, laptops, and most mobile devices contain multiple CPUs. If you want your applications to take advantage of all of the processing power present in a modern system, you must create multithreaded applications.

Unfortunately, creating efficient and error-free multithreaded applications can be a challenge. The low-level threading constructs such as `Thread`, `Runnable`, `wait()`, `notify()`, and synchronized blocks are too primitive for many requirements and force developers to create their own high-level threading libraries. Custom threading libraries can be both error prone and time consuming to create.

The `java.util.concurrent` package provides high-level APIs that support many common concurrent programming use cases. When possible, you should use these high-level APIs in place of the traditional low-level threading constructs (synchronized, wait, notify). Some features (such as the new locking API) provide functionality similar to what existed already, but with more flexibility at the cost of slightly awkward syntax. Using the `java.util.concurrent` classes requires a solid understanding of the traditional Java threading types (`Thread` and `Runnable`) and their use (start, run, synchronized, wait, notify, join, sleep, etc.). If you are not comfortable with Java threads, you should return to the previous chapter before continuing with these high-level concurrency APIs.

CERTIFICATION OBJECTIVE

Apply Atomic Variables and Locks (OCP Objective 11.2)

11.2 Use Lock, ReadWriteLock, and ReentrantLock classes in the java.util.concurrent.locks package to support lock-free thread-safe programming on single variables.

The `java.util.concurrent.atomic` and `java.util.concurrent.locks` packages solve two different problems. They are grouped into a single exam objective simply because they are the only two packages below `java.util.concurrent` and both have a small number of classes and interfaces to learn. The `java.util`

`.concurrent.atomic` package enables multithreaded applications to safely access individual variables without locking, while the `java.util.concurrent.locks` package provides a locking framework that can be used to create locking behaviors that are the same or superior to those of Java's synchronized keyword.

Atomic Variables

Imagine a multiplayer video game that contains monsters that must be destroyed. The players of the game (threads) are vanquishing monsters, while at the same time a monster-spawning thread is repopulating the world to ensure players always have a new challenge to face. To keep the level of difficulty consistent, you would need to keep track of the monster count and ensure that the monster population stays the same (a hero's work is never done). Both the player threads and the monster-spawning thread must access and modify the shared monster count variable. If the monster count somehow became incorrect, your players may find themselves with more adversaries than they could handle.

The following example shows how even the seemingly simplest of code can lead to undefined results. Here you have a class that increments and reports the current value of an integer variable:

```
public class Counter {
  private int count;
  public void increment() {
    count++; // it's a trap!
             // a single "line" is not atomic
  }
  public int getValue() {
    return count;
  }
}
```

A `Thread` that will increment the counter 10,000 times:

```
public class IncrementerThread extends Thread {
  private Counter counter;
  // all instances are passed the same counter
  public IncrementerThread(Counter counter) {
    this.counter = counter;
  }
  public void run() {
    // "i" is local and thread-safe
    for(int i = 0; i < 10000; i++) {
      counter.increment();
    }
  }
}
```

The code from within this application's main method:

```
Counter counter = new Counter();        // the shared object
IncrementerThread it1 = new IncrementerThread(counter);
IncrementerThread it2 = new IncrementerThread(counter);
it1.start(); // thread 1 increments the count by 10000
it2.start(); // thread 2 increments the count by 10000
it1.join();  // wait for thread 1 to finish
it2.join();  // wait for thread 2 to finish
System.out.println(counter.getValue()); // rarely 20000
                                        // lowest 11972
```

The trap in this example is that `count++` looks like a single action when, in fact, it is not. When incrementing a field like this, what *probably* happens is the following sequence:

1. The value stored in count is copied to a temporary variable.
2. The temporary variable is incremented.
3. The value of the temporary variable is copied back to the count field.

We say "probably" in this example because while the Java compiler will translate the `count++` statement into multiple Java bytecode instructions, you really have no control over what native instructions are executed. The JIT (Just In Time compiler)–based nature of most Java runtime environments means you don't know when or if the `count++` statement will be translated to native CPU instructions and whether it ends up as a single instruction or several. You should always act as if a single line of Java code takes multiple steps to complete. Getting an incorrect result also depends on many other factors, such as the type of CPU you have. Do both threads in the example run concurrently or in sequence? A large loop count was used in order to make the threads run longer and be more likely to execute concurrently.

While you could make this code thread-safe with synchronized blocks, the act of obtaining and releasing a lock flag would probably be more time consuming than the work being performed. This is where the `java.util.concurrent.atomic` package classes can benefit you. They provide variables whose values can be modified atomically. An atomic operation is one that, for all intents and purposes, appears to happen all at once. The `java.util.concurrent.atomic` package provides several classes for different data types, such as `AtomicInteger`, `AtomicLong`, `AtomicBoolean`, and `AtomicReference`, to name a few.

Here is a thread-safe replacement for the `Counter` class from the previous example:

```
public class Counter {
  private AtomicInteger count = new AtomicInteger();
  public void increment() {
    count.getAndIncrement(); // atomic operation
```

```
    }
    public int getValue() {
      return count.intValue();
    }
  }
```

In reality, even a method such as `getAndIncrement()` still takes several steps to execute. The reason this implementation is now thread-safe is something called CAS. CAS stands for Compare And Swap. Most modern CPUs have a set of CAS instructions. A basic outline of what is happening now is as follows:

1. The value stored in `count` is copied to a temporary variable.
2. The temporary variable is incremented.
3. Compare the value currently in `count` with the original value. If it is unchanged, then swap the old value for the new value.

Step 3 happens atomically. If step 3 finds that some other thread has already modified the value of `count`, then repeat steps 1–3 until we increment the field without interference.

The central method in a class like `AtomicInteger` is the `boolean compareAndSet(int expect, int update)` method, which provides the CAS behavior. Other atomic methods delegate to the `compareAndSet` method. The `getAndIncrement` method implementation is simply:

```
public final int getAndIncrement() {
  for (;;) {
    int current = get();
    int next = current + 1;
    if (compareAndSet(current, next))
      return current;
  }
}
```

Locks

The `java.util.concurrent.locks` package is about creating (not surprisingly) locks. Why would you want to use locks when so much of `java.util.concurrent` seems geared toward avoiding overt locking? You use `java.util.concurrent.locks` classes and traditional monitor locking (the synchronized keyword) for roughly the same purpose: creating segments of code that require exclusive execution (one thread at a time).

Why would you create code that limited the number of threads that can execute it? While atomic variables work well for making single variables thread-safe, imagine if you have two or more variables that are related. A video game character might have a number of gold pieces that can be carried in his backpack and a number of gold pieces he keeps in an in-game bank vault. Transferring gold into the bank is as simple as subtracting gold from the backpack and adding it to the vault. If we have 10 gold pieces in our backpack and 90 in the vault, we have a total of 100 pieces that belong to our character. If we want to transfer all 10 pieces to the vault, we can first add 10 to the vault count and then subtract 10 from the backpack, or first subtract 10 from the backpack and then add 10 to the vault. If another thread were to try to assess our character's wealth during the middle of our transfer, it might see 90 pieces or 110 pieces depending on the order of our operations, neither being the correct count of 100 pieces.

This other thread that is attempting to read the character's total wealth might do all sorts of things, such as increase the likelihood of your character being robbed, or a variety of other actions to control the in-game economics. It becomes important for all game threads to be able to correctly gauge a character's wealth even if there is a transfer in progress.

The solution to our balance inquiry transfer problem is to use locking. Create a single method to get a character's wealth and another to perform gold transfers. You should never be able to check a character's total wealth while a gold transfer is in progress. Having a single method to get a character's total wealth is also important because you don't want a thread to read the backpack's gold count before a transfer and then the vault's gold count after a transfer. That would lead to the same incorrect total as trying to calculate the total during a transfer.

Much of the functionality provided by the classes and interfaces of the `java.util.concurrent.locks` package duplicates that of traditional synchronized locking. In fact, the hypothetical gold transfer outlined earlier could be solved with either the synchronized keyword or classes in the `java.util.concurrent.locks` package. In Java 5, when `java.util.concurrent` was first introduced, the new locking classes performed better than the synchronized keyword, but there is no longer a vast difference in performance. So why would you use these newer locking classes? The `java.util.concurrent.locks` package provides

- The ability to duplicate traditional synchronized blocks.
- Nonblock scoped locking—obtain a lock in one method and release it in another (this can be dangerous, though).
- Multiple `wait`/`notify`/`notifyAll` pools per lock—threads can select which pool (`Condition`) they wait on.
- The ability to attempt to acquire a lock and take an alternative action if locking fails.
- An implementation of a multiple-reader, single-writer lock.

ReentrantLock

The java.util.concurrent.locks.Lock interface provides the outline of the new form of locking provided by the java.util.concurrent.locks package. Like any interface, the Lock interface requires an implementation to be of any real use. The java.util.concurrent.locks.ReentrantLock class provides that implementation. To demonstrate the use of Lock, we will first duplicate the functionality of a basic traditional synchronized block.

```
Object obj = new Object();
synchronized(obj) {    // traditional locking, blocks until acquired
                       // work
}                      // releases lock automatically
```

Here is an equivalent piece of code using the java.util.concurrent.locks package. Notice how ReentrantLock can be stored in a Lock reference because it implements the Lock interface. This example blocks on attempting to acquire a lock, just like traditional synchronization.

```
Lock lock = new ReentrantLock();
lock.lock();           // blocks until acquired
try {
    // do work here
} finally {            // to ensure we unlock
  lock.unlock();       // must manually release
}
```

It is recommended that you always follow the lock() method with a try-finally block, which releases the lock. The previous example doesn't really provide a compelling reason for you to choose to use a Lock instance instead of traditional synchronization. One of the very powerful features is the ability to attempt (and fail) to acquire a lock. With traditional synchronization, once you hit a synchronized block, your thread either immediately acquires the lock or blocks until it can.

```
Lock lock = new ReentrantLock();
boolean locked = lock.tryLock(); // try without waiting
if (locked) {
  try {
      // work
  } finally {                    // to ensure we unlock
    lock.unlock();
  }
}
```

The ability to quickly fail to acquire the lock turns out to be powerful. You can process a different resource (lock) and come back to the failed lock later instead of just waiting for a lock to be released and thereby making more efficient use of system resources. There is also a variation of the `tryLock` method that allows you to specify an amount of time you are willing to wait to acquire the lock:

```
Lock lock = new ReentrantLock();
try {
  boolean locked = lock.tryLock(3, TimeUnit.SECONDS);
  if (locked) {
    try {
                     // work
    } finally {      // to ensure we unlock
      lock.unlock();
    }
  }
} catch (InterruptedException ex) {
                     // handle
}
```

Another benefit of the `tryLock` method is deadlock avoidance. With traditional synchronization, you must acquire locks in the same order across all threads. For example, if you have two objects to lock against:

```
Object o1 = new Object();
Object o2 = new Object();
```

And you synchronize using the internal lock flags of both objects:

```
synchronized(o1) {
         // thread A could pause here
  synchronized(o2) {
         // work
  }
}
```

You should never acquire the locks in the opposite order because it could lead to deadlock. While thread A has only the `o1` lock, thread B acquires the `o2` lock. You are now at an impasse because neither thread can obtain the second lock it needs to continue.

```
synchronized(o2) {
         // thread B gets stuck here
  synchronized(o1) {
         // work
  }
}
```

Looking at a similar example using a `ReentrantLock`, start by creating two locks:

```
Lock l1 = new ReentrantLock();
Lock l2 = new ReentrantLock();
```

Next, you acquire both locks in thread A:

```
boolean aq1 = l1.tryLock();
boolean aq2 = l2.tryLock();
try{
  if (aq1 && aq2) {
      // work
  }
} finally {
  if (aq2) l2.unlock(); // don't unlock if not locked
  if (aq1) l1.unlock();
}
```

Notice the example is careful to always unlock any acquired lock, but ONLY the lock(s) that were acquired. A `ReentrantLock` has an internal counter that keeps track of the number of times it has been locked/unlocked, and it is an error to unlock without a corresponding successful lock operation. If a thread attempts to release a lock that it does not own, an `IllegalMonitorStateException` will be thrown.

Now in thread B, the locks are obtained in the reverse order in which thread A obtained them. With traditional locking, using synchronized code blocks and attempting to obtain locks in the reverse order could lead to deadlock.

```
boolean aq2 = l2.tryLock();
boolean aq1 = l1.tryLock();
try{
  if (aq1 && aq2) {
      // work
  }
} finally {
  if (aq1) l1.unlock();
  if (aq2) l2.unlock();
}
```

Now, even if thread A was only in possession of the `l1` lock, there is no possibility that thread B could block because we use the nonblocking `tryLock` method. Using this technique, you can avoid deadlocking scenarios, but you must deal with the possibility that both locks could not be acquired. Using a simple loop, you can repeatedly attempt to obtain both locks until successful (Note: This approach is CPU intensive; we'll look at a better solution next):

```
loop2:
while (true) {
  boolean aq2 = l2.tryLock();
  boolean aq1 = l1.tryLock();
  try {
    if (aq1 && aq2) {
      // work
```

```
          break loop2;
        }
      } finally {
        if (aq2) l2.unlock();
        if (aq1) l1.unlock();
      }
    }
```

on the Job

It is remotely possible that this example could lead to livelock. Imagine if thread A always acquires `lock1` at the same time that thread B acquires `lock2`. Each thread's attempt to acquire the second lock would always fail, and you'd end up repeating forever, or at least until you were lucky enough to have one thread fall behind the other. You can avoid livelock in this scenario by introducing a short random delay with `Thread.sleep(int)` any time you fail to acquire both locks.

Condition

A `Condition` provides the equivalent of the traditional `wait`, `notify`, and `notifyAll` methods. The traditional `wait` and `notify` methods allow developers to implement an await/signal pattern. You use an await/signal pattern when you would use locking, but with the added stipulation of trying to avoid spinning (endless checking if it is okay to do something). Imagine a video game character that wants to buy something from a store, but the store is out of stock at the moment. The character's thread could repeatedly lock the store object and check for the desired item, but that would lead to unneeded system utilization. Instead, the character's thread can say, "I'm taking a nap, wake me up when new stock arrives."

The `java.util.concurrent.locks.Condition` interface is the modern replacement for the `wait` and `notify` methods. A three-part code example shows you how to use a condition. Part one shows that a `Condition` is created from a `Lock` object:

```
Lock lock = new ReentrantLock();
Condition blockingPoolA = lock.newCondition();
```

When your thread reaches a point where it must delay until another thread performs an activity, you "await" the completion of that other activity. Before calling `await`, you must have locked the `Lock` used to produce the `Condition`. It is possible that the awaiting thread may be interrupted and you must handle the possible `InterruptedException`. When you call the `await` method, the `Lock` associated with the `Condition` is released. Before the `await` method returns, the lock will be reacquired. In order to use a `Condition`, a thread must first acquire a `Lock`. Part two of the three-part `Condition` example shows how a `Condition` is used to pause or wait for some event:

```
lock.lock();
try {
  blockingPoolA.await(); // "wait" here
                         // lock will be reacquired
    // work
} catch (InterruptedException ex) {
    // interrupted during await()
} finally {              // to ensure we unlock
  lock.unlock();         // must manually release
}
```

In another thread, you perform the activity that the first thread was waiting on and then signal that first thread to resume (return from the `await` method). Part three of the `Condition` example is run in a different thread than part two. This part causes the thread waiting in the second piece to wake up:

```
lock.lock();
try {
  // work
  blockingPoolA.signalAll(); // wake all awaiting
                             // threads
} finally {
  lock.unlock();             // now an awoken thread can run
}
```

The `signalAll()` method causes all threads awaiting on the same `Condition` to wake up. You can also use the `signal()` method to wake up a single awaiting thread. Remember that "waking up" is not the same thing as proceeding. Each awoken thread will have to reacquire the `Lock` before continuing.

One advantage of a `Condition` over the traditional wait/notify operations is that multiple `Conditions` can exist for each `Lock`. A `Condition` is effectively a waiting/ blocking pool for threads.

```
Lock lock = new ReentrantLock();
Condition blockingPoolA = lock.newCondition();
Condition blockingPoolB = lock.newCondition();
```

By having multiple conditions, you are effectively categorizing the threads waiting on a lock and can, therefore, wake up a subset of the waiting threads.

`Conditions` can also be used when you can't use a `BlockingQueue` to coordinate the activities of two or more threads.

ReentrantReadWriteLock

Imagine a video game that was storing a collection of high scores using a non-thread-safe collection. With a non-thread-safe collection, it is important that if a thread is attempting to modify the collection, it must have exclusive access to the collection. To allow multiple threads to concurrently read the high score list or allow a single thread to add a new score, you could use a `ReadWriteLock`.

A `ReentrantReadWriteLock` is not actually a `Lock`; it implements the `ReadWriteLock` interface. What a `ReentrantReadWriteLock` does is produce two specialized `Lock` instances, one to a read lock and the other to a write lock.

```
ReentrantReadWriteLock rwl =
  new ReentrantReadWriteLock();
Lock readLock = rwl.readLock();
Lock writeLock = rwl.writeLock();
```

These two locks are a matched set—one cannot be held at the same time as the other (by different threads). What makes these locks unique is that multiple threads can hold the read lock at the same time, but only one thread can hold the write lock at a time.

This example shows how a non-thread-safe collection (an `ArrayList`) can be made thread-safe, allowing concurrent reads but exclusive access by a writing thread:

```
public class MaxValueCollection {
    private List<Integer> integers = new ArrayList<>();
    private ReentrantReadWriteLock rwl =
        new ReentrantReadWriteLock();

    public void add(Integer i) {
        rwl.writeLock().lock(); // one at a time
        try {
            integers.add(i);
        } finally {
            rwl.writeLock().unlock();
        }
    }

    public int findMax() {
        rwl.readLock().lock(); // many at once
        try {
            return Collections.max(integers);
        } finally {
            rwl.readLock().unlock();
        }
    }
}
```

Instead of wrapping a collection with `Lock` objects to ensure thread safety, you can use one of the thread-safe collections you'll learn about in the next section.

CERTIFICATION OBJECTIVE

Use java.util.concurrent Collections (OCP Objective 11.1) and Use a Deque (OCP Objective 4.5)

11.1 Use collections from the java.util.concurrent package with a focus on the advantages over and differences from the traditional java.util collections.

4.5 Create and use List, Set, and Deque implementations.

Imagine an online video game with a list of the top 20 scores in the last 30 days. You could model the high score list using a `java.util.ArrayList`. As scores expire, they are removed from the list, and as new scores displace existing scores, remove and insert operations are performed. At the end of every game, the list of high scores is displayed. If the game is popular, then a lot of people (threads) will be reading the list at the same time. Occasionally, the list will be modified—sometimes by multiple threads—probably at the same time that it is being read by a large number of threads.

A traditional `java.util.List` implementation such as `java.util.ArrayList` is not thread-safe. Concurrent threads can safely read from an `ArrayList` and possibly even modify the elements stored in the list, but if any thread modifies the structure of the list (add or remove operation), then unpredictable behavior can occur.

Look at the `ArrayListRunnable` class in the following example. What would happen if there were a single instance of this class being executed by several threads? You might encounter several problems, including `ArrayIndexOutOfBoundsException`, duplicate values, skipped values, and null values. Not all threading problems manifest immediately. To observe the bad behavior, you might have to execute the faulty code multiple times or under different system loads. It is important that you are able to recognize the difference between thread-safe and non-thread-safe code yourself, because the compiler will not detect thread-unsafe code.

```
public class ArrayListRunnable implements Runnable {
  // shared by all threads
  private List<Integer> list = new ArrayList<>();
```

```
    public ArrayListRunnable() {
      // add some elements
      for (int i = 0; i < 100000; i++) {
        list.add(i);
      }
    }

      // might run concurrently, you cannot be sure
      // to be safe you must assume it does
    public void run() {
      String tName = Thread.currentThread().getName();
      while (!list.isEmpty()) {
        System.out.println(tName + " removed " + list.remove(0));
      }
    }

    public static void main(String[] args) {
      ArrayListRunnable alr = new ArrayListRunnable();
      Thread t1 = new Thread(alr);
      Thread t2 = new Thread(alr); // shared Runnable
      t1.start();
      t2.start();
    }
  }
```

To make a collection thread-safe, you could surround all the code that accessed the collection in synchronized blocks or use a method such as `Collections.synchronizedList(new ArrayList())`. Using synchronization to safeguard a collection creates a performance bottleneck and reduces the liveness of your application. The `java.util.concurrent` package provides several types of collections that are thread-safe but do not use coarse-grained synchronization. When a collection will be concurrently accessed in an application you are developing, you should always consider using the collections outlined in the following sections.

exam watch

Problems in multithreaded applications may not always manifest—a lot depends on the underlying operating system and how other applications affect the thread scheduling of a problematic application. On the exam, you might be asked about the "probable" or "most likely" outcome. Unless you are asked to identify every possible outcome of a code sample, don't get hung up on unlikely results. For example, if a code sample uses `Thread.sleep(1000)` and nothing indicates that the thread would be interrupted while it was sleeping, it would be safe to assume that the thread would resume execution around one second after the call to sleep.

Copy-on-Write Collections

The copy-on-write collections from the `java.util.concurrent` package implement one of several mechanisms to make a collection thread-safe. By using the copy-on-write collections, you eliminate the need to implement synchronization or locking when manipulating a collection using multiple threads.

The `CopyOnWriteArrayList` is a `List` implementation that can be used concurrently without using traditional synchronization semantics. As its name implies, a `CopyOnWriteArrayList` will never modify its internal array of data. Any mutating operations on the `List` (add, set, remove, etc.) will cause a new modified copy of the array to be created, which will replace the original read-only array. The read-only nature of the underlying array in a `CopyOnWriteArrayList` allows it to be safely shared with multiple threads. **Remember that read-only (immutable) objects are always thread-safe.**

The essential thing to remember with a copy-on-write collection is that a thread that is looping through the elements in a collection must keep a reference to the same unchanging elements throughout the duration of the loop; this is achieved with the use of an `Iterator`. Basically, you want to keep using the old, unchanging collection that you began a loop with. When you use `list.iterator()`, the returned `Iterator` will always reference the collection of elements as it was when `list.iterator()` was called, even if another thread modifies the collection. Any mutating methods called on a copy-on-write–based `Iterator` or `ListIterator` (such as add, set, or remove) will throw an `UnsupportedOperationException`.

on the job

A `for-each` loop uses an `Iterator` when executing, so it is safe to use with a copy-on-write collection, unlike a traditional `for` loop.

```
for(Object o : collection) {}                    // use this
for(int i = 0; i < collection.size(); i++) {} // not this
```

The `java.util.concurrent` package provides two copy-on-write–based collections: `CopyOnWriteArrayList` and `CopyOnWriteArraySet`. Use the copy-on-write collections when your data sets remain relatively small and the number of read operations and traversals greatly outnumber modifications to the collections. Modifications to the collections (not the elements within) are expensive because the entire internal array must be duplicated for each modification.

exam watch

A thread-safe collection does not make the elements stored within the collection thread-safe. Just because a collection that contains elements is thread-safe does not mean the elements themselves can be safely modified by multiple threads. You might have to use atomic variables, locks, synchronized code blocks, or immutable (read-only) objects to make the objects referenced by a collection thread-safe.

Concurrent Collections

The `java.util.concurrent` package also contains several concurrent collections that can be concurrently read and modified by multiple threads, but without the copy-on-write behavior seen in the copy-on-write collections. The concurrent collections include

- `ConcurrentHashMap`
- `ConcurrentLinkedDeque`
- `ConcurrentLinkedQueue`
- `ConcurrentSkipListMap`
- `ConcurrentSkipListSet`

Be aware that an `Iterator` for a concurrent collection is weakly consistent; it can return elements from the point in time the `Iterator` was created **or later**. This means that while you are looping through a concurrent collection, you might observe elements that are being inserted by other threads. In addition, you may observe only some of the elements that another thread is inserting with methods such as `addAll` when concurrently reading from the collection. Similarly, the `size` method may produce inaccurate results. Imagine attempting to count the number of people in a checkout line at a grocery store. While you are counting the people in line, some people may join the line and others may leave. Your count might end up close but not exact by the time you reach the end. This is the type of behavior you might see with a weakly consistent collection. The benefit to this type of behavior is that it is permissible for multiple threads to concurrently read and write a collection without having to create multiple internal copies of the collection, as is the case in a copy-on-write collection. If your application cannot deal with these inconsistencies, you might have to use a copy-on-write collection.

The `ConcurrentHashMap` and `ConcurrentSkipListMap` classes implement the `ConcurrentMap` interface. A `ConcurrentMap` enhances a `Map` by adding the atomic `putIfAbsent`, `remove`, and `replace` methods. For example, the `putIfAbsent` method is equivalent to performing the following code as an atomic operation:

```
if (!map.containsKey(key))
    return map.put(key, value);
  else
    return map.get(key);
```

`ConcurrentSkipListMap` and `ConcurrentSkipListSet` are sorted. `ConcurrentSkipListMap` keys and `ConcurrentSkipListSet` elements require the use of the `Comparable` or `Comparator` interfaces to enable ordering.

Blocking Queues

The copy-on-write and the concurrent collections are centered on the idea of multiple threads sharing data. Sometimes, instead of shared data (objects), you need to transfer data between two threads. A `BlockingQueue` is a type of shared collection that is used to exchange data between two or more threads while causing one or more of the threads to wait until the point in time when the data can be exchanged. One use case of a `BlockingQueue` is called the producer-consumer problem. In a producer-consumer scenario, one thread produces data, then adds it to a queue, and another thread must consume the data from the queue. A queue provides the means for the producer and the consumer to exchange objects. The `java.util.concurrent` package provides several `BlockingQueue` implementations. They include

- `ArrayBlockingQueue`
- `LinkedBlockingDeque`
- `LinkedBlockingQueue`
- `PriorityBlockingQueue`
- `DelayQueue`
- `LinkedTransferQueue`
- `SynchronousQueue`

General Behavior

A blocking collection, depending on the method being called, may cause a thread to block until another thread calls a corresponding method on the collection. For example, if you attempt to remove an element by calling `take()` on any `BlockingQueue` that is empty, the operation will block until another thread inserts an element. Don't call a blocking operation in a thread unless it is safe for that thread to block. The commonly used methods in a `BlockingQueue` are described in the following table.

Method	General Purpose	Unique Behavior
`add(E e)`	Insert an object.	Returns `true` if object added, false if duplicate objects are not allowed. Throws an `IllegalStateException` if the queue is bounded and full.
`offer(E e)`	Insert an object.	Returns `true` if object added, false if the queue is bounded and full.
`put(E e)`	Insert an object.	Returns `void`. If needed, will block until space in the queue becomes available.
`offer(E e, long timeout, TimeUnit unit)`	Insert an object.	Returns `false` if the object was not able to be inserted before the time indicated by the second and third parameters.
`remove(Object o)`	Remove an object.	Returns `true` if an equal object was found in the queue and removed; otherwise, returns `false`.
`poll(long timeout, TimeUnit unit)`	Remove an object.	Removes the first object in the queue (the head) and returns it. If the timeout expires before an object can be removed because the queue is empty, a null will be returned.
`take()`	Remove an object.	Removes the first object in the queue (the head) and returns it, blocking if needed until an object becomes available.
`poll()`	Remove an object.	Removes the first object in the queue (the head) and returns it or returns null if the queue is empty.
`element()`	Retrieves an object.	Gets the head of the queue without removing it. Throws a `NoSuchElementException` if the queue is empty.
`peek()`	Retrieves an object.	Gets the head of the queue without removing it. Returns a null if the queue is empty.

Bounded Queues

ArrayBlockingQueue, LinkedBlockingDeque, and LinkedBlockingQueue support a bounded capacity and will block on put(e) and similar operations if the collection is full. LinkedBlockingQueue is optionally bounded, depending on the constructor you use.

```
BlockingQueue<Integer> bq = new ArrayBlockingQueue<>(1);
try {
  bq.put(42);
  bq.put(43); // blocks until previous value is removed
} catch (InterruptedException ex) {
  // log and handle
}
```

Special-Purpose Queues

A SynchronousQueue is a special type of bounded blocking queue; it has a capacity of zero. Having a zero capacity, the first thread to attempt either an insert or remove operation on a SynchronousQueue will block until another thread performs the opposite operation. You use a SynchronousQueue when you need threads to meet up and exchange an object.

A DelayQueue is useful when you have objects that should not be consumed until a specific time. The elements added to a DelayQueue will implement the java.util.concurrent.Delayed interface which defines a single method: public long getDelay(TimeUnit unit). The elements of a DelayQueue can only be taken once their delay has expired.

The LinkedTransferQueue

A LinkedTransferQueue (new to Java 7) is a superset of ConcurrentLinkedQueue, SynchronousQueue, and LinkedBlockingQueue. It can function as a concurrent Queue implementation similar to ConcurrentLinkedQueue. It also supports unbounded blocking (consumption blocking) similar to LinkedBlockingQueue via the take() method. Like a SynchronousQueue, a LinkedTransferQueue can be used to make two threads rendezvous to exchange an object. Unlike a SynchronousQueue, a LinkedTransferQueue has internal capacity, so the transfer(E) method is used to block until the inserted object (and any previously inserted objects) is consumed by another thread.

In other words, a LinkedTransferQueue might do almost everything you need from a Queue.

Because a `LinkedTransferQueue` implements the `BlockingQueue`, `TransferQueue`, and `Queue` interfaces, it can be used to showcase all the different methods that can be used to add and remove elements using the various types of queues. Creating a `LinkedTransferQueue` is easy. Because `LinkedTransferQueue` is not bound by size, a limit to the number of elements CANNOT be supplied to its constructor.

```
TransferQueue<Integer> tq =
  new LinkedTransferQueue<>(); // not bounded
```

There are many methods to add a single element to a `LinkedTransferQueue`. Note that any method that blocks or waits for any period may throw an `InterruptedException`.

```
boolean b1 = tq.add(1);                     // returns true if added or throws
                                            // IllegalStateException if full
tq.put(2);                            // blocks if bounded and full
boolean b3 = tq.offer(3);                   // returns true if added or false
                                            // if bounded and full
                                            // recommended over add
boolean b4 =
  tq.offer(4, 10, MILLISECONDS);            // returns true if added
                                            // within the given time
                                            // false if bound and full
tq.transfer(5);                       // blocks until this element is consumed
boolean b6 = tq.tryTransfer(6);             // returns true if consumed
                                            // by an awaiting thread or
                                            // returns false without
                                            // adding if there was no
                                            // awaiting consumer
boolean b7 =
  tq.tryTransfer(7, 10, MILLISECONDS);      // will wait the
                                            // given time for
                                            // a consumer
```

Shown next are the various methods to access a single value in a `LinkedTransferQueue`. Again, any method that blocks or waits for any period may throw an `InterruptedException`.

```
Integer i1 = tq.element();    // gets without removing
                              // throws NoSuchElementException
                              // if empty
Integer i2 = tq.peek();       // gets without removing
                              // returns null if empty
Integer i3 = tq.poll();       // removes the head of the queue
                              // returns null if empty
Integer i4 =
  tq.poll(10, MILLISECONDS);  // removes the head of the
```

```
                                  // queue, waits up to the time
                                  // specified before returning
                                  // null if empty
Integer i5 = tq.remove();         // removes the head of the queue
                                  // throws NoSuchElementException
                                  // if empty
Integer i6 = tq.take();           // removes the head of the queue
                                  // blocks until an element is ready
```

Use a `LinkedTransferQueue` (new to Java 7) instead of another comparable queue type. The other `java.util.concurrent` queues (introduced in Java 5) are less efficient than `LinkedTransferQueue`.

CERTIFICATION OBJECTIVE

Use Executors and ThreadPools (OCP Objective 11.3)

11.3 Use Executor, ExecutorService, Executors, Callable, and Future to execute tasks using thread pools.

`Executors` (and the `ThreadPools` used by them) help meet two of the same needs that `Threads` do:

1. Creating and scheduling some Java code for execution and
2. Optimizing the execution of that code for the hardware resources you have available (using all CPUs, for example)

With traditional threading, you handle needs 1 and 2 yourself. With `Executors`, you handle need 1, but you get to use an off-the-shelf solution for need 2. The `java.util.concurrent` package provides several different off-the-shelf solutions (`Executors` and `ThreadPools`), which you'll read about in this chapter.

on the Job

When you have multiple needs or concerns, it is common to separate the code for each need into different classes. This makes your application more modular and flexible. This is a fundamental programming principle called "separation of concerns."

In a way, an `Executor` is an alternative to starting new threads. Using `Threads` directly can be considered low-level multithreading, while using `Executors` can be considered high-level multithreading. To understand how an `Executor` can replace manual thread creation, let us first analyze what happens when starting a new thread.

1. First, you must identify a task of some sort that forms a self-contained unit of work. You will typically code this task as a class that implements the `Runnable` interface.
2. After creating a `Runnable`, the next step is to execute it. You have two options for executing a `Runnable`:
   - **Option one** Call the `run` method synchronously (i.e., without starting a thread). This is probably **not** what you would normally do.

```
Runnable r = new MyRunnableTask();
r.run(); // executed by calling thread
```

   - **Option two** Call the method indirectly, most likely with a new thread.

```
Runnable r = new MyRunnableTask();
Thread t1 = new Thread(r);
t1.start();
```

The second approach has the benefit of executing your task asynchronously, meaning the primary flow of execution in your program can continue executing, without waiting for the task to complete. On a multiprocessor system, you must divide a program into a collection of asynchronous tasks that can execute concurrently in order to take advantage of all of the computing power a system possesses.

Identifying Parallel Tasks

Some applications are easier to divide into separate tasks than others. A single-user desktop application may only have a handful of tasks that are suitable for concurrent execution. Networked, multiuser servers, on the other hand, have a natural division of work. Each user's actions can be a task. Continuing our computer game scenario, imagine a computer program that can play chess against thousands of people simultaneously. Each player submits their move, the computer calculates its move, and finally it informs the player of that move.

Why do we need an alternative to `new Thread(r).start()`? What are the drawbacks? If we use our online chess game scenario, then having 10,000 concurrent players might mean 10,001 concurrent threads. (One thread awaits network connections from clients and performs a `Thread(r).start()` for each player.) The player thread would be responsible for reading the player's move, computing the computer's move, and making the response.

How Many Threads Can You Run?

Do you own a computer that can concurrently run 10,000 threads or 1,000 or even 100? Probably not—this is a trick question. A quad-core CPU (with four processors per unit) might be able to execute two threads per core for a total of eight concurrently executing threads. You can start 10,000 threads, but not all of them will be running at the same time. The underlying operating system's task scheduler rotates the threads so that they each get a slice of time on a processor. Ten thousand threads all competing for a turn on a processor wouldn't make for a very responsive system. Threads would either have to wait so long for a turn or get such small turns (or both) that performance would suffer.

In addition, each thread consumes system resources. It takes processor cycles to perform a context switch (saving the state of a thread and resuming another thread), and each thread consumes system memory for its stack space. Stack space is used for temporary storage and to keep track of where a thread returns to after completing a method call. Depending on a thread's behavior, it might be possible to lower the cost (in RAM) of creating a thread by reducing a thread's stack size.

on the job

To reduce a thread's stack size, the Oracle JVM supports using the nonstandard-`Xss1024k` option to the `java` command. Note that decreasing the value too far can result in some threads throwing exceptions when performing certain tasks, such as making a large number of recursive method calls.

Another limiting factor in being able to run 10,000 threads in an application has to do with the underlying limits of the OS. Operating systems typically have limits on the number of threads an application can create. These limits can prevent a buggy application from spawning countless threads and making your system unresponsive. If you have a legitimate need to run 10,000 threads, you will probably have to consult your operating system's documentation to discover possible limits and configuration options.

CPU-Intensive vs. I/O-Intensive Tasks

If you correctly configure your OS and you have enough memory for each thread's stack space plus your application's primary memory (heap), will you be able to run an application with 10,000 threads? It depends.... Remember that your processor can only run a small number of concurrent threads (in the neighborhood of 8 to 16 threads). Yet, many network server applications, such as our online chess game, would have traditionally started a new thread for each connected client. A system might be able to run an application with such a high number of threads because most of the threads are not doing anything. More precisely, in an application like our online chess server, most threads would be blocked waiting on I/O operations such as `InputStream.read` or `OutputStream.write` method calls.

When a thread makes an I/O request using `InputStream.read` and the data to be read isn't already in memory, the calling thread will be put to sleep ("blocked") by the system until the requested data can be loaded. This is much more efficient than keeping the thread on the processor while it has nothing to do. I/O operations are extremely slow when compared to compute operations—reading a sector from a hard drive takes much longer than adding hundreds of numbers. A processor might execute hundreds of thousands, or even millions, of instructions while awaiting the completion of an I/O request. The type of work (either CPU intensive or I/O intensive) a thread will be performing is important when considering how many threads an application can safely run. Imagine your world-class computer chess playing program takes one minute of processor time (no I/O at all) to calculate each move. In this scenario, it would only take about 16 concurrent players to cause your system to have periods of maximum CPU utilization.

If your tasks will be performing I/O operations, you should be concerned about how increased load (users) might affect scalability. If your tasks perform blocking I/O, then you might need to utilize a thread-per-task model. If you don't, then all your threads may be tied up in I/O operations with no threads remaining to support additional users. Another option would be to investigate whether you can use nonblocking I/O instead of blocking I/O.

Fighting for a Turn

If it takes the computer player one minute to calculate a turn and it takes a human player about the same time, then each player only uses one minute of CPU time out of every two minutes of real time. With a system capable of executing 16 concurrent game threads, that means we could handle 32 connected players. But if all 32 players make their turn at once, the computer will be stuck trying to calculate 32 moves at once. If the system uses preemptive multitasking (the most common type), then each thread will get preempted while it is running (paused and kicked off the CPU) so a different thread can take a turn (time slice). In most JVM implementations, this is handled by the underlying operating system's task scheduler. The task scheduler is itself a software program. The more CPU cycles spent scheduling and preempting threads, the less processor time you have to execute your application threads. Note that it would appear to the untrained observer that all 32 threads were running concurrently because a preemptive multitasking system will switch out the running threads frequently (millisecond time slices).

Decoupling Tasks from Threads

The best design would be one that utilized as many system resources as possible without attempting to over-utilize the system. If 16 threads are all you need to fully utilize your CPU, why would you start more than that? In a traditional system, you start more threads than your system can concurrently run and hope that only a small number are in a running state. If we want to adjust the number of threads that are started, we need to decouple the tasks that are to be performed (our `Runnable` instances) from our thread creation and starting. This is where a `java.util.concurrent.Executor` can help. The basic usage looks something like this:

```
Runnable r = new MyRunnableTask();
Executor ex = // details to follow
ex.execute(r);
```

A `java.util.concurrent.Executor` is used to execute the `run` method in a `Runnable` instance much like a thread. Unlike a more traditional `new Thread(r).start()`, an `Executor` can be designed to use any number of threading approaches, including

- Not starting any threads at all (task is run in the calling thread)
- Starting a new thread for each task
- Queuing tasks and processing them with only enough threads to keep the CPU utilized

You can easily create your own implementations of an `Executor` with custom behaviors. As you'll see soon, several implementations are provided in the standard Java SE libraries. Looking at sample `Executor` implementations can help you to understand their behavior. This next example doesn't start any new threads; instead, it executes the `Runnable` using the thread that invoked the `Executor`.

```
import java.util.concurrent.Executor;
public class SameThreadExecutor implements Executor {
    @Override
    public void execute(Runnable command) {
        command.run(); // caller waits
    }
}
```

The following Executor implementation would use a new thread for each task:

```
import java.util.concurrent.Executor;
public class NewThreadExecutor implements Executor {
    @Override
    public void execute(Runnable command) {
        Thread t = new Thread(command);
        t.start();
    }
}
```

This example shows how an Executor implementation can be put to use:

```
Runnable r = new MyRunnableTask();
Executor ex = new NewThreadExecutor(); // choose Executor
ex.executor(r);
```

By coding to the Executor interface, the submission of tasks is decoupled from the execution of tasks. The result is that you can easily modify how threads are used to execute tasks in your applications.

on the job

There is no "right number" of threads for task execution. The type of task (CPU intensive versus I/O intensive), number of tasks, I/O latency, and system resources all factor into determining the ideal number of threads to use. You should perform testing of your applications to determine the ideal threading model. This is one reason why the ability to separate task submission from task execution is important.

Several Executor implementations are supplied as part of the standard Java libraries. The Executors class (notice the "s" at the end) is a factory for Executor implementations.

```
Runnable r = new MyRunnableTask();
Executor ex = Executors.newCachedThreadPool(); // choose Executor
ex.execute(r);
```

The Executor instances returned by Executors are actually of type ExecutorService (which extends Executor). An ExecutorService provides management capability and can return Future references that are used to obtain the result of executing a task asynchronously. We'll talk more about `Future` in a few pages!

```
Runnable r = new MyRunnableTask();
ExecutorService ex = Executors.newCachedThreadPool(); // subtype of Executor
ex.execute(r);
```

Three types of `ExecutorService` instances can be created by the factory methods in the `Executors` class: cached thread pool executors, fixed thread pool executors, and single thread pool executors.

Cached Thread Pools

```
ExecutorService ex = Executors.newCachedThreadPool();
```

A cached thread pool will create new threads as they are needed and reuse threads that have become free. Threads that have been idle for 60 seconds are removed from the pool.

Watch out! Without some type of external limitation, a cached thread pool may be used to create more threads than your system can handle.

Fixed Thread Pools—Most Common

```
ExecutorService ex = Executors.newFixedThreadPool(4);
```

A fixed thread pool is constructed using a numeric argument (4 in the preceding example) that specifies the number of threads used to execute tasks. This type of pool will probably be the one you use the most because it prevents an application from overloading a system with too many threads. Tasks that cannot be executed immediately are placed on an unbounded queue for later execution.

on the Job

You might base the number of threads in a fixed thread pool on some attribute of the system your application is executing on. By tying the number of threads to system resources, you can create an application that scales with changes in system hardware. To query the number of available processors, you can use the `java.lang.Runtime` class.

```
Runtime rt = Runtime.getRuntime();
int cpus = rt.availableProcessors();
```

ThreadPoolExecutor

Both `Executors.newCachedThreadPool()` and `Executors.newFixedThreadPool(4)` return objects of type `java.util.concurrent.ThreadPoolExecutor` (which implements `ExecutorService` and `Executor`). You will typically use the `Executors` factory methods instead of creating `ThreadPoolExecutor` instances directly, but you can cast the fixed or cached thread pool `ExecutorService` references if you need access to the additional methods. The following example shows how you could dynamically adjust the thread count of a pool at runtime:

```
ThreadPoolExecutor tpe = (ThreadPoolExecutor)Executors.newFixedThreadPool(4);
tpe.setCorePoolSize(8);
tpe.setMaximumPoolSize(8);
```

Single Thread Pools

```
ExecutorService ex = Executors.newSingleThreadExecutor();
```

A single thread pool uses a single thread to execute tasks. Tasks that cannot be executed immediately are placed on an unbounded queue for later execution. Unlike a fixed thread pool executor with a size of 1, a single thread executor prevents any adjustments to the number of threads in the pool.

Scheduled Thread Pool

In addition to the three basic `ExecutorService` behaviors outlined already, the Executors class has factory methods to produce a `ScheduledThreadPoolExecutor`. A `ScheduledThreadPoolExecutor` enables tasks to be executed after a delay or at repeating intervals. Here, we see some thread scheduling code in action:

```
ScheduledExecutorService ftses =
  Executors.newScheduledThreadPool(4);                     // multi-threaded
                                                           // version
ftses.schedule(r, 5, TimeUnit.SECONDS);                    // run once after
                                                           // a delay
ftses.scheduleAtFixedRate(r, 2, 5, TimeUnit.SECONDS);      // begin after a
                                                           // 2sec delay
  // and begin again every 5 seconds
ftses.scheduleWithFixedDelay(r, 2, 5, TimeUnit.SECONDS); // begin after
                                                           // 2sec delay
  // and begin again 5 seconds *after* completing the last execution
```

The Callable Interface

So far, the Executors examples have used a Runnable instance to represent the task to be executed. The java.util.concurrent.Callable interface serves the same purpose as the Runnable interface, but provides more flexibility. Unlike the Runnable interface, a Callable may return a result upon completing execution and may throw a checked exception. An ExecutorService can be passed a Callable instead of a Runnable.

on the Job

Avoid using methods such as Object.wait, Object.notify, and Object .notifyAll in tasks (Runnable and Callable instances) that are submitted to an Executor or ExecutorService. Because you might not know what the threading behavior of an Executor is, it is a good idea to avoid operations that may interfere with thread execution. Avoiding these types of methods is advisable anyway since they are easy to misuse.

The primary benefit of using a Callable is the ability to return a result. Because an ExecutorService may execute the Callable asynchronously (just like a Runnable), you need a way to check the completion status of a Callable and obtain the result later. A java.util.concurrent.Future is used to obtain the status and result of a Callable. Without a Future, you'd have no way to obtain the result of a completed Callable and you might as well use a Runnable (which returns void) instead of a Callable. Here's a simple Callable example that loops a random number of times and returns the random loop count:

```
import java.util.concurrent.Callable;
import java.util.concurrent.ThreadLocalRandom;
public class MyCallable implements Callable<Integer> {

  @Override
  public Integer call() {
    // Obtain a random number from 1 to 10
    int count = ThreadLocalRandom.current().nextInt(1, 11);
    for(int i = 1; i <= count; i++) {
      System.out.println("Running..." + i);
    }
    return count;
  }
}
```

Submitting a Callable to an ExecutorService returns a Future reference. When you use the Future to obtain the Callable's result, you will have to handle two possible exceptions:

- **InterruptedException** Raised when the thread calling the Future's get() method is interrupted before a result can be returned

- **`ExecutionException`** Raised when an exception was thrown during the execution of the `Callable`'s `call()` method

```
Callable<Integer> c = new MyCallable();
ExecutorService ex =
        Executors.newCachedThreadPool();
Future<Integer> f = ex.submit(c); // finishes in the future
try {
  Integer v = f.get(); // blocks until done
  System.out.println("Ran:" + v);
} catch (InterruptedException | ExecutionException iex) {
  System.out.println("Failed");
}
```

on the Job

I/O activities in your `Runnable` and `Callable` instances can be a serious bottleneck. In preceding examples, the use of `System.out.println()` will cause I/O activity. If this wasn't a trivial example being used to demonstrate `Callable` and `ExecutorService`, you would probably want to avoid repeated calls to `println()` in the `Callable`. One possibility would be to use `StringBuilder` to concatenate all output strings and have a single `println()` call before the `call()` method returns. Another possibility would be to use a logging framework (see `java.util.logging`) in place of any `println()` calls.

ThreadLocalRandom

The first `Callable` example used a `java.util.concurrent.ThreadLocalRandom`. `ThreadLocalRandom` is a new way in Java 7 to create random numbers. `Math.random()` and shared `Random` instances are thread-safe, but suffer from contention when used by multiple threads. A `ThreadLocalRandom` is unique to a thread and will perform better because it avoids any contention. `ThreadLocalRandom` also provides several convenient methods such as `nextInt(int,int)` that allow you to specify the range of possible values returned.

ExecutorService Shutdown

You've seen how to create `Executors` and how to submit `Runnable` and `Callable` tasks to those `Executors`. The final component to using an `Executor` is shutting it done once it is done processing tasks. An `ExecutorService` should be shut down once it is no longer needed to free up system resources and to allow graceful application shutdown. Because the threads in an `ExecutorService` may be nondaemon threads, they may prevent normal application termination. In other words, your application stays running after completing its main method. You could perform a `System.exit(0)` call, but it would preferable to allow your threads to complete their current activities (especially if they are writing data).

```
ExecutorService ex =
// ...
ex.shutdown(); // no more new tasks
               // but finish existing tasks
try {
  boolean term = ex.awaitTermination(2, TimeUnit.SECONDS);
    // wait 2 seconds for running tasks to finish
} catch (InterruptedException ex1) {
    // did not wait the full 2 seconds
} finally {
  if(!ex.isTerminated()) // are all tasks done?
  {
    List<Runnable> unfinished = ex.shutdownNow();
    // a collection of the unfinished tasks
  }
}
```

For long-running tasks (especially those with looping constructs), consider using `Thread.currentThread().isInterrupted()` to determine if a `Runnable` or `Callable` should return early. The `ExecutorService.shutdownNow()` method will typically call `Thread.interrupt()` in an attempt to terminate any unfinished tasks.

CERTIFICATION OBJECTIVE

Use the Parallel Fork/Join Framework (OCP Objective 11.4)

11.4 Use the parallel Fork/Join Framework.

The Fork-Join Framework provides a highly specialized `ExecutorService`. The other `ExecutorService` instances you've seen so far are centered on the concept of submitting multiple tasks to an `ExecutorService`. By doing this, you provide an easy avenue for an `ExecutorService` to take advantage of all the CPUs in a system by using a threads to complete tasks. Sometimes, you don't have multiple tasks; instead, you have one really big task.

There are many large tasks or problems you might need to solve in your application. For example, you might need to initialize the elements of a large array with values. You might think that initializing an array doesn't sound like a large complex task in need of a framework. The key is that it needs to be a **large** task. What if you need to fill up a 100,000,000-element array with randomly generated values? The Fork-Join Framework makes it easier to tackle big tasks like this, while leveraging all of the CPUs in a system.

Divide and Conquer

Certain types of large tasks can be split up into smaller subtasks; those subtasks might, in turn, be split up into even smaller tasks. There is no limit to how many times you might subdivide a task. For example, imagine the task of having to repaint a single long fence that borders several houses. The "paint the fence" task could be subdivided so that each household would be responsible for painting a section of the fence. Each household could then subdivide their section into subsections to be painted by individual family members. In this example, there are three levels of recursive calls. The calls are considered recursive because at each step we are trying to accomplish the same thing: paint the fence. In other words, Joe, one of the home owners, was told by his wife, "paint that (huge) fence, it looks old." Joe decides that painting the whole fence is too much work and talks all the households along the fence into taking a subsection. Now Joe is telling himself "paint that (subsection of) fence, it looks old." Again, Joe decides that it is still too much work and subdivides his section into smaller sections for each member of his household. Again, Joe tells himself "paint that (subsection of) fence, it looks old," but this time, he decides that the amount of work is manageable and proceeds to paint his section of fence. Assuming everyone else paints their subsections (hopefully in a timely fashion), the result is the entire fence being painted.

on the Job

When using the Fork-Join Framework, your tasks will be coded to decide how many levels of recursion (how many times to subdivide) are appropriate. You'll want to split things up into enough subtasks that you have enough tasks to keep all of your CPUs utilized. Sometimes, the best number of tasks can be a little hard to determine because of factors we will discuss later. You might have to benchmark different numbers of task divisions to find the optimal number of subtasks that should be created.

Just because you can use Fork-Join to solve a problem doesn't always mean you should. If our initial task is to paint eight fence planks, then Joe might just decide to paint them himself. The effort involved in subdividing the problem and assigning those tasks to workers (threads) can sometimes be more than the actual work you want to perform. The number of elements (or fence planks) is not the only thing to consider—the amount of work performed on each element is also important. Imagine if Joe was asked to paint a mural on each fence plank. Because processing each element (fence plank) is so time consuming, in this case, it might be beneficial to adopt a divide-and-conquer solution even though there is a small number of elements.

ForkJoinPool

The Fork-Join `ExecutorService` implementation is `java.util.concurrent.ForkJoinPool`. You will typically submit a single task to a `ForkJoinPool` and await its completion. The `ForkJoinPool` and the task itself work together to divide and conquer the problem. Any problem that can be recursively divided can be solved using Fork-Join. Anytime you want to perform the same operation on a collection of elements (painting thousands of fence planks or initializing 100,000,000 array elements), consider using Fork-Join.

To create a `ForkJoinPool`, simply call its no-arg constructor:

```
ForkJoinPool fjPool = new ForkJoinPool();
```

The no-arg `ForkJoinPool` constructor creates an instance that will use the `Runtime.availableProcessors()` method to determine the level of parallelism. The level of parallelism determines the number of threads that will be used by the `ForkJoinPool`.

There is also a `ForkJoinPool(int parallelism)` constructor that allows you to override the number of threads that will be used.

ForkJoinTask

Just as with `Executors`, you must capture the task to be performed as Java code. With the Fork-Join Framework, a `java.util.concurrent.ForkJoinTask` instance (actually a subclass—more on that later) is created to represent the task that should be accomplished. This is different from other executor services that primarily used either `Runnable` or `Callable`. A `ForkJoinTask` has many methods (most of which you will never use), **but the following methods are important: `compute()`, `fork()`, and `join()`.**

A `ForkJoinTask` subclass is where you will perform most of the work involved in completing a Fork-Join task. `ForkJoinTask` is an abstract base class; we will discuss the two subclasses, `RecursiveTask` and `RecursiveAction`, later. The basic structure of any `ForkJoinTask` is shown in this pseudocode example:

```
class ForkJoinPaintTask {
  compute() {
    if(isFenceSectionSmall()) {  // is it a manageable amount of work?
      paintFenceSection();       // do the task
    } else {                     // task too big, split it
      ForkJoinPaintTask leftHalf = getLeftHalfOfFence();
      leftHalf.fork();           // queue left half of task
      ForkJoinPaintTask rightHalf = getRightHalfOfFence();
      rightHalf.compute();       // work on right half of task
      leftHalf.join();           // wait for queued task to be complete
    }
  }
}
```

Fork

With the Fork-Join Framework, each thread in the `ForkJoinPool` has a queue of the tasks it is working on; this is unlike most `ExecutorService` implementations that have a single shared task queue. The `fork()` method places a `ForkJoinTask` in the current thread's task queue. A normal thread does not have a queue of tasks—only the specialized threads in a `ForkJoinPool` do. This means that you can't call `fork()` unless you are within a `ForkJoinTask` that is being executed by a `ForkJoinPool`.

Initially, only a single thread in a `ForkJoinPool` will be busy when you submit a task. That thread will begin to subdivide the tasks into smaller tasks. Each time a task is subdivided into two subtasks, you fork (or queue) the first task and compute the second task. In the event you need to subdivide a task into more than two subtasks, each time you split a task, you would fork every new subtask except one (which would be computed).

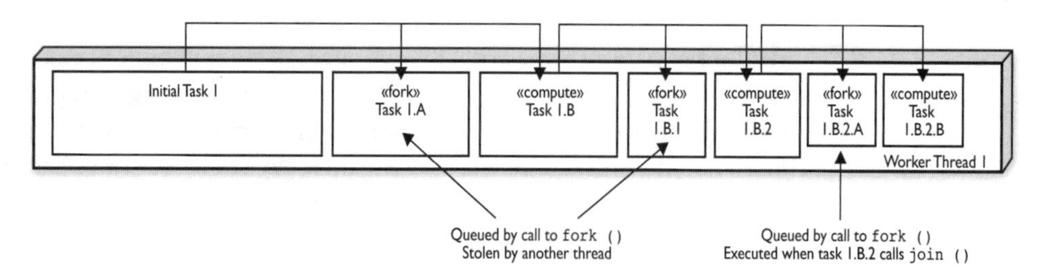

Work Stealing

Notice how the call to `fork()` is placed before the call to `compute()` or `join()`. A key feature of the Fork-Join Framework is work stealing. Work stealing is how the other threads in a `ForkJoinPool` will obtain tasks. When initially submitting a Fork-Join task for execution, a single thread from a `ForkJoinPool` begins executing (and subdividing) that task. Each call to `fork()` placed a new task in the calling thread's task queue. The order in which the tasks are queued is important. The tasks that have been queued the longest represent larger amounts of work. In the `ForkJoinPaintTask` example, the task that represents 100 percent of the work would begin executing, and its first queued (forked) task would represent 50 percent of the fence, the next 25 percent, then 12.5 percent, and so on. Of course, this can vary, depending on how many times the task will be subdivided and whether we are splitting the task into halves or quarters or some other division, but in this example, we are splitting each task into two parts: queuing one part and executing the second part.

The nonbusy threads in a `ForkJoinPool` will attempt to steal the oldest (and therefore largest) task from any Fork-Join thread with queued tasks. Given a `ForkJoinPool` with four threads, one possible sequence of events could be that the initial thread queues tasks that represent 50 percent and 25 percent of the work, which are then stolen by two different threads. The thread that stole the 50 percent task then subdivides that task and places a 25 percent task on its queue, which is then stolen by a fourth thread, resulting in four threads that each process 25 percent of the work.

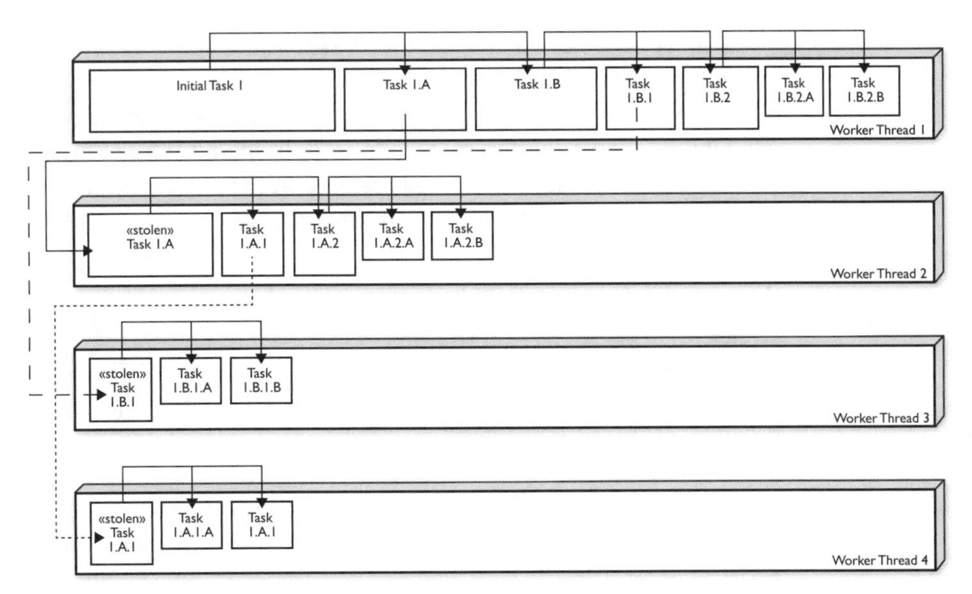

Of course, if everything was always this evenly distributed, you might not have as much of a need for Fork-Join. You could just presplit the work into a number of tasks equal to the number of threads in your system and use a regular `ExecutorService`. In practice, each of the four threads will not finish their 25 percent of the work at the same time—one thread will be the slow thread that doesn't get as much work done. There are many reasons for this: The data being processed may affect the amount of computation (25 percent of an array might not mean 25 percent of the workload), or a thread might not get as much time to execute as the other threads. Operating systems and other running applications are also going to consume CPU time. In order to finish executing the Fork-Join task as soon as possible, the threads that finish their portions of the work first will start to steal work from the slower threads—this way, you will be able to keep all of the CPU involved. If you only split the tasks into 25 percent of the data (with four threads), then there would be nothing for the faster threads to steal from when they finish early. In the beginning, if the slower thread stole 25 percent of the work and started processing it without further subdividing and queuing, then there would be no work on the slow thread's queue to steal. You should subdivide the tasks into a few more sections than are needed to evenly distribute the work among the number of threads in your `ForkJoinPools` because threads will most likely not perform exactly the same. Subdividing the tasks is extra work—if you do it too much, you might hurt performance. Subdivide your tasks enough to keep all CPUs busy, but not more than is needed. Unfortunately, there is no magic number to split your tasks into—it varies based on the complexity of the task, the size of the data, and even the performance characteristics of your CPUs.

Back to fence painting, make the `isFenceSectionSmall()` logic as simple as possible (low overhead) and easy to change. You should benchmark your Fork-Join code (using the hardware that you expect the code to typically run on) and find an amount of task subdivision that works well. It doesn't have to be perfect; once you are close to the ideal range, you probably won't see much variation in performance unless other factors come into play (different CPUs, etc.).

Join

When you call `join()` on the (left) task, it should be one of the last steps in the `compute` method, after calling `fork()` and `compute()`. Calling `join()` says "I can't proceed unless this (left) task is done." Several possible things can happen when you call `join()`:

- The task you call `join()` on might already be done. Remember you are calling `join()` on a task that already had `fork()` called. The task might have been stolen and completed by another thread. In this case, calling `join()` just verifies the task is complete and you can continue on.

- The task you call `join()` on might be in the middle of being processed. Another thread could have stolen the task, and you'll have to wait until the joined task is done before continuing.
- The task you call `join()` on might still be in the queue (not stolen). In this case, the thread calling `join()` will execute the joined task.

RecursiveAction

`ForkJoinTask` is an abstract base class that outlines most of the methods, such as `fork()` and `join()`, in a Fork-Join task. If you need to create a `ForkJoinTask` that does not return a result, then you should subclass `RecursiveAction`. `RecursiveAction` extends `ForkJoinTask` and has a single abstract compute method that you must implement:

```
protected abstract void compute();
```

An example of a task that does not need to return a result would be any task that initializes an existing data structure. The following example will initialize an array to contain random values. Notice that there is only a single array throughout the entire process. When subdividing an array, you should avoid creating new objects when possible.

```
public class RandomInitRecursiveAction extends RecursiveAction {
  private static final int THRESHOLD = 10000;
  private int[] data;
  private int start;
  private int end;

  public RandomInitRecursiveAction(int[] data, int start, int end) {
    this.data = data;
    this.start = start;             // where does our section begin at?
    this.end = end;                 // how large is this section?
  }
  @Override
  protected void compute() {
    if (end - start <= THRESHOLD) {  // is it a manageable amount of work?
      // do the task
      for (int i = start; i < end; i++) {
        data[i] =  ThreadLocalRandom.current().nextInt();
      }
    } else {                        // task too big, split it
      int halfWay = ((end - start) / 2) + start;
      RandomInitRecursiveAction a1 =
```

```
          new RandomInitRecursiveAction(data, start, halfWay);
        a1.fork(); // queue left half of task
        RandomInitRecursiveAction a2 =
          new RandomInitRecursiveAction(data, halfWay, end);
        a2.compute();    // work on right half of task
        a1.join();       // wait for queued task to be complete
      }
    }
  }
```

Sometimes, you will see one of the `invokeAll` methods from the `ForkJoinTask` class used in place of the fork/compute/join method combination. The `invokeAll` methods are convenience methods that can save some typing. Using them will also help you avoid bugs! The first task passed to `invokeAll` will be executed (compute is called), and all additional tasks will be forked and joined. In the preceding example, you could eliminate the three fork/compute/join lines and replace them with a single line:

```
invokeAll(a2, a1);
```

To begin the application, we create a large array and initialize it using Fork-Join:

```
public static void main(String[] args) {
  int[] data = new int[10_000_000];
  ForkJoinPool fjPool = new ForkJoinPool();
  RandomInitRecursiveAction action =
    new RandomInitRecursiveAction(data, 0, data.length);
  fjPool.invoke(action);
}
```

Notice that we do not expect any return values when calling invoke. A `RecursiveAction` returns nothing.

RecursiveTask

If you need to create a `ForkJoinTask` that does return a result, then you should subclass `RecursiveTask`. `RecursiveTask` extends `ForkJoinTask` and has a single abstract compute method that you must implement:

```
protected abstract V compute(); // V is a generic type
```

The following example will find the position in an array with the greatest value; if duplicate values are found, the first occurrence is returned. Notice that there is only a single array throughout the entire process. (Just like before, when subdividing an array, you should avoid creating new objects when possible.)

```
public class FindMaxPositionRecursiveTask extends RecursiveTask<Integer> {
  private static final int THRESHOLD = 10000;
  private int[] data;
  private int start;
  private int end;

  public FindMaxPositionRecursiveTask(int[] data, int start, int end) {
    this.data = data;
    this.start = start;
    this.end = end;
  }

  @Override
  protected Integer compute() {      // return type matches the <generic> type
    if (end - start <= THRESHOLD) { // is it a manageable amount of work?
      int position = 0;             // if all values are equal, return position 0
      for (int i = start; i < end; i++) {
        if (data[i] > data[position]) {
          position = i;
        }
      }
        return position;
      } else { // task too big, split it
      int halfWay = ((end - start) / 2) + start;
      FindMaxPositionRecursiveTask t1 =
        new FindMaxPositionRecursiveTask(data, start, halfWay);
      t1.fork(); // queue left half of task
      FindMaxPositionRecursiveTask t2 =
        new FindMaxPositionRecursiveTask(data, halfWay, end);
      int position2 = t2.compute(); // work on right half of task
      int position1 = t1.join();    // wait for queued task to be complete
      // out of the position in two subsection which is greater?
      if (data[position1] > data[position2]) {
        return position1;
      } else if (data[position1] < data[position2]) {
        return position2;
      } else {
        return position1 < position2 ? position1 : position2;
      }
    }
  }
}
```

To begin the application, we reuse the `RecursiveAction` example to create a large array and initialize it using Fork-Join. After initializing the array with random values, we reuse the `ForkJoinPool` with our `RecursiveTask` to find the position with the greatest value:

```
public static void main(String[] args) {
  int[] data = new int[10_000_000];
  ForkJoinPool fjPool = new ForkJoinPool();
  RandomInitRecursiveAction action =
    new RandomInitRecursiveAction(data, 0, data.length);
  fjPool.invoke(action);
```

```
    // new code begins here
    FindMaxPositionRecursiveTask task =
      new FindMaxPositionRecursiveTask(data, 0, data.length);
    Integer position = fjPool.invoke(task);
    System.out.println("Position: " + position + ", value: " +
data[position]);
}
```

Notice that a value is returned by the call to invoke when using a `RecursiveTask`.

on the Job

If your application will repeatedly submit tasks to a `ForkJoinPool`, then you should reuse a single `ForkJoinPool` instance and avoid the overhead involved in creating a new instance.

Embarrassingly Parallel

A problem or task is said to be embarrassingly parallel if little or no additional work is required to solve the problem in a parallel fashion. Sometimes, solving a problem in parallel adds so much more overhead that the problem can be solved faster serially. The `RandomInitRecursiveAction` example, which initializes an array to random values, has no additional overhead because what happens when processing one subsection of an array has no bearing on the processing of another subsection. Technically, there is a small amount of overhead even in the `RandomInitRecursiveAction`; the Fork-Join Framework and the `if` statement that determines whether or not the problem should be subdivided both introduce some overhead. Be aware that it can be difficult to get performance gains that scale with the number of CPUs you have. Typically, four CPUs will result in less than a 4× speedup when moving from a serial to a parallel solution.

The `FindMaxPositionRecursiveTask` example, which finds the largest value in an array, does introduce a small additional amount of work because you must compare the result from each subsection and determine which is greater. This is only a small amount, however, and adds little overhead. Some tasks may introduce so much additional work that any advantage of using parallel processing is eliminated (the task runs slower than serial execution). If you find yourself performing a lot of processing after calling `join()`, then you should benchmark your application to determine if there is a performance benefit to using parallel processing. Be aware that performance benefits might only be seen with a certain number of CPUs. A task might run on one CPU in 5 seconds, on two CPUs in 6 seconds, and on four CPUs in 3.5 seconds.

The Fork-Join Framework is designed to have minimal overhead as long as you don't over-subdivide your tasks and the amount of work required to join results can be kept small. A good example of a task that incurs additional overhead but still benefits from Fork-Join is array sorting. When you split an array into two halves and sort each half separately, you then have to combine the two sorted arrays, as shown in the following example:

```
public class SortRecursiveAction extends RecursiveAction {
  private static final int THRESHOLD = 1000;
  private int[] data;
  private int start;
  private int end;

  public SortRecursiveAction(int[] data, int start, int end) {
    this.data = data;
    this.start = start;
    this.end = end;
  }

  @Override
  protected void compute() {
    if (end - start <= THRESHOLD) {
      Arrays.sort(data, start, end);
    } else {
    int halfWay = ((end - start) / 2) + start;
    SortRecursiveAction a1 =
      new SortRecursiveAction(data, start, halfWay);
    SortRecursiveAction a2 =
      new SortRecursiveAction(data, halfWay, end);
    invokeAll(a1, a2);  // shortcut for fork() & join()
      if(data[halfWay-1] <= data[halfWay]) {
        return; // already sorted
      }
        // merging of sorted subsections begins here
        int[] temp = new int[end - start];
        int s1 = start, s2 = halfWay, d = 0;
        while(s1 < halfWay && s2 < end) {
          if(data[s1] < data[s2]) {
          temp[d++] = data[s1++];
        } else if(data[s1] > data[s2]) {
          temp[d++] = data[s2++];
        } else {
            temp[d++] = data[s1++];
          temp[d++] = data[s2++];
        }
      }
        if(s1 != halfWay) {
        System.arraycopy(data, s1, temp, d, temp.length - d);
      } else if(s2 != end) {
        System.arraycopy(data, s2, temp, d, temp.length - d);
      }
      System.arraycopy(temp, 0, data, start, temp.length);
    }
  }
}
```

In the previous example, everything after the call to `invokeAll` is related to merging two sorted subsections of an array into a single larger sorted subsection.

on the job

Because Java applications are portable, the system running your application may not have the hardware resources required to see a performance benefit. Always perform testing to determine which problem and hardware combinations see performance increases when using Fork-Join.

CERTIFICATION SUMMARY

This chapter covered the required concurrency knowledge you'll need to apply on the certification exam. The `java.util.concurrent` package and its subpackages form a high-level, multithreading framework in Java. You should become familiar with threading basics before attempting to apply the Java concurrency libraries, but once you learn `java.util.concurrent`, you may never extend `Thread` again.

`Callables` and `Executors` (and their underlying thread pools) form the basis of a high-level alternative to creating new `Threads` directly. As the trend of adding more CPU cores continues, knowing how to get Java to make use of them all concurrently could put you on easy street. The high-level APIs provided by `java.util.concurrent` help you create efficient multithreaded applications while eliminating the need to use low-level threading APIs such as `wait()`, `notify()`, and `synchronized`, which can be a source of hard-to-detect bugs.

When using an `Executor`, you will commonly create a `Callable` implementation to represent the work that needs to be executed concurrently. A `Runnable` can be used for the same purpose, but a `Callable` leverages generics to allow a generic return type from its `call` method. `Executor` or `ExecutorService` instances with predefined behavior can be obtained by calling one of the factory methods in the `Executors` class like so: `ExecutorService es = Executors.newFixedThreadPool(100);`.

Once you obtain an `ExecutorService`, you submit a task in the form of a `Runnable` or `Callable` or a collection of `Callable` instances to the `ExecutorService` using one of the `execute`, `submit`, `invokeAny`, or `invokeAll` methods. An `ExecutorService` can be held onto during the entire life of your application if needed, but once it is no longer needed, it should be terminated using the `shutdown` and `shutdownNow` methods.

We looked at the Fork-Join Framework, which supplies a highly specialized type of `Executor`. Use the Fork-Join Framework when the work you would typically put in a `Callable` can be split into multiple units of work. The purpose of the Fork-Join Framework is to decrease the amount of time it takes to solve a problem by leveraging the additional CPUs in a system. You should only run a single Fork-Join task at a time in an application, because the goal of the framework is to allow a single task to consume all available CPU resources in order to be solved as quickly as possible. In most cases, the effort of splitting a single task into multiple tasks that can be operated on by the underlying Fork-Join threads will introduce additional overhead. Don't assume that applying Fork-Join will grant you a performance benefit for all problems. The overhead involved may be large enough that any benefit of applying the framework is offset.

When applying the Fork-Join Framework, first subclass either `RecursiveTask` (if a return result is desired) or `RecursiveAction`. Within one of these `ForkJoinTask` subclasses, you must implement the `compute` method. The `compute()` method is where you divide the work of a task into parts and then call the `fork` and `join` methods or the `invokeAll` method. To execute the task, create a `ForkJoinPool` instance with `ForkJoinPool pool = new ForkJoinPool();` and submit the `RecursiveTask` or `RecursiveAction` to the pool with the `pool.invoke(task)` method. While the Fork-Join API itself is not that large, creating a correct and efficient implementation of a `ForkJoinTask` can be challenging.

We learned about the `java.util.concurrent` collections. There are three categories of collections: copy-on-write collections, concurrent collections, and blocking queues. The copy-on-write and concurrent collections are similar in use to the traditional `java.util` collections, but are designed to be used efficiently in a thread-safe fashion. The copy-on-write collections (`CopyOnWriteArrayList` and `CopyOnWriteArraySet`) should be used for read-heavy scenarios. When attempting to loop through all the elements in one of the copy-on-write collections, always use an `Iterator`. The concurrent collections included

- `ConcurrentHashMap`
- `ConcurrentLinkedDeque`
- `ConcurrentLinkedQueue`
- `ConcurrentSkipListMap`
- `ConcurrentSkipListSet`

These collections are meant to be used concurrently without requiring locking. Remember that iterators of these five concurrent collections are weakly consistent. `ConcurrentHashMap` and `ConcurrentSkipListMap` are `ConcurrentMap` implementations that add atomic `putIfAbsent`, `remove`, and `replace` methods to the `Map` interface. Seven blocking queue implementations are provided by the `java.util.concurrent` package:

- `ArrayBlockingQueue`
- `LinkedBlockingDeque`
- `LinkedBlockingQueue`
- `PriorityBlockingQueue`
- `DelayQueue`
- `LinkedTransferQueue`
- `SynchronousQueue`

These blocking queues are used to exchange objects between threads—one thread will deposit an object and another thread will retrieve that object. Depending on which queue type is used, the parameters used to create the queue, and the method being called, an insert or a removal operation may block until it can be completed successfully. In Java 7, the `LinkedTransferQueue` class was added that acts as a superset of several blocking queue types; you should prefer it when possible.

The `java.util.concurrent.atomic` and `java.util.concurrent.locks` packages contain additional utility classes you might consider using in concurrent applications. The `java.util.concurrent.atomic` package supplies thread-safe classes that are similar to the traditional wrapper classes (such as `java.lang.Integer`) but with methods that support atomic modifications. The `java.util.concurrent.locks.Lock` interface and supporting classes enable you to create highly customized locking behaviors that are more flexible than traditional object monitor locking (the `synchronized` keyword).

✓ TWO-MINUTE DRILL

Here are some of the key points from the certification objectives in this chapter.

Apply Atomic Variables and Locks (OCP Objective 11.2)

- ❑ The `java.util.concurrent.atomic` package provides classes that are similar to volatile fields (changes to an atomic object's value will be correctly read by other threads without the need for synchronized code blocks in your code).
- ❑ The atomic classes provide a `compareAndSet` method that is used to validate that an atomic variable's value will only be changed if it matches an expected value.
- ❑ The atomic classes provide several convenience methods such as `addAndGet` that will loop repeatedly until a `compareAndSet` succeeds.
- ❑ The `java.util.concurrent.locks` package contains a locking mechanism that is an alternative to synchronized methods and blocks. You get greater flexibility at the cost of a more verbose syntax (such as having to manually call `lock.unlock()` and having an automatic release of a synchronization monitor at the end of a synchronized code block).
- ❑ The `ReentrantLock` class provides the basic Lock implementation. Commonly used methods are `lock()`, `unlock()`, `isLocked()`, and `tryLock()`. Calling `lock()` increments a counter and `unlock()` decrements the counter. A thread can only obtain the lock when the counter is zero.
- ❑ The `ReentrantReadWriteLock` class provides a `ReadWriteLock` implementation that supports a read lock (obtained by calling) and a write lock (obtained by calling).

Use java.util.concurrent Collections (OCP Objective 11.1)

- ❑ Copy-on-write collections work well when there are more reads than writes because they make a new copy of the collection for each write. When looping through a copy-on-write collection, use an iterator (remember, `for-each` loops use an iterator).
- ❑ None of the concurrent collections make the elements stored in the collection thread-safe—just the collection itself.
- ❑ `ConcurrentHashMap`, `ConcurrentSkipListMap`, and `ConcurrentSkipListSet` should be preferred over synchronizing with the more traditional collections.

- `ConcurrentHashMap` and `ConcurrentSkipListMap` are `ConcurrentMap` implementations that enhance a standard Map by adding atomic operations that validate the presence and value of an element before performing an operation: `putIfAbsent(K key, V value)`, `remove(Object key, Object value)`, `replace(K key, V value)`, and `replace(K key, V oldValue, V newValue)`.
- Blocking queues are used to exchange objects between threads. Blocking queues will block (hence the name) when you call certain operations, such as calling `take()` when there are no elements to take. There are seven different blocking queues that have slightly different behaviors; you should be able to identify the behavior of each type.

Blocking Queue	Description
`ArrayBlockingQueue`	A FIFO (first-in-first-out) queue in which the head of the queue is the oldest element and the tail is the newest. An `int` parameter to the constructor limits the size of the queue (it is a bounded queue).
`LinkedBlockingDeque`	Similar to `LinkedBlockingQueue`, except it is a double-ended queue (deque). Instead of only supporting FIFO operations, you can remove from the head or tail of the queue.
`LinkedBlockingQueue`	A FIFO queue in which the head of the queue is the oldest element and the tail is the newest. An optional `int` parameter to the constructor limits the size of the queue (it can be bounded or unbounded).
`PriorityBlockingQueue`	An unbounded queue that orders elements using `Comparable` or `Comparator`. The head of the queue is the lowest value.
`DelayQueue`	An unbounded queue of `java.util.concurrent.Delayed` instances. Objects can only be taken once their delay has expired. The head of the queue is the object that expired first.
`LinkedTransferQueue`	New to Java 7. An unbounded FIFO queue that supports the features of a `ConcurrentLinkedQueue`, `SynchronousQueue`, and `LinkedBlockingQueue`.
`SynchronousQueue`	A blocking queue with no capacity. An `insert` operation blocks until another thread executes a remove operation. A `remove` operation blocks until another thread executes an `insert` operation.

- Some blocking queues are bounded, meaning they have an upper bound on the number of elements that can be added, and a thread calling `put(e)` may block until space becomes available.

Use Executors and ThreadPools (OCP Objective 11.3)

- ❑ An `Executor` is used to submit a task for execution without being coupled to how or when the task is executed. Basically, it creates an abstraction that can be used in place of explicit thread creation and execution.
- ❑ An `ExecutorService` is an enhanced `Executor` that provides additional functionality, such as the ability to execute a `Callable` instance and to shut down (nondaemon threads in an `Executor` may keep the JVM running after your main method returns).
- ❑ The `Callable` interface is similar to the `Runnable` interface, but adds the ability to return a result from its `call` method and can optionally throw an exception.
- ❑ The `Executors` (plural) call provides factory methods that can be used to construct `ExecutorService` instances, for example: `ExecutorService ex = Executors.newFixedThreadPool(4);`.

Use the Parallel Fork/Join Framework (OCP Objective 11.4)

- ❑ Fork-Join enables work stealing among worker threads in order to keep all CPUs utilized and to increase the performance of highly parallelizable tasks.
- ❑ A pool of worker threads of type `ForkJoinWorkerThread` are created when you create a `new ForkJoinPool()`. By default, one thread per CPU is created.
- ❑ To minimize the overhead of creating new threads, you should create a single Fork-Join pool in an application and reuse it for all recursive tasks.
- ❑ A Fork-Join task represents a large problem to solve (often involving a collection or array).
- ❑ When executed by a `ForkJoinPool`, the Fork-Join task will subdivide itself into Fork-Join tasks that represent smaller segments of the problem to be solved.
- ❑ A Fork-Join task is a subclass of the `ForkJoinTask` class, either `RecursiveAction` or `RecursiveTask`.
- ❑ Extend `RecursiveTask` when the `compute()` method must return a value, and extend `RecursiveAction` when the return type is void.
- ❑ When writing a `ForkJoinTask` implementation's `compute()` method, always call `fork()` before `join()` or use one of the `invokeAll()` methods instead of calling `fork()` and `join()`.
- ❑ You do not need to shut down a Fork-Join pool before exiting your application because the threads in a Fork-Join pool typically operate in daemon mode.

SELF TEST

The following questions might be some of the hardest in the book. It's just a hard topic, so don't panic. (We know some Java book authors who didn't do well with these topics and still managed to pass the exam.)

1. The following block of code creates a `CopyOnWriteArrayList`, adds elements to it, and prints the contents:

```
CopyOnWriteArrayList<Integer> cowList = new CopyOnWriteArrayList<>();
cowList.add(4);
cowList.add(2);
Iterator<Integer> it = cowList.iterator();
cowList.add(6);
while(it.hasNext()) {
  System.out.print(it.next() + " ");
}
```

What is the result?

A. `6`

B. `12`

C. `4 2`

D. `4 2 6`

E. Compilation fails

F. An exception is thrown at runtime

2. Given:

```
CopyOnWriteArrayList<Integer> cowList = new CopyOnWriteArrayList<>();
cowList.add(4);
cowList.add(2);
cowList.add(6);
Iterator<Integer> it = cowList.iterator();
cowList.remove(2);
while(it.hasNext()) {
  System.out.print(it.next() + " ");
}
```

Which shows the output that will be produced?

A. `12`

B. `10`

C. `4 2 6`

D. `4 6`

E. Compilation fails

F. An exception is thrown at runtime

3. Which methods from a `CopyOnWriteArrayList` will cause a new copy of the internal array to be created? (Choose all that apply.)

A. `add`

B. `get`

C. `iterator`

D. `remove`

4. Given:

```
ArrayBlockingQueue<Integer> abq = new ArrayBlockingQueue<>(10);
```

Which operation(s) can block indefinitely? (Choose all that apply.)

A. `abq.add(1);`

B. `abq.offer(1);`

C. `abq.put(1);`

D. `abq.offer(1, 5, TimeUnit.SECONDS);`

5. Given:

```
ConcurrentMap<String,Integer> ages = new ConcurrentHashMap<>();
ages.put("John", 23);
```

Which method(s) would delete `John` from the map only if his value was still equal to 23?

A. `ages.delete("John", 23);`

B. `ages.deleteIfEquals("John", 23);`

C. `ages.remove("John", 23);`

D. `ages.removeIfEquals("John", 23);`

6. Which method represents the best approach to generating a random number between one and ten if the method will be called concurrently and repeatedly by multiple threads?

A.
```
public static int randomA() {
    Random r = new Random();
  return r.nextInt(10) + 1;
}
```

B.
```
private static Random sr = new Random();
public static int randomB() {
  return sr.nextInt(10) + 1;
}
```

C.
```
public static int randomC() {
  int i = (int)(Math.random() * 10 + 1);
  return i;
}
```

D.
```
public static int randomD() {
  ThreadLocalRandom lr = ThreadLocalRandom.current();
  return lr.nextInt(1, 11);
}
```

7. Given:

```
AtomicInteger i = new AtomicInteger();
```

Which atomically increment `i` by 9? (Choose all that apply.)

A. `i.addAndGet(9);`

B. `i.getAndAdd(9);`

C. `i.set(i.get() + 9);`

D. `i.atomicIncrement(9);`

E. `i = i + 9;`

8. Given:

```
public class LeaderBoard {
  private ReadWriteLock rwl = new ReentrantReadWriteLock();
  private List<Integer> highScores = new ArrayList<>();
  public void addScore(Integer score) {
    // position A
    lock.lock();
    try {
      if (highScores.size() < 10) {
        highScores.add(score);
      } else if (highScores.get(highScores.size() - 1) < score) {
        highScores.set(highScores.size() - 1, score);
      } else {
        return;
      }
      Collections.sort(highScores, Collections.reverseOrder());
    } finally {
      lock.unlock();
    }
  }
  public List<Integer> getHighScores() {
    // position B
    lock.lock();
    try {
      return Collections.unmodifiableList(highScores);
    } finally {
      lock.unlock();
    }
  }
}
```

Which block(s) of code best match the behavior of the methods in the `LeaderBoard` class? (Choose all that apply.)

A. `Lock lock = rwl.reentrantLock(); // should be inserted at position A`

B. `Lock lock = rwl.reentrantLcock(); // should be inserted at position B`

C. `Lock lock = rwl.readLock(); // should be inserted at position A`

D. `Lock lock = rwl.readLock(); // should be inserted at position B`

E. `Lock lock = rwl.writeLock(); // should be inserted at position A`

F. `Lock lock = rwl.writeLock(); // should be inserted at position B`

9. Given:

```
ReentrantReadWriteLock rwl = new ReentrantReadWriteLock();
rwl.readLock().unlock();
System.out.println("READ-UNLOCK-1");
rwl.readLock().lock();
System.out.println("READ-LOCK-1");
rwl.readLock().lock();
System.out.println("READ-LOCK-2");
rwl.readLock().unlock();
System.out.println("READ-UNLOCK-2");
rwl.writeLock().lock();
System.out.println("WRITE-LOCK-1");
rwl.writeLock().unlock();
System.out.println("WRITE-UNLOCK-1");
```

What is the result?

A. The code will not compile

B. The code will compile and output:

```
READ-UNLOCK-1
READ-LOCK-1
READ-LOCK-2
READ-UNLOCK-2
```

C. The code will compile and output:

```
READ-UNLOCK-1
READ-LOCK-1
READ-LOCK-2
READ-UNLOCK-2
WRITE-LOCK-1
WRITE-UNLOCK-1
```

D. A `java.lang.IllegalMonitorStateException` will be thrown

10. Which class contains factory methods to produce preconfigured `ExecutorService` instances?

A. `Executor`

B. `Executors`

C. `ExecutorService`

D. `ExecutorServiceFactory`

11. Given:

```
private Integer executeTask(ExecutorService service,
                            Callable<Integer> task) {
// insert here
}
```

Which set(s) of lines, when inserted, would correctly use the `ExecutorService` argument to execute the `Callable` and return the `Callable`'s result? (Choose all that apply.)

A.
```
try {
  return service.submit(task);
} catch (Exception e) {
  return null;
}
```

B.
```
try {
  return service.execute(task);
} catch (Exception e) {
  return null;
}
```

C.
```
try {
  Future<Integer> future = service.submit(task);
  return future.get();
} catch (Exception e) {
  return null;
}
```

D.
```
try {
  Result<Integer> result = service.submit(task);
  return result.get();
} catch (Exception e) {
  return null;
}
```

12. Which are true? (Choose all that apply.)

A. A `Runnable` may return a result, but must not throw an Exception

B. A `Runnable` must not return a result nor throw an Exception

C. A `Runnable` must not return a result, but may throw an Exception

D. A `Runnable` may return a result and throw an Exception

E. A `Callable` may return a result, but must not throw an Exception

F. A `Callable` must not return a result nor throw an Exception

G. A `Callable` must not return a result, but may throw an Exception

H. A `Callable` may return a result and throw an Exception

13. Given:

```
public class IncrementAction extends RecursiveAction {
  private final int threshold;
  private final int[] myArray;
  private int start;
  private int end;
  public IncrementAction(int[] myArray, int start, int end, int threshold) {
    this.threshold = threshold;
    this.myArray = myArray;
    this.start = start;
    this.end = end;
  }
  @Override
  protected void compute() {
    if (end - start < threshold) {
      for (int i = start; i <= end; i++) {
        myArray[i]++;
      }
    } else {
      int midway = (end - start) / 2 + start;
      IncrementAction a1 = new IncrementAction(myArray, start,
                                               midway, threshold);
      IncrementAction a2 = new IncrementAction(myArray, midway + 1,
                                               end, threshold);
      // insert answer here
    }
  }
}
```

Which line(s), when inserted at the end of the `compute` method, would correctly take the place of separate calls to `fork()` and `join()`? (Choose all that apply.)

A. `compute();`

B. `forkAndJoin(a1, a2);`

C. `computeAll(a1, a2);`

D. `invokeAll(a1, a2);`

14. When writing a `RecursiveTask` subclass, which are true? (Choose all that apply.)

A. `fork()` and `join()` should be called on the same task

B. `fork()` and `compute()` should be called on the same task

C. `compute()` and `join()` should be called on the same task

D. `compute()` should be called before `fork()`

E. `fork()` should be called before `compute()`

F. `join()` should be called after `fork()` but before `compute()`

SELF TEST ANSWERS

1. ☑ **C** is correct. The `Iterator` is obtained before 6 is added. As long as the reference to the `Iterator` is maintained, it will only provide access to the values 4 and 2.
   ☒ **A, B, D, E,** and **F** are incorrect based on the above. (OCP Objective 11.1)

2. ☑ **C** is correct. Because the `Iterator` is obtained before the number 2 is removed, it will reflect all the elements that have been added to the collection.
   ☒ **A, B, D, E,** and **F** are incorrect based on the above. (OCP Objective 11.1)

3. ☑ **A** and **D** are correct. Of the methods listed, only `add` and `remove` will modify the list and cause a new internal array to be created.
   ☒ **B** and **C** are incorrect based on the above. (OCP Objective 11.1)

4. ☑ **C** is correct. The `add` method will throw an `IllegalStateException` if the queue is full. The two `offer` methods will return false if the queue is full. Only the `put` method will block until space becomes available.
   ☒ **A, B,** and **D** are incorrect based on the above. (OCP Objective 11.1)

5. ☑ **C** is correct; it uses the correct syntax.
   ☒ The methods for answers **A, B,** and **D** do not exist in a `ConcurrentHashMap`. A traditional `Map` contains a single-argument `remove` method that removes an element based on its key. The `ConcurrentMap` interface (which `ConcurrentHashMap` implements) added the two-argument `remove` method, which takes a key and a value. An element will only be removed from the `Map` if its value matches the second argument. A boolean is returned to indicate if the element was removed. (OCP Objective 11.1)

6. ☑ **D** is correct. The `ThreadLocalRandom` creates and retrieves `Random` instances that are specific to a thread. You could achieve the same effect prior to Java 7 by using the `java.lang.ThreadLocal` and `java.util.Random` classes, but it would require several lines of code. `Math.random` is thread-safe, but uses a shared `java.util.Random` instance and can suffer from contention problems.
   ☒ **A, B,** and **C** are incorrect based on the above. (OCP Objective 11.3)

7. ☑ **A** and **B** are correct. The `addAndGet` and `getAndAdd` both increment the value stored in an `AtomicInteger`.
   ☒ Answer **C** is not atomic because in between the call to get and set, the value stored by `i` may have changed. Answer **D** is invalid because the `atomicIncrement` method is fictional, and answer **E** is invalid because auto-boxing is not supported for the atomic classes. The difference between the `addAndGet` and `getAndAdd` methods is that the first is a prefix method (++x) and the second is a postfix method (x++). (Objective 11.2)

8. ☑ **D** and **E** are correct. The `addScore` method modifies the collection and, therefore, should use a write lock, while the `getHighScores` method only reads the collection and should use a read lock.
   ☒ **A, B, C,** and **F** are incorrect, they will not behave correctly. (Objective 11.2)

9. ☑ **D** is correct. A lock counts the number of times it has been locked. Calling lock increments the count, and calling unlock decrements the count. If a call to unlock decreases the count below zero, an exception is thrown.
   ☒ **A, B,** and **C** are incorrect based on the above. (OCP Objective 11.2)

10. ☑ **B** is correct. `Executor` is the super-interface for `ExecutorService`. You use `Executors` to easily obtain `ExecutorService` instances with predefined threading behavior. If the `Executor` interface does not produce `ExecutorService` instances with the behaviors that you desire, you can always look into using `java.util.concurrent.AbstractExecutorService` or `java.util.concurrent.ThreadPoolExecutor` directly.
    ☒ **A, C,** and **D** are incorrect based on the above. (OCP Objective 11.3)

11. ☑ **C** is correct. When you submit a `Callable` to an `ExecutorService` for execution, you will receive a `Future` as the result. You can use the `Future` to check on the status of the `Callable`'s execution, or just use the get method to block until the result is available.
    ☒ **A, B,** and **D** are incorrect based on the above. (OCP Objective 11.3)

12. ☑ **B** and **H** are correct. `Runnable` and `Callable` serve similar purposes. `Runnable` has been available in Java since version 1. `Callable` was introduced in Java 5 and serves as a more flexible alternative to `Runnable`. A `Callable` allows a generic return type and permits thrown exceptions, while a `Runnable` does not.
    ☒ **A, C, D, E, F,** and **G** are incorrect statements. (Objective 11.3)

13. ☑ **D** is correct. The `invokeAll` method is a var args method that will fork all Fork-Join tasks, except one that will be invoked directly.
    ☒ **A, B,** and **C** are incorrect; they would not correctly complete the Fork-Join process. (OCP Objective 11.4)

14. ☑ **A** and **E** are correct. When creating multiple `ForkJoinTask` instances, all tasks except one should be forked first so that they can be picked up by other Fork-Join worker threads. The final task should then be executed within the same thread (typically by calling `compute()`) before calling join on all the forked tasks to await their results. In many cases, calling the methods in the wrong order will not result in any compiler errors, so care must be taken to call the methods in the correct order.
    ☒ **B, C, D,** and **F** are incorrect based on the above. (OCP Objective 11.4)

15 JDBC

CERTIFICATION OBJECTIVES

- Describe the Interfaces that Make Up the Core of the JDBC API (Including the Driver, Connection, Statement, and ResultSet Interfaces and Their Relationship to Provider Implementations)
- Identify the Components Required to Connect to a Database Using the DriverManager Class (Including the JDBC URL)
- Submit Queries and Read Results from the Database (Including Creating Statements; Returning Result Sets; Iterating Through the Results; and Properly Closing Result Sets, Statements, and Connections)
- Use JDBC Transactions (Including Disabling Auto-commit Mode, Committing and Rolling Back Transactions, and Setting and Rolling Back to Savepoints)
- Construct and Use RowSet Objects Using the RowSetProvider Class and the RowSetFactory Interface
- Create and Use PreparedStatement and CallableStatement Objects

✓ Two-Minute Drill

Q&A Self Test

This chapter covers the JDBC API that was added for the Java SE 7 exam. The exam developers have long felt that this API is truly a core feature of the language, and being able to demonstrate proficiency with JDBC goes a long way toward demonstrating your skills as a Java programmer.

Interestingly, JDBC has been a part of the language since JDK version 1.1 (1997) when JDBC 1.0 was introduced. Since then, there has been a steady progression of updates to the API, roughly one major release for each even-numbered JDK release, with the last major update being JDBC 4.0, released in 2006 with Java SE 6. In Java SE 7, JDBC got some minor updates, and is now at version 4.1, which we'll discuss a little later in the chapter. While the focus of the exam is on JDBC 4.x, there are some questions about the differences between loading a driver with a JDBC 3.0 and JDBC 4.x implementation, so we'll talk about that as well.

The good news is that the exam is not going to test your ability to write SQL statements. That would be an exam all by itself (maybe even more than one—SQL is a BIG topic!). But you will need to recognize some basic SQL syntax and commands, so we'll start by spending some time covering the basics of relational database systems and enough SQL to make you popular at database parties. If you feel you have experience with SQL and understand database concepts, you might just skim the first section or skip right to the first exam objective and dive right in.

Starting Out: Introduction to Databases and JDBC

When you think of organizing information and storing it in some easily understood way, a spreadsheet or a table is often the first approach you might take. A spreadsheet or a table is a natural way of categorizing information: The first row of a table defines the sort of information that the table will hold, and each subsequent row contains a set of data that is related to the key we create on the left. For example, suppose you wanted to chart your monthly spending for several types of expenses (Table 15-1).

TABLE 15-1 Chart of Expenses

Month	Gas	EatingOut	Utilities	Phone
January	$200.25	$109.87	$97.00	$45.08
February	$225.34	$121.08	$97.00	$23.36
March	$254.78	$130.45	$97.00	$56.09

From the data in the chart, we can determine that your overall expenses are increasing month to month in the first three months of this year. But notice that without the table, without a relationship between the month and the data in the columns, you would just have a pile of receipts with no way to draw out important conclusions, such as

- Assuming you drove the same number of miles per month, gas is getting pricey—maybe it is time to get a Prius.
- You are eating out more month to month (or the price of eating out is going up)—maybe it's time to start doing some meal planning.
- And maybe you need to be a little less social—that phone bill is high.

The point is that this small sample of data is the key to understanding a relational database system. A relational database is really just a software application designed to store and manipulate data in tables. The software itself is actually called a Relational Database Management System (RDBMS), but many people shorten that to just "database"—so know that going forward, when we refer to a database, we are actually talking about an RDBMS (the whole system). What the relational management system adds to a database is the ability to define relationships between tables. It also provides a language to get data in and out in a meaningful way.

Looking at the simple table in Table 15-1, we know that the data in the columns, Gas, EatingOut, Utilities, and Phone, are grouped by the months January, February, and so on. The month is unique to each row and identifies this row of data. In database parlance, the month is a "primary key." A primary key is generally required for a database table to identify which row of the table you want, and to make sure that there are no duplicate rows.

Extending this a little further, if the data in Table 15-1 were stored in a database, I could ask the database (write a query) to give me all of the data for the month of January (again, my primary key is "month" for this table). I might write something like:

"Give me all of my expenses for January."

The result would be something like:

```
January: Gas: $200.25, EatingOut: $109.87, Utilities: $97.00, Phone: $45.08
```

This kind of query is what makes a database so powerful. With a relatively simple language, you can construct some really powerful queries in order to manipulate your data to tell a story. In most RDBMSs, this language is called the Structured Query

Language (SQL). The same query we wrote out in a sentence earlier, would be expressed like this in SQL:

```
SELECT * FROM Expenses WHERE Month = 'January'
```

which can be translated to "select all of the columns (`*`) from my table named 'Expenses' where the month column is equal to the string `'January'`." Let's look a bit more at how we "talk" to a database and what other sorts of queries we can make with tables in a relational database.

Talking to a Database

There are three important concepts when working with a database:

- Creating a connection to the database
- Creating a statement to execute in the database
- Getting back a set of data that represents the results

Let's look at these concepts in more detail.

Before we can communicate with the software that manages the database, before we can send it a query, we need to make a connection with the RDBMS itself. There are many different types of connections, and a lot of underlying technology to describe the connection itself, but in general, to communicate with an RDBMS, we need to open a connection using an IP address and port number to the database. Once we have established the connection, we need to send it some parameters (such as a username and password) to authenticate ourselves as a valid user of the RDBMS. Finally, assuming all went well, we can send queries through the connection. This is like logging into your online account at a bank. You provide some credentials, a username and password, and a connection is established and opened between you and the bank. Later in the chapter, when we start writing code, we'll open a connection using a Java class called the `DriverManager`, and in one request, pass in the database name, our username, and password.

Once we have established a connection, we can use some type of application (usually provided by the database vendor) to send query statements to the database, have them executed in the database, and get a set of results returned. A set of results can be one row, as we saw before when we asked for the data from the month of January, or several rows. For example, suppose we wanted to see all of the Gas expenses from our Expenses table. We might query the database like this:

```
"Show me all of my Gas Expenses"
```

Or as a SQL query:

```
SELECT Gas FROM Expenses
```

The set of results that would "return" from my query would be three rows, and each row would contain one column.

$200.25
$225.34
$254.78

An important aspect of a database is that the data is presented back to you exactly the same way that it is stored. Since Gas expense is a column, the query will return three rows (one for January, one for February, and one for March). Note that because we did not ask the database to include the Month column in the results, all we got was the Gas column. The results do preserve the fact that Gas is a column and not a row, and in general, presents the data in the same row-and-column order that it is stored in the database.

SQL Queries

Let's look a bit more at the syntax of SQL, the language used to write queries in a database. There are really four basic SQL queries that we are going to use in this chapter, and that are common to manipulating data in a database. In summary, the SQL commands we are interested in are used to perform CRUD operations.

Like most terms presented in all caps, CRUD is an acronym, and means Create, Read, Update, and Delete. These are the four basic operations for data in a database. They are represented by four distinct SQL commands, detailed in Table 15-2.

Here is a quick explanation for the examples in Table 15-2:

- **INSERT** Add a row to the table Expenses, and set each of the columns in the table to the values expressed in the parentheses.
- **SELECT with WHERE** You have already seen the SELECT clause with a WHERE clause, so you know that this SQL statement returns a single row identified by the primary key—the Month column. Think of this statement as a refinement to Read—more like a Find or Find by primary key.
- **SELECT** When the SELECT clause does not have a WHERE clause, we are asking the database to return every row. Further, because we are using an asterisk (*) following the SELECT, we are asking for every column. Basically, it is a dump of the data shown in Table 15-1. Think of this statement as a Read All.

TABLE 15-2 Example SQL CRUD Commands

"CRUD"	SQL Command	Example SQL Query	Expressed in English
Create	INSERT	`INSERT INTO Expenses VALUES ('April', 231.21, 29.87, 97.00, 45.08)`	Add a new row (April) to expenses with the following values....
Read (or Find)	SELECT	`SELECT * FROM Expenses WHERE Month="February"`	Get me all of the columns in the Expenses table for February.
Read All	SELECT	`SELECT * FROM Expenses`	Get me all of the columns in the Expenses table.
Update	UPDATE	`UPDATE Expenses SET Phone=32.36, EatingOut=111.08 WHERE Month='February'`	Change my phone expense and EatingOut expense for February to....
Delete	DELETE	`DELETE FROM Expenses WHERE Month='April'`	Remove the row of expenses for April.

- **UPDATE** Change the data in the Phone and EatingOut cells to the new data provided for February.
- **DELETE** Remove a row altogether from the database where the Month is April.

Really, this is all the SQL you need to know for this chapter. There are many other SQL commands, but this is really the core set. If we need to go beyond this set of four commands in the chapter, we will cover them as they come up. Now, let's look at a more detailed database example that we will use as the example set of tables for this chapter, using the data requirements of a small bookseller, Bob's Books.

on the Job

SQL commands, like SELECT, INSERT, UPDATE, and so on, are case insensitive. So it is largely by convention (and one we will use in this chapter) to use all capital letters for SQL commands and key words, such as WHERE, FROM, LIKE, INTO, SET, and VALUES. SQL table names and column names, also called identifiers, can be case sensitive or case insensitive, depending upon the database. The example code shown in this chapter uses a case-insensitive database, so again, just for convention, we will use upper camel case, that is, the first letter of each noun capitalized and the rest in lowercase.

One final note about case—all databases preserve case when a string is delimited—that is, when they are enclosed in quotes. So a SQL clause that uses single or double quotation marks to delimit an identifier will preserve the case of the identifier.

Bob's Books, Our Test Database

In this section, we'll describe a small database with a few tables and a few rows of data. As we work through the various JDBC topics in this chapter, we'll work with this database.

Bob is a small bookseller who specializes in children's books. Bob has designed his data around the need to sell his books online using a database (which one doesn't really matter) and a Java application. Bob has decided to use the JDBC API to allow him to connect to a database and perform queries through a Java application.

To start, let's look at the organization of Bob's data. In a database, the organization and specification of the tables is called the database schema (Figure 15-1). Bob's is a relatively simple schema, and again, for the purposes of this chapter, we are going to concentrate on just four tables from Bob's schema.

FIGURE 15-1 Bob's BookSeller database schema

TABLE 15-3 Bob's Books Customer Table Sample Data

CustomerID	FirstName	LastName	Email	Phone
5000	John	Smith	john.smith@verizon.net	555-340-1230
5001	Mary	Johnson	mary.johnson@comcast.net	555-123-4567
5002	Bob	Collins	bob.collins@yahoo.com	555-012-3456
5003	Rebecca	Mayer	rebecca.mayer@gmail.com	555-205-8212
5006	Anthony	Clark	anthony.clark@gmail.com	555-256-1901
5007	Judy	Sousa	judy.sousa@verizon.net	555-751-1207
5008	Christopher	Patriquin	patriquinc@yahoo.com	555-316-1803
5009	Deborah	Smith	debsmith@comcast.net	555-256-3421
5010	Jennifer	McGinn	jmcginn@comcast.net	555-250-0918

This is a relatively simple schema that represents a part of the database for a small bookstore. In the schema shown, there is a table for Customer (Table 15-3). This table stores data about Bob's customers—a customer ID, first name and last name, an e-mail address, and phone number. Address and other information could be stored in another table.

The next three tables we will look at represent the data required to store information about books that Bob sells. Because a book is a more complex set of data than a customer, we need to use one table for information about books, one for information about authors, and a third to create a relationship between books and authors.

Suppose that you tried to store a book in a single table with a column for the ISBN (International Standard Book Number), title, and author name. For many books, this would be fine. But what happens if a book has two authors? Or three authors? Remember that one requirement for a database table is a unique primary key, so you can't simply repeat the ISBN in the table. In fact, having two rows with the same primary key will violate a key constraint in relational database design: The primary key of every row must be unique.

ISBN	Title	Author
ABCD	The Wonderful Life	Fred Smith
~~ABCD~~	~~The Wonderful Life~~	~~Tom Jones~~
1234	Some Enchanted Night	Paula Fredrick

TABLE 15-4

Bob's Books Sample Data for the "Books" Table

ISBN	Title	PubDate	Format	Price
142311339X	The Lost Hero (Heroes of Olympus, Book 1)	2010-10-12	Hardcover	10.95
0689852223	The House of the Scorpion	2002-01-01	Hardcover	16.95
0525423656	Crossed (Matched Trilogy, Book 2)	2011-11-01	Hardcover	12.95
1423153627	The Kane Chronicles Survival Guide	2012-03-01	Hardcover	13.95
0439371112	Howliday Inn	2001-11-01	Paperback	14.95
0439861306	The Lightning Thief	2006-03-12	Paperback	11.95
031673737X	How to Train Your Dragon	2010-02-01	Hardcover	10.95
0545078059	The White Giraffe	2008-05-01	Paperback	6.95
0803733428	The Last Leopard	2009-03-05	Hardcover	13.95
9780545236	Freaky Monday	2010-01-15	Paperback	12.95

Instead, there needs to be a way to have a separate table of books and authors and some way to link them together. Bob addressed this issue by placing Books in one table (Table 15-4) and Authors (Table 15-5) in another. The primary key for Books is the ISBN number, and therefore, each Book entry will be unique. For the Author table, Bob is creating a unique AuthorID for each author in the table.

TABLE 15-5

Bob's Books Author Table Sample Data for the "Authors" Table

AuthorID	FirstName	LastName
1000	Rick	Riordan
1001	Nancy	Farmer
1002	Ally	Condie
1003	Cressida	Cowell
1004	Lauren	St. John
1005	Eoin	Colfer
1006	Esther	Freisner
1007	Chris	D'lacey
1008	Mary	Rodgers
1009	Heather	Hatch

To tie Authors to Books and Books to Authors, Bob has created a third table called Books_by_Author. This is a unique table type in a relational database. This table is called a *join* table. In a join table, there are no primary keys—instead, all the columns represent data that can be used by other tables to create a relationship. These columns are referred to as foreign keys—they represent a primary key in another table. Looking at the last two rows of this table, you can see that the Book with the ISBN 9780545236 has two authors: author id 1008 (Mary Rodgers) and 1009 (Heather Hatch). Using this join table, we can combine the two sets of data without needing duplicate entries in either table. We'll return to the concept of a join table later in the chapter.

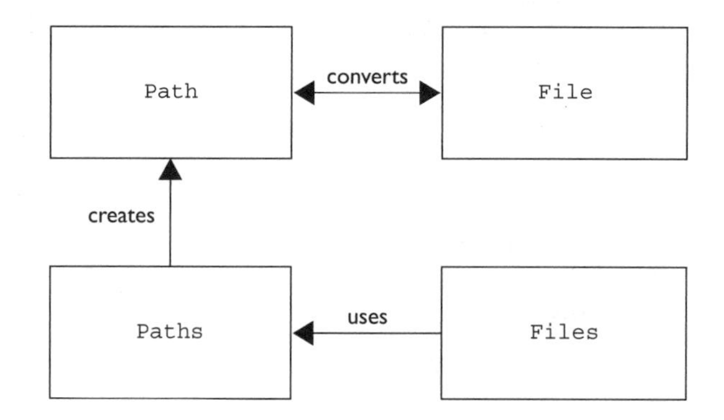

A complete Bob's Books database schema would include tables for publishers, addresses, stock, purchase orders, and other data that the store needs to run its business. But for our purposes, this part of the schema is sufficient. Using this schema, we can write SQL queries using the SQL CRUD commands you learned earlier.

To summarize, before looking at JDBC, you should now know about connections, statements, and result sets:

- A connection is how an application communicates with a database.
- A statement is a SQL query that is executed on the database.
- A result set is the data that is returned from a SELECT statement.

Having these concepts down, we can use Bob's Books simple schema to frame some common uses of the JDBC API to submit SQL queries and get results in a Java application.

CERTIFICATION OBJECTIVE

Core Interfaces of the JDBC API (OCP Objective 9.1)

9.1 Describe the interfaces that make up the core of the JDBC API (including the Driver, Connection, Statement, and ResultSet interfaces and their relationship to provider implementations).

As we mentioned in the previous section, the purpose of a relational database is really threefold:

- To provide storage for data in tables
- To provide a way to create relationships between the data—just as Bob did with the Authors, Books, and Books_by_Author tables
- To provide a language that can be used to get the data out, update the data, remove the data, and create new data

The purpose of JDBC is to provide an application programming interface (API) for Java developers to write Java applications that can access and manipulate relational databases and use SQL to perform CRUD operations.

Once you understand the basics of the JDBC API, you will be able to access a huge list of databases. One of the driving forces behind JDBC was to provide a standard way to access relational databases, but JDBC can also be used to access file systems and object-oriented data sources. The key is that the API provides an abstract view of a database connection, statements, and result sets. These concepts are represented in the API as interfaces in the `java.sql` package: `Connection`, `Statement`, and `ResultSet`, respectively. What these interfaces define are the *contracts* between you and the implementing class. In truth, you may not know (nor should you care) *how* the implementation class works. As long as the implementation class implements the interface you need, you are assured that the methods defined by the interface exist and you can invoke them.

The `java.sql.Connection` interface defines the contract for an object that represents the connection with a relational database system. Later, we will look at the methods of this contract, but for now, an instance of a `Connection` is what we need to communicate with the database. How the Connection interface is implemented is vendor dependent, and again, we don't need to worry so much about the how—as long as the vendor follows the contract, we are assured that the object that represents a Connection will allow us to work with a database connection.

The Statement interface provides an abstraction of the functionality needed to get a SQL statement to execute on a database, and a ResultSet interface is an abstraction functionality needed to process a result set (the table of data) that is returned from the SQL query when the query involves a SQL SELECT statement.

The implementation classes of Connection, Statement, ResultSet, and a number of other interfaces we will look at shortly are created by the vendor of the database we are using. The vendor understands their database product better than anyone else, so it makes sense that they create these classes. And, it allows the vendor to optimize or hide any special characteristics of their product. The collection of the implementation classes is called the JDBC driver. A JDBC driver (lowercase "d") is the collection of classes required to support the API, whereas Driver (uppercase "D") is one of the implementations required in a driver.

A JDBC driver is typically provided by the vendor in a JAR or ZIP file. The implementation classes of the driver must meet a minimum set of requirements in order to be JDBC compliant. The JDBC specification provides a list of the functionality that a vendor must support and what functionality a vendor may optionally support.

Here is a partial list of the requirements for a JDBC driver. For more details, please read the specification (JSR-221). Note that the details of implementing a JDBC driver are NOT on the exam.

- Fully implement the interfaces: java.sql.Driver, java.sql.DatabaseMetaData, java.sql.ResultSetMetaData.
- Implement the java.sql.Connection interface. (Note that some methods are optional depending upon the SQL version the database supports—more on SQL versions later in the chapter.)
- Implement the java.sql.Statement, java.sql.PreparedStatement.
- Implement the java.sql.CallableStatement interfaces if the database supports stored procedures. Again, more on this interface later in the chapter.
- Implement the java.sql.ResultSet interface.

CERTIFICATION OBJECTIVE

Connect to a Database Using DriverManager (OCP Objective 9.2)

9.2 Identify the components required to connect to a database using the DriverManager class (including the JDBC URL)

Not all of the types defined in the JDBC API are interfaces. One important class for JDBC is the `java.sql.DriverManager` class. This concrete class is used to interact with a JDBC driver and return instances of `Connection` objects to you. Conceptually, the way this works is by using a design pattern called `Factory`. Next, we'll look at `DriverManager` in more detail.

exam watch

Let's take this opportunity to see the Factory design pattern we discussed in Chapter 10 in use.

As you recall, in a factory pattern, a concrete class with static methods is used to create instances of objects that implement an interface. For example, suppose we wanted to create an instance of a `Vehicle` object:

```
public interface Vehicle {
  public void start();  // Methods we think all vehicles should
  public void stop();   // support.
}
```

We need an implementation of `Vehicle` in order to use this contract. So we design a `Car`:

```
package com.us.automobile;
public class Car implements Vehicle {
  public void start() { }  // ... do start things
  public void stop() { }   // ... do stop things
}
```

In order to use the `Car`, we could create one:

```
public class MyClass {
  public static void main(String args[]) {
    Vehicle ferrari =
      new com.us.automobile.Car(); // Create a Ferrari
    ferrari.start();               // Start the Ferrari
  }
}
```

However, here it would be better to use a factory—that way, we need not know anything about the actual implementation, and, as we will see later with `DriverManager`, we can use methods of the factory to dynamically determine which implementation to use at runtime.

```
public class MyClass {
  public static void main(String args[]) {
    Vehicle ferrari =
      CarFactory.getVehicle("Ferrari");         // Use a factory to
                                                 // create a Ferrari
    ferrari.start();
  }
}
```

The factory in this case could create a different car based on the string passed to the static `getVehicle()` method; something like this:

```
public class CarFactory {
  public static Vehicle getVehicle(String type) {
    // ... create an instance of an object that represents the
    // type of car passed as the argument
  }
}
```

`DriverManager` uses this factory pattern to "construct" an instance of a `Connection` object by passing a string to its `getConnection()` method.

The DriverManager Class

The `DriverManager` class is a concrete class in the JDBC API with static methods. You will recall that static or class methods can be invoked by other classes using the class name. One of those methods is `getConnection()`, which we look at next.

The `DriverManager` class is so named because it manages which JDBC driver implementation you get when you request an instance of a `Connection` through the `getConnection()` method.

There are several overloaded `getConnection` methods, but they all share one common parameter: a String URL. One pattern for `getConnection` is

```
DriverManager.getConnection(String url, String username, String password);
```

For example:

```
String url
    = "jdbc:derby://localhost:1521/BookSellerDB";    // JDBC URL
String user = "bookguy";  // BookSellerDB user name
String pwd = "$3lleR";    // BookSellerDB password
try {
  Connection conn
    = DriverManager.getConnection(url, user, pwd);  // Get an
                                                    // instance of a
                                                    // Connection
                                                    // object
} catch (SQLException se) { }
```

In this example, we are creating a connection to a Derby database, on a network, at a localhost address (on the local machine), at port number 1521, to a database called `"BookSellerDB"`, and we are using the credentials, `"bookguy"` as the user id, and `"$3lleR"` as the password. Don't worry too much about the syntax of the URL right now—we'll cover that soon.

on the job

It's a horrible idea to hard-code a username and password in the `getConnection()` method. Obviously, anyone reading the code would then know the username and password to the database. A more secure way to handle database credentials would be to separate the code that produces the credentials from the code that makes the connection. So in some other class, you would use some type of authentication and authorization code to produce a set of credentials to allow access to the database.

For simplicity in the examples in the chapter, we'll hard-code the username and password, but just keep in mind that on the job, this is not a best practice.

When you invoke the `DriverManager`'s `getConnection()` method, you are asking the `DriverManager` to try passing the first string in the statement, the driver URL, along with the username and password to each of the driver classes registered with the `DriverManager` in turn. If one of the driver classes recognizes the URL string, and the username and password are accepted, the driver returns an instance of a `Connection` object. If, however, the URL is incorrect, or the username and/or password are not correct, then the method will throw a `SQLException`. We'll spend some time looking at `SQLException` later in this chapter.

How JDBC Drivers Register with the DriverManager

Because this part of the JDBC process is important to understand, and it involves a little Java magic, let's spend some time diagramming how driver classes become "registered" with the `DriverManager`, as shown in Figure 15-2.

First, one or more JDBC drivers, in a JAR or ZIP file, are included in the classpath of your application. The `DriverManager` class uses a service provider mechanism to search the classpath for any JAR or ZIP files that contain a file named `java.sql.Driver` in the META-INF/services folder of the driver jar or zip. This is simply a text file that contains the full name of the class that the vendor used to implement the `jdbc.sql.Driver` interface. For example, for a Derby driver, the full name is `org.apache.derby.jdbc.ClientDriver`.

The `DriverManager` will then attempt to load the class it found in the `java.sql.Driver` file using the class loader:

```
Class.forName("org.apache.derby.jdbc.ClientDriver");
```

When the driver class is loaded, its static initialization block is executed. Per the JDBC specification, one of the first activities of a driver instance is to "self-register" with the `DriverManager` class by invoking a static method on `DriverManager`. The code (minus error handling) looks something like this:

```
public class ClientDriver implements java.sql.Driver{
  static {
    ClientDriver driver = new ClientDriver();
    DriverManager.registerDriver(driver);
  }
  //...
}
```

This registers (stores) an instance of the `Driver` class into the `DriverManager`.

Now, when your application invokes the `DriverManager.getConnection()` method and passes a JDBC URL, username, and password to the method, the `DriverManager` simply invokes the `connect()` method on the registered `Driver`. If the connection was successful, the method returns a `Connection` object instance to `DriverManager`, which, in turn, passes that back to you.

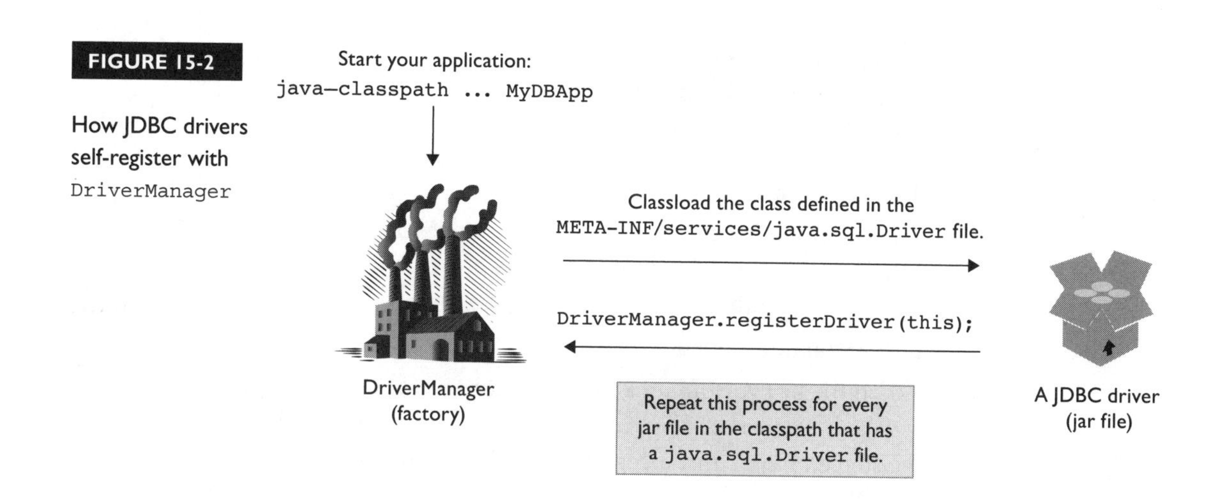
Start your application:
java—classpath ... MyDBApp
Classload the class defined in the
META-INF/services/java.sql.Driver file.
DriverManager.registerDriver(this);
DriverManager
(factory)
Repeat this process for every
jar file in the classpath that has
a java.sql.Driver file.
A JDBC driver
(jar file)

FIGURE 15-2 How JDBC drivers self-register with `DriverManager`

If there is more than one registered driver, the `DriverManager` calls each of the drivers in turn and attempts to get a `Connection` object from them, as shown in Figure 15-3.

The first driver that recognizes the JDBC URL and successfully creates a connection using the username and password will return an instance of a `Connection` object. If

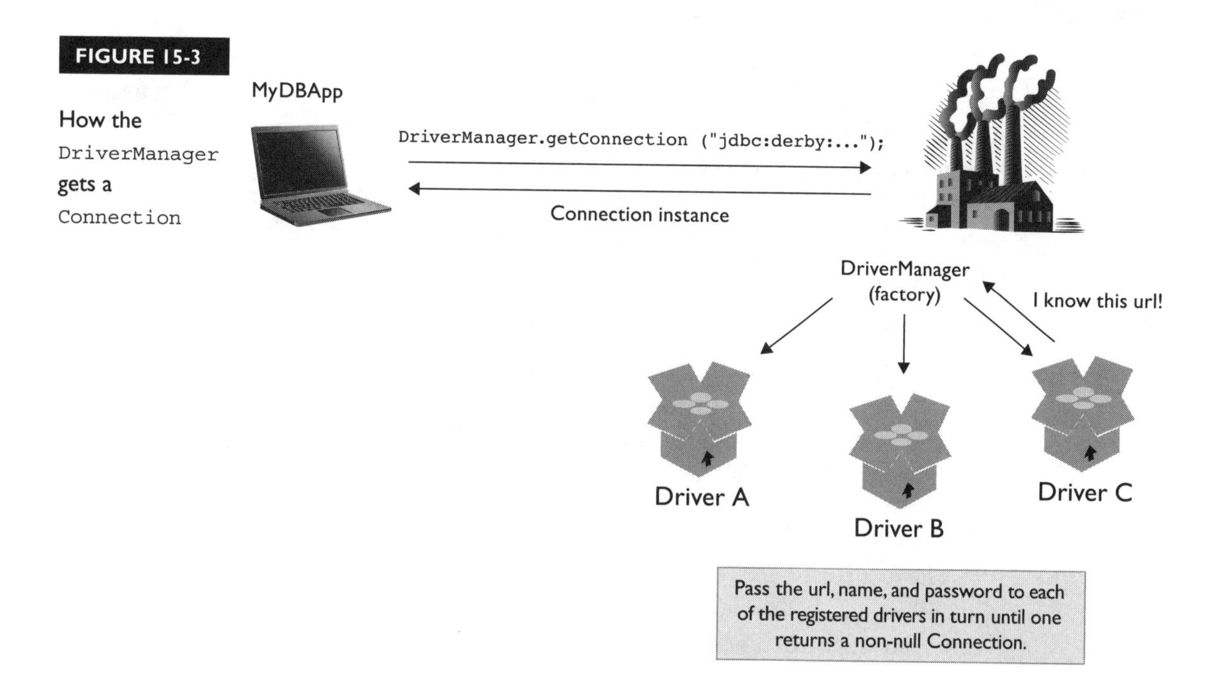
MyDBApp
DriverManager.getConnection ("jdbc:derby:...");
Connection instance
DriverManager
(factory)
I know this url!
Driver A
Driver B
Driver C
Pass the url, name, and password to each
of the registered drivers in turn until one
returns a non-null Connection.

FIGURE 15-3 How the `DriverManager` gets a `Connection`

no drivers recognize the URL, username, and password combination, or if there are no registered drivers, then a `SQLException` is thrown instead.

To summarize:

- The JVM loads the `DriverManager` class, a concrete class in the JDBC API.
- The `DriverManager` class loads any instances of classes it finds in the META-INF/services/java.sql.Driver file of JAR/ZIP files on the classpath.
- Driver classes call `DriverManager.register(this)` to self-register with the `DriverManager`.
- When the `DriverManager.getConnection(String url)` method is invoked, `DriverManager` invokes the `connect()` method of each of these registered `Driver` instances with the URL string.
- The first `Driver` that successfully creates a connection with the URL returns an instance of a `Connection` object to the `DriverManager.getConnection` method invocation.

Let's look at the JDBC URL syntax next.

The JDBC URL

The JDBC URL is what is used to determine which driver implementation to use for a given `Connection`. Think of the JDBC URL (uniform resource locator) as a way to narrow down the universe of possible drivers to one specific connection. For example, suppose you need to send a package to someone. In order to narrow the universe of possible addresses down to a single unique location, you would have to identify the country, the state, the city, the street, and perhaps a house or address number on your package:

```
USA:California://SanJose:FirstStreet/15
```

This string indicates that the address you want is in the United States, California State, San Jose city, First Street, number 15.

JDBC URLs follow this same idea. To access Bob's Books, we might write the URL like this:

```
jdbc:derby://localhost:1521/BookSellerDB
```

The first part, `jdbc`, simply identifies that this is a JDBC URL (versus HTTP or something else). The second part indicates that driver vendor is `derby` driver. The third part indicates that the database is on the `localhost` of this machine (IP address

127.0.0.1), at port `1521`, and the final part indicates that we are interested in the `BookSellerDB` database.

Just like street addresses, the reason we need this string is because JDBC was designed to work with multiple databases at once. Each of the JDBC database drivers will have a different URL, so we need to be able to pass the JDBC URL string to the `DriverManager` and ensure that the `Connection` returned was for the intended database instance.

Unfortunately, other than a requirement that the JDBC URL begin with "jdbc," there is very little standard about a JDBC URL. Vendors may modify the URL to define characteristics for a particular driver implementation. The format of the JDBC URL is

```
jdbc:<subprotocol>:<subname>
```

In general, subprotocol is the vendor name; for example:

```
jdbc:derby
jdbc:mysql
jdbc:oracle
```

The subname field is where things get a bit more vendor specific. Some vendors use the subname to identify the hostname and port, followed by a database name. For example:

```
jdbc:derby://localhost:1521/MyDB
jdbc:mysql://localhost:3306/MyDB
```

Other vendors may use the subname to identify additional context information about the driver. For example:

```
jdbc:oracle:thin:@//localhost:1527/MyDB
```

In any case, it is best to consult the documentation for your specific database vendor's JDBC driver to determine the syntax of the URL.

There are two ways to establish a connection in JDBC. The first way is using one of the few concrete classes in the `java.sql` package, `DriverManager`. The `java.sql.DriverManager` class has been a part of the JDBC implementation since the beginning, and is the easiest way to obtain a connection from a Java SE application. The alternative way is with an instance of a class that implements `javax.sql.DataSource`, introduced in JDBC 2.0.

Since a `DataSource` instance is typically obtained through a Java Naming and Directory Interface (JNDI) lookup, it is more often used in Java applications where there is a container that supports JNDI—for example, a Java EE application server. For the purposes of this chapter (and because `DataSource` is not on the exam), we'll focus on using `DriverManager` to obtain a connection, but in the end, both ways serve to give you an instance of a `Connection` object.

To summarize, `DriverManager` is on the exam and `DataSource` is not.

JDBC Driver Implementation Versions

We talked about how the `DriverManager` will scan the classpath for JAR files that contain the `META-INF/services/java.sql.Driver` file and use a classloader to load those drivers. This feature was introduced in the JDBC 4.0 specification. Prior to that, JDBC drivers were loaded manually by the application.

If you are using a JDBC driver that is an earlier version, say, a JDBC 3.0 driver, then you must explicitly load the class provided by the database vendor that implements the `java.sql.Driver` interface. Typically, the database vendor's documentation would tell you what the driver class is. For example, if our Apache Derby JDBC driver were a 3.0 driver, you would manually load the `Driver` implementation class before calling the `getConnection()` method:

```
Class.forName("org.apache.derby.jdbc.ClientDriver");  // Class loads
                                                      // ClientDriver
try {
  Connection conn
    = DriverManager.getConnection(url, user, pwd);
```

Note that using the `Class.forName()` method is compatible with both JDBC 3.0 and JDBC 4.0 drivers. It is simply not needed when the driver supports 4.0.

Here is a quick summary of what we have discussed so far:

- Before you can start working with JDBC, creating queries and getting results, you must first establish a connection.
- In order to establish a connection, you must have a JDBC driver.
- If your JDBC driver is a JDBC 3.0 driver, then you are required to explicitly load the driver in your code using `Class.forName()` and the fully qualified path of the `Driver` implementation class.
- If your JDBC driver is a JDBC 4.0 driver, then simply include the driver (jar or zip) in the classpath.

exam watch

Although the certification exam covers up through Java SE 7, the exam developers felt that since this was the first time that JDBC was being covered by the Programmer exam, they ought to include some questions about obtaining a connection using both JDBC 3.0 and JDBC 4.0 drivers. So keep in mind that for JDBC 3.0 drivers (and earlier), you are responsible for loading the class using the static `forName()` method from `java.lang.Class`.

CERTIFICATION OBJECTIVE

Submit Queries and Read Results from the Database (OCP Objective 9.3)

9.3 Submit queries and read results from the database (including creating statements; returning result sets; iterating through the results; and properly closing result sets, statements, and connections).

In this section, we'll explore the JDBC API in much greater detail. We will start by looking at a simple example using the `Connection`, `Statement`, and `ResultSet` interfaces to pull together what we've learned so far in this chapter. Then we'll do a deep dive into `Statements` and `ResultSets`.

All of Bob's Customers

Probably one of the most used SQL queries is SELECT * FROM <Table name>, which is used to print out or see all of the records in a table. Assume that we have a Java DB (Derby) database populated with data from Bob's Books. To query the database and return all of the Customers in the database, we would write something like the example shown next.

Note that to make the code listing a little shorter, going forward, we will use `out.println` instead of `System.out.println`. Just assume that means that we have included a static import statement, like the one at the top of this example:

```
import static java.lang.System.*;  // Static import of the
                                   // System class methods.
                                   // Now we can use just 'out'
                                   // instead of System.out.
String url = "jdbc:derby://localhost:1521/BookSellerDB";
String user = "bookguy";
String pwd = "$3lleR";
try {
  Connection conn =
    DriverManager.getConnection(url, user, pwd); // Get Connection
  Statement stmt = conn.createStatement();       // Create Statement
  String query = "SELECT * FROM Customer";
  ResultSet rs = stmt.executeQuery(query);       // Execute Query
  while (rs.next()) {                            // Process Results
    out.print(rs.getInt("CustomerID") + "  ");   // Print Columns
    out.print(rs.getString("FirstName") + "  ");
    out.print(rs.getString("LastName") + "  ");
    out.print(rs.getString("EMail") + "  ");
    out.println(rs.getString("Phone"));
  }
} catch (SQLException se) { }                    // Catch SQLException
```

Again, we'll dive into all of the parts of this example in greater detail, but here is what is happening:

- **Get connection** We are creating a `Connection` object instance using the information we need to access Bob's Books Database (stored on a Java DB Relational database, `BookSellerDB`, and accessed via the credentials `"bookguy"` with a password of `"$3lleR"`).
- **Create statement** We are using the `Connection` to create a `Statement` object. The `Statement` object handles passing `Strings` to the database as queries for the database to execute.
- **Execute query** We are executing the query string on the database and returning a `ResultSet` object.
- **Process results** We are iterating through the result set rows—each call to `next()` moves us to the next row of results.
- **Print columns** We are getting the values of the columns in the current result set row and printing them to standard out.
- **Catch `SQLException`** All of the JDBC API method invocations throw `SQLException`. A `SQLException` can be thrown when a method is used improperly, or if the database is no longer responding. For example, a `SQLException` is thrown if the JDBC URL, username, or password is invalid.

Or we attempted to query a table that does not exist. Or the database is no longer reachable because the network went down or the database went offline. We will look at `SQLException` in greater detail later in the chapter.

The output of the previous code will look something like this:

```
5000  John  Smith  John.Smith@comcast.net  555-340-1230
5001  Mary  Johnson  mary.johnson@comcast.net  555-123-4567
5002  Bob  Collins  bob.collins@yahoo.com  555-012-3456
5003  Rebecca  Mayer  rebecca.mayer@gmail.com  555-205-8212
5006  Anthony  Clark  anthony.clark@gmail.com  555-256-1901
5007  Judy  Sousa  judy.sousa@verizon.net  555-751-1207
5008  Christopher  Patriquin  patriquinc@yahoo.com  555-316-1803
5009  Deborah  Smith  debsmith@comcast.net  555-256-3421
5010 Jennifer McGinn  jmcginn@comcast.net  555-250-0918
```

We'll take a detailed look at the `Statement` and `ResultSet` interfaces and methods in the next two sections.

Statements

Once we have successfully connected to a database, the fun can really start. From a `Connection` object, we can create an instance of a `Statement` object (or, to be precise, using the `Connection` instance we received from the `DriverManager`, we can get an instance of an object that implements the `Statement` interface). For example:

```
String url = "jdbc:derby://localhost:1521/BookSellerDB";
String user = "bookguy";
String pwd = "$3lleR";
try {
  Connection conn = DriverManager.getConnection(url, user, pwd);
  Statement stmt = conn.createStatement();
  // do stuff with SQL statements
} catch (SQLException se) { }
```

The primary purpose of a `Statement` is to execute a SQL statement using a method and return some type of result. There are several forms of `Statement` methods: those that return a result set, and those that return an integer status. The most commonly used `Statement` method performs a SQL query that returns some data, like the SELECT call we used earlier to fetch all the `Customer` table rows.

Constructing and Using Statements

To start, let's look at the base `Statement`, which is used to execute a static SQL query and return a result. You'll recall that we get a `Statement` from a `Connection` and then use the `Statement` object to execute a SQL statement, like a query on the database. For example:

```
Connection conn = DriverManager.getConnection(url, user, pwd);
Statement stmt = conn.createStatement();
ResultSet rs = stmt.executeQuery("SELECT * FROM Customer");
```

Because not all SQL statements return results, the `Statement` object provides several different methods to execute SQL commands. Some SQL commands do not return a result set, but instead return an integer status. For example, SQL INSERT, UPDATE, and DELETE commands, or any of the SQL Data Definition Language (DDL) statements, like CREATE TABLE, return either the number of rows affected by the query or 0.

Let's look at each of the execute methods in detail.

public ResultSet executeQuery(String sql) throws SQLException This is the most commonly executed `Statement` method. This method is used when we know that we want to return results—we are querying the database for one or more rows of data. For example:

```
ResultSet rs = stmt.executeQuery("SELECT * from Customer");
```

Assuming there is data in the `Customer` table, this statement should return all of the rows from the `Customer` table into a `ResultSet` object—we'll look at `ResultSet` in the next section. Notice that the method declaration includes "throws `SQLException`." This means that this method must be called in a `try-catch` block, or must be called in a method that also throws `SQLException`. Again, one reason that these methods all throw `SQLException` is that a connection to the database is likely **to a database on a network**. As with all things on the network, availability is not guaranteed, so one possible reason for `SQLException` is the lack of availability of the database itself.

public int executeUpdate(String sql) throws SQLException This method is used for a SQL operation that affects one or more rows and does not return results—for example, SQL INSERT, UPDATE, DELETE, and DDL queries. These statements do not return results, but do return a count of the number of rows affected by the SQL query. For example, here is an example method invocation where we want to update the Book table, increasing the price of every book that is currently priced less than 8.95 and is a hardcover book:

```
String q = "UPDATE Book SET UnitPrice=8.95
          WHERE UnitPrice < 8.95 AND Format='Hardcover'";
int numRows = stmt.executeUpdate(q);
```

When this query executes, we are expecting some number of rows will be affected. The integer that returns is the number of rows that were updated.

Note that this `Statement` method can also be used to execute SQL queries that do not return a row count, such as CREATE TABLE or DROP TABLE and other DDL queries. For DDL queries, the return value is 0.

public boolean execute(String sql) throws SQLException This method is used when you are not sure what the result will be—perhaps the query will return a result set, and perhaps not. This method can be used to execute a query whose type may not be known until runtime—for example, one constructed in code. The return value is true if the query resulted in a result set and false if the query resulted in an update count or no results.

However, more often, this method is used when invoking a stored procedure (using the `CallableStatement`, which we'll talk about later in the chapter). A stored procedure can return a single result set or row count, or multiple result sets and row counts, so this method was designed to handle what happens when a single database invocation produces more than one result set or row count.

You might also use this method if you wrote an application to test queries—something that reads a `String` from the command line and then runs that `String` against the database as a query. For example:

```
ResultSet rs;
int numRows;
boolean status = stmt.execute("");  // True if there is a ResultSet
if (status) {                        // True
  rs = stmt.getResultSet();          // Get the ResultSet
  // Process the result set...
} else {                             // False
  numRows = stmt.getUpdateCount();   // Get the update count
  if (numRows == -1) {               // If -1, there are no results
    out.println("No results");
  } else {                           // else, print the number of
                                     // rows affected
    out.println(numRows + " rows affected.");
  }
}
```

Because this statement may return a result set or may simply return an integer row count, there are two additional statement commands you can use to get the results or the count based on whether the execute method returned true (there is a result set) or false (there is an update count or there was no result). The `getResultSet()` is used to retrieve results when the execute method returns true, and the `getUpdateCount()` is used to retrieve the count when the execute method returns false. Let's look at these methods next.

on the job

It is generally a very bad idea to allow a user to enter a query string directly in an input field, or allow a user to pass a string to construct a query directly. The reason is that if a user can construct a query or even include a freeform string into a query, they can use the query to return more data than you intended or to alter the database table permissions.

For example, assume that we have a query where the user enters their e-mail address and the string the user enters is inserted directly to the query:

```
String s = System.console().readLine("Enter your e-mail address: ");
ResultSet rs = stmt.executeQuery("SELECT * FROM Customer
                                  WHERE EMail='" + s + "'");
```

The user of this code could enter a string like this:

```
tom@trouble.com' OR 'x'='x
```

The resulting query executed by the database becomes:

```
SELECT * FROM Customer WHERE Email='tom@trouble.com' OR 'x'='x'
```

Because the OR statement will always return `true`***, the result is that the query will return ALL of the customer rows, effectively the same as the query:***

```
SELECT * FROM Customer
```

And now this user of your code has a list of the e-mail addresses of every customer in the database.

This type of attack is called a SQL injection attack. It is easy to prevent by carefully sanitizing any string input used in a query to the database and/or by using one of the other `Statement` ***types,*** `PreparedStatement` ***and*** `CallableStatement`***. Despite how easy it is to prevent, it happens frequently, even to large, experienced companies like Yahoo!.***

public ResultSet getResultSet() throws SQLException If the boolean value from the `execute()` method returns true, then there is a result set. To get the result set, as shown earlier, call the `getResultSet()` method on the `Statement` object. Then you can process the `ResultSet` object (which we will cover in the next section). This method is basically foolproof—if, in fact, there are no results, the method will return a null.

```
ResultSet rs = stmt.getResultSet();
```

public int getUpdateCount() throws SQLException If the boolean value from the `execute()` method returns false, then there is a row count, and this method will return the number of rows affected. A return value of –1 indicates that there are no results.

```
int numRows = stmt.getUpdateCount();
if (numRows == -1) {
  out.println("No results");
} else {
  out.println(numRows + " rows affected.");
}
```

Table 15-6 summarizes the `Statement` methods we just covered.

TABLE 15-6 Important `Statement` Methods

Method (Each Throws SQLException)	Description
`ResultSet executeQuery(String sql)`	Execute a SQL query and return a `ResultSet` object, i.e., SELECT commands.
`int executeUpdate(String sql)`	Execute a SQL query that will only modify a number of rows, i.e., INSERT, DELETE, or UPDATE commands.
`boolean execute(String sql)`	Execute a SQL query that may return a result set OR modify a number of rows (or do neither). The method will return true if there is a result set, or false if there may be a row count of affected rows.
`ResultSet getResultSet()`	If the return value from the `execute()` method was true, you can use this method to retrieve the result set from the query.
`int getUpdateCount()`	If the return value from the `execute()` method was false, you can use this method to get the number of rows affected by the SQL command.

ResultSets

When a query returns a result set, an instance of a class that implements the `ResultSet` interface is returned. The `ResultSet` object represents the results of the query—all of the data in each row on a per-column basis. Again, as a reminder, *how* data in a `ResultSet` are stored is entirely up to the JDBC driver vendor. It is possible that the JDBC driver caches the entire set of results in memory all at once, or that it uses internal buffers and gets only a few rows at a time. From your point of view as the user of the data, it really doesn't matter much. Using the methods defined in the `ResultSet` interface, you can read and manipulate the data, and that's all that matters.

One important thing to keep in mind is that a `ResultSet` is a *copy* of the data from the database from the instance in time when the query was executed. Unless you are the only person using the database, you need to always assume that the underlying database table or tables that the `ResultSet` came from could be changed by some other user or application.

Because `ResultSet` is such a comprehensive part of the JDBC API, we are going to tackle it in sections. Table 15-7 summarizes each section so you can reference these later.

TABLE 15-7 `ResultSet` Sections

Section Title	Description
"Moving Forward in a ResultSet"	How to access each "row" of the result of a query.
"Reading Data from a ResultSet"	How to use `ResultSet` methods to access the individual columns of each "row" in the result set.
"Getting Information about a ResultSet"	How to use a `ResultSetMetaData` object to retrieve information about the result set: the number of columns returned in the results, the names of each column, and the Java type of each column.
"Printing a Report"	How to use the `ResultSetMetaData` methods to print a nicely formatted set of results to the console.
"Moving Around in ResultSets"	How to change the cursor type and concurrency settings on a `Statement` object to create a `ResultSet` that allows the row cursor to be positioned and allows the data to be modified.
"Updating ResultSets"	How to use the concurrency settings on a `Statement` object to create a `ResultSet` that allows you to update the results returned and later synchronize those results with the database.
"Inserting New Rows into a ResultSet"	How to manipulate a `ResultSet` further by deleting and inserting rows.
"Getting Information about a Database Using DatabaseMetaData"	How to use the `DatabaseMetaData` object to retrieve information about a database.

Moving Forward in a ResultSet

The best way to think of a `ResultSet` object is visually. Assume that in our BookSellerDB database we have several customers whose last name begins with the letter "C." We could create a query to return those rows "like" this:

```
String query = "SELECT FirstName, LastName, EMail from Customer
                WHERE LastName LIKE 'C%'";
```

The SQL operator LIKE treats the string that follows as a pattern to match, where the `%` indicates a wildcard. So, `LastName LIKE 'C%'` means "any `LastName` with a `C`, followed by any other character(s)."

When we execute this query using the `executeQuery()` method, the `ResultSet` returned will contain the `FirstName`, `LastName`, and `EMail` columns where the customer's `LastName` starts with the capital letter "C":

```
ResultSet rs = stmt.executeQuery (query);
```

The `ResultSet` object returned contains the data from the query as shown in Figure 15-4.

Note in Figure 15-4 that the `ResultSet` object maintains a cursor, or a pointer, to the current row of the results. When the `ResultSet` object is first returned from the query, the cursor is not yet pointing to a row of results—the cursor is pointing above the first row. In order to get the results of the table, you must always call the `next()` method on the `ResultSet` object to move the cursor forward to the first row of data. By default, a `ResultSet` object is read-only (the data in the rows cannot

FIGURE 15-4 A `ResultSet` after the `executeQuery`

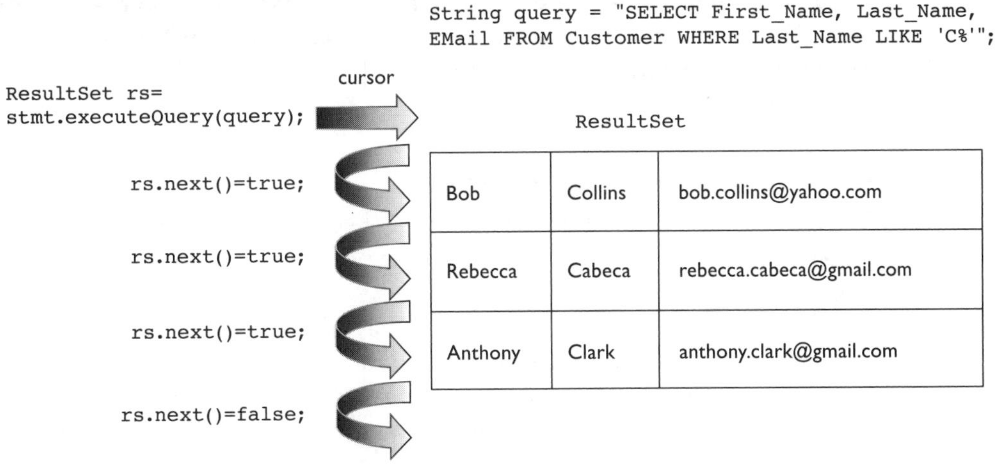

```
String query = "SELECT First_Name, Last_Name,
EMail FROM Customer WHERE Last_Name LIKE 'C%'";
```

cursor

```
ResultSet rs=
stmt.executeQuery(query);
rs.next()=true;
rs.next()=true;
rs.next()=true;
rs.next()=false;
```

ResultSet

Bob	Collins	bob.collins@yahoo.com
Rebecca	Cabeca	rebecca.cabeca@gmail.com
Anthony	Clark	anthony.clark@gmail.com

be updated), and you can only move the cursor forward. We'll look at how to change this behavior a little later on.

So the first method you will need to know for `ResultSet` is the `next()` method.

public boolean next() The `next()` method moves the cursor forward one row and returns true if the cursor now points to a row of data in the `ResultSet`. If the cursor points beyond the last row of data as a result of the `next()` method (or if the `ResultSet` contains no rows), the return value is false.

So in order to read the three rows of data in the table shown in Figure 15-4, we need to call the `next()` method, read the row of data, and then call `next()` again twice more. When the `next()` method is invoked the fourth time, the method will return false. The easiest way to read all of the rows from first to last is in a `while` loop:

```
String query = "SELECT FirstName, LastName, EMail FROM Customer
               WHERE LastName LIKE 'C%'";
ResultSet rs = stmt.executeQuery(query);
while (rs.next()) {  // Move the cursor from the current position
                     // to the next row of data - return true if the
                     // next row is valid data and false if the
                     // cursor has moved past the last row
  // ...
}
```

exam watch

Because the cursor is such a fundamental concept in JDBC, the exam will test you on the status of the cursor in a `ResultSet`. As long as you keep in mind that you must call the `next()` method before processing even one row of data in a `ResultSet`, then you'll be fine. Maybe you could use a memory device, like this one: "When getting results, don't vex, always call next!" Okay, maybe not.

Reading Data from a ResultSet

Moving the cursor forward through the `ResultSet` is just the start of reading data from the results of the query. Let's look at the two ways to get the data from each row in a result set.

When a `ResultSet` is returned, and you have dutifully called `next()` to move the cursor to the first actual row of data, you can now read the data in each column of the current row. As illustrated in Figure 15-4, a result set from a database query is like a table or a spreadsheet. Each row contains (typically) one or more columns, and the data in each column is one of the SQL data types. In order to bring the data from each column into your Java application, you must use a `ResultSet` method to retrieve each of the SQL column values into an appropriate Java type. So SQL INTEGER, for example, can be read as a Java int primitive, SQL VARCHAR can be read as a Java String, SQL DATE can be read as a `java.sql.Date` object, and so on. `ResultSet` defines several other types as well, but whether or not the database or the driver supports all of the types defined by the specification depends on the database vendor. For the exam, we recommend you focus on the most common SQL data types and the `ResultSet` methods shown in Table 15-7.

on the Job

SQL has been around for a long time. The first formalized, American National Standards Institute (ANSI)–approved version was adopted in 1986 (SQL-86). The next major revision was in 1992, SQL-92, which is widely considered the "base" release for every database. SQL-92 defined a number of new data types, including DATE, TIME, TIMESTAMP, BIT, and VARCHAR strings. SQL-92 has multiple levels; each level adds a bit more functionality to the previous level. JDBC drivers recognize three ANSI SQL-92 levels: Entry, Intermediate, and Full.

SQL-1999, also known as SQL-3, added LARGE OBJECT types, including BINARY LARGE OBJECT (BLOB) and CHARACTER LARGE OBJECT (CLOB). SQL-1999 also introduced the BOOLEAN type and a composite type, ARRAY and ROW, to store collections directly into the database. In addition, SQL-1999 added a number of features to SQL, including triggers, regular expressions, and procedural and flow control.

SQL-2003 introduced XML to the database, and importantly, added columns with auto-generated values, including columns that support identity, like the primary key and foreign key columns. Believe or not, other standards have been proposed, including SQL-2006, SQL-2008, and SQL-2011.

The reason this matters is because the JDBC specification has attempted to be consistent with features from the most widely adopted specification at the time. Thus, JDBC 3.0 supports SQL-92 and a part of the SQL-1999 specification, and JDBC 4.0 supports parts of the SQL-2003 specification. In this chapter, we'll try to stick to the most widely used SQL-92 features and the most commonly supported SQL-1999 features that JDBC also supports.

One way to read the column data is by using the names of the columns themselves as string values. For example, using the column names from Bob's Book table

(Table 15-4), in these `ResultSet` methods, the `String` name of the column from the Book table is passed to the method to read the column data type:

```
String query = "SELECT Title, PubDate, UnitPrice from Book";
ResultSet rs = stmt.executeQuery(query);
while (rs.next()) {
    String title = rs.getString("Title");     // Read the data in the
                                              // column named "Title"
                                              // into a String
    Date PubDate = rs.getDate("PubDate");     // Read the data in the
                                              // "PubDate" column into
                                              // a Date object
    float price = rs.getFloat("Price");       // Read the data in the
                                              // column "Price"
                                              // into a float
    // ....
}
```

Note that although here the column names were retrieved from the `ResultSet` row in the order they were requested in the SQL query, they could have been processed in any order.

`ResultSet` also provides an overloaded method that takes an integer index value for each of the SQL types. This value is the integer position of the column in the result set, numbered from 1 to the number of columns returned. So we could write the same statements earlier like this:

```
String title = rs.getString(1); // Title is first column
Date PubDate = rs.getDate(2);   // PubDate is second column
float price = rs.getFloat(3);   // Price is third column
```

Using the positional methods shown earlier, the order of the column in the `ResultSet` does matter. In our query, Title is in position 1, PubDate is in position 2, and Price is in position 3.

exam watch

Remember: Column indexes start with 1.

It is important to keep in mind that when you are accessing columns using integer index values, the column indexes always start with 1, not 0 as in traditional arrays. If you attempt to access a column with an index of less than 1 or greater than the number of columns returned, a `SQLException` will be thrown. You can get the number of columns returned in a `ResultSet` through the result set's metadata object. See the section on `ResultSetMetaData` to learn more.

on the Job

What the database stores as a type, the SQL type, and what JDBC returns as a type are often two different things. It is important to understand that the JDBC specification provides a set of standard mappings—the best match between what the database provides as a type and the Java type a programmer should use with that type. Rather than repeating what is in the specification, we encourage you to look at Appendix B of the JDBC (JSR-221) specification.

The most commonly used `ResultSet get` methods are listed next. Let's look at these methods in detail.

public boolean getBoolean(String columnLabel) This method retrieves the value of the named column in the `ResultSet` as a Java boolean. Boolean values are rarely returned in SQL queries, and some databases may not support a SQL BOOLEAN type, so check with your database vendor. In this contrived example here, we are returning employment status:

```
if (rs.getBoolean("CURR_EMPLOYEE")) {
    // Now process the remaining columns
}
```

public double getDouble(String columnLabel) This method retrieves the value of the column as a Java double. This method is recommended for returning the value stored in the database as SQL DOUBLE and SQL FLOAT types.

```
double cartTotal = rs.getDouble("CartTotal");
```

public int getInt(String columnLabel) This method retrieves the value of the column as a Java int. Integers are often a good choice for primary keys. This method is recommended for returning values stored in the database as SQL INTEGER types.

```
int authorID = rs.getInt("AuthorID");
```

public float getFloat(String columnLabel) This method retrieves the value of the column as a Java float. It is recommended for SQL REAL types.

```
float price = rs.getFloat("UnitPrice");
```

public long getLong(String columnLabel) This method retrieves the value of the column as a Java long. It is recommended for SQL BIGINT types.

```
long socialSecurityNumber = rs.get("SocSecNum");
```

public java.sql.Date getDate(String columnLabel) This method retrieves the value of the column as a Java `Date` object. Note that `java.sql.Date` extends `java.util.Date`. The most interesting difference between the two is that the `toString()` method of `java.sql.Date` returns a date string in the form: "yyyy mm dd." This method is recommended for SQL DATE types.

```
java.sql.Date pubDate = rs.getDate("PubDate");
```

public java.lang.String getString(String columnLabel) This method retrieves the value of the column as a Java `String` object. It is good for reading SQL columns with CHAR, VARCHAR, and LONGVARCHAR types.

```
String lastName = rs.getString("LastName");
```

public java.sql.Time getTime(String columnLabel) This method retrieves the value of the column as a Java `Time` object. Like `java.sql.Date`, this class extends `java.util.Date`, and its `toString()` method returns a time string in the form: "hh:mm:ss." TIME is the SQL type that this method is designed to read.

```
java.sql.Time time = rs.getString("FinishTime");
```

public java.sql.Timestamp getTimestamp(String columnLabel) This method retrieves the value of the column as a `Timestamp` object. Its `toString()` method formats the result in the form: yyyy-mm-dd hh:mm:ss.fffffffff, where fffffffff is nanoseconds. This method is recommended for reading SQL TIMESTAMP types.

```
java.sql.Timestamp timestamp = rs.getTimestamp("ClockInTime");
```

public java.lang.Object getObject(String columnLabel) This method retrieves the value of the column as a Java `Object`. It can be used as a general-purpose method for reading data in a column. This method works by reading the value returned as the appropriate Java wrapper class for the type and returning that as a Java `Object` object. So, for example, reading an integer (SQL INTEGER type) using this method returns an object that is a `java.lang.Integer` type. We can use `instanceof` to check for an `Integer` and get the `int` value:

```
Object o = rs.getObject("AuthorID");
if (o instanceof java.lang.Integer) {
    int id = ((Integer)o).intValue();
}
```

Table 15-8 lists the most commonly used methods to retrieve specific data from a `ResultSet`. For the complete and exhaustive set of `ResultSet` get methods, see the Java documentation for `java.sql.ResultSet`.

exam watch

The exam is not going to test your knowledge of all of the `ResultSet` `get` and `set` methods for SQL types. For the exam, just remember the basic Java types, `String`, and `int`. Each `ResultSet` getter method is named by its closest Java type, so, for example, to read a database column that holds an integer into a Java `int` type, you invoke the `getInt()` method with either the `String` column or the column index of the column you wish to read.

TABLE 15-8 SQL Types and JDBC Types

SQL Type	Java Type	ResultSet get methods
BOOLEAN	`boolean`	`getBoolean(String columnName)` `getBoolean(int columnIndex)`
INTEGER	`int`	`getInt(String columnName)` `getInt(int columnIndex)`
DOUBLE, FLOAT	`double`	`getDouble(String columnName)` `getDouble(int columnIndex)`
REAL	`float`	`getFloat(String columnName)` `getFloat(int columnIndex)`
BIGINT	`long`	`getLong(String columnName)` `getLong(int columnIndex)`
CHAR, VARCHAR, LONGVARCHAR	`String`	`getString(String columnName)` `getString(int columnIndex)`
DATE	`java.sql.Date`	`getDate(String columnName)` `getDate(int columnIndex)`
TIME	`java.sql.Time`	`getTime(String columnName)` `getTime(int columnIndex)`
TIMESTAMP	`java.sql.Timestamp`	`getTimestamp(String columnName)` `getTimestamp(int columnIndex)`
Any of the above	`java.lang.Object`	`getObject(String columnName)` `getObject(int columnIndex)`

Getting Information about a ResultSet

When you write a query using a string, as we have in the examples so far, you know the name and type of the columns returned. However, what happens when you want to allow your users to dynamically construct the query? You may not always know in advance how many columns are returned and the type and name of the columns returned.

Fortunately, the `ResultSetMetaData` class was designed to provide just that information. Using `ResultSetMetaData`, you can get important information about the results returned from the query, including the number of columns, the table name, the column name, and the column class name—the Java class that is used to represent this column when the column is returned as an `Object`. Here is a simple example, and then we'll look at these methods in more detail:

```
String query = "SELECT AuthorID FROM Author";
ResultSet rs = stmt.executeQuery(query);
ResultSetMetaData rsmd = rs.getMetaData();
rs.next();
int colCount = rsmd.getColumnCount();  // How many columns in this
                                       // ResultSet?
out.println("Column Count: " + colCount);
for (int i = 1; i <= colCount; i++) {
  out.println("Table Name:    " + rsmd.getTableName(i));
  out.println("Column Name:   " + rsmd.getColumnName(i));
  out.println("Column Size:   " + rsmd.getColumnDisplaySize(i));
}
```

Running this code using the BookSeller database (Bob's Books) produces the following output:

```
Column Count: 1
Table Name:   AUTHOR
Column Name:  AUTHORID
Column Size:  11
```

`ResultSetMetaData` is often used to generate reports, so here are the most commonly used methods. For more information and more methods, check out the JavaDocs.

public int getColumnCount() throws SQLException This method is probably the most used `ResultSetMetaData` method. It returns the integer count of the number of columns returned by the query. With this method, you can iterate through the columns to get information about each column.

```
try {
  conn = DriverManager.getConnection(...);
  stmt = conn.createStatement();
  String query = "SELECT * FROM Author";
  ResultSet rs = stmt.executeQuery(query);
  ResultSetMetaData rsmd = rs.getMetaData(); // Get the meta data
                                             // for this ResultSet
  int columnCount = rsmd.getColumnCount();   // Get the number
                                             // of columns in this
  ...                                        // ResultSet
} catch (SQLException se) { }
```

The value of `columnCount` for the `Author` table is 3. We can use this value to iterate through the columns using the methods illustrated next.

public String getColumnName(int column) throws SQLException This method returns the `String` name of this column. Using the `columnCount`, we can create an output of the data from the database in a report-like format. For example:

```
String colData;
ResultSet rs = stmt.executeQuery(query);
ResultSetMetaData rsmd = rs.getMetaData();
int cols = rsmd.getColumnCount();
for (int i = 1; i <= cols; i++) {
  out.print(rsmd.getColumnName(i)+ " ");     // Print each column name
}
out.println();
while (rs.next()) {
  for (int i = 1; i <= cols; i++) {
    if (rs.getObject(i) != null) {
      colData = rs.getObject(i).toString();  // Get the String value
                                             // of the column object
    } else {
      colData = "NULL";                      // or NULL for a null
    }
    out.print(colData);                      // Print the column data
  }
  out.println();
}
```

This example is somewhat rudimentary, as we probably need to do some better formatting on the data, but it will produce a table of output:

```
AUTHORID FIRSTNAME LASTNAME
1000 Rick Riordan
1001 Nancy Farmer
1002 Ally Condie
1003 Cressida Cowell
1004 Lauren St. John
1005 Eoin Colfer
...
```

public String getTableName(int column) throws SQLException The method returns the `String` name of the table that this column belongs to. This method is useful when the query is a join of two or more tables and we need to know which table a column came from. For example, suppose that we want to get a list of books by author's last name:

```
String query = "SELECT Author.LastName, Book.Title
                FROM Author, Book, Books_By_Author
                WHERE Author.AuthorID = Books_By_Author.AuthorID
                AND Book.isbn = Books_By_Author.isbn"
```

With a query like this, we might want to know which table the column data came from:

```
ResultSetMetaData rsmd = rs.getMetaData();
int cols = rsmd.getColumnCount();
for (int i = 1; i <= cols; i++) {
  out.print(rsmd.getTableName(i) + ":" +
                    rsmd.getColumnName(i) + " ");
}
```

This code will print the name of the table, a colon, and the column name. The output might look something like this:

```
AUTHOR:LASTNAME BOOK:TITLE
```

public int getColumnDisplaySize(int column) throws SQLException This method returns an integer of the size of the column. This information is useful for determining the maximum number of characters a column can hold (if it is a VARCHAR type) and the spacing that is required between columns for a report.

Printing a Report

To make a prettier report than the one in the `getColumnName` method earlier, for example, we could use the display size to pad the column name and data with spaces. What we want is a table with spaces between the columns and headings that looks something like this when we query the Author table:

```
AUTHORID   FIRSTNAME            LASTNAME
1000        Rick                  Riordan
1001        Nancy                 Farmer
1002        Ally                  Condie
1003        Cressida              Cowell
1004        Lauren                St. John
1005        Eoin                  Colfer
...
```

Using the methods we have discussed so far, here is code that produces a pretty report from a query:

```
ResultSet rs = stmt.executeQuery(query);
ResultSetMetaData rsmd = rs.getMetaData();
int cols = rsmd.getColumnCount();
String col, colData;
for (int i = 1; i <= cols; i++) {
  col = leftJustify(rsmd.getColumnName(i),             // Left justify
                    rsmd.getColumnDisplaySize(i));     // column name
  out.print(col);                                      // padded with
}                                                      // size spaces
out.println(); // Print a linefeed
while (rs.next()) {
  for (int i = 1; i <= cols; i++) {
    if (rs.getObject(i) != null) {
      colData = rs.getObject(i).toString(); // Get the data in the
                                            // column as a String
    } else {
      colData = "NULL";                     // If the column is null
                                            // use "NULL"
    }
    col = leftJustify(colData,
                      rsmd.getColumnDisplaySize(i)));
    out.print(col);
  }
  out.println();
}
```

A couple of things to note about the example code: first, the `leftJustify` method, which takes a string to print left-justified and an integer for the total number of characters in the string. The difference between the actual string length and the integer value will be filled with spaces. This method uses the `String` `format()` method and the "`-`" (dash) flag to return a `String` that is left-justified with spaces. The `%1$` part indicates the flag should be applied to the first argument. What we are building is a format string dynamically. If the column display size is 20, the format string will be `%1$-20s`, which says "print the argument passed (the first argument) on the left with a width of 20 and use a string conversion."

Note that if the length of the string passed in and the integer field length (n) are the same, we add one space to the length to make it look pretty:

```
public static String leftJustify(String s, int n) {
  if (s.length() <= n) n++;  // Add an extra space if the length of
                             // the String s is less than or equal to
                             // the length of the column n
  return String.format("%1$-" + n + "s", s);  // Pad to the right of
                                              // the String by n
                                              // spaces
}
```

Second, databases can store NULL values. If the value of a column is NULL, the object returned in the `rs.getObject()` method is a Java null. So we have to test for null to avoid getting a null pointer exception when we execute the `toString()` method.

Notice that we don't have to use the `next()` method before reading the `ResultSetMetaData`—we can do that at any time after obtaining a valid result set. Running this code and passing it a query like "SELECT * FROM Author" returns a neatly printed set of authors:

```
AUTHORID     FIRSTNAME              LASTNAME
1000         Rick                   Riordan
1001         Nancy                  Farmer
1002         Ally                   Condie
1003         Cressida               Cowell
1004         Lauren                 St. John
1005         Eoin                   Colfer
...
```

Moving Around in ResultSets

So far, for all the result sets we looked at, we simply moved the cursor forward by calling `next()`. The default characteristics of a `Statement` are cursors that only move forward and result sets that do not support changes. The `ResultSet` interface actually defines these characteristics as static int variables: TYPE_FORWARD_ONLY and CONCUR_READ_ONLY. However, the JDBC specification defines additional static `int` types (shown next) that allow a developer to move the cursor forward, backward, and to a specific position in the result set. In addition, the result set can be modified while open and the changes written to the database. Note that support for cursor movement and updatable result sets is not a requirement on a driver, but most drivers provide this capability. In order to create a result set that uses positionable cursors and/or supports updates, you must create a `Statement` with the appropriate scroll type and concurrency setting, and then use that `Statement` to create the `ResultSet` object.

The ability to move the cursor to a particular position is the key to being able to determine how many rows are returned from a result set—something we will look at shortly. The ability to modify an open result set may seem odd, particularly if you are a seasoned database developer. After all, isn't that what a SQL UPDATE command is for?

Consider a situation where you want to perform a series of calculations using the data from the result set rows, then write a change to each row based on some criteria, and finally write the data back to the database. For example, imagine a database table that contains customer data, including the date they joined as a customer, their purchase history, and the total number of orders in the last two months. After reading this data into a result set, you could iterate over each customer record and modify it based on business rules: set their minimum discount higher if they have been a customer for more than a year with at least one purchase per year, or set their preferred credit status if they have been purchasing more than $100 per month. With an updatable result set, you can modify several customer rows, each in a different way, and commit the rows to the database without having to write a complex SQL query or a set of SQL queries—you simply commit the updates on the open result set.

Let's look at how to modify a result set in more detail. There are three `ResultSet` cursor types:

- **TYPE_FORWARD_ONLY** The default value for a `ResultSet`—the cursor moves forward only through a set of results.
- **TYPE_SCROLL_INSENSITIVE** A cursor position can be moved in the result forward or backward, or positioned to a particular cursor location. Any changes made to the underlying data—the database itself—are not reflected in the result set. In other words, the result set does not have to "keep state" with the database. This type is generally supported by databases.
- **TYPE_SCROLL_SENSITIVE** A cursor can be changed in the results forward or backward, or positioned to a particular cursor location. Any changes made to the underlying data are reflected in the open result set. As you can imagine, this is difficult to implement, and is therefore not implemented in a database or JDBC driver very often.

JDBC provides two options for data concurrency with a result set:

- **CONCUR_READ_ONLY** This is the default value for result set concurrency. Any open result set is read-only and cannot be modified or changed.
- **CONCUR_UPDATABLE** A result set can be modified through the `ResultSet` methods while the result set is open.

Because a database and JDBC driver are not required to support cursor movement and concurrent updates, the JDBC provides methods to query the database and driver using the `DatabaseMetaData` object to determine if your driver supports these capabilities. For example:

```
Connection conn = DriverManager.getConnection(...);
DatabaseMetaData dbmd = conn.getMetaData();
if (dbmd.supportsResultSetType(ResultSet.TYPE_FORWARD_ONLY)) {
  out.print("Supports TYPE_FORWARD_ONLY");
  if (dbmd.supportsResultSetConcurrency(
      ResultSet.TYPE_FORWARD_ONLY,
      ResultSet.CONCUR_UPDATABLE)) {
    out.println(" and supports CONCUR_UPDATABLE");
  }
}

if (dbmd.supportsResultSetType(ResultSet.TYPE_SCROLL_INSENSITIVE)) {
  out.print("Supports TYPE_SCROLL_INSENSITIVE");
  if (dbmd.supportsResultSetConcurrency(
      ResultSet.TYPE_SCROLL_INSENSITIVE,
      ResultSet.CONCUR_UPDATABLE)) {
    out.println(" and supports CONCUR_UPDATABLE");
  }
}
if (dbmd.supportsResultSetType(ResultSet.TYPE_SCROLL_SENSITIVE)) {
  out.print("Supports TYPE_SCROLL_SENSITIVE");
  if (dbmd.supportsResultSetConcurrency(
      ResultSet.TYPE_SCROLL_SENSITIVE,
      ResultSet.CONCUR_UPDATABLE)) {
    out.println("Supports CONCUR_UPDATABLE");
  }
}
```

Running this code on the Java DB (Derby) database, these are the results:

```
Supports TYPE_FORWARD_ONLY and supports CONCUR_UPDATABLE
Supports TYPE_SCROLL_INSENSITIVE and supports CONCUR_UPDATABLE
```

In order to create a `ResultSet` with TYPE_SCROLL_INSENSITIVE and CONCUR_UPDATABLE, the `Statement` used to create the `ResultSet` must be created (from the `Connection`) with the cursor type and concurrency you want. You can determine what cursor type and concurrency the `Statement` was created with, but once created, you can't change the cursor type or concurrency of an existing `Statement` object. Also, note that just because you set a cursor type or concurrency setting, that doesn't mean you will get those settings. As you will see in the section on exceptions, the driver can determine that the database doesn't support one or both of the settings you chose and it will throw a warning and (silently) revert to its default settings if they are not supported. You will see how to detect these JDBC warnings in the section on exceptions and warnings.

```
Connection conn = DriverManager.getConnection(...);
Statement stmt =
  conn.createStatement(ResultSet.TYPE_SCROLL_INSENSITIVE,
                       ResultSet.CONCUR_UPDATABLE);
```

Besides being able to use a ResultSet object to update results, which we'll look at next, being able to manipulate the cursor provides a side benefit—we can use the cursor to determine the number of rows returned in a query. Although it would seem like there ought to be a method in ResultSet or ResultSetMetaData to do this, this method does not exist.

In general, you should not need to know how many rows are returned, but during debugging, you may want to diagnose your queries with a stand-alone database and use cursor movement to read the number of rows returned.

Something like this would work:

```
ResultSet rs = stmt.executeQuery(query);  // Get a ResultSet
if (rs.last()) {                          // Move the very last row
    int rowCount = rs.getRow();           // Get row number (the count)
    rs.beforeFirst();                     // Move to before the 1st row
}
```

Of course, you may also want to have a more sophisticated method that preserves the current cursor position and returns the cursor to that position, regardless of when the method was called. Before we look at that code, let's look at the other cursor movement methods and test methods (besides next) in ResultSet. As a quick summary, Table 15-9 lists the methods you use to change the cursor position in a ResultSet.

TABLE 15-9 ResultSet Cursor Positioning Methods

Method	Effect on the Cursor and Return Value
boolean next()	Moves the cursor to the next row in the ResultSet. Returns false if the cursor is positioned beyond the last row.
boolean previous()	Moves the cursor backward one row. Returns false if the cursor is positioned before the first row.
boolean absolute(int row)	Moves the cursor to an absolute position in the ResultSet. Rows are numbered from 1. Moving to row 0 moves the cursor to before the first row. Moving to negative row numbers starts from the last row and works backward. Returns false if the cursor is positioned beyond the last row or before the first row.
boolean relative(int row)	Moves the cursor to a position relative to the current position. Invoking relative(1) moves forward one row; invoking relative(-1) moves backward one row. Returns false if the cursor is positioned beyond the last row or before the first row.
boolean first()	Moves the cursor to the first row in the ResultSet. Returns false if there are no rows in the ResultSet (empty result set).

TABLE 15-9 ResultSet Cursor Positioning Methods *(continued)*

Method	Effect on the Cursor and Return Value
boolean last()	Moves the cursor to the last row in the ResultSet. Returns false if there are no rows in the ResultSet (empty result set).
void beforeFirst()	Moves the cursor to before the first row in the ResultSet.
void afterLast()	Moves the cursor to after the last row in the ResultSet.

Let's look at each of these methods in more detail.

public boolean absolute(int row) throws SQLException This method positions the cursor to an absolute row number. The contrasting method is relative. Passing 0 as the row argument positions the cursor to before the first row. Passing a negative value, like -1, positions the cursor to the position after the last row minus one—in other words, the last row. If you attempt to position the cursor beyond the last row, say at position 22 in a 19-row result set, the cursor will be positioned beyond the last row, the implications of which we'll discuss next. Figure 15-5 illustrates how invocations of absolute() position the cursor.

The absolute() method returns true if the cursor was successfully positioned within the ResultSet and false if the cursor ended up before the first or after the last row. For example, suppose that you wanted to process only every other row:

```
ResultSet rs = stmt.executeQuery(query);
for (int i = 1; ; i += 2) {
  if (rs.absolute(i)) {  // The absolute method moves to the row
                         // passed as the integer value and returns
                         // true if the move was successful
                         // ... process the odd row
  } else {
    break;
  }
}
```

public int getRow() throws SQLException This method returns the current row position as a positive integer (1 for the first row, 2 for the second, and so on) or 0 if there is no current row—the cursor is either before the first row or after the last row. This is the only method of this set of cursor methods that is optionally supported for TYPE_FORWARD_ONLY ResultSets.

public boolean relative(int rows) throws SQLException The relative() method is the cousin to absolute. Get it, cousin? Okay, anyway, relative() will position the cursor either before or after the current position of the number of rows

FIGURE 15-5

Absolute cursor positioning

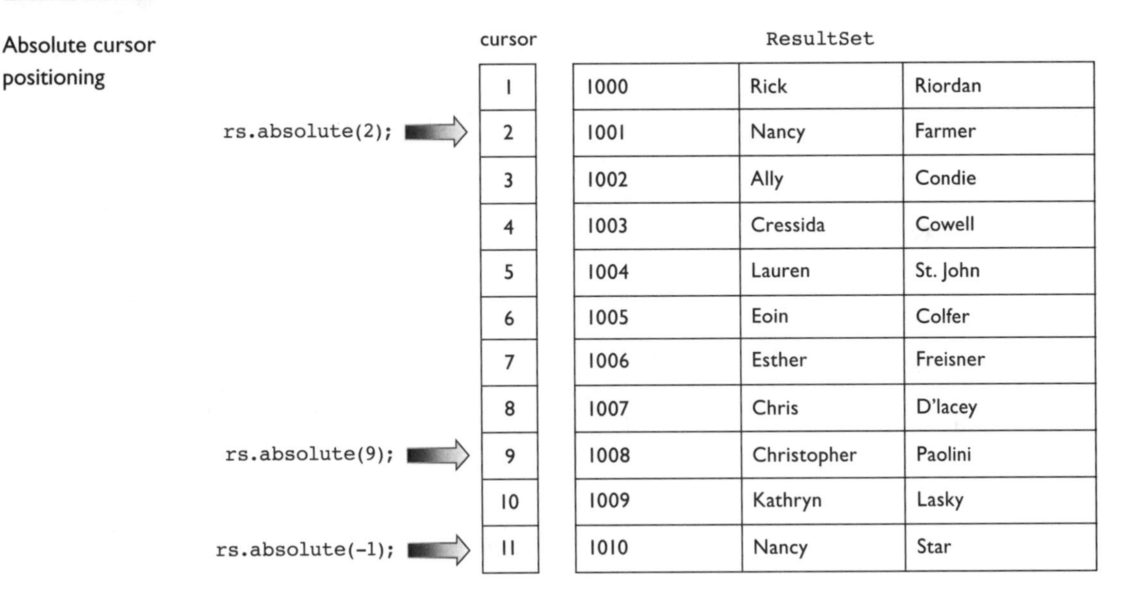

passed in to the method. So if the cursor is on row 15 of a 30-row `ResultSet`, calling `relative(2)` will position the cursor to row 17, and then calling `relative(-5)` positions the cursor to row 12. Figure 15-6 shows how the cursor is moved based on calls to `absolute()` and `relative()`.

Like absolute positioning, attempting to position the cursor beyond the last row or before the first row simply results in the cursor being after the last row or before the first row, respectively, and the method returns false. Also, calling relative with an argument of 0 does exactly what you might expect—the cursor remains where it is. Why would you use relative? Let's assume that you are displaying a fairly long database table on a web page using an HTML table. You might want to allow your user to be able to page forward or backward relative to the currently selected row; maybe something like this:

```
public boolean getNextPageOfData (ResultSet rs, int pageSize) throws
SQLException{
  return rs.relative(pageSize);
}
```

public boolean previous() throws SQLException The `previous()` method works exactly the same as the `next()` method, only it backs up through the

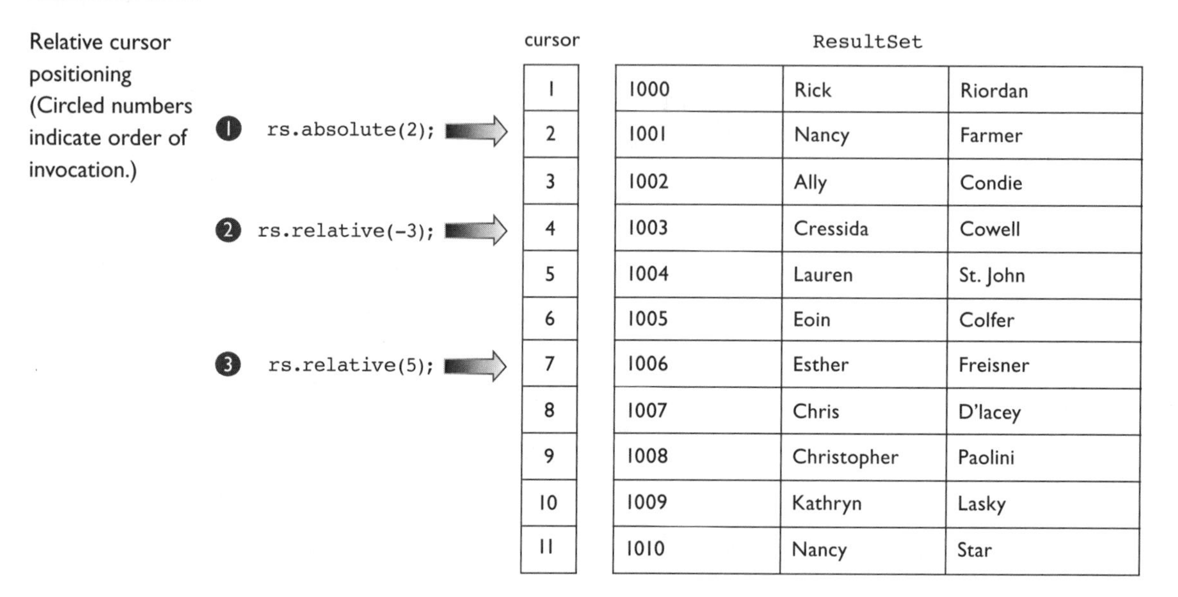

FIGURE 15-6 Relative cursor positioning (Circled numbers indicate order of invocation.)

ResultSet. Using this method with the afterLast() method described next, you can move through a ResultSet in reverse order (from last row to first).

public void afterLast() throws SQLException This method positions the cursor after the last row. Using this method and then the previous() method, you can iterate through a ResultSet in reverse. For example:

```
public void showFlippedResultSet(ResultSet rs) throws SQLException {
  rs.afterLast();            // Position the cursor after the last row
  while (rs.previous()) {    // Back up through the ResultSet
                             // process the result set
  }
}
```

Just like next(), when previous() backs up all the way to before the first row, the method returns false.

public void beforeFirst() throws SQLException This method will return the cursor to the position it held when the ResultSet was first created and returned by a Statement object.

```
rs.beforeFirst(); // Position the cursor before the first row
```

public boolean first() throws SQLException The `first()` method positions the cursor on the first row. It is the equivalent of calling `absolute(1)`. This method returns `true` if the cursor was moved to a valid row, and `false` if the `ResultSet` has no rows.

```
if (!rs.first()) {
  out.println("No rows in this result set");
}
```

public boolean last() throws SQLException The `last()` method positions the cursor on the last row. This method is the equivalent of calling `absolute(-1)`. This method returns `true` if the cursor was moved to a valid row, and `false` if the `ResultSet` has no rows.

```
if (!rs.last()) {
  out.println("No rows in this result set");
}
```

A couple of notes on the exceptions thrown by all of these methods:

- A `SQLException` will be thrown by these methods if the type of the `ResultSet` is TYPE_FORWARD_ONLY, if the `ResultSet` is closed (we will look at how a result set is closed in an upcoming section), or if a database error occurs.
- A `SQLFeatureNotSupportedException` will be thrown by these methods if the JDBC driver does not support the method. This exception is a subclass of `SQLException`.
- Most of these methods have no effect if the `ResultSet` has no rows—for example, a `ResultSet` returned by a query that returned no rows.

The following methods return a boolean to allow you to "test" the current cursor position without moving the cursor. Note that these are not on the exam, but are provided to you for completeness:

- **`isBeforeFirst()`** True if the cursor is positioned before the first row
- **`isAfterLast()`** True if the cursor is positioned after the last row
- **`isFirst()`** True if the cursor is on the first row
- **`isLast()`** True if the cursor is on the last row

So now that we have looked at the cursor positioning methods, let's revisit the code to calculate the row count. We will create a general-purpose method to allow the row count to be calculated at any time and at any current cursor position. Here is the code:

```
public static int getRowCount(ResultSet rs) throws SQLException {
  int rowCount = -1;
  int currRow = 0;

  if (rs != null) {              // make sure the ResultSet is not null
    currRow = rs.getRow();       // Save the current row position:
                                 // zero indicates that there is no
                                 // current row position - could be
                                 // beforeFirst or afterLast
    if (rs.isAfterLast()) {      // afterLast, so set the currRow negative
        currRow = -1;
    }
    if (rs.last()) {             // move to the last row and get the position
                                 // if this method returns false, there are no
                                 // results
      rowCount = rs.getRow();    // Get the row count
                                 // Return the cursor to the position it
                                 // was in before the method was called.
      if (currRow == -1) {       // if the currRow is negative, the cursor
                                 // position was after the last row, so
                                 // return the cursor to the last row
        rs.afterLast();
      } else if (currRow == 0) { // else if the cursor is zero, move
                                 // the cursor to before the first row
        rs.beforeFirst();
      } else {                   // else return the cursor to its last position
        rs.absolute(currRow);
      }
    }
  }
  return rowCount;
}
```

Looking through the code, you notice that we took special care to preserve the current position of the cursor in the `ResultSet`. We called `getRow()` to get the current position, and if the value returned was 0, the current position of the `ResultSet` could be either before the first row or after the last row, so we used the `isAfterLast()` method to determine where the cursor was. If the cursor was after the last row, then we stored a `-1` in the `currRow` integer.

We then moved the cursor to the last position in the `ResultSet`, and if that move was successful, we get the current position and save it as the `rowCount` (the last row and, therefore, the count of rows in the `ResultSet`). Finally, we use the value of `currRow` to determine where to return the cursor. If the value of the cursor is `-1`, we need to position the cursor after the last row. Otherwise, we simply use `absolute()` to return the cursor to the appropriate position in the `ResultSet`.

While this may seem like several extra steps, we will look at why preserving the cursor can be important when we look at updating `ResultSets` next.

Updating ResultSets (Not on the Exam!)

If you have casually used JDBC, or are new to JDBC, you may be surprised to know that a `ResultSet` object can do more than just provide the results of a query to your application. Besides just returning the results of a query, a `ResultSet` object may be used to modify the contents of a database table, including update existing rows, delete existing rows, and add new rows. Please note that this section and the subsections that follow are ***not on the exam***, and are provided to give you some insight into the power of using an object to represent relational data.

In a traditional SQL application, you might perform the following SQL queries to raise the price of all of the hardcover books in inventory that are currently 10.95 to 11.95 in price:

```
UPDATE Book SET UnitPrice = 11.95 WHERE UnitPrice = 10.95
                                  AND Format = 'Hardcover'
```

Hopefully by now you feel comfortable that you could create a `Statement` to perform this query using a SQL UPDATE:

```
// We have a connection and we are in a try-catch block...
Statement stmt = conn.createStatement();
String query = "UPDATE Book SET UnitPrice = 11.95 " +
               "WHERE UnitPrice = 10.95 AND Format = 'Hardcover'";
int rowsUpdated = stmt.executeUpdate(query);
```

But what if you wanted to do the updates on a book-by-book basis? You only want to increase the price of your best sellers, rather than every single book.

You would then have to get the values from the database using a SELECT, then store the values in an array indexed somehow—perhaps with the primary key—then construct the appropriate UPDATE command strings, and call `executeUpdate()` one row at a time. Another option is to update the `ResultSet` directly.

When you create a `Statement` with concurrency set to CONCUR_UPDATABLE, you can modify the data in a result set and then apply your changes back to the database without having to issue another query.

In addition to the `getXXXX` methods we looked at for `ResultSet`, methods that get column values as integers, `Date` objects, `Strings`, etc., there is an equivalent `updateXXXX` method for each type. And, just like the `getXXXX` methods, the `updateXXXX` methods can take either a `String` column name or an integer column index.

Let's rewrite the previous update example using an updatable `ResultSet`:

```
// We have a connection and we are in a try-catch block...
Statement stmt =                                          // Scrollable
  conn.createStatement(ResultSet.TYPE_SCROLL_SENSITIVE, // and
                       ResultSet.CONCUR_UPDATABLE);     // updatable
String query = "SELECT UnitPrice from Book " +
               "WHERE Format = 'Hardcover'";
ResultSet rs = stmt.executeQuery(query);      // Populate the ResultSet
while (rs.next()) {
    if (rs.getFloat("UnitPrice") == 10.95f) { // Check each row: if
                                              // unitPrice = 10.95
        rs.updateFloat("UnitPrice", 11.95f);  // set it to 11.95
        rs.updateRow();                       // and update the row
                                              // in the database
    }
}
```

Notice that after modifying the value of UnitPrice using the `updateFloat()` method, we called the method `updateRow()`. This method writes the current row to the database. This two-step approach ensures that all of the changes are made to the row before the row is written to the database. And, you can change your mind with a `cancelRowUpdates()` method call.

Table 15-10 summarizes methods that are commonly used with updatable `ResultSets` (whose concurrency type is set to CONCUR_UPDATABLE).

TABLE 15-10 Methods Used with Updatable `ResultSets`

Method	Purpose
`void updateRow()`	Updates the database with the contents of the current row of this `ResultSet`.
`void deleteRow()`	Deletes the current row from the `ResultSet` and the underlying database.
`void cancelRowUpdates()`	Cancels any updates made to the current row of this `ResultSet` object. This method will effectively undo any changes made to the `ResultSet` row. If the `updateRow()` method was called before `cancelRowUpdates`, this method will have no effect.
`void moveToInsertRow()`	Moves the cursor to a special row in the `ResultSet` set aside for performing an insert. You need to move to the insert row before updating the columns of the row with update methods and calling `insertRow()`.
`void insertRow()`	Inserts the contents of the insert row into the database. Note that this method does not change the current `ResultSet`, so the `ResultSet` should be read again if you want the `ResultSet` to be consistent with the contents of the database.
`void moveToCurrentRow()`	Moves the cursor back to the current row from the insert row. If the cursor was not on the insert row, this method has no effect.

Let's look at the common methods used for altering database contents through the `ResultSet` in detail.

public void updateRow() throws SQLException This method updates the database with the contents of the current row of the `ResultSet`. There are a couple of caveats for this method. First, the `ResultSet` must be from a SQL SELECT statement on a single table—a SQL statement that includes a JOIN or a SQL statement with two tables cannot be updated. Second, the `updateRow()` method should be called *before* moving to the next row. Otherwise, the updates to the current row may be lost.

So the typical use for this method is to update the contents of a row using the appropriate `updateXXXX()` methods and then update the database with the contents of the row using the `updateRow()` method. For example, in this fragment, we are updating the UnitPrice of a row to $11.95:

```
rs.updateFloat("UnitPrice", 11.95f); // Set the price to 11.95
rs.updateRow();                      // Update the row in the DB
```

public boolean rowUpdated() throws SQLException This method returns true if the current row was updated. Note that not all databases can detect updates. However, JDBC provides a method in `DatabaseMetaData` to determine if updates are detectable, `DatabaseMetaData.updatesAreDetected(int type)`, where the type is one of the `ResultSet` types—TYPE_SCROLL_INSENSITIVE, for example. We will cover the `DatabaseMetaData` interface and its methods a little later in this section.

```
if (rs.rowUpdated()) {             // Has this row been modified?
  out.println("Row: " + rs.getRow() + " updated.");
}
```

public void cancelRowUpdates() throws SQLException This method allows you to "back out" changes made to the row. This method is important, because the `updateXXXX` methods should not be called twice on the same column. In other words, if you set the value of UnitPrice to 11.95 in the previous example and then decided to switch the price back to 10.95, calling the `updateFloat()` method again can lead to unpredictable results. So the better approach is to call `cancelRowUpdates()` before changing the value of a column a second time.

```
boolean priceRollback = ...;  // Price rollback set somewhere else
while (rs.next()) {
  if (rs.getFloat("UnitPrice") == 10.95f) {
    rs.updateFloat("UnitPrice", 11.95f);
```

```
    }
    if (priceRollback) {          // If priceRollback is true
      rs.cancelRowUpdates();      // Rollback changes to this row
    } else {
      rs.updateRow();             // else, commit this row to the DB
    }
  }
```

public void deleteRow() throws SQLException This method will remove the current row from the `ResultSet` and from the underlying database. The row in the database is removed (similar to the result of a DELETE statement).

```
rs.last();
rs.deleteRow();  // Delete the last row.
```

What happens to the `ResultSet` after a `deleteRow()` method depends upon whether or not the `ResultSet` can detect deletions. This ability is dependent upon the JDBC driver. When a `ResultSet` can detect deletions, the deleted row is removed from the `ResultSet`. When the `ResultSet` cannot detect deletions, the columns of the `ResultSet` row that was deleted are made invalid by setting each column to null.

The `DatabaseMetaData` interface can be used to determine if the `ResultSet` can detect deletions:

```
int type = ResultSet.TYPE_SCROLL_INSENSITIVE; // Scrollable ResultSet
DatabaseMetaData dbmd = conn.getMetaData();   // Get meta data about
                                              // the driver and DB
if (dbmd.deletesAreDetected(type)) {          // Returns false if deleted rows
                                              // are removed from the ResultSet
  while (rs.next()) {                         // Iterate through the ResultSet
    if (rs.rowDeleted()) {                    // Deleted rows are flagged, but
      continue;                               // not removed, so skip them
    } else {
     // process the row
    }
} else {
  // Close the ResultSet and re-run the query
}
```

In general, to maintain an up-to-date `ResultSet` after a deletion, the `ResultSet` should be re-created with a query.

Deleting the current row does not move the cursor—it remains on the current row—so if you deleted row 1, the cursor is still positioned at row 1. However, if the deleted row was the last row, then the cursor is positioned after the last row. Note that there is no undo for `deleteRow()`, at least, not by default. As you will see a little later, we can "undo" a delete if we are using transactions.

public boolean rowDeleted() throws SQLException As described earlier, when a `ResultSet` can detect deletes, the `rowDeleted()` method is used to indicate a row has been deleted, but remains as a part of the `ResultSet` object. For example, suppose that we deleted the second row of the Customer table. Printing the results (after the delete) to the console would look like Figure 15-7.

So if you are working with a `ResultSet` that is being passed around between methods and shared across classes, you might use `rowDeleted()` to detect if the current row contains valid data.

Updating Columns Using Objects An interesting aspect of the `getObject()` and `updateObject()` methods is that they retrieve a column as a Java object. And, since every Java object can be turned into a `String` using the object's `toString()` method, you can retrieve the value of any column in the database and print the value to the console as a `String`, as we saw in the section "Printing a Report."

Going the other way, toward the database, you can also use `Strings` to update almost every column in a `ResultSet`. All of the most common SQL types—integer, float, double, long, and date—are wrapped by their representative Java object: `Integer`, `Float`, `Double`, `Long`, and `java.sql.Date`. Each of these objects has a method `valueOf()` that takes a `String`.

FIGURE 15-7

A `ResultSet` after `delete()` is called on the second row

```
String query = "SELECT * FROM Customer";
ResultSet rs = stmt.executeQuery(query);
rs.next();
rs.next();
rs.delete();
```

ResultSet

5000	John	Smith	john.smith@verizon.net	555-340-1230
null	null	null	null	null
5002	Bob	Collins	bob.collins@yahoo.com	555-012-3456
5003	Rebecca	Mayer	rebecca.mayer@gmail.com	555-205-8212
5006	Anthony	Clark	anthony.clark@gmail.com	555-256-1901
5007	Judy	Sousa	judy.sousa@verizon.net	555-751-1207
5008	Christopher	Patriquin	patriquinc@yahoo.com	555-316-1803
5009	Deborah	Smith	deb.smith@comcast.net	555-256-3421
5010	Jennifer	McGinn	jmcginn@comcast.net	555-250-0918

The `updateObject()` method takes two arguments: the first, a column name (`String`) or column index, and the second, an `Object`. We can pass a `String` as the `Object` type, and as long as the `String` meets the requirements of the `valueOf()` method for the column type, the `String` will be properly converted and stored in the database as the desired SQL type.

For example, suppose that we are going to update the publish date (`PubDate`) of one of our books:

```
// We have a connection and we are in a try-catch block...
Statement stmt =
  conn.createStatement(ResultSet.TYPE_SCROLL_INSENSITIVE,
                       ResultSet.CONCUR_UPDATABLE);
String query = "SELECT * FROM Book WHERE ISBN='142311339X'";
ResultSet rs = stmt.executeQuery(query);
rs.next();
rs.updateObject("PubDate", "2005-04-23"); // Update PubDate using
                                          // a String date
rs.updateRow();                           // Update this row
```

The `String` we passed meets the requirements for java.sql.Date, "yyyy-[m]m-[d]d," so the `String` is properly converted and stored in the database as the SQL Date value: 2005-04-23. Note this technique is limited to those SQL types that can be converted to and from a `String`, and if the `String` passed to the `valueOf()` method for the SQL type of the column is not properly formatted for the Java object, an `IllegalArgumentException` is thrown.

Inserting New Rows Using a ResultSet

In the last section, we looked at modifying the existing column data in a `ResultSet` and removing existing rows. In our final section on `ResultSets`, we'll look at how to create and insert a new row. First, you must have a valid `ResultSet` open, so typically, you have performed some query. `ResultSet` provides a special row, called the insert row, that you are actually modifying (updating) before performing the insert. Think of the insert row as a buffer where you can modify an empty row of your `ResultSet` with values.

Inserting a row is a three-step process, as shown in Figure 15-8: First (1) move to the special insert row, then (2) update the values of the columns for the new row, and finally (3) perform the actual insert (write to the underlying database). The existing `ResultSet` is not changed—you must rerun your query to see the underlying changes in the database. However, you can insert as many rows as you like. Note that each of these methods throws a `SQLException` if the concurrency type of the result set is set to CONCUR_READ_ONLY. Let's look at the methods before we look at example code.

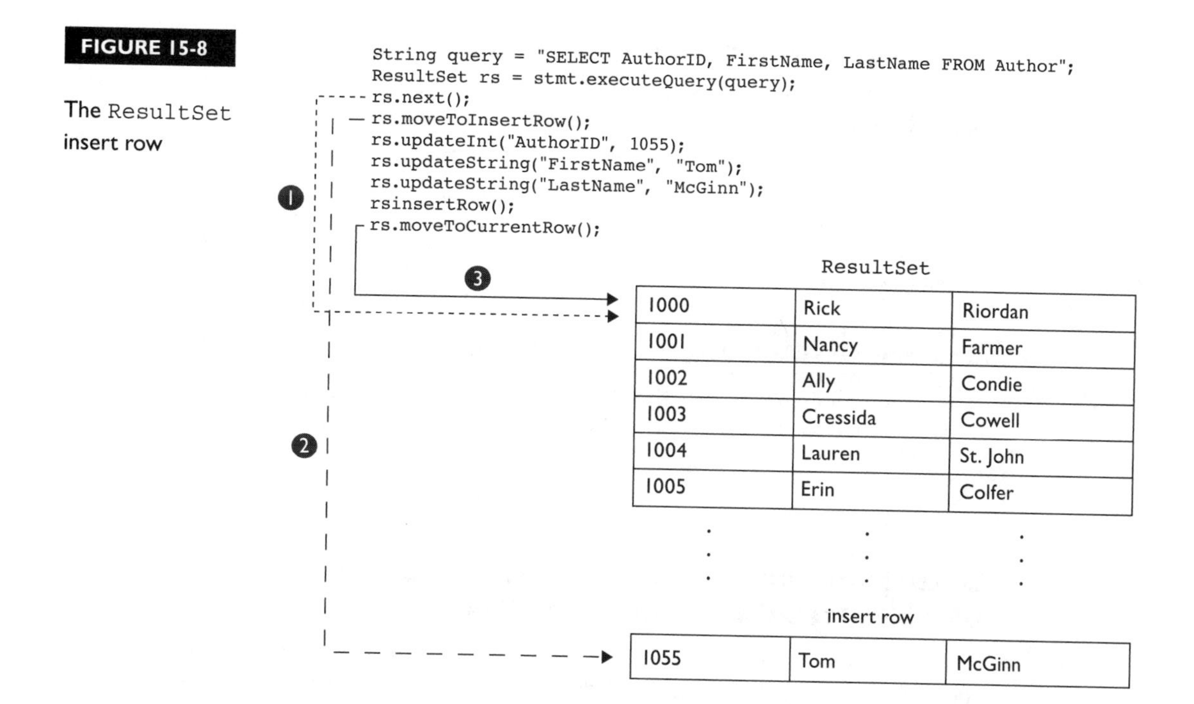
String query = "SELECT AuthorID, FirstName, LastName FROM Author";
ResultSet rs = stmt.executeQuery(query);
rs.next();
rs.moveToInsertRow();
rs.updateInt("AuthorID", 1055);
rs.updateString("FirstName", "Tom");
rs.updateString("LastName", "McGinn");
rsinsertRow();
rs.moveToCurrentRow();
1
2
3
ResultSet
1000
Rick
Riordan
1001
Nancy
Farmer
1002
Ally
Condie
1003
Cressida
Cowell
1004
Lauren
St. John
1005
Erin
Colfer
insert row
1055
Tom
McGinn

FIGURE 15-8 The `ResultSet` insert row

public void moveToInsertRow() throws SQLException This method moves the cursor to insert a row buffer. Wherever the cursor was when this method was called is remembered. After calling this method, the appropriate updater methods are called to update the values of the columns.

```
rs.moveToInsertRow();
```

public void insertRow() throws SQLException This method writes the insert row buffer to the database. Note that the cursor must be on the insert row when this method is called. Also, note that each column must be set to a value before the row is inserted in the database or a `SQLException` will be thrown. The `insertRow()` method can be called more than once—however, the `insertRow` follows the same rules as a SQL INSERT command—unless the primary key is auto-generated, two inserts of the same data will result in a `SQLException` (duplicate primary key).

```
rs.insertRow();
```

public void moveToCurrentRow() throws SQLException This method returns the result set cursor to the row the cursor was on before the `moveToInsertRow()` method was called.

Let's look at a simple example, where we will add a new row in the Author table:

```
// We have a connection and we are in a try-catch block...
Statement stmt = conn.createStatement(ResultSet.TYPE_SCROLL_INSENSITIVE,
                                      ResultSet.CONCUR_UPDATABLE);
ResultSet rs = stmt.executeQuery("SELECT AuthorID, FirstName, LastName
                                  FROM Author");
rs.next();
rs.moveToInsertRow();                     // Move the special insert row
rs.updateInt("AuthorID", 1055);           // Create an author ID
rs.updateString("FirstName", "Tom");      // Set the first name
rs.updateString("LastName", "McGinn");    // Set the last name
rs.insertRow();                           // Insert the row into the database
rs.moveToCurrentRow();                    // Move back to the current row in
                                          // ResultSet
```

Getting Information about a Database Using DatabaseMetaData (Not on the Exam!)

In the example we are using in this chapter, Bob's Books, we know quite a lot about the tables, columns, and relationships between the tables because we had that nifty data model earlier. But what if that were not the case? This section covers `DatabaseMetaData`, an interface that provides a significant amount of information about the database itself. This topic is fairly advanced stuff and is not on the exam, but it is provided here to give you an idea about how you can use metadata to build a model of a database without having to know anything about the database in advance.

Recall that the `Connection` object we obtained from `DriverManager` is an object that represents an actual connection with the database. And while the `Connection` object is primarily used to create `Statement` objects, there are a couple of important methods to study in the `Connection` interface. A `Connection` can be used to obtain information *about* the database as well. This data is called "metadata," or "data about data."

One of `Connection`'s methods returns a `DatabaseMetaData` object instance, through which we can get information about the database, about the driver, and about transaction semantics that the database and JDBC driver support. We will spend more time looking at transactions in another section.

To obtain an instance of a `DatabaseMetaData` object, we use `Connection`'s `getMetaData()` method:

```
String url = "jdbc:derby://localhost:1521/BookSellerDB";
String user = "bookguy";
String pwd = "$3lleR";
try {
  Connection conn = DriverManager.getConnection(url, user, pwd);
  DatabaseMetaData dbmd = conn.getMetaData(); // Get the database
                                              // meta data
} catch (SQLException se) { }
```

`DatabaseMetaData` is a comprehensive interface, and through an object instance, we can determine a great deal about the database and the supporting driver. Most of the time, as a developer, you aren't coding against a database blindly and know the capabilities of the database and the driver before you write any code. Still, it is helpful to know that you can use `getObject` to return the value of the column, regardless of its type—very useful when all you want to do is create a report, and we'll look at an example.

Here are a few methods we will highlight:

- **`getColumns()`** Returns a description of columns in a specified catalog and schema
- **`getProcedures()`** Returns a description of the stored procedures in a given catalog and schema
- **`getDriverName()`** Returns the name of the JDBC driver
- **`getDriverVersion()`** Returns the version number of the JDBC driver as a string
- **`supportsANSI92EntryLevelSQL()`** Returns a boolean true if this database supports ANSI92 entry-level grammar

It is interesting to note that `DatabaseMetaData` methods also use `ResultSet` objects to return data about the database. Let's look at these methods in more detail.

public ResultSet getColumns(String catalog, String schemaPattern, String tableNamePattern, String columnNamePattern) throws SQLException This method is one of the best all-purpose data retrieval methods for details about the tables and columns in your database. Before we look at a code sample, it might be helpful to define catalogs and schemas. In a database, a schema is an object that enforces the integrity of the tables in the database. The schema name is generally the name of the person who created the database. In our examples, the BookGuy database holds the collection of tables and is the name of the schema. Databases may have multiple schemas stored in a catalog.

In this example, using the Java DB database as our sample database, the catalog is null and our schema is "BOOKGUY", and we are using a SQL catch-all pattern "%" for the table and column name patterns, like the "*" character you are probably used to with file systems like Windows. Thus, we are going to retrieve all of the tables and columns in the schema. Specifically, we are going to print out the table name, column name, the SQL data type for the column, and the size of the column. Note that here we used uppercase column identifiers. These are the column names verbatim from the JavaDoc, but in truth, they are not case sensitive either, so "Table_Name" would have worked just as well. Also, the JavaDoc specifies the column index for these column headings, so we could have also used `rs.getString(3)` to get the table name.

```
String url = "jdbc:derby://localhost:1521/BookSellerDB";
String user = "bookguy";
String pwd = "$3lleR";
try {
  Connection conn = DriverManager.getConnection(url, user, pwd);
  DatabaseMetaData dbmd = conn.getMetaData();
  ResultSet rs
   = dbmd.getColumns(null, "BOOKGUY", "%", "%"); // Get a ResultSet
                                                  // for any catalog (null)
                                                  // in the BOOKGUY schema
                                                  // for all tables (%)
                                                  // for all columns (%)
  while (rs.next()) {
    out.print("Table Name:  " + rs.getString("TABLE_NAME") + " ");
    out.print("Column_Name: " + rs.getString("COLUMN_NAME") + " ");
    out.print("Type_Name:   " + rs.getString("TYPE_NAME") + " ");
    out.println("Column Size  " + rs.getString("COLUMN_SIZE"));
  }
} catch (SQLException se) {
   out.println("SQLException: " + se);
}
```

Running this code produces output something like this:

```
Table Name:  AUTHOR Column_Name: AUTHORID Type_Name:   INTEGER Column Size  10
Primary Key
Table Name:  AUTHOR Column_Name: FIRSTNAME Type_Name:   VARCHAR Column Size  20
Table Name:  AUTHOR Column_Name: LASTNAME Type_Name:   VARCHAR Column Size  20
Table Name:  BOOK Column_Name: ISBN Type_Name:   VARCHAR Column Size  10 Primary
Key
Table Name:  BOOK Column_Name: TITLE Type_Name:   VARCHAR Column Size  100
Table Name:  BOOK Column_Name: PUBDATE Type_Name:   DATE Column Size  10
Table Name:  BOOK Column_Name: FORMAT Type_Name:   VARCHAR Column Size  30
Table Name:  BOOK Column_Name: UNITPRICE Type_Name:   DOUBLE Column Size  52
Table Name:  BOOKS_BY_AUTHOR Column_Name: AUTHORID Type_Name:   INTEGER Column
Size  10
```

```
Table Name:  BOOKS_BY_AUTHOR Column_Name: ISBN Type_Name:   VARCHAR Column Size
10
Table Name:  CUSTOMER Column_Name: CUSTOMERID Type_Name:   INTEGER Column Size
10 Primary Key
Table Name:  CUSTOMER Column_Name: FIRSTNAME Type_Name:   VARCHAR Column Size  30
Table Name:  CUSTOMER Column_Name: LASTNAME Type_Name:   VARCHAR Column Size  30
Table Name:  CUSTOMER Column_Name: EMAIL Type_Name:   VARCHAR Column Size  40
Table Name:  CUSTOMER Column_Name: PHONE Type_Name:   VARCHAR Column Size  15
```

public ResultSet getProcedures(String catalog, String schemaPattern, String procedureNamePattern) throws SQLException Stored procedures are functions that are sometimes built into a database and often defined by a database developer or database admin. These functions can range from data cleanup to complex queries. This method returns a result set that contains descriptive information about the stored procedures for a catalog and schema. In the example code, we will use null for the catalog name and schema pattern. The null indicates that we do not wish to narrow the search (effectively, the same as using a catch-all "%" search). Note that this example is returning the name of every stored procedure in the database. A little later, we'll look at how to actually call a stored procedure.

```
try {
  Connection conn = ...
  DatabaseMetaData dbmd = conn.getMetaData();
  ResultSet rs =
       dbmd.getProcedures(null, null, "%");     // Get a ResultSet of all
                                                // the stored procedures
                                                // in any catalog (null)
                                                // in any schema (null)
                                                // with wildcard name (%)
  while(rs.next()) {
    out.println("Procedure Name: " + rs.getString("PROCEDURE_NAME"));
  }
} catch (SQLException se) { }
```

Note that the output from this code fragment is highly database dependent. Here is sample output from the Derby (JavaDB) database that ships with the JDK:

```
Procedure Name: INSTALL_JAR
Procedure Name: REMOVE_JAR
Procedure Name: REPLACE_JAR
Procedure Name: SYSCS_BACKUP_DATABASE
Procedure Name: SYSCS_BACKUP_DATABASE_AND_ENABLE_LOG_ARCHIVE_MODE
Procedure Name: SYSCS_BACKUP_DATABASE_AND_ENABLE_LOG_ARCHIVE_MODE_NOWAIT
Procedure Name: SYSCS_BACKUP_DATABASE_NOWAIT
Procedure Name: SYSCS_BULK_INSERT
```

public String getDriverName() throws SQLException This method simply returns the name of the JDBC driver as a string. This method would be useful to log in the start of the application, as you'll see in the next section.

```
System.out.println("getDriverName: " + dbmd.getDriverName());
```

Obviously, the name of the driver depends on the JDBC driver you are using. Again, with the Derby database and JDBC driver, the output from this method looks something like this:

```
getDriverName: Apache Derby Network Client JDBC Driver
```

public String getDriverVersion() throws SQLException This method returns the JDBC driver version number as a string. This information and the driver name would be good to log in the start-up of an application.

```
Logger logger = Logger.getLogger("com.cert.DatabaseMetaDataTest");
Connection conn = ...
DatabaseMetaData dbmd = conn.getMetaData();
logger.log(Level.INFO, "Driver Version: {0}", dbmd.getDriverVersion());
logger.log(Level.INFO, "Driver Name: {0}", dbmd.getDriverName());
```

Statements written to the log are generally recorded in a log file, but depending upon the IDE, they can also be written to the console. In NetBeans, for example, the log statements look something like this in the console:

```
Sep 23, 2012 3:55:39 PM com.cert.DatabaseMetaDataTest main
INFO: Driver Version: 10.8.2.2 - (1181258)
Sep 23, 2012 3:55:39 PM com.cert.DatabaseMetaDataTest main
INFO: Driver Name: Apache Derby Network Client JDBC Driver
```

public boolean supportsANSI92EntryLevelSQL() throws SQLException This method returns true if the database and JDBC driver support ANSI SQL-92 entry-level grammar. Support for this level (at a minimum) is a requirement for JDBC drivers (and therefore the database.)

```
Connection conn = ...
DatabaseMetaData dbmd = conn.getMetaData();
if (!dbmd.supportsANSI92EntryLevelSQL()) {
    logger.log(Level.WARNING, "JDBC Driver does not meet minimum
                requirements for SQL-92 support");
}
```

When Things Go Wrong—Exceptions and Warnings

Whenever you are working with a database using JDBC, there is a possibility that something can go wrong. A JDBC connection is typically through a socket to a database resource on the network. So already we have at least two possible points of failure—the network can be down and/or the database can be down. And that assumes that everything else you are doing with your database is correct, that all your queries are perfect! Like other Java exceptions, `SQLException` is a way for your application to determine what the problem is and take action if necessary.

Let's look at the type of data you get from a `SQLException` through its methods.

public String getMessage() This method is actually inherited from `java.lang.Exception`, which `SQLException` extends from. But this method returns the detailed reason why the exception was thrown. Note that this is not the same message that is returned from the `toString()` method, i.e., the method called when you put the exception object instance into a `System.out.println` method. Often, the message content `SQLState` and error code provide specific information about what went wrong.

public String getSQLState() The `String` returned by `getSQLState` provides a specific code and related message. `SQLState` messages are defined by the X/Open and SQL:2003 standards; however, it is up to the implementation to use these values. You can determine which standard your JDBC driver uses (or if it does not) through the `DatabaseMetaData.getSQLStateType()` method. Your implementation may also define additional codes specific to the implementation, so in either case, it is a good idea to consult your JDBC driver and database documentation. Because the `SQLState` messages and codes tend to be specific to the driver and database, the typical use of these in an application is limited to either logging messages or debugging information.

public int getErrorCode() Error codes are not defined by a standard and are thus implementation specific. They can be used to pass an actual error code or severity level, depending upon the implementation.

public SQLException getNextException() One of the interesting aspects of `SQLException` is that the exception thrown could be the result of more than one issue. Fortunately, JDBC simply tacks each exception onto the next in a process called chaining. Typically, the most severe exception is thrown last, so it is the first exception in the chain.

You can get a list of all of the exceptions in the chain using the getNextException() method to iterate through the list. When the end of the list is reached, getNextException() returns a null. In this example, the SQLExceptions, SQLState, and vendor error codes are logged:

```
Logger logger = Logger.getLogger("com.example.MyClass");
try {
  // some JDBC code in a try block
  // ...
} catch (SQLException se) {
  while (se != null) {
    logger.log(Level.SEVERE, "------ SQLException ------");
    logger.log(Level.SEVERE, "SQLState: " + se.getSQLState());
    logger.log(Level.SEVERE, "Vendor Error code: " +
                             se.getErrorCode());
    logger.log(Level.SEVERE,"Message: " + se.getMessage());
    se = se.getNextException();
  }
}
```

Warnings

Although SQLWarning is a subclass of SQLException, warnings are silently chained to the JDBC object that reported them. This is probably one of the few times in Java where an object that is part of an exception hierarchy is not thrown as an exception. The reason is that a warning is not an exception per se. Warnings can be reported on Connection, Statement, and ResultSet objects.

For example, suppose that we mistakenly set the result set type to TYPE_SCROLL_SENSITIVE when creating a Statement object. This does not create an exception; instead, the database will handle the situation by chaining a SQLWarning to the Connection object and resetting the type to TYPE_FORWARD_ONLY (the default) and continue on. Everything would be fine, of course, until we tried to position the cursor, at which point a SQLException would be thrown. And, like SQLException, you can retrieve warnings from the SQLWarning object using the getNextWarning() method.

```
Connection conn =
  DriverManager.getConnection("jdbc:derby://localhost:1527/BookSellerDB",
 "bookguy", "$3lleR");
Statement stmt =
  conn.createStatement(ResultSet.TYPE_SCROLL_SENSITIVE,
                       ResultSet.CONCUR_UPDATABLE);
String query = "SELECT * from Book WHERE Book.Format = 'Hardcover'";
ResultSet rs = stmt.executeQuery(query);
SQLWarning warn = conn.getWarnings();    // Get any SQLWarnings
```

```
while (warn != null) {                    // If there is a SQLWarning, print it
  out.println("SQLState: " + warn.getSQLState());
  out.println("Message: " + warn.getMessage());
  warn = warn.getNextWarning();           // Get the next warning
}
```

Connection objects will add warnings (if necessary) until the Connection is closed, or until the clearWarnings() method is called on the Connection instance. The clearWarnings() method sets the list of warnings to null until another warning is reported for this Connection object.

Statements and ResultSets also generate SQLWarnings, and these objects have their own clearWarnings() methods. Statement warnings are cleared automatically when a statement is reexecuted, and ResultSet warnings are cleared each time a new row is read from the result set.

The following sections summarize the methods associated with SQLWarnings.

SQLWarning getWarnings() throws SQLException This method gets the first SQLWarning object or returns null if there are no warnings for this Connection, Statement, or ResultSet object. A SQLException is thrown if the method is called on a closed object.

void clearWarnings() throws SQLException This method clears and resets the current set of warnings for this Connection, Statement, or ResultSet object. A SQLException is thrown if the method is called on a closed object.

Properly Closing SQL Resources

In this chapter, we have looked at some very simple examples where we create a Connection and Statement and a ResultSet all within a single try block, and catch any SQLExceptions thrown. What we have not done so far is properly close these resources. The reality is that it is probably less important for such small examples, but for any code that uses a resource, like a socket, or a file, or a JDBC database connection, closing the open resources is a good practice.

It is also important to know when a resource is closed automatically. Each of the three major JDBC objects, Connection, Statement, and ResultSet, has a close() method to explicitly close the resource associated with the object and explicitly release the resource. We hope by now you also realize that the objects have a relationship with each other, so if one object executes close(), it will have an impact on the other objects. The following table should help explain this.

Method Call	Has the Following Action(s)
`Connection.close()`	Releases the connection to the database. Closes any `Statement` created from this `Connection`.
`Statement.close()`	Releases this `Statement` resource. Closes any open `ResultSet` associated with this `Statement`.
`ResultSet.close()`	Releases this `ResultSet` resource. Note that any `ResultSetMetaData` objects created from the `ResultSet` are still accessible.
`Statement.executeXXXX()`	Any `ResultSet` associated with a previous `Statement` execution is automatically closed.

It is also a good practice to minimize the number of times you close and re-create `Connection` objects. As a rule, creating the connection to the database and passing the username and password credentials for authentication is a relatively expensive process, so performing the activity once for every SQL query would not result in highly performing code. In fact, typically, database connections are created in a pool, and connection instances are handed out to applications as needed, rather than allowing or requiring individual applications to create them.

`Statement` objects are less expensive to create, and as we'll see in the next section, there are ways to precompile SQL statements using a `PreparedStatement`, which reduces the overhead associated with creating SQL query strings and sending those strings to the database for execution.

`ResultSets` are the least expensive of the objects to create, and as we looked at in the section on `ResultSets`, for results from a single table, you can use the `ResultSet` to update, insert, and delete rows, so it can be very efficient to use a `ResultSet`.

Let's look at one of our previous examples, where we used a `Connection`, a `Statement`, and a `ResultSet`, and rewrite this code to close the resources properly.

```
Connection conn = null;
String url, user, pwd;      // These are populated somewhere else
try {
  conn = DriverManager.getConnection(url, user, pwd);
  Statement stmt = conn.createStatement();
  ResultSet rs = stmt.executeQuery("SELECT * FROM Customer");
  // ... process the results
  // ...
  if (rs != null && stmt != null) {
    rs.close();             // Attempt to close the ResultSet
    stmt.close();           // Attempt to close the Statement
  }
} catch (SQLException se) {
```

```
    out.println("SQLException: " + se);
  } finally {
    try {
      if (conn != null) {
        conn.close();         // Close the Connection
      }
    } catch (SQLException sec) {
      out.println("Exception closing connection!");
    }
  }
```

Notice all the work we have to go through to close the `Connection`—we first need to make sure we actually got an object and not a null, and then we need to try the `close()` method inside of another `try` inside of the `finally` block! Fortunately, there is an easier way....

Using try-with-resources to Close Connections, Statements, and ResultSets

As you'll recall from Chapter 7, one of the most useful changes in Java SE 7 (JDK 7) was a number of small modifications to the language, including a new `try` statement to support the automatic resource management. This language change is called `try`-with-resources, and its longer name belies how much simpler it makes writing code with resources that should be closed. The `try`-with-resources statement will automatically call the `close()` method on any resource declared in the parentheses at the end of the `try` block.

There is a caveat: A resource declared in the `try`-with-resource statement must implement the `AutoCloseable` interface. One of the changes for JDBC in Java SE 7 (JDBC 4.1) was the modification of the API so that `Connection`, `Statement`, and `ResultSet` all implement the `AutoCloseable` interface and support automatic resource management. So we can rewrite our previous code example using `try`-with-resources:

```
String url, user, pwd;  // These are populated somewhere else
try (Connection conn = DriverManager.getConnection(url, user, pwd)){
  Statement stmt = conn.createStatement();
  ResultSet rs = stmt.executeQuery("SELECT * FROM Customer");
  // ... process the results
  // ...
  if (rs != null && stmt != null) {
    rs.close();        // Attempt to close the ResultSet
    stmt.close();      // Attempt to close the Statement
  }
} catch (SQLException se) {
  out.println("SQLException: " + se);
}
```

Notice that we must include the object type in the declaration inside of the parentheses. The following will throw a compilation error:

```
try (conn = DriverManager.getConnection(url, user, pwd);) {
```

The try-with-resources can also be used with multiple resources, so you could include the Statement declaration in the try as well:

```
try (Connection conn = DriverManager.getConnection(url, user, pwd);
     Statement stmt = conn.createStatement()) {
```

Note that when more than one resource is declared in the try-with-resources statement, the resources are closed in the reverse order of their declaration—so stmt.close() will be called first, followed by conn.close().

It probably makes sense that if there is an exception thrown from the try block, the exception will be caught by the catch statement, but what happens to exceptions thrown as a result of closing the resources in the try-with-resources statement? Any exceptions thrown as a result of closing resources at the end of the try block are suppressed if there was also an exception thrown in the try block. These exceptions can be retrieved from the exception thrown by calling the getSuppressed() method on the exception thrown.

For example:

```
} catch (SQLException se) {
  out.println("SQLException: " + se);
  Throwable[] suppressed = se.getSuppressed(); // Get an array of
                                               // suppressed
                                               // exceptions
  for (Throwable t: suppressed) {  // Iterate through the array
    out.println("Suppressed exception: " + t);
  }
}
```

CERTIFICATION OBJECTIVE

Use PreparedStatement and CallableStatement Objects (OCP Objective 9.6)

9.5 *Create and use PreparedStatement and CallableStatement objects.*

So far, we used Statement object instances to pass queries as strings directly to the JDBC driver and then to the database. But as we mentioned earlier, the JDBC

API provides two additional interfaces that JDBC driver vendors implement. These are `PreparedStatement` and `CallableStatement`. These interfaces extend the `Statement` interface and add functionality.

A `PreparedStatement` can improve the performance of a frequently executed query because the SQL part of the statement is *precompiled* in the database. In order to understand what precompiled means, we need to explain SQL execution at a high level. When a SQL string is sent to a database, the string goes through a number of processing steps. First, the string is parsed and all of the SQL keywords are checked for proper syntax. Next, the table and column names are checked against the schema to make sure they all exist (and are properly spelled). Next, the database creates an execution plan for the query, choosing between several options for the best overall performance. Finally, the chosen execution plan is run.

The steps leading up to the execution of a query plan can be done in advance using a `PreparedStatement` object. Parameters can be passed to a `PreparedStatement`, and these are inserted into the query just before execution. This is why `PreparedStatement` is a good choice for a frequently executed SQL statement.

Databases also provide the capability for developers to write small programs directly to the database. Each program is named, compiled, and stored in the database itself. These named programs are generally developed and added to the database when the tables are created. There are three types of these small programs: procedures, functions, and triggers. Because triggers are only invoked by the database itself and are not accessible by SQL queries or directly from an external application, we will not cover triggers. We will focus on stored procedures and functions.

The advantage of stored procedures and functions is that they are completely self-contained. You can think of a stored procedure as a method for a database. You call the stored procedure using its name and pass it arguments. The stored procedure may or may not return results, as you will see in the section on `CallableStatements`.

The `CallableStatement` is used to execute a named stored procedure or function. Unlike prepared statements, stored procedures and functions must exist before a `CallableStatement` can be executed on them. Like `PreparedStatements`, parameters can be passed to stored procedures and functions.

PreparedStatement

Because PreparedStatements are precompiled, they excel at reducing overall execution time for frequently executed SQL queries. For example, an online retailer like Bob's Books may make frequent changes to price and quantity of the inventory based on seasonal demand and stock on hand. When the number of update operations with the database is in the thousands per day, the savings that a precompiled SQL statement affords is significant.

PreparedStatement objects are obtained from a Connection object in the same way that Statement objects are obtained, but through the prepareStatement() method instead of a createStatement() method. There are several forms of the prepareStatement method, including those that take the result set type and result set concurrency, just like Statement, so a ResultSet returned from a PreparedStatement can be scrollable and updatable as well.

One difference between the Statement and PreparedStatement is the execution sequence. Recall that for a Statement object, we created a Statement and then passed a String query to it to obtain a result, perform and update, or perform a general-purpose query. In order to construct a dynamic query using Statement, we had to carefully concatenate Strings to create the SQL query. Any parameters were added to the query before the String was passed as an argument to Statement's execute method.

To create a PreparedStatement object instance, you pass a String query to the prepareStatement() method. The string passed as an argument is a parameterized query. A parameterized query looks like a standard SQL query, except the query takes an argument—for example, in the WHERE clause, we simply add a placeholder character, a question mark (?), as a parameter that will be filled in before we execute the query. Thus, the PreparedStatement object instance is constructed before the final query is executed, allowing you to modify the parameters of the query without having to construct a new Statement object every time.

Parameters passed into the query are referred to as IN parameters. In this example, we create a parameterized query to return the price of all books that have a title, such as the string we will pass into the query as a parameter:

```
try (Connection conn = DriverManager.getConnection(url, user, pwd)){
  String pQuery = "SELECT UnitPrice from Book WHERE Title LIKE ?";
  PreparedStatement pstmt = conn.prepareStatement(pQuery);
  pstmt.setString(1, "%Heroes%");  // Substitute this String for the
                                   // first parameter (?)
  ResultSet rs = pstmt.executeQuery();
  // ... process rows ....
} catch (SQLException se) {}
```

Let's take this apart. First, we created the `PreparedStatement` with a string that contained a parameter, indicated by the question mark in the string. The question mark represents a parameter that this query is expecting. Attempting to execute a query without setting a parameter will result in a `SQLException`.

The Java type of the parameter, `String`, `int`, `float`, etc., is entirely up to you. For this query, the type of the parameter expected is a `String`, so the `PreparedStatement` method used to insert a string value into the query is the `setString()` method. Note that we did not have to construct the `String` with single quotes, as you would typically have to do for a `String` query passed to a `Statement`:

```
SELECT UnitPrice FROM Book WHERE Title LIKE '%Heroes%'
```

This is an additional benefit of a `PreparedStatement`. Since the type expected by the `setString()` method is a `String`, the method replaces non-string characters by "escaping" them. Characters like `'` (single quote) are converted to `\'` (slash-single quote) in the string. Strings that could be executed as commands in SQL are converted to a single SQL string.

The `setString()` method takes two parameters: the index of the placeholder and the type expected by the set method. Just like the `updateXXXX` methods we looked at in `ResultSet` earlier, `PreparedStatement` has a `setXXXX` method for each of the Java types JDBC supports.

Again, as we mentioned earlier, the power of a `PreparedStatement` is that once the object is created with the parameterized query, the query is precompiled. When bind parameters are passed in the query, the query is stored in its post-plan state in the database. When parameters are received, the database simply has to substitute them into the plan and execute the query.

Where this makes the most sense is with a set of queries that is likely to be executed many times over the life of an application. For example, here is a `PreparedStatement` query used to add a record to the `Purchase_Item` table by adding another book to an existing customer's order:

```
INSERT INTO Purchase_Item (CustomerID, ISBN, Quantity) VALUES (?, ?, ?)
```

Queries like this one would be created by the application developer and used to create `PreparedStatements` available for execution at any point in the application lifecycle.

CallableStatement

The `CallableStatement` extends the `PreparedStatement` interface to support calling a stored procedure or function using JDBC. By the way, the only difference between a stored procedure and a function is that a function is designed to return an argument. So for the rest of this chapter, we will refer to stored procedures and functions collectively as stored procedures.

Stored procedures offer a number of advantages over straight SQL queries. Most stored procedure languages are fairly sophisticated and support variables, branching, looping, and if-then-else constructs. A stored procedure can execute any SQL statement, so a single stored procedure can perform a number of operations in a single execution.

One use case for a stored procedure is to encapsulate specific tables in the database. Just like a Java class can encapsulate data by making a field private and then only providing access to the field through a method, a stored procedure can be used to prevent a user from having access to the data in a table directly. For example, imagine that an employee database contains very sensitive information, such as salary, Social Security numbers, and birth dates. To protect this information, a stored procedure can perform several checks on the user executing the stored procedure before making any changes or allowing access to the data.

There are two drawbacks to stored procedures. First, stored procedures are typically developed in a proprietary, database-specific language, requiring a developer to learn yet another set of commands and syntax. Second, once in the database, how they were written and what they actually do can be difficult to figure out since they are "compiled" into the database. And we all know how much developers like to create detailed documentation for their code!

Recently, more and more database vendors have moved to allowing Java to run in the database, making it easier to write stored procedures, although this doesn't address the documentation issue. **The bottom line from a performance standpoint is that stored procedures rule (just not so much from a maintainability standpoint).** Regardless, how to write a stored procedure is really beyond the scope of this chapter, but some resources are available on the Internet—just do a search for "java stored procedures."

Because stored procedures can be a proprietary language with a unique syntax, the JDBC API provides JDBC-specific escape syntax for executing stored procedures and functions. The JDBC driver takes care of converting the JDBC syntax to the database format. This syntax has two forms: one form for functions that return a result, and another form for stored procedures that do not return a result.

```
{? = call <procedure-name>[(<arg1>,<arg2>, ...)]}  // Return a result
{call <procedure-name>[(<arg1>,<arg2>, ...)]}      // No result
```

Like `PreparedStatements`, `CallableStatements` can pass arguments in to the stored procedure using an IN parameter. However, as shown in the first form earlier, functions return a value, as shown by the question mark to the left of the equals sign. The result of a function is returned to the caller as a parameter registered as an OUT parameter. Finally, stored procedures also support a third type of parameter that can be used to pass values into a stored procedure and return a result. These are called INOUT parameters. We will look at examples using these three types of parameters next.

`CallableStatement` objects are created using a `Connection` object instance and the `prepareCall()` method. Like `PreparedStatement`, the `prepareCall()` method takes a `String` as the first argument that describes the stored procedure call and uses one of the two forms shown earlier. Let's look at an example. A stored procedure named "getBooksInRange" takes three arguments: a customer ID and two dates that represent the range to search between. The stored procedure returns all of the books purchased by a customer (the customer ID is used to identify the customer) between the two dates as a `ResultSet`.

Each of the parameters is an IN parameter and is inserted into the `CallableStatement cstmt` object using the appropriate `setXXXX` method before executing the stored procedure and returning the `ResultSet`:

```
// We have a Connection object and are in a try block
int customerID = 5001;
java.sql.Date fromDate = ...;  // The start date for the search
java.sql.Date toDate = ...;    // The end date for the search
String getBooksInDateRange  = "{call getBooksDateRange(?, ?, ?)}";
CallableStatement cstmt =
  conn.prepareCall(getBooksInDateRange,
                   ResultSet.TYPE_SCROLL_INSENSITIVE,
                   ResultSet.CONCUR_UPDATABLE);
cstmt.setInt(1, customerID);  // IN parameter 1 for customerID
cstmt.setDate(2, fromDate);   // IN parameter 2 for fromDate
cstmt.setDate(3, toDate);     // IN parameter 3 for toDate
ResultSet rs = cstmt.executeQuery();
```

Note that the `executeQuery()` command does not take a string (just like the `PreparedStatement executeQuery()` method). If you attempt to call `executeQuery()` on a `CallableStatement` with a `String` argument, a `SQLException` is thrown at runtime.

When a callable statement takes an OUT parameter, the parameter must also be registered as such before the call. For example, suppose we had a simple stored procedure that calculates the total of all orders placed by a customer. In this example, the stored procedure will return the result of the calculation as a SQL DOUBLE:

```
// We have a Connection object and are in a try block
int customerID = 5001;
double customerTotal;
CallableStatement cstmt =
  conn.prepareCall("{? = call customerTotal (?)}");
cstmt.registerOutParameter(1, java.sql.Types.DOUBLE);  // register
                                                        // the OUT
                                                        // parameter
cstmt.setInt(2, customerID);
cstmt.execute();  // Note we are not returning a ResultSet,
                  // so execute is the appropriate method
customerTotal = cstmt.getDouble(1);
```

A stored procedure that takes a parameter that doubles as an INOUT parameter is passed the IN parameter first and then registered as an OUT parameter—for example, an imaginary stored procedure that takes the customer ID and simply counts the orders and returns them in the same parameter.

```
// We have a Connection object and are in a try block
int customerID = 5001;
int numberOfOrders;
CallableStatement cstmt =
  conn.prepareCall("{call customerOrderCount (?)}");     // INOUT
cstmt.setInt(1, customerID);  // set the IN part of the parameter
cstmt.registerOutParameter(1, java.sql.Types.INTEGER);  // the OUT
                                                         // part
cstmt.execute();
numberOfOrders = cstmt.getInt(1);
```

Because stored procedures are code that you, as a JDBC developer, may not have insight or control over, you may or may not know if a stored procedure returns a `ResultSet`. In fact, invoking `executeQuery()` on a stored procedure that does not return a `ResultSet` object will throw a `SQLException`. So if you are not sure, a good practice is to use the `execute()` method instead and test for a `ResultSet` after executing a stored procedure by using the method `getMoreResults()`; for example:

```
cstmt.execute();                  // we executed some stored procedure
if (cstmt.getMoreResults()) {  // returns true if the next result is
                                  // a ResultSet
    // ... process the ResultSet
}
```

CERTIFICATION OBJECTIVE

Construct and Use RowSet Objects (OCP Objective 9.5)

9.5 Construct and use RowSet objects using the RowSetProvider class and the RowSetFactory interface.

One of the changes for Java SE 7 was a minor update to JDBC. The version number of the API went from 4.0 to 4.1, and there were changes to the `javax.sql.rowset` package, including the addition of an interface, `RowSetFactory`, and a class, `RowSetProvider`. This interface and this class provide a convenient way for a developer to either use the default reference implementation of `RowSet` objects, or use a custom implementation using a factory pattern. These changes are referred to as RowSet 1.1.

What this means to you is two things: First, `RowSetFactory` and `RowSetProvider` are on the exam, and second, as a consequence, there is some coverage of `RowSet` interfaces on the exam as well. So this section will look at how to use `RowSet` interfaces.

First, know that a `RowSet` is a `ResultSet`. The `RowSet` interface extends the `ResultSet` interface. `RowSet` objects fall into two categories: those that are connected to the database and therefore stay in sync with the data in the database, and those that can be disconnected from a database and synchronized with the database later.

A connected `RowSet` provides you with the opportunity to keep state synchronized with data in a database table—so you might use a connected `RowSet` object to keep a shopping cart or other type of cache without needing to translate changes in your cart object into SQL update or insert queries. A disconnected `RowSet` is created with some initial state read from the database and can then be disconnected and passed to other objects and later synchronized with the database with changes.

Note there is no magic associated with data synchronization—a `RowSet` is a `ResultSet`, and therefore has the ability to update, remove, and insert new rows in the database. The difference between a `ResultSet` and `RowSet` is that a `RowSet` can maintain state so that when the underlying `ResultSet` object is changed, the data changes are reflected in the database—either synchronously, in the case of a connected `RowSet`, or asynchronously, in the case of a disconnected `RowSet`.

You might use a disconnected `RowSet` to pass an object containing a result set to a completely different application. For example, imagine that you have an application that builds a customer profile for an insurance policy using a workflow application.

The initial data read may contain information about the customer: name, address, phone, and e-mail. This record is then passed as an object to another part of an application that fills in medical information: blood pressure, cholesterol, and blood sugar. When the disconnected `RowSet` object finally returns, it is synchronized with the database and any new and changed data is automatically written to the database without having to construct another SQL query.

Prior to RowSet 1.1, to create an instance of a `RowSet` object, you needed to know the full path name to the reference implementation class. So, to create an instance of a `JdbcRowSet` with the Sun reference implementation, you would need to include the full name of the implementation class (or make sure you imported the class) and include the implementation API in your classpath. For example:

```
JdbcRowSet jrs = new com.sun.rowset.JdbcRowSetImpl();
```

Now, in Java SE 7, the `RowSetProvider` class, which is part of the core API, manages access to the reference implementation and returns a factory object (`RowSetFactory`) that can be used to generate instances of `RowSet` objects. Hopefully, this sounds very familiar to you—this factory pattern is similar to the one used to create `Connection` objects. The `RowSetProvider` class will return a reference to a `RowSetFactory`, which in turn can be used to create instances of `RowSet` objects. For example:

```
RowSetFactory rsf = RowSetProvider.newFactory();  // The no-arg
     // newFactory() method returns an instance of a factory that
     // will create RowSet objects from the reference implementation
JdbcRowSet jrs = rsf.createJdbcRowSet();
```

While this additional code may seem unnecessary, it allows you, the developer, to work with a well-defined factory interface in the API rather than a specialized implementation object. As a result, the implementation could be swapped out, and you would need only change one line of code:

```
RowSetFactory rsf =
   RowSetProvider.newFactory("com.example.MyRowSetProvider", null);
JdbcRowSet jrs = rsf.createJdbcRowSet();
```

Working with RowSets

The `javax.sql` package (and several subpackages) were introduced in Java SE 1.4 as an important part of supporting J2EE (Java EE 1.4). Although the bulk of the work for 1.4 was the introduction of `DataSource` as an alternative to

`DriverManager`, `Connection` and `Statement` pooling in a J2EE container, and distributed transactions, what we are interested in in this section is `RowSet`.

The `RowSet` interface was developed to wrap a `ResultSet` as a JavaBeans component; in fact, the `RowSet` interface extends `java.sql.ResultSet`. So you may think of `RowSet` as a JavaBeans version of `ResultSet`. JavaBeans components have two important characteristics. One, they have a well-defined pattern for accessing fields in a class through getters and setters (properties), and two, they support and can participate in the JavaBeans event notification system.

Properties in a JavaBeans component are represented by a pair of methods, one to get the value of the property and one to set the value of the property. We often think of a property as a getter/setter pair for a class instance field, but the value of the property can also be computed. What is important about the getter/setter methods is consistency, because a requirement for a JavaBeans component is support for introspection. So, given these methods from the `RowSet` interface, we can infer that there is a String URL property associated with this component:

- `public String getUrl()` throws `SQLException`
- `public void setUrl(String url)` throws `SQLException`

The JavaBeans notification system allows `RowSets` to register themselves as listeners for events. A `RowSet` registers for an event by adding an instance of a class that implements the `RowSetListener` interface, which has three event methods that are invoked when one of the following events occurs on an instance of a `RowSet` object:

- A change in the cursor location
- A change to a row in this `RowSet` (inserted, updated, or deleted)
- A change to the `RowSet` contents (a new `RowSet`)

As we mentioned earlier, `RowSet` objects come in two flavors: connected and disconnected. A connected `RowSet` maintains its connection to the underlying database. A disconnected `RowSet` can be connected to a database to get its initial information and then disconnected. While disconnected, changes can be made to the `RowSet`: Rows can be added, updated, or deleted and when reconnected to the database, the changes will be synchronized. Let's look at each of these `RowSet` types.

Connected RowSets: JdbcRowSet

The `JdbcRowSet` interface extends `RowSet` and provides a connected JavaBeans-styled `ResultSet` object. A `JdbcRowSet` instance is created from the `RowSetFactory` and then populated with a `ResultSet` returned from executing a SQL query. `JdbcRowSet` is a fairly thin wrapper around `RowSet`, so many of the methods shown in the examples are actually `RowSet` methods. Let's start by creating a `JdbdRowSet` object:

```
String url = "jdbc:derby://localhost:1527/BookSellerDB";
String user = "bookguy";
String pwd = "$3lleR";
  // Construct a JdbcRowSet object in a try-with-resources statement
try (JdbcRowSet jrs = RowSetProvider.newFactory().createJdbcRowSet()) {
  String query = "SELECT * FROM Author";
  jrs.setCommand(query);    // Set the query to build the RowSet
  jrs.setUrl(url);          // JDBC URL
  jrs.setUsername(user);    // JDBC username
  jrs.setPassword(pwd);     // JDBC password
  jrs.execute();            // Execute the query stored in setCommand
  while (jrs.next()) {      // Get the next row
    // ... process the rows ...
  }
} catch (SQLException) {
}
```

Notice that we used the `JdbcRowSet` object to perform all of the tasks we did previously with a `Connection`, `Statement`, and `ResultSet`. Once we obtained the object from the factory, we simply set the values of the connection (URL, username, and password) and then execute the query statement. The `JdbcRowSet` object takes care of creating the connection, creating a statement, and executing the query. One of the nice features of a `JdbcRowSet` is that a number of characteristics are set by default. The default values and the setter methods are listed in the following table:

Property Method	Default Value
`setType(int type)`	`ResultSet.TYPE_SCROLL_INSENSITIVE`
`setConcurrency(int concurrency)`	`ResultSet.CONCUR_UPDATABLE`
`setEscapeProcessing(boolean enable)`	`true` (escape processing is performed by the driver)
`setMaxRows(int max)`	`0` (no limit on the number of rows in this `RowSet`)
`setMaxFieldSize(int max)`	`0` (no limit on the number of bytes for a column value of BINARY, VARBINARY, LONGVARBINARY, CHAR, VARCHAR, LONGVARCHAR, NCHAR, and NVARCHAR columns
`setQueryTimeout(int seconds)`	`0` (no time limit)
`setTransactionIsolation(int level)`	`Connection.TRANSACTION_READ_COMMITTED` (this is in the section on transactions)

exam watch

Note that the property setter methods and their default values are provided here for completeness. This level of detail is not on the exam.

Once the execute statement completes, we have a connected `JdbcRowSet`. From there, the rest of the code should look familiar. We used `next()` to get to the next row in the result set and then printed the results to the console.

An important difference between how `RowSet` objects work and `ResultSet` objects work is evident in the `execute()` method. The `execute()` method is really the equivalent of `executeQuery()` and is intended to populate the `JdbcRowSet` object with data. There are no `executeQuery()` or `executeUpdate()` methods, and attempting to use the `execute()` method to perform an UPDATE, INSERT, or DELETE query will result in a `SQLException`. Instead, to perform an update, you simply need to update the data in your `JdbcRowSet` object. For example, assuming that we have populated the `JdbcRowSet` object `jrs` with all of the Author data, here we will change the first name of the last author in the set:

```
jrs.last();                                // Position to the last row of Authors
jrs.updateString("FirstName", "Raquel");   // Update the first name
jrs.updateRow();                           // Apply the change (write to the
                                           // database)
```

To delete a row, we move the cursor to the desired row and delete it. Here, for example, we will delete the fifth row of the current `RowSet`:

```
jrs.absolute(5);
jrs.deleteRow();
```

To insert a new row into the `JdbcRowSet`, the methods are similar to those in `ResultSet`. In this example, we will add a new author to the `JdbcRowSet`:

```
jrs.moveToInsertRow();
jrs.updateInt("AuthorID", 1032);
jrs.updateString("FirstName", "Michael");
jrs.updateString("LastName", "Crichton");
jrs.insertRow();
jrs.moveToCurrentRow();
```

Note that like `ResultSet`, updating, deleting, and inserting affect the underlying database, but have varying effects on the current `RowSet`. Deleting a row from a `RowSet` leaves a gap in the current `RowSet` data, and inserting a row has no effect on the current `RowSet` data. The way to keep the data in the `JdbcRowSet` current is to re-execute the original query that populated the RowSet. You could simply add the execute command after every update, delete, or insert, like this:

```
jrs.execute();
```

But a more elegant way is to use the event model that JdbcRowSet implements. RowSet has a method to register a RowSetListener object:

```
public void addRowSetListener(RowSetListener listener)
```

The RowSetListener interface has three methods that are invoked by the implementation, depending upon the event:

- **public void cursorMoved(RowSetEvent event)** Receives an event for every movement of the cursor. This method is called a lot, for example, once for every invocation of next(), so be judicious of its use.
- **public void rowChanged(RowSetEvent event)** Receives an event when a row is updated, inserted, or deleted. This is a good method to use to refresh the RowSet.
- **public void rowSetChanged(RowSetEvent event)** Receives an event when the entire RowSet is changed, so for every invocation of execute().

Each of the methods listed here is passed a RowSetEvent object, which is simply a wrapper around the RowSet object that created the event. To create a listener that will automatically update our JdbcRowSet each time we delete, update, or insert a row, we need to create a class that implements RowSetListener and implement a rowChanged() method to refresh our RowSet:

```
public class MyRowSetListener implements RowSetListener {
  @Override
  public void rowChanged(RowSetEvent event) {   // A row changed:
                                                // updated, inserted
                                                // or deleted.
    if (event.getSource() instanceof RowSet) {
      try {
        ((RowSet) event.getSource()).execute(); // Re-execute the
                                                // query, refreshing
                                                // the results
      } catch (SQLException se) {
        out.println("SQLException during execute");
      }
    }
  }

  @Override
  public void cursorMoved(RowSetEvent event) {  // Cursor moved
  }
```

```
    @Override
    public void rowSetChanged(RowSetEvent event) { // Entire RowSet
                                                   // changed
    }
}
```

Now we simply need to register this listener with our `JdbcRowSet`:

```
jrs.addRowSetListener(new MyRowSetListener());
```

Now, whenever a row is updated, deleted, or inserted, the `rowChanged()` method in `MyRowSetListener` will be invoked and execute the current query set in the `RowSet` object to refresh the data in the `RowSet`.

Disconnected RowSets: CachedRowSet

There are several disconnected `RowSets`: `WebRowSet`, `FilteredRowSet`, and `JoinRowSet`. These `RowSets` are descendants of `CachedRowSet`, with some additional specialization in each. So once you understand `CachedRowSet`, we can describe the other interfaces in a few sentences. Working through each of the `RowSets` is really beyond the scope of this chapter, and is not covered on the exam.

A disconnected `RowSet` operates without requiring a connection to a database. Of course, in order to start with data, a disconnected `RowSet` typically *does* make a connection and gets a `ResultSet`, but immediately after, it is disconnected and can operate even if the database is offline. This is really the definition of a cache, after all—it is data held in memory and only synchronized with its data source when required.

To create a `CachedRowSet`, you create one from the `RowSetFactory`:

```
CachedRowSet crs = RowSetProvider.newFactory().createCachedRowSet();
```

To initially load a `CachedResultSet`, you follow the same sequence as a `JdbcRowSet`: by setting the JDBC URL, username, password, and an execute query to populate the initial results:

```
String query = "SELECT * FROM Author";
crs.setCommand(query);    // Set the query to build the RowSet
crs.setUrl(url);          // JDBC URL
crs.setUsername(user);    // JDBC username
crs.setPassword(pwd);     // JDBC password
crs.execute();            // Populate the CachedRowSet with data
```

Once you have made some changes (updated, inserted, or deleted) and are ready to push those changes to the database, you need to call the `acceptChanges()` method:

```
crs.acceptChanges();
```

The difference between a connected `RowSet`, `JdbcRowSet`, and a disconnected `RowSet` is what happens behind the scenes for the `execute()` and `acceptChanges()` methods. `CachedRowSet` relies on another class, `SyncProvider`, to perform the synchronization with the underlying database. `SyncProvider` is implemented for you in the reference implementation. `SyncProvider` has two additional interfaces to perform reading (`RowSetReader`) and to perform writing (`RowSetWriter`). The implementation of these classes performs the following functions:

- **`RowSetReader`** Makes a connection to the database, executes the query set in the `RowSet`, populates the `CachedRowSet` object with the data, and closes the connection.
- **`RowSetWriter`** Makes a connection, updates the database with the changes made to the `CachedRowSet` object, and closes the connection.

If there are conflicts between the changes made to the disconnected `RowSet` object and the database (i.e., someone else altered the database while the `CachedRowSet` was disconnected), then `SyncProvider` will throw a `SyncProviderException`. You can use the exception thrown to get an instance of a class called `SyncResolver` to manage the conflicts. As your head is surely spinning by now, don't worry—this is not on the exam and really beyond the scope of what this chapter is meant to cover.

Just to wrap up our discussion on the remaining `RowSet` objects, here is a summary of the `RowSet` objects in RowSet 1.1 and some benefits and features of each.

RowSet Object	Description
`JbdcRowSet`	A connected `RowSet`; acts as JavaBeans component by providing a thin wrapper around a `ResultSet`; useful for applications that benefit from the event model supported by `JdbcRowSet`.
`CachedRowSet`	A disconnected `RowSet`; provides an offline representation of a `RowSet`; useful for applications where the data needs to be available when the database is not (for example, in a portable device).
`WebRowSet`	A `CachedRowSet` that can write itself as an XML file and read an XML file to re-create a `WebRowSet`. Useful in applications where XML data is a requirement.
`FilteredRowSet`	A `WebRowSet` that provides the additional capability of filtering its contents. `FilteredRowSets` can use a `Predicate` object to control what data is returned.
`JoinRowSet`	A `WebRowSet` that can combine related data from multiple `RowSets` into a single `JoinRowSet`. A useful alternative to the use of a SQL JOIN statement.

CERTIFICATION OBJECTIVE

JDBC Transactions (OCP Objective 9.4)

9.4 Use JDBC transactions (including disabling auto-commit mode, committing and rolling back transactions, and setting and rolling back to savepoints).

Transactions are a part of our everyday life. The classic transaction example involves two parties attempting to alter the same piece of data at the same time. For example, using the Figure 15-9, imagine we have two hopeful concert-goers, both interested in seats at the nearly sold-out Coldplay concert. Person A, on the top computer, wants five seats, all together, as close to center stage as possible. So in step 1 in the figure, the system returns information that it read from the concert-seating database, that yes, there are five seats together in row 12!

Person B on another computer (which looks suspiciously like Person A's computer) is interested in three seats together, close to center stage. Again, in step 2, the database returns information that indicates that yes, there are three seats in row 12. So we arrive at the critical point—who will get the tickets?

Person B enters her credit card information and presses the buy button to purchase three tickets. The system begins a transaction to purchase the three seats. The system checks the credit card, gets a preliminary okay for the charge, updates the records of three seats to mark them unavailable, and charges the credit card. Finally, the transaction is committed and the system returns a confirmation message to Person B.

FIGURE 15-9 A transaction problem

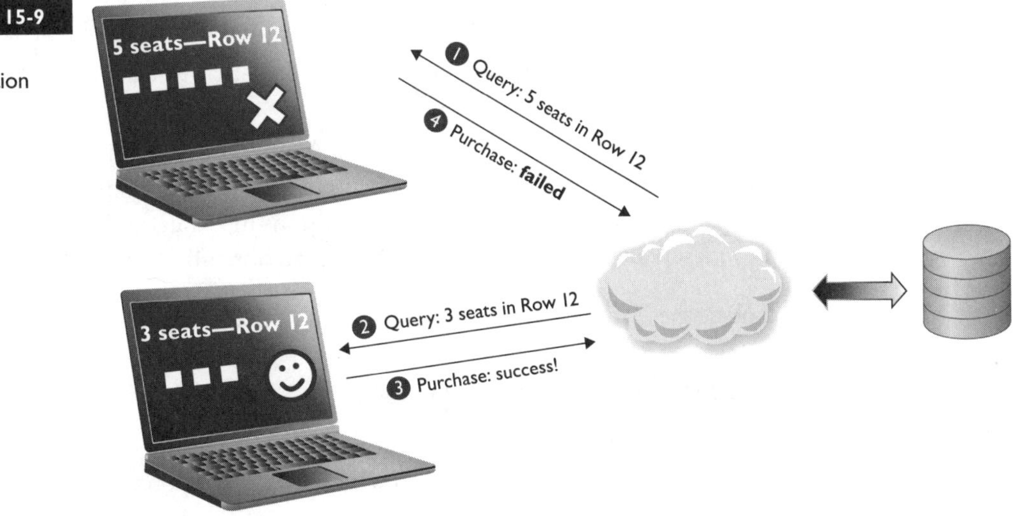

Meanwhile, Person A has finished entering his credit card information and started a transaction for the five seats. The system begins a transaction to purchase five seats. The system checks the credit card, gets a preliminary okay for the charge, and attempts to update the records of the five seats, but now three of the five seats are already marked taken. (By the way, as you will see a little later, this is called a dirty read.) At this point, the system must roll back the entire transaction, issue a credit request to the credit card, and return an error message to Person A.

This is the way transactions are supposed to work. What we would not want (or expect) to happen is that the system goes ahead and charges Person A for the five seats anyway, or conversely, for Person B to get the three seats even if her card was rejected. A transaction for the tickets is all or nothing—the desired seats have to be available, and the credit card must be valid and capable of being charged the amount of the tickets. This is the criteria for a successful transaction: all of them have to happen together, or none of them happens. And if any part of the transaction should fail—a bad credit card number or not enough seats—then everything must go back to the way it was before the transaction began. As it is, Person A may not be going to see Coldplay, but he is also not being charged for the tickets.

Fundamentally, in the world of transactions, it comes down to making sure that everything we wanted to happen in a transaction does, and that if there is a problem, everything goes back to the way it was before the transaction started.

JDBC Transaction Concepts

JDBC support for transactions is a requirement for compliance with the specification. JDBC support for transactions includes three concepts:

- All transactions are in auto-commit mode unless explicitly disabled.
- Transactions have varying levels of isolation—that is, what data is visible to the code executing in a transaction.
- JDBC supports the idea of a savepoint. A savepoint is a point within a transaction where the work that occurred up until that point is valid. A savepoint is useful when there are conditions in a transaction that you wish to preserve even if other parts of the transaction fail.

Let's look at these three concepts in more detail in the next few sections.

Starting a Transaction Context in JDBC

Transactions are typically started with some type of `begin` statement. However, the JDBC API does not provide a `begin()` method for transactions, and by default, the

JDBC driver or the database determines when to start a transaction and when to commit an existing transaction. When a SQL statement requires a transaction, the JDBC driver or database creates a transaction and commits the transaction when the statement ends. In order for you to control transactions with JDBC, you must first turn off this auto-commit mode:

```
Connection conn = DriverManager.getConnection(url, username, password);
conn.setAutoCommit(false);  // The JDBC equivalent of
                            // begin transaction
```

Note the comment in the code—**when you turn off auto-commit mode, you also explicitly begin a transaction.**

A transaction includes all of the SQL queries you execute until either

- You explicitly commit the current transaction.
- You explicitly roll back the current transaction.
- There is a failure that forces an automatic rollback.

As an example, we are going to add a book to Bob's Bookstore. A book has a three-part relationship in our schema: There is an entry in the Authors table for the author's name (first and last), and an entry in the Books table for the book, and a relationship between the two in the Books_by_Author table. If one of these three tables is not updated, we would end up with a phantom author or book. So when we add a book to Bob's Bookstore, we need all three tables to be populated in a single transaction (all of the insert statements happen as a unit):

```
Connection conn = DriverManager.getConnection(url, username,
                  password);
conn.setAutoCommit(false); // Start a transaction
Statement stmt = conn.createStatement();
stmt.execute("INSERT INTO Author VALUES(1031, 'Rachel', 'McGinn')");
stmt.execute("INSERT INTO Book VALUES('0554466789',
             'My American Dolls', '2012-08-31','Paperback', 7.95)");
stmt.execute(("INSERT INTO Books_by_Author
              VALUES(1031,'0554466789')");
conn.commit();  // Commit the current transaction and
                // start another
```

This is a perfect opportunity to use a set of prepared statements or, better yet, a stored procedure, since this is likely something that would happen a lot in a bookstore! As an application developer, if you find yourself cutting and pasting code, even if you are modifying it, think about being a DRY programmer. Andy Hunt and Dave Thomas formulated this principle in

their book** The Pragmatic Programmer **(Addison-Wesley Professional, 1999). DRY stands for Don't Repeat Yourself. What? I said, don't... ah, you got me—very funny. Fundamentally, the DRY principle is about looking for every opportunity to apply code reuse by creating other methods or classes instead of copying and pasting. (As a counterpoint, programmers who cut and paste are sometimes called WET programmers: "Write Everything Twice," or perhaps "We Enjoy Typing"?)

This example illustrates the concept of a transaction demarcation—where and when a transaction is started, and where and when a transaction is committed. Notice that we start a transaction on a `Connection` object by turning auto-commit off (false). This means that `Connection` can only have one transaction active at any one time. And without going into a lot of details about the different transaction models, this means that transactions in JDBC are *flat*. A flat transaction can include a number of different SQL statements, but there is only one transaction, and it only has one beginning and one end (at commit).

The other point is that as soon as the `commit()` method returns, we have started another transaction. Now what happens to our database if we don't invoke the `commit()` method? If for, example, in the code fragment earlier, we left off the `conn.commit()` and just closed the `Connection`? Well, because invoking `commit()` changes the database, and JDBC is required to make sure that any statements are completely executed, the driver will not perform a commit implicitly, and the driver and database simply roll back the transaction as if nothing happened.

Rolling Back a Transaction

In the example we used to open this section on transactions, we mentioned that when Person A's attempt to get five seats for Coldplay fails, the credit card transaction that was started is rolled back—in fact, short of remembering that he attempted to buy the tickets, there is no record of the credit transaction at all; it is as if it never happened.

A transaction rollback is simply a way to indicate, "These operations aren't working out, I want everything back the way it was." Transactions can be rolled back explicitly in code by invoking the `rollback()` method on the `Connection` object, or implicitly if a `SQLException` is thrown during any point of the transaction. As an example of an explicit rollback, in the code example where we added a new book to the database, we might want to check to make sure that each SQL INSERT was successful and, if there was a problem, roll back the entire transaction. The modified code looks like this:

```
Connection conn = DriverManager.getConnection(url, username, password);
conn.setAutoCommit(false); // Start a transaction
Statement stmt = conn.createStatement();
int result1, result2, result3;
try {
  result1 = stmt.executeUpdate("INSERT INTO Author
            VALUES(1031, 'Rachel', 'McGinn')");
  result2 = stmt.executeUpdate("INSERT INTO Book
            VALUES('0554466789', 'My American Dolls',
            '2012-08-31','Paperback', 7.95)");
  result3 = stmt.executeUpdate("INSERT INTO Books_by_Author
            VALUES(1031,'0554466789')");
  conn.commit();       // No exception: commit the entire transaction
} catch (SQLException ex) {

    conn.rollback();   // Rollback the entire transaction
                       // if an exception thrown


}
```

Note that both `commit()` and `rollback()` are transaction methods, and if either of these methods is invoked when a `Connection` is not in a transaction (for example, when a `Connection` is in auto-commit mode), these methods will throw a `SQLException`.

exam watch

One final point on the `setAutoCommit()` method. If auto-commit is turned back on during a transaction, i.e., `setAutoCommit(true)`, any current transaction is committed and auto-commit mode is then turned back on. Turning auto-commit on and off is not something likely to happen a lot in actual code, but it is something that the exam developers thought you ought to know in the context of transactions with JDBC.

on the job

One thing that is important to remember when using transactions is that it is extremely rare for an application to have only one user. As a result, there is a strong likelihood that two users will attempt to access the same data at the same time. An important aspect of transactions is isolation level—the visibility of one transaction to the changes being made by another transaction. Most databases (and therefore their drivers) have some default isolation level, and you can determine what isolation support is available

using `DatabaseMetaData` and set the isolation level using the Connection `setTransactionIsolation()` method.

However, choosing the appropriate isolation level is an important task because with too little isolation, you run the risk of incorrect results, and with too much isolation, application performance suffers. Typically, you would work with your DBA to learn what the default isolation level is for your database and whether customizing the level would be appropriate for your application.

Using Savepoints with JDBC

A savepoint is some point in a transaction where you want to place a virtual marker, indicating that everything is good up until this point. As a practical example of a transaction savepoint, imagine a situation in which a customer places an order for several books. The order application checks the availability of the requested books and finds that one of the books is out of stock. Rather than roll back the entire transaction, the application may place a savepoint on the order (for some limited amount of time) to allow the customer to decide if they want either the order all at once or a partial shipment now of the available titles and the rest later. If the customer agrees to receive a partial shipment, the transaction could then continue from the savepoint and ship part of the order.

In the JDBC API, a Savepoint is an object returned by a Connection in a transaction. A Savepoint object can be named or unnamed (created with a String name or not). The benefit of a Savepoint is that it represents a point in a transaction that you can roll back to. For example, let's look at our sample code where we add a book to Bob's Books. Suppose that we decide that while we must have an entry in the Book and Author table, we are okay if the entry in the join table fails, because we can make the connection between a book and its authors later.

We decide to use a Savepoint to identify that point when the Book and Author tables are set, and we can roll the transaction back to that point and commit it there if necessary:

```
Connection conn = DriverManager.getConnection(url, username,
                  password);
conn.setAutoCommit(false); // Start a transaction
Statement stmt = conn.createStatement();
int result1, result2, result3;
String query1 = "INSERT INTO Author " +
                "VALUES(1031, 'Rachel', 'McGinn')";

String query2 = "INSERT INTO Book " +
                "VALUES('0554466789', " +
                "'My American Dolls', '2012-08-31'," +
                "'Paperback', 7.95)";
```

```
try {
  result1 = stmt.executeUpdate(query1);
  result2 = stmt.executeUpdate(query2);
  Savepoint sp1 = null;

  sp1 = conn.setSavepoint();           // Create a Savepoint
                                       // for the two inserts so far
} catch (SQLException ex) {
  conn.rollback();                     // If we did not successfully insert
  throw new SQLException("fail"); // one record in author and book,
                                       // rollback the transaction and
                                       // throw an exception
}
String query3 = "INSERT INTO Books_by_Author " +
                "VALUES(1031,'0554466789')";
try {
  result3 = stmt.executeUpdate(query3);

  conn.commit();         // If the whole thing worked, commit
} catch (SQLException ex) {
  conn.rollback(sp1);    // If the join table insert failed, that's
                         // ok, rollback to the Savepoint (rollback
                         // the insert into Books_by_Author)
  conn.commit();         // and commit from there.
}
```

There are a few important things to note about Savepoints:

- When you set Savepoint A and then later set Savepoint B, if you roll back to Savepoint A, you automatically release and invalidate Savepoint B.
- Support for Savepoints is not required, but you can check to see if your JDBC driver and database support Savepoints using the `DatabaseMetaData.supportsSavePoints()` method, which will return true if Savepoints are supported.
- Because a Savepoint is an actual point-in-time state of a transaction context, the number of Savepoints supported by your JDBC driver and database may be limited. For example, the Java DB database does support Savepoints, but only one per transaction.

There is good news and bad news as well. The bad news is that there is no method to determine the number of Savepoints supported by your JDBC driver and database. The good news is that if you only get one, you can reuse it. `Connection` provides a `releaseSavepoint()` method, which takes a Savepoint object. After the Savepoint is released, you can set another Savepoint, sort of like moving your pebble forward in hopscotch!

CERTIFICATION SUMMARY

Core JDBC API

Remember that the JDBC API is a set of interfaces with one important concrete class, the `DriverManager` class. You write code using the well-defined set of JDBC interfaces, and the provider of your JDBC driver writes code implementations of those interfaces. The key (and therefore required) interfaces a JDBC driver must implement include `Driver`, `Connection`, `Statement`, and `ResultSet`.

The driver provider will also implement an instance of `DatabaseMetaData`, which you use to invoke a method to query the driver for information about the database and JDBC driver. One important piece of information is if the database is SQL-92 compliant, and there are a number of methods that begin with "supports" to determine the capabilities of the driver. One important method is `supportsResultSetType()`, which is used to determine if the driver supports scrolling result sets.

DriverManager

The `DriverManager` is one of the few concrete classes in the JDBC API, and you will recall that the `DriverManager` is a factory class—using the `DriverManager`, you construct instances of `Connection` objects. In reality, the `DriverManager` simply holds references to registered JDBC drivers, and when you invoke the `getConnection()` method with a JDBC URL, the `DriverManager` passes the URL to each driver in turn. If the URL matches a valid driver, host, port number, username, and password, then that driver returns an instance of a `Connection` object. Remember that the JDBC URL is simply a string that encodes the information required to make a connection to a database.

How a JDBC driver is registered with the `DriverManager` is also important. In the current version of JDBC, 4.0, and later, the driver jar file simply needs to be on the classpath, and the `DriverManager` will take care of finding the driver's `Driver` class implementation and load that. JDBC, 3.0, and earlier, require that the driver's `Driver` class implementation be manually loaded using the `Class.forName()` method with the fully qualified class name of the class.

Statements and ResultSets

The most important use of a database is clearly using SQL statements and queries to create, read, update, and delete database records. The `Statement` interface provides the methods needed to create SQL statements and execute them. Remember that there are three different `Statement` methods to execute SQL queries: one that returns a result set, `executeQuery()`; one that returns an affected row count, `executeUpdate()`; and one general-purpose method, `execute()`, that returns a boolean to indicate if the query produced a result set.

`ResultSet` is the interface used to read columns of data returned from a query, one row at a time. `ResultSet` objects represent a snapshot (a copy) of the data returned from a query, and there is a cursor that points to just above the first row when the results are returned. Unless you created a `Statement` object using the `Connection.createStatement(int, int)` method that takes `resultSetType` and `resultSetConcurrency` parameters, `ResultSets` are not updatable and only allow the cursor to move forward through the results. However, if your database supports it, you can create a `Statement` object with a type of `ResultSet.TYPE_SCROLL_INSENSITIVE` and/or a concurrency of `ResultSet.CONCUR_UPDATABLE`, which allows any result set created with the `Statement` object to position the cursor anywhere in the results (scrollable) and allows you to change the value of any column in any row in the result set (updatable). Finally, when using a `ResultSet` that is scrollable, you can determine the number of rows returned from a query—and this is the only way to determine the row count because there is no "`rowCount`" method.

`SQLException` is the base class for exceptions thrown by JDBC, and because one query can result in a number of exceptions, the exceptions are chained. To determine all of the reasons a method call returned a `SQLException`, you must iterate through the exception by calling the `getNextException()` method. JDBC also keeps track of warnings for methods on `Connection`, `Statement`, and `ResultSet` objects using a `SQLWarning` exception type. Like `SQLException`, `SQLWarning` is silently chained to the object that caused the warning—for example, suppose that you attempt to create a `Statement` object that supports scrollable `ResultSet`, but the database does not support that type. A `SQLWarning` will be added to the `Connection` object (the `Connection.createConnection(int, int)` method creates a `Statement` object). The `getWarnings()` method is used to return any `SQLWarnings`.

One of the important additions to Java SE 7 is the `try`-with-resources statement, and all of the JDBC interfaces have been updated to support the new `AutoCloseable` interface. However, bear in mind that there is an order of precedence when closing `Connections`, `Statements`, and `ResultSets`. So when a `Connection` is closed, any `Statement` created from that `Connection` is also closed, and likewise, when a `Statement` is closed, any `ResultSet` created using that `ResultSet` is also closed. And attempting to invoke a method on a closed object will result in a `SQLException`!

PreparedStatement and CallableStatement

SQL provides the ability to create a prepared statement query that is "precompiled." This means that the syntax of the statement has been checked; any table names and column names are checked against the schema and, finally, an execution plan for the query is created. Note that JDBC's `PreparedStatement` performs this precompilation during the first execution of the `PreparedStatement`. When you pass parameters to a prepared statement, the database substitutes the values you pass in for placeholders in the precompiled query. This makes the execution of the prepared query much faster than a regular query.

JDBC's `PreparedStatement` object uses this mechanism to pass parameters into the precompiled query from your Java code. This approach makes it difficult to create a SQL injection attack because each `PreparedStatement` doesn't allow strings passed in as parameters to contain non-string characters—these are "escaped" by prepending backslashes to them to make them into string characters.

Parameters passed into `PreparedStatements` are called IN parameters—these are set into the prepared statement and passed to the database for execution. Each IN type parameter corresponds to a specific placeholder (indicated by a question mark character).

`CallableStatement` is the JDBC object used to invoke database stored procedures. Unlike prepared statements, stored procedures use a database-dependent language that may or may not resemble SQL. Like prepared statements, stored procedures are compiled into the database and can accept parameters passed to them. However, stored procedures also allow values to be returned to the caller through OUT type parameters, using the same "?" syntax. Finally, parameters can be passed into a stored procedure *and* return a new value as a result through an INOUT type parameter.

RowSet, RowSetProvider, and RowSetFactory

Remember that as a result of a minor change to JDBC for version 4.1, the way that `RowSet` objects were created was changed, and thus, `RowSetFactory` and `RowSetProvider` are covered on the exam. Further, this means that you should understand the major differences between the various `RowSet` interfaces as well.

In previous versions of JDBC, an instance of a `RowSet` was created using the new keyword on a specific implementation, and you had to include the implementation in your classpath. In Java SE 7, using the `RowSetProvider` class and `newFactory()` method, you get an instance of a `RowSetFactory` object. Finally, `RowSet` objects are created using the factory. This approach hides the implementation details and eliminates changes in your code for different `RowSet` implementations.

The key to understanding `RowSet` objects is the difference between a connected and unconnected `RowSet`. A connected `RowSet` object, like `JdbcRowSet`, is created using an instance of `RowSetFactory` and then populated through a SQL query. Once populated, changes to a `JdbcRowSet` (updates, deletes, and inserts) are automatically reflected in the underlying database. To keep the `JdbcRowSet` in sync with the underlying database contents, you can re-execute the initial `JdbcRowSet` query or implement a `RowSetListener` to manage synchronization by tracking changes to the `RowSet`.

There are several disconnected `RowSets`, all descendants of `CachedRowSet`, so if you learn this one, you will be in good shape. Like connected `RowSets`, a disconnected `RowSet` is initially populated with a `ResultSet`. However, immediately after the `RowSet` is populated, it is disconnected from the database. Any changes made to the underlying results are cached (thus the aptly named class!). You are responsible for synching the changes you made with the underlying database by calling the `acceptChanges()` method.

JDBC Transactions

The key takeaway for this certification objective is that JDBC transactions are in auto-commit mode by default, and you must explicitly start a transaction by calling `Connection.setAutoCommit()` with a boolean false parameter. This starts a transaction context. Within a transaction context, any changes made to the current `ResultSet` are not made to the underlying database until you explicitly call the `commit()` method. If you wish to undo changes made during a transaction, the transaction can be rolled back by calling the `rollback()` method. If a method invoked during a transaction results in a `SQLException`, the transaction is rolled back automatically. Finally, remember that the `setAutoCommit()` method is tricky—if you are in the middle of a transaction and call `setAutoCommit(true)`, the equivalent of turning auto-commit back on, then the current transaction context is immediately committed.

Transactions in JDBC are flat, meaning there can be only one transaction context per `Connection` at any one time. However, some databases allow you to mark spots in your transaction called savepoints. If, partway through a transaction with multiple changes (inserts, deletes, updates), you create a Savepoint object by calling the `setSavepoint()` method, and if there is a problem further on in the transaction, you can roll the transaction back to your savepoint instead of all the way to the beginning.

TWO-MINUTE DRILL

Here are some of the key points from the certification objectives in this chapter.

Core Interfaces of the JDBC API (OCP Objective 9.1)

- ❑ To be compliant with JDBC, driver vendors must provide implementations for the key JDBC interfaces: `Driver`, `Connection`, `Statement`, and `ResultSet`.
- ❑ `DatabaseMetaData` can be used to determine which SQL-92 level your driver and database support.
- ❑ `DatabaseMetaData` provides methods to interrogate the driver for capabilities and features.

Connect to a Database Using DriverManager (OCP Objective 9.2)

- ❑ The JDBC API follows a factory pattern, where the `DriverManager` class is used to construct instances of `Connection` objects.
- ❑ The JDBC URL is passed to each registered driver in turn in an attempt to create a valid `Connection`.
- ❑ Identify the Java statements required to connect to a database using JDBC.
- ❑ JDBC 3.0 (and earlier) drivers must be loaded prior to their use.
- ❑ JDBC 4.0 drivers just need to be part of the classpath, and they are automatically loaded by the `DriverManager`.

Submit Queries and Read Results from the Database (OCP Objective 9.3)

- ❑ The `next()` method must be called on a `ResultSet` before reading the first row of results.
- ❑ When a `Statement execute()` method is executed, any open `ResultSets` tied to that `Statement` are automatically closed.
- ❑ When a `Statement` is closed, any related `ResultSets` are also closed.

- `ResultSet` column indexes are numbered from 1, not 0.
- The default `ResultSet` is not updatable (read-only), and the cursor moves forward only.
- A `ResultSet` that is scrollable and updatable can be modified, and the cursor can be positioned anywhere within the `ResultSet`.
- `ResultSetMetaData` can be used to dynamically discover the number of columns and their type returned in a `ResultSet`.
- `ResultSetMetaData` does not have a row count method. To determine the number of rows returned, the `ResultSet` must be scrollable.
- `ResultSet` fetch size can be controlled for large data sets; however, it is a hint to the driver and may be ignored.
- `SQLExceptions` are chained. You must iterate through the exception class thrown to get all of the reasons why an exception was thrown.
- `SQLException` also contains database-specific error codes and status codes.
- The `executeQuery` method is used to return a `ResultSet` (SELECT).
- The `executeUpdate` method is used to update data, to modify the database, and to return the number of rows affected (INSERT, UPDATE, DELETE, and DDLs).
- The `execute` method is used to perform any SQL command. A boolean `true` is returned when the query produced a `ResultSet` and `false` when there were no results, or if the result is an update count.
- There is an order of precedence in the closing of `Connections`, `Statements`, and `ResultSets`.
- Using the `try`-with-resources statement, you can close `Connections`, `Statements`, and `ResultSets` automatically (they implement the new `AutoCloseable` interface in Java SE 7).
- When a `Connection` is closed, all of the related `Statements` and `ResultSets` are closed.

Use PreparedStatement and CallableStatement Objects (OCP Objective 9.6)

- `PreparedStatements` are precompiled and can increase efficiency for frequently used SQL queries.

- `PreparedStatement` is a good way to avoid SQL injection attacks.
- `PreparedStatement setXXXX` methods are indexed from 1, not 0.
- `CallableStatements` are executed using a stored procedure on the database.
- The actual language used to create the stored procedure is database dependent.

Construct and Use RowSet Objects (OCP Objective 9.5)

- `JdbcRowSet` provides a JavaBean view of a `ResultSet` (getters and setters).
- Understand `CachedRowSet`, `FilteredRowSet`, `JdbcRowSet`, `Joinable`, `JoinRowSet`, `Predicate`, and `WebRowSet`.
- `RowSetProvider` is a factory class used to obtain a `RowSetFactory` to generate `RowSet` object types.
- `RowSetFactory` provides a way to create instances of `RowSet` objects. Prior to JDBC 4.1 (Java SE 7), the developer was required to provide the class name of the implementation of the `RowSet` interface.

JDBC Transactions (OCP Objective 9.4)

- Transactions in JDBC are flat—that is, there is only one transaction active at any one time per `Connection` instance.
- All transactions in JDBC are in auto-commit mode by default—you must explicitly turn transactions on by calling `Connection.setAutoCommit(false)`.
- Invoking `setAutoCommit(true)` explicitly commits the current transaction (and reverts to auto-commit mode).
- A rollback method throws an exception if `Connection` is set to auto-commit mode.
- A savepoint is a point within a current transaction that can be referenced from a `Connection.rollback()` method.
- A rollback to a savepoint only rolls the transaction back to the last savepoint created.

SELF TEST

1. Given:

```
String url = "jdbc:mysql://SolDBServer/soldb";
String user = "sysEntry";
String pwd = "fo0B3@r";
// INSERT CODE HERE
Connection conn = DriverManager.getConnection(url, user, pwd);
```

Assuming `"org.gjt.mm.mysql.Driver"` is a legitimate class, which line, when inserted at `// INSERT CODE HERE`, will correctly load this JDBC 3.0 driver?

A `DriverManager.registerDriver("org.gjt.mm.mysql.Driver");`

B. `Class.forName("org.gjt.mm.mysql.Driver");`

C. `DatabaseMetaData.loadDriver("org.gjt.mm.mysql.Driver");`

D. `Driver.connect("org.gjt.mm.mysql.Driver");`

E. `DriverManager.getDriver("org.gjt.mm.mysql.Driver");`

2. Given that you are working with a JDBC 4.0 driver, which three are required for this JDBC driver to be compliant?

A. Must include a `META-INF/services/java.sql.Driver` file

B. Must provide implementations of `Driver`, `Connection`, `Statement`, and `ResultSet` interfaces

C. Must support scrollable `ResultSets`

D. Must support updatable `ResultSets`

E. Must support transactions

F. Must support the SQL99 standard

G. Must support `PreparedStatement` and `CallableStatement`

3. Which three are available through an instance of `DatabaseMetaData`?

A. The number of columns returned

B. The number of rows returned

C. The name of the JDBC driver

D. The default transaction isolation level

E. The last query used

F. The names of stored procedures in the database

G. The current Savepoint name

4. Given:

```
try {
  Statement stmt = conn.createStatement();
  String query =
         "SELECT * FROM Author WHERE LastName LIKE 'Rand%'";
  ResultSet rs = stmt.executeQuery(query);  // Line X
  if (rs == null) {                         // Line Y
    System.out.println("No results");
  } else {
    System.out.println(rs.getString("FirstName"));
  }
} catch (SQLException se) {
  System.out.println("SQLException");
}
```

Assuming a `Connection` object has already been created (conn) and that the query produces a valid result, what is the result?

A. Compiler error at line X

B. Compiler error at line Y

C. No result

D. The first name from the first row that matches 'Rand%'

E. `SQLException`

F. A runtime exception

5. Given the SQL query:

```
String query = "UPDATE Customer SET EMail='John.Smith@comcast.net'
                WHERE CustomerID = 5000";
```

Assuming this is a valid SQL query and there is a valid `Connection` object (conn), which will compile correctly and execute this query?

A.
```
Statement stmt = conn.createStatement();
stmt.executeQuery(query);
```

B.
```
Statement stmt = conn.createStatement(query);
stmt.executeUpdate();
```

C.
```
Statement stmt = conn.createStatement();
stmt.setQuery(query);
stmt.execute();
```

D.
```
Statement stmt = conn.createStatement();
stmt.execute(query);
```

E.
```
Statement stmt = conn.createStatement();
ResultSet rs = stmt.executeUpdate(query);
```

6. Given:

```
try {
  ResultSet rs = null;
  try (Statement stmt = conn.createStatement()) {  // line X
    String query = "SELECT * from Customer";
    rs = stmt.executeQuery(query);                 // line Y
  } catch (SQLException se) {
    System.out.println("Illegal query");
  }
  while (rs.next()) {
    // print customer names
  }
} catch (SQLException se) {
  System.out.println("SQLException");
}
```

And assuming a valid `Connection` object (conn) and that the query will return results, what is the result?

A. The customer names will be printed out

B. Compiler error at line X

C. Illegal query

D. Compiler error at line Y

E. `SQLException`

F. Runtime exception

7. Given this code fragment:

```
Statement stmt = conn.createStatement();
ResultSet rs;
String query = "<QUERY HERE>";
stmt.execute(query);
if ((rs = stmt.getResultSet()) != null) {
  System.out.println("Results");
}
if (stmt.getUpdateCount() > -1) {
  System.out.println("Update");
}
```

Which query statements entered into `<QUERY HERE>` produce the output that follows the query string (in the following answer), assuming each query is valid? (Choose all that apply.)

A. `"SELECT * FROM Customer"`
   `Results`

B. `"INSERT INTO Book VALUES ('1023456789', 'One Night in Paris', '1984-10-20', 'Hardcover', 13.95)"`
   `Update`

C. `"UPDATE Customer SET Phone = '555-234-1021' WHERE CustomerID = 101"`
   `Update`

D. `"SELECT Author.LastName FROM Author"`
   `Results`

E. `"DELETE FROM Book WHERE ISBN = '1023456789'"`
   `Update`

8. Given:

```
String q = "UPDATE Customer SET Last_name=? WHERE Customer_id=?";
try {
  PreparedStatement pstmt = conn.prepareStatement(q);
  pstmt.setString(0, "Smith");                  // Line X
  pstmt.setString(1, "5001");                   // Line Y
  int result = pstmt.executeUpdate();
  if (result != 1) System.out.println ("Error - update failed");
} catch (SQLException se) {
  System.out.println("Exception");
}
```

Assuming the table name and column names are valid, what is the result?

A. The last name of the customer with id 5001is set to `"Smith"`

B. Error – update failed

C. Exception

D. Compilation fails

9. Given:

```
try {
  String[] searchPair = {"%lacey", "%Fire%", "R%", "%Lost Hero%"};
  String query = "SELECT Book.Title, Author.FirstName, " +
                 "Author.LastName FROM Author, Book, " +
                 "Books_by_Author WHERE Author.LastName LIKE ? " +
                 "AND Book.Title LIKE ? " +
                 "AND Books_by_Author.AuthorID=Author.AuthorID " +
                 "AND Books_by_Author.ISBN = Book.ISBN";
  PreparedStatement pstmt = conn.prepareStatement(query);
```

```
    for (int i = 0; i < searchPair.length; i += 2) {
      pstmt.setString(i+1, searchPair[i]);     // line X
      pstmt.setString(i+2, searchPair[i+1]);  // line Y
      ResultSet rs = pstmt.executeQuery();     // line Z
      while (rs.next()) {
        System.out.print("Yes ");
      }
    }
  } catch (SQLException se) {
    System.out.println("SQLException");
  }
```

And assuming that each pair of query elements in the array `searchPair` will return two rows and assuming a valid `Connection` object (conn), what is the result?

A. `SQLException`

B. `Yes Yes SQLException`

C. `Yes Yes Yes Yes`

D. Compiler error at line X

E. Compiler error at line Y

F. Compiler error at line Z

10. Given:

```
String call = "{CALL REMOVEBOOKS(?, ?)}";
String titleToRemove = null;
int maxBooks = 0;
CallableStatement cstmt = conn.prepareCall(call);
String titles = "%Hero%";
int numBooksRemoved;
// Code added here
```

If REMOVEBOOKS is a stored procedure that takes an INOUT integer parameter as its first argument and an IN `String` parameter as its second argument, which code blocks, when placed at the line `// Code added here`, could correctly execute the stored procedure and return a result?

A.
```
cstmt.setInt(0, maxBooks);
cstmt.setString(1, titleToRemove);
cstmt.registerOutParameter(0, java.sql.Types.INTEGER);
cstmt.execute();
numBooksRemoved = cstmt.getInt(0);
```

B.
```
cstmt.setInt(1, maxBooks);
cstmt.setString(2, titleToRemove);
cstmt.registerOutParameter(1, java.sql.Types.INTEGER);
cstmt.executeQuery(query);
numBooksRemoved = cstmt.getInt(1);
```
C.
```
cstmt.setInt(1, maxBooks);
cstmt.setString(2, titleToRemove);
cstmt.execute();
cstmt.registerOutParameter(1, java.sql.Types.INTEGER);
numBooksRemoved = cstmt.getInt(1);
```
D.
```
cstmt.setInt(1, maxBooks);
cstmt.setString(2, titleToRemove);
cstmt.registerOutParameter(1, java.sql.Types.INTEGER);
ResultSet rs = cstmt.executeQuery();
rs.next();
numbBooks = rs.getInt(1);
```
E.
```
cstmt.setInt(1, maxBooks);
cstmt.setString(2, titleToRemove);
cstmt.registerOutParameter(1, java.sql.Types.INTEGER);
cstmt.execute();
numBooksRemoved = cstmt.getInt(1);
```

11. Which creates a connected `RowSet` object?

A. `WebRowSet wrs = RowSetProvider.newFactory().createWebRowSet();`

B. `CachedRowSet crs = RowSetProvider.newFactory().createCachedRowSet();`

C.
```
try(JdbcRowSet jrs = RowSetProvider.newFactory().createJdbcRowSet()) {
  // assume the rest of the try-catch is valid
```
D.
```
try(RowSetFactory rsf = RowSetProvider.newFactory()) {
RowSet rws = rsf.createRowSet();
  // assume the rest of the try-catch is valid
```
E. `JoinRowSet jrs = RowSetProvider.newFactory().createJoinRowSet();`

F.
```
ResultSet rs = Statement.execute("SELECT * FROM Customer");
JdbcRowSet jrs = RowSetProvider.newFactory().setResultSet(rs);
```

12. Given:

```
try (CachedRowSet crs =
        RowSetProvider.newFactory().createCachedRowSet()) {
    String query = "SELECT * FROM Employee";    // Line Q
    crs.setCommand(query);
    crs.setUrl(url);
    crs.setUsername(user);
    crs.setPassword(pwd);
    crs.execute();
    crs.last();                  // Line V
    crs.updateString("LastName", "Sullivan-McGinn");
    // DATABASE GOES OFFLINE HERE
    crs.moveToInsertRow();  // Line W
    crs.updateInt("ID", 101);
    crs.updateString("FirstName", "Michael");
    crs.updateString("LastName", "Fuller");
    crs.updateFloat("Salary", 101234.56f);
    crs.insertRow();         // Line X
    crs.moveToCurrentRow();
    crs.absolute(10);        // Line Y
    crs.deleteRow();         // Line Z
    // DATABASE BACK ONLINE
} catch (SQLException se) {
    System.out.println ("SQLException");
}
```

Assuming that the query produced a result set in Line Q and that the database goes offline on or before the line OFFLINE and comes back online on or before the line ONLINE, which statements are true?

A. `SQLException` will print out due to Line V

B. `SQLException` will print out due to Line Z

C. `SQLException` will print out due to Line X

D. `SQLException` will print out due to Line Y

E. `SQLException` will print out due to Line W

F. One row is updated, one row is inserted, and one row is deleted

G. The database will be unchanged

13. Given:

```
boolean businessRule = true;
try {
  Connection conn = DriverManager.getConnection(url, username, password);
  String query1 = "INSERT INTO Order VALUES(20, 200.50,
                  'Panasonic Stereo Receiver')";
  String query2 = "UPDATE Order SET Price = 35.20 WHERE ID = 21";

  Statement stmt = conn.createStatement();
  stmt.executeUpdate(query1);  // Line X
  stmt.executeUpdate(query2);  // Line Y
  if (businessRule) {
    conn.rollback();           // Line Z
  }
} catch (SQLException se) {
  System.out.println("SQLException");
}
```

And assuming the two queries are valid, what is the result of executing this fragment?

A. Query 1 and Query 2 are rolled back (no change to the database)

B. Query 1 is executed and Query 2 is rolled back

C. Query 1 is executed, Query 2 is executed, and `SQLException`

D. `SQLException`

E. A runtime exception is thrown

14. Given:

```
try (Connection conn = DriverManager.getConnection(url, username, password)) {
  conn.setAutoCommit(false);
  String query1 = "INSERT INTO Order VALUES (22, 99.99, 'Winter Boots')";
  String query2 = "INSERT INTO Order VALUES (24, 39.99, 'Fleece Jacket')";
  Statement stmt = conn.createStatement();
  stmt.executeUpdate(query1);
  Savepoint sp1 = conn.setSavepoint();
  stmt.executeUpdate(query2);
  conn.rollback(sp1);
} catch (SQLException se) {
  System.out.println ("SQLException");
}
```

And given that the queries are valid, what is the result of executing this fragment?

A. Two new rows are added to the database

B. The row from query 1 is added to the database

C. The row from query 2 is added to the database

D. No rows are added to the database

E. A `SQLException` is thrown

15. Given:

```
try (Connection conn = DriverManager.getConnection(url, username, password)) {
  conn.setAutoCommit(false);
  String q1, q2, q3;
  q1 = "INSERT INTO Order VALUES(23, 99.99, 'Winter Boots')";
  q2 = "INSERT INTO Order VALUES(24, 39.99, 'Fleece Jacket')";
  q3 = "INSERT INTO Order VALUES(25, 29.99, 'Wool Scarf')";
  Statement stmt = conn.createStatement();
  stmt.executeUpdate(q1);
  Savepoint sp1 = conn.setSavepoint("item1");
  stmt.executeUpdate(q2);
  Savepoint sp2 = conn.setSavepoint("item2");
  conn.rollback(sp1);
  stmt.executeUpdate(q3);
  Savepoint sp3 = conn.setSavepoint("item3");
  conn.commit();
} catch (SQLException se) {
  System.out.println ("SQLException");
}
```

Assuming that the Order table was empty before this code fragment was executed and that the database supports multiple savepoints and that all of the queries are valid, what rows does Order contain?

A. `23, 99.99, 'Winter Boots'`

B. `23, 99.99, 'Winter Boots'`
   `25, 29.99, 'Wool Scarf'`

C. `23, 99.99, 'Winter Boots'`
   `24, 39.99, 'Fleece Jacket'`

D. `24, 39.99, 'Fleece Jacket'`
   `25, 29.99, 'Wool Scarf'`

E. No rows

SELF TEST ANSWERS

1. ☑ **B** is correct. Prior to JDBC 4.0, JDBC drivers were required to register themselves with the `DriverManager` class by invoking `DriverManager.register(this);` after the driver was instantiated through a call from the classloader. The `Class.forName()` method calls the classloader, which in turn creates an instance of the class passed as a `String` to the method.
   ☒ **A** is incorrect because this method is meant to be invoked with an instance of a `Driver` class. **C** is incorrect because `DatabaseMetaData` does not have a `loadDriver` method, and the purpose of `DatabaseMetaData` is to return information about a database connection. **D** is incorrect because, again, while the method sounds right, the arguments are not of the right types, and this method is actually the one called by `DriverManager.getConnection` to get a `Connection` object. **E** is incorrect because while this method returns a `Driver` instance, one has to be loaded and registered with the `DriverManager` first. (OCP Objective 9.2)

2. ☑ **A, B,** and **E** are correct. To be JDBC 4.0 compliant, a JDBC driver must support the ability to autoload the driver by providing a file, `META-INF/services/java.sql.Driver`, that indicates the fully qualified class name of the `Driver` class that `DriverManager` should load upon start-up. The JDBC driver must implement the interfaces for `Driver`, `Connection`, `Statement`, `ResultSet`, and others. The driver must also support transactions.
   ☒ **C** and **D** are incorrect. It is not a requirement to support scrollable or updatable `ResultSets`, although many drivers do. If, however, the driver reports that through `DatabaseMetaData` it supports scrollable and updatable `ResultSets`, then the driver must support all of the methods associated with cursor movement and updates. **F** is incorrect. The JDBC requires that the driver support SQL92 entry-level grammar and the SQL command DROP TABLE (from SQL92 Transitional Level). **G** is not correct. While JDBC 4.0 drivers must support `PreparedStatement`, `CallableStatement` is optional, and only required if the driver returns true for the method `DatabaseMetaData.supportsStoredProcedures`. (OCP Objective 9.2)

3. ☑ **C, D,** and **F** are correct. `DatabaseMetaData` provides data about the database and the `Connection` object. The name, version, and other JDBC driver information are available, plus information about the database, including the names of stored procedures, functions, SQL keywords, and more. Finally, the default transaction isolation level and data about what transaction levels are supported are also available through `DatabaseMetaData`.
   ☒ **A** and **B** are incorrect, as they are really about the result of a query with the database. Column count is available through a `ResultSetMetaData` object, but a row count requires that you, as the developer, move the cursor to the end of a result set and then evaluate the cursor position. **E** is incorrect. There is no method defined to return the last query in JDBC. **G** is not correct. The Savepoint information is accessed through a Savepoint instance and is part of a transaction. (OCP Objective 9.1)

4. ☑ **E** is correct. When the `ResultSet` returns, the cursor is pointing before the first row of the `ResultSet`. You must invoke the `next()` method to move to the next row of results *before* you can read any data from the columns. Trying to read a result using a `getXXXX` method will result in a `SQLException` when the cursor is before the first row or after the last row.
   ☒ **A, B, D,** and **F** are incorrect based on the above. Note about **C**: the `ResultSet` returned from `executeQuery` will never be null. (OCP Objective 9.3)

5. ☑ **D** is correct.
   ☒ Note that answer **E** is close, but will not compile because the `executeUpdate(query)` method returns an integer result. **A** will compile correctly, but throw a `SQLException` at runtime—the `executeQuery` method cannot be used on INSERT, UPDATE, DELETE, or DDL SQL queries. **B** will not compile because the `createStatement` method does not take a `String` argument for the query. **C** is incorrect because `Statement` does not have a `setQuery` method and this fragment will not compile. (OCP Objective 9.3)

6. ☑ **E** is correct. Recall that the `try`-with-resources statement on line X will automatically close the resource specified at the close of the `try` block (when the closing curly brace is reached), and closing the `Statement` object automatically closes any open `ResultSets` associated with the `Statement`. The `SQLException` thrown is that the `ResultSet` is not open. To fix this code, move the `while` statement into the `try`-with-resources block.
   ☒ **A, B, C, D,** and **F** are incorrect based on the above. (OCP Objective 9.3)

7. ☑ All of the answers are correct (**A, B, C, D, E**). SELECT statements will produce a `ResultSet` even if there are no rows. INSERT, UPDATE, and DELETE statements all produce an update count, even when the number of rows affected is 0. (OCP Objective 9.3)

8. ☑ **C** is the correct answer. Parameters are numbered from 1, not 0. When the program executes, a `SQLException` will be thrown by Line X.
   ☒ **D** is incorrect because the compiler cannot detect that the value of the method should be a 1 and not a zero. The compiler can only determine that the type of the argument is correct, and in this case, the type is correct as an integer. **A** and **B** are incorrect based on the above. (OCP Objective 9.6)

9. ☑ **B** is correct. In the first iteration of the `for` loop, `i = 0` and the `pstmt.setString` method index (the first parameter) is `1` and the second index is `2`. But in the second iteration of the loop, the index value is now `3` and `4`, respectively. It would be better to hard-code these two values as `1` and `2`, respectively.
   ☒ **A, C, D, E,** and **F** are incorrect based on the above. (OCP Objective 9.6)

10. ☑ **E** is correct. Recall that to specify an IN parameter, you use a `setXXXX` method, and for an OUT parameter, you must register the parameter as an OUT before the call, and then use a `getXXXX` method to return the result from the stored procedure after executing the method.

☒ A is incorrect because parameter indexes are numbered from 1, not from 0. **B** is incorrect because the `executeQuery` method includes the `String` query passed in as a parameter. This method will throw a `SQLException`. **C** is incorrect because the OUT parameter was not registered before the execute call, but after the execute method. **D** is incorrect because this stored procedure does not return a `ResultSet`. So while a `ResultSet` will be returned as a result of the `executeQuery` call, the call to `rs.getInt` will throw a `SQLException`. (OCP Objective 9.6)

11. ☑ **C** is the correct answer. This code fragment is creating an instance of a `JdbcRowSet` object—the only `RowSet` that is a connected `RowSet` object. This is the proper way to use the `RowSetProvider` static `newFactory()` method or obtain a `RowSetFactory` instance that is then used to create a `JdbcRowSet` instance.
☒ **A, B,** and **E** are incorrect. These are disconnected `RowSet` objects, although the syntax to acquire these objects is correct. **D** is incorrect and will not compile. The reason is that `RowSetFactory` does not extend `AutoCloseable`; thus, the compiler will complain about the use of `RowSetFactory` in a `try`-with-resources. **F** is incorrect because this is not the proper way to initialize a `RowSet` object. The factory method is used to create an instance, and the instance must be used to execute a query and populate the `RowSet` with results. (OCP Objective 9.5)

12. ☑ **G** is correct. First, the database being offline at any point after the `execute()` method is invoked is irrelevant, since this is a disconnected `RowSet` object (`CachedRowSet`). Thus, the results are cached in the object and changes can be made to the results, regardless of the status of the database. However, there is a critical error in this code: to write the changes made to the data due to the update, insert, and delete, the `acceptChanges()` method must be called in order to make a connection to the database and reconcile the results in the `CachedRowSet` with the database. Since this line of code is missing, the changes were only made to the in-memory object and not reflected in the database.
☒ **A, B, C, D, E,** and **F** are incorrect based on the above. (OCP Objective 9.5)

13. ☑ **C** is correct. Because the `Connection` object conn was never set to `setAutoCommit(false)`, there is no transaction context to rollback. All transactions are in auto-commit mode, so the first transaction is executed and completed, the second transaction is executed and completed, and when the `conn.rollback()` method is executed on line Z, a `SQLException` is thrown because there is no transaction to rollback.
☒ **A, B, D,** and **E** are incorrect based on the above. (OCP Objective 9.4)

14. ☑ **D** is correct. Because there is no commit statement, the `Connection` closes when the `try` block completes, and the transaction created by setting `setAutoCommit` to false is rolled back.
☒ **A, B, C,** and **E** are incorrect based on the above. (OCP Objective 9.4)

15. ☑ **B** is correct. The statement `conn.rollback(sp1);` rolls back the insertion of the row that contains the `'Fleece Jacket'`. Then the transaction continues and processes the insertion of the row that contains `'Wool Scarf'`.
☒ **A, C, D,** and **E** are incorrect based on the above. (OCP Objective 9.4)

Appendix

About the CD

The CD-ROM included with this book comes complete with Oracle Press Practice Exam Software that simulates the OCA 1Z0-803 and OCP 1Z0-804 exams, additional content in PDF format, including the book's glossary and other bonus content such as serialization, and a free electronic version of the book. The software is easy to install on any Mac or Windows computer and must be installed to access the Practice Exam feature. You may, however, browse the electronic book or additional PDF content directly from the CD without installation.

System Requirements

The software requires Microsoft Windows XP, Windows Server 2003, Windows Server 2008, Windows Vista Home Premium, Business, Ultimate, or Enterprise (including 64-bit editions) with Service Pack 2, or Windows 7 or Mac OS X 10.6 and 10.7 with 512MB of RAM (1GB recommended). The electronic book requires Adobe Acrobat Reader.

Installing the Practice Exam Software

Follow the instructions for Windows or Mac OS.

Windows

Step 1 Insert the CD into your CD-ROM drive.

Step 2 After a few moments, the installer will open automatically. If the installer does not open automatically, check the following note.

Step 3 Follow the onscreen instructions to install the application.

NOTE If the installer does not automatically open, from the Start menu, select Run and enter:

X:\Installer.exe

(where "X" is the letter of your CD-ROM drive). Then click OK.

Mac OS

Step 1 Insert the CD into your CD-ROM drive.

Step 2 After a few moments, the contents of the CD will be displayed.

Step 3 Double-click Installer to begin installation.

Step 4 Follow the onscreen instructions to install the application.

***NOTE** If you get an error while installing the software, please ensure your antivirus or Internet security programs are disabled and try installing the software again. You may enable the antivirus or Internet security program again after installation is complete.*

Running the Practice Exam Software

Follow the instructions after you have completed the software installation.

Windows

After installing, you can start the application using *either* of the two following methods:

1. Double-click the Oracle Press Java Exams icon on your desktop *or*
2. Go to the Start menu and click Programs or All Programs. Click Oracle Press Java Exams to start the application.

Mac OS

Open the Oracle Press Java Exams folder inside your Mac's Application folder and double-click the Oracle Press Java Exams icon to run the application.

Practice Exam Software Features

The Practice Exam Software provides you with a simulation of the actual exam. The software also features a custom mode that can be used to generate quizzes by exam objective domain. Quiz mode is the default mode. To launch an exam simulation, select one of the OCA or OCP exam buttons at the top of the screen, or select the

Exam Mode check box at the bottom of the screen and select the OCA or OCP exam in the custom window.

The number of questions, types of questions, and the time allowed on the exam simulation are intended to be a representation of the live exam. The custom exam mode includes hints and references, and in-depth answer explanations are provided through the Feedback feature.

When you launch the software, a digital clock display will appear in the upper-right corner of the question window. The clock will continue to count unless you choose to end the exam by selecting Grade The Exam.

Removing Installation

The Practice Exam Software is installed on your hard drive. For best results for removal of programs using a Windows PC, use Control Panel | Uninstall a Program option and then choose Oracle Press Java Exams to uninstall.

For best results for removal of programs using a Mac, go to the Oracle Press Java Exams folder inside your applications folder and drag the Oracle Press Java Exams icon to the trash.

Help

A help file is provided through the Help button on the main page in the top-right corner. A readme file is also included in the Bonus Content folder that provides more information about the additional content available with the book.

Bonus Content (Including Coverage for the OCP 7, OCPJP 5, and OCPJP 6 Exams)

The Bonus Content folder on the CD-ROM includes the glossary. You will also find the following content to complete exam-specific coverage:

- Serialization for the OCP 7 exam
- Chapter 10 from the previous edition, which covers topics such as classpaths and JAR files for the OCPJP 5 and OCPJP 6 exams
- Eight chapters for the Java SE 6 Developer exam

These are provided in PDF format and can be viewed using Adobe Acrobat. The Readme file on the CD-ROM provides more information on how to navigate the Bonus Content folder.

Glossary

The glossary for the book is included in the Bonus Content folder on the CD-ROM. The glossary is provided in PDF format and can be viewed using Adobe Acrobat.

Free PDF Copy of the Book

The entire contents of the Study Guide are provided in PDF format. Adobe's Acrobat Reader has been included on the CD-ROM.

Technical Support

Technical support information is provided in the following sections by feature.

Windows 8 Troubleshooting

The following known errors on Windows 8 have been reported. Please see the following for information on troubleshooting these known issues.

If you get an error while installing the software, such as "The application could not be installed because the installer file is damaged. Try obtaining the new installer from the application author," you may need to disable your antivirus or Internet security programs and try installing the software again. You may enable the antivirus or Internet security program again after installation is complete.

For more information on how to disable antivirus programs in Windows, please visit the web site of the software provider of your antivirus program. For example, if you use Norton or MacAfee products, you may need to visit the Norton or MacAfee web site and search for "how to disable antivirus in Windows 8." Antivirus programs are different from firewall technology, so be sure to disable the antivirus program, and be sure to re-enable the program after you have installed the Practice Exam Software.

Although Windows doesn't include default antivirus software, it can often detect antivirus software installed by you or the manufacturer of your computer, and typically displays the status of any such software in the Action Center, which is located in the Control Panel under System and Security (select Review Your Computer's Status). Windows' help feature can also provide more information on how to detect your antivirus software. If the antivirus software is on, check the Help feature that came with that software for information on how to disable it.

Windows will not detect all antivirus software. If your antivirus software isn't displayed in the Action Center, you can try typing the name of the software or the publisher in the Start menu's search field.

McGraw-Hill Education Content Support

For questions regarding the glossary, PDF copy of the book, or the additional bonus content, e-mail techsolutions@mhedu.com or visit http://mhp.softwareassist.com.

For questions regarding book content, e-mail customer.service@mheducation.com. For customers outside the United States, e-mail international_cs@mheducation.com.

INDEX

B

C

D

E

F

J

K

M

P

Q

R

S

U

V